MW01058688

DIVORCE AND FAMILY MEDIATION

Divorce and Family Mediation
Models, Techniques, and Applications

Edited by
Jay Folberg
Ann L. Milne
Peter Salem

THE GUILFORD PRESS
New York   London

© 2004 The Guilford Press
A Division of Guilford Publications, Inc.
72 Spring Street, New York, NY 10012
www.guilford.com

Printed in the United States of America

This book is printed on acid-free paper.

Last digit is print number: 9 8 7 6 5 4 3 2 1

Library of Congress Cataloging-in-Publication Data

Divorce and family mediation : models, techniques, and applications /
edited by Jay Folberg, Ann L. Milne, Peter Salem.
    p. cm.
Includes bibliographical references and index.
  ISBN 1-59385-002-6 (hardcover : alk. paper)
  1. Divorce mediation—United States.   2. Family mediation—United
States. I. Folberg, Jay, 1941–   II. Milne, Ann.   III. Salem, Peter.
  KF535.D558 2004
  346.7301´66—dc22

                                              2003026727

About the Editors

Jay Folberg, JD, is Professor of Law and former Dean at the University of San Francisco School of Law. He has been an active mediator since 1974 and is a dispute resolution consultant and trainer for alternative dispute resolution (ADR) provider organizations and courts in the United States and abroad. He has served as president of the Association of Family and Conciliation Courts and the Academy of Family Mediators, as well as chair of the Alternative Dispute Resolution Section of the Association of American Law Schools. Professor Folberg is currently chair of the Ethics Committee of the Dispute Resolution Section of the American Bar Association. In 1998, he was appointed by the Chief Justice of the California Supreme Court to chair a California Judicial Council Task Force on Alternative Dispute Resolution and in 2001 to chair the Judicial Council's Blue Ribbon Panel on Arbitration Ethics. He was honored in 2003 with the Judicial Council's Bernard Witkin Amicus Curiae Award "for his leadership in the field of alternative dispute resolution and his outstanding contributions to the California courts." Professor Folberg is also the recipient of the Academy of Family Mediators' Distinguished Mediator Award and the Mediation Society's Distinguished Contribution to Mediation Award. He has practiced law in Portland, Oregon, and has taught law at Northwestern School of Law at Lewis and Clark College and at the University of Washington. His many books and articles include *Joint Custody and Shared Parenting, Second Edition.*

Ann L. Milne, ACSW, is in private practice in Madison, Wisconsin, as a family and divorce mediator. She served as Executive Director of the Association of Family and Conciliation Courts for 13 years and is currently on the faculty of the Department of Professional Development and Applied Studies at the University of Wisconsin. She has been a trainer and guest lecturer for a number of agencies and courts across the United States and in Canada. She has also written a number of articles on mediation and was coeditor (with Jay Folberg) of *Divorce Mediation: Theory and Practice.*

Peter Salem, MA, is Executive Director of the Association of Family and Conciliation Courts as well as Adjunct Professor at Marquette University Law School, where he teaches mediation. He formerly served as director and mediator at Mediation and Family Court Services in Rock County, Wisconsin, and has been in practice since 1986, providing mediation, training, and consulting services. Mr. Salem has published several articles on mediation and domestic violence and divorce education, and has written and produced educational and training videotapes on mediation and divorce.

Contributors

Allan E. Barsky, JD, MSW, PhD, School of Social Work, Florida Atlantic University, Boca Raton, Florida

Connie J. A. Beck, PhD, Psychology and Law Program, Department of Psychology, University of Arizona, Tucson, Arizona

Robert D. Benjamin, MSW, JD, Mediation and Conflict Management Services, Portland, Oregon; Straus Institute for Dispute Resolution, Pepperdine University School of Law, Malibu, California

Emily M. Brown, MSW, Key Bridge Therapy and Mediation Center, Arlington, Virginia

Robert A. Baruch Bush, JD, Hofstra University School of Law, Hempstead, New York

Robert E. Emery, PhD, Department of Psychology, University of Virginia, Charlottesville, Virginia

Peggy English, BScN, MEd, Cert. FRM (FMC), mediation practitioner, assessor, and trainer, Vancouver, British Columbia, Canada

Stephen K. Erickson, JD, Erickson Mediation Institute, Bloomington, Minnesota

Jay Folberg, JD, University of San Francisco School of Law, San Francisco, California

Lynn Carp Jacob, MSW, Chicago Center for Family Health, University of Chicago, Chicago, Illinois

Janet R. Johnston, PhD, Department of Administration of Justice, San Jose State University, San Jose, California

Michael Lang, JD, The Graduate School at Sullivan University, Louisville, Kentucky

L. Randolph Lowry, MPA, JD, Straus Institute for Dispute Resolution, Pepperdine University School of Law, Malibu, California

Bernard Mayer, PhD, CDR Associates, Boulder, Colorado

Marilyn S. McKnight, MA, Erickson Mediation Institute, Bloomington, Minnesota

Nina R. Meierding, MS, JD, Mediation Center for Family Law, Ventura, California

James C. Melamed, JD, Oregon Mediation Center, Inc., Eugene, Oregon

Ann L. Milne, ACSW, Ann L. Milne and Associates, Madison, Wisconsin

Forrest S. Mosten, JD, Mediator, family lawyer, and trainer, Los Angeles, California

Linda C. Neilson, LLB, PhD, Department of Sociology/Law in Society, University of New Brunswick, Fredericton, New Brunswick, Canada

Sally Ganong Pope, MEd, JD, Sally Pope and Associates, New York, New York

Marsha Kline Pruett, PhD, MSL, Division of Law and Psychiatry, Department of Psychiatry, Yale University School of Medicine, and the Yale Child Study Center, New Haven, Connecticut

Joan K. Raisner, MS, MA, Marriage and Family Counseling Service, Chicago, Illinois

Isolina Ricci, PhD, New Family Center, Tiburon, California

Chip Rose, JD, The Mediation Center, Santa Cruz, California

Peter Salem, MA, Association of Family and Conciliation Courts, Madison, Wisconsin

Bruce D. Sales, PhD, JD, Psychology and Law Program, Department of Psychology, University of Arizona, Tucson, Arizona

Donald T. Saposnek, PhD, Department of Psychology, University of California, Santa Cruz, Santa Cruz, California

Andrew Schepard, MA, JD, Hofstra University School of Law, Hempstead, New York

Arnold Shienvold, PhD, Central Pennsylvania Mediation Services, Inc., Harrisburg, Pennsylvania

Nancy A. Welsh, JD, Dickinson School of Law, Pennsylvania State University, Carlisle, Pennsylvania

Preface

The growth and acceptance of divorce and family mediation over the past several decades has been stunning. When Jay Folberg and Ann Milne prepared their previous volume, *Divorce Mediation: Theory and Practice*, there were few books available on the subject. As the field has matured, there is now a wide selection of books and articles on different approaches and applications of mediation to family dissolution. The chapters prepared for this new book are collectively the state of the art in family mediation. We are pleased to showcase in this one volume the writings of leading authors, educators, trainers, researchers, and practitioners in the field. Peter Salem joins us as an editor to add his extensive experience to this collaborative project that brings together an all-star cast of those influencing the development of divorce and family mediation.

This book is written for two audiences. First, for those who are new to the field of divorce and family mediation, it will serve as a comprehensive, all-in-one volume of work that will enhance their understanding and mastery of the field. Second, it will benefit seasoned practitioners who are searching for a collection of the work of some of the best theorists and practitioners in the field.

The chapters examine emerging models of mediation techniques and applications for specific populations of clients; the influence and demands of different practice settings, such as court-based mediation; and some of the most hotly debated policy questions that will have an impact on the future of the profession. In Part I, Introduction to Divorce and Family Mediation, the editors provide their own perspectives on the evolution of divorce and family mediation—past, present, and future.

As the practice of mediation has matured, it has been shaped by the diversity of practitioners who have been drawn to the field as well as by clients, the courts, and the changes that have occurred in the law. We have moved from the question "Should we mediate?" to the question "*How* should we mediate?" Several models of practice have emerged, and there is debate about the most appropriate style of mediation and the values represented by each model. Some would argue that the descriptive labels attached to these models serve to help us define who we are as mediators and to educate the public about the variety of mediation practices from which they can choose. Given that mediation is intended to be a flexible process designed to meet the needs of the client, others suggest that strict adherence to any single model of mediation is unwise. Part II, Models of Practice, presents several of the most prominent models of mediation, with chapters addressing facilitative, evaluative, transformative, therapeutic, and hybrid practices, by those who shaped these models of practice.

Part III, Mediation Techniques and Interventions, provides guidance on some of the core issues that family and divorce mediators must address with clients. Chapters on parenting plans, the inclusion of children in mediation, financial issues, power, communication, and impasse provide new ways to look at these challenges.

The emergence of family and divorce mediation has been accompanied by significant changes in society and in the families who must make decisions about the dissolution of their existing relationship. Our clients are no longer limited to married biological fathers and mothers. The families with whom we work have changed, and the practice of mediation reflects the expanded relationships for which mediation holds great promise. Part IV, Special Applications and Considerations, includes chapters on mediation with same-sex couples, never-married parents, and stepfamilies. In addition, it examines mediation in the challenging contexts of cases involving domestic violence and extramarital affairs.

In 1980 California mandated mediation in child custody disputes and revolutionized the way the court system addresses disputes between divorcing parents. Today, jurisdictions in most states require disputing parents to attend mediation. Court-connected mediation services must deal with a multiplicity of issues—mandated services, limited resources, high conflict, multiproblem families, and time constraints—issues not always present in other settings. Part V, Mediation in the Court Context, addresses these challenging issues.

Part VI, Developing the Profession, looks at some of the macro and micro policy and practice issues regarding professionalizing the field. It includes an overview of research as well as chapters on mediator certification, standards of practice, establishing a private mediation practice, and the use of the Internet in mediation.

One of the hallmarks of mediation is collaboration. It is our pleasure to have had the opportunity to facilitate the collaborative effort that has resulted in this book, which could not have been written by any single practitioner or scholar. Although we are pleased to include chapters written by so many of the leaders and innovators in family mediation, no one volume can include all those who are helping to shape the field or cover all nuances and refinements of the practice. This book provides the foundation for understanding the evolution of mediation theory and current techniques, as well as the professional issues that have emerged to face the next generation of mediation professionals.

Acknowledgments

First, we thank all the authors who have graciously shared their experience, insight, and wisdom by writing original chapters for this book. All are highly respected colleagues who, by sharing their work here, continue to contribute to the profession they have helped to create.

We are very appreciative of the professionals at The Guilford Press who helped to bring this work to fruition. Editor-in-Chief Seymour Weingarten encouraged us to again put pen to paper (or fingers to keyboard) and tap into our network of colleagues who have ushered the divorce and family mediation field to the next level. We have worked with Senior Editor Jim Nageotte on several projects over the years, and he continues to guide and shape our ideas and our writing with patience and aplomb. The copy editor, Margaret Ryan, polished up our grammar, punctuation, and writing to a point where our English teachers would be proud, and Anna Nelson, production editor, kept the project on track.

Jay would like to thank his spouse, Diana Taylor, whose love and understanding prevent him from experiencing divorce mediation as a client, and Allyson Ukishima for her multifaceted assistance and good cheer.

Ann would like to thank her clients and mediation students who over the years have helped her to appreciate the promise of mediation, and her husband, Bill Bablitch, who is always there when life's natural and normal conflicts seem otherwise.

Peter would like to thank his wife, Susanne Daering, his son, Daniel, and stepson, Sam, who provide firsthand experience parenting in a blended family, and his father, Richard Salem, for making possible the pleasure of sharing our work as mediators.

Contents

DIVORCE AND FAMILY MEDIATION

PART I
Introduction to Divorce and Family Mediation

CHAPTER 1

The Evolution of Divorce and Family Mediation

An Overview

ANN L. MILNE
JAY FOLBERG
PETER SALEM

The current practice of divorce and family mediation has developed from the juncture of law, counseling, and social work, as structuring and terminating family relationships have increasingly become a matter of private decision. In this chapter the editors of the book lay the foundation for subsequent material by providing an overview of the origins, evolution, theory, emerging models of practice, and critical issues facing the field.

Creating a family relationship and ending it have recently evolved from strict statutory requirements and judicial scrutiny to more private choice (Mnookin, 1985). As the state allows individuals more choice in creating and ending domestic relationships, the potential use of mediation increases as a means to facilitate decisions about parenting, financial support, and the division of acquired property.

Making divorce easier legally does not make it easier emotionally. Divorce entwines legal considerations with emotional dynamics; family dissolution is a matter of the heart as well as the law (Gold, 1992). The field of mediation is unique in its recognition of both the emotional and legal dimensions of family dissolution. The practice of mediation has matured into a new profession to meet the needs of individuals ending or restructuring a family (Folberg, 2003). This chapter examines the evolution of family and divorce mediation, defines and distinguishes the practice from other professional services, provides an overview of several models of practice, and outlines some of the critical issues facing the continued development of the field.

A BRIEF HISTORY

The increase in, and growing acceptance of, divorce in our society has led to sweeping changes in the substantive law of divorce, the most significant being the adoption of no-fault grounds for divorce. All states now provide some form of no-fault divorce (Ellman, Kurtz, & Scott, 1998), which shifts the responsibility for determining whether or not a divorce is warranted from the court to the parties involved. Other substantive legal changes include legislative provisions for shared parenting and joint custody, as well as the requirement in some states that parents submit parenting plans for how responsibility for children will be allocated. Alimony based on fault and entitlement has given way to financial arrangements based on need and ability to pay. Rigid rules of property division have been replaced in many states by considerations of equity and fairness based on the unique circumstances of the parties.

In addition to these substantive legal reforms are changes in the procedural aspects of divorce. Traditional divorce embodied adversarial norms intended to minimize direct communication and maximize third-party decision making. Divorce actions were initiated by a lawsuit naming a plaintiff and a defendant, and settlement negotiations were conducted under the threat of a trial that only reinforced the competitive underpinnings of the "winner-takes-all" mentality. In the early 1970s a handful of attorneys took to heart the emerging no-fault divorce philosophy and began offering "nonadversarial legal services" (Elson, 1988; Folberg, 1983). These attorneys risked bar association sanctions by meeting with both spouses to help settle financial, property, and child custody issues (Oregon State Bar Ethics Opinion 488, July 1983, *In re* Folberg). The concept of a neutral attorney set the stage for other members of the legal profession to promote the principles of mediation in divorce-related matters.

About this same time, mental health professionals began offering new options for divorcing family members. Historically, divorce was viewed by mental health professionals as lying outside the domain of psychotherapy. The psychodynamic model, with its focus on an individual's unconscious conflicts and intrapsychic pathology, did not allow couples in conflict to be treated together in a clinical setting. The more traditional schools of therapy (e.g., psychoanalytic, Adlerian, Jungian, Eriksonian) did not direct themselves to the psychological and emotional issues of the divorcing family. These practitioners saw divorce solely as a legal process that begins at the point of separation (Milne, 1986).

As more therapists began to identify themselves as divorce counselors specializing in services directed toward the mental health concerns of the divorcing family, they created therapeutic interventions that combined an insight approach with the action-oriented focus of the behaviorists. Divorcing spouses enlisted the help of clinicians in an attempt to resolve conflicts to effect a satisfactory postdivorce adjustment. Out of these efforts emerged a body of theory that addressed the emotional–psychological aspects of divorce (Federico, 1979; Brown, 1976; Kessler, 1975; Weiss, 1975; Wiseman, 1975; Bohannon, 1970). This divorce theory moved professionals from the one-dimensional view of divorce as a legal process to a more integrated view of divorce as a multidimensional process involving both legal and psychological matters (Kaslow, 1979–1980). Some mental health professionals began offering mediation as a means of helping the divorcing family with both the psychological dissolution of the marriage and with working out a contractual agreement on parenting responsibilities, property division, and finances (Kelly, 1983, 1995).

California first established court-connected conciliation services in 1939. The initial focus of these services was to provide marriage counseling aimed at reconciliation (Folberg & Milne, 1988). Conciliation court personnel were probably the first to offer mediation services, as the focus of conciliation shifted from reconciliation to divorce counseling and custody mediation (Brown, 1982). In 1980 California became the first state to mandate all parents with custody or visitation disputes to participate in family mediation prior to a court hearing. Disputants could choose to use either court-based or private mediators (see Ricci, Chapter 18, this volume). Most states today have statutes and court policies governing family mediation and selected jurisdictions in at least 38 states mandate mediation when there are disputes over custody or visitation (Tondo, Coronel, & Drucker, 2001).

The first private-sector family mediation center was established in 1974 in Atlanta, Georgia, by O. J. Coogler, an attorney and marriage and family counselor. Spurred by his own emotionally and financially costly divorce, Coogler helped popularize the idea of divorce mediation through the publication of his book *Structured Mediation in Divorce Settlement* (1978). To assist couples in contractually resolving issues of finances, property division, support, and child custody, Coogler proposed a structured framework for third-party mediators, using communication and intervention techniques borrowed from labor mediation and the social sciences. In 1975 Coogler established the Family Mediation Association (FMA), an interdisciplinary organization of individuals interested in the development and advancement of divorce mediation. Like many pioneers, Coogler and his "structured mediation model" were harshly criticized. Bar associations declared mediation by nonlawyers to be the unauthorized practice of law and attempted to discourage lawyers from mediating through the threat of ethical sanctions (Silberman, 1988).

Nonetheless, the practice of divorce mediation continued, encouraged by judges who welcomed both the reduction of cases on their dockets and relief from making difficult decisions about the best interests of children. Court administrators supported legislation that compelled family mediation, as evidence mounted that mediation was less expensive than court hearings and resulted in less postdivorce litigation and enforcement problems. The divorcing population, through a number of grassroot organizations, began demanding reform. Legislative changes supporting co-parenting, joint custody, and shared parenting set the stage for the institutionalization of divorce mediation.

Following a dispute within the leadership of FMA over organizational direction, John Haynes, Stephen Erickson, and Samuel Marguiles founded the Academy of Family Mediators (AFM), in 1982. AFM became the professional association for family and divorce mediators. The organization sponsored mediation training programs, addressed public policy issues (including diversity, standards of practice, and supervision qualifications), and published a newsletter and journal for its members. In 2001 AFM merged with the Society of Professionals in Dispute Resolution (SPIDR) and the Conflict Resolution Education Network (CREnet) to form the Association for Conflict Resolution (ACR)—a membership organization dedicated to "enhancing the practice and public understanding of conflict resolution" (Association for Conflict Resolution Mission Statement, 2000).

Other national organizations, including the Association of Family and Conciliation Courts, the American Arbitration Association, and the American Bar Association, began to encourage divorce and child custody mediation and added mediation topics and programs to their conferences, newsletters, and journals.

Today, the largest dispute resolution membership organization, with more than 9,000 members, is the American Bar Association Section of Dispute Resolution. In April 1999, the Section Council called for the inclusion of people from all backgrounds as neutral participants, regardless of whether they are lawyers, and in 2002 passed a resolution stating that mediation is not the practice of law (Hanna, 2003).

The early years of the divorce mediation field focused on attempting to establish a foothold of credibility. Research, limited as it was, established the benefits of mediation over lawyer-assisted negotiation, custody evaluation, and litigation (Kelly, 1991; Pearson & Thoennes, 1984). Funding for court mediation programs—through the use of filing fees dedicated to support these programs—was established in some jurisdictions (McIsaac, 1981).

Since its inception in the early 1970s, the landscape of the mediation field has evolved as more programs and services have been established. Mediation is now used in thousands of divorce-related disputes annually (Cole, Rogers, & McEwen, 2001). The field has matured, as evidenced by current professional issues and controversies. Topics such as the use of mediation in cases involving allegations of domestic abuse (Milne, Chapter 14, this volume), same-sex partners (Barsky, Chapter 16, this volume), and members from blended families (Jacob, Chapter 15, this volume) as well as unmarried parents (Raisner, Chapter 13, this volume) have moved our professional discourse beyond the benefits of mediation.

Model Standards of Practice for Family and Divorce Mediation were developed through a cooperative effort of the Association of Family and Conciliation Courts, the Family Law Section of the American Bar Association, the Dispute Resolution Section of the American Bar Association, the Academy of Family Mediators, the Conflict Resolution Education Network, the National Association for Community Mediation, the National Conference on Peacemaking and Conflict Resolution, and the Society of Professionals in Dispute Resolution (Schepard, Chapter 22, this volume; Milne & Schepard, 2002; Milne, 1984).

The training and education of mediators have expanded from 1- to 5-day programs with no entrance or exit requirements to academic programs that confer a degree in conflict resolution upon completion of course work and a field practicum (e.g., Marquette University, Antioch University, University of Missouri Law School, George Mason University, Pepperdine University).

New models of mediation that extend beyond the traditional problem-solving, facilitative approach are being touted together with accompanying training curricula. Some blanch at these new approaches and decline to call them *mediation* (Boskey, 1995), whereas others welcome them and point to the benefits of having a diversity of tools in the mediator's tool kit (Linden, 2001; Zumeta, 2000); Chapters 2–6 discuss several of these emerging models of practice and their applications.

A look back at the historical footnotes and a look forward at the more recent developments in the field help us to understand the unique roots and traditions of divorce mediation. As specialized as divorce mediation is within the broad field of dispute resolution, the evolution of its conceptual framework rests upon the early theories of human conflict and conflict resolution.

EVOLUTION OF THE CONCEPTUAL FRAMEWORK

In 1973, social psychologist Morton Deutsch presented his theories on the nature of human conflict and described the constructive use of a third party in conflict resolution (Deutsch, 1973). Legal scholars, most notably Lon Fuller, Frank Sander, and Roger Fisher, all of Harvard Law School, have helped to shape professional and public thought on the procedures, application, and techniques of mediation (Folberg, 2003).

Rubin and Brown described mediation as a means of

> reducing irrationality in the parties by preventing personal recrimination
> by focusing and refocusing on actual issues; by exploring alternative solu-
> tions and making it possible for the parties to retreat or make concessions
> without losing face or respect; by increasing constructive communication
> between the parties; by reminding the parties of the costs of conflict and
> the consequences of unresolved disputes and by providing a mediator
> model of competence, integrity and fairness. (in Brown, 1982, p. 14)

Mediation is not *arbitration.* In arbitration, a designated third person holds the responsibility for making a finding or providing a decision for the parties. The arbitration process is adjudicatory but typically less formal than the traditional court process. In mediation a neutral third party is used, but the parties do not authorize the mediator to make decisions for them (Folberg & Taylor, 1984).

Mediation is also distinguishable from a *negotiation* process, which is typ-ically a sounding-out and bargaining process and does not normally include a neutral third party.

Mediation is not *therapy.* No diagnoses are made, and the parties do not analyze past behaviors but attempt to reach agreements that provide for the future. Unlike traditional forms of therapy, mediation does not focus on ob-taining insight into the history of the conflict, nor does it attempt to change personality patterns. Although insights and changes may occur, they are fringe benefits of the mediation process (Kelly, 1983; Milne, 1982).

Mediation provides a personalized approach to dispute resolution in which spouses have an opportunity to learn about each other's needs. Media-tion can help the parties solve problems together and recognize that cooper-ation is mutually advantageous. Mediation is bound neither by rules of proce-dure and substantive law nor by other assumptions that dominate the adversarial process of the law. The ultimate authority in mediation belongs to the parties. With the help of the mediator, the parties may consider a comprehensive mix of individual needs, interests, and whatever else they deem relevant, irrespective of rules of evidence or legal precedent. Unlike the adjudicatory process, the emphasis is not on who is right and who is wrong but on establishing a workable resolution that best meets the needs of the participants (Folberg, 1985).

Mediation is a private and, in most cases, confidential process, so the most personal of matters may be freely discussed without concern that the information disclosed will become part of a public record. Participants for-mulate their own agreement and emotionally invest in its success. They are thus more likely to support the agreement than if the terms were negotiated or ordered by others.

Family and divorce mediation has emerged as distinct from commercial and civil claims mediation. Attorneys are not usually present during the mediation session, although they may advise and coach their clients, as well as draft the settlement agreement or, at least, review it prior to the clients formally signing it. *Caucusing*, or separate meetings between the mediator and each party, is less frequently utilized in family and divorce contexts than in commercial and civil case settlement mediations. Unlike commercial and personal injury mediation, family mediation strives to provide a model of interaction and communication for resolution of future disputes, particularly involving children.

EVOLUTION OF THE PRACTICE

The practice of divorce mediation is largely dependent on who is doing the mediating, where the mediation is offered, and what is being mediated (Folberg, 1982). Mediation in a mandatory court-based setting may differ from a private, voluntary process. Some mediators adhere to a model that focuses on client interaction (see Mayer, Chapter 2, and Bush & Pope, Chapter 3, this volume), whereas others emphasize settlement and outcome (see Lowry, Chapter 4, this volume). Others may integrate therapeutic or arbitrative components into the mediation process (see Pruett & Johnston, Chapter 5, and Shienvold, Chapter 6, this volume). A number of authors describe mediation as a series of stages (Moore, 1996; Folberg & Taylor, 1984; Haynes, 1981), whereas Bush and Pope eschew the notion of stages altogether (see Chapter 3, this volume). Mayer (Chapter 2, this volume) identifies a set of tasks to be accomplished rather than stages.

Who Are the Mediators?

Early research indicated that mental health professionals, including social workers, marriage and family therapists, psychologists, and psychiatrists, accounted for 78% of family mediators in the private sector and 90% in the public sector. Lawyers comprised 15% of private-sector family mediators and only 1% of those in public-sector service (Pearson, Ring, & Milne, 1983). Although more recent data are not available, public-sector court-connected mediation programs report that they continue to employ primarily mental health professionals (Milne & Salem, 2000).

Terms such as "court-connected mediator," "private mediator," and "lawyer/nonlawyer mediator" are often used as a means of describing and distinguishing divorce mediation services. These dichotomous labels, although useful for drawing distinctions, add to the territorial competitiveness between the divisions and may stereotype practices. A description of the settings of practice is a more productive way of viewing the range of organizational entities and approaches to divorce mediation.

Settings of Practice

Because family mediation has not developed a distinct academic tradition of its own and most practitioners approach the field from their previous professional orientation, it is difficult to present a singular picture of family mediation. Family mediation services are typically offered in one of four settings: (1) court-connected venues, (2) private practice, (3) agencies and clinics, and (4) community mediation centers.

Court-Connected Mediation

Court-connected mediation programs have moved beyond the traditionally offered services of reconciliation counseling, divorce counseling, and custody and visitation evaluations to include mediation. Approximately one-tenth of the nation's domestic relations courts have mediation programs, and the vast majority of them authorize the courts to compel parents to attempt to mediate their custody and visitation disputes (Cole et al., 2001). Mediation may be initiated through mandatory or voluntary procedures. Mediators in court-connected settings are, for the most part, mental health practitioners, primarily social workers and psychologists, who are supervised by a director reporting to the chief judge of the family/domestic court (Comeaux, 1983).

It is important to avoid sweeping generalizations about court-connected mediation programs. However, it is equally important to highlight the significant impact of the court setting. The most notable features of court-based mediation services are (1) the limitation of the issues being mediated, (2) the limitations of staff resources, and (3) the mediator's symbiotic relationship with the court system.

Most court-connected mediation services limit themselves, or are limited by statute, to mediating parenting plans. A few court-connected programs use mental health mediators to mediate limited financial matters, such as child support and property division, upon the consent of the parties and their attorneys (Milne & Salem, 2000). Most often, if financial issues are mediated in a court-based program, the mediation is conducted by a court-employed commissioner, referee, or volunteer lawyer.

"Issue-focused mediation" (Johnston & Roseby, 1997), wherein mediators isolate child custody and visitation issues from the other issues in the divorce, has drawn both support and criticism (Pearson & Thoennes, 1984; Saposnek, 1983; Folberg, 1982). Concerns have been expressed by the legal community that mental health professionals lack the expertise to mediate financial and property issues. Isolating these issues helps to alleviate these concerns and reinforce the bar's support for court mediation programs. Iso-lating parent–child issues from financial and property issues may also pre-clude using the children as pawns and leveraging money for children in the mediation process.

Others note that the isolation of parenting from property and financial issues artificially limits the mediation process, in which decisions made in one area may affect decisions in other areas (Milne & Folberg, 1988). Isolat-ing child-related issues places limits on the scope of the parties' decision making, may create an impediment to reaching an agreement, and can cause tentative agreements to unravel later, when parents face the financial impli-cations of custody decisions (e.g., payment and the amount of child support).

Many court-connected mediation programs are challenged by limited re-sources, including budgets, staff, and office space. Court-connected pro-grams are increasingly underfunded and understaffed due to the number of high-conflict cases being referred and the growing number of unrepresented parties. There is often significant pressure on these mediators to bring par-ties to an agreement, typically within one or two sessions (Milne & Salem, 2000). This pressure to quickly settle cases may lead to what has been re-ferred to as a "muscle mediation" process in which the mediator substan-tively shapes the agreement rather than empowering the parties to do so (Milne, 1981; Lande, 1997).

The often symbiotic relationship between a court-connected program and the judiciary can muddy the expectation of mediator neutrality in these settings. In California, the statute allows the mediator to make a recommen-dation to the court, pursuant to local court rules, if the parties do not reach an agreement (California Family Code, Section 1383); and in Hennepin County, Minnesota, parties that reach an impasse in mediation may opt for their mediator to continue as the custody evaluator (Dennis, 1994).

Some court-connected mediators agree that this combined mediation/ evaluation process is not "pure" mediation; however, they argue that it does create an effective process, given the resource limitations of the courts (Chavez-Fallon, 2002). They note that court-based mediators are often work-ing with high-conflict families who otherwise may have little likelihood of reaching an agreement. An aggressive mediation approach, in some cases bordering on arbitration, may provide the structure necessary to allow these parties to reach a settlement and that precludes destructive and costly litiga-tion. Allowing the mediator to make a custody recommendation to the par-ties or to the court may conserve resources, eliminate duplication of effort, and save time. Some parties prefer this course over an impasse (see Ricci, Chapter 18, this volume).

Critics of this practice contend that it dramatically changes the dynam-ics of the mediation process when parents know that the mediator may be-come the evaluator (McIsaac, 1985; Cohen, 1991). Clients will be advised by their attorneys to carefully measure what they discuss in mediation and to approach the mediator as a potential witness for or against them in a court trial if mediation comes to an impasse.

Restricting the mediation process to those clients who consent to participate may underestimate the coercive pressure this practice can place on a reluctant participant. This symbiotic relationship with the court and the judicial decision-making process is not a factor in other mediation settings and may influence the decision of some consumers to opt out of court-connected mediation. Certainly, the practice will continue to be debated among mediators.

Private Practice

The private practice of family and divorce mediation is not limited to those with legal and mental health backgrounds; however, professionals from these fields comprise the most significant number. Mediators in private practice typically operate on a fee-for-service basis and rely on referrals from the courts and other professionals. Most private mediators offer comprehensive services that encompass financial, property, and parenting issues. In contrast to those mediating in court-connected programs, private mediators may offer parties as many sessions as are needed. The number of sessions generally depends on the number and complexity of issues; typically, private mediators complete a comprehensive mediation in 4 to 8 sessions, with each session lasting between 1 and 2 hours (Milne & Salem, 2000).

Services provided by these individuals vary according to the issues mediated, the mediation model used, and the professional orientation of the mediator. Most common is the mental health mediator working as a sole proprietor or as part of a private mental health clinic. Private mental health mediators may offer divorce mediation in conjunction with counseling, custody evaluation, parent coordination, or other divorce-related services. Many mental health mediators are drawn to the field because of their background in family therapy and their conviction that mediation is a healthy alternative to the adversarial system.

Although mental health mediators have historically outnumbered lawyer mediators, the number of lawyer mediators has grown significantly as the organized bar has become more supportive of mediation and as lawyers look for less adversarial ways to practice law. Many lawyer mediators offer mediation services in addition to their legal practices and may specialize in disputes over property and financial issues. Lawyers who provide mediation services attempt to make it clear that they are not serving as a representational lawyer or providing individual legal advice. Like mental health mediators, lawyer mediators encourage parties to obtain representation by independent legal counsel. Some mediators with a legal background are willing to provide legal information and evaluate possible outcomes (see Lowry, Chapter 4, this volume).

Some mediators hold degrees in both the legal and mental health fields. These cross-trained individuals draw upon their legal expertise to assist couples with the legal and financial issues and use their counseling skills to assist with the communication process and underlying emotional issues.

Although many private mediators have thriving practices, others struggle to make private mediation a full-time practice. Many private practitioners supplement their mediation practice with other professional services, such as counseling, legal services, and mediation training.

Agencies and Clinics

A third setting for divorce mediation are agencies or clinics that offer a range of services and employ a number of professionals, one or two of whom specialize in divorce mediation. Agencies may specifically market divorce mediation as one of several available services that include individual and family counseling, parent education, financial planning, and other services. Most agencies or clinics view mediation as a logical add-on to their existing community services and as a potential source of income for the agency. Mediators in these settings are usually mental health professionals; services are often offered on a sliding-fee scale and may be limited to parent–child issues.

Community Mediation Centers

Some community mediation centers also provide limited divorce mediation services. These neighborhood dispute resolution centers were established to provide mediation services as part of their mandate to offer an alternative to the court for a broad range of disputes, including criminal misdemeanor offenses, landlord–tenant, business–consumer, neighborhood, and family conflicts (Shonholtz, 1984). These centers are most often staffed by trained volunteers and administered by an executive director and board of directors. The services are usually free or low cost and tend to be short-term in nature.

MODELS OF PRACTICE

As the divorce mediation field has evolved, so too have various models or styles of practice. These models of practice are not venue specific as described in the earlier discussion, but rather tend to present views about the mission of the mediation process as adhered to by their proponents. These different approaches—including facilitative, transformative, evaluative, therapeutic, narrative, and other hybrids—are all referred to as *mediation*. However, they each have a different focus, different goals, different training programs, and sometimes even different outcomes. It is these differences that have elicited some concerns for the field and for the consumer. Although the emergence of different mediation models marks the maturing nature of family mediation practice (Folberg, 2003), there are also a number of noted leaders in the field who believe that "it is important that the alternative dispute resolution profession achieve greater clarity regarding the variety of dispute resolution processes and the boundaries that distinguish them" (Peace, 2003, p. 2).

The chapters that follow explain the basis, rationale, and application of the most prominent mediation models by the authors who are closely identified with each process. A summary of several of these approaches highlights the evolution of the field and the development of distinctive practices.

Facilitative Mediation

Facilitative mediation is where the family and divorce mediation field began. The writings of the earliest practitioners and authors would today be described as facilitative mediation (Moore, 1996; Milne, 1986; Lemmon, 1985; Folberg & Taylor, 1984; Haynes, 1981; Coogler, 1978). Many of these early mediation proponents described what we would now call a facilitative model of divorce mediation offered as a multistage process.

Facilitative mediators would agree that this model of practice is first and foremost a *process* that emphasizes the participants' responsibility for making the decisions that affect their lives. Furthermore, it is intended to be an empowering process. Facilitative mediators would agree that the process consists of systematically isolating points of agreement and disagreement, exploring interests, developing options, and considering accommodations with the help of a neutral third-party mediator, who serves as a facilitator of communications, a guide toward the definition of issues, and a settlement agent who assists the disputants in their own negotiations (Folberg, 1983; Milne, 1982).

In this model of practice the parties typically are seen together, so that the mediator can more effectively facilitate a collaborative communication and problem-solving process. The facilitative mediator does not make recommendations to the parties, give advice, or predict what a court would do (Zumeta, 2000). The mediator is in charge of the process, whereas the parties retain responsibility for the product. Consequently, substantive expertise about money, property, or children is not considered a prerequisite for the facilitative mediator.

Mayer (Chapter 2, this volume) notes that all mediators use some facilitative techniques, and he identifies four key characteristics common to facilitative mediation:

1. *Facilitative mediation is process oriented, not focused on outcomes.* Mediators serve as process guides to assist the parties in their own deliberations.

2. *Facilitative mediation is client centered.* The job of the mediator is to help the clients communicate and problem solve effectively.
3. *Facilitative mediation is communication focused.* The mediator facilitates, or in some instances restricts, communication between the parties.
4. *Facilitative mediation is interest based.* Mediators help parties understand the interests and concerns that they each have and work together to look for solutions that address those areas.

Critics of the facilitative model state that the inability to provide substantive expertise may protract the mediation process, cause additional expense if the parties have to consult other experts, and agreements may be contrary to standards of fairness (Zumeta, 2000).

Evaluative Mediation

In contrast to the facilitative model described above, evaluative mediators offer their substantive knowledge and experience to the disputants. Settlement is a central goal and tends to trump process.

Evaluative mediation is modeled on a settlement conference format (Kovach & Love, 1996; Zumeta, 2000). An evaluative mediator helps the disputants evaluate their positions in light of what would likely happen if they were not to settle. This "reality test" can be very useful for some clients when the issues are of a more legal nature (Linden, 2001). Face saving is often an issue for a client in an evaluative mediation process. Individual sessions, caucuses, and shuttle mediation are more often used in the evaluative model compared to other approaches.

Lowry (Chapter 4, this volume) contends that all mediators use evaluation at some level, given that "a mediator makes a judgment about the dispute at hand and expresses that judgment to the parties" (p. 72). Some mediators directly propose outcomes or ask questions that imply an outcome—for example, "Do you *really* think it is good for the children to go back and forth between homes every other day?"

Lowry notes that an evaluative process (1) may be more effective and efficient in helping parties reach an agreement, (2) provides the opportunity to integrate needed substantive expertise, (3) may empower a weaker party, and (4) may allow parties to save face while reaching an agreement.

Evaluative mediation has been the target of significant criticism. Detractors contend that this model is favored by lawyers and retired judges because they are more comfortable being in the decision-making role than empowering the clients. Of greater concern is probably the worry about the legitimacy of any prediction of a courtroom outcome and the vulnerability of substantive expertise. Proponents of other mediation models point to concerns about mediator impartiality and neutrality that they believe this model raises.

The Model Standards of Practice for Family and Divorce Mediation (Schepard, 2000) caution the mediator about giving opinions and making recommendations (see also Schepard, Chapter 22, this volume). Florida's Rules of Conduct for Mediators state that a mediator can provide information and advice that he or she is qualified to provide as long as he or she does not violate mediator impartiality or the self-determination of the parties (Zumeta, 2000). In contrast, a Wisconsin statute mandates that disputing parents attempt to mediate their conflict and requires that the mediator certify that the agreement is in the best interests of the child (761.11 [12] [a]).

Transformative Mediation

In the transformative model, first developed by Bush and Folger (1994), mediation is defined as "a process in which a third party works with the parties to help them change the quality of their conflict interaction from negative and destructive to positive and constructive, as they explore and discuss issues and possibilities for resolution" (Bush & Pope, Chapter 3, this volume, p. 59).

The purpose of transformative mediation is to effect a changed and more pacific relationship between the parties. The focus is on the interactions and communications of the parties that will lead them to "moral growth" (Currie, 2001). Settlement of the dispute is a welcome by-product. The focus on the relationship requires that a transformative mediator meet conjointly with the parties.

Bush and Pope (Chapter 3, this volume) contend that conflict propels people into feelings of weakness and self-absorption. As these vulnerable states reinforce one another, conflict escalates. To reverse this escalation, the mediator must foster a shift in the parties from weakness to empowerment and self-absorption to recognition. The cumulative impact of these shifts transforms the interaction between the parties.

Unlike other models of mediation, the transformative mediator is not a process guide but follows the parties by using supportive skills such as reflection, summary, and "checking in." Directive interventions—such as setting an agenda, normalizing, pointing out common ground, probing for underlying issues, or keeping parties focused on a discussion topic—are avoided. Proponents of transformative mediation believe that this approach creates the opportunity for the parties to reverse the negative conflict spiral and move toward positive interactions, and that this reversal is the greatest value that mediation offers to families in conflict.

Criticism of transformative mediation ranges from those who contend that it is therapy, not mediation, to others who question the appropriateness of assuming that clients are seeking a transformation. Furthermore, this model of mediation may not lend itself to disputes that involve domestic abuse or power imbalances.

Hybrid Models of Mediation

Hybrid mediation processes combine different models of mediation with other interventions such as therapy and arbitration. Pruett and Johnston (Chapter 5, this volume) present several hybrid mediation models that combine mediation with therapeutic processes. Using multiple sessions, they combine a therapeutic or counseling stage, which prepares parents for negotiation, with a sociopsychological assessment of the child. The mediator plays many roles, including facilitator, educator, child advocate, and counselor to the parents.

Shienvold (Chapter 6, this volume) discusses an evaluative mediation model in which the mediator conducts a child custody evaluation and then uses those findings as the basis for the subsequent mediation process with the parents. The parties are informed that if no agreement is reached, the evaluator/mediator will make a recommendation to the court.

Processes that blend mediation with other techniques have the potential to create confusion as to what "real" mediation is. Furthermore, these models of practice blur some of mediation's fundamental tenets, such as neutrality, confidentiality, empowerment, and self-determination. One can imagine a conversation between two divorcing couples who are comparing their experiences in mediation and the confusion that may arise as they describe two dramatically different processes—each called *mediation*. However, both couples may conclude that what they experienced as mediation was beneficial and appropriate for their situation.

The development of new models of practice will continue to create controversy in the field and will raise questions regarding training, certification, and standards of practice. A Michigan court rule allows a judge to order parties to participate in a facilitative mediation process but not an evaluative one (Zumeta, 2000). While there may be room in the field for many styles and models of practice, it is argued that when parties are required to participate in a mediation process, they ought to be clearly informed about the different models and allowed to select the one that they prefer (Peace, 2003).

CRITICAL ISSUES SHAPING THE FUTURE OF THE FIELD

As the practice of family and divorce mediation continues to grow, the field faces a number of critical developmental issues. These include confidentiality, domestic abuse, power imbalances, mandatory mediation, and the unauthorized practice of law, in addition to those discussed below. Some of these are addressed in depth in subsequent chapters of this book.

Certification and Credentialing

Certification and credentialing of mediators as a condition to practice is seen by some as the path to public acceptance, enhanced confidence in mediation, and the maturation of a profession. Others see credentialing as an obstacle to the development of new approaches as well as a way to shut the gates behind first-generation mediators (Folberg, 2003). Some note that until a level of consensus can be reached on theory, practice, and proficiency, the basis on which to credential would-be practitioners remains elusive (Milne, 1984).

The absence of certification and licensure provisions also makes it difficult to enforce ethical standards—a prerequisite to the recognition of mediation as a full-fledged profession. Efforts by mediation organizations on both statewide and national levels have resulted in a great deal of interesting discussion but little in the way of certification processes. As of this writing, Florida, Georgia, and Virginia have developed and implemented a comprehensive process for training, certifying, and administering grievances for both court-connected and private mediators who accept court referrals (S. Press, personal communication with A. L. Milne, May 2003).

A system of sanctions may provide some assurance for the public against the practice of mediation by unqualified individuals and may promote more uniformity of service (Milne, 1983a, 1983b). To establish a set of qualifications for practice, however, requires a consensus on definitions, minimum qualifications, and standards. At this stage in the developmental process of divorce mediation, such a consensus may not be realistic.

Then there is the question of who will provide the certification of proficiency. Should the certifying body be a professional organization that provides divorce mediation training, or an independent, interprofessional board that reflects the multidisciplinary practice of divorce mediation, or a government agency, or the courts?

Yet another arena is the legal liability of divorce mediators, which has not been well defined or tested (Folberg, 1988). How best to assure quality without unreasonably restricting choice and needed experimentation is problematic in a field that is still developing.

Canada's experience with voluntary certification of family mediators is proving very valuable (see English & Neilson, Chapter 21, this volume). The development of practice parameters that cross professional boundaries will also assist in the convergence of disciplines and allow divorce mediation to become a profession in its own right (see Schepard, Chapter 22, this volume).

Training

In the absence of required certification, there is great variation and little control over mediation training. Although the number of academic degree programs has increased, these programs have not yet become the established path to mediation practice. Training programs ranging from 1 to 5 days provide the initial starting point.

Credible mediation training must be supported by credible theoretical underpinnings and supporting research and experience. Academic institutions can help to fill this void by rigorously examining the nature of conflict and the emerging conflict resolution tools and techniques. The William and Flora Hewlett Foundation has provided significant and instrumental financial support to the development of these theory centers (Alfini, Press, Sternlight, & Stulberg, 2001). Changes within the Hewlett Foundation's areas of support will require that other sources of financial support be sought. More is needed.

The thirst for the 1- to 5-day mediation training programs may be abating, as many trainees learn that mediation jobs are not plentiful and apprenticeship opportunities are even scarcer. Mentoring and supervised opportunities for mediators to practice their skills are rare and need to be expanded.

Diversity of Practice Models

John Cooley (2000) eloquently wrote, "Let us develop our own paradigm and not let the paradigms of any other profession, be it law, psychology or any other discipline, determine who we are and how we practice" (cited in Peace, 2003, p. 2). Yet we cannot ignore that the field of divorce mediation drew its first breath from law and the behavioral sciences.

New models of practice will continue to be added to the traditional facilitative school of mediation. Disputes between mediators about the legitimacy of each new model of mediation can be uncomfortable (Bellman, 1998). However, conflict is the mother of invention and the field of mediation must move forward. To do this in a manner that does not confuse the public and the consumer is our greatest challenge.

As mediators we understand the importance of clear communication and the conflicts that result from miscommunications and misperceptions. We need to take great care that the innovative techniques and practices that we are adding to our mediator's tool kit are not misidentified. Mediators need a variety of tools to deal with the diversity of disputes and disputants. On the other hand, "let us not paint it green and call it grass" (H. Bellman, personal communication with A. L. Milne, May 2003).

Financial Realities

The dollars and cents of mediation are often overlooked. Honeyman's *Financing Dispute Resolution* (1995) is one of the few efforts made in the field to examine this critical issue. Although many people have been trained in mediation, comparatively few have the luxury of giving up their "day job." The growth of fee-for-service mediation appears to have occurred more in civil litigation and commercial cases—the purview of lawyer-trained mediators—than in family and divorce cases. Commercial mediators have had the benefit of well-organized and well-financed groups, such as JAMS (formerly Judicial Arbitration and Mediation Services) and the American Arbitration Association (AAA), actively pursuing and educating the marketplace. Newly trained family mediators find themselves unprepared for the business of setting up and marketing a practice. Forrest Mosten (Chapter 23, this volume) provides helpful advice on how to establish a profitable, full-time mediation practice.

Divorcing spouses are accustomed to having their health insurance pay for individual and marital counseling, and clients resignedly accept that legal fees may put them in debt. Mediation is rarely covered by insurance. Fees for mediation services range from free to $400+ per hour, depending upon the setting of the service. How can the same service vary so dramatically in cost? Some mediators have lamented that the free or low-cost community mediation services are taking away business and that courts that contract for services unfairly set fees below a market rate (Honeyman, 1995).

A few large self-insured corporations, such as Oscar Mayer, have offered employee benefit plans that cover the costs of divorce mediation services. These companies view mediation as an investment in employee productivity. Time would be well spent encouraging other large entities to support mediation services. Perhaps the mediation field could borrow a strategy from the arts community and encourage business and government to designate 1% of funding to be set aside for dispute resolution programs (Honeyman, 1995).

The other side of this critical issue is the lack of appreciable client demand. While the court-connected mediator is overwhelmed with court-ordered referrals for mediation, many agencies and private practitioners are underutilized. And, unlike McDonald's, there is not a lot of repeat business in divorce mediation.

Funding for court-connected mediation programs has generally come from tax revenue. Oregon initiated the dedication of filing fee increases for court mediation programs, and California as well as a number of other states followed suit (McIsaac, 1981) This "pot of gold" may become less of an annuity for these court programs as governments struggle with budget shortfalls and look to raid these funds. Staff cuts and consolidation and reduction of services have already penetrated court programs throughout the country (Milne & Salem, 2000).

Nearly all of the national organizations that serve family and divorce mediation members have received funding from the William and Flora Hewlett Foundation. The funding has supported these organizations' capacity-building efforts as well as individual projects, such as the design of a certification examination and increasing diversity in the field. As the Hewlett Foundation redirects its funds to areas other than dispute resolution, these membership organizations and other beneficiaries of these funds face the critical issue of finding new benefactors for the field. While this may seem like a remote concern to the individual practitioner, the work of these organizations is critical for the growth and sustenance of divorce mediation as a professional entity.

Public Education

Many divorcing individuals indicate that they want a dignified, fair, and co-operative divorce but do not connect the mediation process with those goals. The public needs to be educated about mediation—what it is, its benefits, and how it is different from other services. An individual mediator can help to educate the public and potential users of mediation services by appearing on programs, workshops, and media events and discussing the benefits of mediation and how it works. If nearly one out of every two marriages ends in divorce, then it could be said that wherever two people gather there are potential mediation clients.

Public education efforts must also be a priority for the field's national and local membership organizations. Market-building efforts have been lacking. Name-branding concepts, *de rigueur* for most businesses, have been absent in mediation—where the public still confuses mediation with *meditation.* A few organizations have initiated "Mediation Week" or "Mediation Month" projects (e.g., Wisconsin Association of Mediators; Florida Association of Professional Mediators), which could have a much broader application and could lead to a concerted, coordinated public education effort. Billboards, grocery store bags, basketball game marquees, movie theater preview trailers, public access cable TV, airplane banners, rock concerts à la Farm AID—the opportunities are endless. Given the enthusiasm that most divorce mediators have for the process, someone must have hit the MUTE button when it comes to public education. Not addressing this critical issue may well leave the field open to others who wish to claim the turf.

Professionalizing the Practice

Because divorce mediation practice is still relatively new and crosses traditional professional boundaries, there are interdisciplinary turf struggles concerning professional dominance: Debates over who can mediate, who should be certified, and what models of mediation should be practiced abound.

Questions of certification, licensure, and control of mediation training have yet to be answered. Should professional associations engage in training, accreditation, or certification? Will professional organizations of mediators perform a public-interest role or function as a guild to protect existing practitioners? Will the established organizations and leaders "colonize" development of the field by requiring only their approved trainings and ways of practicing (Landau, 2002)? The need to determine professional qualifications for divorce mediators, the establishment of a code of ethics, and the establishment of some form of regulatory control over the practice have been discussed since the early days of family mediation (Coogler, 1978; Crouch, 1982; Elkin, 1982; Folberg, 1982; Harbinson, 1981; Haynes, 1981; Milne, 1983a, 1983b; Silberman, 1981). These concerns center on the need to establish some form of quality control to protect both the consumer and the credibility of a developing profession (Milne, 1983a, 1983b).

Divorce mediators no longer have an association that speaks solely for their interests. The merger of the Academy of Family Mediators with two other more generic dispute resolution organizations has left the field of divorce mediation without an exclusive association identity and with decreased resources to carry out public and professional education efforts. The Association for Conflict Resolution has a broad mission to speak for its constituents under challenging times of decreased foundation support, a lagging economy, and national and international events that have turned away from cooperative dispute resolution practices and philosophy.

Other fields of practice, including collaborative law and traditional legal practices, are looking to establish or reestablish a place on the map. It is unlikely that divorce is going to go away. The question is, will the field of divorce mediation be able to address these and other critical issues in the future?

LOOKING FORWARD

The following chapters, written by the founders, leaders, and emerging stars of family and divorce mediation, address many of the issues raised here. Collectively they define the practice, provide a comprehensive view of our field, and foreshadow the future.

REFERENCES

Alfini, J., Press, S., Sternlight, J., & Stulberg, J. (2001). *Mediation theory and practice.* Charlottesville, VA: Lexis.

Association for Conflict Resolution Mission Statement. (2000). Available: *www.acrnet.org*

Bellman, H. S. (1998). Some reflections on the practice of mediation. *Negotiation Journal, 14*(3), 205–210.

Bohannon, P. (Ed.). (1970). *Divorce and after: An analysis of the emotional and social problems of divorce.* New York: Doubleday.

Boskey, J. (1995, March). Books in review. *Alternative Newsletter,* p. 1.

Brown, D. (1982). Divorce and family mediation: History, review, future directions. *Conciliation Courts Review, 20*(2), 1–44.

Brown, E. (1976). A model of the divorce process. *Conciliation Courts Review, 14*(2), 1–11.

Bush, B., & Folger, J. (1994). *The promise of mediation.* San Francisco: Jossey-Bass.

Chavez-Fallon, P. (2002, August). *Family court mediation: Respective roles and relationship of mediator and court.* Presentation at the meeting of the Association for Conflict Resolution, San Diego, CA.

Cohen, H. (1984). Mediation in divorce: Boon or bane? *Women's Advocate, 5*(2), 1–2.

Cohen, L. (1991). Mandatory mediation: A rose by any other name. *Mediation Quarterly, 9*(1), 33–46.

Cole, R., Rogers, N., & McEwen, C. (2001). *Mediation: Law, policy and practice.* St. Paul, MN: West.

Comeaux, E. (1983). A guide to implementing divorce mediation in the public sector. *Conciliation Courts Review, 21*(2), 1–25.

Coogler, O. J. (1978). *Structured mediation in divorce settlement: A handbook for marital mediators.* Lexington, MA: Heath.

Crouch, R. (1982). Mediation and divorce: The dark side is still unexplored. *Family Advocate, 4*(27), 33–35.

Currie, C. (2001, January). Transformation to what? Available: *www.mediate.com*

Dennis, D. (1994, Spring). The advantages of having mediators conduct custody evaluations. *Association of Family and Conciliation Courts Newsletter, 13*(6), 6.

Deutsch, M. (1973). *The resolution of conflict.* New Haven, CT: Yale University Press.

Elkin, M. (1982). Divorce mediation: An alternative process for helping families to close the book gently. *Conciliation Courts Review, 20*(1), iii–iv.

Ellman, I., Kurtz, P., & Scott, E. (1998). *Family law.* Charlottesville, VA: Lexis.

Elson, H. (1988). Divorce mediation in a law office setting. In J. Folberg & A. Milne (Eds.), *Divorce mediation: Theory and practice* (pp. 143–162). New York: Guilford Press.

Federico, J. (1979). The marital termination period of the divorce adjustment process. *Journal of Divorce, 3*(2), 93–106.

Folberg, J. (1982). Divorce mediation: A workable alternative. In J. Davidson, L. Ray, & R. Horowitz (Eds.), *Alternative means of family dispute resolution* (pp. 11–41). Washington, DC: American Bar Association.

Folberg, J. (1983). Divorce mediation: Promises and pitfalls. *The Advocate of Northwestern School of Law of Lewis & Clark College, 3*(1), 4–7.

Folberg, J. (1985). Mediation of child custody disputes. *Columbia Journal of Law and Social Problems, 19*(4), 1–36.

Folberg, J. (1988). Liability of divorce mediators. In J. Folberg & A. Milne (Eds.), *Divorce mediation: Theory and practice* (pp. 341–357). New York: Guilford Press.

Folberg, J. (2003). The continuing history of conflict resolution practice. *ACResolution, 2*(2), 13–15.

Folberg, J., & Milne, A. (Eds.). (1988). *Divorce mediation: Theory and practice.* New York: Guilford Press.

Folberg, J., & Taylor, A. (1984). *Mediation: A comprehensive guide to resolving conflicts without litigation.* San Francisco: Jossey-Bass.

Gold, L. (1992). *Between love and hate: A guide to a civilized divorce.* New York: Plenum Press.

Hanna, J. (2003). Beyond ACR: Partners with a common mission. *ACResolution, 2*(2), 21–25.

Harbinson, K. (1981). Family law–attorney mediation of marital disputes and conflict of interest considerations. *North Carolina Law Review, 60,* 171–184.

Haynes, J. (1981). *Divorce mediation: A practical guide for therapists and counselors.* New York: Springer.

Honeyman, C. (1995). *Financing dispute resolution.* (NIDR Report No. 1042). Washington, DC: National Institute for Dispute Resolution.

Johnston. J., & Roseby, V. (1997). *In the name of the child.* New York: Free Press.

Kaslow, F. (1979–1980). Stages of divorce: A psychological perspective. *Villanova Law Review, 25*(4–5), 718–751.

Kelly, J. (1983). Mediation and psychotherapy: Distinguishing the difference. *Mediation Quarterly, 1,* 33–44.

Kelly, J. (1991). Parent interaction after divorce: Comparison of mediated and adversarial divorce processes. *Behavioral Science and the Law, 9,* 387–398.

Kelly, J. (1995). Power imbalance in divorce and interpersonal mediation: Assessment and intervention. *Mediation Quarterly, 13*(2), 85–98.

Kessler, S. (1975). *The American way of divorce: Prescription for change.* Chicago: Nelson-Hall.

Kovach, K. K., & Love, P. L. (1996). "Evaluative" mediation is an oxymoron. *Alternatives to the High Costs of Litigation, 14,* 31–35.

Landau, B. (2002, January). Remarks: Ontario Bar Association, ADR Award of Excellence Dinner, Toronto, Canada.

Lande, J. (1997). How will lawyering and mediation practices transform each other? *Florida State University Law Review, 24,* 839–901.

Lemmon, J. (1985). *Family mediation practice.* New York: Free Press.

Linden, J. (2001). Mediation styles: The purists vs. the "toolkit." Available: *www.mediate.com*

McIsaac, H. (1981). Mandatory conciliation custody/visitation matters: California's bold stroke. *Conciliation Courts Review, 19*(2), 73–77.

McIsaac, H. (1985). Confidentiality: An exploration of issues. *Mediation Quarterly, 8,* 57–66.

Milne, A. (1981). *Divorce mediation: An overview of current approaches.* Paper presented at the winter meeting of the Association of Family and Conciliation Courts, Ft. Lauderdale, FL.

Milne, A. (1982). Divorce mediation: An idea whose time has come. *Wisconsin Journal of Family Law, 2*(2), 1–10.

Milne, A. (1983a). Divorce mediation: The state of the art. *Mediation Quarterly, 1,* 15–31.

Milne, A. (1983b). Divorce mediation: Shall we sanction the practice? In H. Davidson, L. Ray, & R. Horowitz (Eds.), *Alternative means of family dispute resolution* (pp. 1–8). Washington, DC: American Bar Association.

Milne, A. (1984). The development of parameters of practice for divorce mediation. *Mediation Quarterly, 4,* 49–59.

Milne, A. (1986). Divorce mediation: A process of self-definition and self-determination. In N. Jacobson & A. Gurman (Eds.), *Clinical handbook of marital therapy* (pp. 197–216). New York: Guilford Press.

Milne, A., & Folberg, J. (1988). The theory and practice of divorce mediation: An overview. In J. Folberg & A. Milne (Eds.), *Divorce mediation: Theory and practice* (pp. 3–25). New York: Guilford Press.

Milne, A., & Salem, P. (2000). *Report on capacity building for Connecticut support services division.* Unpublished manuscript.

Milne, A., & Schepard, A. (2002). Does your mediator measure up? *Family Advocate, 24*(4), 22–27.

Mnookin, R. (1985). Children, divorce and the legal system. *Columbia Journal of Law and Social Problems, 19*(4), 1–5.

Moore, C. (1996). *The mediation process.* San Francisco: Jossey-Bass.

Oregon State Bar Ethics Opinion. (July 1983). 488, *In re* Folberg.

Peace, N. (2003). Developing our own paradigm. *ACResolution, 2*(2), 2.

Pearson, J., Ring, M., & Milne, A. (1983). A portrait of divorce mediation services in the public and private sector. *Conciliation Courts Review, 21*(1), 1–24.

Pearson, J., & Thoennes, N. (1984). A preliminary portrait of client reactions to three court mediation programs. *Mediation Quarterly, 3,* 21–40.

Saposnek, D. (1983). *Mediating child custody disputes.* San Francisco: Jossey-Bass.

Schepard, A. (2000). Model standards of practice for family and divorce mediation. *Family Court Review, 39*(1), 121–134.

Shonholtz, R. (1984). Neighborhood justice systems: Work structure and guiding principles. *Mediation Quarterly, 5,* 3–30.

Silberman, L. (1981). Professional responsibility problems of divorce mediation. *Family Law Reporter, 7,* 4001–4012.

Silberman, L. (1988). Ethical constraints: A legal perspective. In J. Folberg & A. Milne (Eds.), *Divorce mediation: Theory and practice* (pp. 359–384). New York: Guilford Press.

Tondo, C., Coronel, R., & Drucker, B. (2001). Mediation trends: Survey of the states. *Family Court Review, 39*(4), 431–453.

Weiss, R. (1975). *Marital separation.* New York: Basic Books.

Wisemann, R. (1975). Crisis theory and the process of divorce. *Social Case Work, 56*(4), 205–212.

Zumeta, Z. (2000, Fall). Styles of mediation: Facilitative, evaluative, and transformative mediation. *National Association for Community Mediation Newsletter,* pp. 4–5, 8.

PART II
Models of Practice

CHAPTER 2

Facilitative Mediation

BERNARD MAYER

Facilitative mediation can be highly structured, very open ended, and either process or outcome oriented with an interventionist or passive mediator. Bernard Mayer offers a flexible
approach to facilitative mediation, suggesting that rigid adherence to any model is seldom
wise. This chapter examines definitions and characteristics as well as values and assumptions of facilitative mediation, challenges to facilitative mediation in family mediation, behaviors of facilitative mediators, and critiques of the facilitative process.

We mediators, like everybody else, seem to need labels to identify our approach to our work. These identifiers let the world know how we view ourselves, but they also have a way of limiting our thinking and constraining our
flexibility. Most of us who identify ourselves as *facilitative mediators* have chosen this descriptor (or had it applied to us by others) in order to distinguish
our approach from other styles of mediation and to place ourselves within a
broad category of approaches to its practice. But it is unlikely that we arrived
at this descriptor by consciously studying the concept of facilitation as it applies to mediation or by investigating the underlying assumptions or values
of this approach. Most of us came to facilitative mediation in quite the opposite way. That is, we looked at our own practice, identified what we do, what
we believe, and how we think, and then looked for an appropriate label to
distinguish our work from other approaches and decided that the facilitative
label was the most apt. In this sense *facilitative mediation* is more a description than a prescription, more a statement of values and goals than an articulation of a thoroughly formulated approach to mediation. Most of the mediation literature, and probably most practitioners, roughly fall within this
broadly defined category (e.g., Folberg & Taylor, 1984; Haynes, 1994; Moore,
1996). As a result, there are many different approaches to mediation that

could be loosely defined as facilitative. Some approaches are very structured, some very open ended, some more oriented toward outcome, others toward process, some more interventionist, others more passive. Facilitative mediators may focus on problem solving, dialogue, storytelling, or the potential for personal transformation.

What are the conceptual frameworks, values, assumptions, structure, and techniques of facilitative mediation? How does it look in practice, and how, in particular, does it work in family mediations? Can facilitative mediation be usefully distinguished from other approaches to mediation, and if so, how? In this chapter, I address these questions, raise some others, and suggest a framework for thinking about facilitative mediation and a range of practices that might fall within that framework.

I do not intend to suggest that there is a single approach to mediation that can be called *facilitative* or that there is a particular set of techniques or actions that reflect what "true" facilitative mediators do. Many approaches to mediation have the potential to assist families in dealing with their conflicts constructively. I believe that most effective mediators—whether they consider themselves to be transformative, evaluative, eclectic, or narrative mediators— are effective facilitators of a communication process as part of their work. In this sense they are facilitative mediators at least some of the time. So to some extent, we can think of facilitative mediation as the baseline approach out of which most practices of mediation have emerged. If mediators are not at all facilitative, they may not be providing mediation in the sense that most of us understand the concept. However, a clear set of values and assumptions characterize a facilitative approach to mediation. The more our work embodies these values and assumptions, the more accurate it is to describe ourselves as facilitative mediators.

WHAT IS FACILITATIVE MEDIATION?

Who invented the term "facilitative mediation" and what does it mean? In trying to describe what makes mediation work, Debra Kolb, in her classic work *The Mediators* (Kolb, 1983), broadly defined two types of mediators: the "deal-makers" and the "orchestrators." This is one of the first categorizations that suggests the approximate division we would later label *evaluative* and *facilitative. Orchestration* is a metaphor for what we can think of as facilitative mediation. It implies guiding people through a communication process in which the parties' voices, thoughts, feelings, and ideas are the important factors. The orchestrating mediator supplies the process that allows these voices to come together in an effective and harmonious way. Such a mediator does not attempt to persuade parties to accept an agreement that he or she has determined to be workable or fair. Compare this sketch to Lande's description of the difference between facilitative and evaluative mediation:

Mediators using a facilitative style focus on eliciting the principals' opinions and refrain from pressing their own opinions about preferable settlement options. Mediators using an evaluative style develop their own opinions about preferable settlement options and may try to influence principals to accept them. (Lande, 2000, pp. 322–323)

Leonard Riskin, who may have actually coined the term *facilitative mediation,* has developed a grid for classifying mediators' orientations (Riskin, 1994). The grid is based on whether a mediator takes a narrow or broad definition of the problem to be solved and whether the mediator defines his or her role as evaluative or facilitative. Riskin says that "the facilitative mediator assumes that his principal mission is to enhance and clarify communications between the parties in order to help them decide what to do" (p. 111). Interestingly, Riskin identifies broad differences in what facilitative mediators actually do. At the narrow end of the facilitative spectrum, mediators are more likely to focus on positions, help parties develop proposals, and ask parties to consider their alternatives. In a sense, narrow-based facilitative mediators, in Riskin's view, emphasize helping parties carry out their own evaluative, position-based process. At the broad end of the spectrum, mediators focus more on understanding the underlying interests of the parties, developing a range of options, and helping parties consider how to arrive at integrative solutions.

Most of the classic definitions of mediation include some reference to the mediator's facilitative role, even if the word is not used. Moore (1996) defines mediation as "the intervention in a negotiation or a conflict of an acceptable third party who has limited or no authoritative decision-making power but who assists the involved parties in voluntarily reaching a mutually acceptable settlement of issues in dispute" (p. 15). Folberg and Taylor (1984) say that mediation

can be defined as a process by which the participants, together with the assistance of a neutral person or persons, systematically isolate disputed issues in order to develop options, consider alternatives, and reach a consensual settlement that will accommodate their needs. Mediation is a process that emphasizes the participants' own responsibility for making decisions that affect their lives. (pp. 7–8)

Leeson and Johnston (1998) simply define mediation as "facilitated negotiation" in which "an impartial third party (the mediator) facilitates negotiations between disputants" (pp. 133–134, cited in Yard, 1999, p. 275). Brown (1997) defines comprehensive divorce mediation as a "facilitated decision-making process for couples whose relationship is ending or has ended, and who need help making decisions about financial matters, parenting arrangements, or other 'business aspects' of their relationship" (p. 37). These definitions of mediation are very similar to definitions of both fa-

cilitation and facilitative mediation. Schwarz (1994) defines group facilitation as

> a process in which a person acceptable to all members of the group, sub-
> stantively neutral, and has no decision-making authority, intervenes to help
> a group improve the way it identifies and solves problems and makes deci-
> sions, in order to increase the group's effectiveness. (p. 5)

Phillips (2001) describes facilitative mediation as being "free of advice"
and says that facilitative mediators' essential expertise is about the process
(p. 170).

In one of the clearest summaries of facilitative mediation, Zumeta
(2000) described it as an approach in which

> the mediator structures a process to assist the parties in reaching a mutu-
> ally agreeable resolution. The mediator asks questions, validates and nor-
> malizes parties' points of view; searches for interests underneath the posi-
> tions taken by parties; and assists the parties in finding and analyzing
> options for resolution. The facilitative mediator does not make recommen-
> dations to the parties, give his or her own advice or opinion as to the out-
> come of the case, or predict what a court would do in the case. The media-
> tor is in charge of the process, while the parties are in charge of the
> outcome. (p. 1)

FOUR HALLMARKS OF FACILITATIVE MEDIATION

When most authors define *mediation,* they are essentially describing what has
become labeled as *facilitative mediation.* Four elements seem to be present in
most definitions of facilitative mediation:

1. *Facilitative mediation is process oriented.* Facilitative mediators concentrate on the process of the interaction and do not present themselves as substantive experts even if they are. Furthermore, the facilitative mediator does
not focus on the most desirable outcome, the likely outcome should the case
be adjudicated, or any outcome at all. Instead the mediator conducts a process
to assist the parties in their own deliberations. Facilitative mediators may
make process recommendations (although there is a wide variety of practice in
this regard), but they do not make settlement or outcome recommendations—
at least, to the extent that they remain within a facilitative mode.

2. *Facilitative mediation is client centered.* Facilitative mediators may vary
in how passive or interventionist they are, but they all see their job as helping
the parties themselves do the hard work of understanding the issues, interests, options, and implications of their situation. The mediator's job is to
help clients be effective communicators and problem solvers. Furthermore,

in facilitative mediation, the clients are clearly in charge. They determine the purpose, approve the process, evaluate the issues and the information, generate options, consider the implications of those options, and decide how they wish to proceed. If attorneys are present, their role is to assist and advise the parties, not to conduct the negotiations for them. The facilitative mediator works with the attorneys to help them operate in this manner.

3. *Facilitative mediation is communication focused.* Facilitative mediators see their role as enabling an effective communication process among the parties. The ultimate goal is to help the parties find a way to communicate with each other about the concerns they have and the issues they wish to resolve. This focus often requires mediators to first establish effective communication between themselves and each of the parties. Occasionally it means restricting direct communication among the parties until they are ready to engage directly with each other in an effective way. There is no more important skill for a facilitative mediator than communication and no more central dynamic to address than how the parties communicate.

4. *Facilitative mediation is interest based.* Facilitative mediators are oriented towards helping clients examine their needs at an appropriate level of depth (Mayer, 2000, p. 207). They want to help the parties understand their own needs and concerns more clearly, as well as those of the other parties, and they work with parties to identify ways in which these needs can be adequately met. Mostly, facilitative mediators focus on the integrative (rather than the distributive) dimension of the conflict—that is, on how to identify options that will increase the degree to which all parties can obtain their goals (see Thomas, 1983; Walton & McKersie, 1980). However, facilitative mediators also help parties negotiate the distribution of limited resources when necessary. The way in which most facilitative mediators describe this approach, in keeping with the work of Fisher and Ury (1981), is as an interest-based focus in mediation.

These hallmarks of facilitative mediation are not all exclusive to the facilitative approach, and few mediators are completely facilitative at all times. However, the four general characteristics describe the essence of facilitative mediation. To the degree that mediators embrace these elements, they can be described as *facilitative mediators.*

CHALLENGES TO FACILITATIVE MEDIATION IN A FAMILY CONTEXT

What does it mean to be a facilitative mediator in a family mediation context? Few family mediators are purely facilitative in all cases, because the realities they face in helping families arrive at workable agreements pose many challenges to such an approach. The more mediators adhere to these hallmarks, however, the more they operate from a facilitative orientation.

Process versus Substance

To say that family mediators are process focused means that they see their role as creating a process that allows family members to address the issues that have brought them to mediation. Facilitative mediators do not take on the role of educators, option generators, advisors, or information providers. Instead, they help the participants assume these roles for themselves. The particular challenge here is that many family mediators have expertise in child development, family dynamics, child support guidelines, finances, tax laws, etc., and often parties to family disputes are very much in need of such information to make effective and informed decisions. A purely facilitative mediator, however, resists the temptation to fall into the roll of the educator or advisor, because to do so tends to undermine the focus on the process of interaction, communication, negotiation, and decision making that is his or her key responsibility. Once mediators begin to play the role of educator or expert, it can be very difficult for them to maintain their focus on process. Experts or educators tend to be more oriented toward providing information to families than to guiding them through their own decision-making process. Although it is possible to provide some education and still be facilitative, the more mediators drift into the role of the educator, the harder it is for them to remain focused on their role as facilitators.

Information versus Advice

Many facilitative mediators make the distinction between providing information and giving advice or making recommendations. For example, a mediator might explain how child support guidelines work or what the range of custody options might be in a particular jurisdiction without recommending what is appropriate or advisable in any particular situation. However, the line between information provision and advice giving is a subtle one. Once family members see the mediator as the source of information, his or her role as a process facilitator can quickly become undermined. The more mediators provide information, offer substantive advice, or correct misinformation, the more families will look to the mediator for such assistance. Although this dynamic may be very helpful in crafting workable agreements, such interventions tend to draw mediators away from their focus on process and into a focus on content.

Facilitative mediators see their responsibility more as one of helping parents identify the information they need to make informed decisions and consider how they might obtain it rather than acting as the primary providers of that information. The substantive expertise of family mediators helps them ask useful questions, frame issues in a constructive and meaningful way, and suggest areas that their clients may want to consider. For example, inquiring whether parents understand child support guidelines or the implications of different custodial arrangements suggests that these are important areas about which parents should be knowledgeable. Discussing with them possible sources of information and directing them to these sources is a second key approach. Many mediators maintain a library that parents can use to become informed. Often, parents have much of this information already, and by conducting a discussion between them, the mediator can help them inform each other and discover what they themselves already know. Raising the question of when and how parties wish to consult their attorneys or other advisors is also important. Many mediators recommend, sometimes quite adamantly, that divorcing clients consult their attorneys before committing to an agreement. This recommendation is, in itself, a deviation from a strictly facilitative approach, but it does address concerns many mediators have about the provision of legal or financial information. Clients are usually somewhat aware of the information they need and where they might get it. Often the most important action a mediator can take is to help structure the mediation sessions in such a way that clients have the opportunity to become informed before they commit to certain agreements that are information sensitive.

Communication

Family mediation presents a particular challenge to the mediator with regard to focusing on communication. Often the mediator is faced with couples who have communicated intensely in the past, have experienced severely disrupted communication as a result of the breakup of their relationship, and now need to reestablish better communication if they are to cooperate successfully in the parenting of their children. A facilitative mediator attends to how family members can constructively communicate with each other, given the history of their relationship and the intensity of their conflict. Helping parents to articulate their concerns and hopes and to genuinely listen to and understand each other are central to effective family mediation for a facilitative mediator. If there is no way to establish effective and productive communication, then facilitative mediation may not be appropriate.

Staying Family Focused

To work in a *family-focused* manner means that the mediator helps the parents (or other involved family members) identify the issues they wish to discuss, obtain and digest the needed information, discuss their own concerns, and generate options they wish to consider themselves. Most importantly, it means that the mediator assumes that the parents are the most equipped agents to make good decisions about the needs of their children. In divorce, the state suddenly becomes involved in decisions that otherwise are the prerogative of the family. The facilitative mediator's goal is to give that power back to the family, to the greatest extent possible, and within certain ethical limitations. This goal means that even if parents want to make child-rearing decisions with which the facilitative mediator does not personally agree, his or her job is not to interfere. The parents are the center of the decision-making process, not the mediator. Nor are attorneys normally central to this process; they may have a critical role to play, but it is as advisors and technical assistants, not as chief negotiators.

This stance of noninterference poses an emotional and occasionally an ethical challenge to the mediator. What if parents are agreeing to an arrangement that does not seem optimal for the child—too much back and forth, too elaborate a visitation schedule, not enough time with one of the parents, or disruption to the child's schooling? Does the mediator raise his or her concerns, offer other suggestions, ask questions that are designed to expose the problems such an arrangement may raise, or offer explicit advice against the agreement? Of course, certain extreme circumstances pose ethical demands on even the most facilitative of mediators (e.g., agreements that would allow for the neglect of a child). Short of these obvious situations, the facilitative mediator maintains a focus on ensuring that both parents have articulated their issues, evaluated their options, and arrived at a genuine agreement that they are prepared to enact. Most mediators ask questions that help parents consider the implications of their agreements, for example: "What is the impact of that parenting schedule likely to be on your ability to establish a parenting routine with your child?" or "Do you think your child will be able to understand this schedule, and do you think it is important that [he or she] be able to understand it?" This kind of questioning can be very effective. Still, the more mediators focus on raising their own concerns in this way, the less they will be focused on helping parents articulate their needs and views, and ultimately the less facilitative their contribution.

Sometimes parents agree to something that is unrealistic, illegal, or unethical. This is where a purely facilitative approach can break down. What happens, for example, if parents agree to waive child support? Mediators are not doing families or children a service by letting such agreements pass in the name of maintaining a facilitative approach. However, how they raise the issue with the parents can vary greatly. To the extent that mediators handle this situation by informing parents that what they are proposing is not legal or will not be acceptable to a court, they are opting out of a facilitative approach. Often, the same purpose can be accomplished by asking parents thought-provoking questions, by raising concerns that the parents should check out, or by bringing experts into the mediation process. Few family mediators, even those operating from a facilitative perspective, are likely to knowingly allow an illegal or unethical agreement to pass unchallenged. The critical question is *how* the mediator raises his or her concerns about such an agreement.

Perhaps the biggest challenge to the facilitative approach is any indica-

tion of domestic violence. Most mediators understand the critical importance of screening for domestic violence and ensuring that the mediation
process does not contribute to the cycle of violence or further endanger victims. Admittedly, it is difficult to accomplish this goal from within a purely
facilitative stance. Nevertheless, it is here that the underlying values of
facilitative mediation are particularly important. Mediators must screen for
domestic violence, assess the appropriateness of mediation, and proceed accordingly. This does not mean that the mediator suddenly takes over the proceedings, however, and assumes an authoritarian role. Victims of domestic
violence can feel easily disempowered by well-meaning professionals who
think they know what is best. Instead, facilitative mediators conduct this
screening and assessment process in partnership with the parties (although
generally in individual meetings), and they decide how to proceed in a similar manner. If a victim or potential victim wants to proceed with mediation
against the mediator's best judgment, the mediator may have to make a difficult and independent decision, but such an action is normally the last resort
for how to deal with this situation. Of course, regardless of mediators' orientation to their work, they are obligated by statute and codes of ethics to
report child abuse and to provide appropriate warnings when they have
information that someone may be physically endangered.

From Positions to Interests

Parents enter mediation with ideas, options, demands, proposals, positions,
and requirements. Facilitative mediators (particularly those who operate
from a broader definition of the issues, to use Riskin's [1994] typology) dig
for the underlying interests or needs that these proposals represent. Most
facilitative mediators want parents who have proposed a particular parenting
agreement to explain what this arrangement is intended to accomplish: how
it will meet their needs as divorced parents and the children's needs. The
challenge is that parents tend to identify the issues that need to be decided
as distributive in nature; that is, they see their task as claiming the most they
can for themselves from what is perceived to be a limited amount of available
resources. Parents often define parenting arrangements as if they were a matter of dividing up a fixed amount of parenting time between them. There is
only so much time in the week, and whatever time one parent has with a
child, the other will *not* have. When parents are struggling over dividing a
limited amount of time, they are likely to disagree, to take a rigidly positional
stance, and to act heavy-handedly in how they try to exert their power. This is
also the case when they are struggling over what they perceive to be a limited
amount of financial resources or assets.

   Of course, time and resources are not unlimited, but such an emphasis is
not usually the most productive way of approaching these issues. A more
productive question to pose about parenting time, for example, is to ask each

parent what kind of needs the child has and how these needs can best be met. When divorcing parents remember that there is a very strong *integrative* aspect to rearing children—that in most circumstances the child needs both parents as well as their cooperation and mutual participation—then a very different type of discussion can take place. Likewise, when parents start focusing on how they can work together to provide for the financial needs and future of their children, a different conversation ensues as well. Although it is not always possible to create this kind of dialogue, facilitative mediators strive to create the framework that will allow an integrative view to develop to the greatest extent possible or practical. They do this by focusing on the essential interests or needs of the parents and on the parents' understanding of the needs of their children. According to Macfarlane (1999):

> Interests are the essence of the mediation alternative. . . . A focus on interests reflects a complex set of values about how we understand disputes and how best to resolve them. These values can be contrasted with the assumptions underpinning the adjudicative rights model of dispute resolution. . . . Instead of assuming that conflict must have arisen over incompatible ethical positions, an interests-based approach to dispute resolution challenges the parties to consider whether their conflict is really over the sharing of resources in which they have a common interest. . . . Mediation is much more than simply the introduction of a non-partisan third party into disputing contexts; it represents a paradigm shift in how disputants think about the resolution of their conflict. (p. 259)

Facilitative mediators are not passive mediators who remain emotionally uninvolved. Indeed, they exert considerable influence, just as do all types of mediators. But their energy is guided by the overarching commitment to conducting a *process*, promoting effective *communication*, creating a framework that *empowers* the parties to take control over their lives, and focusing parties on the most salient interests and concerns affecting them *and* their children. They do not take on the role of substantive experts, deal makers, advisors, or evaluators. Why? What are the underlying values and presumptions that motivate this type of mediator to act from a facilitative stance?

VALUES AND ASSUMPTIONS OF FACILITATIVE MEDIATION

Facilitative mediation operates from the assumption that the parties themselves are the ones who are best able to make decisions and arrive at productive resolutions to their disagreements. The mediator's role is to provide a forum and process that allows them to accomplish these goals. In particular, facilitative family mediators believe that families should be empowered to make the decisions that govern family life and that the help they need to do so is more procedural than substantive in nature. Following are some of the values and assumptions that facilitative family mediators make (although other types of mediators may share some of these as well):

- Parents are the most equipped to decide what is in their children's interests.
- The self-determination of the parties should be preserved to the maximum extent possible.
- Families coming to mediation need help communicating more than they need the mediator to provide substantive advice or information.
- Empowering people to make decisions for themselves is a worthwhile social goal.
- Plenty of experts, relatives, and friends are usually available to advise families about what they should do, but very few opportunities or forums exist to help parents communicate directly and responsibly with each other.
- Voluntarily and freely arrived at agreements are more powerful, durable, and effective than those that are attained under pressure or by way of deference to the opinion of experts.
- Good process leads to good communication.
- Good communication leads to good agreements.
- Even when people are upset, distrustful, angry, or grieving, they can still be helped to communicate with each other effectively and constructively.
- The issues that are on the table in family mediation ought not to be decided simply by reference to legal standards or court practices but on the basis of the specific needs and concerns of each individual family (although they should not violate legal standards either).
- There are effective and appropriate ways for dealing with power inequities in mediation. The best way for a mediator to deal with power inequities is not to act as an advocate or power broker but to arrange for a process that allows for effective communication, access to important information, and when necessary, the support of advocates other than the mediator.

These values often rest on a generally unarticulated assumption about the nature of democracy and the role of conflict and adjudication within a democracy. Facilitative mediators may not always be aware of the societal implications of their values. Nevertheless, these values are closely related to a desire many mediators have to deepen the nature of democracy. Facilitative mediators strive to empower families to be able to make tough decisions under difficult circumstances. Adjudicatory systems are necessary when people cannot make these decisions or when one party exercises oppressive power over the other. However, if every time a family experienced a crisis, the state stepped in to make decisions (or professionals empowered by the state took over that role), or if families were encouraged to rely on outside experts to recommend the best decisions to them, as opposed to supporting the families in making their own best decision, then democracy would be weakened and possibly eroded.

The deeper roots underlying the values of facilitative mediation, however, need not override the essential role that facilitative mediators assume when they enter into a case. The goal of facilitative mediators is to help parties work their way through a conflict constructively by orchestrating an effective communication and problem-solving process among the parties. If mediators attend to this task as their first and foremost goal, then the value of deepening democracy, empowering families, and broadening our societal understanding of how conflicts can be handled will follow over time.

WHAT DO FACILITATIVE MEDIATORS DO?

Facilitative mediation does not require following a particular set of steps or stages so much as employing a way of thinking about mediation and conflict resolution. Many works on mediation have outlined the stages that mediators tend to follow (Moore, 1996; Folberg & Taylor, 1984; Haynes, 1994; CDR Associates, 1986), and these stages or steps are often, in fact, how the process proceeds. Nevertheless, facilitative mediation is not about following a particular template or set of procedures. Instead it may be more useful to consider the tasks that need to be accomplished and the tools used to accomplish them.

Setting the Stage

How mediation begins and the arena in which it is conducted are critical to the creation of a facilitative atmosphere. At the very outset the mediator faces several key tasks to accomplish:

- Determining the appropriateness of mediation
- Clarifying the goals of mediation
- Defining roles
- Building rapport

Determining the Appropriateness of Mediation

The first question to consider is whether mediation should occur at all. Who should assess this and how should it be decided? The mediator has an ethical obligation to ascertain whether mediation is appropriate, whether it is safe, whether parties should be brought together in the same room, and who ought to be at the table. But these assessments can be conducted in a number of significantly different ways. To begin with, selling people on the advantages of mediation or trying to convince them to utilize mediation is not really consistent with a facilitative approach. Instead, the facilitative mediator informs potential clients about how mediation works, answers their questions, and helps them think through whether it is the right approach for them. Of course, in some settings (e.g., court-based mediation programs) divorcing parents may not have a choice as to whether to engage in mediation. Most facilitative mediators handle this absence of choice by giving clients plenty of opportunity to voice their concerns about mediation and discontinue the process if they do not want to proceed. When facilitative mediators believe that mediation is not advisable, they generally discuss their concerns with their clients and, unless there is an ethical problem with continuing, the decision as to whether to proceed remains with the parties.

Clarifying the Goals of Mediation

Often the nature of a mediation is determined by how the goals for mediation are defined. Bush and Folger (1994) suggest that mediators have a tendency to assume that the most important goals of mediation clients involve arriving at an agreement of some sort, and they discuss how this assumption can become a self-fulfilling prophecy. Facilitative mediation makes no supposition about what parties want or need to accomplish, other than that of communicating about the issues that have brought them to mediation. Arriving at a clear understanding of the purpose of a mediation is not always an easy task, and the goals parties set can change as mediation progresses. Nonetheless, it is the parties' task to define their own goals, not the mediator's. Although most people come to family mediators because they want to work out an agreement about parenting and financial issues, this is not always the case. Some parents may simply need help in discussing their situation and may want assistance in communicating with the other parent, even though they have no need or desire to arrive at an agreement or change an existing agreement.

Defining Roles

Similarly, how mediators define their role and describe the process is key to establishing a facilitative context. Facilitative mediators normally identify their role in terms of the four hallmarks of facilitative mediation. They explain their role as neutral agents who help parents communicate with each other about the issues and concerns they wish to discuss but who do not act as substantive experts or advisors. They also present their intention to help people explore their interests and the various choices that they face. If this role and process description works for the parties, then the stage has been set for a facilitative process to begin. Often, however, parties come to the table expecting something different from mediation. They may want substan-

tive advice, an explanation of their options, help with structuring a complicated financial agreement, or assistance in convincing the other side to
behave more flexibly. What usually ensues is a sort of negotiation (prefera-
bly, interest based) between the mediator and clients about exactly how the
process will look. Facilitative mediators are flexible, but they are not without
parameters.

Building Rapport

Key to all forms of mediation are the trust and rapport that the mediator is
able to establish with the parties. How trust is built between a mediator and
two or more parties who generally have little trust in one another is actually
quite subtle and one of the genuine arts to the practice of mediation. No
matter what type of mediation is practiced, the use of self, the projection of
competence, evenhandedness, consistency, follow-through, and empathy are
critical to the development of a safe and productive atmosphere. The mediator must be skilled in dealing with the common presumption that someone
who is attentive and empathic with one side in a conflict cannot also be attentive and empathic with the other side. In other words, the mediator has to
contend with the belief that "my enemy's friend is my enemy." Instead, all
mediators must attempt to help their clients understand that "because the
mediator is my 'friend,' he or she must also be my opponent's 'friend.' "
   Facilitative mediators have the additional challenge of developing trust
without relying on a demonstration of their substantive expertise. *Process* is a
subtle concept that many find difficult to grasp. Generally, parties come to
divorce mediation wanting to know that the mediator understands the issues
involved in divorce proceedings and also wanting to know the mediator's orientation to those issues. Facilitative mediators need to understand these basic divorce-related issues and to know both the regulatory and psychological
framework within which divorce negotiations proceed, as well as the needs
of children in divorce. However, if they rely on too overt a demonstration of
this knowledge (e.g., through elaborate discussions of the legal or child development aspects of divorce) or discuss their own views about what constitutes a fair divorce agreement, then it is likely they will lose their facilitative
focus.
   Most mediators do not take a purist view in this area and are willing to
discuss some of these substantive issues. If this shift in focus is not done in a
measured way, however, the mediator can easily turn into an advisor, coach,
or substantive expert and thereby lose his or her crucial facilitative function.
Facilitative mediators are confronted with the challenge of establishing their
foundational knowledge but explaining their role as process guides to parties
who may not understand this concept very clearly. Facilitative mediators establish trust by showing the parties that they can (1) help them examine the

issues in a productive way, (2) guide them through a tricky substantive process without functioning as the source of all information and education, and (3) accomplish both tasks without taking sides or acting as an advocate. In the early stages of the process, the facilitative mediator must especially rely on his or her ability to connect with each party, establish rapport, and explain the process in terms that make sense to both participants.

Helping People Tell Their Story

At some point in family mediation, people usually need to tell their story. If people do not tell their story, the context for problem solving does not get clearly established and the emotional and cognitive aspects of the situation are not be expressed, understood, or addressed (Mayer, 2000). An important part of a mediator's work involves setting the framework for this storytelling to occur and guiding parties through this process. The mediator faces the question of whether people need to tell their story directly to each other or whether it is better to discuss it with the mediator alone, at least as a preliminary step. As much as facilitative mediators want to help parties communicate directly with each other, they also must recognize that sometimes people are afraid (often, with good reason) to tell their story in front of the other party(ies). Or they may be too upset or angry to tell their story in a way that the other party is likely to be willing to listen to—and they may not be prepared to listen to the stories that others have to tell. Sometimes, in order to give people the opportunity they need to tell their story, mediators choose to work with the parties separately, at least in the beginning. Facilitative mediators want to help parties listen to each other's stories with an open mind and to respond honestly but constructively. This often requires individual work, preparation, coaching, and ground rules.

Often mediators think that storytelling should occur first, after the contractual aspects are completed, and often this is the case. Frequently, however, the storytelling process has to emerge over time through the course of mediation. Sometimes the key elements of the story do not surface until after some initial problem solving, information gathering, and issue framing have occurred. Occasionally, the real storytelling may not occur until almost all aspects of the parenting plan and financial arrangements have been completed. Only then do some parties feel safe enough or emotionally ready to discuss how they view the situation that led them to the divorce and what their deepest hopes and fears for the future are. Of course, in many divorce mediations, this level of storytelling never occurs (or never ends!). The absence of storytelling does not mean that the mediation was a failure or that the agreements reached did not have integrity, but it is a sign that the mediation process only dealt with one dimension of the conflict.

Identifying Issues and Interests

Often, mediators seek to identify the issues and understand the interests of the parties very early in the mediation process. Taking this approach may be appropriate, but, as with storytelling, issues and interests are likely to continue to emerge throughout the mediation. Facilitative mediators are always seeking to understand the issues from the point of view of the parties, to frame these issues in a genuine, meaningful, and constructive manner, and to find a formulation of the issues that all parties can accept. For example, if one parent articulates an issue as "wanting more time with my children" and the other parent sees it as "not wanting to disrupt the children's lives more than necessary," then the mediator has at least two tasks to accomplish. First, the underlying meaning of this issue to each parent must be understood at least enough so that the real concerns of the parent are on the table. Second, the issue must be articulated or reframed in a way that makes it possible for the parents to talk about it with each other. The facilitative mediator does not necessarily sit back, listen to the discussion, and produce a beautifully reframed issue formulation that the parties gratefully accept. Reframing is an interactive, iterative, and sometimes messy process that evolves throughout the mediation.

The mediator is always listening for the interests or needs that are motivating parties and seeking to put these on the table in a constructive way. Here mediators contend with two potential dangers: They can fail to probe deeply enough, or they can go too deep—beyond where the parties are willing or needing to go. If the mediator does not ask the first parent in the above example to say more about the kind of time he or she wants to spend with the children, then the real concerns may not emerge and the discussion will not focus on what is genuinely important to that parent. Perhaps the issue really is about the overall amount of time, but it could also be about the type of time, the frequency of contact, the length of any given contact, the connection with school, or the ability to participate in certain activities with the children. So exploring each parent's interests further is essential, and finding a way to put those interests on the table is critical.

Underneath any interest are always other interests, and under these, still others. Where to go and where not to go are decisions that mediators make continually. Returning to the parent who wants more frequent contact with the children, the first probe may elicit the first layer of motivation—for example, to keep up with their schoolwork, maintain a sense of continuity, and be part of their development. Probing deeper, it may turn out that this parent grew up with an absent parent and does not want to repeat that experience with his or her own children. To go deeper still and explore the nature of those needs the parent has for not wanting to repeat that experience may be going too far. As with reframing, eliciting reasons for a particular interest is not something that the mediator sits back and decides alone, but rather does so in partnership with the parties to the mediation.

One of the dilemmas faced by mediators is that not all interests are "nice" or constructive. Parents may have an interest in limiting each other's contact, in gaining revenge, in staying involved in the other's life, and so forth. Sometimes, it is best to leave some of these interests alone, but at other times it is critical to find some way of putting them on the table or the real issues will never get aired. Underneath the second parent's concern for minimizing disruption to the children may be a concern that the other parent is a bad influence, not skilled in dealing with the children, or prone to making poor decisions about what activities are appropriate for the children. Finding a way to raise these difficult concerns for discussion may be critical to dealing with the issues with which the parents are struggling. This is one of the many ways in which facilitative mediation requires very active involvement of the mediator and involves what Cloke (2001) calls "mediating dangerously."

Facilitating Communication

Almost everything that a facilitative mediator does is about facilitating communication. Hence the mediator must be an excellent listener (the most overtalked-about and underdeveloped skill of human relations professionals), a skilled reframer, and an effective communication coach. The real art is in helping people in conflict communicate effectively with each other. Often this means that the mediator first has to establish effective communication with each of the parties and then use the rapport and understanding gained through this process to enable them to communicate more directly with each other. Knowing when to direct the parties toward each other is another key art in the practice of facilitative mediation. At some point the mediator has to get out of the middle position, but he or she must first set the stage for effective communication. Sometimes people are able to discuss issues almost immediately, sometimes it takes a great deal of work before they are ready for it, and sometimes it never happens.

As noted, a key task of mediators is to help people express their concerns, articulate their needs, and give voice to their feelings in a way that is both powerful and constructive. A second key task is to help people listen to each other. A third is to help people respond to what they have heard in an honest and constructive way. There are many techniques that mediators can use to accomplish these tasks: reflective listening, rehearsing specific communication with people, asking them to paraphrase, providing feedback on their communication, as well as simply letting the communication flow. The salient focus for the mediator tends to be less the technique than the awareness of the importance of enhancing the flow of communication between the parties. As with all aspects of facilitative mediation, facilitating dialogue is something the mediator does *with* the parties, not *to* them—they are the best allies the mediator has in overcoming the obstacles to communication that they themselves may present.

Gathering Information

If parties do not have the essential information they need to make wise decisions, they cannot be truly empowered. One of the challenges for facilitative mediators is to help parties become informed without losing their process-focused role. Family mediators face a challenging question when they consider whether they can or should provide their clients with needed information in the course of mediation. For example, should they provide information about the needs of children, the tax implications of options under consideration, the different ways in which custody or parenting agreements can be reached, or the ways in which a retirement account can be handled? Parties often want this information, do not want to pay additional fees to lawyers, accountants, or child development experts to get it when they know that mediators can provide it, and are willing to accept this information without placing the mediator in the role of decision maker. Yet the more mediators take on the role of information provider, the less able they will be to focus on process, communication, and the other tasks that are essential to the facilitative mediator's task. This is a matter of degree and judgment. Too rigid an insistence on not being the information provider is probably counterproductive, but falling into this role to too great a degree can disempower clients and interfere with the communication process.

Dealing with Impasse

Facilitative mediators are often put to the test when parties appear to be deadlocked or at an impasse. This is when it is most tempting to offer an evaluation of the likely alternatives should resolution not be reached, or suggestions and advice, or to turn up the pressure. I do not mean to suggest that such interventions are never advisable, but to the extent that mediators employ them, they are deviating from a facilitative approach. The facilitative mediator has several essential tools available when parties appear to be at an impasse. First and foremost, the mediator can remain patient, calm, and persistent. Projecting confidence and ease is often the greatest gift we can give to people who feel stuck. Second, the mediator can find a constructive formulation of the problem, give it back to the parties, and then help them work on it. Articulating the interests or concerns that have led the parties to their blocked position and putting these on the table are often useful interventions as well. Paradoxically, giving parties permission to be at an impasse and urging them not to move off their position until they are clear that their concerns are being adequately addressed can also help. Enlarging the issue, narrowing the issue, breaking the problem down into a variety of different issues, asking people to evaluate their choices, giving them an opportunity to consult advisors, obtaining more information, bringing in other parties, and addressing the possibility that mediation is not the best way for people to get their needs met are all alternatives that facilitative mediators may choose to use. Approaches to impasse (e.g., providing evaluative comments, confronting parties about their behavior, or offering suggestions about solutions to their differences) that fall outside the facilitative framework may be warranted at times, but they are frequently less effective than mediators might think.

Solidifying Agreements

Facilitative mediators do more than guide a communication process. They help people craft and arrive at agreements, then nail them down. These are areas, however, in which it is easy to lose the facilitative focus and start taking the process away from the clients. Mediators are often tempted, as agreements are committed to writing, to start crafting them in a way that inserts their ideas into a document. Most mediators have done this at one time or another; sometimes doing so can help parties come to closure. But to the degree that mediators rely on this approach, they are deviating from a facilitative framework. Ideally, facilitative mediators use the drafting of an agreement to try to capture the meaning of the understandings that have been arrived at during the course of mediation and to use the actual concepts—and, when possible, the actual words—of the parties. Often, it is helpful early in mediation and throughout the process to put in writing the agreements people have reached as they reach them, even if these are very general or procedural in nature. When people work from a document, they often are able to communicate or process issues in a very different, and sometimes more constructive, way then when they are engaging in verbal interchanges. This is the concept behind the single text negotiating documents proposed by Fisher and Ury (1981) and a variety of other techniques for conceptualizing issues and potential avenues of resolution in writing. Of course, it is important not to let this approach interfere with people's need to communicate verbally with each other. Likewise, using such an approach to drive parties toward a premature or inappropriate focus on outcomes should be avoided.

Agreements can be reached or articulated at any time during the mediation process. Indeed, sometimes very important agreements are reached early in the process. Mediators try to help parties recognize when they have agreed upon something—when an agreement is implied by what has been said and which avenues for resolution have been suggested. Mediators also work to gain the parties' acknowledgment of agreements that have, in fact, been reached. Often facilitative mediators help parties engage in their own analysis of what has been agreed to, what the outstanding issues are, and what avenues for resolution might be productive. Another technique that mediators use is that of "successive reframing" (Mayer, 2000), a process of framing an issue in a tighter and tighter way, based on the parties' discussions, until an agreement emerges. For example, an initial framing of a parenting issue may be how much time the children will be spending with each parent. Upon further discussion, the issue may become one of how to allocate an approximately equal time division so that the children spend both weekend and weekday time in each parent's home. Upon still further discussion, the issue emerges in terms of how to minimize the number of times the children must pass back and forth between the two homes, while at the same time ensuring that they do not go for too long a period without seeing one of the parents. After each reframing, the issue becomes more tightly formulated and the outlines of an agreement more clearly defined. Mediators also try to make sure that agreements are specified to the degree necessary to ensure that everyone understands the nature of the agreement and how it is to be implemented.

Although facilitative mediators emphasize the integrative aspects of disputes, at some point in most negotiations, it is necessary to look at the distributive aspects of the conflict as well. This point is reached when the integrative potential has been utilized as far as possible or when the parties really feel the need to focus on the distributive aspects (in the parlance of some conflict theorists, the place where *Pareto optimality* [that is, the point at which no further gain can be achieved for one party other than by diminishing the benefits to another] is being approached [Lax & Sebenius, 1986]). For example, as much as parents may benefit from a discussion of creative parenting arrangements, time schedules, holidays, and vacations, at some point they may disagree about how many days each week the children should be with each of them. Perhaps a thoroughgoing discussion of the relevant interests and principles has already occurred, and it has come down to a difference in what each of them wants and feels is acceptable. This is yet another point where it is tempting (and, again, sometimes helpful) to offer evaluative comments, to suggest a compromise, or to turn up the pressure on each of the parties. However, there are facilitative approaches to this situation as well.

The mediator can employ many of the same approaches relevant to impasses, because at this juncture the process can again reach such a point. The mediator can also find a constructive way to put the distributive nature of the problem on the table. It is often helpful to redefine the issue from that of a single issue to multiple issues. For example, parents may define a disagreement as being about how many school days per week the children are in each of their homes, but this issue can often be expanded to include consideration about the duration of the agreement, the possibility of different arrangements for different children, or how the agreement might change over time. The question then becomes what arrangements should they agree to now, for each child, and when might these be revisited using what criteria? Most issues can be broken apart, opening up the possibility for new consideration of the parents' interests, new attempts to look for exchanges, and new principles of agreement. Often parents can agree on the overriding principles that should govern the decision but disagree on how to apply these to a particular situation. Sometimes people can agree on a process for arriving at an agreement, even if they cannot agree on the agreement itself (e.g., referral to a third party, application of a set of criteria, or use of a decision-making tree). Sometimes, out-and-out compromise is necessary, and the mediator can certainly raise this possibility with the parties without abandoning a facilitative stance. Suggesting to parties that they may have reached the point at which compromise is necessary if an agreement is to be struck is not, in itself, a contradiction to a facilitative approach. However, the mediator starts to deviate from this framework when he or she pressures parties to compromise or takes responsibility for suggesting what a reasonable compromise might be.

CRITIQUES OF FACILITATIVE MEDIATION

Although facilitative mediation has long been identified as the baseline approach of most mediators (or perhaps *because* it has been identified in that way), it has been criticized from a number of angles. Perhaps the two most cogent criticisms have come from the opposite ends of the continuum. Proponents or defenders of a more evaluative approach have suggested that facilitative mediators often fail to provide parties with information they need or an awareness of the legal alternatives that might be open to them. Some critics have suggested that a facilitative approach can, in fact, serve to disempower people and exacerbate the power differential between parties (e.g., Hart, 1990; Lerman, Kuehl, & Brygger, 1989). They point to the critique of family mediation by women's advocates who are concerned that mediation may further disempower women because structural sources of inequality are actually increased in the absence of strong advocates. The most thorough critique from this perspective has been offered by Stempel (2000), who is particularly concerned that the evaluative–facilitative debate presents a false dichotomy that leads to an "almost evangelical view that there is but one 'true way' of practicing mediation" (p. 248). He goes on to argue that "even in the most facilitative of mediations, disputants should ordinarily come to a resolution with at least a rudimentary knowledge of their options under the legal regime outside mediation" (Stempel, 2000, p. 248).

In a response to Stempel's critique, Lande (2000) has pointed out that although there are overly zealous advocates of purely facilitative mediation, the debate has been important and useful. He also says that the advantages of a facilitative approach should not be overlooked:

> Facilitation by mediators emphasizes the principals' abilities to do their own critical evaluation and creative problem-solving. While this may not be the best approach for every person in every problem that is mediated, mediation truly offers a distinctive opportunity for parties to exercise responsibility over their own disputes and their own lives. This is an important so-

cial value that other dispute resolution processes generally do not
promote. (Lande, 2000, p. 325)

Lande (2000) also points out that evaluative approaches to mediation do not
necessarily counteract the possibility that the less powerful party is at a disadvantage, because the evaluation may, in fact, tend to side with the stronger
party. Despite whatever flaws there may be in Stempel's critique, there is no
question that he raises important points and gives voice to concerns many people have about mediation, in general, and facilitative mediation, in particular.
There is no one correct, true, or right approach to mediation. Different circumstances and different clients require different approaches, and no one
owns the copyright on any mediation approach. Furthermore, the overly rigid
application of any one approach is problematic, at best, and likely to represent
a case of the mediator putting his or her needs before those of the parties.
However, there are consequences to the decisions that we make about which
approach to take, and it is important for mediators to consider these. Furthermore, many mediators give lip service to a facilitative approach but deviate
from it the moment the road to resolution becomes bumpy.

A second major critique comes from those who feel that what normally
passes for facilitative mediation is really not, because it is more focused on
achieving an outcome than on empowering the clients. The most important
articulation of this point of view is by Bush and Folger (1994) and their associates, who are proponents of a transformative approach (see Bush & Pope,
Chapter 3, this volume). They believe that by focusing on the satisfaction of
client interests, mediators inevitably become focused on outcomes and
thereby fail to achieve the transformative potential of mediation. Although
many people have taken issue with this criticism (cf. Williams, 1997), there is
no doubt that many facilitative mediators have been lured away from the
facilitative approach by pushing too hard for an agreement or by automatically assuming that what clients want from mediation is to achieve a
particular kind of outcome.

I believe it would go against the spirit of the facilitative approach to mediation to become defensive, rigid, or reflexively critical in response to these
arguments. There is some truth in all of them, and it can only help mediators improve their thinking—and therefore their practice—if they take these
concerns seriously and consider how to address them.

CONCLUSION: A FLEXIBLE APPROACH TO FACILITATIVE MEDIATION

This chapter has both described the facilitative approach to family mediation
and emphasized that it is not the only valid approach. It is doubtful that most
mediators, even those who identify themselves with this method, follow a

strictly facilitative model. Stempel (2000) argues that, in practice, almost all mediators follow an eclectic approach that involves some evaluative components. He is clearly looking at this from the point of view of a lawyer and is talking about legal evaluation. But whether we are talking about evaluation, legal information, tax advice, or a child development perspectives, at some point all mediators have to decide whether it is in their clients' best interest to stay within a strictly facilitative framework. A rigid adherence to one approach is seldom wise. Sometimes we may need to provide information to clients, sometimes advice, sometimes coaching, and sometimes an evaluation of what their alternatives are likely to be. However, we probably err more often by deviating from the facilitative approach unconsciously or prematurely then by sticking to it too rigidly.

The facilitative approach continues to offer a powerful way to promote self-determination and client empowerment in the face of considerable pressures to turn over significant decisions, with their lifelong implications, to professionals, the courts, or other agents outside the family. When applied flexibly, wisely, and compassionately, facilitative mediation continues to be a powerful way to guide families through a very difficult time in a more humane way than would otherwise be available to them.

REFERENCES

Brown, E. (1997). Comprehensive divorce mediation. In E. Kruk (Ed.), *Mediation and conflict resolution in social work and the human services.* Chicago: Nelson-Hall.

Bush, R., & Folger, J. (1994). *The promise of mediation: Responding to conflict through empowerment and recognition.* San Francisco: Jossey-Bass.

CDR Associates. (1986). *The mediation process training manual.* Boulder, CO: Author.

Cloke, K. (2001). *Mediating dangerously: The frontiers of conflict resolution.* San Francisco: Jossey-Bass.

Fisher, R., & Ury, W. (1981). *Getting to yes.* Boston: Houghton Mifflin.

Folberg, J., & Taylor, A. (1984). *Mediation: A comprehensive guide to resolving conflicts without litigation.* San Francisco: Jossey-Bass.

Hart, B. J. (1990). Gentle jeopardy: The further endangerment of battered women and children in custody mediation. *Mediation Quarterly, 7*(4), 317–330.

Haynes, J. (1994). *Fundamentals of family mediation.* Albany, NY: State University of New York Press.

Kolb, D. (1983). *The mediators.* Cambridge, MA: MIT Press.

Lande, J. (2000). Toward more sophisticated mediation theory. *Journal of Dispute Resolution, 2000*(2), 321–334.

Lax, D., & Sebenius, J. (1986). *The manager as negotiator.* New York: Free Press.

Leeson, S. M., & Johnston, B. M. (1998). *Ending it: Dispute resolution in America: Descriptions, examples, cases, and questions.* Cincinnati, OH: Anderson.

Lerman, L. G., Kuehl, S. J., & Brygger, M. P. (1989). *Domestic abuse and mediation: Guidelines for mediators and policymakers.* Washington, DC: National Woman Abuse Prevention Project.

Macfarlane, J. (1999). *Dispute resolution: Readings and case studies.* Toronto: Montgomery.

Mayer, B. (2000). *The dynamics of conflict resolution: A practitioner's guide.* San Francisco: Jossey-Bass.

Moore, C. W. (1996). *The mediation process: Practical strategies for resolving conflict* (2nd ed.). San Francisco: Jossey-Bass.

Phillips, B. A. (2001). *The mediation field guide: Transcending litigation and resolving conflicts in your business or organization.* San Francisco: Jossey-Bass.

Riskin, L. (1994). Mediator orientations, strategies, techniques. *Alternatives, 12.*

Schwarz, R. M. (1994). *The skilled facilitator: Practical wisdom for developing effective groups.* San Francisco: Jossey-Bass.

Stempel, J. (2000). The inevitability of the eclectic: Liberating ADR from ideology. *Journal of Dispute Resolution, 2000*(2), 247–294.

Thomas, K. W. (1983). Conflict and conflict management. In M. D. Dunnette (Ed.), *Handbook of industrial and organizational psychology.* Chicago: Rand McNally.

Walton, R. W., & McKersie, R. B. (1980). *A behavioral theory of negotiations.* New York: McGraw Hill.

Williams, M. (1997). Can't I get no satisfaction?: Thoughts on *The promise of mediation. Mediation Quarterly, 15*(2), 143–154.

Yard, D. (Ed.). (1999). *Dictionary of conflict resolution.* San Francisco: Jossey-Bass.

Zumeta, Z. (2000). Styles of mediation: Facilitative, evaluative, and transformative mediation. Retrieved January 17, 2002, from *www.Mediate.com*

CHAPTER 3

Transformative Mediation

Changing the Quality of Family Conflict Interaction

ROBERT A. BARUCH BUSH
SALLY GANONG POPE

One of the most significant mediation developments in the last decade is the emergence of transformative mediation as a distinct, theoretically based model. In this chapter, Robert A. Baruch Bush and Sally Ganong Pope, two of the founders of this model, explain the principles underlying transformative mediation and answer questions about why it is used, its nature, and how it changes the mediator's role and work with the parties. The authors apply transformative theory to the practice of divorce mediation and discuss the use of empowerment and recognition principles to help couples address family conflicts.

This chapter on transformative mediation is organized as an answer to three questions about divorce mediation:

1. Why is this process used?
2. What is the basic nature of this process, especially the mediator's role?
3. How does a mediator work with the parties in this process?

Answering these three questions—why, what, and how—provides a good overview of the transformative model in theory and practice.

TRANSFORMATIVE CONFLICT THEORY: THE WHY AND WHAT
OF TRANSFORMATIVE MEDIATION IN DIVORCE CASES

Why do parties come to divorce mediators and how can mediators best serve them? The parties themselves, as they enter mediation, give varied reasons for their choice of mediation, but most fall into the following categories. Saving money and time and avoiding the legal system are at the top of most lists. Reducing hostility and conflict (for their own sake and the sake of their children) and developing effective parenting plans are also important. One party may be more interested in the time savings and the other in protection of the children. Most, however, agree that staying out of the legal system is essential. With few exceptions, all hope to achieve a fair divorce settlement agreement. More generally, parties are looking for "closure"—for an outcome that allows them to move beyond the conflict and get on with their lives.

Mediators express goals that mirror the reasons expressed by their clients for choosing mediation. Some mediators emphasize protection of children, others the avoidance of the court process, and others the cost and time savings. Look at the Yellow Pages for your community to see what mediators believe are the important "selling points" for mediation—you will probably find all of these.

However, in our view, all the above examples of party expectations reflect a common, and deeper, set of concerns that motivate parties to try mediation. That is, these goals reflect the parties' underlying desire to find a different mode of dealing with their conflict—different from the one they have experienced in their private negotiations and that they believe they would find in the legal system. They are clearly looking for a better alternative to "doing it themselves" or having lawyers (and perhaps a judge) do it for them. They want to feel more in control of themselves and the process. They do not want to be victimized or to victimize the other party. Rather, they want to come out of the process feeling better about themselves and each other than they do at the point of frustration or impasse that led them to seek help from a divorce mediator in the first place.

What we regularly hear when parties talk about their personal experience of conflict, in divorce cases and others, is this: What people find hardest about conflict is not that it frustrates the satisfaction of their rights or interests, no matter how important these are, but that it leads—and sometimes even forces them—to behave toward themselves and others in ways that they find uncomfortable and even repellent. It alienates them from their sense of their own strength and their sense of connection to others, and thus it disrupts and undermines the interaction between them as human beings. In short, conflict precipitates a crisis in human interaction that parties find profoundly disturbing, and help in overcoming that crisis is a major part of what parties want from a mediator.

This view of why parties seek mediation is supported not only by our own experience but also by what theory tells us about conflict and its escalation. Insights from the fields of communication (McCorkle & Mills, 1992), cognitive psychology (Beck, 1999), neurophysiology (Goleman, 1995), and social psychology (Lind & Tyler, 1988), among others, all support this view of what conflict "means" to people, and what kinds of processes they find most helpful in responding to it. According to what we and our colleagues call the "transformative" theory (Bush & Folger, 1994; Folger & Bush, 2001), conflict as a social phenomenon is not only—or even primarily—about rights, interests, or power. Although it implicates all of those areas, conflict is most importantly about people's interaction with one another as human beings.

Certainly there are problems to be solved at the end of a marriage—the assets to be divided, the parenting plan to be created—and parties do want to solve those problems. The reality is, however, that they want to do so in a way that enhances their sense of their own competence and autonomy without taking advantage of the other. They want to feel proud of themselves for how they handled this life crisis, and this means making changes in the difficult conflict interaction that is going on between them, rather than simply coming up with the "right" answers to the specific problems. The corollary, explored below, is that in order to be useful to parties, conflict intervention must directly address the interactional crisis itself; it cannot be limited to problem solving and satisfaction of interests.

The Downward Spiral of Conflict

Figure 3.1 represents this phenomenon, as transformative theory understands it. Conflict, along with whatever else it does, affects people's experience of both self and other. First, conflict generates, for almost anyone it touches, a sense of his or her own *weakness* and incapacity. For each party involved, conflict brings a sense of relative weakness, compared to the preconflict state, in

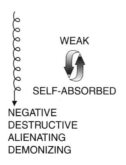

FIGURE 3.1. Negative conflict interaction.

his or her experience of self-efficacy: a sense of lost control over the situation, accompanied by confusion, doubt, uncertainty, and indecisiveness. This overall sense of "weakening" is something that occurs as a very natural human response to conflict; almost no one is immune to it, regardless of their initial "power position." At the very same time, conflict generates a sense of *self-absorption*: each party becomes more focused on self alone—more protective of self, and more suspicious, hostile, closed, and impervious to the perspective of the other person (Beck, 1999; Goleman, 1995).

In sum, no matter how strong people are, conflict propels them into relative weakness. No matter how considerate of others people are, conflict propels them into self-absorption and self-centeredness. None of this occurs because human beings are "defective" in any way. It is rather because conflict has this power to affect our experience of ourselves and others, in the context of marriage and divorce as in any other conflict arena.

However, there is more to the picture. As the cycling arrows in Figure 3.1 suggest, the experiences of weakness and self-absorption do not occur independently. Rather, they reinforce each other in a feedback loop: The weaker I feel myself becoming, the more hostile and closed I am toward you; and the more hostile I am toward you, the more you react to me in kind, the weaker I feel, the more hostile and closed I become, and so on. This vicious circle of disempowerment and demonization is exactly what scholars mean when they talk about "conflict escalation" (Rubin, Pruitt, & Kim, 1994). The transformative theory regards it in terms of "interactional degeneration." Before the conflict, there is some decent human interaction going on, whatever the context—between people in a family, a workplace, a community. Even divorcing couples were once engaged in some form of decent, even loving, human interaction. Then the conflict arises and, propelled by the vicious cycle of disempowerment and demonization, what started as a decent interaction spirals down into one that is negative, destructive, alienating, and demonizing on all sides.

The spiraling line descending at the left of Figure 3.1 is meant to represent this degeneration. The interaction in question does not end when conflict begins, but it degenerates to a point of mutual alienation and destruction. That is the conflict escalation or degeneration spiral. When nations get caught up in that spiral, the outcome is what we have seen all too often in the last decades—war, or even worse than war, if that is possible. When families get caught up in that negative conflict spiral, the home becomes a battleground and the result is family disintegration.

Where does conflict intervention come into the picture? In particular, what are divorcing couples looking for when they seek the services of a mediator? The answer follows from the above discussion. What bothers parties most about conflict is the interactional degeneration itself. Therefore, what they most want from an intervener—even more than help in resolving specific issues—is help in reversing the downward spiral and restoring a more humane quality to their interaction. Perhaps no one can avoid the negative conflict spiral, but what can be done to reverse it?[1]

In the transformative model, reversing the downward spiral is the primary value that mediation offers to parties in family conflict. That value goes beyond the dimension of helping parties reach agreement on disputed issues. With or without the achievement of agreement, the help many parties want most in family conflict (and probably in all conflict) involves helping them end the vicious circle of disempowerment, disrespect, and demonization—alienation from both self and other. Because without ending or changing that cycle, the parties cannot move beyond the negative interaction that has entrapped them and cannot escape its crippling effects.

As stated at the beginning of this chapter, divorcing parties often explain that they want to reach not simply agreement but "closure," to let go of their bitter conflict experience, and to move on with their lives. But if the negative conflict cycle is not reversed—if divorcing parties don't regenerate some sense of their own strength and some degree of understanding of the other—it is unlikely they can move on and be at peace with themselves, much less each other. In effect, without a change in the conflict interaction between them, parties are left disabled, even if an agreement on concrete issues has been reached. Their confidence in their own competence to handle life's challenges remains weakened, and their ability to trust others in relationships remains compromised. The result can be lasting damage to the parties' ability to function, not only in family relationships but in general. "Moving on," therefore, necessarily means moving out of their negative conflict interaction itself, and parties intuitively know this and want help in doing it.

The Relational Theory of Human Nature

How do parties in conflict reverse the destructive conflict spiral? Out of what resource is that transformation generated, and—of greatest salience to this chapter—what is the mediator's role in facilitating that transformation? The critical resource is the parties' own basic humanity: their essential strength and their essential decency and compassion as human beings. As discussed earlier, the transformative theory of conflict recognizes that conflict tends to escalate because of our susceptibility to experience weakness and self-absorption in the face of sudden challenge. However, based on what many call a "relational" theory of human nature, the theory also posits that human beings have inherent capacities for strength (agency/autonomy) and responsiveness (connection/compassion), and an inherent moral resiliency that allows these capacities to overcome the tendencies toward weakness and self-absorption (Bush & Folger, 1994; Della Noce, 1999). When these capacities are activated, the conflict spiral can reverse and interaction can regenerate—often, without the presence of a mediator.

Figure 3.2 expands the picture presented earlier and illustrates this positive potential of conflict interaction. Conflict is not static. It is an emergent, dynamic phenomenon in which parties can and do move and shift in remarkable ways. They move from weakness to strength, becoming (in more specific terms) calmer, clearer, more confident, more articulate, and more decisive. They shift from self-absorption to responsiveness, becoming more attentive, open, trusting, and responsive toward the other party (Beck, 1999; Goleman, 1995).

The arrows moving from left to right in Figure 3.2 represent these shifts that parties make—from weakness to strength, and from self-absorption to responsiveness to one another. In transformative conflict theory, these two dynamic shifts are called "empowerment" and "recognition" (Bush, 1996; Bush & Folger, 1994). Moreover, as the figure suggests, there is a reinforcing feedback effect on this side of the picture too. The stronger I become, the more open I am to you. The more open I am to you, the stronger you feel, the more open you become to me, and the stronger I feel. (Indeed, the more open I become to you, the stronger I feel in myself, simply because I am more open. That is, openness both requires and creates a sense of strength and magnanimity.) So there is also a cycling between strength and responsiveness, once they begin to emerge, which we think of as a virtuous cycle of conflict transformation.

Why conflict *transformation*? Because as the parties make empowerment and recognition shifts and as those shifts are gradually reinforced in a virtuous cycle, the interaction as a whole begins to turn the corner and regenerate. It changes from a negative, destructive, alienating, and demonizing interaction to one that becomes positive, constructive, connecting, and humanizing, even

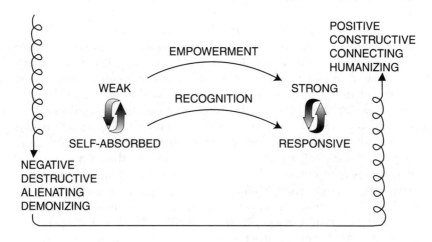

FIGURE 3.2. Changing conflict interaction. Copyright 2001 by R. A. B. Bush.

while conflict and disagreement are still continuing. This reversal of the conflict cycle from negative and destructive to positive and constructive is indicated by the upward spiraling line at the right of Figure 3.2.

The keys to this transformation of conflict interaction are the empowerment and recognition shifts that the parties themselves make. No matter how small and seemingly insignificant, these shifts can transform the entire interaction as they continue and accumulate. Is it difficult to make these shifts? It most certainly is, especially for parties who have been overcome by the sense of weakness and self-absorption that conflict initially engenders. In the transformative model, facilitating these shifts in the dimensions of empowerment and recognition is the "value-added" that mediators bring to the table (Antes, Folger, & Della Noce, 2001; Bush, 1996).

Defining Transformative Mediation

What many divorcing parties want most from mediators, and what mediators can, in fact, provide—with the proper focus and skills, as discussed below—is help and support in making these critical shifts from weakness to strength and from self-absorption to responsiveness. Figure 3.2 reflects the effects of the mediation process on conflict interaction: the transformation and regeneration of the human interaction between the parties, from negative and destructive to positive and constructive, even as the conflict continues to unfold. In this figure, the mediator stands, as it were, at the bottom of the picture offering support that helps the parties make empowerment and recognition shifts when and as they choose to do so. This overall picture leads us to a definition of mediation and the mediator's role in the transformative model that differs markedly from the descriptions typically found in training materials and literature on mediation. In the transformative model:

- *Mediation* is defined as a process in which a third party works with the parties to help them change the quality of their conflict interaction from negative and destructive to positive and constructive, as they explore and discuss issues and possibilities for resolution.
- The *mediator's role* is to help the parties make positive interactional shifts (i.e., empowerment and recognition shifts) by supporting the exercise of their capacities for strength and responsiveness through deliberation, perspective taking, communication, and decision making.
- The *mediator's primary goals* are (1) to foster empowerment shifts by supporting, but never supplanting, each party's deliberation and decision making, at every point in the session where choices arise (regarding either process or outcome); and (2) to foster recognition shifts by encouraging and supporting, but never forcing, each party's freely chosen efforts to achieve new understandings of the other's perspective. (Specific practices tied to these goals are discussed below.)

The transformative model does not ignore the significance of resolving specific issues, but it assumes that, if mediators do the job just described, the parties themselves will very likely make positive changes in their interaction and, as a result, find acceptable terms of resolution for themselves if such terms genuinely exist. More important, they will have reversed the negative conflict spiral and begun to reestablish a positive and connecting mode of interaction that allows them to move forward on a different footing, both while and after specific issues are resolved—and, indeed, even if they cannot be resolved.

The transformative model posits that this is the greatest value that many families in conflict will find in mediation: It can help them conduct conflict itself in a different way. It can help them find and take the small but meaningful opportunities for empowerment and recognition shifts as they arise. It can support the virtuous cycle of personal empowerment and interpersonal recognition that de-escalates and de-embitters conflict (so that, with the bitterness drained out, even if there may still be conflict, it's no longer dehumanizing and demonizing). It can turn conflict interaction away from alienation, from both self and other, toward a restored connection to both—strength of self and appreciation of other—even while conflict continues. Mediation can thus help divorcing parties to "move on with their lives," with the capacities for living those lives restored—including both the sense of their own competence, and the confidence in their ability to connect with others.

The transformative view of mediation is both practically and theoretically based. From the insights of psychology, communication, and other fields, we have understood in theoretical terms why conflict transformation is important and how it can occur through mediation. From the parties that we have worked with and studied over these years, we have learned that this theoretical promise of what mediation can offer is real. Transformative mediators allow and trust the parties to find their own way through the conflict, and even more important, find themselves and each other, discovering and revealing the strength and compassion within themselves. In the following section, we discuss some of the specific practices that mediators can use to accomplish these goals

TRANSLATING THEORY INTO PRACTICE: HOW DOES THE TRANSFORMATIVE MEDIATOR WORK?

How do we translate transformative conflict theory into specific mediation practices? The first skill of the transformative mediator is to keep in mind the "why and what" of divorce mediation from this perspective. As noted, the transformative mediator supports the parties as they discuss the issues between them, supporting shifts from weakness to strength and self-absorption to responsiveness—empowerment and recognition shifts. Understanding and embracing this perspective, and being confident in its value to the parties, is essential to everything the mediator does. Holding this perspective in mind, the transformative mediator is finely attuned to the kind of interaction the parties are having and to indications of weakness and self-absorption. When weakness and self-absorption are present, the mediator views those states as opportunities for facilitating their reversal through empowerment and recognition. She responds, at appropriate points, with several simple but effective kinds of interventions, all of which are used throughout the session to support conflict transformation—which she always sees as the essence of the process.

Learning the Vocabulary of Empowerment and Recognition

In order to notice the opportunities for supporting empowerment and recognition, the mediator pays close attention to the parties' conversational cues in the immediate interactions between them—what they say and do. The mediator stays "in the moment" of the conversation in order to see and hear what they are saying. He understands that, when the mediation first begins, parties may not be able to talk about the issues or listen to each other effectively and productively, and they may be confused about what they want. As a result, the mediator initially focuses on listening and observing for indications of weakness and self-absorption, because these are the points of opportunity for interactional transformation.

The mediator must know how to recognize these opportunities; in other words, the mediator must know what he is listening and looking for. In effect, the mediator is learning to listen to the exchanges between the parties in a whole new way, on a new level, and in a new language—the language of conflict transformation. Therefore, the mediator must master the vocabulary of empowerment and recognition, starting with the ability to recognize signifiers of either weakness or self-absorption (Moen, Hudson, Antes, Jorgensen, & Hendrikson, 2001). For example, asking "What should I do?" shows that the party sees the mediator as the decision maker and feels dependent on his guidance. "I'm really confused" expresses lack of clarity and probably uncertainty. "I've had enough of this!" expresses strong emotions and feelings and shows a sense of helplessness or frustration. "What do you expect from someone like that?" indicates a negative view of the other party and, hence, self-absorption. "It's not like me" and "You don't understand what it's been like for me" are requests for understanding that suggest the experience of nonrecognition.

A mediator listening with a transformative ear does not ignore or dismiss statements of this nature as "resisting" or merely "venting." Such statements are viewed as important markers of opportunities for shifts in the conflict interaction. In this new language, every expression that conveys the message "I feel weak" is an opportunity for an empowerment shift toward greater strength. Every expression that conveys the message "I am trapped in my own perspective and cut off from the other" is an opportunity for a recognition shift toward increased responsiveness.

Once able to work in the language of conflict transformation, the mediator also needs to provide supportive responses that assist the parties in making empowerment and recognition shifts, and to do this without pushing, directing, or having any agenda for the parties.

Supportive Responses

With the understanding that one of the hallmarks of transformative mediation (Folger & Bush, 1996) is that "small steps count," the mediator must be able to observe and listen closely as the conversation unfolds. *Close listening,* combined with observation of what the parties are conveying through body language, is thus a foundational skill that is used continuously throughout the mediation. Nuances in the language used by the parties as they move through the discussion are crucial indicators of shifts, and body language is as important as the actual words spoken. Close listening is done with no other goal in mind except to hear what is being said or trying to be said (O'Reilly, 1998). It requires being fully present to the person speaking. Deep listening makes possible the effective use of other key skills, such as reflection, summary, and "checking in." Without close listening, effective transformative mediation is impossible.

Reflection is another primary supportive response. In reflecting a party's statement, the mediator simply says what she hears the party saying, using words close to the party's own language, even (or especially) when the language is strong, loud, negative, or strongly expressive. The mediator does not soften the party's language or remove its "sting." For example, the mediator does not turn anger into a request for change but simply acknowledges the anger by saying what she has heard. By using the exact or similar language, without distortion or softening, the mediator leaves room for the party to choose to expand on the angry or negative statement, to explain it further, or to rethink it and amend it to reduce hostility or exaggeration. Reflection is particularly helpful in assisting a party to think through something that seems unclear or complex, or to help the party who seems uncertain or ambiguous about what he or she is saying. In these ways, reflection allows a party to "listen and talk to him- or herself," thereby gaining clarity and confidence about what he or she is saying. It also may give the other party an opportunity to hear something he or she may not have heard or understood when it was first being said. The overall effect of reflection is to amplify the conversation for both parties—to make what is being said more audible so the parties can understand themselves, and each other, better.

Here is a short example of reflection in practice, in a portion of a divorce mediation that concerned division of assets:

> The husband, John, says, "Our house in the country is mine. I bought it before we got married. After we got married and spent more time there, I completely renovated it myself. I gutted the inside to open it up, put in windows, and added a new room. Oh, and a new roof and cedar shingles on the outside walls. It's worth a lot more now, and there is no way she is going to share in the value!"

> The mediator's reflection could be: "So, you feel strongly that the country house is entirely yours and that Lois should not share in its value at all. You bought the house before you married, and after your marriage you spent more time there, and you did extensive renovations. You gutted the inside, put in new windows, added a new room, a new roof, and shingles. You are saying that it's worth a lot more now, and you put a lot of personal labor into making the value increase, and you see the house as yours."

Even in this brief example, it is evident that the mediator's reflection can help John himself hear and think about what he is saying, consider whether he wants to elaborate or modify it in any way, and decide what to say or do next. It can also help Lois listen in and consider what John is saying, without immediate pressure to respond, and decide what she thinks about it. In short, it can support empowerment for both parties in a significant way.

Practicing this sort of reflection may sound simple and easy: just listen and say what you heard the party say. In fact, it is not easy at all. Really listening to what is being said and accurately reflecting it all, without editing or judging its validity or likely impact, is actually very difficult. First, the mediator does not want to simply reinforce or harden a party position, or be seen as agreeing with that position; nor does she want to implicitly dismiss consideration of legal or other standards that contradict the position. Additionally, the mediator may be concerned that the listening party will object to the other party "getting so much attention," in a climate where all subjects are personal and emotional. To avoid these pitfalls, the reflection must be given in a properly tentative tone and demeanor, indicating that the mediator is simply trying to "get" what is being said, in order to assist decision making and communication, without introducing any standards for judging the comment, legal or otherwise. Furthermore, the mediator must not be distracted from her close focus on what is being said by the speaking party, even by a sense that the other party is waiting impatiently for his or her turn. The calmness and presence of mind required for this kind of focus is far from easy to maintain.

Once the parties start talking directly with each other, *summary* may be the preferred response rather than reflection. In fact, in the transformative mediation model, the parties often begin talking directly to each other early on, and for extended lengths of time. Mediator participation in the discussion may be quite minimal for those periods, but the mediator's intense focus on listening continues. In this situation, summarizing is the more likely response used when the mediator enters the conversation. The difference between reflection and summary is important. In a reflection, the mediator is speaking to, and with, one of the parties, engaging that party directly and allowing the other to "listen in" from a safe distance. In a summary, the mediator speaks to, and with, both parties and includes larger blocks, or "chunks," of the party conversation and interactions. For this very reason, it is harder to give a realistic example of summary in a short space.

Nevertheless, for purposes of illustration, consider the following continuation of the conversation started above, concerning the country house. Suppose that the husband responds to the mediator's reflection by saying, "You got it. She's not getting that house. No way, no how. No matter what she says."

Now Lois jumps into the conversation: "I can't believe your attitude! When we were together, it was *my* home. You let *me* keep it clean. You wanted *me* to decorate. You call it our country house, but it was our primary *home*. I put my heart and soul into that home!" The exchange then continues:

JOHN: You got to live there! It's all I've got. I intended it as my retirement asset. You can't just take it away from me.

LOIS: If you had a pension, you would have to share it with me. What makes the house different?

JOHN: I did the work. It was mine. I bought it.

LOIS: But I was there, too. I worked along with you. Who did the wallpaper? Who did the plans for the construction? Are you conveniently forgetting that?

JOHN: You're just out to get me.

LOIS: Oh, it's no use talking to you.

Assuming the conversation reached a lull at this point, the mediator might offer this summary:

"It's clear you both have strong feelings about the house, but you also have some strong differences about it. First of all, you have different views about who put what effort into the house. John, you're saying that you really did all the significant construction renovations and that your work is what increased its value; but Lois, you're saying that you both put effort into making it what it is today, that you also worked on the renovations, by preparing plans, decorating, putting up the wallpaper, keeping it clean.

"And then, besides the work done, you also seem to have pretty different views of how to see the house today, or what it represents to you. Lois, you're attached to it as your primary home, you 'put your heart and soul into it,' to use your words. You also see the house as a valuable asset to divide between you in some way (like a pension). In contrast, John, you see the house as entirely yours and actually 'all you've got,' as you put it, what you've been counting on for your retirement. So you have very different views about who should get what value from the house."

This example illustrates both the value and the difficulty of using a summary as a mode of response. Summarizing is often used when there have been long periods of direct party exchange, and the parties come to a natural break. It is also helpful when the parties don't know "where to go next" or seem stuck. Since a good stretch of ground will have been covered during the conversation, the summary provides a review of what they have been talking about and what each has been saying. It helps the parties remember what they were discussing and make more informed choices about where they want to go next. However, for this very reason, offering a good summary can be difficult: The mediator must be able to track, recall, and describe the whole stretch of ground covered, and this, in itself, is a difficult skill to develop.

Moreover, like reflection, a summary is inclusive. The mediator does not select from what has been said, does not "soften" what was said, and does not drop any issues, particularly intangible ones. The summary is not an educational monologue by the mediator and has no built-in agenda or direction. It is an especially powerful tool for supporting empowerment and recognition shifts when it highlights the differences between the parties and the choices they face. For all these reasons, it is a challenging skill to hone. It requires the mediator to resist emphasizing superficial "common ground" and to highlight instead the deeper "fault lines" in the parties' conversations—because that is where the greatest potential for empowerment and recognition lies.

Without any other skills, the mediator could effectively mediate in a supportive way using only listening, reflection, and summary. *Checking in,* however, is an important and effective addition to these essential skills and is frequently coupled with reflection and summary. Checking in can be used to end a summary, when the mediator asks the parties, "Where do you want to go from here?" It is often used as a process intervention when it seems the parties have come to a choice point in the mediation; checking in provides them with the opportunity to make a clear decision. When there is a fork in the road, it is helpful for the mediator to point it out and ask the parties which direction they want to take. For example, if the parties began talking about one subject and moved on to two or three others, the mediator may summarize the discussion and ask the parties whether they want to talk further about any of the subjects already mentioned, or move on to other matters.

Questions are obviously used for checking in. Questions are also used in many other supportive ways, provided that they do not lead or direct a party in any way. The risk is that questions can put the mediator ahead of the parties, leading the discussion and requiring the parties respond to her, rather than allowing the parties to have their own conversation about the matters important to them. In transformative mediation, questions are used to open doors or invite further discussion. "Is there more you want to say about that?" is one such question. The mediator does not use questions for her own purposes, such as to gather information or to understand what the parties are discussing. The parties have the information they need, and if they need more information, they will discover that for themselves in due course.

There are still other responses that can be used to support empowerment and recognition shifts. Silence is a natural response of parties to intense conversation. Allowing time for silence is an important mediator response. When something powerful has been said or has happened during the parties' interaction, it is helpful to simply let the parties decide how they want to respond, even if there is a long period of silence. The mediator does not need to *do* something just because there is silence. Moreover, eye contact, facial expression, and gestures are also part of the mediator's communication. Just by looking at the other party when one party seems to be finished speaking, the mediator may unwittingly send the message that she is asking the second party to speak, which may put pressure on a party who is not really ready to respond. In other words, since silence and nonverbal messages can be used in directive as well as supportive ways, the mediator needs to consider them as carefully as any verbal communication.

All the above mediator responses—reflection, summary, checking in, questions, and allowing silence—are used over and over again throughout the mediation. They are also used steadfastly, resisting the temptation to substitute other responses that are inconsistent with transformative theory. The model asks the mediator to go beyond simply "trying out" transformative moves but then abandoning the approach when the "going gets tough." This approach to mediation requires the courage that comes from convictions—courage to allow and help the parties to deal with differences, even differences expressed in chaos, confusion, and high conflict. She must be able to summarize the chaos, confusion, and differences, as well as any negative views of each other that parties might express. The courage to do so comes from trusting that the parties have the ability to make empowerment and recognition shifts and to make the best decisions for themselves and their families.

This approach also requires a certain degree of tentativeness in the use of responses. An "in charge" mediator will interfere with the parties' empowerment and undermine the potential for shifts. Instead, the transformative mediator realizes that her reflections or summaries may not be entirely accurate and that they should therefore be presented in ways that allow and encourage correction by the parties. Similarly, questions should be asked in ways that allow parties to refrain from answering them if they so choose. The message in both words and mediator "style" should be that this is the parties' process, not the mediator's.

The preceding paragraphs describe the primary skills needed to practice effective transformative mediation in divorce cases. Mediator personality and conversational style have an impact on how responses are implemented; still, consistency in the use of the responses discussed here will identify the transformative mediator and make her an effective practitioner. The mediator does not act differently in a divorce mediation than in any other substantive area of practice. No new skills or special techniques are used in a divorce mediation compared to a workplace or business mediation. Whether the parties are in high conflict or not, the transformative mediator continues to use the basic responses summarized here. All the mediator's decisions—whether to speak or be silent, whether to summarize what has been happening or to ask a question—are guided by and based on the transformative theory discussed earlier.

Avoiding Directive Responses

Using the essential skills of reflection, summary, and checking in, the mediator "follows" or "accompanies" the parties (Della Noce, 2001; Pope, 2001); he does not have a set agenda of steps to accomplish in a divorce mediation. The parties begin where they choose to begin, and in the course of the discussion, they talk about anything of importance to them. The mediator does not rule out any subject as inappropriate or unhelpful, nor does the mediator tell the parties how to have their conversation or when to continue or end it.

Directive impulses arise when the mediator has his own view of what the parties should accomplish, such as reducing conflict or avoiding unfairness (Grillo, 1991). Such impulses almost certainly get in the way of the mediator's continuing ability to "follow" the parties. For example, interrupting an argument about past events by turning the focus to the future, or by asking a question about another subject, substitutes the mediator's judgment for the parties' as to the proper focus for discussion. Why a husband walked out of a marriage with no notice to the wife may be a crucial subject for discussion when the parties first appear for a divorce mediation. If the mediator stops the interchange and refuses to "allow" discussion of what went wrong with the marriage, or discussion of an "old argument" about money, he is not following the parties or helping them have the discussion they choose. If it transpires that only one person wants to have a particular discussion and the other refuses, then that difference becomes the subject for discussion and mediation.

The transformative mediator is not the director of the discussion. He does not tell the parties how to talk to each other or direct the course of their discussion or its content in any way. Some divorce mediators use checklists of "usual topics for discussion" and forms for gathering information. Doing so does not necessarily undermine the transformative model if this is done carefully, in a manner consistent with the model, and not in order to direct the conversation or influence party choices. The transformative divorce mediator positions himself as a reflective and helpful "conversational companion," regardless of what the parties choose to discuss.

The transformative mediator supports, *but never supplants,* party decision making. He assists the parties with their decisions by helping them identify choice points throughout the conversation and by restraining himself from making any decisions for the parties about the process or the substantive results (Folger, 2001). He respects the parties and their choices. He trusts the parties. He has confidence in them: the confidence that they know best, that they know what is right for them and their children. He will not attempt to substitute his judgment for theirs. He will not try to steer them in the direction of what he thinks is the best arrangement for them and their children. Indeed, how could he know this, as an outsider to their lives? He will not decide what is fair for them, or what is unfair. He respects and trusts the parties to make those decisions for themselves. The transformative mediator is not trying to "get" the parties to do anything—whether to talk to each other, to stop arguments for the sake of the children, or even to stay out of court.

While intensely engaged in listening, observing, and enacting supportive responses, the mediator constantly maintains an awareness of—and represses—his directive impulses. One of the parties may say, "I just don't know what to do. I'm afraid to be on my own." An almost automatic response would be to explain that most people feel that way when going through a divorce and then to move on with the "real business" of the mediation. To do so, however, minimizes the feeling of the confused party by making the confusion normal, usual, and therefore ripe for ignoring—perhaps with a referral to a popular book on divorce. It is also a directive response in that the mediator is attempting to control the content of the discussion by characterizing the feeling and then changing the topic. In contrast, a supportive response that utilizes the opportunity for empowerment being presented would be to simply reflect the statement and then allow time for the party to respond as he or she chooses. A party might choose to move on to other business, or comment that "It's just normal, I guess," or request more time to deal with the shock, or elaborate on how he feels, how the other party is behaving, or what he wants to do about it. Any of these possible responses would be empowering for the party who is feeling weak and confused at the moment.

Another example: Even if many women going through divorce fear they will end up as "bag ladies on the street," it does not help a particular woman dealing with these circumstances to be told that "Everyone feels that way." Rather than offering empathy and assurance, it is dismissive of a very real fear. Instead, the transformative mediator simply reflects the fear, using words close to those used by the party. The mediator might say, "So you are scared and worried about becoming destitute and, to use your words, 'winding up on the street.' " That kind of reflective statement allows the woman to know the subject is, in essence, now on the table for discussion if she chooses to pursue it and that the others in the room are now aware of how she feels and the depth of that feeling. She can then choose where to take the discussion at that moment.

There are many other kinds of directive impulses. Trying to keep the parties "on track" or to "move the discussion along" interferes with the natural cycles of conversation between the parties. Pointing out "common ground," by saying, for example, "You both really care about your child" or "You both have fears about financial security," does little, if anything, to bring parties together and probably obscures the real and important differences between them. In this model, differences are not downplayed in the attempt to find and stress the common ground. In the transformative view, probing for what the mediator believes are the "real underlying issues" is directive, and disregarding of parties' autonomy. Following the parties in their discussion highlights all of the issues they choose to put out on the table. Pushing them, probing and asking questions to get them to do more, is experienced as just that. The parties feel they are being pushed, and opportunities for empowerment and recognition are almost certainly lost. "Hypothesizing" by the mediator about what is important to one of the parties, or what would be an acceptable settlement, detracts from the intense focus needed to pay attention to what is actually going on right in front of the mediator. Hypothesizing requires the mediator to develop a line of questioning to follow up on and test the accuracy of the hypothesis; the result is the pursuit of the mediator's agenda, not the parties', and the loss of focus on transforming the conflict interaction.

The skills employed by the transformative divorce mediator are simple to describe but difficult to employ: (1) listening, (2) reflecting, (3) summarizing, and (4) questioning to invite further discussion on a subject raised by the parties or to "check in" on what the parties want to do at a choice point in the discussion. It is much easier to allow our directive impulses to steer us into leading and guiding the discussion—and, as a result, the outcome. Although it is difficult to stay with the parties through their cycles of conversation as they develop

strength and understanding, doing so is the work of the transformative mediator, and it is the help that many parties in conflict value most.

CONCLUSION: PRACTICE BASED ON PRINCIPLES

As discussed above, the "how" of transformative practice in divorce mediation flows from the "why and what" of transformative conflict theory. In
sum, it is all a matter of principles and the theories to which they give rise
concerning what mediation is and why it is conducted. Extraordinary differences in mediation practice occur as a result of the varying principles of mediators. Personality and conversational style do have an impact on mediator
responses, but the most powerful impact on practice comes from the mediator's principles—what the mediator believes and values about conflict, mediation, and the human beings who are his or her clients. Clear articulation and
understanding of the principles of mediation are essential to a mediator's
understanding of effective, responsible practice (Della Noce, Bush, & Folger,
2002). Once a foundation of principles and purpose is clearly established, an
understanding of how to practice flows from that foundation and can be
tested for its consistency with those foundational principles.

ACKNOWLEDGMENTS

We acknowledge the collaboration of the Fellows and Associates of the Institute for the
Study of Conflict Transformation in the generation of ideas summarized here. We also acknowledge Bonny Adams, a graphic designer and volunteer at the Dayton Mediation Center in Dayton, Ohio, for the computer designs of Figures 3.1 and 3.2.

NOTE

1. Of course, what is done to "resolve conflict" can sometimes make that downward
spiral even worse, as is often the case with the adversarial legal process (Wexler & Winick,
1996). If conflict tends to position the parties as both victims and victimizers, why become
immersed in a process that only reinforces that state of affairs? Even though the formal adversarial process does help divorcing parties claim and vindicate important rights, that
process itself often leaves the participants wounded and, in some cases, permanently so
(Wexler & Winick, 1996). Many are not comfortable paying that price, even for victory,
and even when they feel they are clearly "in the right." Indeed, even the lawyers who represent them do not escape the harshness of the process in which they work. This does not
mean that the adversarial process is not a necessary institution. We firmly believe in the
importance of the law, lawyers, legal rights, and vindication of those rights in court and
similar venues, because all of these are sometimes necessary. Yet even as we affirm the
value of formal legal processes, we also suggest that they serve as a last, not a first, resort
in most cases, because the costs of using the legal process are very high, not just in the material terms we normally think of, but in the human terms: the negative impact of the
process on human interaction.

REFERENCES

Antes, J. R., Folger, J. P., & Della Noce, D. J. (2001). Transforming conflict in the workplace: Documented effects of the USPS REDRESS program. *Hofstra Labor and Employment Law Journal, 18,* 429–467.

Beck, A. T. (1999). *Prisoners of hate: The cognitive basis of anger, hostility, and violence.* New York: HarperCollins.

Bush, R. A. B. (1996). "What do we need a mediator for?": Mediation's value-added for negotiators. *Ohio State Journal of Dispute Resolution, 12,* 1–36.

Bush, R. A. B., & Folger, J. P. (1994). *The promise of mediation: Responding to conflict through empowerment and recognition.* San Francisco: Jossey-Bass.

Della Noce, D. J. (1999). Seeing theory in practice: An analysis of empathy in mediation. *Negotiation Journal, 15*(3), 271–301.

Della Noce, D. J. (2001). Mediation as a transformative process: Insights on structure and movement. In J. P. Folger & R. A. B. Bush (Eds.), *Designing mediation: Approaches to training and practice within a transformative framework* (pp. 71–95). New York: Institute for the Study of Conflict Transformation.

Della Noce, D. J., Bush, R. A. B., & Folger, J. P. (2002). Clarifying the theoretical underpinnings of mediation: Implications for practice and policy. *Pepperdine Dispute Resolution Law Journal, 3,* 39–65.

Folger, J. P. (2001). Who owns what in mediation?: Seeing the link between process and content. In J. P. Folger & R. A. B. Bush (Eds.), *Designing mediation: Approaches to training and practice within a transformative framework* (pp. 55–60). New York: Institute for the Study of Conflict Transformation.

Folger, J. P., & Bush, R.A.B. (1996). Transformative mediation and third-party intervention: Ten hallmarks of a transformative approach to practice. *Mediation Quarterly, 13*(4), 263–278.

Folger, J. P., & Bush, R. A. B. (Eds.). (2001). *Designing mediation: Approaches to training and practice within a transformative framework.* New York: Institute for the Study of Conflict Transformation.

Goleman, D. (1995). *Emotional intelligence.* London: Bloomsbury.

Grillo, T. (1991). The mediation alternative: Process dangers for women. *Yale Law Journal, 100,* 1545–1610.

Lind, E. A., & Tyler, T. (1988). *The social psychology of procedural justice.* New York: Plenum Press.

McCorkle, S., & Mills, J. (1992). Rowboat in a hurricane: Metaphors of interpersonal conflict. *Communications Reports, 5,* 57–66.

Moen, J. K., Hudson, D. T., Antes, J. R., Jorgensen, E. O., & Hendrikson, L. H. (2001). Identifying opportunities for empowerment and recognition in mediation. In J. P. Folger & R. A. B. Bush (Eds.), *Designing mediation: Approaches to training and practice within a transformative framework* (pp. 112–132). New York: Institute for the Study of Conflict Transformation.

O'Reilley, M. R. (1998). *Radical presence: Teaching as contemplative practice.* Portsmouth, NH: Boynton/Cook.

Pope, S. G. (2001). Beginning the mediation: Party participation promotes empowerment and recognition. In J. P. Folger & R. A. B. Bush (Eds.), *Designing mediation: Approaches to training and practice within a transformative framework* (pp. 85–95). New York: Institute for the Study of Conflict Transformation.

Rubin, J. Z., Pruitt, D. G., & Kim, S. H. (1994). *Social conflict: Escalation, stalemate, and settlement* (2nd ed.). New York: McGraw-Hill.

Wexler, D. B., & Winick, B. J. (Eds.). (1996). *Law in a therapeutic key.* Durham, NC: Carolina Academic Press.

CHAPTER 4

Evaluative Mediation

L. RANDOLPH LOWRY

Evaluative mediation is commonly used to help resolve commercial and insurance disputes but is more controversial when applied to family conflicts. This chapter explains the evaluative process and assesses concerns about its use in custody and divorce cases. Randolph Lowry reframes the question of whether or not a mediator should evaluate by noting that all mediators form judgments but not all mediators share their evaluations with the parties. Professor Lowry then offers a strategic approach for when and how to use evaluations in family mediations and identifies areas on which evaluations can be focused. Evaluative techniques are explained along with how evaluations can best be communicated.

There are few issues in professional mediation that evoke more passion than the use of evaluation. The use of evaluation—in which a mediator makes a judgment about the dispute at hand and expresses that judgment to the parties—is enthusiastically embraced by some and severely criticized by others (Kovach & Love, 1996). It is one technique that mediators use, among many others, to move parties toward settlement. It reflects an approach to the mediation process that is fraught with dangers, yet its influence on parties is great. This chapter focuses on the evaluative approach to mediation and advocates its use as a legitimate and helpful mediation tool (Marks, 1996).[1]

A PERSPECTIVE ON THE DEBATE

The emergence of mediation as a prominent dispute resolution process in the last two decades has revealed that it is a process that can be defined and conducted in a variety of ways. Some professionals advocate, quite strongly, for an approach that "transforms" the participants as the conflict is resolved

(Bush & Folger, 1994). Others contend that the true (and only legitimate) role of the mediator is as a facilitator of the parties' dialogue (Love, 1997). Still others embrace a perspective that portrays evaluation by the mediator as an appropriate and often necessary task (Aaron, 1996).[2] These divergent views and practices frame mediation work as it takes place today.

Different approaches to mediation practice have merit, and each of the approaches has limitations. It is in considering the benefits and dangers of any technique that practitioners find the most productive debate (Alfini, 1996).[3] Family mediation needs strong advocacy. Passionate perspectives and reflective thinking benefit the field of family mediation and help develop the best that can be offered by dedicated mediators to those in conflict.

One side of the debate is discussed in this chapter; the evaluative approach to mediation. The perspective offered here is the product of my experience as a teacher, mediator, and observer of the mediation field for the last 20 years. Yet I recognize that these perspectives may not reflect readers' work or experience. My hope is that the subject of using the tool of evaluation in family mediation will be given a fair hearing and the judgment of it will be thoughtful.

DEFINITION OF EVALUATION

The evaluative approach to the mediation process either allows or, in many cases, establishes an expectation that the mediator will make assessments about the conflict as well as its resolution and communicate those assessments to the parties. It is an analytical process that focuses the mediator's attention on the substance of the conflict and what would be necessary in order to achieve a settlement. It gets the mediator "knee deep" in the content of the matter at hand and assumes that the mediator is capable of not only facilitating the mediation process but also making judgments about its content.

Riskin (1996) suggests that evaluation involves at least three activities: (1) first assessing the strengths and weaknesses of the parties' case; (2) then developing and proposing options to resolve the case; and (3) predicting the outcome at trial if a dispute, not settled in mediation, were to be fully litigated. Notice the activity included in his definition—*assessing, developing, proposing,* and *predicting.* Evaluation in mediation assumes the mediator's involvement in the substance as well as the process. It is active, decisive, and involved.

Evaluative activity contrasts starkly with the purely facilitative approach to mediation. Although facilitation does not exclude critical analysis and certain strategic moves designed to help parties reach a settlement, it does not address the substance of the case or provide a deliberate communication regarding the merits of the case to the parties (Furey, 1995). Likewise, the transformative approach avoids all content issues and pursues its goal of facilitating the transformation of the parties in the mediation (Bush & Folger, 1994, p. 81; see also Kolb & Kressel, 1994).[4] It sees conflict as an opportunity for parties to change the way they interact with one another. Often, the transformative mediator has the agenda of change within and between people, and the evaluative mediator, while not opposed to such change, simply sees the goal as resolving the issues faced by the parties.

THE DANGERS OF EVALUATION

Perhaps the best way to begin an examination of evaluative mediation is to describe the perspectives of professionals in the mediation field who do not support its use (Love, 1997). The dangers or cautions about evaluation in mediation are described first so that they can be considered as the benefits are presented. Admittedly, there is a tinge of advocacy for evaluation in this overall presentation, but even those who are advocates for evaluation (such as myself) and use it successfully must be cognizant of the thoughtful concerns expressed by colleagues in the field. The criticisms put forth by those professionals are listed without substantial comment as a place to begin consideration of this technique.

In considering the criticisms, it might be helpful to bear in mind what may be thought of as stereotypical evaluative mediation. The evaluative mediator is one who is highly experienced, focuses narrowly on the issues at hand, listens to both parties to understand the issues involved, and then draws upon expertise and a healthy dose of confidence to tell the parties what to do, perhaps in no uncertain terms. This mediator is not reluctant to address the strengths and weaknesses of the situation, as he or she sees them, and then use that evaluation to get the matter resolved. To the evaluative mediator, the focus is on the deal and doing whatever is necessary to get parties to resolution. This stereotype may be a bit exaggerated, but it is not unrealistic.[5]

Those who oppose evaluation and embrace a more facilitative model have much to say, and it is worth considering. Eight arguments in favor of a more facilitative approach are offered for consideration here:

1. It is suggested that an evaluative approach takes away from the ability of the parties to reach independent conclusions regarding the appropriate resolution for their case.[6] The concern is that the parties could be influenced by the power of the mediator and persuaded to settle based upon the mediator's evaluation rather than the parties' own judgment. The parties

then may experience greater dissatisfaction with both the result and the process.

2. Those considering the impact of evaluation suggest that the evaluation itself could be wrong (Menkel-Meadow, 1996).[7] It is a particularly talented individual who always has complete understanding of these complex situations, knows all of the right answers, and is in a position to tell others what to do. There is a chance that the evaluative mediator may simply be wrong in the evaluation or perspective shared. The consequences for the parties, the success of the process, as well as the mediator's own reputation could be dramatic.

3. The evaluation, even if correct, could bring closure too quickly. Moving hastily to a clear evaluative moment may deprive the parties of the opportunity to share their stories or describe their case. As Johnston concludes, "The right answer at the wrong time is the wrong answer!"[8] The right answer at the wrong time may result in dissatisfaction with the mediation dynamic and may decrease its usefulness in relation to resolution.

4. Evaluative mediation may damage, perhaps beyond repair, the negotiation between the parties. If the core of mediation is negotiation—a communication process used to achieve deals or resolve conflicts—then activities that would inhibit the communication process have the potential to affect, negatively, the negotiation. Experienced mediators know that evaluation often inhibits, or ends, the negotiation between parties once the mediator has determined the "right" result in the matter and communicated that perspective to the parties. In that circumstance, it is a challenge for one side to be more generous than what is suggested by the mediator. At the same time, it is difficult for the other side to take less than what the mediator suggests is the right substantive outcome. A definite "chill" envelopes the negotiation process as a third party expresses an opinion on the issues in the case.

5. The focus of the evaluation may result in the conflict being too narrowly defined. While some legal disputes involve only a single issue, most family cases involve a variety of issues, many of which do not have purely quantifiable solutions. Gravitation toward the more tangible legal issues may miss the unique opportunity in mediation to address the broader, but perhaps less tangible, conflicts between the parties. The mindset of what is "relevant" in court—which is often the object of a mediator's evaluation—may not include important matters that are relevant in the more collaborative process of mediation.

6. Evaluation necessitates that people with the requisite background or training for such evaluation (often lawyers and judges) carry out the role of the mediator. If the evaluation involves predicting what the court will do with a particular issue, then only those familiar with the law and the courts could perform the evaluative mediator function. This requirement would limit the diversity of backgrounds now found among family mediators and

ultimately provide a diminished resource for those needing mediation assistance.

7. Evaluation confuses the role of the third party. If evaluation takes place after the parties have been educated about mediation as a cooperative problem-solving experience, parties may experience substantial confusion. Parties hear the introductory comments about the facilitative nature of the mediator's work and the fact that the parties are allowed to control the process as well as the outcome. Then, sometime later, the same mediator suggests what the parties should do, or what will happen if they do not do it, and the parties become confused as to the nature of the process in which they are engaged. The role of the mediator and the operation of the mediation process have become a source of additional confusion.

8. Finally, the use of evaluative techniques in mediation blurs the line between consensual dispute resolution processes, such as negotiation, and adjudicative dispute resolution processes, such as trial. Some would contend that each type of dispute resolution process is needed, and diluting either would necessarily affect the other. In essence, it is argued that evaluation, if needed by the parties to resolve their conflict, ought to be provided as part of adjudicative forums and not the mediation process.

Each of the above viewpoints merits consideration, particularly by those who are in favor of using evaluation in family mediation. The limitations described and the precautions implied should help those who engage in evaluation to do so with a complete understanding of the dynamics of family mediation.

THE BENEFITS OF EVALUATION

Those who advocate for the evaluative technique do so with a sense of commitment and based on experiences that confirm, for them, its value. The primary arguments in favor of using evaluation in the mediation process follow:

1. Those who favor evaluative mediation cite its value in achieving the most important objective of mediation: getting an agreement (Bickerman, 1996).[9] They point to the many cases in which the moment in the mediation that was most influential and persuasive occurred when the mediator formulated and expressed an opinion about how the parties should view the case. It was at that moment that hard news was delivered to one, or both, of the parties that reconsideration of positions took place and that parties were motivated to move toward each other in the negotiation. That moment took place because the mediator formulated and expressed an opinion that was intended to influence how the parties viewed their own position and the ulti-

mate resolution of their case. The evaluation was persuasive, and the parties settled the dispute.

In the family area, as is the case in civil mediation, the legal alternative to a mediated agreement is a trial. Although courtroom adjudication may be a major motivator for settlement, it is not the only one. Stopping the hemorrhaging of legal costs, eliminating the emotional investment in conflict, and finding a sense of personal relief when the divorce issues are resolved are all benefits of settlement. Evaluation, if offered to and accepted by each party, may get them to resolution more quickly and more efficiently than other mediation approaches. Evaluation is simply a tool to settle cases.

2. Those asserting the value of an evaluative form of mediation suggest that the evaluation represents the integration into the mediation process of expertise not available among the parties or perhaps even their advocates (Alfini & Clay, 1994).[10] Conflict generally takes place in the context of relationships. The conflict being experienced by those involved is probably not unique. Often the very employment of a mediator, either by the court or the parties themselves, is a decision to bring additional expertise to the table. Evaluative mediation embraces that expertise and gives the parties more information with which to work.

Although at one time in the mediation field there seemed to be an exclusive emphasis on the skill of the mediator in managing the mediation process, times have changed and now there is a growing expectation that mediators of family disputes possess the traditional process skills as well as substantive expertise (Stark, 1996).[11] The need for additional expertise is evident in many substantive areas in which mediation is used and certainly illustrated in the family law arena. Most parties in a divorce context are experiencing the trauma of that event for the first time. By definition, they have only limited experience with it. They cannot be expected to know all of the issues that will need to be resolved, the range of possible options, or the preferences of the court in resolving the conflicts. Their emotion is certainly very real, but their knowledge of the law may be nonexistent. Those represented by lawyers may be more informed; still, additional expertise is often necessary for the resolution of the issues at hand. The mediator could be that resource if he or she is willing to move from a purely facilitative role to a more evaluative role.

3. Evaluation benefits the mediation process by making it more efficient. In essence, evaluation expressed at the appropriate point shortens the time of dialogue and moves the mediation toward settlement. There rarely is an end to the parties' advocacy of their own perspective. In moments of advocacy they seem to have an unrelenting desire to express themselves, even long after the story has been told and the arguments made. At some point, someone has to encourage a transition from unrelenting advocacy to problem solving. Often the expression of an opinion encourages such movement. When that movement occurs, the evaluation has served the parties well.

Most family advocates and mediators have encountered a party who has redefined life around the conflict. The hurt is so deep, the emotions so raw, and the anger so great that the conflict becomes the end. As illustrated effectively in the movie *The War of the Roses,* conflict can be consuming and an investment in it can be for life. Although the mediator may not be equipped to handle the deeper psychological dimensions of family conflict, he or she is able to see each party's investment in the conflict and begin moving them toward resolution. Evaluation of the process dynamics at an appropriate time can be helpful in resolving the issues and allowing the parties to move on in their lives.

4. Parties who have little or no influence on the opposing party benefit from the evaluation approach. The lack of influence might concern a perspective on the conflict, a particular solution to the conflict, or the consequences likely to occur if an agreement is not reached. The "reality testing" offered in the form of evaluation by the mediator is often influential in affecting the opposing party. When it comes to convincing the opposing party, the neutral third party has the platform from which to express a perspective and have it taken more seriously than if the same perspective were expressed by the other party.

In reality, each party would like the mediator to evaluate the *other party's* position using his or her most analytical thinking. One can easily imagine a husband and wife in family mediation as they look for signs that confirm the position each has taken. Few, however, relish the moment when the reality testing is turned their way.

5. Evaluation by the mediator is a benefit because it gives the parties an excuse to agree. In highly entrenched family disputes, neither party may see the possibility of agreement on a particular issue. There are many circumstances that lead to entrenchment. Sometimes the lack of agreement is related to bargaining on one side—a negotiation between a lawyer and the lawyer's client. For a variety of personal and professional considerations, the lawyer-advocate might find it difficult to suggest to the client that a case be settled. The lawyer cannot look "soft." Yet that same lawyer might recommend that the client carefully consider "what the mediator has said" and be thrilled that an outsider has said it. In that moment, the evaluation benefits the parties by allowing a socially acceptable way to move toward one another.

The psychological dynamics of conflict are complex. Parties resist agreement for a variety of reasons, but one of them is certainly because they just do not have a way to move toward agreement. After hours of often heated conversation, family disputants may have some idea of the right answer, but after years of conflict it is just not easy to embrace. The mediator who evaluates the situation and expresses an educated opinion regarding the attractiveness or appropriateness of a settlement may give the parties a neutral platform for agreement.

Ury suggests that one way to overcome an impasse in a negotiation is to "build [the disputants] a golden bridge" (1991, p. 105). The golden bridge could be built by one of the parties; it could also be engineered by the mediator. The golden bridge is the means by which parties can cross over the gulf of conflict to the shore of agreement. An evaluation can serve as a resource that allows the parties to agree with each other. Their psychological integrity is maintained because it was the mediator, after all, who suggested a particular course of action. They can point to the evaluation as the reason for making a deal that, until that point in time, was unacceptable.

Consider a child custody case wherein the father has openly expressed to friends and family that his former wife "will never see the kids again!" His position is clear, and it is expressed in a very public way. Now, months later, in the second session of a court-mandated mediation process, he realizes that the probability of the mother of his children never seeing her children again is a ridiculous position to have taken, no doubt resulting from his anger during a difficult moment. And yet he has taken that position. What does he do now? There may be little that he can do and save face (in his own mind), but there is a great deal that an evaluative mediator can do for him. Moving to accept the mediator's evaluation of what needs to be agreed upon (coincidentally consistent with what the judge will order) is something that the former husband and current father can do. We can imagine how he will explain it: It may never be what he thinks should be the case, but he is yielding to the mediator's judgment. He is greatly benefited by the evaluation that allows him to *move* while, at the same time, blaming that movement on someone else.

6. The quality of the analysis and advice given by the mediator may be greater than most other information received (Stulberg, 1997).[12] Who is to say that the parties know more about the application of law or the probable outcome of a matter in litigation than someone who might have mediated hundreds of cases with the same issues? Is it not a benefit to the party to receive the evaluation? Whereas the traditional view would be to defer to the party's expertise in mediation, those supportive of an evaluative model point to the value of correct information as an asset to the parties involved.

Take, for instance, a case in which unrepresented parties seek to resolve a child custody matter through the process of mediation. Assume that the mother is seeking full legal and physical custody of the couple's adolescent daughter who, at age 15, has an excellent relationship with her biological father and is willing to express a preference for continued joint physical custody. Also assume that there is information learned during the mediation that the mother is engaging in a battle for sole custody because she is angry at the father for an entirely different set of circumstances. While the mediator might approach the mediation in a purely facilitative way that focuses solely on the process, the mother is likely to benefit by listening to the mediator's evaluation of the likelihood of success in changing the custody arrangement. An evaluation of the likelihood of that course of action could save money and protect her relationship with her daughter. The potential benefit of outside information, drawn from the mediator's evaluation of the case, is an important resource for parties in conflict.

The benefits related to the use of evaluative techniques in mediation are substantial; they reflect an understanding of one way that a third party can be helpful. Not all professionals will agree with the importance of evaluation in mediation, nor will all who practice the art of mediation incorporate these strategies into their arsenal of techniques. Yet it is hoped that some recognition of value is accorded to the evaluative capabilities of a neutral third party.

THE FOCUS OF EVALUATION

Experience suggests that there is a variety of directions an evaluative mediator might take in seeking to understand, analyze, and then share a perspective with the parties in mediation. This section offers five areas of focus for the family mediator who is considering using evaluative techniques:

1. The mediator might *focus on the status of the negotiation* between the parties. If the role of the parties in mediation is to negotiate and the role of the mediator is to facilitate the negotiation, then one focus of evaluation might be the negotiation itself. As a trained third party, the mediator can evaluate the negotiation in a more objective and educated manner. The mediator can evaluate the dynamics between the parties, their movement or lack of movement toward a negotiated resolution, and identify barriers that might impede success. The evaluating mediator can also categorize the work of the parties in the negotiation in terms of their contribution, or lack of contribution, to progress as the communication process unfolds. In essence, the mediator who is not afraid to evaluate the negotiation and share that evaluation with the parties offers substantial guidance to the mediation process.

In a recent family case I mediated, the call for mediation came jointly from lawyers representing a divorcing husband and wife. The pending divorce, like many, occurred after more than 20 years of marriage. Although the children were grown, the dynamics of their relationships still affected the entire family. Complicating the matter were assets that included a large family business and the need to dispose of substantial real estate holdings. During the first mediation session, the parties needed to understand the impasse in the negotiations between their lawyers and recognize that if the negotiations did not move forward, the issues would be decided by someone with much less understanding of their circumstances and less concern for those involved. It was not until the state of the negotiation was diagnosed and the reality of the impasse made explicit to the parties that either party was willing to engage in more creative work to find solutions. This is not a negative comment about the lawyers involved; they were enthusiastic advocates. It is an illustration that the evaluation of the negotiation between the parties can be helpful in clarifying the impasse they are experiencing. The negotiation itself is an appropriate focus of the mediator's evaluation.

2. Evaluation in mediation might *focus on the behavior of parties*, both during the negotiation and outside the moments when more formal negotiation is taking place. This kind of focus can be especially helpful in divorce mediations where "acting out" behavior is prominent. Parties in divorce mediation are not necessarily in counseling at the same time they are participating in mediation. In fact, the mediation may be the only forum where the husband and wife talk to each other. If willing to evaluate behavior, the mediator is in a unique position to point out those actions or behaviors that may lead to an agreement or may keep an agreement from occurring. In this case, the evaluation does not replace psychotherapy in any sense of that resource. It focuses only on *the behavior that impacts the success of the mediation process*. At the same time, it can be a valuable aid to parties who cannot see the impact of their behavior on the negotiation process and therefore may miss getting what they ostensibly want—which is a deal.

In the case noted above, the husband was so uptight and angry about the situation that he simply would not participate in the conversation. He sat in the negotiation hour after hour, staring at his about-to-be-ex-wife and saying nothing. As it turned out, he sensed that he could avoid the divorce (which he did not want) if he simply refused to discuss its terms in the mediation process. His behavior, while not overtly disruptive, brought the negotiation to a standstill. Eventually, the mediator, after evaluating the husband's behavior, confronted him about it in a private session. Slowly, ever so slowly, the husband began to trust the mediator and discuss the issues that were important to him. Evaluating the behavior led to change in the behavior in a way that contributed to the negotiation.

3. The mediator's evaluation might *focus on the priorities of the parties*. Although difficult to ascertain in many mediations, understanding the priorities of the parties in terms of the resolution of the issues at hand, and in terms of life more generally, is an important aspect of the mediator's work. The move from understanding to evaluating such priorities may be important in achieving an agreement that maximizes for the parties what they can receive in the settlement. I am not advocating substitution of the mediator's priorities for the priorities of the parties; rather I am calling for the mediator's understanding of the parties' priorities so that they can be evaluated in light of what is actually achievable in a legal forum.

The parties in the divorce mediation described above had diametrically opposed priorities when it came to the involvement of the children in the family business. One parent prioritized the ongoing involvement of the children in the business and had the confidence that they could run it success-fully. The other parent wanted to get "the kids" out of the business so that the business could be more effectively operated; that parent had far less con-fidence in the ability of the children to run it. Those priorities, stated early in the mediation, created substantial challenge for those negotiating. The lawyers had to advocate for their client's wishes. The clients had invested in the stance each had taken. The mediator was the only one in the room who could evaluate the priorities in light of the success of the mediation process and talk with the parties about them. It was a challenging strategy because, in one sense, peoples' priorities are what they are. Yet if each held to the pri-orities articulated, then it would not be possible to handle the business in a way that continued to successfully support several families. The mediator's evaluation became the key to progress.

4. The evaluation of a mediator might *focus on particular plans* pro-posed as solutions to the conflict. Not all plans proposed by parties are equal in their usefulness or applicability to the conflict. Not all plans are viewed the same by courts (if an agreement must be approved by the court). Not all plans are equally durable or evoke the same level of com-mitment from the parties to the agreement. As a result, particularly in a case where the parties do not have other outside resources for evaluation, the evaluative mediator may be a key resource in helping the parties con-sider a particular plan in the most realistic and helpful way. The evaluative mediator may have handled hundreds of similar cases, seen how lasting particular plans might or might not be, and understand the court's view of particular issues. The willingness to share an evaluation of a plan being proposed may be critically important to the success of that plan and to the best interests of the parties being served. Some would claim that the re-fusal to evaluate in such a way might itself impede the conflict resolution work of those in mediation.

The need to evaluate a proposed plan was certainly evident in the above case. At the end of the first 8 hours of mediation, the husband asked the me-diator, "Do you know what would solve these problems? My wife just needs to come home." That was a plan that would solve things in his mind, but there was no indication from his wife, who at that point had been living apart from him for months, that she wanted or intended to "come home." The husband thought this suggestion was a solution, but it was not one that appeared to have any possibility of success. Deep into denial and caught up in wishful thinking, his lawyer could not move him to look at a future any different from what he wished it to be. It was the job of the mediator to evaluate the husband's idea and then to encourage him to reevaluate it. Making a judg-ment about a proposed plan that is totally unworkable is one contribution that an evaluative mediator can make.

5. The mediator who evaluates might *focus on the alternatives* outside the mediated negotiation. Just as every legal case is settled in the shadow of the law, every negotiation is conducted in the shadow of its alternative. In effect,

knowing, understanding, and correctly perceiving the alternative to a negoti-ated agreement in divorce or family mediation are central to the potential willingness of parties to agree to the terms proposed. In many cases, the only reason to agree to what is being proposed in a negotiated setting is its attrac-tiveness when compared to a less attractive alternative. If the alternative is more attractive, then the terms offered in the mediated settlement would usually not be accepted. A mediator experienced in divorce and family law, or in the specific subject of dispute, can evaluate proposed solutions in the context of real-world alternatives. The evaluation directs the mediator either to encourage the acceptance of the proposed agreement or to consider the dangers in accepting the terms proposed. The mediator's experience or ex-pertise is most helpful in that evaluative moment, whether that experience is in child development, financial planning, real estate, or another subject in dispute.

In the above case study, the parties needed to focus on the reality of how their case would be handled if they were not successful in negotiating a reso-lution. While their lawyers painted optimistic pictures of their potential suc-cess in court, the reality was that if the court disposed of their multimillion dollar properties or ordered them to do it on the court's timetable, rather than transitioning the tangible assets into separate property over time, it would cost the couple millions of dollars. Selling the properties for their cur-rent business value would have brought only limited amounts. Selling the properties for their land development value over the next decade or so would have brought millions more to the table. Someone needed to evaluate the varying costs of resolving the real estate issue in mediation versus litiga-tion. The clients could not make such an evaluation, because they did not have the knowledge of what the court would do. Their lawyers could not do so objectively, because each was predicting success in that alternative forum. It was up to the neutral third party to evaluate the alternative and interject that evaluation into the mediation.

Each of the areas identified above may be an appropriate focus for an evaluative mediator. If positioned on a continuum, from left to right, the ar-eas of potential focus move from less onerous to more onerous.

Some mediators may feel comfortable with work that focuses in one or more of those areas but not comfortable embracing all of them. For in-stance, engaging in evaluation related to the status of negotiation and the party's behavior may be acceptable, but moving to evaluating the parties' pri-

Status of negotiation ———— Behavior of parties ———— Priorities of parties ———— Proposed plans ———— Alternatives to agreement

Less onerous ————————————————————————————————→ More onerous

orities, plans, or alternatives may not be comfortable for the mediator. In essence, the continuum suggests areas of possible evaluative work while recognizing that, even within the evaluative context, there may be different areas of focus chosen by each mediator.

THE EVALUATION GRID

In considering evaluative techniques in mediation, many mediators question whether or not evaluation should occur at all, as previously discussed. This may be the wrong question. In looking closely at the work of a mediator, most observers would conclude that, on some level, all mediators evaluate. Mediators make informed decisions based upon the information presented. They mentally process information, formulate judgments, and respond according to their theoretical framework. They even decide what they think of the parties involved and what the outcome should be. If mediators did not evaluate (at least internally), it would be difficult to move the parties toward a settlement.

Perhaps the question is not *whether* to evaluate but, rather, should the evaluation by the mediator be expressed and, if so, how? If one considers the reality of at least the mediator's internal evaluation, then the focus becomes on what and how any of it might be shared. Does the mediator react to evidence, reveal a feeling about the case, or share an idea about what a settlement might look like? Does the mediator understand the reality of the circumstance and test the parties' understanding as well? Does the mediator ask questions with the intention of affecting the parties' perspectives? Many mediators, even those who would consider themselves more facilitative in approach, carry out those tasks without violating their commitment to the process and to the parties.

If the question moves beyond the willingness to evaluate, the focus must be centered on *what* to evaluate and *how* to express that evaluation. It might be helpful to view the nature of evaluation in terms of the evaluation grid, which is a tool used to help illustrate the choices available to effective mediators in evaluating their work.

The vertical line on the grid reflects *what* the mediator does. The top end of the line represents the expression of the evaluation as a direct instruction to the parties. The bottom end of the line represents the expression of the evaluation as a suggestion to the parties. Both ends reflect the thinking of the mediator and a decision to share that evaluation with the parties. There is, however, a range in the directness of the expression. Similarly, a counselor determines how direct or suggestive a message needs to be communicated to someone in therapy. It is not a question *that* something will be communicated but, rather, the *degree of directness* in that communication.

Experienced mediators, as well as legal advocates, are often able to determine the degree of directness required after meeting with the client for only a few minutes. For clients who are particularly attentive, a mere suggestion could send them down a new path. Once the suggestion is made (however subtly presented), they pick up the cue and proceed in a way that the mediator or advocate believes would be beneficial.

Unfortunately, not all parties or clients are in tune with what is suggested to them. They might be caught in the drama of the moment and miss the subtle cues that were expressed. They might be so invested in a particular solution or outcome that their ability to consider different ideas is limited. They might not understand the subtleties of less direct communication and need more direct guidance.

At the Straus Institute for Dispute Resolution at Pepperdine University School of Law, staff meetings involve many people who are well trained in the art of mediation. Often, each person is both a teacher of the skill and a practitioner as well. You can imagine the delicate nature of the conversation when each person is trying to facilitate the conversation of everyone else at the table! Sometimes the conversation is so diplomatic that those around the table just do not understand what is being communicated. Often, a person will prompt a colleague to "just say it!" The parties may want communication to be more direct.

On the evaluation grid, the vertical line indicates the directness in communicating an evaluation with a range from instruction (telling the party what to do) to suggestion (merely bringing an idea to the attention of the party). Each could be more or less extreme and communicated with a variety of feelings, intensity, and emotion. Obviously, both are assertive and active in that the decision has been made to share an evaluative perspective. It is solely the manner of doing so that is under consideration.

The choice of communicating in an instructive or suggestive format is the choice of the mediator, the one engaging in the communication. The mediator's experience, judgment, and wisdom may contribute to the decision. In addition, the mediator uses his or her perception of the party receiving the information to guess at, or intuit, the level of directness most needed.

The recipient of the communication obviously influences the success of the mediator's communication choice. The party decides if the message feels like, or is interpreted as, an instruction or a suggestion. What was intended by the communicator may not be the same as what is perceived by the recipient. However, that ambiguity is inherent in all communication, and in the often delicate communication in mediation, it is especially present.

The horizontal continuum below represents how the evaluative mediator communicates his or her perspective. One end of this continuum involves making statements and the other relies, almost exclusively, on asking questions. Each is a very different approach to communicating.

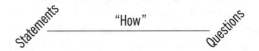

Making statements may be a more succinct, clear, and overall efficient method of conveying information. Some people benefit from the clarity of knowing "where one stands" because it allows them to make their own judgments in that context. At the same time, however, such an approach may evoke reaction rather than responsiveness and thereby create its own conflict. Some people are offended and resistant when they feel they are being told what to do by others.

In contrast, asking questions—which is the core technique offered by many counselors and mediators—has the advantage of being the more widely accepted mediational approach. Asking questions conveys respect and regard to the parties and allows them to "buy in" to a message or course of action. At the same time, however, questions tend to hide the message, take considerably longer to move people in one direction or another, and perhaps may never fully communicate the precise information embedded in the question. The frustration caused by the failure to communicate may not be worth the effort to "bring people around" through a long and laborious series of questions.

The two lines form a grid that may be useful in understanding the choices underlying the work of an evaluative mediator. The degree of direction chosen (from instruction to suggestion) and the technique chosen (statements or questions) position the mediator's work on the grid. In considering where to position one's mediation work on the grid, it may be worthwhile to consider it more likely that mediators give instructions by making statements and make suggestions by asking questions. However, it is possible for accomplished mediators to give strong instructions in a carefully worded question and to make gentle suggestions in the form of a statement. The art of mediation is the art of communicating. In the expression of a mediator's evaluation, that communication can be raised to a level of great sophistication.

To illustrate the evaluation grid, consider the mediator's evaluation of one divorced parent's lack of involvement in the lives of his or her children. Assume that there are no extenuating circumstances that would prevent the parent from carrying out normal parenting responsibilities; the parent is simply not willing to do so. Also assume that the mediator feels that the children would benefit by the involvement of both parents in their lives and views the mediation session as one of the few places where this level of involvement can be discussed.

If the mediator chooses to be instructive through a statement, it might sound something like "I have had a great deal of experience with children going through their parents' divorce, and you need to be continuously involved in their lives!" If the mediator chooses to be instructive through a question, it might sound something like "Don't you think that more involvement in your children's lives at this critical time of transition would be helpful?"

If the mediator chooses to be suggestive through a statement, it might sound something like "I would hope that you would consider your children during this difficult time and how your contact with them might contribute to their ability to manage this transition." If the mediator chooses to be suggestive through a question, it might sound something like "Have you considered the positive impact your involvement with your children might have during this time of transition?" While the wording in the examples might be improved when in practice, it seeks merely to illustrate that the "what" and "how" of an evaluative mediator's work can be strategically decided, as illustrated on the evaluator's grid below:

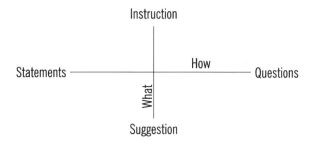

A STRATEGIC APPROACH TO EVALUATION

If there is perceived merit in the use of evaluation as a mediation technique, the challenge for the mediator is to determine how to use it strategically. Its effective use is not as simple as the stereotype described earlier suggests. Like much of the mediation dynamic, the tool of evaluation demands the mediator's careful understanding, insight, and sensitivity to the parties involved. The following ideas identify *times* when evaluation might be appropriate and *types* of evaluation that might be useful. The implementation of the ideas should occur within a philosophy of mediation that values the dynamics of the process as a continuing negotiation between the parties.

Evaluative mediators should not lose sight of the *process* they are conducting:

1. If evaluation is to be utilized, it should take place at a time when it is most influential. Evaluation is not a tool with which the mediator demonstrates his or her competence, nor one whereby the mediator manipulates a case in such a way that it comes out as he or she designates. Rather, evaluation is a technique used to move the parties from their entrenched positions, which have resulted in an impasse, to a mutually agreeable settlement.

Experienced family mediators know that the timing of evaluation is critical in the context of divorce. The anger of the moment and the residue of hard feelings, disappointment, and hurt often prevent reason from prevailing. When parties are working through the dynamics of separation and change, there may be moments when a third party's perspective is not even heard, let alone considered, and other moments when it will be greatly influential in facilitating resolution. If expressed too early, evaluation falls on deaf ears. If expressed at the right time, the parties move toward an agreement. As in much of life, timing is everything!

The "right time" can occur at various stages of the mediation process. It might occur during the initial conversation with the parties, when the only task is to set the agenda for the mediation process. Evaluating what is and is not relevant to the process might be helpful in focusing precious time on the most important issues. Alternatively, the right time might not occur till the end of the process, when the parties are deciding who gets the last of the relatively small value. Although no one can specify in the abstract when evaluation should occur, it is wise to bear in mind that timing is a critical factor in helping the parties reach an agreement.

2. The style of evaluation is important. Mediators vary tremendously in the way they express their perspectives or evaluations. There are those who, in almost a self-effacing way, softly suggest through questions an extremely tentative perspective on a particular issue. If a map of the United States were superimposed on the evaluation grid, they "live" near Orlando, Florida—a location that reflects suggestions made via questions.

On the other hand, there are those who, with tremendous self-confidence and egocentric focus, express their evaluation on how a particular issue should be resolved in a dogmatic and perhaps abrasive way. On the same map, those individuals would be located somewhere close to Seattle, Washington, where instruction is provided via explicit, even emphatic, statements. Mediators at both extremes seem to continue to be busy in the world of professional mediation. Why some people pay for an evaluation that is so tentative that it may not influence them at all and others pay for an evaluation that results in discomfort and embarrassment is a mystery. But individuals do so voluntarily, and on a daily basis, because it is helpful for them and their particular personalities.

3. The nature of the evaluation is affected by the type of relationship the mediator forms with the parties. Again, there is great diversity in the field. Some mediators want to be liked and perceived as colleagues in the grand problem-solving process, and who, having established excellent relationships with the parties, will draw upon the sense of trust and regard to provide an evaluative perspective. Alternatively, there are those individuals who seemingly do not care about their personal relationship with the parties and who are more interested in putting a notch on their mediation success belt. Clearly, the kind of relationship the mediator fosters (or does not foster) with the parties influences the nature and approach to evaluation. Although such a relationship is important to some, it is far less important to others.

The structure of family mediation may influence the mediator's interest in his or her relationship with the parties. Private mediators who depend on referrals to support a professional practice may feel a high degree of concern that the relationship be as positive as possible. Those who engage in family mediation as volunteers or in the context of a public agency have less interest in "future business" and therefore may not seek that aspect of a relationship for practice development purposes. This observation is not made to denigrate the latter group; their work is particularly helpful to society and the people they serve. It is made simply to point out that the nature of the professional relationship sought in mediation may be different.

4. There may be a connection between the use and nature of evaluation and the type of issue that is the subject of the mediation process. For instance, if it is very clear how a court would decide an issue, the mediator may be more willing to provide an evaluative perspective. In the family context, a dispute about whether the noncustodial parent who is earning sufficient income should contribute to child support is not a question in most jurisdictions. Even the amount may be clearly set out in a court-approved schedule. The mediator's evaluation of a plan that would contradict the clear court mandate would be perceived by most as helpful in establishing a child support agreement that would be approved by the court and acceptable to the parties.

On the other hand, there are issues whose court outcome is far less clear, and as a result mediators are less likely to be evaluative. For instance, the selection of which school a child should attend may be quite controversial between the parents, and the court's willingness to decide or even consider the issue may be unclear. As a result, the mediator may be far less willing to suggest direction to the parties on this substantive issue and choose instead to focus on helping the parties articulate their own assessments. It is *predictability* that provides the mediator with confidence in deciding to act in an evaluative manner.

5. The focus of the evaluation should be considered carefully. Earlier in this chapter, choices were presented relating to the focus of evaluative activities. Oftentimes, evaluating the merits of a party's position or the likelihood of prevailing in an adversarial forum is needed in order to move people from

a position they have taken previously. Sometimes, even in a family law context, the focus of the evaluation is a numerical settlement on items that have quantifiable values. At other times the attitudes, actions, and behavior of the parties need to be evaluated by a neutral third party. Or the evaluation may be directed to the state of the parties' negotiation and what needs to be done to expedite it. The counsel in this chapter has not suggested what the focus should be; rather, the intent has been to expand the range of directions an evaluative mediator might take.

6. Finally, the method of the evaluation might make a difference in the mediator's work. The methods largely concern the degree of directness and communication techniques described earlier in this chapter. Selecting the right method, using it at the right time, and using it with people who would be affected beneficially by it are the keys to successful evaluative efforts.

CONCLUSION

The debate continues regarding the most controversial technique in mediation—evaluation. Perhaps the perspective in this chapter, advocating for the use of more evaluative techniques, will add to the dialogue in a way that broadens the menu of approaches considered by mediators to assist parties during their time of conflict. In the end, it is not about those professionals who have chosen the family mediation field for their work; it is about clients who allow mediators entrance into the intimate area of their conflict in hope that resolution will be reached. Professional mediators should be expansive in their consideration of techniques that contribute to resolution. When mediators assist clients in reaching an effective, efficient, and respectful resolution of their family matters, they are fulfilling the high calling of the peacemaker.

NOTES

1. Marks (1996) contends there are cases in which the mediator's responsibility is to "step over the threshold from facilitator to evaluator," (p. 48A).

2. According to Aaron (1996), evaluation is a last step, but in many cases skipping that step means missing the sole opportunity for settlement.

3. An example of the debate is the Fifth Annual Conference for Mediators and Arbitrators sponsored by the Florida Dispute Resolution Center in 1996.

4. Bush and Folger (1994) assert that the mediator's goal of swift and secure settlements often fail to meet the parties' needs for a transformative process.

5. Although this description is necessarily exaggerated and stereotypical, it is a reflection of one aspect of the mediation marketplace. That aspect of practice was clearly evident to me when I spent 5 years as vice-president of one of the most successful dispute resolution firms in the United States.

6. Mediator Lawrence Watson observed, "You must take this evaluation issue in light of the issue of self determination. If you're evaluating in a way that interferes with the par-

ties' consensual agreement, with their independent decision about the settlement, I don't care if you're 'evaluating' or 'hypothesizing'; whatever you're doing, it's wrong" (in Alfini, 1996, p. 928).

7. As Professor Carrie Menkel-Meadow (1996) points out, the possibility that the evaluation might be "wrong" raises ethical and practical concerns.

8. Professor Johnston is a former Director of the Center for Dispute Resolution at Willamette University College of Law. He uses that statement in training programs conducted for mediators around the world.

9. Mediator John Bickerman (1996) suggests that evaluation may be the only way an agreement in some mediations can be achieved.

10. In a dialogue with Professor James Alfini (Alfini & Clay, 1994), mediator Gerald Clay contends that many mediators are hired precisely for their technical expertise.

11. Professor James Stark (1996) points out that in studies of court-annexed and lawyer-controlled mediations, lawyers expect mediators to firmly guide the mediation toward appropriate grounds for settlement.

12. Professor Josh Stulberg (1997) contends that evaluation is often sought as parties to a litigated matter prepare for trial. In that circumstance, experienced mediators may have better information than most litigants.

REFERENCES

Aaron, M. C. (1996). ADR toolbox: The highwire act of evaluation. *Alternatives to the High Cost of Litigation, 14,* 62–64.

Alfini, J. J., & Clay, G. S. (1994, Spring). Should lawyer mediators be prohibited from providing legal advice or evaluations? *Dispute Resolution Magazine,* p. 8–9, 11.

Alfini, J. J. (1996). Evaluative versus facilitative mediation: A discussion. *Florida State University Law Review, 24,* 919–935.

Bickerman, J. (1996). Evaluative mediator responds. *Alternatives to the High Cost of Litigation, 14,* 70.

Bush, R., & Folger, J. (1994). *The promise of mediation.* San Francisco: Jossey-Bass.

Furey, K. (1995). Mediators cannot be both mediators and evaluators. *Advocate (Idaho), 38,* 11–14.

Kolb, D., & Kressel, K. (1994). The realities of making talk work. In D. Kolb & Associates, *When talk works: Profiles of mediators.* San Francisco: Jossey-Bass.

Kovach, K. K., & Love, L. P. (1996). "Evaluative" mediation is an oxymoron. *Alternatives to the High Cost of Litigation, 14,* 31–32.

Love, L. P. (1997). The top ten reasons why mediators should not evaluate. *Florida State University Law Review, 24,* 937–948.

Marks, J. B. (1996, May). Evaluative mediation—oxymoron or essential tool? *The American Lawyer,* p. 48A.

Menkel-Meadow, C. (1996). Is mediation the practice of law? *Alternatives to the High Cost of Litigation, 14,* 57–61.

Riskin, L. L. (1996). Understanding mediators' orientations, strategies and techniques: A grid for the perplexed. *Harvard Negotiation Law Review, 1,* 7–51.

Stark, J. H. (1996). Preliminary reflections on the establishment of a mediation clinic. *Clinical Law Review, 2,* 457–521.

Stulberg, J. P. (1997). Facilitative versus evaluative mediation orientations: Piercing the "grid" lock. *Florida State University Law Review, 24,* 985–1005.

Ury, W. (1991). *Getting past no.* New York: Bantam.

CHAPTER 5

Therapeutic Mediation with High-Conflict Parents

Effective Models and Strategies

MARSHA KLINE PRUETT
JANET R. JOHNSTON

High-conflict parents present special challenges for mediators. For these parents, a more intensive intervention is often needed to help them maintain boundaries that protect their children from ongoing conflict. This chapter explores the individual and couple dynamics of high-conflict divorce and presents two models that integrate mediation and therapeutic strategies to effectively assist high-conflict parents resolve parenting disputes. Results of research that support the efficacy of these models are presented.

Over the past 25 years divorce mediation has slowly emerged as an increasingly popular alternative to adversarial dispute resolution when child custody issues are in dispute. Its purported goals are to help parents cooperate, communicate, and shield their children from involvement in parental disputes inside and outside of court. From the outset, mediation attracted and proved successful with couples that desired to avoid the adversarial process and maximize the possibilities of co-parenting after divorce. Clinical descriptions and early evaluation research indicated that couples whose concerns were successfully mediated (1) made progress in dealing with the emotional aspects of divorce, (2) exhibited manageable levels of anger toward their ex-spouses, (3) demonstrated a willingness to compromise, and (4) claimed no gross psychopathology or physical abuse between the parties (Milne, 1983; Kressel, 1987). Research also revealed differences between mediating couples and their adversarial counterparts. Mediating couples reported higher levels of perceived fair-mindedness by their spouses, perceived themselves as more capable of cooperating about children's issues, and viewed the other parent as more competent than did adversarial ex-spouses (Kelly, 1991). A review of numerous studies found mediation to be superior to the traditional adversarial process for custody and visitation disputes among couples with moderate levels of conflict, relatively limited issues, and reasonable negotiation capacities (Emery, 1994; Kelly, 1996; Sprenkel & Storm, 1983). Moreover, mediation was philosophically appealing in its emphasis on empowering parents to make their own decisions and avoiding unnecessary state interference in family affairs. As a rational, issue-focused, and problem-solving process, regular divorce mediation assumed that parents themselves are the ones who are best able to identify and advocate on behalf of the needs of their children.

Court-based mediation, a model that generally encompasses higher-conflict parents, has drawn more mixed reactions from mediation supporters. Concerns focus on the potential abuse of confidentiality by mediators who, in accord with their contract with the courts and with clients, report to the judge and/or legal counsel (Milne, 1983). Another concern is whether the mediator can and will influence an agreement because of the power invested in him or her by the court to help reach resolution (Milne, 1983).

Concerns about the mediator's power and role in the context of high-conflict mediations raise further questions. One especially sensitive issue is that of power imbalances between highly conflictive spouses, and the mediator's role in protecting each client and managing the power imbalances. The question of mediation's efficacy and advisability for couples that report episodes of domestic violence, for example, is receiving increased research attention as a result of heated debates from professionals and consumers with varying perspectives. Specifically, it is argued by women's advocates that mediators cannot remedy the power imbalances between couples in an abusive relationship in order to protect victims and reach fair agreements (Girdner, 1990). One study reported that compared to couples that used attorney negotiation to reach agreements, mediation made a greater contribution toward reducing couples' postdivorce verbal and physical abuse (Ellis, 1995; Ellis & Stuckless, 1996). Other research findings concur that mediation may be helpful and beneficial for certain ex-partners between whom domestic violence has occurred, particularly when (1) both spouses were aggressive, not particularly fearful of the other, and were interactively violent in the marriage, or (2) there were one, or at most two, separation-specific incidents after a nonviolent marriage, and particular safeguards were put in place during the mediation process (see Hahn & Kleist, 2000; Kelly, 1996).

However, research also indicates that some children of divorced parents with ongoing conflict suffer as much after mediation as before, indicating the need for more intensive intervention to help parents maintain boundaries that protect their children from ongoing marital/parental conflict (Kitzmann & Emery, 1994). It is evident from studies that high levels of anger and marital conflict do not necessarily preclude couples from reaching agreements. However, more session hours, experienced and highly trained mediators, and a specific focus on areas of relational issues are all elements that improve the likelihood of success in high-conflict cases (see Ezzell's, 2001 review). Amid ongoing debate and investigation about the potential effectiveness of mediation for higher-conflict families, mounting evidence suggests that the original premises of mediation can be expanded to include higher-conflict families but that new, creative methods of intervention are needed.

This chapter examines two individual models of impasse-directed therapy. The models are replicable, empirically tested, and offer encouraging results about the efficacy of such models for use with very-high-conflict families with children.

INDIVIDUAL AND COUPLE DYNAMICS OF HIGH-CONFLICT DIVORCE

Mediation-type interventions with high-conflict couples require special knowledge and skills in order to have any chance of being effective. Interventions with divorcing families that are entrenched in conflict and chronic custody disputes should be grounded in a basic understanding of the psychological and systemic dynamics that generate and sustain the disputes. (See Johnston, in press, for a full discussion.) In brief, Johnston describes how high-conflict parents are susceptible, to varying degrees, to the stresses of loss and rejection that are inherent in the divorce process and its aftermath. A relatively small but highly vulnerable group of separating spouses are especially susceptible to continuing conflict as a result of having experienced previous traumatic losses, such as the untimely death of a parent, child, or sibling. More often, members of this group are vulnerable as a result of never having separated or individuated from their own primary caretakers because of early emotional deprivation and childhood trauma. For them, the marital separation can trigger panic and intense anxiety about being alone again; when this happens, parents may cling to the child as a substitute for the ex-spouse or other lost person in their life (Johnston, in press).

Many of these parents are emotionally fragile individuals who manifest chronic difficulty in maintaining a positive and stable sense of self. Old feelings of shame, failure, or "badness" are evoked by the separation and become part of the response to the ex-spouse's rejection and the threatened loss or perceived "betrayal" of the child. These feelings produce overwhelming anxiety that is typically managed by psychological processes of splitting and projective identification: Painful, unwanted feelings are associated solely with the former spouse, in order to attain relief from anxiety and the disturbing feelings that accompany it. These persons tend to view the other parent as irresponsible, even dangerous, while they view themselves as the essential, responsible, and safe caretaker. Among the most narcissistically vulnerable people, one partner may experience the other's rejection and custody demands as a devastating attack and, in defense, develop rigid ideas of betrayal, conspiracy, and exploitation at the hands of the ex-mate. The children are pressured to mirror the rejected parents feelings and perceptions in order to assure themselves that they will continue to derive nurturance and caretaking without being rejected, in turn.

The problems presented by such parents begin intrapsychically but are reinforced by the social world of the divorcing family. In most cases, and to varying degrees, the negative views of one or both spouses have some basis in fact, as part of their real experience of the other spouse's violent, neglectful, or substance-abusing behavior. The goal for the mediator/clinician is to help parents distinguish unrealistic from realistic fears about the other parent's capacity to safely and competently care for the child.

To achieve this goal, the mediator must combine therapeutic counseling with mediation techniques in order to assist the parents in making use of mediation, and to provide additional psychological supports that assist the family in reaching a higher level of functioning. The mediator helps the family problem solve and contain the parental conflict. In doing so, the mediator also takes an active educational and advocacy role around the developmental needs of the child. The parents receive intensive support and assistance in separating their own issues from the needs of their child and in viewing their child as a separate person, capable of experiencing his or her own individual relationship with both parents. In this way, the mediation stays child focused throughout its course. Only in such an environment can the divorce settlement be finalized and the longer-term well-being of the child fostered.

IMPASSE-DIRECTED MEDIATION

The term "therapeutic mediation" describes the nature of the mediation; it also implies the specialized training and skills required by the mediator. The description to follow is best applied by a skilled mediator/clinician who has considerable experience working with fragile, vulnerable, narcissistic, and potentially volatile people. Without such experience and training, the family is likely to best the mediator, adding to the considerable load of problems already plaguing the family during divorce.

Although a number of therapeutic mediation approaches have been described (e.g., Irving & Benjamin, 1995; Saposnek, 1998), the most comprehensive model is that of impasse-directed mediation with high-conflict couples. This model is composed of three phases of therapeutic work after the initial intake (Johnston & Campbell, 1988; Roseby & Johnston, 1997). At intake, parents are informed about the 12-week length of their program. They agree to the complete confidentiality of proceedings, including the unavailability of the mediation to the court, and a sliding scale (familiar to clinicians) is assessed. The therapeutic mediation work described below is depicted in Figure 5.1.

Three Phases of Impasse-Directed Mediation

Prenegotiation Counseling Phase

The therapeutic mediation begins with an information-gathering phase that sets up the potential to work with the family during the next two phases. Each parent, child, and parent–child dyad are seen separately in order to emphasize the process of separation on which the parents are, or must begin, embarking. A history of the marriage and separation are obtained from each parent as well as a developmental sketch of each child, along with an assessment of each child's response to the separation and divorce. This focus assists the mediator/clinician in beginning to unravel the nature and potency of the impasse and to identify any available family resources that might be enlisted to support their behavioral change and settle major aspects of the dispute.

Impasse-related strategies aim to raise the parents' level of awareness of the psychological motivations underlying their disputes. Some parents are able to use their insights to better comprehend their own personal and couple dynamics, typically resulting in more rational behavior. A father begins to understand that his motivation for complaining about the mother's parenting emanates from his wish that she would be unable to parent their children without him and therefore reconsider her decision to divorce him. For others, such insights are not sufficient, and the parents cannot face their understanding without feeling blamed, attacked, or exposed. A deeply humiliated mother, whose husband fell in love with a secretary at his office, seeks to reassure herself of her own self-worth by proving him to be an irresponsible, "bad" parent. As she is supported and reassured about how special she is to her children and what a good job she has done in protecting them from the hurt of the divorce, her need to attack him in court (e.g., a public arena) and to view him as a lousy father decreases. For these parents, careful redirection of their defenses is necessary to help them design and maintain successful divorce arrangements. Indirect support, rather than insight or supportive confrontation, helps some parents to shore up their confidence and sense of self. The mediator points out the parent's strengths and reframes conflicts as emanating from positions of strength, such as protective feelings for his or her children. Another indirect tack may be useful for a parent so afraid of loss and abandonment that he or she cannot tolerate letting go of the marital relationship. Encouraging new adult relationships that

Phases	Court Referral
I.	Intake Center ⇓
Information Gathering and Assessment	Parents are informed about the service: Its counseling–mediation nature and separation from legal proceedings are highlighted. A sliding-fee scale is assessed. ⇓
	Information-Gathering Interviews
	One or two interviews are conducted with each parent and each child, seen separately. Significant others are invited to participate in counseling. Standardized measures and questionnaires are completed. ⇓
	Strategy Conference
	Service providers develop a dispute-specific assessment of each family and formulate an individual or group intervention plan. ⇓
II.	Individual Family Impasse-Directed Mediation Model
Prenegotiation Counseling Phase (preparation for negotiation)	Each family member is seen in individual and, when appropriate, conjoint interviews.
	Length of service depends on the family's individual needs.
	One counselor/mediator sees the entire family.
III.	Conjoint interviews are conducted (if appropriate) with parents to finalize plans and draft access agreements.
Negotiation or Conflict Resolution Phase	
IV.	The last session reviews insights gained and settlements reached; referrals are made for counseling or to court. ⇓
Implementation Phase	On-Call Consultation
	A counselor mediator is available to the family for emergencies and continued mediation. ⇓
	6-Month and 24-Month Follow-Up

FIGURE 5.1. Flowchart and structure of impasse-directed mediation.

shift the parent's focus also supports readiness for separation from the past relationship.

Another strategy is to ask parents whether their problem-solving efforts are producing desired effects, indirectly inviting them to acknowledge that their current strategies are unfruitful. The more reflective parent may absorb more of the mediator's efforts, as he or she is coached to resolve conflicts without provoking the other parent's vulnerabilities. The parent who is the lesser equipped to work through his or her conflicts may require an intervention that includes someone in the parent's external world: the former spouse, a new spouse, a grandparent of the children, etc.

As the mediator endeavors to penetrate the parental impasse, he or she also works to enhance parents' understanding of their children's developmentally appropriate needs as separate from their own. As the mediation progresses and the parents are better able to tolerate such interventions, the mediator moves from sensitizing parents to the children's needs to actual counseling. Through a sequence of questions, the mediator elicits parental awareness of the children's perspectives, the risks of continued fighting to their continued development and the pain the children experience as a result of the conflict. The mediator/clinician draws on knowledge gleaned from each child's sessions, and with permission from the child, he or she may share, for example, the child's artwork with the parents, a powerful medium for demonstrating the child's inner world and response to family events. For example, a boy's drawing depicting himself crouched in a corner of the paper, looking away from everyone else in the family, may vividly illustrate to his parents how frightened, alone, and unable to share his suffering he perceives himself to be. If needed, the mediator eventually begins confronting parents with examples of ways they prolong their children's suffering by entangling him or her in their disputes.

Finally, the mediator lays the groundwork for establishing a workable agreement between the parties. This requires clarification of legal realities, distinguishing what the law can enforce from the parents' illusions about the law. For example, parents often want an agreement that makes the other parent more responsible or that punishes him or her for being a disappointing spouse and/or parent. Through confrontation, education, encouragement that parents obtain legal consultation, and interviews with child protective workers and court personnel, the mediator helps the parents define and limit their options, preparing them for planning a specific parenting agreement.

Negotiation or Conflict Resolution Phase

In this subsequent phase, the couple meets together for the first time for the purpose of specifying their parenting plan. Sometimes parents induce a crisis at this juncture, indicating their lack of readiness to move ahead in a straightforward manner. This crisis may entail an incident of verbal abuse that escalates to shoving or snatching the child at the time of transfer between parental residences, or a refusal to allow the child to make a scheduled transition to the other parent's home, prompting a screaming match on the telephone, in front of the child. Predicting such regressions can help forestall them, as they lose some of their power. Alternatively, the mediator can intervene directly as the parents describe a recent incident, reminding them verbally or with a gesture that they are becoming mired in their impasse and escalating again.

Although the mediator may occasionally confront parents directly, people who are most frightened or psychologically vulnerable often need reassurance, rather than a confrontation that serves only to deepen their fears and maladaptive behaviors. It is part of the clinician's art to know when direct confrontation will be effective versus counterproductive. Parents for whom the separation is a narcissistic wound of major proportion, evoking profound shame and rage, generally do not respond well to direct descriptions of their maladaptive behaviors or interpretations of the underlying causes. Reframing their negative behaviors in terms of more benign or positive intentions and supporting their developing capacity to maintain self-control reinforces their incipient ability to deescalate the conflict. For example, say the father does not return the mother's phoned request to talk about the child. The mediator might reframe his refusal to communicate as a way of trying to avoid a predictable fight with the other parent and commend him on his efforts—misplaced though they may be.

Paradoxical injunctions are useful, especially when control is an issue with ex-spouses and they are locked into bitter power struggles with each other and/or the mediator. The mediator can acknowledge the parents' need to fight, help them develop a forum, and identify topics over which to continue their battles. For example, the mediator might suggest that the parents meet for coffee at the local doughnut shop to fight some more about which parent actually bought most of the child's winter clothes. For couples who experience shock and perhaps great shame around the events of the separation, some attention may need to be given to reworking the events, giving each parent an opportunity to discuss his or her views of critical incidents. A woman might wish to discuss, once again, how she happened to learn about her husband's infidelity, and whether or not there was evidence that he had planned to tell her, as he insists he did. Apologies carry remarkable power to help heal old wounds, and the mediator should encourage them whenever possible.

Finally, for those couples that have difficulty dealing with the final task of creating a viable parenting plan, use of stories or analogies are particularly helpful to preserve face and steer the couple clear of the old impasses. The mediator might choose a myth or folk tale; for example, the tale could describe an animal that rushes into everything and hurries to complete tasks, only to make careless mistakes, in interaction with an animal that delays completing everything that has to be done, to the annoyance of everyone around.

Once the couple is able to move forward in developing a parenting plan, the actual plan specifications usually become clear rapidly. Issues get defined, options get discussed and evaluated, specific alternatives selected, details clarified, and agreements drafted. For all couples, but especially high-conflict ones, careful attention to wording and language prevents the emergence of prior impasses. The agreement must be specific enough that the couple can have positive interactions and slowly build mutual trust. At the same time, it must satisfy both parents' particular fears. For example, a father wants it specified to the school that both parents are primary parents for the sake of notification in case of emergency. A mother who has felt dominated wants some openness in the agreement, so that she can make minor modifications without feeling boxed into a "final" agreement that may not meet her work schedule over the long term.

Implementation Phase

The final agreement is taken to attorneys for review. The attorneys specify who will draft the documents and how they will be filed with the court. During this final phase, the mediator takes a clinical consulting role and remains present to the family when crises arise or unanticipated glitches are encountered.

OUTCOMES OF THE IMPASSE-DIRECTED MODEL

A 2- to 3-year follow-up was conducted to assess the effectiveness of the impasse-directed mediation model with high-conflict couples (Johnston & Campbell, 1988). Success was determined by how many people mediated agreements; the number who maintained, or were able to renegotiate, the agreements over the follow-up period; and the number who returned to court during the same period. In addition, instruments were used in interviews to assess the extent of improvement in the co-parenting relationship, satisfaction with the agreement, and amount of sharing the children. Furthermore, the children's adjustment was assessed. Finally, the relative cost-effectiveness of the model, compared to a group model of impasse-directed mediation and counseling, was evaluated.

Eighty couples with a total of 100 children between the ages of 2 and 12 years participated in the interventions, referred from family courts after having failed the regular mediation that is mandated in California for families disputing custody matters. Seventy-seven (94%) of them were located for the 30-month follow-up: 85% of the mothers, 74% of the fathers, and 70% of the children were interviewed.

At the end of the mediations, 82.5% of the families had reached agreement. Two years later, 44% of them were maintaining their original agreements, 16% had renegotiated on their own, and 3% had sought another mediator. Nearly two-thirds, in all, were managing on their own. These statistics parallel outcomes reported across countries and populations for court-based and community-based services and voluntary as well as mandatory mediations. The studies show that 50–85% of couples reach agreements, with most studies reporting mid- to upper-range figures (see Ezzell, 2001, for a review).

Thirty-six percent of the 80 couples returned to court, 13% of them only once, and 23% two or more times over custody and access matters. Thus, all but approximately one-fourth of the sample was successfully helped from impasse-directed mediation.

At follow-up, parents reported a marked diminution of hostility and conflict, according to the Conflict Tactics Scale (Straus, 1979). Both verbal and physical aggression decreased to levels consistent with the normal divorcing population.

WHEN IMPASSE-DIRECTED MEDIATION IS INADEQUATE FOR THE NEEDS OF THE FAMILY

Any success with this difficult and intransigent population must be appreciated as a minor victory—but it is often a victory with a downside. Many of these families resolved their disputes but at great cost, especially to their children, who endured the rancor, chaos, and volatility of their interchanges. The success of the intervention does not erase the troubling image we hold of the quarter of the people who could not benefit, or could not sustain benefits, from brief treatment in the form of impasse-directed mediation. Despite the agreements, 15% of the sample described above actually deteriorated over the follow-up period. Some of the children who were symptom free at the conclusion of the intervention began to show signs of stress and distress by follow-up. Whether stable or no longer in conflict, some families continued to function at a disturbed level that raised concerns for the children's longer-term psychological and social development. Family restructuring among this subgroup must occur in a fuller sense in order to safeguard the futures of these children. These families require a more intensive intervention—a two-stage therapeutic endeavor.

FOSTERING STRUCTURAL FAMILY AND INDIVIDUAL CHANGE IN ENTRENCHED CUSTODY DISPUTES

Several elements separate mediation with couples involved in long-term, chronic conflict from traditional mediation procedures, or even from those used in briefer impasse-directed mediation model described above. The mediator may choose a more intensive counseling model because it seems necessary to effect an agreement and because the destructive nature of the family dictates that additional interventions are needed to safeguard the child's well-being. Counseling within the mediation aims to foster structural changes in family dynamics and within the individual parents (Johnston, in press).

The first rule governing work with these most chronic and chaotic families is to create a legally defined framework that helps constrain the conflict through external controls. A legal contract or court order specifies each of the following: (1) the goals of the intervention; (2) who is seen in sessions; (3) the limits of confidentiality with the court; (4) the permissible lines of communication among parties and collaterals; (5) a timely procedure for resolving crises; (6) payment for services; and (7) a process for terminating the intervention or effecting a transfer to another clinician.

The mediator/clinician obtains permission to speak with all family members involved in the dispute. Both parents are required to pay for sessions, sharing the cost of the mediation. As noted in impasse-directed mediation, parties are asked to stipulate confidentiality and that the mediator will not be asked or subpoenaed to testify in court. At the same time, the mediator must obtain permission to confer with other professionals and extended family members involved in the dispute—most importantly, parents' and children's therapists. Teachers and day-care providers are equally essential. The mediator communicates that he or she will exchange information between parents given in separate interviews. The children's confidentiality is fully maintained.

The time commitment for these cases is often startling to novice clinicians. More severely conflicted families may require 3–5 hours per week for 2 months or so, accompanied by frequent phone calls and crisis points. The commitment generally tapers off to 1–2 hours per week for the next 2–6 months, followed by a follow-up period that generally requires 1–2 hours per month, with additional telephone counseling.

Initial Referral and Contract Formation

When the family is first referred, both parties' acceptance of involvement must be obtained. Otherwise, parents do not begin the mediation and treatment from an equal position in terms of motivation and power in regard to each person's desire to reach an agreement. Temporary custody and access orders must be in place. All agreed-upon terms and conditions are put in writing to minimize misunderstandings or manipulations. Parents are seen individually, then each brings a child for separate play interviews and for parent–child observation sessions. This aspect of the mediation resembles processes used in custody evaluations, except that the meetings are confidential.

Once the counseling and mediation are underway, the phases of impasse-directed mediation can be followed as described above. However, additional considerations of the children's role in the conflict and what each child needs from the mediator characterize the work with this subpopulation of highly disputing families. The mediator assists not only in helping parents to identify, understand, and resolve psychological and interpersonal conflicts, but the advocacy role of the mediator is intensified, much like the role of *guardian ad litem*,[1] but with a strictly therapeutic focus and bent.

The Stance of the Mediator

The mediator's stance in the face of the parents' pathology plays a large role in uncovering the parents' impasses. The mediator endeavors to relate empathically to feelings expressed by both parents, is careful not to take sides, and makes it clear, repeatedly, that there are two sides to every story. The mediator can easily be seduced into making promises that cannot possibly be kept regarding the expected success of the mediation. Rescue fantasies are common, as the mediator hopes he or she will be more effective than the string of defeated professionals the family dispute has already left in its wake. On the other hand, maintaining a too-distant demeanor from the parents in the name of emotional neutrality may serve to evoke the parents' anxiety or even paranoia.

Child Advocacy

As the parents work through the phases of mediation, focus is created and maintained on the children's needs more than the parents' problems. Leverage for change emerges out of parental concern for the effect the disputes are having on their children. The mediator/clinician's approach takes a radical departure from traditional methods of mediation, as the mediator calls on his or her understanding of the children's experience, and interpretations are framed with the aim of heightening parents' ability to feel empathy for the children's plight in the divorce.

A common scenario involves the ubiquitous fights over the children's clothes and possessions during transitions from one parental home to the other. One or both parents maintain that they provide clothes or toys that are taken to the other home and never returned. Parents react in a variety of ways to this situation—all of them stressful to the children. They scream and yell, frightening the children; they order the children to retrieve the items; they refuse to let the children take treasured items to the other home; some even strip their children at the point of transfer, making them dress in ill-fitting or scruffy clothes. All of these actions serve to further burden the children and undermine their sense of safety, continuity, and control. The mediator acknowledges to the parents the symbolic and monetary value of the items, then points out the far more costly expense to the children's lowered self-esteem and diminished well-being.

The mediator also advocates on behalf of the children by conveying to the parents, in actions and words, that no matter how bad the problems get, the mediator will not give up on the family. Such expressions and actions of steadfastness model the parents' need to stand by their children, however difficult that is to do at times. In the process, the mediator confronts his or her own feelings of impotence, rage, exhaustion, and distress that such angry couples arouse. By not acting on such feelings and, instead, making clear repeatedly what can and cannot be done realistically to end the dispute, the mediator conveys to the parents that they will not be abandoned in their struggles. The mediator/clinician turns the discussion back, yet again, to the children—for example, what outcomes are desirable for a child of a certain age and character. This containment and reframing facilitate a deeper trust in vulnerable and frightened parents in both the mediational and the psychological processes unfolding during this phase. For many high-conflict couples, this experience of intensive working through is unique, as they have become so adept at getting professionals to give up on them. Often their early experience of abandonment by an important caretaker is relived and reworked until the mediator breaks the pattern.

Core activities with parents in the negotiation phase of this type of mediation include educational child guidance work, counseling, and coaching in how to communicate with each other about the children, all while reaching agreements and breaking impasses. Ideally, the mediator/clinician is accepted by the parents as someone profoundly interested in working toward the children's benefit. The parents begin to trust that the mediator does not become co-opted by either parent in their disputes, thereby abandoning the children's welfare the way the parents have done in response to their conflicts in the past. As parents become better able to remain committed to meeting their children's needs, the mediator's role becomes less crucial and parents resolve more disputes themselves, with little or no dependence upon the mediator.

Working with the Children

In order for the mediator to become an advocate for the children, he or she must know about each child's behaviors and inner experience. Close contact with an outside therapist should be initiated and maintained if the child is already in treatment. If the child does not have a therapist, the clinician sees the child, on occasion, as part of the family intervention. Children are often wary about talking to a mediator directly, so providing opportunities for projective play is crucial. Drawings, puppet play, sand tray play, and storytelling are all useful media. With their permission, the children's stories and artwork can be shared with the parents. The mediator/clinician then uses the material to discuss each child's reality and ways of helping the child cope with the parents.

During the mediation, the clinician also works directly with the children, using projective play themes and materials. Akin to more traditional play therapy, stories and play that symbolize the family situation are used to help children understand and redefine their understanding of changing family relationships. Typically, the therapist tells a story about characters that are neither villains nor heroes, just real people with strengths and weaknesses. The story illustrates how two people got together, had children, then discovered they had irreconcilable differences. The story draws out dilemmas the child faces in his or her family and potential coping strategies and solutions to problems. The main character loves both parents and finds the good qualities in each one. The sense of relief in children at hearing a realistic but comforting ending to conflict—one that speaks to the children's wishes and needs—is usually palpable.

Moreover, the mediator's relationship to the children models acceptance of them and both parents as well as the possibility of having a respectful relationship with all family members. This positive modeling relieves some of the children's fears and reinforces their increasing capacity to convey to each parent their needs for acceptance, as well as for civility between the parents.

In sum, this form of intervention weds the mediation process to a longer-term therapeutic model of intervention, backed by a legal contract. This kind of work with highly disputing, chaotic, and/or violent families has two primary purposes: (1) to fashion a workable parenting agreement, and (2) to temper the destructive emotional climate of the family into a better functioning postdivorce structure that rests squarely on the needs of the children. Attitudinal and behavioral changes in the parents, including the containment of neurotic and destructive tendencies, are ultimate goals. This process also is detailed in Johnston's (in press) psychoanalytically oriented discussion of this type of intervention.

OUTCOMES OF COUNSELING MEDIATION

The outcome effectiveness of this longer counseling mediation model was assessed in a study of divorcing families referred by family courts, all of whom had been in ongoing custody disputes, three-fourths of whom had experienced domestic violence (Johnston, 1994). This more intensive counseling model, like the impasse-directed model, can be structured in various ways. Two variations of the counseling model are compared and discussed below: parents-only counseling, and parents and child/family counseling. A third model, group counseling for children and parents, was implemented and evaluated as well (described in Roseby & Johnston, 1997) but is beyond the scope of the present chapter.

In the first 2 years of the project, 60 families were randomly distributed between the individual and family group models. Coping and distress were assessed for 89 of the children (ages 3–12 years) before and after treatment, using two symptom checklists with 5-point scales: Child's Reaction to Transitions (21 items) and Child's Reaction to Witnessing Parental Conflict (24 items). Children's emotional and behavioral distress observed at the time of transition from one parent to the other decreased significantly; that is, they were less likely to be quiet/withdrawn, tense, resistant, regressive, or to manifest somatic and aggressive reactions.

The parents and child/family counseling was as effective, and in some areas more effective, than parents-only counseling. With respect to coping with parental disputes, children showed more active coping responses and less passivity and distress after treatment. They were less likely to act submissively distressed and more likely to deflect and divert the parental disputes. Unfortunately, children were not able to strategically avoid the parental conflict—the best possible outcome—probably because of their age and dependent status.

A study of the parents in the parents-only and parents and child/family models at a 30-month follow-up was conducted by inspecting family court records and mailing questionnaires to parents. There was a dramatic decrease in the rates of litigation in family court over custody, visitation, and domestic violence issues. Court filings were reduced to one-sixth of their former rates: 66% did not refile concerning visitation, 76% did not refile concerning custody, and 84% did not refile for domestic violence matters. Thirty-nine of the original 120 parents responded to a 41-item mailed questionnaire, with each item measured on a 5-point scale. Responses showed significant positive shifts between baseline and follow-up, from high levels of negativity and hostility toward the ex-spouse, distrust of the ex-spouse's parenting, and dissatisfaction with the custody and visitation arrangements, to more moderate attitudes about these issues. Outcomes were similar for both models.

Although these are gratifying results, it is important to note that considerable hostility, distrust, and dissatisfaction remain between many of the parents—a finding that is, in general, corroborated by clinical impressions. The negativity and conflict in the family environment for these children may be muted by intervention, but the children remain at risk because the relative peace or truce is likely to be quite fragile.

ENHANCING SUCCESS OF THE INTERVENTION
THROUGH COOPERATIVE WORK WITH ATTORNEYS

Until now, mediators have not explicated the very important role nonmediating attorneys play in these interventions. Legal professionals' attitudes are increasingly more inclusive toward mental health professional's collaborative efforts in managing high-conflict parents and supporting the children caught in the middle. Despite this dramatic sea change in attorney attitudes, there are still many traditional lawyers, and family law is still practiced in very traditional ways in many parts of the country. Attorney involvement can either support or undermine mediators' attempts to bring high-conflict families to agreement. One of the barriers encountered in this work occurs when the parents consult their attorneys about the progress they are making toward resolution. The attorney may suggest tactics that potentially undermine mutual trust and the spirit of mediation. An example is the not-infrequent practice for the attorney to advise a client to seek sole custody of the children so that a 50/50 split in the children's residential time will be effected as a compromise. Even if such a compromise is reached, the damage done between the couple in terms of distrust, wasted resources, and intensified anxiety and fear render the compromise meaningless, as the couple typically experiences greater difficulty than ever in sharing their children.

More frequently, the attorneys introduce a new vantage point or a different perspective from that of the clients, with the best intentions of legitimately representing their client's legal interests. The attorney directs the client in ways that foster change in the direction of some aspect of the mediation. The client then backs away from aspects of the agreement or compromises, and the other party feels betrayed, with the outcome again fueling the distrust that is already rampant and destructive between the couple.

With high-conflict couples, in particular, including attorneys as legal consultants in the mediation process and partners in the intervention *before* an agreement is drafted is key. Often the clients resist mediators' attempts to do so, in order to save money. The mediator must not collude with the client, since the money saved will be paid later if an agreement falls apart. The attorney, not unlike mental health professionals working in the courts, symbolically represents the authority of the court. He or she carries a significant influence and weight with the client. Bringing in the attorney as a collaborator provides an additional means of assisting high-conflict couples in constraining their dispute through boundaries created by the attorney's participation. Another person, associated with the authority of the court, interprets what is realistic and expectable, and distinguishes such realities from the fights wrapped up in intrapsychic or interpersonal conflicts.

The Collaborative Divorce Project (CDP) being piloted in Connecticut, (Pruett, 1998; Pruett, Ebling, & Insabella, 2004; Pruett, Williams, Insabella, & Little, 2003) incorporated Johnston's principles and techniques into a brief therapeutic intervention in the court system that was designed for families with children 6 years old or younger. The impasse-directed mediation model was extended by specifying roles for attorneys that support the resolution of conflict.

First, the mediator/clinician helps the clients evaluate, early on, whether they have found a legal advocate that will protect their interests without intensifying conflict. During the prenegotiation phase, clients in the CDP receive information about what to expect from an attorney–client relationship, what questions to ask a prospective attorney, and how to determine whether their advocate is, in fact, a good choice given their high-conflict situation. The mediators are careful not to give legal advice, nor do they recommend or dissuade clients from using any particular attorney. The parents are only guided to evaluate for themselves whether they have selected an attorney who will best suit their interests.

Second, when clients agree to participate in the project, attorneys are notified about the intervention. They are asked to support the client's participation and to work with the mediator/clinicians throughout the intervention. Once attorneys in a judicial district understand the nature of services being provided, they can be notified with a faxed form letter of a particular client's participation. If the services offered are new to a district, a number of steps can be taken to familiarize attorneys with the program. Effective strategies in the CDP included: brief descriptions posted at the courthouse; informational brown bag luncheons at the court for attorneys appearing that particular day; attending a Family Law section meeting and making a presentation; having brochures available; and having judges introduce the program to attorneys present in the courtroom prior to the day's hearings. The selection of a specific strategy or combination thereof should be determined by the particular culture of a judicial district.

During the CDP, a six-way meeting (two parents, two attorneys, and a male–female mediator/clinician team) is used to accomplish several purposes. The timing of the meeting depends on the parents' needs. If the parents have difficulty getting started and are far apart on their goals for a parenting agreement, then the meeting is called after the family has passed the halfway mark of the negotiation phase. The mediators speak to the attorneys ahead of time, clarifying the goals of the meeting and identifying those aspects of impasse the attorneys can best address. Thus, the attorneys become part of the voice of reality, helping clients understand their options and counseling them about the options that are not realistic in their circumstance. Together, the mediators and attorneys lead the clients into accepting what is possible and realistic (as opposed to pursuing their fantasies), thereby reducing the distance between the parents to agreement. When it becomes clear that one parent is stalling the work more than another, the parent's attorney may speak with the parent in private during a break. The attorney can then help guide the parent without the parent's losing face. In most cases, it is important for parents to be present in the negotiations so that they feel they have an important voice in their own problem resolution and thereby learn to be part of solutions as well as creators of conflict. If the parents have inordinate difficulty in controlling themselves in each other's presence, each attorney might have his or her client remain silent while he or she speaks for the client temporarily. This works best when the attorney–client alliance is strong.

For parents who have made significant headway toward developing a parenting agreement, the attorneys are invited into a group meeting toward the end of the mediation. Their function is to verify the progress that has been made, clarify some of the more minor points that are "sticky wickets," and determine with both parties who will be responsible for writing the draft agreement. With the attorneys' help, all aspects of the agreements are more likely to be put into court orders—which is especially helpful for parents in highest conflict, who fare best when agreements are very specific and detailed.

For parents who are having difficulty resolving their impasses around particular issues, the meeting can be used at several other points during the mediation. At certain sticking points, attorneys can be asked to participate for the express purpose of working through one or two issues. This technique is used sparingly, since it can become costly. However, sometimes these consultations are cost-effective and efficient. Some parents have difficulty resolving a number of issues because they introduce a new issue that is interlocked with previously introduced issues every time a resolution point is reached. The attorneys can assist in unbundling the decisions, when appropriate. In addition, they can suggest creative ways of bundling several decisions so that progress can advance unimpeded.

Some attorneys are understandably reluctant to participate in these meetings without knowing how the mediation will progress and whether it will break down. They express concerns that the other lawyer will misuse information for data gathering later in court. They fear that the joint negotiations along the way will "tip their hand" about potential litigation strategies. It is our experience that while these fears may be founded, the risk is well worth the success usually achieved.

Perhaps more important from clients' perspectives is the problem of how to include attorneys without violating the confidentiality of the mediation. The mediator's skill is critical here, as he or she must guide the meeting and, when necessary, gently confront parents to move along in the process, without doing the therapeutic work that would expose either parent's vulnerabilities to the attorneys. The therapeutic work is put on hold as the mediator's focus switches to the attorneys to maximize the use of their expertise, thus helping to break an impasse with the provision of legal information and guidance. Sometimes the parents express relief at dealing solely with legal realities, while shelving their psychological issues for a brief time. The meeting serves to model the importance and practicality of maintaining a specific, reality-based focus for a brief time period to accomplish a measure of resolution. The meeting also fosters exchanges of information and views needed to pursue resolution with less impasse in the next session.

CONCLUSIONS

Impasse-directed and therapeutic mediation strategies for high-conflict couples rely on techniques from traditional mediation procedures while incorporating psychodynamic (e.g., object relations) and family systems knowledge (e.g., symptomatology manifested in poorly functioning triads within the family across generational lines) into informed interventions. Impasse-directed mediation enables mediators/clinicians to work with the psychological conflicts presented within and between parents in order to help them reach parenting agreements that are sustainable and to refocus their energies on the needs of their children. For some disputing parents, however, such brief mediation treatment is insufficient. Couples whose high levels of conflict are marked by severe character pathology in one or both parents, such as narcissistic vulnerabilities that stem from deeply rooted early experience and previous unsuccessful relationships, may require a longer-term, more intensive intervention model. The model presented here expands upon impasse-directed treatment to offer intensive counseling and case coordination for parents until they are able to integrate new internal constructs about their ex-spouse and the relationship. Such work takes time, patience, and strict boundaries and is characterized by additional education and advocacy regarding the developmental needs of the children. The children's emotional suffering in response to the family conflict, as well as developmental risks posed if the conflict continues, become the focus for helping parents to reorganize their focus and behavior around the needs of their children.

Attorneys may function as an important potential foil and cooperative partner to mediators in these endeavors. Techniques for including attorney input during the process and utilizing the authority inherent in the attorney role to resolve impasses bring the level of collaboration between legal and mental health professionals to new heights.

No longer do mediation and therapeutic strategies need to be divorced from one another, creating confused layers of service providers for families who need integration and consolidation of services and management. In the impasse model, the mediators and attorneys form alliances that operate, as all good marriages should, to foster the future health and well-being of the children, first and foremost, as well as the parents who are raising them.

NOTE

1. *Guardian ad litem* is a legal term that refers to a guardian (a lawyer or mental health professional) appointed by the court to ensure that a child's legal rights and interests are represented.

REFERENCES

Ellis, D. (1995). *Family mediation pilot project.* North York, Ontario, Canada: Hamilton Unified Family Court.

Ellis, D., & Stuckless, N. (1996). *Mediating and negotiating marital conflicts.* Thousand Oaks, CA: Sage.

Emery, R. E. (1994). *Renegotiating family relationships: Divorce, child custody and mediation.* New York: Guilford Press.

Ezzell, B. (2001). Inside the minds of America's family law courts: The psychology of mediation versus litigation in domestic disputes. *Law and Psychology Review, 25,* 119–143.

Girdner, L. (Ed.). (1990). Mediation triage: Screening for spousal abuse in divorce mediation—special issue on "mediation and spousal abuse." *Mediation Quarterly, 7,* 365–376.

Hahn, R. A., & Kleist, D. M. (2000). Divorce mediation: Research and implications for family and couples counseling. *Family Journal, 8,* 165–172.

Irving, H. H., & Benjamin, M. (1995). *Family mediation: Contemporary issues.* Thousand Oaks, CA: Sage.

Johnston, J. R. (1994). *Developing preventative interventions for children of severe family conflict and violence: A comparison of three treatment models.* Technical report available from Protecting Children from Conflict, P.O. Box 2483, Menlo Park, CA 94026.

Johnston, J. R. (in press). Clinical work with parents and children of families in entrenched custody disputes. In L. Gundsberg & P. Hymowitz (Eds.), *Divorce and custody: Contemporary developmental psychoanalytic perspectives.* Hillsdale, NJ: Analytic Press.

Johnston, J. R., & Campbell, L. G. G. (1988). *Impasses of divorce: The dynamics and resolution of family conflict.* New York: Free Press.

Kelly, B. (1996). A decade of divorce mediation research: Some answers and questions. *Family and Conciliation Courts Review, 34,* 373–385.

Kelly, J. B. (1991). Parent interaction after divorce: Comparison of mediated and adversarial divorce processes. *Behavioral Science and the Law, 9,* 387–398.

Kitzmann, K. M., & Emery, R. E. (1994). Child and family coping one year after mediated and litigated child custody disputes. *Journal of Family Psychology, 8,* 150–159.

Kressel, K. (1987). Clinical implications of existing research on mediation. *American Journal of Family Therapy, 15,* 69–74.

Milne, A. (1983). Divorce mediation: The state of the art. *Mediation Quarterly, 1,* 15–31.

Pruett, M. K. (1998). Divorce in legal context: Outcomes for children. *Connecticut Family Lawyer, 13*(1), 1–11.

Pruett, M. K., Ebling, R., & Insabella, G. (2004). Critical aspects of parenting plans for young children: Interjecting data into the debate about overnights. *Family Court Review, 42*(1), 39–59.

Pruett, M. K., Williams, T. Y., Insabella, G., & Little, T. D. (2003). Family and legal indicators of child adjustment to divorce among families with young children. *Journal of Family Psychology, 17*(2), 169–180.

Roseby, V., & Johnston, J. R. (1997). *High conflict, violent and separating families: A group treatment model for school-age children.* New York: Free Press.

Saposnek, D. T. (1998). *Mediating child custody disputes: A strategic approach* (rev. ed.). San Francisco: Jossey-Bass.

Sprenkel, D. H., & Storm, C. L. (1983). Divorce therapy outcome research: A substantive and methodological review. *Journal of Marital and Family Therapy, 9,* 239–258.

Straus, M. A. (1979). Measuring intrafamily conflict and violence: The Conflict Tactics (CT) Scales. *Journal of Marriage and the Family, 41,* 71–86.

CHAPTER 6

Hybrid Processes

ARNOLD SHIENVOLD

Mediation, according to Arnold Shienvold, may be viewed as a "hybrid process," combining elements from psychotherapy, negotiation, facilitation, and other services. Once the "impure" origins of mediation are recognized, the use of mixed techniques within mediation may be more acceptable to practitioners. There are times when a rights-based approach, rather than an interest-based approach, is more useful in helping parents resolve dispute. The two techniques might be combined in a way that keeps interests in focus while incorporating processes that deal with rights and power issues. This chapter reviews several mixed processes used to help resolve disputes within the family. Dr. Shienvold includes evaluative mediation, mediation followed by arbitration ("med-arb"), and arbitration followed by mediation ("arb-med"). Examples of the use of each of these processes are provided along with a discussion of some of the ethical issues raised.

One of the more controversial issues involving the use of alternative dispute resolution procedures is the mixing of various processes when attempting to resolve a single dispute. Such use of "mixed" or "hybrid processes" has stirred much debate. Practitioners who believe that alternative dispute resolution (ADR) processes should be pure (i.e., never combined with another process conducted by the same neutral) consider the use of a mixed process to be heretical and, perhaps, unethical. There are, however, practitioners who design and offer multitiered ADR systems who consider the use of mixed processes both practical and essential.

The continuum of ADR processes runs from simple negotiation on one end to adjudication on the other end. In between these two extremes are processes of facilitation, mediation, neutral evaluation, and arbitration, which take place in ascending order, depending on the degree of third-party intervention and decision-making power of the neutral. The assumption of a "purest"—that is, a professional who believes that processes should not be mixed (Bush & Folger, 1994; Gould, 1998; L. Marlowe, personal communication, April 2002; Williams, 1998) is that each process consists of its own set of techniques, skills, and values. Based on that assumption, the purists would argue that associated with each process are specific positive and negative factors that make it more or less valuable in resolving a particular dispute. The particular process chosen in a given conflict should be utilized to a conclusion, either resolution or impasse, to avoid confusion and ethical traps.

However, it is equally plausible to conceive the continuum of dispute resolution processes as composed of an infinite number of points. As we move from a particular, defined process to another, we pass through a variety of associated skills in which the emphasis gradually shifts toward techniques that are more related to the next point on the continuum (Murray, Rau, & Sherman, 1996). For example, if we move from facilitation toward neutral evaluation, the emphasis of the skills and techniques utilized by the neutral party will be initially related to the facilitative process, with its goal of assisting in the negotiation process. As we move further along the continuum toward mediation, facilitative techniques remain important, but the neutral party may also place increasing emphasis on problem solving and utilize a more structured approach. As we proceed up the continuum toward neutral evaluation, the nature of the mediation begins to shift in such a way that the mediator may employ more evaluative techniques until, in fact, he or she is conducting "evaluative mediation." Finally, the neutral party is no longer using the mediation process at all. The next point on the continuum is the use of a neutral evaluation to aid the disputants in the resolution of their conflict, and so on.

In stark contrast to the purist's opinion, it could be argued that there are no pure processes, that each process developed through the incorporation of techniques or skills from other processes. It was only after these other skills were incorporated into a specific set of procedures and universally accepted that a new process, such as mediation, was labeled and given its own standing on the ADR continuum. Even in the purest forms of mediation, the skills of active listening, facilitation, and negotiation are utilized as part of the basis of the process. However, active listening is not a unique skill of mediation; indeed, it is more commonly associated with therapeutic interventions in psychotherapy. Similarly, facilitation is a defined "process" that stands alone on the ADR continuum. Consequently, mediation may be viewed as a mixed process that combines some nondirective psychotherapeutic skills, significant negotiation skills, heaping amounts of facilitation skills, and an array of other techniques as well. In the end, the process is uniquely "mediation." At the same time, however, recognition of the "impure" origins of these so-called pure processes makes us far more accepting of the use of mixed processes.

The danger in not recognizing that all dispute resolution processes are mixed is the tendency to assume that mixed processes are somehow unacceptable, unhelpful, and unethical. It is easy to forget that ADR techniques have acquired popularity because they help parties accomplish a number of important goals: they (1) allow individuals to better control the outcomes of their conflict, (2) create more rapid access to resolution, (3) provide a lower-cost system of resolution when compared to litigation, and (4) facilitate the discovery of more creative and satisfying solutions to many conflicts. Generally speaking, disputants are less concerned about the specific mix or relative purity of techniques and are more concerned that the process allows them a fair chance to resolve their conflict.

Whether perceived as pure or mixed, it is important to understand the particular strengths and weaknesses of any process that is being used to help resolve a dispute. It is also necessary to be able to communicate those strengths and weaknesses to the disputant so that they can make informed decisions about using a specific process. The task is particularly important when "mixed processes" are used, since the pitfalls increase as the number of processes used increases.

An important aspect of the use of mixed processes involves the understanding that not all disputes can be settled by an interest-based approach. Disputes are resolved along one of three dimensions: *interests, rights,* or *power* (Mayer, 2000). Mediation is generally accepted as the best approach to resolving conflict and reaching an interest-based solution. There are times, however, when a rights-based approach must be considered. In some cases, the rights-based approach may be used as a preliminary step to an interest-based approach. At other times, the rights-based or power approaches may be more effective in resolving conflicts. Instead of using a simple and pure process, it may be more beneficial to combine an approach that keeps interests in focus *and* incorporates processes that address rights and power issues.

With respect to family mediation, another issue of importance arises. Since all family members are not at the bargaining table, who represents the children in interest-based negotiation? Can the parents be relied upon to objectively consider the needs and interests of their children? Additionally, can the needs and interests of the children be dealt with in a timely fashion, especially within the pure mediation setting or a mediation that occurs during the process of litigation, when there is a high degree of conflict between the parents? The answer to the latter two questions is probably "no." With respect to the first question, if there is an expectation that the mediator should take on the responsibility of ensuring that the children's needs and interests are considered, then the mediator is adding an additional dimension to his or her traditional role. To some extent, this mediator would have to employ techniques that lay the groundwork for the incorporation of a mixed process into the mediation. The model standards recently adopted by the Association of Family and Conciliation Courts, the American Bar Association Section of Dispute Resolution, and the Association for Conflict Resolution explicitly state that one of the responsibilities of the family mediator is to ensure that the best interests of the children are being considered in the final resolution of a dispute. Therefore, these questions take on added significance.

Often, a mixed process is one that includes two conflict resolution processes that differ in the degree to which the third party directly intervenes with the parties and/or the decision-making authority given to the neutral party by the client or taken on by the neutral party. It is clear that the goal of combining the roles is to help ensure the resolution of the particular conflict. The primary question is whether the parties will have the final say in determining that resolution, and if so, with how much "help" from the facilitator; or whether the third party will be given the power to determine the outcome. These aspects of mixed processes shift the degree of authority given to the neutral party and generate the greatest amount of caution within the field. Some professionals find it completely unacceptable to give a neutral party any evaluative or decision-making authority (Phillips, 2002; Bush & Folger, 1994).

Having laid the groundwork for the debate over mixed processes, the remainder of this chapter reviews several of the so-called mixed processes that are most frequently used to help resolve disputes within the family context. It should be kept in mind that such processes as "therapeutic mediation"—and even litigation—entail a mixture of techniques that are all aimed at bringing about the resolution of a conflict. However, the only processes to be considered in the remainder of this chapter are evaluative mediation and mediation–arbitration.

EVALUATIVE MEDIATION

It may be surprising to think of evaluative mediation as a mixed process. Some juxtapose evaluative mediation as the polar opposite of facilitative mediation. Evaluative mediation is a mediation process because the mediator does not have decision-making power and, it is hoped, does not try to coerce a settlement from the participants. As with all mediation, the mediator tries to facilitate settlement through empowerment of the parties (see Lowry, Chapter 4, this volume).

However, within the process of evaluative mediation, the mediator performs an evaluation of the relative merits of each of the parties positions and provides them with feedback regarding some dimension of their case. Thus, the mediator actually plays two roles in relation to the parties. The first role is to serve as a traditional mediator attempting to facilitate a settlement through the relatively structured techniques typically employed in mediation. The second role is as a neutral evaluator. If the parties request a neutral evaluation of their case in order to gain some insight from an individual with expertise in the area over which the dispute has arisen, it is the neutral evaluator's role to provide an analysis of the issues in conflict, give feedback regarding the strengths of the positions held by the parties, especially around their legal rights, and, if the mediator has legal expertise, to make recommendations regarding possible ways of settling the dispute. The fact that the evaluative mediator plays two roles (i.e., as traditional mediator and as neutral evaluator) gives strength to the conclusion that evaluative mediation is a mixed process.

A variation of evaluative mediation is used both in private practice and the court system with families in conflict over custody of their children. The process entails the sequential use of neutral evaluation, followed by mediation. An individual practitioner begins the process by conducting a custody evaluation of the family. The evaluation leads to custodial recommendations regarding the best interests of the children. However, before the family proceeds with the litigation process, the same practitioner changes roles and becomes a mediator in an attempt to facilitate the parties' settlement of their own dispute. This approach is similar to evaluative mediation in that the neutral evaluator is also a mediator. It differs from evaluative mediation in that the evaluator often has authority from the court, or from the parties, to send their evaluation and/or recommendations to the court. This process also parallels the process of arbitration followed by mediation ("arb-med"), as described below.

A case illustration might be helpful at this point. Ralph and Anita have two children, Ben and Alicia, ages 2 and 4, respectively. Ralph and Anita were referred from the court for a "comprehensive custody evaluation," with the additional direction from the judge to "settle if possible." In essence, the court was requesting that a custody evaluation be completed and that at the end of the evaluation component, the evaluator meet with the parties to attempt to mediate the custody conflict. If the mediation brings about settlement of the custodial issues, the court has little need for further intervention. However, if the mediation reaches an impasse and the parties are unable to agree upon an appropriate parenting plan for their children, then the evaluative mediator is free to report to the court his or her findings and recommendations regarding the "best interests" of the children.

In this particular case, Ralph and Anita are invited to an orientation session where the entire process is explained to them in detail. Distinctions between traditional facilitative mediation, including its emphasis on self-determination and confidentiality, and this evaluative process in which the "evaluator/mediator" assesses the best interests of the children and makes recommendations directly to the parties and, if necessary, to the court are clearly explained. Only with the agreement of the parties and their attorneys does the process continue.

Assuming that the parties have agreed to the process, a traditional custody evaluation is performed, wherein the evaluator interviews caretakers, observes the children and their interaction with the parents and other family members, conducts psychological testing of pertinent parties, and reviews any collateral information that is important to the understanding of the family. Typically, a report is written at the conclusion of the evaluation, which contains recommendations that will be sent to the court regarding the best interests of the children.

However, in the evaluation/mediation process, the evaluator changes roles and attempts to help facilitate an agreement between the parents regarding the custodial arrangements. The evaluator is in an ideal position, having extensively interviewed the parents, to understand their positions regarding custody. He or she is familiar with the concerns they have expressed about various types of arrangements, the strengths of each parent's skills with the children, the desires of the children (if they are old enough, in legal terms, to have a considered voice in the proceedings—usually 12 years old, depending on the state) regarding parenting arrangements, the history of the relationship and subsequent parenting responsibilities, the developmental needs of the children, and the relative strengths of each parent in meeting those needs. Utilizing this knowledge and skill as a mediator, the evaluator attempts to help the parents reach an agreement while they still maintain some control over the final outcome of the conflict, as opposed to going into court and submitting to the judge's final decision.

If the mediative component of the process fails, a report is sent to the court. The evaluator has the duty to testify at any subsequent hearing regarding the custodial evaluation. With full knowledge of their attorneys, the parties waived their right to confidentiality in the orientation session at the initiation of the process. On the other hand, if the mediation is successful, the evaluator/mediator writes a memorandum of understanding, which the attorneys for the parties then reduce to a stipulated custody agreement. The evaluator does not send a final report but may keep his or her written recommendations in the event that problems subsequently arise and his or her testimony is necessary.

Thus, in the case of Ralph and Anita, a comprehensive custody evaluation was initially completed. During the course of that evaluation, it became obvious that the parents were seeking "assistance" in determining what course of action would be best for their children, and they appeared capable of negotiating an agreement as long as they trusted the feedback they were receiving regarding the best interests of the children. The parents demonstrated a desire to attempt to work out their differences together and an ability to communicate with one another in a meaningful manner. The evaluator now changed roles to facilitate that process. The parties were aware that the evaluator had made a "judgment" as to what she felt was best, and the parties were interested in her feedback. The feedback they received laid out for the parents the pros and cons of custodial arrangements, especially as they would impact children the ages of Ben and Alicia and in light of the skills and availability of Ralph and Anita. However, a final recommendation was withheld in lieu of the parents reaching their own conclusion. In this particular instance, the parents arrived at their own agreement, which was not the same as the recommendations of the evaluator but which they believed better met the needs of their children.

In the case of another family—Dave and Maria and their three children— the mediation component of the process did not bring about a mutually agreed-upon arrangement for custody. In that case, Maria was completely against allowing David any time beyond weekends with "her" children, in spite of the fact that they had been utilizing a relatively traditional custodial arrangement for close to a year prior to the evaluation. The evaluation revealed that Maria's concerns regarding neglect of the children by David were exaggerated and that the children were safe while in his care. Although Maria seemed to accept those findings, she would not alter her position regarding custody. Therefore, after two attempts at reaching a settlement, the evaluator gave his recommendations to the parents and the court regarding the most appropriate parenting arrangements for the children. Interestingly, after the release of the recommendations and one day of court testimony, the parents requested a return to the mediation table and the parties reached an agreement.

These two cases raise important questions about the process and timing by which the evaluator decides to share his or her assessment of the case with the parties and/or the court. There are several ways in which practitioners approach the problem. Some practitioners share their assessment of the parties' positions and concerns prior to any negotiation between the parties. The assessment may be shared in a formal "report" to the parties that is prepared by the evaluator, or it may be informally shared during the early parts of the negotiation. Generally, a report is not shared with the court until the negotiation process has proved unsuccessful in resolving the dispute.

The timing in sharing the assessment varies depending upon the situation. When parties' positions and disagreements are not extremely disparate, they may not need the specific recommendations of the evaluator regarding a resolution. Rather, the clarifications the evaluator provides, without making a specific assessment or recommendation, may be all the facilitation needed to lead to a conclusion. On the other hand, when positions are more disparate and entrenched, the parties may benefit from a more direct assessment and recommendation from the evaluator to move them from their invested positions to a greater awareness of the needs of their children. Finally, if the parties are unable to move beyond impasse in the conflict, they know that a formal report to the court will be submitted and is essential if the litigation process is to continue. It should be noted that occasionally the formal report may be written, but not shared, prior to the initiation of the settlement process.

There is little question that the type of mediation that occurs following the release of a formal report by the evaluator differs from the type of mediation that occurs when assessment of the positions is not known by the parties. If the parties perceive the evaluator as "powerful" and strongly attached to the decision maker in court, they are likely to adjust their genuine desires and accept compromises (based on the results of the evaluation) that they would not have accepted if there were no formal report to the court. Obviously, the mediators in these scenarios are given considerably greater "power" than in traditional mediation. Many of the concerns expressed in the mediation literature regarding "muscle mediation" (Folberg & Milne, 1988) and power imbalance apply in these cases (Stulberg, 1981). However, as is emphasized later in this chapter, the parties should be informed of these differences between processes prior to engaging in them.

Evaluative mediation raises several significant questions about mixed processes. First, is a process a "mixed" one if separate individuals perform the processes? In other words, are the disputants in a case involved in the use of a mixed process if one neutral party conducts the mediation and another performs the neutral evaluation? Some practitioners believe that early neutral evaluation—med-arb and other similar forms of hybrid processes—are mixed processes, regardless of whether they are performed by one or more individuals (Phillips, 2002). The opinion of these writers appears to be related to their overall view of the legal process and, therefore, the place of alternative dispute resolution within that process. Within that view, the use of any other process during the adjudication process constitutes a mixed process. Consequently, when early neutral evaluation is used to help attorneys or judges settle a case during a subsequent settlement conference, it is considered a mixed or hybrid process. In this view, the client is the central definitional element—that is, if the client is exposed to more than one process, then mixed processes are involved.

Another perspective on defining a mixed process views the neutral party's role as the determining factor in whether a mixed process is being used; that is, the process is mixed if the same neutral party intentionally combines two or more processes to settle a dispute. It does not seem persuasive to argue that if two participants try to settle their dispute by obtaining a neutral evaluation from one expert and take that opinion to another expert who mediates for them, then the individuals have taken part in a mixed process. It is more logical to state that the parties have utilized two distinct processes to settle their dispute. If both of those processes were unsuccessful and they ultimately used litigation to settle their disagreement, then they would simply be adding a third process to the dispute resolution activity in which they were engaged.

However, if the two parties had a single evaluative mediator who, while mediating their dispute, conducted an evaluation of their cases and suggested possible outcomes, then they would be utilizing a mixed process. Furthermore, if the evaluative mediator were, in fact, a judge who was likely to hear the case, the process would be further mixed. Thus, this perspective

holds that if processes are kept distinct and employed by different professionals, then they are not being mixed. The parties are simply engaging in a relatively extensive dispute resolution system that has multiple processes available to aid in settlement. Part of the importance of this distinction comes
about from an analysis of the pros and cons of using mixed processes, which
is addressed later in this chapter.

MED-ARB

A second mixed process that is gaining more attention and use in the area of
family disputes is mediation followed by arbitration ("med-arb"). *Med-arb* is a
generic term that refers to the sequencing of mediation and arbitration processes in order to bring about the resolution of a dispute. The term is generally applied to this sequence regardless of whether the same neutral performs the two processes. There are variations on the med-arb process, such
as "shadow mediation" or "co-med-arb," whereby different professionals
serve in different capacities during the settlement of the dispute but with
varying degrees of overlap. Finally, as previously discussed, *arb-med* reverses
the sequence of the process, beginning with arbitration and then mediation.
Regardless of the sequencing of the processes, the most important characteristic of this mixed process is that the mediator is given authority to make a
binding decision regarding some aspects of the parties' dispute.

When med-arb is utilized, the parties agree that they will first attempt to
resolve their dispute using mediation prior to beginning any active settlement phase. However, if they are unable to reach agreement using the mediation process and an impasse is declared, then an arbitration process is used
to bring about a final, binding settlement. The final settlement includes
agreements reached during the mediation phase of the process along with
the decisions rendered by the mediator/arbitrator. The initial agreement by
the parties to utilize the med-arb process should include the areas of dispute
the arbitrator will be deciding, the ground rules of the processes, and how
much authority the mediator/arbitrator will possess.

There are many benefits to the med-arb process. The primary advantage
is that a final resolution of the conflict is guaranteed. Unlike traditional mediation (wherein an impasse can be declared and the parties may leave the
process without having reached a settlement), in med-arb, settlement is guaranteed as a function of the preexisting agreement to employ arbitration. The
nature of the agreement is likely to be different in cases where arbitration is
necessary as opposed to using only mediation. When an agreement is
reached through the mediation process, the parties are likely to feel that they
have had significant input and control in the final outcome. On the other
hand, an arbitrator's decision is more likely to be viewed as one that has
been imposed upon the disputants. Many of the problems associated with

resolutions decided through litigation are inherent in those reached through arbitration. Therefore, the parties may be less willing to voluntarily comply with the decision. Furthermore, the process may push the parties to focus on proving themselves right as opposed to finding ways to create a process of ongoing communication and conflict resolution.

Proponents of med-arb believe that using a single professional in both roles (i.e., as mediator and as arbitrator) provides a more efficient and less expensive alternative to the more cumbersome technique of first utilizing a mediator and then employing a new neutral for the arbitration phase. The time and expense consumed in bringing a different neutral party "up to speed" in the case is not necessary in a med-arb situation that engages a single professional. It is noted that even when only one neutral party is used, additional fact-finding or presentation of evidence may be necessary as the individual switches from mediation to arbitration, which certainly increases the time and expense of the process. However, the timeline in preparing to make the arbitration decision is shortened considerably by having first served during the fact-finding and discussion phases of the mediation.

Not surprisingly, there are potential disadvantages associated with the med-arb process. As noted above, the nature of the agreement and potential compliance with that agreement are changed when the arbitration process is included. Thus, the nature of the discussions between the parties during the mediation phase may change as a function of the parties' understanding that the mediator will become a decision maker. The parties may be less candid about their situations and positions, and they may do more posturing during this type of mediation than they would in a single-process mediation. This added factor makes the course of the mediation phase more difficult and may result in fewer settlements.

Given these potential problems, why is med-arb gaining popularity and being used more frequently by families in divorce-related conflict? Part of the answer lies in the fact that working with high-conflict families is extremely difficult, especially because their ability to communicate is so poor. Traditional mediation with these difficult situations is, at best, an extremely slow and frustrating process. Additionally, access to the court system is slow, expensive, and fraught with many of its own problems for these families. Court-designated solutions to their problems are often inadequate, because of the lack of time and attention that can be given to creating individualized resolutions. Finally, when there is both a slow process and ongoing parental conflicts, the parties that suffer the most are the children—which many parents recognize and hope to minimize.

Because the parents often fail to make timely decisions to resolve these problems due to their lack of skill, entrenched positions, and vested interests, the children typically suffer multiple consequences. The immediate consequences can include missed educational or extracurricular opportunities, delayed medical or dental treatment, failure to obtain counseling or therapy, and inhibited social growth and development. Longer-term consequences can include significant emotional distress, including anxiety, depression, and anger, especially at their parents, who are supposed to be their primary source of safety and security. The use of med-arb in the face of an impasse between the parents can result in an instantaneously binding decision that is certainly beneficial to the children. The purpose of the initial mediation phase of the process is to teach parents to communicate effectively and problem solve with continued guidance. If, however, med-arb is unsuccessful, the children are not forced to suffer the far-ranging consequences that may accrue from indecision.

Another case example might help in understanding the med-arb process. Eric and Shana were both born in Syria. They had been living in the United States for 8 years when they separated. They have one daughter, Tasha, who is 4 years old. Eric and Shana have been in a constant battle about custodial issues since the time of the separation. The court determined that Shana would have primary physical custody of Tasha, with liberal partial custody afforded to Eric. The parents have been experiencing repeated conflicts over the "interpretation" of the physical and legal custodial rights since the court's ruling. Multiple contempt petitions have been filed over what appeared to be even the most trivial decisions.

The parents agreed to the use of a med-arb process to deal with their ongoing conflicts. One such dispute arose last summer when Eric wanted to take Tasha to Syria for an extended summer vacation to visit relatives. The custody agreement allowed for extended time and did not restrict travel as long as each party was given the same opportunity. The problem was not related to whether or not it was acceptable under the agreement to take that type of vacation. Rather, Shana felt strongly that the political atmosphere and world setting (i.e., terrorism) would place Tasha in danger. Eric felt that U.S. news reports were exaggerating the problems and that he should be allowed to take his daughter "home."

After repeated attempts to mediate their differences, an impasse was reached and the mediator/arbitrator was asked to make the decision. The mediator/arbitrator felt that there was too great a risk of danger (the mediator/arbitrator called the U.S. State Department and received notice of warnings regarding travel in the Middle East) and "ruled" not to allow Tasha to go with her father. The entire process took 1 week from the beginning of the mediation to the decision. The end result was more beneficial for all three parties, who then had plenty of time to make different arrangements. It should be noted that Eric and Shana are now working harder to make the simpler decisions together, including the use of clothing, timing of transfers, and sharing of medications.

Contrary to the belief that the use of med-arb leads to fewer settlements, a research study by Pruitt (1995) suggests that the opposite is true. Pruitt specifically evaluated the med-arb process and its impact on the mediation phase of the settlement. Three approaches were evaluated for their effect on the mediation process: med-arb same (one neutral party), med-arb different (two neutral parties), and traditional mediation. Pruitt analyzed the data to assess in which approach mediation proceeded most "smoothly" and to evaluate the disputants' motivational levels during the process.

The results were somewhat surprising: According to the study by Pruitt (1995), instead of following the course of straight mediation, the mediation process worked better for disputants under med-arb (same). Another finding was that the disputants were more motivated to reach settlements under both of the med-arb conditions than when using only mediation. One finding that seemed to support a fundamental criticism of med-arb was that mediators in the med-arb (same) approach used the most "heavy pressure tactics" in trying to reach an agreement. The author conjectured that mediator power was a contributing factor in helping disputants resolve their conflict under med-arb (same). Another finding was that, under the med-arb (same) approach, disputants seemed to be more engaged in creative, problem-solving strategies during their mediation. It is hypothesized that the inevitability of arbitration following mediation influenced the parties' motivation to reach their own settlements during the mediation phase of the process. (Anecdotally, that is what appears to be happening with Eric and Sasha, albeit gradually.)

Nevertheless, it must also be acknowledged that the med-arb approach and evaluative mediation raise several ethical dilemmas. The first—and perhaps the largest—is related to the issue of mediator neutrality. In reality, this ethical problem permeates every mixed process that includes the use of mediation. One of the cornerstones of the mediation process is the necessity of mediator neutrality, at least with respect to the outcome of the mediation. A mediator is ethically bound not to direct or coerce the disputants toward a particular outcome. How can a mediator "switch" roles during the settlement process to become a fact-finding decision maker and not violate his or her ethical obligations as a mediator to remain neutral?

Before attempting to answer that question, we must consider the other major ethical problem that arises through the use of the med-arb process. Confidentiality is another cornerstone of the mediation process. Many states have enacted statutes specifically related to the confidentiality privilege that exists for mediation and its participants. A significant ethical dilemma arises with respect to confidentiality in a case where a single neutral party serves as both mediator and arbitrator or evaluator. It is practically impossible for the information that is obtained during the mediation phase to be separated and "disregarded" during the decision-making or arbitration phase. Thus, the confidentiality that is considered imperative in the mediation process cannot be upheld in the single neutral, med-arb scenario. Admittedly, the parties have preexisting knowledge that their settlement negotiations during mediation will, in fact, have an impact on the decision making of the arbitrator. As noted, the parties are informed of the limits of confidentiality in this process and consequently may not negotiate as openly and creatively during the mediation phase, while they are in the "shadow" of the arbitration, as they would have, were there no arbitration looming or were the arbitrator a different person.

So, how are these ethical problems overcome? From the standpoint of pure mediation standards and guidelines, they cannot be overcome. If I call myself a mediator, then I cannot breach the confidentiality of the process without the express waiver of all involved or unless the information received is subject to some exception to the rules of confidentiality and privilege. Even then, it is questionable as to whether breaching confidentiality is appropriate or best for the clients. Similarly, I cannot have the authority to act as a decision maker and a mediator at the same time. The role of mediator is mutually exclusive from that of arbitrator. However, does the role of an arbitrator necessarily preclude the ability or wisdom to use mediation skills and techniques while attempting to assist parties in reaching resolutions of their disputes?

The only approach to resolving the ethical dilemmas inherent in the use of med-arb, or any other mixed process, is to be sure to use appropriate and clear terminology regarding the process that is being used and to ensure that the parties understand the differences between the various processes. Only with a clear understanding of the processes and the risks and benefits involved can participants make informed decisions as to which process to use. In addition, the neutral party feels more comfortable (or *should* feel more comfortable) in the use of a particular process after honest disclosure. We should never consider ourselves to be doing mediation when, in fact, we are serving as an arbitrator or some other kind of decision maker. To use the label of *mediator* in such a situation is inaccurate and sets the stage to engage in the unethical practice of mediation. However, if we clearly describe the process (including the fact that in this particular process we are not serving as a mediator), indicate the advantages and disadvantages, risks and benefits, associated with it and then allow the parties to make an informed choice, we have taken the minimal but yet necessary steps to overcome the ethical pitfalls associated with the use of any mixed process.

ARB-MED

As the name implies, *arb-med* is the inverse process of med-arb. In the arb-med process, one individual serves as both arbitrator and mediator, but the sequence is reversed such that the process starts with the arbitration phase.

In many ways, the evaluative mediation process (described earlier) used in family disputes is a variation of the arb-med process, since the evaluative phase leads to a "judgment" that may or may not be acknowledged until after the mediation process has been attempted. Of course, the evaluator is not allowed to make a binding decision, but his or her recommendations and testimony to the court tend to greatly influence the judicial decision in most courts.

By reversing the order of the mediation and arbitration processes, some of the disadvantages of the med-arb are avoided. First, since there are no open "negotiations" and settlement offers in the arbitration hearing (i.e., evaluation phase), there are no expectations that what is disclosed in that hearing will be confidential and not used in the decision-making process. In fact, the expectations are just the opposite. The whole proceeding is structured to produce a decision. Therefore, issues around confidentiality are initially sidestepped. Secondly, there is less chance of parties becoming confused about the "power" of the decision maker. When mediation precedes arbitration, parties may question the ultimate power held by the mediator. However, when arbitration occurs first, the power of the arbitrator is recognized by all and should not be confused during the mediation phase.

This latter point raises one of the disadvantages of the arb-med process. Since the arbitrator (evaluator) has already made his or her decision about what would constitute the "right" settlement, there might be a tendency to push the mediation in the direction of that decision. The parties may negotiate more openly since there is nothing to lose, but they also recognize that there is already a potential decision on hand if they do not settle. The parties are likely to be influenced by the arbitrator (evaluator) and "settle" for an alternative that they might not have accepted in a "pure" mediation. All of the pitfalls associated with a "powerful" or "muscle" mediator are present in this type of process.

As noted in the section on evaluative mediation, a variation within this process is to have the decision sealed at the end of the arbitration phase without sharing that decision with the parties. The advantage of this particular approach is to allow the parties to continue their negotiation without the influence of the arbitrator's decision. The parties still have the opportunity to reach their own resolution without feeling "muscled" into the decision that the arbitrator has already made. However, if the arbitrator is also the mediator, he or she is likely, whether unconsciously or consciously, to move the parties in the direction that he or she believes is best. An arbitrator who is able to remain distanced from his or her own decision and who believes that solutions reached by the parties are ultimately best is less likely to attempt to "muscle" the parties in the direction of his or her decision.

CONCLUSION

Mixed processes have evolved in the resolution of family disputes because there has been a need for them. The common goal that is part of all of these processes is to bring about a speedier, less expensive, and *final* resolution to a conflict. Each of the different processes described in this chapter is appropriate for certain disputes and not for others. Their very multiplicity demonstrates the great number of variations that can be applied creatively to disputes in order to meet the needs of the disputants with respect to outcomes. It is imperative that, as conflict resolvers, we remain open to the use of these hybrids and recognize the important role that each can play in assisting individual families to resolve their conflicts in the most expedient and just ways possible.

REFERENCES

Bush, R. A. B., & Folger, J. P. (1994). *The promise of mediation: Responding to conflict through empowerment and recognition.* San Francisco: Jossey-Bass.

Folberg, J., & Milne, A. (Eds.). (1988). *Divorce mediation: Theory and practice.* New York: Guilford Press.

Gould, J. W. (1998). *Conducting scientifically crafted child custody evaluations.* Thousand Oaks, CA: Sage.

Mayer, B. (2000). *The dynamics of conflict resolution.* San Francisco: Jossey-Bass.

Murray, J. S., Rau, A. S., & Sherman, E. F. (1996). *Processes of dispute resolution: The role of lawyers* (2nd ed.). Westbury, NY: Foundation Press.

Phillips, G. E. (2002, April). *Ethical implications of med-arb.* Institute conducted at the meeting of the American Bar Association Section of Dispute Resolution, Seattle, WA.

Pruitt, D. (1995). Process and outcome in community mediation. *Negotiation Journal, 11,* 365–377.

Stulberg, J. B. (1981). The theory and practice of mediation: A reply to Professor Susskind. *Vermont Law Review, 6*(1), 85–117.

Williams, M. (1998). *Mediation: Why people fight and how to help them to stop.* Dublin: Poolbeg Press.

PART III
Mediation Techniques and Interventions

CHAPTER 7

The Plan to Separately Parent Children after Divorce

MARILYN S. MCKNIGHT
STEPHEN K. ERICKSON

The traditional adversarial system can fuel a competitive and conflictual relationship between divorcing parents. This chapter presents a parent planning model that mediators can use with parents to focus on the future and address the day-to-day details of raising children, rather than the win–lose aspects of who gets custody. Marilyn S. McKnight and Stephen K. Erickson provide specific suggestions and useful examples to utilize when mediating this parenting plan. This chapter not only adds to the mediator's repertoire but may also be a useful handout for parents.

As 9-year-old David leaves Mom's car at a neutral exchange site to enter Dad's waiting vehicle, he kisses his mother goodbye and says, "Mommy, if I were dead, maybe then you and Daddy wouldn't fight over me so much." David's parents are now on their second round of appeals to the Minnesota Supreme Court over the issue of custody. Beginning with the report of the custody investigator, the guardian ad litem's report, the testimony of the expert psychologists hired by both sides, and continuing with the countless motions, hearings, and endless rounds of appeals, it never seems to end for David. David's parents have each spent in excess of $150,000 on legal fees fighting over custody of him. They may soon realize that they have nothing left to fight over. They will certainly be awarded damaged goods once the hearings are over. David's parents are wealthy and have the means to carry on the custody battle as long as they can find attorneys who are willing to take their money. Even though many jurisdictions have passed legislation attempting to limit this type of continual litigation, all jurisdictions permit recourse to the court upon a showing of child endangerment. This change usually allows an opening for yet more litigation, as each parent can allege that the other parent's conduct is endangering the child. As we know from the research and our own observations, each parent's conduct *is* definitely endangering the child. But now, David on his own may have figured out a way to truly end the battle that is so deeply affecting him.

THE CUSTODY CONTEST

There are many more Davids in this country than we, as a society, are willing to acknowledge and they all have something in common. Children such as David have parents who have sufficient funds to engage in legal battles, and they have a legal system willing to give parents the weapons with which to wage the battle. Most observers want to blame the parents, but in reality the genesis of David's problem is a system of adversarial conflict resolution that provides fuel for more conflict by forcing parents to compete with each other instead of encouraging parents to cooperate. The adversarial assumptions are deeply ingrained. They are subtle but powerfully damaging to families and children, because these assumptions create a contest mentality.

One of the more destructive impacts of this contest mentality is the relentless need to evaluate. This demand for evaluation is created by a faulty premise that says, in essence, "Well, if they can't live together as husband and wife, then we certainly can't expect them to raise their children together, and we'd best put one of them in charge." In order to determine who should be in charge, it becomes necessary to evaluate each parent's past behavior in light of a set of standards, called the "best interest tests" and then apply these standards to the past conduct of the parents. This focus has three major flaws that create unfairness and suffering:

1. It assumes that people cannot and will not change.
2. It assumes that circumstances are static and will never change, in that past conduct is evaluated in light of the past circumstances—which are always certain to change, once two homes have been established and the children begin to move between those homes.
3. It ignores the high cost of the contest. The transaction cost of evaluating past conduct and assigning it a score is always exponentially greater than the process of building a Parenting Plan in mediation.

Moreover, a custody evaluation approach diminishes the likelihood of future parental cooperation by virtue of the destructive impact of the contest itself.

The evaluative approach has been at the center of divorce in the United States from the beginning. It is now time to change the view, because we know that the process of determining who should be in charge only creates more turmoil on top of existing turmoil. A custody trial and all that is involved in preparing for it is just the beginning of parents' problems, not the end. The hurt created by the contest fuels the anger in a vicious circle that nourishes continual conflict. We must finally conclude that custody trials do not serve a useful purpose. Furthermore, we must conclude that evaluating past conduct serves no useful purpose. All that a custody evaluation can accomplish is to intensify the parents' conflict and create thousands of children who experience what David has experienced.

Beginning with Kelly and Wallerstein's (1980) earliest research about the harmful effects of custody battles, all subsequent research has reached the same conclusion: that children's negative adjustment to their parents' divorce is directly related to the level of the parents' conflict.[1] If we were really willing to accept the truth of this research, we would dismantle the custody trial apparatus that exists in this country and start teaching people how to cooperate. However, the courts cannot do this, and as a result, the adversarial process continues to encourage parents to fight by holding on to the notion that it is necessary to put one parent in charge and call the other less qualified.

CHANGING THE GAME

If we can remove divorcing parents' fear of losing their children, we will end the need to have custody battles. The most constructive way to accomplish this goal is by changing the game from a *contest* to a *process of future planning.* Parents fear losing when each parent is advised that it is necessary to compete with the other parent to win custody of the children. Parents do not fear losing their children when they are assured that no one is trying to minimize their importance by attempting to turn them into a second-class visitor. Removing the fear can be accomplished in the mediation room, and it is beginning to happen in the legislatures of the 21 states that have passed, or are considering passage of, Parenting Plan legislation (Alabama, Arizona, California, Colorado, Idaho, Kansas, Minnesota, Missouri, Montana, Nebraska, New Mexico, North Carolina, Oregon, South Dakota, Tennessee, Utah, Virginia, Washington, Washington, DC, West Virginia, and Wisconsin).[2] The impetus for such an approach comes from research and simple observation of children's suffering in the course of custody battles.

Ricci (1997) has pointed out that children can easily adapt to moving between two loving homes; the struggle begins with the need to fight over which home is better. Her book, *Mom's House, Dad's House* (Ricci, 1997), has been read by millions. She observed an 8-year-old simply say, "I'm going to be at my dad's house this weekend," or "I'm going to be at my mom's house this weekend." He does not say to his friend on Friday afternoon that he is going to spend the weekend with his noncustodial, nonprimary, nonpsychological, nonresidential, secondary, nonmanaging, Disneyland, deadbeat, visitation parent.

Mediators who practice a facilitative rather than an evaluative method of intervention have seen the pain children experience at the hand of their parents' conflict. After 25 years of observing couples in our own daily mediation practice, we have come to the only conclusion possible: that most of the battle created in the minds of parents and their advocates is more a result of the statutory adversarial process we impose on divorcing couples and less a result of their own misfortunes and tribulations. As mediators, we have also learned that the battle is fueled by two other forces in addition to the evaluative force: (1) a focus on the past, and (2) the impact of words. Think of the associative differences between the word *custody* and the word *parenting*:

Impact of, and assumptions associated with, the word *custody*	Impact of, and assumptions associated with, the word *parenting*
Ownership	Sharing
Control, power over other parent	Empowering each parent
Possession	Cooperation
Static situation; signifies a position won at trial and assumes the ruling solves all problems; does not address future interaction	Evolving and changing relationship in light of future tasks; *to parent* is a verb and assumes an ongoing relationship and ongoing interaction between the parents
Requires evaluations of past conduct to determine who wins custody	Requires discussion about future changes needed and parenting ground rules, to be observed jointly
Used by proponents of an adversarial approach	Used by mediators in an attempt to create a cooperative approach
Serves the judicial system's need for simple outcomes dictated by evaluating the weight of the evidence as applied to the case	Serves parents' needs to remain parents; does require more complex discussion and planning than simply determining who is better or worse
Creates losers who are branded noncustodial visitation parents	Creates new status for parents, who are then viewed equally in the eyes of their children
Establishes a number of "prizes" or benefits that accompany the parent who is anointed as the custodial winner	Disconnects the award of child support, possession of the house, and other normal spoils of custody, and requires fairness on all issues
Emphasizes rights of parents	Emphasizes obligations of parents
Past focused and evaluative	Future focused and task oriented

THE EVOLUTION OF PARENTING PLANS

The approach outlined in this chapter follows the understandings first discovered by a small group of mediators in the early 1980s who noticed that it was much easier to reach resolution of the custody issues when the entire content of the parenting arrangements were first agreed upon prior to engaging in discussions about custody labels. This approach attempted to neutralize the framework of the adversarial system of divorce by eliminating the connection between winning custody as the key to so many other "prizes" that are attached to the custody label. Although at the time we did not think of it in terms of building a Parenting Plan, the approach essentially called for the mediator to refuse to mediate *custody* and to instead mediate schedules, housing, even how the clothes would be exchanged or handled.

When following such an approach, the mediator's responsibility is to provide a cooperative environment wherein the couple can begin to experience positive progress and improvement. The mediator moves beyond each parent's claim that he or she is entitled to be the primary custodial parent by asking each to flesh out the details of proposed schedules for exchanges and other important conditions and ground rules for future parenting. This approach moves parents, almost exclusively, into future planning arrangements, even though the parents may still be caught in the pain of the past and prone to ruminate about the other's past misconduct.

It is a well-known fact that many mediators do not practice the Parenting Plan approach but use a law-centered approach and make evaluative determinations about who should have custody—which, of course, then imposes the role of *visitor* upon the parent deemed less likely to prevail in a custody trial. The public may think this is mediation, but it mediates the wrong issue. It mediates the winning or losing of custody. Our focus is on mediating a Parenting Plan, not a custody dispute, and it calls for asking an entirely different question of the parents. Instead of asking who is a better or worse parent, the parents are asked if they wish to build a plan detailing the future parenting of the children that views the parents as significantly involved in their children's lives after divorce.

The following sample language used in our practice may be helpful in understanding how a Parenting Plan is mediated. The plan itself is essentially a series of detailed agreements about each parent's conduct in the future. Most Parenting Plans include some statement about the processes and philosophies by which parenting decisions will be made, a schedule of time that each parent spends with the children, a mechanism for sharing the costs of raising the children, rules that address concerns specific to the particular couple, and a method of dispute resolution for use if the parents are unable to resolve future parenting conflicts on their own. In those jurisdictions that do not follow a Parenting Plan approach, the person awarded custody is generally presumed to be in charge of determining the scope and content of these ground rules, often without any input from the other parent, other than perhaps active or passive resistance to the wishes of the custodial parent.

SAMPLE PARENTING PLAN AGREEMENT USED AT THE ERICKSON MEDIATION INSTITUTE

The following Parenting Plan language has been developed from our experiences with clients as well as our work with mediators throughout the United States. This Parenting Plan includes the best of what we have learned from, and shared with, parents and mediators. The Parenting Plan is presented first with an explanation of some of the topics, followed by optional language (in *italics*) to be used by our fictional parents, John and Mary Doe.

Agreements Regarding Parental Responsibilities

Custody Options

In developing a Parenting Plan, parents have many choices about the legal definitions of their arrangement. They may choose to use custody labels that are consistent with the laws of their state, or they may choose not to use any such labels. When they are deciding whether or not to use the labels, their most important consideration is the legal consequence of the labels. In those states that designate two gradations of custody, *legal custody* relates to the legal incidents of parenthood, such as access to school records, signing for medical emergencies, and other legal rights; *physical custody* generally relates to parental control of the children, which parent is presumed to be in charge, who will receive child support, and what kind of a visitation schedule will be imposed upon the parent losing custody.

Legal Custody

The label of *legal custody* relates to the legal rights and responsibilities of parents. Generally, most states encourage both parents to continue to have joint legal custody of their children after a divorce. This gives them the same legal rights and responsibilities that they had while married. In those cases where a parent does not have legal custody, that parent relinquishes the right to share in the major decision making concerning the children's education, medical care, and religious upbringing. When creating a Parenting Plan, almost all parents consider these important decisions as their joint responsibility. Legal custody language in a Parenting Plan varies from state to state but generally follows language that, in this case, incorporates much of the Minnesota statute with a presumption in favor of joint legal custody:

Joint Legal Custody

John and Mary have agreed that they will share joint legal custody of their children. Joint legal custody means that John and Mary both have equal rights and responsibilities regarding their children's upbringing, including education, health care, and religious training. Neither of their rights is superior to those of the other parent. Neither John nor Mary will do anything that would lead to estrangement between their children and the other parent, nor will either parent perform any act that would interfere with the natural development of love and affection between the children and either of them. Both John and Mary recognize that children have emotional and psychological needs to establish a healthy and satisfying relationship with both parents.

Major decision making. On important matters relating to the health, welfare, and/or education of the minor children, John and Mary will discuss and work toward a mutually acceptable determination of the issues, including, for example, but not limited to, the following:

- *In the event of illness or injury to the children, the parent first learning of the illness or injury will notify the other parent immediately.*
- *The parents will consult with each other regarding the schooling of the children.*
- *Each parent will promptly inform or consult with the other in the event of any serious medical problem of the children.*
- *Each parent will have equal access to the information relating to the children, including, but not limited to, access to school, governmental, law enforcement, and medical records, and access to all teachers, governmental officials and officers, doctors, and other professionals having contact with the children.*
- *Both parents may participate, individually or jointly, with the children in special activities including, but not limited to, Scouts, music, sports, school conferences and other activities, etc. Such information and contacts will be available to each parent without notice or any further consent of the other parent.*
- *Each parent is authorized to consent to emergency medical care for the children at the time when the other parent is not easily accessible to give such consent.*
- *Each parent will continue to play a full and active role in providing a sound moral, social, economic, religious, and educational environment for the children. Each parent will inform the other of the children's social and educational activities and appointments, so that both parents might participate, when possible and appropriate, and each parent will further advise the other of the children's emergency situations, illnesses, and problems which may occur when the children are in his or her care.*
- *Both parents agree to resolve all conflicts in a manner consistent with the best interests of the children and, when necessary, to use the conflict resolution mechanisms described in this Parenting Plan.*

Physical Custody

The *physical custody* label described earlier creates difficulties for parents building a Parenting Plan. Parents generally remove the contest assumption of this label in their Parenting Plan by choosing Joint Physical Custody. This choice nullifies the power of the label and frees parents to make practical, workable decisions about how they will address specific concerns in the future, should they present themselves:

Sole Physical Custody

John and Mary agree that [one of them] will have sole physical custody of their children.

Joint Physical Custody

John and Mary agree that they will share joint physical custody of their children.

No Designation of Physical Custody

Parenting Plan laws in Minnesota have provided parents with the opportunity to refrain from designating the physical custody of their children in a divorce.[3] Many parents choose not to designate a custodial parent and use the following language:

No Designation of Physical Custody

John and Mary agree not to designate a physical custodian of the minor children. For purposes of travel to states or countries that do not recognize Parenting Plans, this arrangement may be considered Joint Legal and Joint Physical Custody.

In Minnesota, when courts still required a specific finding of physical custody, we were able to help couples avoid a custody battle by including language in the final decree that stated, for example, *John will have physical custody of the minor children when he is on duty and caring for the children, according to their parenting schedule of exchanges, and Mary will have physical custody of the minor children during the time that she is on duty and scheduled to care for the children, according to their parenting schedule of exchanges.* Of course, this language was essentially a scam upon the entire system, but many innovative lawyers and judges accepted it as a way of avoiding a custody designation. Such an approach may be valuable in those states that currently resist the notion of Parenting Plans.

The following paragraphs are examples of the form and language of a Parenting Plan for parents to consider as they create their own plan. Not all of these topics are included by parents in their Parenting Plans, of course, but we offer them here as language that other parents have used for their situations.

General Understandings

As parents, John and Mary are committed to cooperating with each other to provide future parenting of their children that is in the children's best interests. They recognize that they are each very important to the physical, social, and psychological development of their children and that their children need each of them to be actively involved in their lives in the future. John and Mary agree to respect each other's individual parenting role with the children and to be supportive of each other as parents.

John and Mary further understand that sending messages to the other parent through the children places the children in the middle of their conflict and that it is their responsibility to communicate with each other directly. They also know that disrespecting the other parent is harmful to the children's sense of self, and so they each agree to refrain from these behaviors. Instead, they will encourage the children's relationship with the other parent and give each child clear permission to love, and be proud of, the other parent.

Separate Parenting[4]

John and Mary agree that they no longer have a relationship as marriage partners and that they have only.a relationship as separate parents with separate lives and homes. As separate parents, they agree to the following:

- *The children will have a meaningful relationship with each of them.*
- *They will communicate with each other directly–either verbally, in writing, or by e-mail–and will refrain from sending any messages to each other through the children.*
- *When the children complain to one of them about the other parent, the parent receiving the complaint will ask the child(ren) to discuss it with the other parent. If the child is uncomfortable doing so, the parent receiving the complaint will help the child(ren) communicate with the other parent. Each parent will try to understand the complaint without making a judgment, interfering, or taking sides.*
- *They each understand that their parenting styles may be different and that the differences will enhance their children's growth. They each agree to accept and respect each other's differences.*

- *They will each be supportive of the other's parenting and positively encourage the children in their relationship with the other parent.*
- *When parenting problems arise, they agree that they will deal with the problems as parents, just between them.*
- *They agree that they will refrain from discussing their personal lives and parenting problems or differences with the children.*
- *When they have parenting problems between them that they are unable to resolve, they will seek the services of a professional family mediator, or a professional neutral expert in family and/or child therapy, to assist them in resolving the matter.*
- *They agree to respect each other's boundaries. They agree that their separate lives and private lives are no longer joined. They each agree not to enter the other parent's home or private space without being invited.*
- *Finally, they agree that if either or them enters a new significant relationship that may affect the children, each will inform the other parent of this new relationship. They further agree that they will each assist the children in understanding and adjusting to the new relationship.*

Residential Arrangements

The first question parents ask when divorcing is "Where will the children live?" This issue is at the core of the Parenting Plan. The answer is that the children will live with each parent at separate times. The best way to determine these times is for parents to develop a schedule of times the children will spend at each of their homes and when the children will move from one home to the other.

The earliest type of schedule that was commonly used by courts in the United States before the introduction of joint physical custody statutes was a very unequal schedule that assumed children would remain with their custodial parent in the family home and the other parent would have the privilege of having the children visit every other weekend, from Friday evening to Sunday evening, and every other Wednesday from 5:00 to 7:00 P.M.

States began to legislate the concept of joint custody at the same time divorce mediation was beginning to be offered, and more and more parents began to consider different ways they could both be more involved with their children after divorce. Parents in mediation often chose to create more equivalent time-sharing schedules of when the children would be with each parent. This was especially appealing to parents who chose to continue to reside in close proximity after the divorce. In our practices, parents have designed a variety of schedules that meet the needs of the children, their activities, and the parents' work schedules. We found that most parents wanted to have equal time with the children on weekends, and so they alternated weekends routinely. They would often, however, add Sunday night as an overnight; in this event, children would be exchanged at school or at after-school programs on Fridays and at school or at before-school programs on Mondays. Some parents then added the Monday and Tuesday nights to the schedule, creating a half-time parenting schedule, in which one parent has the children overnight on Mondays and Tuesdays and the other parent has them overnight Wednesdays and Thursdays:

(M, Mom; D, Dad)

	Mon.	Tues.	Wed.	Thurs.	Fri.	Sat.	Sun.
Wk. 1	D/M	M	M/D	D	D/M	M	M
Wk. 2	M	M	M/D	D	D	D	D
Wk. 3	D/M	M	M/D	D	D/M	M	M
Wk. 4	M	M	M/D	D	D	D	D

For infants and toddlers, who need more frequent contact with each parent, parents have used the above schedule and added "touch-base" times when the other parent would spend time with children over a meal to break up the longer periods of time.

Some parents wanted longer periods of time, especially with teenage children. These parents frequently chose 1-week periods of time with and without the children, with the exchange time being Fridays after school:

(M, Mom; D, Dad)

	Mon.	Tues.	Wed.	Thurs.	Fri.	Sat.	Sun.
Wk. 1	D	D	D	D	D/M	M	M
Wk. 2	M	M	M	M	M/D	D	D
Wk. 3	D	D	D	D	D/M	M	M
Wk. 4	M	M	M	M	M/D	D	D

Many parents find that they have to help each other out because of their unique work schedules. Pilots, flight attendants, air traffic controllers, physicians, nurses, U.S. armed services personnel, servers, and professional athletes, are examples of parents who find that they have to create unique parenting schedules and plan them out a year in advance. They also need to build flexibility into their agreements, so that either parent can make changes, as necessary, while not misusing the flexibility as a means to manipulate a schedule for other than parenting purposes.

Some parents chose to have special one-on-one time between a child and a parent and scheduled this into their Parenting Plan so that it would occur regularly. This "one-on-one time" may also be scheduled for a period of time, based on a special need of a child.

Parents often begin this approach by trying out a parenting schedule for a few months to see how it works for themselves and the children. They may find it necessary to make adjustments to the schedule so that both parents can make a commitment to maintain it. Parents find that the parenting schedules tend to keep the separate homes organized around the children. When a parenting schedule is part of an entire Parenting Plan, the parents make agreements that enhance the entire parenting experience for them and their children. Children generally like parenting schedules once they have adjusted to residing in two homes with separate parents. Children also like to have the parenting calendar displayed where they have access to it at each home. Once the family has adjusted to a parenting schedule, the arrangements tend to go quite smoothly for everyone.

Residential Arrangements

John and Mary realize that their children's needs play a most important role in how they plan their living arrangements, and also that those needs will change as the children grow older. John and Mary will be sensitive to each child's process of adjusting to their divorce and separate parenting in the future. They recognize that their children will adjust better to the changes if they know what will be happening and the schedule of when they will be with each parent. Therefore, John and Mary will clearly communicate to their children the regular schedule for spending time with each parent and the schedule for their holidays. They will make the schedule available to the children at each of their homes or on the Internet.

John and Mary will try to keep the schedules predictable, specific, and routine, and when either of them needs to make an exception to the normal schedule, he or she will first ask the other parent to care for the children. They will give each other as much advance notice as possible about a need to make a schedule change. If the other parent is unable to care for the children, the scheduled parent will make other arrangements.

From time to time, John and Mary may experiment with different schedules in order to try to find an exchange routine that does not unduly disrupt the children's daily schedule and still allows for significant parenting involvement by each of them. They will follow an initial parenting schedule, as follows:

(M, Mom; D, Dad)

	Mon.	Tues.	Wed.	Thurs.	Fri.	Sat.	Sun.
Wk. 1	M/D/M*	M	M/D	D	D/M/D*	D	D
Wk. 2	D/M	M	M/D	D	D/M	M	M
Wk. 3	M/D/M*	M	M/D	D	D/M/D*	D	D
Wk. 4	D/M	M	M/D	D	D/M	M	M

*Touch-base time from 5:00 to 7:00 P.M. for dinner.

Summer Parenting and Vacations—Options

- *During the summer, John and Mary may make different parenting arrangements. They will agree on a summer schedule at least a month prior to the end of the school year.*
- *John and Mary will have a preliminary discussion about summer plans, camps, and vacations each year by February with the final plans being decided upon by May.*
- *John and Mary agree that they may each have up to 2 weeks of vacation with the children each year. This time may be in 1-week blocks or a full 2-week block. They agree to discuss their vacation plans with the other parent as soon as each is considering vacation times.*

Holiday Schedule

A few decades ago it would have seemed strange to have to create a schedule of when children would be with their parents on holidays. Now it is commonly known as an area of great conflict for divorced parents. A judge once called our office on December 24 to ask if he could order parents to meet with us on *that day* to mediate where their children would spend Christmas Eve and Christmas Day. We agreed to see them, and the parents came directly to us from the courtroom to mediate this issue. After some time wrestling with the issue of where the children would be that evening, Christmas Eve, and the next day, Christmas Day, the parents refused to cooperate and continued to find fault with the other's ideas. Finally the mediator said, "Well, I guess you will just have to return to court and have the judge decide." They both became extremely upset, with one of them protesting, "We *can't* go back to court! The judge told us if we did, he would place our children in foster care today!" Needless to say, they reached an agreement. Had they had a schedule in place, if only as a fallback in the event they could not agree upon holiday plans, they would not have been in court or mediation on the day of Christmas Eve. Parents understand that when they make a holiday schedule, they are engaging their best effort to plan how the holidays with the children will be celebrated in the future. It also gives parents time to consider how they might create new traditions with their children after divorce. We make an assumption that all families celebrate holidays, though by no means the same holidays. A holiday schedule must be based upon the family's beliefs and traditions. A typical holiday schedule follows on p. 142.

Holiday Schedule

John and Mary agree to the following holiday schedule, in which holidays will be treated as an exception to the regular weekly parenting schedule, without the need to have makeup time. The children will spend holidays as follows on p. 143:

Holiday	Even-numbered years	Odd-numbered years
Spring break		
Passover		
Easter		
Memorial Day		
Fourth of July		
Labor Day		
Rosh Hashanah		
Yom Kippur		
Sukkoth		
Teachers' convention		
Halloween		
Thanksgiving		
Thanksgiving Fri.–Sun.		
Chanukah		
First half-winter break		
Christmas Eve		
Christmas Morning		
Christmas Day		
Second half-winter break		
New Year's Eve		
New Year's Day		
Children's birthdays	According to schedule, and the other parent may have some contact as requested by that parent.	
Parents' birthdays	Time to celebrate with each parent	
Mother's Day	Mom	Mom
Father's Day	Dad	Dad

Holiday	Even-numbered years	Odd-numbered years
Spring break	Dad	Mom
Easter	Dad	Mom
Memorial Day	Mom	Dad
Fourth of July	Mom	Dad
Labor Day	Dad	Mom
Teachers' convention	Mom	Dad
Halloween	Dad	Mom
Thanksgiving	Mom	Dad
Thanksgiving Fri.–Sun.	Mom	Dad
First half-winter break	Dad	Dad
Christmas Eve	Dad	Dad
Christmas Morning	Mom	Dad
Christmas Day	Mom	Mom
Second half-winter break	Mom	Mom
New Year's Eve	Dad	Mom
New Year's Day	Mom	Dad
Children's birthdays	According to schedule, and the other parent will have some contact as requested by that parent	
Parents' birthdays	Time to celebrate with each parent	
Mother's Day	Mom	Mom
Father's Day	Dad	Dad

Some parents make some special agreements about Monday holidays, adding the Monday holiday to the on-duty parent's weekend, thereby extending it through Monday. Others acknowledge that the parent normally scheduled for the Monday of the holiday will be responsible for planning the children's activities on that day.

Monday Holidays

When Mondays are a holiday, John and Mary agree that the parent on duty on the Sunday before the holiday may have the children for an extended weekend.

Optional Parenting Agreements

Conflict Resolution about Parenting Schedules

If John and Mary disagree about scheduling changes or have disputes about the holiday schedule, they agree to first try to resolve such disagreements on their own but will return to mediation if they have difficulties in resolving these new issues on their own. The future costs of returning to mediation will be shared equally.

On-Duty, Off-Duty Parenting

John and Mary recognize that decision making is an important part of their parenting role. They agree that the parent with whom the children are residing on a particular day will be the on-duty parent and, in that capacity, will make decisions about the care and control of the children on that day.

This means that if the children are ill, or either parent had other obligations during their on-duty time with the children, it will be the responsibility of the on-duty parent to make arrangements for the care of the children. John and Mary each expect the on-duty parent to first request assistance from the off-duty parent, but they both understand that if the off-duty parent is not able to assist the on-duty parent during the scheduled time, it will be the responsibility of the on-duty parent to make alternative arrangements for the children.

Relationships Important to the Children

John and Mary recognize that the children will benefit from maintaining their ties with grandparents, relatives, and people important to them. They will each help the children maintain their relationships with these people and spend time with them periodically. John and Mary further agree that they will ask their friends and relatives to refrain from saying negative or disrespectful things about the children's other parent in the presence of the children or within their range of hearing such remarks.

Education

John and Mary agree that unless the present school boundaries change, the children will continue to attend Washington Elementary School, Jefferson Junior High, and Lincoln High School. Mary and John will each reside within easy access of the schools. They will each attend school conferences and will receive copies of report cards. Each parent will communicate with the children's schools to remain informed about each child's needs, progress, and pertinent special events, including parent–teacher conferences. John and Mary also agree to share with each other any information they receive separately about the children's school progress, behavior, and events.

Higher Education

John and Mary further agree that college or technical training is important for their children, and they will encourage and support each child's efforts for further education. Costs associated with pre-college expenses will be shared. These costs include books, field trips, school supplies, and miscellaneous fees, as well as trips to visit campuses and application fees. Both will jointly share in transportation of the children and are committed to strong support of, and involvement in, the children's education.

Removal from School

John and Mary agree to obtain the other parent's advance approval if they wish to remove the children from a day of school. They agree that it is acceptable for the children to miss occasional elementary school days for a special event; however, they also agree that at middle and high school levels, the children may not miss school except for family emergencies or for some very special reason to which they each agree in advance.

Religious Training and Religious Activities

John and Mary agree that the children will continue to be raised in the Presbyterian Church, even though John is Muslim. They will each be supportive of the children's religious upbringing and "agree to agree" regarding all religious activities in advance. All costs associated with religious activities that are agreed to in advance will be shared. While each parent will be respectful of the children's wishes, John and Mary will first agree on travel costs and other matters that require cooperation. Since each parent will have the children for half of the weekends, they agree to communicate frequently about organized religious activities, so that each parent may be aware of the children's schedule. Mary and John agree that John may introduce the children to his religious faith; however, both agree that John will not indoctrinate the children in his own particular religious beliefs.

Communication

When the children are with one parent, John and Mary agree that the children will have open access to the parent with whom they are not staying. They will each also encourage and help the children communicate frequently with the other parent. They agree to give the other parent the address and phone number where the children can be reached any time they are away from home for more than 24 hours.

Sunday Night Phone Call

John and Mary agree that they will talk to each other every Sunday evening at 9 P.M. to discuss the children. The parent who is on duty with the children will initi-

ate the phone call. They will only discuss issues regarding the children. If either John or Mary becomes uncomfortable with the conversation, that parent has only to say that he or she is uncomfortable with the conversation, that they will need to resume it next Sunday, and then gently hang up the phone. The other parent will respect that response, and they will talk to each other the following Sunday evening at 9 P.M.

Safety

John and Mary each agree not to compromise the safety of the children. They will not leave a child unattended for more than 2 hours, until each child is 12 years old.

Special Safety Concerns

Swimming, jet skiing, and snowmobiling activities require the constant supervision of a parent. John and Mary agree to prohibit the children from riding all ATVs and motorcycles. Both recognize the special danger to children from jet skis and snowmobiles. John and Mary agree that they will each closely monitor and supervise the children's use of jet skis or snowmobiles.

Alcohol or Chemical Abuse

John and Mary agree that neither of them will ever care for the children nor transport them while impaired. If either of them believes that the other parent is about to, or has violated, this agreement, that parent may ask for an immediate chemical dependency test for drugs or alcohol. This test may be requested up to two times per month. Should the test result not show impairment, as defined by the state's DUI laws, the parent requesting the test will pay for the cost of the test. However, should the test show impairment, that parent will enter a 30-day inpatient chemical dependency treatment program and follow the recommendations for aftercare. The parenting schedule will be altered temporarily during the treatment program. The other parent will cooperate with requests by the chemical dependency treatment program for participation of the children in the program. The regular parenting schedule will resume immediately upon the recommendation of the chemical dependency treatment program.

Authorized Caregivers

John and Mary will exchange a list of authorized caregivers for the children, and both agree that they will not allow any babysitters or child-care workers to provide care for the children who are not on the list without the prior consent of each.

Transportation for the Exchanges of the Children

John and Mary each agree that the parent whose home the children are coming to will pick them up. That parent will pick up the children's belongings at the same time he or she picks up the children. In addition, John and Mary will cooperate to help the children remember to take their belongings with them, so each child will have the personal belongings and school supplies they need.

Joint Rules at Each Home

John and Mary recognize that they have different parenting styles and agree that the children will be enhanced by the different experiences at each home. However, they agree there are certain ground rules that should be enforced at both homes. Therefore, they agree to the following:

1. *Bedtimes at both homes will be between 8:30 and 9:30 P.M. on school nights and 10:00 and 11:00 P.M. on weekends.*
2. *Curfew at both homes on weeknights will be 9:30 P.M., and on weekends curfew will be 11:30 P.M., unless there is a special event to which both parents agree in advance.*
3. *Discipline for minor problems will be limited to time-outs and withdrawal of a privilege. Discipline for more serious problems will be limited to greater lack of privilege or grounding; still more serious problems will require consultation between John and Mary. They will cooperate with and support the other in carrying out discipline at each of their homes for serious infractions.*
4. *Mary and John will support each other when a child calls to complain about the other parent. They will help the child discuss the matter, but they will support the other parent and encourage the child to work out the problem with the other parent.*
5. *John and Mary agree that the goal is for the children's entertainment to be beneficial, safe, educational, and expansive. If either is unsure about any entertainment, they agree to consult the other parent in advance. There will be no PG-13 movies allowed for a child until age 13, or any R movies for a child unless one parent is supervising the viewing of the movie.*
6. *John and Mary agree that, in general, the on-duty parent is responsible for the supervision of children's activities and entertainment, and he or she will ensure safety, cleanliness, and appropriate behavior.*
7. *John and Mary will each encourage healthy activities for the children, including attendance at children's museums, reading clubs, Scouts, and church youth groups, and once the specifics are agreed upon, each of them will share in the associated costs. If no agreement can be reached concerning the activity, the initiating parent may enroll the child in the activity and pay for and arrange the transportation. If the activity impacts the other parent's*

schedule with the children, John and Mary agree to consult and obtain agreement from the other parent before enrolling the child in the activity.

Location of Parents' Homes

John and Mary agree to reside no more than 10 miles from the other parent's home. As the children reach school age, they will attend the school that serves Mary's residence, and each parent will be responsible for transporting the children to school when they are on duty.

Parent's Move from Current Home

If John or Mary anticipates a move from a current residence that will make it impossible to continue the parenting schedule, John and Mary agree to renegotiate the parenting schedules prior to a move. They will focus on how they can still be significantly involved as parents in a way that would meet the needs of the children.

Travel Out of the Country

John and Mary agree to not take the children out of the country without prior written agreement of the other parent. Each will respond reasonably when the other parent requests to take the children out of the country for vacations or travel. They will keep the children's passports in a safe deposit box, with joint access by Mary and John.

Access to Information about the Children

John and Mary agree that they will each have access to information about the children, either through the use of The Children's Book *[Erickson & McKnight Erickson, 1992], a notebook,* ourfamilywizzard.com,[5] *or another means to record all information necessary to meet the needs of the children (i.e., medical records, doctors' and dentists' names and phone numbers, medical I.D. cards, names and phone numbers of the children's teachers, coaches, friends, the parenting and holiday schedules, and any other information they may need to effectively and efficiently meet the children's needs at any given time the children are with them). They will exchange the information with the children. They will also write notes to each other about the children. John and Mary further agree that the comments contained in their information or notes may not be admissible in any court proceeding in the future.*

Duration of the Parenting Plan

John and Mary understand that this Parenting Plan will be in effect until they make changes to it, and the court subsequently issues a new court order reflecting the new changes. They agree that all changes to the Parenting Plan will be in writing and dated and signed by both of them. Until their divorce decree is amended to reflect written changes, they realize agreements made in this Parenting Plan will legally govern any dispute.

Future Conflict Resolution

In the future, John and Mary agree to behave flexibly and cooperatively, and to communicate with each other in order to meet the changing needs of their children. When John and Mary cannot agree about the meaning of a part of the Parenting Plan, or if a significant change (such as a move or remarriage) causes conflict, they will make a good faith effort to resolve their differences through mediation, before petitioning the court. Should they be unable to resolve their differences in mediation, they will select and share the cost of a neutral child expert who will meet with the children and with each parent. Then, the neutral expert will present a plan in mediation that will allow the parents to overcome their differences. The costs of the neutral party shall be shared, and the neutral party may not be called as a witness in any court proceeding.

Child Support

When parents create a Parenting Plan, they often also want to make agreements about how they will financially support the budgetary needs of their children. Accommodating this need frequently results in a deviation from the statutory Child Support Guidelines in favor of a child support plan agreed to by the parents. With the increasing number of couples deciding to engage in equivalent time sharing, it is necessary to develop new ways of sharing the costs of raising the children. It can no longer be presumed that the custodial parent pays for all of the children's costs and, therefore, is entitled to receive child support. In mediation, it is possible to identify all the costs of raising a child and construct a much more detailed child support arrangement. Upon reviewing their budgets of personal living expenses and children's expenses, most couples agree that the higher income spouse should carry a greater portion of the children's expenses.

Child Support–Deviation from Child Support Guidelines/ No Exchange of Support

Amount of Support

John and Mary have agreed to an arrangement for sharing the costs of raising their children that calls for itemizing all expenses related to the children and sharing these costs on a pro rata basis, according to their gross incomes. Each will contribute and pay child support toward the expenses listed below of the children by contributing a percentage of their own income, which will then be deposited each month into a joint children's checking account. This percentage will be calculated on the basis of the percentage of each of their gross incomes in relation to their combined gross incomes.

The joint checking account checkbook will be exchanged each time the children are exchanged, and the on-duty parent will have the use of the checkbook for the authorized shared expenses, to be paid from the checking account, as outlined below:

Shared Expenses	
Description	*Monthly cost*
Lunches at school	55
Clothing	125
Medical insurance	136
Uncovered medical expenses	25
Prescriptions	5
Eye care	15
Therapy and counseling	30
Uncovered dental expenses	10
Orthodontia	150
Gas/oil children's car	45
Maintenance and repairs	50
Auto insurance	75
License	10
Personal items/incidentals	50
Hair care	10
Child care	325
Tuition	125
Books/supplies	20
Allowances	25
Extracurricular activities	25
Sports fees	120
Dance lessons	55
Pet expenses	10
Gifts	15
Total	**1,521**

John and Mary will each pay separately for food, recreation, entertainment, and travel expenses, which will not be shared as a part of the joint checkbook arrangement.

From time to time, and at least once every 12 months, John and Mary will meet and review the budgeted expenses for the children. Should the unused balance reach $2,000, or should there be a shortfall in the checkbook for a period of 2 consecutive months, both agree this will be a trigger to review the expenditures now budgeted for the children. John and Mary agree that neither will purchase items using the checkbook account other than those in the above-authorized categories. Should there be expenses for the children that are unusual, not anticipated, and not part of their projected expense costs, they agree to meet and discuss whether or not to incur the expense, and if they agree, the item will be purchased using the joint account.

Beginning [date], John will contribute the sum of $ ___ per month to the children's checkbook account, and Mary will contribute the sum of $ ___ per month to the checkbook account. This contribution is based upon a pro rata calculation of their incomes. John's gross income is $ ___ per year, and Mary's income is $ ___ per year. Therefore, John earns ___% of their combined incomes, and he will contribute $ ___ toward the children's itemized expenses, to be paid from the joint checkbook. Mary earns ___% of their total income, and she agrees to contribute $ ___ toward the itemized children's expenses, to be paid from the joint checkbook. They agree that for the first year, John will receive the checks and bank statements and will balance the checkbook. In February of each year, John and Mary will exchange W-2 income verification or tax returns in order to adjust their pro rata contribution toward the children's checking account. Should there be any dispute about what their current gross income is, they will submit the dispute to _____, CPA, or some other mutually agreed-upon CPA.

In the event they change their equal time-sharing schedule or in the event either one of them believes the checkbook arrangement is no longer workable, either may return to mediation to request a different child support arrangement. Should they be unable to reach agreement in mediation, they may ask the court to set a formula for child support.

Duration of Support

John and Mary will be responsible for the financial support of their children until each child reaches the age of 18 years, enters the Armed Forces of the United States, is emancipated, self-supporting, or deceased, or until each child reaches the age of 20 years if the child is still attending secondary school, or until further order of the court.

Cost-of-Living Adjustments

There will be no cost-of-living increases in child support, as they will conduct a yearly review of expenses as part of the children's checkbook agreement.

Day-Care Support

John and Mary will be responsible for the day-care or after-school program expenses of their minor children through the use of the checkbook.

Medical and Dental Health Insurance

Mary currently maintains health and dental insurance coverage for the minor children through the coverage maintained from her employment. Mary will continue to be responsible for said coverage, and for payment of the cost of said coverage, which is deducted from her paycheck, and be reimbursed by payment from John to the children's checking account. In the event such coverage will no longer be available, they will confer and reach agreement concerning alternate coverage.

Uninsured Expenses

Uninsured medical, dental, and optical expenses of the children will be paid from the children's checkbook account.

Extraordinary Expenses

Before arranging for any elective uncovered health-related procedures, John and Mary will agree on the procedure before assuming that the other parent will share in the costs of the procedure.

Security for Support

John and Mary will provide security for the financial support of their children in the form of life insurance coverage. In order to fund future child support payments, John and Mary will each maintain life insurance coverage in an amount sufficient to guarantee the payment of remaining child support for the benefit of the children until they reach the age of 18 years or graduate from secondary school. Both Mary and John will give the other the right to receive information from the insurer concerning the status of his or her life insurance policy. Presentation of a copy of the judgment to the applicable insurer will entitle both to receive information concerning the existence of coverage, the status of payments, etc. In the event of failure to pay life insurance premiums, either John or Mary will have a claim against the estate in probate of the other parent, but only to the extent of the balance of the remaining unpaid child support.

CONCLUSION

When Dan Rather asked Senator Wayne Morse of Oregon, in 1971, how the United States could extricate itself from the horrendous conflict in Vietnam, Senator Morse replied simply, "We leave." As we all know, this straightforward departure is indeed how we removed ourselves from that war. If we applied Senator Morse's advice to the war waged in divorce courts, we would say to all parents that we do not conduct custody battles anymore, that no one is permitted to encourage parents in any way to act hostilely toward each other. Such a stance is too hard on the children—*all* the children. Every divorce court in the country would display a sign at its entrance that reads: WE DO NOT ALLOW CUSTODY BATTLES ANYMORE. WE BUILD PARENTING PLANS.

Parenting Plans are only the beginning. It is our hope that professionals will continue to bring forth ideas about how we can teach cooperation to, rather than create more conflict in, divorcing families. In the end, if we can diminish the chance of creating more Davids, and if we can help heal the wounds of each breakup, we will have served the children who are at the heart of what we do.

NOTES

1. See also Amato (1994) and Amato and Keith (1996) for a detailed discussion of the behavioral and psychological problems, maladjustment, lower academic achievement, poorer self-concepts, and greater social difficulties that children of divorce experience. See Lamb, Sternberg, and Thompson (1997); Hetherington (1989); Emery (1982); Maccoby and Mnookin (1992); and Ahrons (1994).

2. For Alabama, see Code of Ala. §30-3B-102 (2003); for Arizona, A.R.S. §25-403 (2003); for California, Cal Fam Code §2040 (2003); for Colorado, C.R.S. 14-10-124 (2002); for Washington, DC, D.C. Code §16-914 (2003); for Idaho, Idaho Code §32-1402 (2003); for Kansas, K.S.A. §60-1607 (2002); for Minnesota, Minn. Stat. §518.1705 (2002); for Missouri, §210.853 R.S.Mo. (2003); for Montana, Mont. Code Ann., §25-1-201 (2002); for Nebraska, R.R.S. Neb. §43-2903 (2002); for New Mexico, N.M. Stat. Ann. §40-4-9.1 (2002); for North Carolina, N.C. Gen. Stat. §50A-102 (2003); for Oregon, ORC Ann. 3109.04 (2003); for South Dakota, S.D. Codified Laws §25-7-6.14 (2003); for Tennessee, Tenn. Code Ann. §36-6-403; for Utah, Utah Code Ann. §30-3-10.9 (2003); for Virginia, Va. Code Ann. §20-146.1 (2003); for Washington, Rev. Code Wash. (ARCW) §26.09 (2003); for West Virginia, W. Va. Code §48-1-235 (2003); for Wisconsin, Wis. Stat. §767.24

3. Minn. Stat. §518.1705 (2002).

4. See Erickson and McKnight Erickson (1992).

5. *Ourfamilywizzard.com* is an Internet subscription program that facilitates communication and planning between divorced parents. It contains a calendar, whiteboard, tools for tracking children's expenses, space for keeping records on the children, and resources for divorced parents.

REFERENCES

Ahrons, C. (1994). *The good divorce.* New York: HarperCollins.

Amato, P. R. (1994). Life-span adjustment of children to their parents' divorce. *Future of Children, 4,* 143–164.

Amato, P. R., & Keith, B. (1996). Parental divorce and adult well-being: A meta-analysis. *Journal of Marriage and the Family, 53,* 43–58.

Emery, R. E. (1982). Interparental conflict and the children of discord and divorce. *Psychological Bulletin, 92,* 310–330

Erickson, S. K., & McKnight Erickson, M. (1992). *The children's book: For the sake of the children.* West Concord, MN: CPI.

Hetherington, E. M. (1989). Coping with family transitions: Winners, losers, and survivors. *Child Development, 60,* 1–14.

Kelly, J. B., & Wallerstein, J. S. (1980). *Surviving the breakup: How children and parents cope with divorce.* New York: Basic Books.

Lamb, M. E., Sternberg, K. J., & Thompson, R. A. (1997). The effects of divorce and custody arrangements on children's behavior, development, and adjustment. *Family and Conciliation Courts Review, 35,* 393–404.

Maccoby, E. E., & Mnookin, R. H. (1992). *Dividing the child: Social and legal dilemmas of custody.* Cambridge, MA: Harvard University Press.

Ricci, I. (1997). *Mom's house, Dad's house.* New York: Simon & Schuster.

CHAPTER 8

Working with Children
in Mediation

DONALD T. SAPOSNEK

How can "the best interests of the child" be ensured in mediation when no one is present to speak for the children and parents cannot separate their own needs from those of the children? Some advocate that children should be allowed to speak for themselves. However, including children in the mediation process is not without its critics and acknowledged pitfalls. Following a summary of each side of the issue, Donald T. Saposnek discusses a variety of ways to include children in the mediation process, how to prepare the children and the parents for the children's participation, and how to interpret the information provided by the children "in the best interests of the child."

The "best interests of the child" continues to be the legal standard and guiding principle in developing parenting plans in all family law proceedings, including mediation, litigation, and custody evaluations (Kelly, 1997). However, only a minority of divorce mediators interview the children to assess their best interests. The few published studies on this issue indicate that child custody mediators included the children's direct input in only 4–47% of all mediations completed (depending on the particular research sample), whether in the public or private sectors, and across the United States, the United Kingdom, and Australia (Garwood, 1990; Lansky, Swift, Manley, Elmore, & Gerety, 1996; McIntosh, 2000; Ogus et al., 1989; Paquin, 1988; Pearson, Ring, & Milne, 1983; Pearson & Thoennes, 1988). Most notably, the 1996 Client Baseline Study, conducted across all California family courts, found that less than 16% of its mediators interviewed the children (California Administrative Office of the Courts, 1996).

These findings are particularly striking given that it is the official state policy of California's family court services to proactively assert the best interests of the child. Similarly, Smart (2002, p. 308) notes that in the United Kingdom, the Children Act of 1989 emphasized "ascertaining the wishes and feelings of children." Furthermore, the Honorable Claire L'Heureux-Dube (1998, p. 389) of Canada commented, "The best interests principle thus requires us to listen attentively to the voices of the children involved about these and other concerns."

In a 25-year follow-up study of the responses of children and adolescents to parental separation and divorce, Wallerstein and Lewis (1998) found that these adults recalled "feeling that they had been silenced and expected, without recourse, to follow visiting or custody plans that had not been made with their wishes in mind" (p. 381). Moreover, they reported that the "court-created child is a passive vessel . . . is given no formal opportunity to express her views or even a preference among plans" (pp. 381–382). "But the real children of this study were not at all content to be silent . . . they wanted to be consulted about dual residence . . . wanted their concerns heard" (p. 382).

Although working within a somewhat different context, most custody evaluators also see the importance of interviewing the children in attempting to ascertain the best interests of the child (Ackerman, 1995; Ackerman & Ackerman, 1997; Hynan, 1998; Stahl, 1994). Thus, it would seem essential to include the independent input from the children whenever feasible, especially since it is widely known that parents in dispute about custody and/or visitation often have difficulty separating their own respective interests from those of their children. In practice, however, each mediator typically decides whether and how to involve the children, and if involved, how extensively (Pearson & Thoennes, 1988).

The decision to include children in the mediation process is a function of many personal, professional, and contextual variables. Mediators are more likely to include children if they are personally comfortable with, and knowledgeable about, children at different ages, have had positive experiences interacting with a wide range of children, and have had professional training in interviewing children of various ages. Moreover, mediators from a mental health background are more likely than those from a legal background to interview children (Lansky et al., 1996).

Temporal or financial restraints may also determine whether children are involved in the mediation process. Mediators who work under time restraints (e.g., as in many larger court systems), with heavy caseloads and impending court dates, and/or who work with private clients who can only afford to pay for a minimal amount of time to complete mediation are less likely to include children than those with more time and economic resources.

The mediator's theoretical orientation and style of mediating also contribute to the decision of whether or not to include children. Child custody mediators tend to range along a continuum on this issue. At one end are those who see the mediator's role as a neutral facilitator of negotiations between two parents. At the other end are those who believe that mediators should serve as strong advocates for children. Facilitative mediators would be less likely to include children in the sessions, contending that mediation is a process of self-determination by the parents and that the mediator must not contaminate his or her neutrality with the influence of the children's wishes. Mediators who view themselves as strong advocates for children cite clinical and research evidence that documents the frequent inability of parents going through divorce to consider clearly the needs of their children (Wallerstein & Kelly, 1980) and their tendency to project their own needs onto their children (Young, 1997).

Finally, underlying all of these variables are the values and social attitudes regarding children that exist within the particular culture in which the mediator practices. Not all cultures support children's rights to participate integrally in the decision-making aspects of family life. In some cultures, the needs of children are presumed to be duly satisfied by their parents' assertions of their own rights. "Moreover, there may be a concern that to empower children is to disempower their parents" (Saposnek, 1991, p. 334). Other cultures place a primary value on the autonomy of the individual child and "children are duly empowered to assert their own needs via enacted legislation that assigns them legal rights or legal representation if too young or otherwise incompetent to assert their own rights directly" (Saposnek, 1991, p. 335).

ARGUMENTS IN FAVOR OF INCLUDING CHILDREN IN MEDIATION

Numerous authors have provided compelling reasons for including children directly in the mediation process. Drapkin and Bienenfeld (1985) insist that it is never superfluous and always functional to include children in the mediation process. They identify the following benefits of including children:

- The mediator acts as a nonaligned confidant for the child during the crisis of divorce, a time when parents frequently exhibit diminished capacity to parent (cf. Wallerstein, 1985). Presumably, the presence of such a confidant could help reduce a child's fears and anxieties about divorce.

- Children frequently disclose their real feelings to the mediator, whereas they only tell their parents what they believe their parents want to hear.
- Children feel that someone cares about their needs.
- Children will feel more comfortable talking to a therapist, if therapy is needed later.
- By including the children's perspectives, the mediator can reinforce and maintain the parenting focus of the mediation.
- By gaining firsthand knowledge of the children's needs, the mediator can further educate parents about their children's specific developmental, emotional, and psychological needs—which is usually more compelling than global remarks about the general impact of divorce on children.
- By observing the children, both alone and with each parent, much information can be gleaned about their coping skills, personality styles, tolerances, temperament, relationships, emotional bonds, special needs, and so forth.

Garwood (1990) presents further reasons:

- Children have a right to know what is happening.
- Children are often confused during times of family dissolution and could be helped by hearing what agreements their parents have reached.
- Children can cope better with changes if they know and understand the reasons for them.
- Children can be helped to adjust emotionally to the divorce and the restructuring of the family.
- Parents' roles can be reinforced and directed away from continuing marital disputes.

Landau (1990) further notes:

- Children are the most affected by separation and divorce and by the outcome of mediation proceedings and should have a voice in the process.
- Including children gives them some sense of input or limited control when their lives feel totally out of control. If their voice and concerns can be heard, then parents can offer reassurance, planning, and guidance appropriate to each child's level of development.
- If children participate, there will be better compliance with agreements reached.
- Since children process experiences more by their feelings than by their thoughts, their feelings need to be listened to in making such important decisions as postdivorce parenting plans.

• Sometimes children already have their own plan fully worked out, which could work quite well for all concerned and could serve as an impasse breaker.

From her research on "child-inclusive divorce mediation," McIntosh (2000, p. 67) concluded the following about involving children in the mediation process:

• It encouraged honesty.
• Children benefited in their own right.
• The focus for the parents changed ("Let's behave like parents").
• Parents learned.
• It defused arguments.
• Blaming was reduced.
• It reinforced care in the family system.

In prior publications (Saposnek, 1983, 1998) I have discussed the circumstances in which it is valuable to include children. These circumstances include:

• When children have consistently expressed a preference for a certain type of time-sharing arrangement to one of the parents, a preference that is disputed by the other parent, interviewing the children can often help to resolve the discrepancy and bring the parents to a common view about their children's desires.
• If children have specifically requested to speak with the mediator, that request should be honored to validate their feelings, concerns, and opinions.
• When the parents have been unable to comprehend the destructive consequences to the children of their continued hostility, having the children present in a joint session with the parents—one that is carefully guided and directed by the mediator—can give the parents important direct feedback.
• Most adolescents should be interviewed because of their cognitive ability to formulate abstract plans, and the relative independence of their lives, and because they usually have clear preferences about how they wish to divide their time.

Including adolescents demonstrates respect for their growing independence and contributes to their compliance with the agreement. An exception to their inclusion would be when the parents agree to give each adolescent wide latitude of discretion as to his or her schedule between the parents.

ARGUMENTS OPPOSED TO INCLUDING CHILDREN IN MEDIATION

Generally, there is agreement on the circumstances in which children should *not* be included in the mediation process. These include the following circumstances:

- When both parents agree upon their children's needs and share developmentally appropriate ideas as to what type of parenting plan would best fit them.
- When the children are under approximately 3 years of age, since their immaturity precludes meaningful or reliable communications about custody matters (Drapkin & Bienenfeld, 1985; Garwood, 1990; Saposnek, 1983, 1991, 1998).
- When one or both parents do not want to include the children in mediation.
- When the children are too anxious (e.g., when they tell their parents that they are too scared to talk with the mediator and strongly protest attending the sessions; or when they have nightmares, stomachaches, or stress-related insomnia the night before or day of the session).
- When the children might be manipulated by their parents to such an extent as to cause significant stress to the children. This is the case when the parents are unable to consider their own needs as different from those of their children (Garwood, 1990).

Wallerstein and Kelly (1980) more broadly asserted that children below the stage of adolescence are not reliable judges of their own best interests and their preferences and therefore should not be relied on in making decisions about postdivorce parenting arrangements. These authors cite evidence of young children's erratic emotional reactions, decisions, and judgments regarding their parents, which lead to the formulation of unstable opinions. Yet, more recently, Wallerstein and Lewis (1998) issued a strong plea for listening to, and including, the input of children at any age who are going through a parental separation or divorce.

Likely there is validity to both of these positions. The ultimate decision about whether to include children in the mediation process must be made individually, for each specific child in each specific case. Children under the age of 5 or 6 generally abide by the joint decisions of their parents and seldom need to be included in the mediation process (excluding certain exceptions, stated above; for example, when a young child expresses an enduring preference for one parent). And, although it is true that children between the ages of 6 and 12 vary both in their desires for input and in their tactical usefulness to the mediation process, children as young as 7 or 8 years may have well-thought-out reasons for preferring one parent's home over the other. These reasons need to be considered by parents in making the final decisions.

WAYS TO INCLUDE CHILDREN IN MEDIATION

Children may be included in mediation in several different ways:

- The mediator may interview the children *early* in the process to gather their views, concerns, feelings, and spontaneously stated or implied preferences. The mediator can introduce this information into the negotiations between the parents and can advocate on behalf of the children's needs.
- Children may be brought into the mediation sessions *periodically* throughout the process, whenever an issue comes up that might gain clarity from their input.
- Children may be present *throughout* the mediation process and participate in decision making as an equal party to the proceedings (particularly true in the case of adolescents).
- The mediator and parents may consult with the children regarding their opinions about the agreement *after* agreements between the parents have been reached but before they are finalized. The children's input may prompt the parents to modify the agreement.
- Children may be brought in at the *end* of the final mediation session, simply to be informed of the agreements reached by their parents.

A promising model currently being developed in mediation work engages a child therapist *who is not the mediator* to interview the children separately and then give feedback about each child to both parents and the mediator together. This is the method used in Fagerstrom's (1997) *Collaborative Divorce* model, McIntosh's (2000) *Child-Inclusive Divorce Mediation* model, and in a model suggested by Beck and Biank (1997). Furthermore, Beck and Biank (1997) note that their referral of the child to a child therapist for an assessment is not the same as referring the child to a therapist to help deal with problems resulting from the divorce. Rather, their specific goal is a brief assessment of the child's developmental needs through the parental separation and divorce period in order to give feedback directly to the parents so as to inform their negotiations of a parenting plan. To reach that end, they use a standardized assessment protocol based on the work of Judith S. Wallerstein and her staff at the Center for Families in Transition. (It is of interest to note that Beck and Biank also allow the mediator to conduct this assessment, if he or she is properly trained as a child therapist, and at the parents' request.)

According to Fagerstrom (1997) and McIntosh (2000), referring the child out to an independent assessor may make it easier for the mediator to maintain the appearance of neutrality between the parents, as well as providing the children with a neutral and skilled child interviewer who may help them feel safer in talking out their feelings and concerns. However, I concur with Beck and Biank: parents prefer having their already trusted mediator (if trained as a child therapist) conduct the interviews with the children.

RECOMMENDED PROTOCOL WHEN INCLUDING
CHILDREN IN THE MEDIATION PROCESS

While there may be numerous reasons to interview children during the mediation process, the rationale for choosing to interview a particular child must be carefully considered. Children interviewed in the context of their parents' separation and divorce may experience significant stress, which the mediator must take the appropriate steps to minimize. This stress reduction can be accomplished by (1) affirming that the benefits of including the children in the mediation interview will outweigh the risks (at least, in the long run, even if questionable in the short run); (2) obtaining both parents' permission to conduct the interview; and (3) preparing and instructing both parents about how to set the context for the children prior to coming to the interview.

The following protocol is used when including the children early in the mediation process in order to better inform the parents of their children's needs. Although including the children at other times in the mediation process can be useful (as discussed above), the best integration of their input is achieved when it is obtained early in the process. It is at this point when the greatest skills of the mediator are needed.

Preparing the Parents for the Children's Interview

When the mediator has determined that there is sufficient reason to interview the children, the issue should be raised first with both parents together. It is particularly important to elicit agreement between the parents for the interview if a child has requested to speak with the mediator alone. Interviewing a child without the agreement of both parents is a certain formula for the escalation of conflict and the drafting of lawsuits (especially against the mediator!). Moreover, a parent who did not want the child interviewed may later invalidate what the child said by accusing the other parent of having "primed the child."

If a parent is concerned that the interview will be too stressful for the child, the mediator may reassure that parent (1) of the sensitive manner in which he or she will conduct the interview of the child, and (2) that the mediator will place any expressed preferences of the child into an appropriate developmental context within the particular dynamics of the parents' relationship (e.g., the mediator would be aware that a 5-year-old child who says that he wants to alternate months between his parents would not really understand the implications of such a schedule or that an 8-year-old child of parents in very high conflict and no communication would not do well switching homes every day).

Some parents may only be comfortable with the assurance that they can be in the room while the mediator interviews the children, with the option to leave as the children become more comfortable. This format can serve as an alternate (albeit less desirable) plan by which the mediator can gather data directly from the children.

Occasionally, *both* parents ask the mediator to interview the children. Sometimes this request comes from two loving and rational parents who genuinely want to learn what their children are experiencing and needing, and they are soliciting the mediator's objective expertise. Other times, and perhaps more commonly, each parent believes that the children will express a preference for that parent to the mediator.

To prevent a child from being subtly or overtly criticized and/or rejected by the parent who "loses out" as a result of the child's revelations, it is useful for the mediator to prepare parents by discussing the range of possible outcomes from the child's interviews and then asking each parent to imagine his or her reaction to each outcome. The mediator can ask something like the following:

> "If I go ahead and interview Kevin, what would you agree to do with the findings? For example, Dad, what would you do if Kevin convincingly tells me that he really wants to spend more time with his mother and to see you only every other Saturday, and that he has been afraid to tell you because you might get mad at him or stop loving him?"

After the father answers this question (usually by stating that he would want to understand the child's feelings further but would ultimately accept the child's request), the converse question is then posed to the mother:

> "Mom, what would you do if Kevin convincingly tells me that he wants to live with his dad full-time and see you every other weekend, and that he hasn't told you this because he doesn't want to hurt your feelings, especially since he knows how angry you are at his dad?"

Again, the mother typically responds by agreeing to accept the child's wishes. The advisability of interviewing the children is questionable if both parents cannot come to terms with accepting the needs of their children over their own.

It is also important to help the parents understand how to deal with a child after the child has been interviewed. Parents should be counseled not to ask the child what he or she said to the mediator, and if the child spontaneously tells the parent what he or she said to the mediator, not to question, criticize, get angry at, or subtly reject the child by giving the "cold shoulder." The parents must be encouraged to behave maturely and with appropriate restraint, in spite of what the child may have revealed to the mediator. They should be told that any negative reactions by a parent toward a child would diminish the child's trust in talking with professionals in the future. A child entering an interview with a professional generally has an expectation that the professional will somehow improve things in his or her life. However, if things get worse after the interview because the beleaguered child is confronted by an angry, critical, or rejecting parent, the child loses trust and hope. Most children going through their parents' divorce do not need any extra stress in their lives.

Should Siblings Be Interviewed Together or Separately?

When there is more than one child in the family, the mediator must decide whether to interview the siblings together or separately. Interviewing siblings together offers the benefits of sibling support in talking about difficult topics, gives the mediator data on the children's interactions and relationships with one another, and is a more efficient use of mediator time. However, individual interviews should be conducted when there is a wide age gap between the children, when they have previously expressed different preferences for time-sharing arrangements, or when one child is extremely talkative and/or overpowering of the others.

Preparing a Child for the Interview

The way in which the parents frame the request to a child to come for an interview can make a big difference in the validity of the child's report. For example, imagine the effect on a child whose parent prepares him for the interview with something like the following:

> "Next Tuesday, I'm taking you to the mediator that Mom and Dad are seeing. He's going to ask you to tell him who you want to live with. Honey, don't forget to tell him that you want to live with me or the judge might take you away from me and not let me see you ever again. I really love you, so be sure to tell the mediator that you want to live with me."

This child is likely to believe that he will be asked to choose which parent he loves more—a very scary proposition that generates a forced conflict of loyalty and much resulting anxiety. The child will likely feel frightened, intimidated, and reluctant to reveal honest feelings or opinions to the mediator.

In contrast, consider the effect of the following statement:

"Your [mother/father] and I have been talking with a mediator about how we're going to share our time with you when we live separately. We both love you very much, and we would like you to help us understand your feelings about the arrangements for spending time with each of us so that we can make better decisions for you. Our mediator is really nice and easy to talk with. He talks with lots of children and helps lots of moms and dads who are getting divorced understand their children's feelings. So we'd both like for you to talk with him so he can help us."

A child presented with this frame will likely feel supported and helpful. She will feel relatively calmer, more confident and secure, and may look forward to the opportunity to talk with a knowledgeable divorce professional about her feelings and views regarding her parents' separation or divorce.

Before setting the appointment to interview a child, the mediator should stress to the parents the importance of the wording they use in talking with their child. Ideally, the parents have already presented to the children a mutual story of the divorce (Saposnek, 2002), but even if they have not, rehearsing, at this point, with the parents together how they will tell the child about the interview appointment can be useful. Role playing with both parents gives them the opportunity to practice the exact words that they will use—which also increases the chances that both parents will present a consistent style of invitation. I also find it useful, strategically, to let the parents know that when I interview a child, it usually becomes obvious to me if the child has been influenced to report what a parent wants the child to say. This warning serves as a preemptive move to persuade both parents to try hard to remain neutral when talking with their child about the appointment.

The Unique Thinking and Language of Children

Classic child development research (Flavell, 1985; Inhelder & Piaget, 1964; Piaget, 1929/1979; Piaget & Inhelder, 1969) as well as more recent developmental research (Feldman, 1994; Fischer, Bullock, Rotenberg, & Raya, 1993; Gelman, 2001) have demonstrated that, in many areas of cognition, children process information in a qualitatively different way from adults. In addition, they process information differently *at each stage* of their development until about 11 or 12 years of age, when they are finally capable of engaging in full abstract reasoning "like an adult" (*sans* the life experience and, therefore, the judgment abilities of an adult). For example, young children below the age of approximately 7 years have a very limited grasp of abstract concepts such as *time*, even though they know how to use the "adult" words related to time that convey the false impression that they actually understand the concept behind the word. A 4-year-old child may correctly be able to say, "I'm going to see my Mommy on Monday," but when probed for his or her understanding of the concept, the child has no idea *what* "Monday" is or *when* it is.

A child slowly comes to understand that "seeing Daddy tomorrow" is different from "seeing Daddy next week." Prior to the preschool period, "tomorrow" and "in a year" indicate indistinguishable time periods, since all that exists for the young child is "now." Hodges (1986, p. 159) explains:

> For the young child, "tomorrow" is an undefined, infinite time away, yet the child slowly learns the meaning of tomorrow. "The day after tomorrow" is a far more complex concept. . . . The concept of "tomorrow" is seldom understood by 3 year olds, but 4 year olds understood the idea. By age 5, "the day after tomorrow" is conceptually understood, but a "week" may be a vaguely conceived time period. By age 6 or 7, the child can count and can understand the concept of "a week" or "a month." By age 7 or 8, an infinite time sense develops so that the child understands the concept of "forever."

Children also have different—and much more limited—vocabularies than do adults. This difference is true not only for expressive language but for receptive language as well. Therefore, it is important to understand whether a child who is expressing a preference is really expressing her own ideas (using typical child's language) or those of her parent. When a 5-year-old says, "I want a 5/2 split—I want weekdays with my daddy and weekends with my mommy," the mediator should take pause. It is extremely unlikely that a 5-year-old child even knows what a *weekday* or a *weekend* is, let alone the meaning of a patterned schedule. Moreover, children do not use this type of language on their own. Listening for concepts and phrasing that are highly improbable for a young child to use can provide cues that the child may well have been influenced to please a particular parent.

Furthermore, in talking with a child, the mediator must use language that matches the appropriate stage of the child's receptive language development. For example, when talking with a 6-year-old, the mediator would not say, "Kevin, can you tell me what sort of schedule preferences you'd like to consider?" but would use more simplified language, such as "Kevin, what do you and [Daddy/Mommy] like to do together?" or "What does it feel like when you are with [Mommy/Daddy]?"

Developing Rapport

The mediator's first focus once the child enters the office is to help him or her feel safe, connected, and comfortable in talking freely. Rapport with children can best be developed by interacting with them in play at an appropriate developmental level. Play is a mode that is familiar to children, relaxes them, and eases their tensions. With adolescents, verbal play (i.e., joking around) is a natural way for dealing with new and tense situations; however, humor must be used with discretion, since it may backfire with teens who are very sad or depressed, hypersensitive, or very scared. With younger children, movement activities are generally more relaxing. Playing a quick game of catch, shooting hoops with a Nerf ball, juggling, or drawing are good ways to ease them into the more serious talking that lies ahead.

For mediators not used to talking with children, several facts are important to bear in mind:

• Children do not automatically feel safe or confident talking with an adult, even if the adult is quite nice.

• Children typically need a "warm-up" time before they are willing to talk about important, emotionally laden topics, so patience is an essential characteristic for mediators to nurture. Children feel at ease in knowing that they will not be pressured into revealing emotional content until they are comfortable and ready. Less experienced child interviewers, and/or children who are temperamentally "slow to warm up to new situations" (Thomas & Chess, 1977, p. 23), may need two sessions for the interview—one for the child to get comfortable, and the other for talking about the important content.

• Children need to feel respected, especially when they do *not* give you what you seek in the interview. This may be the case when, for example, a child does not want to talk about the divorce at all and frustrates all the mediator's kind attempts to elicit the child's feelings and preferences. Adults show respect for children by displaying honesty, empathy, compassion, understanding, kindness, noncriticalness, acceptance, helpfulness, and, of course, patience. Interestingly, this is the same list of core qualities that characterizes effective parents. When an adult shows such respect for a child, the child feels protected and safe from humiliation, ridicule, and shame—those feelings that suppress a child's comfort in sharing information with an adult.

• In easing a child into the content of the interview, it is important to begin with benign questions, proceeding to questions of significance only when the child gives signs that he or she is ready. Good rapport-building questions include time-honored favorites such as the following:

"What kinds of things do you like to do for fun?"
"What are the things that you are good at?"

"Do you have any pets? What are their names?"

"Do you have a best friend? What's [his/her] name? What do you like about him/her?"

Most children warm up easily to such questions because they are innocuous, nonthreatening, positive, and show interest in the child's world.

Setting the Context for a Child

After rapport is clearly established, as indicated by the child appearing more relaxed and perhaps smiling, the mediator may begin to prepare him or her for the interview. (A relaxed state can be maintained with younger children by letting them continue to hold and manipulate play materials, such as plastic building blocks, or to draw with crayons and paper throughout the interview.)

It is useful to begin by inquiring what the child already knows about coming to the interview. The mediator can ask questions such as "Who told you that you were coming here today?" After the child answers, the mediator can follow up with "What did [Mom/Dad] say you were going to do here?" The answers to these questions give important clues as to how clear and honest the parents have been and how the child has interpreted the intent of the session. If, for example, the child says, "Both my parents told me that I'm here because they want to know how I feel about their divorce and they want the best for me," you can usually rest assured that the parents are truly child focused, and that the child most likely will be well taken care of, and respected by, both parents, regardless of the schedule developed.

On the other hand, if the child says "My dad told me I had to talk to you about who I wanted to live with. My mom didn't tell me anything," or if the child says something like "My mom told me we were going out to buy milk!" then it is important to spend more time reassuring the child and clarifying the intent of the session. Divisive or evasive answers typically indicate parental discomfort with their child's feelings. It is likely that such parents will not accept what their child says to the mediator unless the child's views happen to correspond with the particular parent's needs. Therefore, when meeting later with the parents, the mediator needs to be particularly careful about what information he or she presents to them regarding the child's preferences (discussed further later in this chapter).

Next, in clarifying the context for the interview, the mediator should explain the purpose of the interview in developmentally appropriate language:

"As you know, your mom and dad are having trouble talking with each other and making decisions together about how to share time with you. It would help them to know how you feel about these plans, so that your parents can make the best plans for you. The final decision about how your parents share time with you will be made by your parents, not by you, but it would be helpful if your parents understood your feelings. Even if you don't have any strong feelings one way or another, that would be helpful for your parents to know, too."

Assessing a Child's Awareness of the Parents' Separation or Divorce

Prior to assessing any time-sharing preferences of a child, it is useful for the mediator to ask what the child knows about his or her parents' separation and/or divorce. Just as each spouse goes through an "emotional process of divorce," in which over time he or she gradually detaches emotionally from the other spouse (Saposnek & Rose, 1990), so do the children detach from the past reality of living with *both* parents together. Learning the degree to which a child has accepted the divorce decision can help a mediator establish his or her degree of credibility regarding any expressed preferences for time sharing. For example, a child who has not been told much about the marital separation may maintain a very strong belief that the parents will soon reunite and therefore patiently accepts any schedule of time sharing set out by the parents (since he or she believes it is only temporary). On the other hand, a child who has been kept well apprised of the status of the parents' decision to divorce throughout the divorce process and has come to terms with the finality of the divorce decision will have more credible preferences about time sharing. Because this child better understands the permanence of the divorce decision, he or she is more likely to have thought about the longer-term consequences of time-sharing schedules and may be able to express valid points to support his or her preferences.

Questions that are useful in assessing a child's awareness of the divorce include:

"Do you know why your mom and dad live in separate houses?"
"How did you find out? Who told you?"
"What did your [mom/dad] say about it?"

Answers to these simple questions give the mediator a sense of what the parents have explained to the child about the marital separation and any discrepancies between the parents in what the child was told. (Such discrepancies invariably lead to confusion in the child.) If the child answers the first question with "No," then the mediator can ask, "What's your guess of why they split up?" Often, the child actually knows a feasible answer to this question but may hesitate to offer it, since the parents have never formally presented an explanation.

Further questions that pursue a child's awareness include:

"Were you surprised when your [mom or dad] left?"
"Did you know it was going to happen?"
"How did you know?"

Answers to these questions give the mediator a sense of the kind and scope of preparation given to the child by the parents prior to the separation. It also gives the mediator some indication of how overt the marital conflict was prior to the separation and how tuned into the marital dynamics the child may be. A child who had no idea that his parents were about to split up will have a much more difficult time coming to terms with the divorce, given the absence of perceived conflict or problems between the parents. When there is an absence of overt conflict, it is often very difficult for children—especially young children—to understand why their parents had to part.

On the other hand, if a child reports having had a strong suspicion over several months (or even years) that her parents were going to get a divorce some day, then the child has already begun the emotional process of detaching from the idea of both parents continuing to live together and will likely have an easier time understanding—and perhaps accepting—the reality of the divorce. Unfortunately, in families with more than one child, the child who is particularly sensitive to the spousal dynamics also tends to get caught up in custody battles, as the parents unwittingly draw in the child. Moreover, because most children of divorcing parents hang on to reconciliation fantasies, often for many years after the divorce, "only" children and more sensitive children among siblings may develop reuniting strategies that functionally contribute to custody fights later (Saposnek, 1983, 1998). An example of a reuniting strategy would be a child who regularly and provocatively tells her dad about her mom's new boyfriend, knowing that it gets her father upset; she hopes that he will come over to Mom's house, get rid of her new boyfriend, and get back together with her.

In order to assess for a child's utilization of reuniting strategies, the following questions are suggested:

"Do you think there is a chance that your mom and dad might get back together?"
"Have you tried anything to get them back together?"
"What have you tried?"

The answers to these questions give the mediator a sense of the child's investment in reuniting his parents and his progress toward emotionally accepting the divorce decision. For example, if the child says, "No! My parents are *not* getting back together—I'm sure of that!" the mediator can assume that current conflicts between the parents are mostly occurring independent of the child's actions and that the parents do not need to offer any further clarifications of their marital status to this child.

On the other hand, suppose that a child tells the mediator, "I'm *sure* they will get back together. I've tried a lot of things to get them together. I told Mommy I'm not going to see her anymore until she comes back home. I also have other things I'm going to try." This child is clearly actively involved in a reuniting strategy and may actually be contributing to the dispute between her parents. It is important for the mediator to help diffuse this triangulation by talking with the parents about their daughter's very strong need to try to reunite her parents and by working directly with the child on this issue.

An effective way to intervene in this situation is by asking the child this question:

"What do you think it will take to get your parents back together?"

This question gives the child an opportunity to test the limits of her imagination, persistence, and intentions. Sometimes, upon hearing this question, a child sighs deeply, thinks long and hard, and finally says, "I guess, nothing. I guess they're just gonna get a divorce."

It is easy to understand how, without knowing the motives behind their child's actions, parents could easily misinterpret these actions as bad or resistant behaviors that are caused by the *other* parent. Blaming, finger-pointing, and filing of court declarations and restraining orders are typical outcomes of such misinterpretations of a child's reuniting strategies. However, with knowledge of the child's intentions and actions, the mediator can inform and educate the parents about these actions and responses of their child, thereby reducing the interparental conflict and redirecting the parents' focus into more constructive discussions.

The line of questioning suggested above can also serve as a therapeutic adjunct to the mediation process, since it is often the case that children of separation have never talked with anyone about their feelings regarding this event in their lives. The children's answers also serve as a poignant source of feedback for the parents, who often think that their children have easily accepted the divorce just because they have not asked about it or expressed any feelings one way or another. Parents need to know that children who believe the separation is only temporary can often restrain expressing their feelings about it, since they believe it will soon end. By learning of a discrepancy between their children's belief that the separation is only temporary and the adults' reality that it is permanent, the parents are able then to discuss the matter with their children, facilitating their children's emotional process in relation to their divorce.

Assessing Children's Time-Sharing Preferences

The mediator needs to explore the children's feelings and preferences regarding the co-parenting arrangement, in order to inform the parents about their children's needs regarding time-sharing schedules. Although it might appear obvious to some, it cannot be overstated that the questions asked by the mediator should be *indirect*. The mediator should not ask children to identify a specific preference about the time-sharing arrangements, since children often hear this as a request to choose which parent they love more. There are some rare exceptions to this guideline, such as the situation of interviewing an older teenager who is very clear, confident, forthright, and comfortable in stating his or her preferences (whether requested or not). Helpful, indirect questions include:

> "How would you describe your [mom/dad/siblings]?"
> "What do you like most about your [mom/dad]?"
> "If you could change one thing about your [mom/dad], what would that be?"
> "How does your [mom/dad] want you to share your time between your parents?"

These questions give a child wide latitude to reveal a range of feelings (both positive and negative) without feeling disloyal to either parent. The balanced arrangement of the questions and their indirect focus help children express their emotions without feeling that they are being asked which parent they love more.

If a child expresses positive feelings about both parents, does not indicate that he was primed to please a particular parent, and has no particular concerns about either parent, then the mediator can feel comfortable informing the parents that the child will likely be able to tolerate whatever plan they develop. On the other hand, suppose a child says something like "My mom is mean and angry and always makes me feel bad when I'm around her. I'd also like her to stop drinking so much. And she told me to tell you that I should be with her full-time. But I would rather be with my dad, 'cause he's nice, and I can always talk with him. He never yells at me." When a child expresses such a parental preference, a good follow-up question (and another example of an exception to the general rule) is:

> "What schedule do *you* think would work best for you?"

In such a circumstance, it is appropriate to ask this kind of a direct question because the child seems less focused on a loyalty conflict and more focused on emotional survival. When a child expresses this kind of discrepancy in parental preference, the mediator needs to facilitate a parental discussion that can ensure greater protection for the child when with the mother and that builds in a plan to improve the mother–child relationship, perhaps through a recommendation for counseling.

There are occasions when the mediator is not sure whether a child's preference for one parent over the other is based on comfort with that parent or comfort with the physical residence in which that parent lives. An excellent question to ask is the following:

"If your mom and dad switched houses, where would you want to be most of the time?"

This question typically elicits clarification of the basis for the child's preference. Some children pick the parent, regardless of the house in which that parent lives, whereas other children pick the house itself and are then faced with the clarifying insight that results. Often, the child has not realized previously the basis of his or her preference.

In questioning a child about preferences (as well as about other topics), the mediator should gently probe while listening for information about all aspects of the child's functioning, including his or her temperament style (e.g., degree of adaptability and potential ease in handling transitions between homes, change of schools, and friends), tolerances, attachments to each parent, comfort level with each parent over short and extended periods, degrees of attachment to neighbors, friends, and relatives, and rapport with siblings. The mediator should listen for any special needs (e.g., physical limitations, medical conditions, or developmental, psychological, or academic problems) and for any reasonable suspicion of child abuse (mediators in most jurisdictions are required by law to report any suspicions of abuse to the appropriate authorities). Because such personality and situational variables can have a tremendous impact on the child's adjustment to a particular parenting plan, they must serve as the context for considering the feasibility of the child's stated preferences.

Presenting a Child's Input to the Parents

Once the information from the children is gathered, the mediator must plan the most effective way to present the feedback to the parents. The manner in which the feedback is presented to the parents is very important, since the parents may feel vulnerable to criticism or rejection by their children. It is much easier on a child if the mediator is able to serve as his or her advocate and to frame this feedback to the parents in a way that they are able to listen and respond to constructively.

In general, and as much as possible, the mediator should try to remain neutral and nonjudgmental toward the parents, framing the information received from a child in terms of the child's feelings. For example, in the discussion presented earlier, when the child gave divisive or evasive answers to being asked why he was being interviewed, the mediator could say something like the following to the parents:

> "It seems that Kevin feels caught in the middle between the two of you and strongly pressured to say what he thinks you each want to hear. He seems afraid to express his own feelings for fear of disappointing or angering you two. Can you help me understand why he might be feeling that way?"

In addition to eliciting more helpful information about the interparental dynamics, this last question can also present a golden opportunity for a discussion that further reinforces the importance of keeping the child *out* of the middle.

If a child expresses confusion about, or lack of awareness of, the reasons for the divorce, the mediator can also utilize this opportunity to help the parents formulate and clarify for their child the reasons for the divorce in the form of a "mutual story of their separation and divorce" (Saposnek, 2002). The story should be "true enough" for each parent, worded to reflect an appropriate stage of language development, and show the parents as sharing the responsibility for the actual decision to separate or divorce. Such a story can often help facilitate a child's process of accepting the split-up. It can also better ensure the child's cooperation in implementing the future co-parenting plan by reducing the tendency to polarize the parents into one good parent and one bad parent, to align with the parent who was left or betrayed, and to blame the leaving parent for breaking up the family.

In giving more specific feedback, the mediator may choose to meet with the parents together, either with or without the children. This decision should largely be based upon whether the children expressed feelings or preferences that would likely imbalance the negotiations. For example, if a child said that he loves his father more than his mother, or if the child's preferences seemed to be based on coaching by one of the parents, then the child should not be present during the feedback session. On the other hand, if a child expressed equal comfort with both parents, no particular residential preferences, and a willingness to accept anything the parents come up with, then the child can be present to deliver the news directly to the parents. If a child is not comfortable doing so, then the mediator can either do the talking for the child while the child is in the room or present the child's feelings by proxy.

If the feedback is critical of a particular parent, it is best to meet with each parent separately in order to allow face saving for the criticized parent. In such a difficult situation, the mediator must take supportive reframing to its highest art form. The mediator's skill is most challenged here, as the needs of the child should be presented and discussed in a way that minimizes backlash on the child (Hysjulien, Wood, & Benjamin, 1994).

For example, in meeting with a father alone, whose child expressed fear of his anger, the mediator can say:

> "Gregory really loves both you and his mother, and he wants and needs a relationship with both of you. However, I'm puzzled about something. Since the separation, it seems that he has some real concerns about getting you upset. He gets really scared whenever he feels like you're angry at him. And, although it would be understandable for you *not* to believe this, he also said that his mom *does* encourage him to go over to your house when it's his time with you, but he resists. This seems to me to be an issue between you and him, and we need to figure out a way to improve his relationship with you. I wonder if you can help me understand why you think he might be feeling this way."

If the father is willing to account satisfactorily for and discuss and accept responsibility for his behavior with regard to the child (e.g., He might acknowledge that his depression during the crisis of the divorce led to bursts of anger that must have really scared his child. He might also admit that he is now in therapy working on controlling his feelings toward the mother and that he wants to apologize to and help his child become more trusting of him), the mediator can follow through with:

> "If you're up for it, I'd like to have him come in and talk with you and me about his concerns to see if we can make things better between the two of you."

However, if the father is unable (or unwilling) to account satisfactorily for his behavior and/or his child's feelings (e.g., He might deny that the child really feels scared and continue relentlessly to blame the mother for all of the child's negative feelings) and the mediator is unable to persuade him otherwise, the child should not be invited into the session. Rather, the mediator needs to proceed with the parental negotiations and attempt to include in the parenting plan an agreement for co-parent counseling, with the hopes that the father will come to terms with his part in fueling the child's negative feelings toward him. In either case, if, in fact, the mother's role in the child's fears is minimal or absent, then a referral for brief, focused counseling between the father and child is often helpful for normalizing their relationship. If it appears that the mother may have been fueling the child's fear, then an individual discussion with the mother would be in order, aimed at exploring and sensitizing her to the negative consequences of this behavior for her child.

Another example: The child has expressed the desire to live primarily with her father but is worried about her mother's well-being if left alone. In an individual meeting with the mother, the mediator could say:

"Your daughter really loves you, and she really loves her dad, too. For some reason, she expressed having a hard time talking with you about her feelings. She's really worried about you and your sadness over the divorce, and she's feeling responsible for keeping you happy. Can you help me understand why she might be feeling like you won't be OK if she spent time with her father and you were left alone, and that she needs to take care of you?"

After this discussion, a follow-up communication could be offered:

"Although she loves her dad just as she loves you, for some reason she feels like she doesn't have your permission to be with her dad. She feels like she is supposed to be just as angry at her dad as you are. I'm sure you must know how unhealthy it is for a child to be dealing with that kind of anger. If we bring her in here, I wonder if you could reassure her that you will be OK being alone for the periods of time she's with her dad—and would you be able to give her your explicit permission for her to spend time with, and to love, her dad?"

Usually, this kind of a discussion brings to the mother's awareness the subtle double messages that she may have been giving to her child and helps motivate her to free the child to share time with her father.

After the feedback is given to the parents, they are ready to negotiate their parenting plan, informed by the actual stated needs of their child. Younger children generally should not remain in the room during these negotiations, since they are too likely to misinterpret things said during the parents' discussions. Adolescents, however, often choose to participate in the negotiations, since they usually have clear ideas about what they want and are often able to negotiate directly with each parent for their needs. Regardless of who remains in the room, the mediator's task is to integrate the children's needs, preferences, and best interests into the parental negotiations. It is at this point in mediating parenting plans when the mediator is truly the children's representative in the negotiations, continually guiding the parents back to their children's needs, whenever they stray.

CONCLUSIONS

If a mediator is to take seriously the standard of achieving what is in the "best interests of the child," an understanding of the needs of each child involved is paramount. However, because parents' expressed views of their child's needs are frequently polarized, such reports are only questionably valid. Information about a child's needs is usually best gathered directly from the child. But, in doing so, mediators must observe an important caveat: *Mediators who interview children must be adequately qualified.* Education in normal child development and family dynamics and current knowledge of children's typical early reactions to divorce and the longer-term effects of divorce on them are essential. Moreover, training and supervised experience in developing skills for interviewing children are equally important. Mediators who are inexperienced, lack knowledge of child development issues, or are insensitive to the needs and ways of children can cause them damage by including them in mediation. If the mediator is not duly qualified, it is best for him or her to exclude children from the process.

Because of children's unique sensitivities, mediators have a responsibility to be informed, responsive, and careful as they intervene with children going through the separation or divorce of their parents.

REFERENCES

Ackerman, M. J. (1995). *Clinician's guide to child custody evaluations.* New York: Wiley.

Ackerman, M. J., & Ackerman, M. C. (1997). Custody evaluation practices: A survey of experienced professionals (revisited). *Professional Psychology: Research and Practice, 28,* 137–145.

Beck, P., & Biank, N. (1997). Broadening the scope of divorce mediation to meet the needs of children. *Mediation Quarterly, 14*(3), 179–199.

California Administrative Office of the Courts, Center for Families, Children and the Courts. (1996). *Statewide uniform statistical reporting system: Client Baseline Study.* San Francisco: Author.

Drapkin, R., & Bienenfeld, F. (1985). The power of including children in custody mediation. *Journal of Divorce, 8*(3/4), 63–95.

Fagerstrom, K. (1997). *Divorce: A problem to be solved, not a battle to be fought.* Orinda, CA: Brookwood.

Feldman, D. H. (1994).*Beyond universal in cognitive development* (2nd ed.). Norwood, NJ: Ablex.

Fischer, K. W., Bullock, D. H., Rotenberg, E. J., & Raya, P. (1993). The dynamics of competence: How context contributes directly to skill. In R. H. Wozniak & K. W. Fischer (Eds.), *Development in context: Acting and thinking in specific environments* (pp. 93–117). Hillsdale, NJ: Erlbaum.

Flavell, J. H. (1985). *Cognitive development* (2nd ed.). Englewood Cliffs, NJ: Prentice-Hall.

Garwood, F. (1990). Children in conciliation: The experience of involving children in conciliation. *Family and Conciliation Courts Review, 28*(1), 43–51.

Gelman, S. A. (2001). Categories in young children's thinking. In E. N. Junn & C. J. Boyatzis (Eds.), *Child growth and development* (8th ed., pp. 47–53). Guilford, CT: McGraw-Hill/Dushkin.

Hodges, W. F. (1986). *Interventions for children of divorce: Custody, access, and psychotherapy.* New York: Wiley.

Hynan, D. J. (1998). Interviewing children in custody evaluations. *Family and Conciliation Courts Review, 36*(4), 466–478.

Hysjulien, C., Wood, B., & Benjamin, G. A. H. (1994). Child custody evaluations: A review of methods used in litigation and alternative dispute resolution. *Family and Conciliation Courts Review, 32*(4), 466–489.

Inhelder, B., & Piaget, J. (1964). *The early growth of logic in the child.* New York: Norton.

Kelly, J. B. (1997). The best interests of the child: A concept in search of meaning. *Family and Conciliation Courts Review, 35*(4), 377–387.

Landau, B.(1990, July). *Involvement of children in the mediation process: An international perspective.* Paper presented at the International Mediation Forum of the Academy of Family Mediators, Danvers, MA.

Lansky, D. T., Swift, L. H., Manley, E. E., Elmore, A., & Gerety, C. (1996). The role of children in mediation. *Mediation Quarterly, 14*(2), 147–154.

L'Heureux-Dube, C. (1998). A response to remarks by Dr. Judith Wallerstein on the long-term impact of divorce on children. *Family and Conciliation Courts Review, 36*(3), 384–391.

McIntosh, J. (2000). Child-inclusive divorce mediation: Report on a qualitative research study. *Mediation Quarterly, 18*(1), 55–69.

Ogus, K. A., Walker, J., Jones-Lee, M., Cole, W., Corlyon, J., McCarthy, P., Simpson, R., & Wray, S. (1989). *Report of the Conciliation Project Unit on the costs and effectiveness of conciliation in England and Wales.* London: Lord Chancellor's Department.

Paquin, G. (1988). The child's input in the mediation process: Promoting the best interests of the child. *Mediation Quarterly, 22,* 69–82.

Pearson, J., Ring, M. L., & Milne, A. (1983). A portrait of divorce mediation services in the public and private sector. *Conciliation Courts Review, 21*(1), 1–24.

Pearson, J., & Thoennes, N. (1988). Mediating parent–child post-divorce arrangements. In C. A. Wolchik & P. Karoly (Eds.), *Children of divorce: Empirical perspectives on adjustment* (pp. 267–298). New York: Gardner Press.

Piaget, J. (1979). *The child's conception of the world.* New York: Harcourt Brace. (Original work published 1929)

Piaget, J., & Inhelder, B. (1969). *The psychology of the child.* New York: Basic Books.

Saposnek, D. T. (1983). *Mediating child custody disputes: A systematic guide for family therapists, court counselors, attorneys, and judges.* San Francisco: Jossey-Bass.

Saposnek, D. T. (1991). The value of children in mediation: A cross-cultural perspective. *Mediation Quarterly, 8*(4), 325–342.

Saposnek, D. T. (1998). *Mediating child custody disputes: A strategic approach* (rev. ed.). San Francisco: Jossey-Bass.

Saposnek, D. T. (2002, Fall). What should we tell the children?: Developing a mutual story of the divorce. *Family Section Editorial.* Available: *www.mediate.com*

Saposnek, D. T., & Rose, F. W. (1990). The psychology of divorce. In D. L. Crumbley & N. G. Apostolou (Eds), *Handbook of financial planning for divorce and separation* (pp. 28–48). New York: Wiley.

Smart, C. (2002). From children's shoes to children's voices. *Family Court Review, 40*(3), 307–319.

Stahl, P. M. (1994). *Conducting child custody evaluations: A comprehensive guide.* Thousand Oaks, CA: Sage.

Thomas, A., & Chess, S. (1977). *Temperament and development.* New York: Brunner/Mazel.

Wallerstein, J. S. (1985). The overburdened child: Some long-term consequences of divorce. *Social Work, 30,* 116–123.

Wallerstein, J. S., & Lewis, J. (1998). The long-term impact of divorce on children: A first report from a 25-year study. *Family and Conciliation Courts Review, 36*(3), 368–382.
Wallerstein, J. S., & Kelly, J. B. (1980). *Surviving the breakup: How children and parents cope with divorce.* New York: Basic Books.
Young, I. M. (1997). *Interesting voices.* Princeton, NJ: Princeton University Press.

CHAPTER 9

Mediating Financial Issues

Theoretical Framework and Practical Applications

Chip Rose

The dissolution of a long-term relationship, whether the parties are married or not, necessitates decisions about the division of financial and property interests. Mediating financial and property issues involves clarification of goals, which Chip Rose refers to as "macro concepts," and satisfying specific needs, which he refers to as "micro applications." The mediation of financial matters often begins with a crisis scenario, which can be defused by focusing on the macro goals and remembering that the responsibility of the mediator is to manage the process, not solve the problem. The specific substantive financial issues to be resolved may include allocation of the family residence, child and spousal support, retirement benefits, stock options, and business interests. This chapter provides strategies to assist the mediator in analyzing the information needed to develop choices for the parties as well as the questions they must answer to assist them in making financial decisions together.

In mediating financial issues, as in mediating other issues, the most important initial assessment is that of the clients: *who they are, what they need, what they seek to achieve, and what the mediator can do to respond to their circumstances.* A subset of this assessment involves individuating the needs of each party and assisting both to establish the connection between self-interest and mutuality. Understanding and applying these concepts are critical steps to achieving a mutually acceptable, maximized outcome (Saposnek & Rose, 1990).

180

This chapter explores strategies and interventions on the broadest level (e.g., "Is it a goal of yours to resolve these issues in a manner that would bring maximum benefit to each of you?") and their applications on the specific level (e.g., "What do you think you could offer your spouse to obtain agreement on this particular issue?"). I focus on the financial issues that must be decided in divorce, after touching on the process requirements necessary to set the stage for this substantive work.

SETTING THE STAGE

Bringing order to the particular kind of interpersonal and financial chaos that most clients experience at the onset of a divorce is both an appropriate and a necessary task for the mediator. The more well developed the conceptual framework for the process, the greater the mediators capacity to respond effectively to the wide variety of needs that clients present (Saposnek, 1998).

An effective conceptual framework of assessment and process development in relation to the clients is one that establishes the relationship in terms of broad concepts and their specific application. As a process tool, imagine the broadest to the most specific on this vertical continuum to be a stairway of wide steps leading down to progressively narrower steps. The narrowest bottom level portion of the stairway represents the specific applications and details—the *micro* level. At the uppermost portion of the stairway are broad concepts, goals, and principles—the *macro* level. This stairway serves as a kind of *break-glass-in-case-of-emergency* tool that a mediator can employ to orient him or her in the face of any type of impasse. When the parties begin to calcify around micro positions, the mediator can begin moving their attention up the steps toward the broader goals that they share, until a goal is identified that brings about two positive responses from them. This simple intervention of redirecting their focus to a shared goal, value, or objective either moves the parties off the point of potential impasse or, at least, gives the mediator additional time and information (i.e., their responses) with which to develop the process further. Then you can lead the parties back down the stairs to help them shape the application details. For example, in response to a challenging statement by a client, such as "I'm not willing to agree to any arrangement for the children but 50–50 custody," the mediator might respond with a macro observation such as "What I'm hearing is how very important the children are to each of you. Perhaps you could tell me more about what parenting means to you in terms of your relationship with your children."

The micro objective for the end of the process—best possible agreement on particulars—flows from the macro concepts established at the beginning of the process—a fair division of property that comes closest to meeting the financial needs of both parties. This same stairway analogy can be used in relation to eliciting specific desired behaviors—for example, cooperation in obtaining financial records in the possession of the other or in filing a joint tax return—by starting with broader process macros, such as agreeing to respectful communication rules, before attempting to address particular behavioral requirements. Clients begin to change their behavior when they understand that it is in their self-interest to do so. Connecting success in achieving their objectives at the end of the process with their attitudes and behaviors at the beginning of the process reinforces the concept of client responsibility and frames a practical guide for satisfying that responsibility (Rose, 2001). The use of the terms *macro* and *micro* suggests the interconnectedness of all elements involved in the dispute resolution process. The process is a continuum of time and effort. The end (a maximally beneficial agreement on the particulars) is more than conceptually connected to the beginning (integrating process structure with client need). The readily used reference to "winning the battle but losing the war" well describes a financial settlement that disregarded the macro level, leaving in its wake two destroyed people and too often their very battered children.

With these concepts in mind, let us take a look at their application to the following specific financial issues in divorce mediation: the family residence, support, retirement, and business interests. Prior to examining these basic substantive categories, however, I address the dynamic that characterizes the beginning of so many case situations—the crisis case.

STRATEGIZING THE CRISIS CASE

A crisis case begins with one or both of the parties issuing an ultimatum to the other and/or the mediator (e.g., "If I don't get an agreement for temporary support by the end of this meeting, then I'm going to court to get one!"). In some cases, the gauntlet has been thrown down even before the mediator has finished the introductions. With inadequate time to establish rapport and little information with which to work, the challenge for effective process facilitation is at its maximum. Anticipating these types of situations, a mediator needs to be prepared with a variety of possible strategic responses and concepts. Of primary importance is to remember that the mediator's responsibility is to manage the process effectively, not solve the clients' problems (Rose, 2002). It is always a safe strategy to enter the issue at the *macro* level. For example, the mediator might acknowledge the stated need for a temporary agreement for support by highlighting the specific need while creating a context for a broader subject matter—agreements, in general. In this context, introducing concepts that create a framework for agreements serves three strategic purposes:

- It creates a framework for characterizing the type and purpose of any agreement (e.g., immediate or "Band-Aid" agreements, transition agreements, renegotiable agreements, confidential agreements).
- It expands the focus of the discussion beyond the stated positions the parties have been taking.
- It demonstrates the need for education and understanding while creating additional opportunities for negotiating.

A common approach that frequently leads to an *un*productive discussion is enacted when the mediator joins a client-generated dialogue and tries to facilitate the process from *inside the frame the clients have created.* In contrast, embracing the conversation from the outside by wrapping it with an introductory discussion of a conceptual topic, such as agreement making, lessens the effect of the clients' stranglehold on their respective positions. For example, the mediator might say, "Before we tackle the specific issue of temporary support, let's discuss the various types of agreements you can create such as temporary, intermediate, settlement, and postsettlement. This will enable you to better understand the consequences of any agreement that you wish to make with each other."

Immediate or *"Band-Aid" agreements* are generally threshold issues for one or both parties. One party's willingness to continue with mediation is made contingent on achieving an immediate objective that would solve a pressing and paramount need. For example, a wife states that she is not willing to go forward with mediation without an agreement for temporary support. Two considerations may create resistance for the husband upon whom the demand is being made. The first is the emotional consequence of yielding to the threat, and the second is the concern about entering into a binding agreement on one issue prior to discussion or negotiation of any of the other (and frequently related) issues.

The first concern can be solved by asking questions that identify something of interest or importance to either party which could be exchanged in consideration for making an agreement (Stoner, 1999). For example, agreeing that a "Band-Aid" agreement would be revisited or renegotiated when more complete information is gathered, or agreeing that the temporary agreement could be modified retroactively to adjust for the facts as they emerge later, can give the payor enough exchange value to avoid the sense of capitulation to the demand.

This approach is regularly employed by attorneys in the adjudicatory model under the concept of *reserving jurisdiction.* The parties can stipulate, or agree in writing, that if they are unsuccessful in resolving all their issues by mutual agreement, the court having jurisdiction to review the voluntary temporary arrangements will ensure that each party's rights are protected and will stipulate retroactive orders when it is necessary and appropriate to establish that protection.

In these temporary crisis cases, the clients frequently come into the first session with such a vise-like grip on one particular "tree" that they are unable to see the rest of the forest. When the mediator invites them to loosen their grip and take a metaphorical journey up the hill to gaze at the entire financial forest, they can begin to see the difference between very temporary agreements ("Band-Aids" to stop the bleeding), transition agreements (mutually acceptable agreements that will be superseded by the settlement), and postsettlement agreements that will govern their continued financial relationship after the divorce is completed. In framing the concept for a temporary agreement, the goal is to *develop a solution that is big enough to solve the immediate problem but small enough so as not to create any new problems.* In the example used here, such an agreement might be to provide *X* amount of dollars to the recipient spouse as an uncharacterized advance and defer the task of resolving future temporary support until the next session.

Another useful macro concept is the description of the three major financial periods in a marriage and divorce. The first is the period from the date of marriage to the date of separation. In many states this is the period marked by acquisition of marital or community property. Skipping ahead for a moment, the third is the period that follows the settlement and judgment, in which the financial relationship of the parties is finite, specific, and defined by their agreement or judgment. It is the second period, beginning with the date of separation and continuing through to the settlement, which the parties experience as a financial tornado.

Following separation, everything in both parties' worlds generally feels uprooted and swirling about, unconstrained by the conscious design or control of the parties. It is in this stage of the process that needs can be categorized as *immediate* and *transitional issues.* The mediator explains that the parties' willingness to work for temporary solutions will be rewarded with the acquisition of more time to work on solving their long-range problems. Time is needed to sort out the issues; time is necessary to gather information thoroughly; time will allow them to explore all possible options, including those that are most valuable to each in settlement. The greatest reward of their willingness to work for interim solutions is the control they retain over their circumstances and the outcomes that will govern their lives (Mayer, 2000).

A FRAMEWORK FOR ADDRESSING SUBSTANTIVE ISSUES

The substantive phase of the mediation can be divided into four stages or tasks: gathering information, identifying options and consequences, developing a proposal, and negotiating a resolving agreement. These stages continue the task of creating reference points for the inevitable status checks the clients need. For example, the mediator might begin each session with a reference to the state of the work accomplished to date, such as "In the previous sessions we have completed the discussion of assets and liabilities, but we have yet to discuss child support or alimony. Would those be appropriate subjects to discuss today?" Each stage is a direct function of the macro goal of achieving a maximized outcome for each party, in a process characterized by empowerment, education, voluntary negotiation, and informed consent. We can identify the strategic progression of these stages by working backward from the ultimate goal.

To prepare clients for this initial process, it is always beneficial to alleviate some of the emotional pressure they generally feel at the outset by the use of metaphors that describe the pragmatic aspect of the preparation that goes on in these early stages. For example, characterizing the preparation as *domestic archeology*—picking up the marital things and examining them for what can be known and observed—helps normalize the process and free it from the influence of emotions. Consider this style of introduction by the mediator:

> "During this preparation phase of the process, imagine we are taking a walk around the boundaries of the marital estate, opening up boxes of issues, taking out the contents to examine what we can learn about them, identifying how you each feel about them, and discovering what interests you each have in them. Many boxes contain smaller boxes inside, which we will open and examine for choices and values. Consistent with our commitment to respect each other's process, differences in your opinions (about value issues, for example) will not be viewed as a problem. Rather, the differences are simply the circumstances we work with in reaching mutually acceptable agreements.
>
> "We will continue to circle the estate until each of you feels ready to move into the negotiating stage. Neither of you can negotiate by yourself, so we will move forward at the speed of the slower party. The most effective thing either of you can do to accelerate the process is to consider in what ways you can remove impediments that would slow the process of the other."

In order to achieve a mutually optimal outcome, the parties must be able to negotiate to their maximum capability. As a precondition to this negotiating capacity, each party must develop settlement proposals that create a balance between those things that he or she will concede and those things he or she will secure in the agreement. In order to have the capacity to develop proposals that balance the values of the offeror with the perceived values of the offeree, clients need to be certain that they have understood all of the possible choices for solutions.

Possible Solution Categories

Choices can be described as coming from three different categories. First, there is the *law model*. Outcomes that are readily predictable from statute or case law can be viewed as an option. There are many legal models for resolution of issues that may be attractive to one or the other of the parties. That being said, the law model becomes unpredictable when the collection of mental issues is put before the court. How any given judge comes to decisions on all of the issues submitted in any particular divorce proceeding may be no more ascertainable than next month's weather. Of equal significance to the client may be the awareness that the law model is primarily designed to give judges criteria by which they can issue rulings to stop litigation, not to ensure that any given divorce litigants get their best and most satisfying outcome. Nonetheless, it is an option and can be considered for its value as an alternative to a negotiated settlement.

The second source may be termed choices that come from the *marketplace* or *business world*, in which the parties have connections. Retirement plans, stock options, mortgages, insurance policies, and lease agreements for small businesses are all examples of connections the parties have to the real world. The distinguishing characteristic of this category of choices is the fact that they exist independent of any family code. For example, Wife wants to retain the family residence in the settlement, and Husband is not opposed to this outcome, as long as he is able to remove his name from the ongoing mortgage obligation. The power to release him from the obligation resides exclusively with the lender, GMAC Mortgage Co. The willingness of that business entity to allow the withdrawal or transfer of one party's name will impact the negotiating process profoundly. If GMAC allows Husband to remove his name from the obligation, then Wife can accomplish her objective with minimal cooperation from Husband, and as a result she will spend minimal negotiating capital. If, on the other hand, the lender will not allow the removal of Husband's name, he may demand a higher level of negotiating consideration in exchange for his cooperation in leaving his name on the mortgage. Characteristics of this market-business consideration can be an important source of bargaining power and capacity.

The third source of choices is the most important. This is the category of *client-generated options*. The most satisfying and acceptable solutions are the ones that only the parties themselves can introduce as negotiating possibilities. Two characteristics give maximum value to the choices generated within this category. First, client-generated solutions incorporate options that the law model would not consider. For example, one party relinquishing equity in the family residence in exchange for future alimony or spousal support is not a procedure most courts have the authority to designate as part of a judgment decision. Second, by making customized offers, the parties can target the specific interests of the other party and attempt to identify consideration received in return for the barter or exchange. For example, Wife might propose her willingness to accept a reduced length on the duration of her support in exchange for Husband's willingness to leave his name on the mortgage until such time as she may qualify for a refinance of the encumbrance.

Analysis of Consequences

Concurrent with the development of options or choices regarding possible solutions is the need for analysis of each choice's consequences. Without this analysis and the understanding it facilitates, there can be no meaningful comparison between competing choices for either party. This need brings us back to the beginning stage of the process. It is not possible to guarantee that all options have been considered unless all material facts, information, or interests have been fully identified, examined, and considered. The definition of *material*, in this context, is determined by asking the question: *Would the information, directly or indirectly, affect the choices of either party?* If the answer is affirmative, then the information should be processed. Consider the information necessary to divide the contents of the kitchen versus that needed to divide stock options—clearly, there are significantly varying needs for information. The imperative of the substantive conceptual framework is to be sure that these needs are strategically evaluated and processed. For example, the parties should know that as long as Husband is named on the mortgage, his ability to borrow funds to purchase another piece of real property, or even an automobile, may be affected by a credit report showing his continued liability on the home mortgage, notwithstanding the divorce agreement that obligates Wife to assume sole responsibility for the debt and indemnify Husband from any liabilities.

It is in these two stages of the process—gathering information and developing choices—that the parties can identify the need for additional information or records, the need for independent valuation, the need for tax advice or financial planning, and the need for legal analysis (Friedman, 1993).

THE FAMILY RESIDENCE

Among the various financial issues, the family residence presents uniquely challenging psychological and emotional considerations. As perceived by the clients, the home represents many things: It is the "nest" where the children reside; the known present (as opposed to the unknown future); the repository of most of the marital equity and savings; the emotional heart of the family; cost-effective housing; a deductible housing expense; and security. The mediator must respond to these and other concerns in building an appropriate framework for resolving issues relating to this unique asset (Rose, 1995).

When we open the family residence "box," we find three smaller "boxes" or issues inside: use issues, disposition issues, and tax issues.

1. *Use issues.* These are issues that relate to the temporary use of the house during the period between separation and settlement. They include

exclusive occupancy, management and control, responsibility for debt service, access to contents and personal belongings, and access to files and records, equipment and tools, and in some instances the children.

2. *Disposition issues.* This category addresses the ultimate determination of the family residence as it will be described in the settlement. Basically, there are four potential outcomes: the property is sold to a third party; the wife retains it in the settlement; the husband retains it in the settlement; or the parties agree to co-own the house until some date in the future (e.g., the high school graduation of a child).

3. *Tax issues.* This category spans the other two. Tax issues are associated with the temporary use of the home, such as the tax deductions available for the monthly mortgage interest and property taxes. These considerations may have a meaningful impact on the temporary support calculations. Additionally, there are tax considerations associated with the disposition of the property in terms of capital gains or losses. These considerations are necessary to identify if the parties are to be assured that they have considered all aspects of their decision to sell to one another, sell to a third party, or continue to co-own the house and defer the sale to a future date.

Categorizing and framing the discussion of the family residence serves several strategic purposes. The most obvious purpose is to organize the asset and liability information in a manner that facilitates the education of the parties, that identifies areas in which the gathering of additional information is necessary, and that points to areas where expert assistance is needed (e.g., an accountant, appraiser, or attorney).

The more subtle strategic purpose is to reframe the discussion (more likely, the arguments) the parties have been having about the same subject. Most clients come into the process having tried some negotiating and experienced various levels of frustration over their inability to make significant progress on the major issues. The problem is not that they are incapable of achieving success; it is that they are incapable of achieving success *in the manner in which they have gone about it.* This stalemate is often sufficient cause for them to cooperate with the development of a new approach in mediation, giving the mediator latitude to shape the process.

EQUITY AND GAIN

The two most important financial issues involved in the family residence are the fair market value (the estimated sale price) and the capital gain (the net increase in market value above its basis, which may be subject to taxes on sale). Although it may seem premature, making some cursory estimates of these two financial categories during the initial discussion of the role of the family

residence can help create an awareness of how these values may be determined, while underlining the caveat that the exercise is simply aimed at creating a sense of scale or approximation. The actual values that may be used in negotiation should be calculated by an accountant and based on appropriate data.
This initial type of "quick and dirty" calculation is simply intended to give a
sense of scale and demonstrate for the parties the process of "domestic
archeology."

An equity calculation begins with an assumed fair market value, or FMV.
For this exercise in the mediation process, it is sufficient if the parties feel
comfortable agreeing on a hypothetical amount, with the understanding that
they are primarily creating a conceptual formula for determining values that
they can use to plug in "real" numbers when they have been determined.
The mortgage and any additional loans, equity lines, or lines of credit that
are secured by the real property or by a deed of trust would be deducted
from the assumed FMV. The resulting figure represents the gross equity of
the property. It is a *gross* figure in the sense that there is no way to access this
sum without refinancing the property or selling it, and each of those actions
has associated costs that would further reduce the gross number. Whether
the buyout figure of a purchase between the spouses should, or should not,
include a reduction for estimated sales or refinance costs is an issue that typically separates the parties around their calculations of financial self-interest.

With a process structure in place that encourages the identification of
individual values, interests, and perspectives, these financial differences can
simply be acknowledged at this point and reserved for use in the larger negotiation context. A sample worksheet for the calculation of equity looks like
this:

Calculation of Equity:

Fair market value: _____ (estimated or actual)

Less mortgage 1st: [   ]

Less equity line: [   ]   (or any other encumbrances)

Gross equity: (without reduction for sales costs)

Less sale costs (±7%):   [   ]

Net equity: (an estimate as realized from a sale)

In considering these two financial concepts, equity and gain, it is very
important to understand that they may bear little resemblance to one another. *Capital gain* is a state and federal tax category that describes the taxable profit the owner has realized on the sale of a piece of property. It is
measured by deducting from the sales price the costs of the sale, the purchase price, and any capital improvements made to the asset. The resulting

figure is the profit or capital gain on the sale of the asset. The resulting tax that will be owed on the sale of the asset varies depending on how long the asset was held from the date of purchase to the date of sale, as well as the individual state tax rate on such items. It is quite possible for clients to have borrowed on most of the equity of a particular asset, so that it has little net value at the time of divorce. They may now discover that there is a significant taxable capital gain attached to the property, with little or no equity in the property to pay it.

The significance of any calculation of capital gain was lessened enormously in 1997 when Congress enacted the tax reform package that eliminated any tax on the capital gain accruing from the sale of a residence for gains of the first $250,000 for an individual and the first $500,000 per married couple. Nonetheless, the parties need to be aware of the status of the gain in any asset they contemplate retaining in the settlement, if they want to be able to make financial decisions based on full knowledge of facts that affect both the present use of the asset and its future disposition.

As an example of how easy it is to overlook the significance of this information, consider the following hypothetical situation. The parties have a home worth $450,000, on which they hold a refinanced mortgage of $200,000, leaving a gross equity in the amount of $250,000. The parties will focus on this figure, which represents the approximate amount of cash in the house. Furthermore, the tax basis (purchase price + capital improvements) of the residence is $175,000 ($125,000 + $50,000). The capital gain in the property (without factoring in the effect of sales costs, for the sake of simplicity) is $275,000 (net sale price − purchase price + improvements). The spouse who retains the house in the settlement will be entitled to exclude the first $250,000 of gain from any taxes. However, the financial facts of this hypothetical scenario are that, based on present values, the seller will incur a tax on that part of the gain not exempted by the exclusion ($275,000 − $250,000 = $25,000). Furthermore, *any* additional growth in the value of the residence will be taxed as a capital gain when the property is sold.

Such information may not be a controlling factor in arriving at a decision for either spouse. The parent negotiating to retain the house may be committed to minimizing disruption to the children, and the associated financial consequence is less consequential. The home may be more valued as a parenting center than as a financial investment for that parent. However, in light of the objectives of empowerment and informed consent, the process question becomes: *Did the parties have knowledge of these financial facts, and were these facts considered by each party in negotiating the agreement?*

A sample worksheet for estimating the capital gain and tax looks like this:

Calculation of Capital Gain:

Net sale price	_____	(sales price less costs of sale)
Less purchase price	[ ]	
Less improvements	[ ]	
Plus gain from sale of prior residence*		
Equals capital gain		
Less exclusion	[$250,000.00]	(per person)
Equals taxable gain		
Multiply by tax rate	X	
Equals capital gains tax (estimated)	_____	

*If prior house was sold before the new tax law took effect in 1997.

The approach to dealing with the family residence is no different from all other financial issues at the macro level: Organize the substantive process into stages or phases that reflect the needs and concerns of the clients. The broadest macro issue is the division of the four stages into two halves: those that facilitate *preparation* and those that facilitate *negotiation*. The former break down into the processes of gathering information and identifying options/choices and their consequences. The latter half breaks down into the development of settlement proposals, in which the participants must consider not only the priority of competing personal choices (assuming each party is not going to get everything he or she wants) but also the interests and values of the party to whom the proposal will be made.

The first two phases (gathering of information and identifying options and consequences) are maximally beneficial when shared by the participants. The development of a settlement model is a much more personal and subjective a part of the process. The more well developed the mediator's strategies for facilitation of the process and substantive issues are, the more constructive and progressive the experience of the clients will be. This specifically includes the ability of each party to become as capable for negotiation as each is able. The process strategy of individuating these phases for each party includes eliciting the parties' commitment to allow each other to move through the stages in his or her own style and stay out of each other's metaphorical backyard.

SUPPORT ISSUES

Next to custody, the support category is at the top of the list of difficult mediation issues. One reason support issues are so difficult is the continued interdependent financial connection they require at a time when most clients want to be as disconnected and far removed from one another as possible. Add to that baseline setting the emotions associated with being the "abandoned spouse." When it is the husband, he perceives that he is not only losing his wife and children but is also being told *to pay for it.* When it is the wife, she may have primary responsibility for several young children and is now faced with the loss of a spouse, partner, and source of financial security. Regardless of the particular circumstances, the support issues are decidedly different from the property issues.

At least in the area of marital property, the parties experienced common interests in furthering the growth of their estate, and each will benefit from that growth when they divide it. To that extent, their interests could be said to be on parallel tracks. On the issue of support, however, their interests are more like two locomotives heading directly at one another on the same track. One strategic approach is to begin by normalizing their fears and concerns, while assuring them that a path for successful resolution of this issue can be developed. It may be comforting for parties to hear that any capacities for empathic behavior regarding the needs and concerns of the other are predictably diminished for most and nonexistent for some. They need to be assured that a consuming self-interested focus is entirely appropriate; it is particularly useful to distinguish between the efficacy of egocentrism and the counterproductivity of selfishness.

A context can be created that begins to provide comparisons between judicially determined support models and negotiated agreements that respond to their particular needs in more meaningful ways. It is unfortunate that in many jurisdictions across the United States and in Canada, the courts do not accept support arrangements that do not conform to the guidelines of particular jurisdictions, even when the parties were fully represented by counsel and willingly made the agreement. Rigid as these jurisdictions may be, the opportunity still exists for the parties to pay homage to the statutory requirements and expand on them with other, more elaborate financial agreements. For example, a jurisdictional requirement that child support must adhere to a mandatory guideline would not necessarily preclude the parties trading an agreement for the payment of other expenses relating to the children (other than those presumed covered by the guideline, such as private school tuition) in exchange for other agreements in other parts of the settlement (e.g., the disproportional division of some tax-deferred savings account).

In this context, a seemingly self-evident question can begin to shed light on another approach to resolution: *Would it be a goal of yours to meet the needs of your children to the best of your abilities, and to do so while minimizing the potential for conflict between the two of you, now and in future negotiations?* Predictably, the clients nod their heads in affirmation; their perspectives have been subtly realigned by a focus on broad common objectives. The real significance of so seemingly obvious a question is revealed in the follow-up query: *Would it be meaningful for you to know that the judicial model is not concerned with either of these goals? Rather, its primary objective is providing criteria that can be used by judges to issue orders that answer the disputes regarding support that are brought in front of them.* The reality is that most parties who seek judicial resolution of support disputes return to court at a future date to litigate changes to the original order. Adjudicated support orders typically fail to end the financial disputes that create them and rarely reflect goals that are of greatest importance to the parties.

The lesson for most mediation participants is to recognize the fundamental common interest they share: the goal of achieving an agreement that eliminates the likelihood that the parties will engage in conflict over finances during the period of the agreement. It is also likely that the parties will share the objective of forging a stable and predictable agreement that extends the necessity of renegotiating the issue as far out as possible. This simple strategic intervention highlights the value of developing common goals and interests—an exercise which is completely counterintuitive when set against the predominant psychological landscape of emotional estrangement.

In the next section we consider the characteristics of cash flow that may shape support-related outcomes.

CASH FLOW CHARACTERISTICS

The discussion of any support issue typically begins with a determination of the income, earnings, or earning capacity of each party. Income analysis begins with an understanding of the wages, salary, or self-employment income of each party. The exact amount of a party's net paycheck from wages or salary may change significantly as a result of divorce. The existing withholdings declaration—the employee's W-4 form—likely reflects a joint income tax return with all the deductions, dependents, and tax deductible contributions included. As a result of the divorce and property division, these elements may change significantly.

A calculation of temporary support that assumes the parties would file a joint tax return at year's end will not necessarily net the parties the same amount of income when carried over into a year in which the parties file separate returns. The change in tax status for the recipient spouse also needs to be considered when the support arrangement is based on the allocation of net (or after-tax) income.

Two separate tax considerations are associated with the children: head of household filing status for the parent who has the children the majority of time in a given tax year, and the dependent exemption for each child of the marriage. The head of household tax filing status is not assignable—the person either satisfies the criteria or does not. The dependency exemption, however, is assignable and can even be traded from one tax year to the next. A parent who qualifies for head of household filing status may elect to assign the dependent exemption for that same child to the other parent in order to realize the greater tax savings.

For self-employed parties, the issues associated with the veracity of the income and expense summaries that are reported on the Schedule C of their federal tax return are almost always a source of dispute. One model for dealing with these issues is represented by the litigation approach. The parties each retain accountants to support their positions and compromise on the amount of income to be calculated for support—after expending substantial sums for professional fees to argue the issue. Typically, the final number is more than the payor initially acknowledged and less than the recipient spouse claimed was available. When these types of circumstances arise, the mediator has an opportunity to explore what likely will occur if the parties choose to limit their negotiation to challenging each other with competing conclusions and threats. In the alternative, the preparation stage of mediation, they have the opportunity to explore safely which of their various interests and objectives will be available as currency for the larger negotiation that will result when each is ready to move toward resolution.

Let us now consider strategies for discussing support issues that will lead to postsettlement arrangements for support. The two basic types of support—child and spousal support (or alimony)—have elements that are unique to each and for which the parties may have significantly different goals and interests.

CHILD SUPPORT

In many respects, child support is the easier of the two support categories to facilitate, because the issue is typically framed by the principled commitment of each parent to see to it that the needs of the children are met. The debate, of course, is how to achieve this goal.

Potentially contentious discussions can be transformed into very constructive dialogues and exploration if two elements are in place. The first is each party's commitment to allowing the other to voice his or her concerns, perspectives, and interests free from the challenge or emotional reaction of the other. The second is the process agreement, established by the mediator, to distinguish preparation from negotiation and to remain in the preparation phase until each party is ready to move into the negotiation phase. These two preliminary processes contribute to the elimination of any responses other than a dialogue focused on examining the elements of the future support relationship, including the sources of income and the expenses to be addressed.

Most clients in jurisdictions that have support guidelines come into the mediation process aware that there is some type of state guideline or schedule, and some are already armed with calculations that have been run for them indicating what they now believe is the appropriate amount of support. Schedules or guidelines are typically based on a number of assumptions, such as net income of one or both of the parents, the number of children, and the amount of time each parent has responsibility for the child or children. When the clients come to the session hauling printouts of calculations run by their attorneys, it is likely that the clients will not agree on the other party's calculations, because each attorney is likely to have adopted the differing assumptions of his or her clients—with the predictable deadlocked outcome. In this case, the clients must ascertain which option they prefer: to seize the opportunity to eliminate the uncertainties and risks associated with a judicial determination by negotiating a settlement via the mediation process, or to relinquish control over the outcome of this issue and take their chances on the court's determination.

Assuming the clients opt to explore the opportunities for negotiation, developing an agreement that is sufficiently thorough that it addresses all of the expense items that might otherwise create disagreement is presented as the goal. In contrast, many state-established guidelines have no detailed annotation to indicate every child expense item that is covered by the order. As a result, parties may find themselves arguing over who is responsible for soccer registration, dance lessons, tutoring costs, summer camp, or any number of other child expense items.

The best way to avoid this pitfall is to identify each and every category of child expense that will likely appear on the financial horizon over the next 12-month cycle and decide what role that expense plays in the agreement. The following is a sample list of various categories of expense that may arise in the course of the child support period:

Employment- or school-related child care	Counseling/therapy expenses
	Tuition expenses
Summer child-care expenses	Tutoring expenses
Health care insurance premiums	Preschool expenses
Health care expenses not covered by insurance	Religious training and church activity expenses
School clothes	Summer camp
School supplies (materials, backpacks, etc.)	Driving lessons and permits
	Auto insurance
Computer supplies	Auto expenses
School activities	College application and test fees

School projects and field trips

Sport activities

Major gifts (bicycle, computer, skis, surfboard, etc.)

Major pet expenses (horses, farm animals, etc.)

Lessons and classes (piano, dance, art, etc.)

College inspection travel costs

College tuition, books, living expenses, and travel

Birthday presents for other children

Special needs (developmental, medical, educational, etc.)

Once these categories have been identified (allowing for differences of opinion as to the necessity of any specific category) and/or the amount of money associated with any particular expense, the parties can experiment with different approaches to subsidizing the agreed-upon categories. The approaches can include the following:

• *Child support.* The expenses in these categories would be deemed to be included in the child support payment each month, and the amount agreed upon would include these additional expenses.

• *Shared expenses.* These expenses will be split by the parties either in addition to any regular monthly child support payment or as an alternative to a traditional support calculation. This approach works well when the parties both (1) have the children significant amounts of time, and (2) have only moderate disparities in their earnings.

• *Dad's/Mom's expenses.* In conjunction with (or as an alternative to) some monthly child support, the parties allocate whole categories to one another, with each parent assuming the expenses of that category. This approach works well when the parties want to minimize the need for reimbursement from one another and when one has greater interest than the other in a particular activity.

• *Discretionary expenses.* Even after a thoughtful discussion and analysis of all the categories of likely expenses, some still pop up unplanned (e.g., a best friend invites the child to go skiing with a church youth group, and it costs $100). This category recognizes that (1) these kinds of expenses are exceptions to the agreement, (2) it is permissible to ask the other parent if he or she might contribute, and (3) it is permissible to decline to contribute.

• *Special expenses.* There are a number of purchases in the life of a child that represent special moments (e.g., the first tricycle or bike, a computer, or a prom dress). This category recognizes that there may be expenses for which neither parent would want to be *excluded,* and for which the parties might include a commitment to discuss such purchases with one another before either acts unilaterally.

When the thorough preparation work has been completed, the clients can consider strategies for negotiating child support. Negotiating exchanges solely inside the child support "box" (e.g., proposing one parent pay all the routine medical expenses not covered by insurance in exchange for the other parent paying for piano lessons) is only one, and perhaps the most limited, approach. Broadening the categories available for negotiation would consider trading interests in the larger "box" of support issues—the one containing both child support and spousal support (or alimony). For example, one spouse might offer to accept a reduced obligation for spousal support in exchange for an agreement to pay a disproportionately greater share of college expenses for the child. The next level of negotiation would consider trading interests in both the child support and alimony categories, and still another level would consider support trades for property or debt items of interest. In the negotiating frame, it is even possible to include agreements regarding support in consideration for agreements on parenting arrangements. For example, if Wife would agree to allow expanded parenting time for Husband, he would agree not to seek a reduction in child support as a result of his having more time with the children. This particular area of exchange must be approached carefully, because some parents might experience it as "negotiating their children" and feel deeply offended at the suggestion. The mediator can reframe this option as one of trading "wants" or "desired outcomes," not the children themselves; for example, "If your concern, Wife, is that Husband's desire for more time, with the children is merely a pretext for reducing his child support obligation, would you be willing to consider adjusting the time if he agreed to continue to pay at the same current level and that he would not seek a reduction? In other words, your desire for economic stability can be exchanged for his desire for more quality time with the children." To ensure that the agreement is enforceable and not in violation of any judicial policy, any consideration given in trade for a particular support agreement must be viewed in light of the support laws in that particular jurisdiction.

ALIMONY OR SPOUSAL SUPPORT

As with child support issues, it is helpful to begin the process by acknowledging the common difficulties inherent in both positions. For example, it may help clients to be reminded that what it feels like to be obligated for the support of another is very different from what it feels like to be dependent on another for support. Reiterating how challenged they may be to tolerate the needs and concerns of the other is a normalizing strategy that tends to depotentiate the "short fuses" that characterize reactions to this category. In another similarity with child support issues, clients may be surprised to find significant common goals and objectives on the horizon, notwithstanding the fact that they are staring at horizons that are 180 degrees apart from one another. In spite of their very different perspectives on this issue, affirmative responses are almost guaranteed to the query, "Would you like to create an agreement that would provide a support arrangement that is stable and predictable for the term of the agreement?"

Another shared circumstance for both types of support is the likelihood that the clients are preoccupied by what they believe to be the "law model" or state guidelines. Depending on the jurisdiction, these guidelines may be known and reasonably predictable, or they may be predictable only in their ambiguity, as is the case in states such as California. If the mediator is not comfortable describing the characteristics of the jurisdictional law model, the issue can be handled by asking counsel for each party to provide statements summarizing the client's perspective and supporting analysis of the law. To the extent that the interpretations of counsel are diametrically opposed, the uncertainty of the law is reinforced, and incentive is generated for the exploration of parties' underlying interests and objectives.

The longitudinal axis of the support equation is the *length of time,* and the latitudinal axis is the *amount of monthly support.* Viewed in the one-dimensional law model, there appears to be little to negotiate. However, viewed through the lens of interest-based negotiation, there are unlimited possibilities. Inside the support "box," trades can be made between length-of-time issues and amount-of-money issues. When support issues are linked to property issues, the proposals are likely to trade limitations on support for greater property in the division, or less value in property for increases in the amount or time of support. When limitations on support are proposed in exchange for greater value in property, many different approaches can be considered by either party:

• *Ceilings on support.* One proposal suggests enforcing contractual ceilings on the amount of support that could be paid in any given month, or in an aggregate total over the length of the obligation, in exchange for consideration in some other part of the negotiation. For example: *In consideration for receiving 100% of husband's 401(k) account, wife agrees that beginning in the third year of support and for the duration of the obligation thereafter, support shall never exceed the sum of $500 per month, regardless of the circumstances of either party.*
• *Restrictions on the source of support.* Instead of limiting the amount of support, this approach would exclude certain portions of the payor's income from being used to calculate or pay support. For example: *In consideration for* . . . [same as above], *wife agrees that any order or agreement for support shall exclude consideration of, or payment from, husband's income that derives from* . . . [bonuses, overtime income, stock option income, employee profit sharing, etc., any of the above].
• *Restrictions on circumstances.* Aside from negotiating limitations on the support itself, another category of negotiation is restrictions on the circumstances that affect the obligation itself. For example: *In consideration for* . . . [same as above], *the parties agree that wife's acquisition of part-time income while*

she attends school shall not be the basis for a reduction of the monthly support amount, unless her employment exceeds 30 hours per week.

These types of negotiating possibilities only emerge in an environment in which parties feel safe to discuss their thoughts and feelings. The key to success in facilitating an effective process for resolving support issues begins with the core principles and agreements that establish mutual respect for each party's process needs and boundaries during the preparation stage of the mediation. When the foundational guidelines are embraced by the clients and applied with consistency by the mediator, the substantive issues can then be introduced with expanded potential for creative accord.

RETIREMENT ISSUES

As experienced by clients, retirement assets often place a spotlight on the allocations of labor in the marriage. For illustration, consider the gender stereotypic family. The husband may feel very possessive about the lifetime of savings that derived from the daily grind of a job that held little satisfaction other than the accumulated financial remuneration. By contrast, the wife looks at her labor as the homemaker and child rearer and is horrified by the absence of any financial acknowledgment for her efforts on behalf of the marriage—no retirement savings or social security contributions to her name. She has only a marital interest in *his* retirement, as provided under the law. Even where Wife is the second wage earner, as is typical in the contemporary household unit, the income differential that discriminates in favor of men deprives most women of achieving comparable retirement contributions where employment generated tax-deferred savings are calculated as a percentage of annual earnings.

Once again, it is necessary to reframe the subject and open up the conversation to expand the outcome possibilities. This situation is an opportunity to apply two of the process concepts discussed earlier for substantive issues. The first is to reaffirm the exercise of *domestic archeology* as an approach to gathering information as effectively and pragmatically as possible. Use of this metaphor is a benign way to frame the education of each spouse regarding his or her retirement assets and to change any negative dynamic that may have existed between them in their discussions of this issue.

The second process concept applied here is the reminder that choices for making agreements with this and any other issue can be viewed as coming from three sources: the law model, the market/business model, and the model based on client-generated choices and criteria. In the case of retirement assets, the first two categories have a significant impact on the available options for disposition. The limitations on choices derive from the employer (and the rules for the retirement plan it has provided for its employees) and the Internal Revenue Service (through the tax laws it enforces regarding the division, distribution, and withdrawal of the retirement funds).

There are basically two types of retirement assets (Campbell, 1990). The most common in the contemporary corporate world is known as the *defined contribution* type of tax-deferred savings program. Although the employer might co-contribute or match percentages of pretax savings, the employee also makes contributions, which are deducted from the employee's gross annual income. The tax on the savings is deferred until the retirement dollars are withdrawn at the prescribed age allowed by the federal tax laws. The most common type of account for this type of plan is the 401(k) account, the 403(b) (in the case of nonprofit organizations), 457 accounts, and similar accounts with creative company names but based on the same IRS sections. When an employee with a defined contribution account leaves one employer, he or she can simply take the tax-deferred savings to the new employer and roll the accrued savings into the new 401(k) account.

The other major type of benefit is the *defined benefit* retirement plan. However, this type of benefit program is disappearing rapidly in an age when employee mobility and employee/employer self-interests make the funding and administering of such plans too expensive for the modern corporation. Defined benefit programs have become an "endangered species" in the contemporary workplace, as companies are faced with an increasingly mobile work force. Furthermore, the commitment to company loyalty that was the hallmark of employee–employer relations a generation ago has evolved into a prototypic relationship that is more driven by an intersection of self-interests—the employees' concern for compensation and benefits, and the employers' concern for productivity and profitability. The evolution of migratory employees, who freely move from one company to another, has made the administration of defined benefit retirement plans a bureaucratic nightmare that is not cost-effective for companies to maintain. Thus arose the primary focus on compensation plans based on defined contributions.

The development of this issue in mediation involves many considerations. Valuation is one major consideration. A defined benefit plan, such as CalPERS or IBM-type plans, can be viewed as providing future streams of income, to be divided between the parties when each reaches the appropriate age; or the present value of that future stream of income can be calculated by an accountant, actuary, or financial planner and turned into a lump sum that can be traded against some other lump-sum asset, such as the equity in the family residence. Of course, the parties must be careful to consider apples for apples—and not apples for oranges. In this example, the equity in the family residence may be tax free because of the capital gains exclusion (making it an apple), whereas the present value of the defined benefit plan is based on pretax calculations and is therefore not "net" of taxes (making it an orange). Nonetheless, the desire of one party to acquire all of one type of asset opens up creative possibilities for negotiating all the others.

Another major consideration is the allocation of the asset. Most retirement plans or tax-deferred savings programs allow for the apportionment of the asset between divorcing spouses in any proportion or specific amount that the plan administrator is instructed to calculate and distribute. It need not be equal allocations. This flexibility is necessary because in almost all jurisdictions, contributions to the marital interest that come from the employee's continued employment, stop after the date of separation (or some comparable date that ends the accumulation of a marital interest). That the employee will continue to contribute to the plan with postdivorce savings, which are the separate property of the employee, means that the plan administrator for the asset must make pro-rated calculations of the marital and separate property interests.

The IRS's mandated document of instructions for the division of the marital interest is called a *Qualified Domestic Relations Order,* or *QDRO,* as it is commonly known. Any qualified retirement plan or tax-deferred savings plan (meaning, governed by the Employees Income Retirement Security Act, or ERISA) *must* be divided pursuant to a QDRO if the tax-deferred status of the funds is to be preserved after the division.

The initial emotion associated with the potential division of retirement assets in a divorce mediation can be constructively channeled into the development and understanding of all the complexities and characteristics of the assets themselves. If the parties feel safe in the mediational process, their personal value issues and complementary interests can lead the way to a positive outcome for both.

STOCK OPTIONS

Over the last decade, the widespread use of stock options as a method of employee compensation has created a unique set of problems for the clients who must address them as marital assets (Internal Revenue Service, 1999). Within the limits of this chapter it is not possible to develop the issues associated with this topic fully; therefore, a brief overview must suffice. The complexity of the stock option asset derives from the second category of circumstances that create or affect the options of the parties: namely, the market/business model choices. This particular asset can be used as a good example to help the clients understand that an important source of option considerations can come from this second category.

In most jurisdictions, the law model may simply define the parties' generic interests in the asset (e.g., community property, equitable distribution, separate property) without specifying the method or manner of division. Then, too, this asset may get "double treatment" in jurisdictions such as California, where it is first viewed as a property asset, for purposes of dividing the marital estate, and then viewed as a source of income, for purposes of determining the income of the parties for child and spousal support/alimony purposes. Although most employee-spouses view this guideline as mandating an unwanted "double-dip," it is nonetheless a fundamental part of many statutory schemes for divorce.

The wave of corporate accounting scandals in 2002 has shed some light on the complex bookkeeping methodologies that allowed options to serve corporate purposes. The media focused on those activities that are best characterized as poor management decisions and, in some cases, criminal conduct. Nonetheless, the more positive policies behind the implementation of the stock option programs have given employees incentives that encourage loyalty (through 3-, 4-, and 5-year vesting requirements) and productivity (employees share in the wealth of the company with any increase in the value of its shares).

The most challenging circumstances arise from the interface between the corporate rules that govern the grant and exercise of the options, on the one hand, and the limitations on their disposition that flow from the rules of the IRS, on the other. Because the options represent a form of deferred compensation (earned through continued employment and subject to the limits of the grant, exercised at a future date determined by the employee), the employers must abide by IRS governing requirements, which are strictly interpreted. One requirement is that the options must remain in the name of the employee, even though the nonemployee spouse owns a marital interest in them. The desire to divide the marital interest coupled with the employer and IRS requirement that the funds remain in the name of the employee mandate a continuing cooperation between the parties that would otherwise be an undesirable connection.

Additionally, regardless of whose options are being exercised, they will be reported to the Social Security number of the employee-spouse. From the gross profit of the transaction (i.e., the difference between the option purchase price and the market value sales price), income taxes, Social Security taxes, and other state and federal obligations will be withheld in the name of the employee-spouse. Likely, the mandatory withholding will not cover the full extent of the tax obligations that will be due, as calculated in that spouse's tax return, necessitating additional cooperation to set aside sufficient funds from the exercise of the options to indemnify and hold the employed-spouse harmless from these liabilities. This continuing connection also requires the assistance of an accountant to estimate the appropriate amount of withholding to neutralize the transaction to the employee. Complicating factors such as these—deriving, as they do, from the market/business model rather than family law rules—may motivate one party to consider proposing a trade of this asset for the property interest of the employed-spouse in another asset. There is enormous risk arising from the vagaries of an uncertain stock market, and *risk* is simply another dynamic value for parties to assess and weigh when reaching a decision.

In summary, the stock option assets represent a trap for the unwary. Significant tax and legal information is necessary for the parties to move forward on the basis of informed consent. From the mediator's perspective, the tasks are the same. Assist the parties in the process of acquiring all the information necessary to make an informed decision. Help the parties assess their own values relative to the competing choices for disposition. Reframe the issues around their positive intentions and shared goals. Support them in the differing process needs (e.g., access to information, education regarding the nature of the assets, analysis as to the disposition possibilities and the use of experts for valuation and financial planning, to name a few) that must be met for them to become capable negotiators.

BUSINESS INTERESTS

The last set of financial issues considered in this chapter is the multifaceted category of business interests, which can take many forms (Lipman, 1990): publicly owned corporations, privately held corporations, partnerships, limited partnerships, and joint ventures, to name a few. Complex corporate ownership, stock options, and other forms of deferred executive compensation raise issues of valuation, division, and taxation that are beyond the scope of this chapter. Addressing these corporate issues usually requires expertise provided by experienced counsel for each spouse, as well as the services of accountants.

The most challenging business-related issues for most divorce mediators are those accompanying the small single-owner or partnership enterprise, in which the marital interest is either 100% or a major percentage of the ownership. The further removed the spouses are from management and control over the business activity, the more likely the asset will be viewed as nothing more than an investment like many others. However, it is more complicated when one or both of the marital partners actively participate in management and control, and the breach of trust that terminated the interpersonal relationship is paralleled by fear and mistrust with regard to the functioning of the business interest.

Following the first stage of laying the conceptual foundation for the development of the substantive issues comes the "archeological dig," whose first components are the assets and liabilities—the primary elements—that make up the business:

- *Assets:* inventory, fixtures, equipment, bank accounts, real estate, improvements, leasehold interests, accounts receivable, trademarks, patents, copyrights, investments, intellectual property, contracts, work in progress, among others.

- *Liabilities:* accounts payable, payroll, short-term debt, long-term debt, interest, contingent liabilities, leasehold obligations, state and federal taxes, payroll taxes, sales taxes, to name a few.
- *Balance sheet:* an accounting tool that allows a snapshot comparison of the assets of the business offset by the liabilities; the balance sheet equalizes the excess value of assets compared to liabilities (or the reverse) with the category of *owner's equity,* which is sometimes called *goodwill.*

An important fact about the various accounting categories associated with a business is that there are a number of approved methods for keeping track of the finances of a business, each of which satisfies the requirements of what is referred to in the business world as "generally accepted accounting practices" (or GAP). It is important to note that there are enough variables in GAP to allow two different accountants to validly produce significantly differing assessments of the worth or value of the business. The consequence of this variability for divorce purposes is the fact that there is no precise way of determining one value of a business to the exclusion of another value. Furthermore, in many jurisdictions, a business interest that is a professional service, such as an independent consultant (i.e., an expert who sells his or her time and advice), may have no "market value" because there is no tangible product to sell to a buyer. Nonetheless, the laws controlling the disposition of marital assets may approve a formula for determining a "goodwill" value for the enterprise, based on reputation and continued business.

Clients seem to approach this issue from one of two categories of experience. There are those circumstances where both spouses have participated in the creation, development, and running of the business, and each has a good understanding of how the business operates and a firm opinion of its value. In the second circumstance, only one of the parties has actively managed and controlled the business (typically, the husband). In these cases, it is not uncommon for the other spouse (typically, the wife) to have little or no understanding of the nature of the business, the circumstances relating to its cash flow, and the worth or value of the enterprise as a marital asset.

In developing a conceptual framework for addressing the capacity of either party to maximize his or her decisions about the business interest in a divorce mediation, the mediator can organize the issues by identifying the two major macro categories. These are *cash flow,* which includes the income it produces, and *valuation,* which considers the worth of the business. Metaphorically, it's a chicken and egg proposition. The eggs are the income that the business generates, and the chicken that is laying the eggs represents the worth of the enterprise. The use of such a cartoon metaphor can frequently provide a kind of comic release that also serves to demystify the specialized business vocabulary of "accountant-speak" that makes the subject so intimidating to those unfamiliar with the business world.

Assessing the needs of the parties regarding the preparation phase of the process means developing a path for the education of each of the spouses as to the cash flow and valuation issues. In cases where there is an imbalance in the business experience of the parties, the issue of information and business records must be addressed. Typically, one party may not know what to ask for or how to interpret the business records, and the other, managing party feels threatened and accused of improprieties when asked to produce routine financial information about the running of the business.

The mediator can preempt these concerns by normalizing clients' experiences as they deal with these issues. Since they are dealing with a business asset, consider asking them if it would be appropriate to approach the development of the issue in a manner consistent with good business principles. Having the more experienced spouse describe what he or she would do to become educated about a business they were considering for purchase can subtly engage the managing spouse in describing a template for the nonmanaging spouse to follow in becoming educated about the asset at hand.

For example, in a routine business transaction, each side would likely be getting both legal and accounting advice about the "chicken and the eggs" elements of the business. Viewed in this frame, the nonmanaging spouse's request for records is simply good business practice, in preparation for participating in a developing sale, and should not be seen as an attack on the integrity of the managing spouse.

Cash flow issues invariably bring up the "shadow" side of the business, such as unreported cash withdrawn from the business, and personal purchases or payments written off the profit-and-loss statement as business expenses. The likelihood that the business has provided these types of "untaxed" income benefits to the family is practically guaranteed. To describe the size or significance of personal benefits written off through the business, some accountants use the metaphor of looking for "golf balls, volleyballs, or beach balls." The proportioning suggests that some expensed items matter a great deal, whereas others are of no great significance. For example, personal cell phone expenses written off through the business would be considered a golf ball. Writing off a monthly car payment would be a volleyball. Writing off the remodeling of part of one's home would be a beach ball. Most likely, the parties will disagree energetically about the amount of income that was filtered through these tax-free channels.

One approach to this particular dispute is to ask the parties to consider the risks associated with taking this issue public in a court hearing. Some family law judges in this country advise clients coming into court to argue about the scope of each other's attempts to defraud the IRS that they (the judges) may feel a duty to report the facts to that agency. This possibility provides a strong incentive for the parties to come to some agreement about the inclusion of untaxed income for both support and valuation purposes.

The key to framing the valuation issue is to remind the parties of the safety that comes from knowing that no value will be applied without first being agreed upon by each of them. It may be necessary to repeat this assurance time and again to overcome the emotional weight of the fears about their financial futures. The options for developing information regarding valuation create a range of considerations:

• *Business valuation.* One or both of the clients are likely to assume that it will be necessary to obtain a full-blown business valuation, and it may turn out to be so. However, before the decision is made, and in light of the potential expense of many thousands of dollars (for which there is already an inadequate amount to meet the expenses of the separated family), the party may want to consider other options.

• *Business assessment.* A creative mediator works with accountants to develop a range of services that assists clients in this circumstance. The assessment approach limits the CPA's services to a set number of billable hours (4 or 5, for example), in which the parties meet with the CPA, provide summary financial information (tax returns, profit-and-loss statements, balance sheets, etc.), and listen to the CPA explain the various elements and formulas that are used in formal valuations, concluding with a conditional range of possible values for their business (e.g., "probably no higher than and no lower than [$X]"). In this manner, expense is minimized and clients are empowered to come to their own number for settlement purposes.

• *Client determined.* It may be surprising how often clients prefer to come to some subjective determination of the value of a business, based on goals that are realized by a trade or exchange involving another consideration. For example, an agreement that allows one spouse to retain the family residence and be ensured an acceptable level of support may be exchanged for a value assigned to the business that is acceptable to the spouse retaining the business asset. In essence, clients choose to ignore the assumption that the business has an intrinsic value separate from the other issues in the case. Instead they see their best interests being served by coordinating the resolution of all the issues with the particular value determination used in the disposition of the business interest. Thus, in our example, the peace of mind that results from the parties mutually achieving their underlying interests (i.e., preservation of a home and business accompanied by a predictable support arrangement) is preferred to the anxiety produced by competing and opposing expert opinions on the value of the business.

Regardless of the approach, it is the mediator's duty to assess the capacity of each party to move through the various stages of preparation (i.e., identification of facts, gathering of information and records, and analysis of options and their corresponding consequences), negotiation, and resolving agreement. The concept of informed consent does not mandate a particular approach to the determination of consensus valuations. However, it does mandate that the client understand the following:

- Available options and their associated risks and consequences
- The proposal for the tradeoffs necessary to resolve the issues
- The worth or value to the client of the things given up in the exchange
- The worth or value to the client of the things acquired in the exchange

These are the characteristics of informed consent that work to ensure an acceptable and enduring agreement.

CONCLUSION

The effective mediation of financial issues is based on the same qualities of any type of skillful mediation. Critical elements include well-developed process structures and a wide variety of intervention strategies. A mediator should consider what it is about the desired end of the process that informs us as to what must occur at the beginning, and what it is about how we begin the process that informs us as to how it will end (Rose, 2001). There is no better macro value for the mediation process than *safety*. The need for safety is universal, the experience of it is critical, and the provision of it is a mediator's most essential macro task. From the broadest meaning of the word ("a general sense of security") to its most micro application (clients' agreement not to interrupt one another), the experience of safety makes the mediation possible. Every word spoken and every action taken by parties during the process affects their perception of safety—which, in turn, has a commensurate impact on the outcome. It is the mediator's responsibility to help the clients understand this interconnection between the experience of safety and the outcome of resolution and to facilitate constructive and progressive decision making that is possible when both clients feel safe.

REFERENCES

Campbell, E. V. (1990). Retirement plans. In D. L. Crumbley & N. G. Apostolou (Eds.), *Handbook of financial planning for divorce and separation* (pp. 361–379). New York: Wiley.

Friedman, G. J. (1993) *A guide to divorce mediation.* New York: Workman.

Internal Revenue Service. (1999, Nov. 1). U.S. government, letter ruling no. 200005006.

Lipman, J. H. (1990). Valuation of closely held businesses, professional practices, and interests in rental real estate partnerships. In D. L. Crumbley & N. G. Apostolou (Eds.), *Handbook of financial planning for divorce and separation* (pp. 297–359). New York: Wiley.

Mayer, B. (2000). *The dynamics of conflict resolution.* San Francisco: Jossey-Bass.

Rose, C. (1995). The family residence. *Family Mediation News, 14*(3), p. 8.

Rose, C. (2001, Spring). Endings/beginnings. *Family Mediation News,* pp. 4–5.

Rose, C. (2002, Summer). Show me the money. *Family Mediation News,* p. 3.

Saposnek, D. T. (1998). *Mediating child custody disputes.* San Francisco: Jossey-Bass.

Saposnek, D. T., & Rose, F. (1990). Psychology and divorce. In D. L. Crumbley & N. G. Apostolou (Eds.), *Handbook of financial planning for divorce and separation* (pp. 28–48). New York: Wiley.

Stoner, K. E. (1999). *Using divorce mediation.* Berkeley, CA: Nolo Press.

CHAPTER 10

Understanding and Responding to Power in Mediation

MICHAEL LANG

Dealing with power differences between divorcing spouses is a controversial subject in the mediation field. Should a mediator balance power between the parties or manage the power to effect an agreement acceptable to both parties? A mediator's view of power as a threat or an opportunity and as something to be managed or utilized will influence the choice of mediator interventions. This chapter provides a comprehensive examination of how parties manifest power and how the mediator's personal belief system can influence the strategic choices that he or she must make in order to effectively intervene.

Twenty years ago family mediators were discussing whether a mediator had responsibility for balancing power between parties. Arguing in favor of a proactive approach were those who believed that without intervention by the mediator, the exercise of power by one party might result in an untenable and unworkable agreement. Others who challenged this approach asserted that parties in mediation have developed a unique balance of power between them, and mediators are ill equipped to alter that balance. In their view mediators should focus on helping parties find workable solutions to their conflict, not on adjusting the balance of power. Mediators should neither defang the lion nor give claws to the lamb. Rather, they should work with existing power relationships.

In the subsequent two decades, family mediators have continued to weigh in with intensity and passion on the issue of balancing power. This heightened attention to the mediator's responsibility regarding power issues is apparent in the mediation literature. Much of the literature dealing with power issues focuses on mediator interventions: how mediators can use their position and influence to affect the power relationship between disputing parties and thereby assist parties to achieve an agreement that is based on a balance of power. These authors present an array of analytical tools and practice skills that are indispensable to a mediator concerned about the impact and influence of power on the parties' decision making. Competent mediators become adept at employing this assortment of techniques and strategies to deal with displays of power.

Absent from considerations of power in family mediation are responses to two key questions: "Why am I intervening at all?" and "What do I hope to accomplish?" This chapter describes how a mediator decides whether and why it would be helpful to address the application of power in family mediation. In addition, the chapter offers a simple and sensible method for making effective practice decisions when faced with expressions (direct or implied) of power in family cases.

Specifically, this chapter addresses the following questions:

• *What is power?* As a context for the discussion about power, I explore experienced mediators' descriptions of the characteristics and most common expressions of power in mediation contexts.

• *How do parties in mediation express their power?* A number of analytical tools have been developed to assess and evaluate the presence and application of power in mediation. Typically, mediators use these frameworks to identify power imbalances and to determine which strategies to employ. Exploring these tools and frameworks (or models) illustrates the importance of using a clear theoretical foundation when making practice decisions.

• *How do mediators respond to displays of power?* A broad array of techniques has been developed to balance or manage the display or threat of power. Choosing among these skills and strategies is influenced by a mediator's understanding of power and its impact on the parties.

• *How does a mediator's beliefs about power affect practice decisions?* The assumption implicit in these models is that a mediator has an obligation to balance power inequities. A mediator's beliefs about power—whether it is a threat or an opportunity, as something to be managed or utilized—determines the strategies and techniques used to deal with power. The relationship between beliefs and practices is demonstrated by a case example that illustrates how a mediator's beliefs about the nature, use, and impact of power affect practice decisions.

• *How does a mediator use beliefs about power to design and implement interventions?* A model of "reflective practice" is presented and a description provided of how mediators can make use of this model's principles and methods in deciding whether and how to respond to expressions of power in mediation. Applying these methods and principles to a sample case shows the benefit of the reflective practice model when dealing with issues of power.

WHAT IS POWER?

Practitioners, educators, and theorists have expressed widely differing views about the nature of power and the responsibility of a mediator to intervene and counteract the possibly negative effects of the use of power. Consider the following definitions of power:

Picard defines power as "the ability to influence other people or groups. . . . It can be used to dominate others, or to enhance a sense of our own power" (1998, p. 106).

To Davis and Salem, power is "the ability to influence or control others" (1984, p. 18). Therefore, power might be seen as a force applied intentionally in order to achieve one's objectives.

Mayer notes that "power is sometimes viewed as a dirty word . . . equated with coercion, a non-cooperative agreement" (1987, p. 75). Indeed, much of the literature dealing with power and power imbalances assumes this posture. Yet on a more positive note, Mayer observes that "power also provides the motivation for collaboration and defines the range of settlement options available to the parties" (1987, p. 75). The will to settle, the motivation to participate in problem-solving negotiation, and the desire to reach a workable solution are all affected by the presence and application of power.

Folberg and Taylor view power as the expression of "long-standing patterns of dominance and submission, deference and competition, dependence and competence" (1984, p. 184). In their view, parties in mediation rely on these "power patterns" under the stress of dealing with their conflicts. Power is embedded in the relationship of the parties and the learned behaviors that characterize their interactions.

Others, such as Kelly (1995), Moore (1996), and Haynes (1988), see power as an "attribute of a relationship" (Kelly, 1995, p. 87). Power exists in relation to others and has significance only if it results in attainment of goals or the prevention of another's objectives.

As becomes apparent later in this chapter, a mediator's understanding of, and beliefs about, power directly affect how he or she answers the questions posed above: "Why am I intervening at all?" and "What do I hope to accomplish?"

HOW DO PARTIES IN MEDIATION EXPRESS THEIR POWER?

Mayer (2000), Kelly (1995), Moore (1996), Haynes (1988), and Neumann (1992) describe the facets, characteristics, elements, and sources of power as well as the ways in which parties display power in mediation. Mayer (2000), for example, enumerates types of individual power, including:

- Formal authority
- Legal prerogative
- Information
- Association
- Resources
- Rewards and sanctions
- Nuisance
- Procedural power
- Habitual power
- Moral power
- Personal characteristics
- Definitional power

Each source of power has unique characteristics and forms of expression. Each has the potential for building cooperative relationships or erecting barriers to reaching an equitable agreement.

Neumann (1992) identified 10 variables that contribute to, or detract from, expressions of power:

1. Belief system
2. Personality
3. Self-esteem
4. Gender
5. Selfishness
6. Force
7. Income/assets
8. Knowledge
9. Status or age
10. Education

Kelly (1995, p. 88) describes eight "factors or conditions that may create the potential for power inequities in the course of a mediation." These include:

1. Economic self-sufficiency
2. Knowledge base
3. Cognitive style and capabilities
4. Personality and character traits
5. History and dynamics of disputant relationship
6. Institutionalized hierarchies
7. Cultural and societal stereotypes and training
8. Gender and age differences

These typologies of power provide a basis for analyzing the nature and sources of power and developing appropriate intervention strategies to balance power differences. For these authors, understanding the nature and expressions of power provide the mediator with vital information with which to ascertain the relationship of the parties, how they will bargain, and where the mediator may need to intervene to keep the process on an even keel.

Implicit in these descriptions is the notion of power as a resource within the relationship. It is a commodity—something that can be identified, used, traded, suppressed, or ignored. To Haynes (1988) power involves the "control of or access to emotional, economic and physical resources desired by other person(s)" (p. 278). Mayer states that power is "the currency of conflict. Whether its exercise is intentional or not, when people are engaged in conflict, their power is in play" (2000, p. 50). Boulding (1989) observes that the term *power* is often used synonymously with the word *force* and is thereby linked to the idea of domination and control over another person, animal, or thing. For these authors power is a highly sought-after commodity—a resource assiduously developed and carefully applied in the attainment of one's prized objectives. Accepting this notion of power leads to the conclusion that

> some people possess more or less power than other people. In other words, power is viewed as a commodity or property that can be possessed in finite quantities that are distributed (unevenly) among people . . . those at the top possess the largest amount of power and have the greatest influence in a conflict. (Winslade & Monk, 2000, p. 49)

A mediator who subscribes to this view—that power equates with control, influence, or force and that the distribution of power is always unequal—may make practice decisions that respond to the issue of control and result in the redistribution of power.

HOW DO MEDIATORS RESPOND TO DISPLAYS OF POWER?

Much of the literature on power balancing emphasizes techniques and tools needed to bring the relationship into relative symmetry as a means of promoting productive and effective negotiations. Moore (1996, p. 327), for example, believes that "mistrust and power imbalances" often interfere with the parties' ability to resolve their disputes by "rational dialogue and good will." To counteract these negative forces he proposes that mediators "manage the means of influence and power the parties exercise" (p. 327). This approach requires the application of leverage or pressure, expressed through the careful management of the mediation process. Among the approaches Moore suggests are managing communication between and within the parties, arranging the physical environment, encouraging and, at times, directing the exchange of information, adjusting the pace of the sessions, and raising questions that create doubt.

Picard (1998) suggests that mediators lessen the impact of power imbalances by supporting the weaker party—for example, by managing the mediation so that parties have equal time to tell their stories and present proposals, adjusting the pace of mediation and assisting weaker parties to express their ideas, needs, and proposals. According to some, mediators should use their influence to increase the flow of information, provide approval, support the legitimacy of a participant's views, express an expert opinion, interrupt coercive behavior, and encourage cooperative interactions (Mayer, 1987; Moore, 1996). Others propose similar types of active mediator intervention in the process of managing, balancing, and controlling parties' expressions of power (Neumann, 1992; Kelly, 1995; Coulson, 1996). Kelly (1995) lists a number of factors that "may create the potential for power inequities in the course of a mediation" (p. 88). This analytical framework provides mediators with a valuable tool for making a thoughtful and effective assessment of the impact of power within the mediation. Kelly (1995) then correlates these factors with intervention techniques that temporarily "level the playing field." The goal of this approach is to provide parties with "an opportunity to fully participate in shaping the mediation process and outcomes" (p. 96).

Haynes (1988) presents a "power relationship assessment form"—a tool for analyzing the areas in which the mediator should intervene—in order to "empower the less powerful partner so he or she may deal more effectively with the spouse" (p. 285). Haynes also states that power is distributed throughout a marital relationship and is expressed in a pattern of interactions, not as a single incident. Using Haynes's (1988) assessment form, a mediator identifies areas of power and powerlessness to determine "whether power in one area can compensate for powerlessness in another" (p. 285). Having concluded this assessment, the mediator can intervene where and when necessary to shore up the weaker party or limit the impact of the stronger party's power.

Both Kelly and Haynes agree that interventions should be limited to the mediation session to provide a more level field on which the parties can conduct their negotiation of the substantive issues in dispute. Based on the belief that disparities of power "invariably exist at the mediation table," Davis and Salem encourage a similar role for dealing with such imbalances by relying on "existing skills to address the problem" (1984, p. 18). They offer a set of principles as well as practice suggestions to guide mediators in addressing the presence and application of power in mediation. A distinctive feature of their approach is their underlying belief that mediation is inherently capable of balancing power between the parties. The structure and goals of the mediation process, together with the parties' desire to resolve their conflict, offer parties an opportunity to deal with each other directly and in a dignified manner, sharing knowledge in the search for workable and mutually supportive agreements.

HOW DOES A MEDIATOR'S BELIEFS ABOUT POWER AFFECT PRACTICE DECISIONS?

As noted previously, the literature dealing with power and power balancing generally addresses the mediator's responsibility to balance power between the parties as a means of assuring that the resulting agreement is fair and just (Kelly, 1995; Moore, 1996; Haynes, 1988). Most of the authors describe power as a force or influence that has the potential to alter the parties' ability to negotiate effectively. For example:

> When the power balance interferes with the couple's ability to negotiate a fair agreement, I believe the mediator has a responsibility to act to correct that imbalance. (Haynes, 1988, p. 281)

> Practical experience and social psychological experimentation indicate that when negotiators have an equal or symmetrical power relationship, they behave more cooperatively, function more effectively, and behave in a less exploitative or manipulative manner than when there is an asymmetrical power relationship. (Moore, 1996, p. 334)

> As a divorce mediator, I believe that assessing and addressing power differences [are] central to the mediation process. The professional mediator can, indeed must, be able to affect those imbalances in order to arrive at a fair and lasting agreement. (Neumann, 1992, p. 228)

The notion that power symmetry influences the ability to negotiate effectively seems to have led these authors to conclude that a mediator is therefore responsible for balancing power. A link between the standard of negotiation fairness and the role of the mediator has been forged in the minds of many mediators (and expressed in the literature on power), resulting in a belief that mediators are obliged to manage power relationships.

Three alternate views regarding the nature of power support different approaches for dealing with expressions of power. Davis and Salem (1984) contend that the mediation process itself creates the opportunity for parties to seek and attain a natural balance of power. In their view, a mediator should not apply unique or specially tailored techniques when faced with the display of power. In contrast to the proactive management of the process proposed by others, they advocate that a mediator should rely on existing skills. A mediator who adopts Boulding's optimistic notion that power represents the potential for change might not feel the obligation to balance its display, preferring to engage the parties' power as an advantageous force that leads to solutions. Furthermore, practice decisions might differ considerably from those that advocate intervention to balance power, if mediators accepted the views of Winslade and Monk (2000) that power "is constantly shifting and fluctuating as we offer each other positions . . . and supplement the positions offered to us by others in return" (p. 118). If power is a variable force, then a mediator would do well to observe and monitor its altering patterns between parties prior to instigating any comment, question, or other intervention.

These examples are offered to illustrate how beliefs inevitably shape a mediator's understanding of interactions between parties and the resulting practice decisions. To make effective and meaningful choices about an intervention, a mediator must be aware of the underlying beliefs that guide and influence his or her choices. A mediator achieves excellence in practice by first identifying and then making purposeful use of the beliefs that shape his or her interpretation of, and response to, the events and circumstances in the mediation. For example:

> The mediator perceived a possible power imbalance between Dorothy and John with regard to parenting decisions. Dorothy had been the primary parent, staying at home to be with their three children, while John built his accounting practice. In mediation, Dorothy presented a detailed plan for co-parenting, to which John readily acceded without modification or discussion. The mediator was concerned that this exchange might represent the application of Dorothy's power (her greater knowledge about the children's needs and emotional closeness to them) and John's lack of power (awareness that he had spent less time with the children and was less familiar with their needs, interests, and activities). The mediator asked John to talk about his hopes and concerns for parenting the children and encouraged him to ask questions of Dorothy about her proposal.

In this scenario the family mediator, believing a power imbalance existed (significant differences in spouses' experience with, and information about, the children), acted to help John reflect on, and possibly assert his interests in, parenting the children. Why would a mediator conclude that John's ready acceptance of Dorothy's proposal represented a power imbalance? What might cause the mediator to interpret John's response as indicating that differences in their information about the children was adversely affecting their ability to reach a mutually acceptable and workable parenting plan—even though agreement was given?

The mediator's assumptions may be correct. However, simply because one party has more power—in this case, knowledge about and experience with the children—does not necessarily result in a flawed agreement. In fact, it is equally plausible that Dorothy's proposal reflects long-standing patterns in their marital relationship and with their children, with which she and John are both comfortable. Alternatively, their behavior may signify that they based their marriage on the belief that mothers should nurture and attend to children, and fathers should provide financial stability for the family. It is also possible that Dorothy proposed a parenting plan that was more generous than John would have requested, hoping, perhaps, to encourage him to take a more active parenting role.

As these alternative explanations suggest, there may be no power imbalance, or the power dynamic may be consistent with the way in which the parties structured their relationship. If any of these explanations is accurate, there is no basis for a mediator to take action in an attempt to redress a power imbalance.

What beliefs shaped the mediator's perception of, and response to, the exchange between Dorothy and John? For a mediator who believes that (1) fair and workable agreements can only be reached when power is relatively equally balanced between parties, and (2) that the mediator is responsible for managing that balance, one of the following interventions would be appropriate:

- Invite John to take time to think about the agreement.
- Ask Dorothy to explain her reasoning in structuring the parenting plan.
- Encourage John to ask Dorothy questions about how she developed the agreement and how it will operate.
- Ask John to talk about his goals for parenting the children.

In contrast, a mediator who "trusts the parties to make the decision about how much power they have, how much they want, and how much they are willing to use in a particular situation" (Davis & Salem, 1984, p. 25) might respond by taking the following action:

- Acknowledge Dorothy's proposal and encourage the parties to talk about its impact on the children and them as parents.
- Ask whether the proposal reflects their past experience as well as the future—in essence, asking them to consider whether there is value in doing things the same way or is a potential benefit to be gained by changing their approach to parenting.
- Invite Dorothy and John to talk about the process by which they reached agreements in the past and ask whether this agreement was reached in a similar fashion.

The response of a mediator who believes that women have historically had less access to power and fewer resources and that the mediator should support an effort by the wife to assert her interests, needs, concerns, and aspirations might look like this:

- Affirm Dorothy's initiative in generating a proposal.
- Ask Dorothy to consider whether she has adequately considered her own needs in developing the proposal.
- Acknowledge that they have reached an agreement.

These varying response patterns illustrate the notion that practice decisions are shaped by a mediator's beliefs. To be effective in responding to expressions of power, a mediator must first acknowledge the beliefs about power that influence his or her perception and interpretation of the parties' interactions and what response might be constructive and appropriate. Mediators achieve excellence in practice by first identifying and then making intentional use of their beliefs to guide their interpretation of, and response to, the events and circumstances that unfold within a mediation.

HOW DOES A MEDIATOR'S BELIEFS ABOUT POWER ASSIST IN ASSESSING POWER RELATIONSHIPS AND DESIGNING APPROPRIATE INTERVENTIONS?

Practice decisions follow beliefs (Lang & Taylor, 2000); this simple yet fundamental assumption underlies all practice decisions. As used in this chapter, the word *belief* is a generic term that includes learned theories, foundational values derived from early experience, cultural and familial heritage, and philosophy of mediation. Taken together, a mediator's beliefs form a constellation of theories, "the sum of all the mediator knows, regardless of how that knowledge was acquired" (Lang & Taylor, 2000, p. 93). Whether tacitly or intentionally, a mediator's beliefs shape how the mediator understands, interprets, and responds to parties' interactions, governing a mediator's selection of strategy and technique. In the context of power and power balancing, a mediator's beliefs about power and the role of the mediator in relation to power directly affect the extent to which the mediator intervenes—if at all. The method used to make this critical connection between belief and action is a process known as "reflective practice" (Lang & Taylor, 2000; Schön, 1983, 1987). Lang and Taylor (2000) explain:

> Unless mediators understand the underlying theoretical principles that influence and shape their practices, they are merely talented mechanics trying out one tool after another without understanding why one tool might be useful and what results are likely to flow. They are skilled mimics who apply techniques and interventions without fully considering the reasons behind the approaches, without understanding the likely consequences, without the ability to evaluate the success or failure of those interventions, and without the tools and resources to learn from each experience. (p. xii)

By developing the habits and methods of reflective practice, a mediator can learn to make use of his or her experience to improve the quality, relevance, and impact of interventions. The cycle of reflection, described below, provides an intelligible and useful approach that enables a mediator to make purposeful and effective practice decisions and to evaluate whether and why such interventions were or were not helpful to the parties.

Discussion of reflective practice frequently evokes questions about its rationale and usefulness, such as:

- When talking about power balancing, why is it necessary or useful to deal with the concept of reflective practice?
- What is the relevance and value of this concept in situations in which the application of power (direct or implied) challenges the ability of the mediator and the parties to move toward a resolution of the issues in dispute?
- Why should a mediator be concerned about beliefs, values, and theories when a more useful approach would be to identify and describe a comprehensive array of strategies, techniques, and skills that can be brought to bear on the imbalance of power?

Applying a matrix that correlates types of power with mediator techniques appears on the surface to be a simple and practical way to address the problem of power balancing. Despite its organizational attractiveness, however, a matrix of generalities cannot acknowledge the unique features of each dispute or the idiosyncratic nature of the parties' interactions. To achieve excellence in practice, a mediator requires a method for dealing with power that accounts for the unique relationship between the parties and the distinctive characteristics of the conflict. Following the path of the reflective cycle offers a mediator the opportunity to tailor interventions to the distinctive responses of the parties. The mediator engaging in reflective practice follows this five-step process:

1. *Wonder.* Remaining continually curious is the starting point of effective practice. Particularly when parties respond in an unexpected manner, it is important for the mediator to stop and take notice, staying alert to the challenge of making sense of what occurred. The mediator cultivates a sense of wonder by observing "nuances in the parties' behavior and their reactions to one another, and . . . subtle shifts in language or tone of voice" (Lang & Taylor, 2000, p. 25).

2. *Reflection.* The thoughtful mediator takes a moment to reflect on the possible explanations for the parties' interactions. By slowing down and *not* simply reacting, the mediator takes time to consider a variety of explanations for the parties' behavior. "Like the photographer who surveys a scene, takes in the entire view and then selects one portion as the subject for the photograph, the mediator maintains an awareness of the larger picture while simultaneously shifting focus between particular aspects of the interaction" (Lang & Taylor, 2000, p. 26).

3. *Hypothesize.* At this point, the mediator generates a hypothesis, a plausible explanation for the parties' behavior. It is natural to seek an explanation for events or behaviors. We want to give them meaning, to place them within familiar and well-understood categories. The process of generating meaning involves the filtering of experience through the lens of belief. How we interpret behavior depends upon our beliefs, as the examples in the Dorothy and John scenario illustrate. A hypothesis is *not* a conclusive interpretation; rather, "it is an intelligent guess or hunch that will be either confirmed or modified depending on the information gathered by the mediator" (Lang & Taylor, 2000, p. 71).

4. *Experiment.* Now the mediator designs and implements an intervention that helps test his or her assumptions (i.e., explanations) of the parties' interactions and to learn more about their experience of, and reactions to, the conflict. Every intervention is an opportunity to learn about the parties and their conflict by observing and thinking about their responses to a carefully constructed intervention. "Experimentation has two principal forms: implementing an intervention and observing the responses of the parties, and asking questions of the parties to elicit their view of the conflict situation" (Lang & Taylor, 2000, p. 32).

5. *Reflect.* Finally, the mediator observes the parties' response to the intervention. As in the first stage of the reflective cycle, he or she wonders about their responses and lets the process continue. "The mediator's discipline is to test, examine, and rework the formulation of the conflict in conjunction with and in response to the way the disputants view the dispute" (Lang & Taylor, 2000, p. 33).

The cycle of reflection described above provides an elegant, simple, and accessible method for learning from experience. The following example illustrates the application of reflective practice to the expression of certain types of power in a parent–teen conflict. Here we consider how a reflective practitioner might address the interaction between Sally and Bob.

The school guidance counselor in the regional high school referred Sally and her father for mediation. Until recently Sally, age 17, had been an above-average student. However, in the past few months her grades have declined, her teachers have reported inattentiveness in class, and she has pulled away from her friends.

Sally's parents are separated. Her mother lives 40 miles away. She lives with her father in the family home and sees her mother occasionally. Bob is a reasonable, even-tempered man who loves Sally and has tried to make up for the loss of her mother.

Recently Sally told her father she wanted to move out of the house and live in an apartment with friends who are 2 years older than she. Her father is frightened, angry, and confused: Sally is too young; he doesn't know these friends; she has no money; she'll end up dropping out of school—all these fears have been voiced, often in anger.

Sally can legally live on her own. She has a job that can provide most—but not all—of her living expenses. She loves her father but wants her independence. Bob has always had a good relationship with Sally. The mediator asks Sally whether she has considered options other than moving in with these friends. She replies, angrily, "I'm moving. He can't keep me there." Immediately, Bob interjects, "You can't make it without my support, and I won't help if you do this!"

Competent mediation demands more than the ability to apply skills and techniques capably; it requires an understanding of the purpose and impact of those interventions. Often a mediator focuses on the technique, strategy, or skill to be used—the *what* of mediation. Excellence in practice, however, cannot be achieved without also considering the purpose and potential value of an intervention—the *why* of mediation. Reflective practice methods give a mediator the tools to address both the *what* and the *why*. A mediator engaging in the reflective cycle might respond to the example above in the following way:

Wonder

In response to Sally's and Bob's threats, the mediator becomes curious about the parties' motivations and patterns of interaction and (internally) considers answers to questions such as: What caused this outburst? Why now? What set it off? How is each responding to the other's threat? What in their relationship might have produced this exchange? At this stage, the mediator does not form a definite explanation for the behavior but merely generates possible interpretations.

Reflect

The sense of wonder, curiosity, and interest leads a mediator to derive hypotheses by filtering the events and interactions of the mediation through the lens of beliefs (theories). Lang and Taylor (200) explain:

> Mediators are trained to listen to disputants, to observe their interactions, to develop formulations (hypotheses), and then to design a process that will constructively respond to the conflict. . . . Generating a coherent structure of meaning out of what the senses experience is a common practice. (p. 32)

The mediator might wonder whether Sally's strong statement is a means of exercising control over her life, asserting her independence, and claiming her right to make decisions for herself. Another way to understand her behavior is to see it as an attempt to overcome Bob's dominance in making decisions for her, resist his influence, and create distance—in the language of mental health professionals, *individuate*. Another possible explanation for Sally's behavior is that she is exerting leverage—namely, the power to move out—as a means of convincing Bob that she is an adult and needs her independence. Bob's behavior might be explained as an effort to use financial power to take charge of the decision making, or he may simply be reacting to the potential loss of another loved one. These are only a few of the many possible explanations for what occurred. How does the mediator then select a hypothesis to guide subsequent interventions?

Hypothesize

Beliefs form the lenses through which a mediator generates and evaluates hypotheses. Thus a mediator who believes that power is a commodity or resource held and exercised by an individual against another in order to attain goals might interpret Sally's and Bob's comments as an effort to influence or coerce one into acceding to the demands of another. Based on this view, the mediator might respond to Sally's threat to leave home (or Bob's threat to withdraw financial support) by investigating (perhaps even questioning) the seriousness of their threats.

A mediator who believes that "power is not a characteristic of a person, exercised in a vacuum, but is instead an attribute of a relationship" (Kelly, 1995, p. 87; Winslade & Monk, 2000) might consider the possibility that Sally's decision to move out of her father's home and Bob's resistance are developmentally appropriate. That hypothesis could lead the mediator to consider separate meetings with Sally and Bob in order to further investigate this possible dynamic.

The response would differ significantly if a mediator believes that "power . . . provides the motivation for collaboration and defines the range of settlement options available to the parties" (Mayer, 1987, p. 75). Responses might include acknowledging that each has power to affect the other and inviting the parties to think about how they might use their power to achieve a mutually agreeable solution to their conflict.

Experiment

The next step in the cycle of reflection is experimentation: applying an intervention based on a hypothesis and observing the parties' response. The object of experimentation is to test whether the mediator's hypothesis accurately captures the experience and perceptions of the parties (Lang & Taylor, 2000). Because the hypothesis represents a mediator's best understanding of the situation, and not a conclusion or diagnosis, experimentation is an opportunity to obtain feedback and information from the parties. With this new information, the mediator can assess the accuracy and appropriateness of the hypothesis and determine a strategy for additional interventions. The success of the experimentation aspect of reflective practice rests on the mediator's commitment to receiving *and acting upon* the parties' feedback.

Returning to the Beginning: Inclusion and Transcendence

The cycle of reflection is an ongoing process that functions like a spiral, circling around and moving upward. Information gathered from each iteration of the cycle is included in, and shapes, the next movement. A mediator uses what has been learned to generate new hypotheses and develop new experiments. The mediation unfolds in this manner, one cycle providing ideas and proposals for the next. As the mediator and the parties gain a clearer understanding of the parties' use of power through each iteration of the cycle, the mediator's and the parties' understanding of the dispute advances and deepens their awareness of the sources of, and solutions to, their conflict. They transcend what is known and explore the undiscovered aspects of the conflict more deeply; *they include the known and seek the unknown.*

CONCLUSION

This chapter set out to answer a number of questions about power and power balancing. Power is a compelling issue; in any venue its presence is provocative and its expression seems fraught with risk for parties and mediators alike. Because expressions of power are perceived as potentially perilous, a mediator's responses are too often limited to prescriptive techniques and strategies—the management and control of the application of power. Relying on these techniques and strategies, as well as frameworks that prescribe interventions, does not necessarily lead to effective practice. Instead, a mediator must look within the self to identify beliefs about power and the mediator's role in balancing power to serve as the foundation for designing and implementing strategies that appropriately respond to expressions of power. Making use of beliefs to guide practice enriches mediation practice and heightens mediator effectiveness. To achieve the connection between beliefs and action, a mediator uses the methods of reflective practice (i.e., the cycle of reflection). In this way, a mediator acts purposefully and with clarity, knowing not just whether and how to act but also *why.*

The debate that caused a tempest 20 years ago continues today. Whether mediators should balance power remains a burning issue. The discussion needs to move from a debate over strategy and technique to a thoughtful consideration of the underlying assumptions and beliefs that support various perspectives on whether and how to intervene in matters of power. Examining these assumptions and beliefs produces a more constructive conversation, creates more effective practice habits, and ultimately leads to excellence in practice.

REFERENCES

Boulding, K. E. (1989). *The three faces of power.* Newbury Park, CA: Sage.

Coulson, R. (1996). *Family mediation: Managing conflict, resolving disputes* (2nd ed.). San Francisco: Jossey-Bass.

Davis, A. M., & Salem, R. A. (1984). Dealing with power imbalances in interpersonal mediation. *Mediation Quarterly, 6,* 17–26.

Folberg, J., & Taylor, A. (1984). *Mediation: A comprehensive guide to resolving conflicts without litigation.* San Francisco: Jossey-Bass.

Haynes, J. (1988). Power balancing. In J. Folberg & A. Milne (Eds.), *Divorce mediation theory and practice* (pp. 277–296). New York: Guilford Press.

Kelly, J. B. (1995). Power imbalance in divorce and interpersonal mediation: Assessment and intervention. *Mediation Quarterly, 13*(2), 85–98.

Lang, M. D., & Taylor, A. (2000). *The making of a mediator: Developing artistry in practice.* San Francisco: Jossey-Bass.

Mayer, B. (1987). The dynamics of power in mediation and negotiation. *Mediation Quarterly, 16,* 75–86.

Mayer, B. (2000). *The dynamics of conflict resolution: A practitioner's guide.* San Francisco: Jossey-Bass.

Moore, C. W. (1996). *The mediation process: Practical strategies for resolving conflict* (2nd ed.). San Francisco: Jossey-Bass.

Neumann, D. (1992). How mediation can effectively address the male–female power imbalance in divorce. *Mediation Quarterly, 9*(3), 227–239.

Picard, C. A. (1998). *Mediating interpersonal and small group conflict.* Ottawa: Golden Dog Press.

Schön, D. A. (1983). *The reflective practitioner: How professionals think in action.* New York: Basic Books.

Schön, D. A. (1987). *Educating the reflective practitioner.* San Francisco: Jossey-Bass.

Winslade, J., & Monk, G. (2000). *Narrative mediation: A new approach to conflict resolution.* San Francisco: Jossey-Bass.

CHAPTER 11

Managing the Communication
Process in Mediation

Nina R. Meierding

Effective communication can be the cornerstone of the mediation process. It can establish a
safe environment, model respectful behavior, and empower parties to express themselves.
This chapter helps mediators to assess their own communication styles and explores communication and processing styles, strategic use of questions in mediation, listening skills,
anger, and reframing skills.

Communication is the heart and soul of the mediation process. Regardless
of profession of origin, training, personal values, or mediation style, a mediator must possess excellent communication skills and be able to effectively
assist disputing parties in communicating with one another.

Determining what constitutes effective communication, however, is a
highly subjective matter. Some divorce mediators believe that effective communication occurs when parties are able to fully express their hurt, anger,
frustrations, and other feelings to one another in a safe environment, such as
a joint mediation session. These mediators may help parties share their feelings and listen to each other, enabling a deeper understanding of the issues
and an exploration of underlying interests and needs. Communication in
this context serves as a vehicle for understanding, which may well lead to
agreement between the parties on the substantive issues in dispute. If parties
do not reach an agreement, however, they may still gain important information and insights into one another's perspectives, which will be helpful in
their future relationship.

Other mediators are very uncomfortable with significant expressions of
emotion in mediation and feel that encouraging such expression borders on

the practice of therapy. For these mediators, effective communication involves a clear articulation and organization of the many practical and legal issues at hand, such as options for child placement, property distribution, financial support, and the tax implications of divorce. Mediators who view communication in this manner may use separate sessions or frequent caucuses to discourage open conflict or expression of emotions and keep disputing parties focused on the task at hand: reaching agreement on the substantive matters.

In fact, most mediators probably fall somewhere between these examples, using a combination of strategies to allow for some expression and management of emotions while also addressing the substantive disagreements. This chapter does not advocate a particular point of view. Rather, the focus is to examine the *strategic use of communication in mediation*. Instead of viewing communication in mediation as a "one-size-fits-all" process, mediators should use their communication strategies flexibly, in response to each client's unique needs, to enhance the mediation process.

SELF-ASSESSMENT OF PERSONAL COMMUNICATION STYLE

Facilitating effective communication between parties requires that the mediator understand the relationship between her personal communication style and how it interacts with, and affects, the conflict. While self-assessment should be ongoing, it is helpful for the mediator to take stock when she first receives training and begins to practice.

Consideration of the following questions can heighten a mediator's awareness of her patterns of communication and their origin:

- How was communication about conflict handled in my family of origin? Was conflict expressed openly (either through constructive conversation or yelling and arguing), discussed outside of the presence of children, or never discussed at all?
- Were emotions openly and easily expressed? Was the expression of "positive" emotions, such as joy and love, encouraged, while expression of "negative" feelings, such as anger and hostility, discouraged?
- What was my role as a communicator within my family of origin? Was I the carrier of messages, the mediator for misunderstandings, the quiet and avoidant bystander, or the active instigator?
- How has my communication style changed as I have grown? If I have changed patterns of communicating and addressing conflict, what are the events that led to this change?
- As a mediator, how do I react when others communicate in a style that is inconsistent with my own? Do I address my own discomfort with open expressions of emotion by establishing ground rules that pro-

hibit interruptions, hostile language, profanity, etc.? If parties wish to communicate with one another in a style different from mine, how do I react?

Considering the answers to these questions helps the mediator begin to assess her own propensities and biases. For example, evaluating the origins of personal preferences for managing communication and conflict helps the mediator understand why she is uncomfortable when one of the parties bursts into tears . . . or why she instinctively feels the need to intervene when voices are raised in anger. This level of understanding can serve as a springboard for the mediator to become more knowledgeable about, and comfortable with, other communication and conflict styles, which will enhance her skill as a mediator.

COMMUNICATION AND PROCESSING STYLES

A fundamental component of communication is how information is organized and processed as it is communicated by and between parties and between the parties and the mediator. Hall (1983) describes two primary approaches to time and the processing of information. The *monochronic individual* thinks in a linear and sequential manner and is organized and focused in her approach to time. The *polychronic individual* thinks in more global terms, has a flexible concept of time and its importance, and feels comfortable processing multiple information sources and tasks at the same time.

Hall's framework is helpful to the mediator who is exploring her own primary mode of processing, as well as how she views time and the sharing of information. Questions for mediators to ask themselves include:

- Do I usually think and process in a linear, organized way? Do I tackle one subject at a time, exploring each issue before leaving that area and moving on? Do I structure my conversations in a way that "makes sense" to me? Do I like to make an agenda for a mediation that prioritizes the issues and encourages the parties to "stay on task" in order to work more effectively? Am I thinking of time as finite, that we are "wasting," "spending," or "using it" effectively?
- Do I process a lot of seemingly unrelated information at one time? Do I interweave multiple topic areas when trying to help the parties solve a problem? If we are working from an outline, am I comfortable deviating from that agenda as new issues are discovered, even if the new issues seem unrelated to the area being discussed? Do I keep all issues open for discussion, even if we have moved on to a new issue? Do I actively encourage brainstorming that is not structured? Am I comfort-

able with overlapping conversations and people speaking at the same time? Am I flexible and open with how time is utilized?

After exploring her most comfortable style of processing interactions and information, the mediator should then evaluate if this style affects how she structures conversations in the mediation, both between the parties and between herself and the parties. Questions to ask include:

- Do I automatically utilize my natural processing style, or do I attempt to ascertain what style would be most helpful to the parties? How do I respond to others who process ideas differently than I do? Do I gravitate to the party whose process is the most similar to my style? Do I send conscious or inadvertent signals to the other party that he or she needs to change his or her style, either by reinforcing the other person's compatible style or by urging the "incompatible party" to change? Am I comfortable switching processing styles, or is it difficult?
- As a focused, linear (monochronic) mediator, do I tell a polychronic party that we need to "stick to the agenda" or "finish up one topic before we move on"?
- As a more polychronic mediator, am I irritated when someone does not want to go "outside the box" or explore many areas at one time? Do I tell the monochronic party to "be more flexible" or to "brainstorm a lot of possibilities" rather than "just focusing on this one issue"? Do I encourage this person to see many possible interconnections among areas of settlement, when he or she seems to be focused on just one area?

Hall's research indicates that, although individuals certainly vary in their styles within each culture, it is nevertheless possible to characterize particular culture as monochronic or polychronic in style. For example, Hall identifies Germany as a monochronic culture and Mexico as a polychronic culture. Although different processing styles and different concepts of time may not occur in every mediation, the parties' inability to communicate may still be due to how they are processing and communicating, not to their disagreement on a substantive issue. Therefore, one of the mediator's tasks is to take note of discordant processing styles and assist the parties in communicating more effectively.

For example, if a polychronic party is discussing many issues at one time, the mediator could "linearize" the information by making columns and lists of the discussed topics on a flip chart or large sheet of paper. The mediator can add notes to each column as the party moves back and forth between different topics. The more monochronic party (who may have habitually ignored the other party's previous conversations because they were too "scattered" or "disorganized") sees the mediator compartmentalizing the information into a more organized and structured format. Rather than stopping the polychronic party midstream, thereby frustrating that party's natural style, the mediator instead formats the information in a visual system that may be far more comfortable for, and intelligible to, the monochronic party. In addition to clarifying the communication, the mediator validates both processing styles with this intervention.

The mediator may also educate the parties about different processing styles and the very real advantages of bringing both styles to the negotiating table. In all likelihood each party is thinking, "If only [he or she] would approach these issues like I do!" In actuality, having similar styles could actually work against them. For example, consider two highly monochronic parties in a mediation session. It is probable that the divorce mediation will start in a timely manner and proceed according to a prioritized agenda, and that the multiple areas of discussion will be tackled sequentially. The parties will pick a topic area, such as the disposition of the house, and analyze it thoroughly before discussing the pension plan. However, this approach may limit the opportunity for creative problem solving; the parties may have difficulty linking different areas and oppose moving from one topic to another. A typical response might be, "I don't care if the value of the pension plan is the same as the house. We're not talking about the pension plan right now! That is just confusing the issue! Let's just deal with the house first."

In contrast, if both parties are highly polychronic, the mediation session may involve a lot of creative and flexible brainstorming. Furthermore, the parties may deal more with relational issues in addition to the substantive or legal issues. However, the parties may have difficulty seeing "the trees for the forest." They may not use their time in mediation as effectively, and if their goal is to reach a settlement, they may feel frustrated at the end of the session if progress has not been made. For example, David and Pam spent much of their mediation session discussing the cause of their divorce and relationship issues. At the end of the session, David said, "I don't know what happened to all our mediation time. We really need to talk about our house. It's in foreclosure! That's what we were supposed to talk about! Now what do we do?" While their discussion was important in addressing their underlying needs and interest, they didn't focus on an immediate and pressing issue, which they had intended to discuss. Their flexible concept of time worked against them. They couldn't see the "tree" for the "forest." In this example, the mediator could assist them by asking questions, such as "This discussion seems very important to both of you. However, I just want to touch base as to where we are with our time together today. You have about 15 minutes left. Would you like to continue to discuss this area today or talk about the situation with the house, which you have indicated is somewhat urgent?"

While acknowledging that different styles can be frustrating, the mediator can underscore the benefits to each party by demonstrating how it is in their self-interest to utilize both styles. The monochronic party holds the focus, and the polychronic party may come up with a creative solution that is "outside of the box." The monochronic party may be more of a timekeeper, ensuring that the most pressing issues are discussed, whereas the polychronic person may be able to weave the issues together and craft a multidimensional solution. Therefore, it is not simply that one party must be patient, understanding, and respectful of the other party's style (emotions and behaviors that may be difficult to encourage, much less realize, if the divorce is highly adversarial), but it is in each party's own interest to have both styles available.

THE STRATEGIC USE OF QUESTIONS

Mediators are trained in the importance of asking questions. Often, the value of the open-ended question is acclaimed, whereas the closed-ended question is scorned. This, however, is an overly simplistic, nonstrategic perspective. Every type of question—whether it be open or closed, clarifying, hypothesizing, confronting, or validating—has its place in mediation. The art of asking questions is to understand the value of each type of question and to utilize each question strategically to gain the desired result.

Few would argue with the premise that the common purpose of open-ended questions is to elicit a narrative or story from the party. Such a question often becomes the vehicle for a husband or wife to express underlying needs and interests, in addition to proffering an explanation of the presenting problem. The mediator asks "how" and "what" questions in order to encourage longer answers and avoids the "why" questions that can trigger defensive reactions.

However, the specific purpose of asking open-ended questions may vary for each mediator and each mediation session. The mediator might use the open-ended question in a joint session to empower the less assertive party to express him- or herself to the other party (e.g., "Tell me about your relationship with your children. What kinds of activities do you share with them?"). The actual substantive information that is shared may be secondary to the feelings or emotions expressed by the speaker to the other party. In this way, the mediator encourages "rapport talk" (i.e., relational communication) rather than "report talk" (i.e., informational communication) (Tannen, 1984) with a goal of establishing a more honest and complete communication pattern between the parties.

Another specific purpose of the open-ended question may be to elicit the underlying interests that must be met if any agreement is to be reached. For example, the question "You have indicated that keeping the family residence is very important to you. Can you tell me more about what it represents to you?" elicited from the wife a heartfelt description of leaving her home when her parents divorced when she was 6 years old. The mediator thereby gains knowledge and flexibility in working with the parties to craft an agreement that meets these underlying needs. If the divorcing parties are hostile, the mediator may ask the question in a private caucus in order for each party to feel comfortable in revealing more information. Since the goal at this point and *for this mediator* is not necessarily facilitation of direct communication between the parties but information gathering for the mediator, the presence of the other party may be inhibiting.

THE MEDIATOR'S STYLE REFLECTED IN QUESTIONS

The manner of asking questions may also reflect the style of the mediator. A more evaluative mediator may utilize more leading or confrontational questions that reflect a reality-testing model. If the mediator is very focused and pragmatic in her approach—dealing primarily with the factual and practical issues of the divorce rather than the emotional or interest-based aspects—she is likely to ask more clarifying or closed-ended questions. She may have a specific agenda that addresses key topics (e.g., custody, child and spousal support, and property division) in a sequential manner.

A facilitative mediator, in contrast, who encourages direct conversation between the parties, may ask more open-ended questions in order to promote active listening by the parties, understanding of, and empathy for, each other's stories, creative exploration of options, and improved communication skills.

For example, while John and Jane are discussing the disposition of their house, the mediator might ask an open-ended question such as "Can you tell me about your residence—when you bought it, what loans you've taken out on it, etc.?" A short narrative usually results and tends to be relatively nonthreatening. The purpose of the question is primarily to elicit information for the mediator (and perhaps to the less knowledgeable party as well) and to establish an open-ended format of questioning. Such questioning may facilitate a dialogue that is broad in scope and in which both parties feel comfortable sharing and exchanging information.

However, if the mediator asks a very focused question—such as "Did either of you use any separate property for the down payment on your house?"—one or both parties may feel a pang of anxiety. After all, this issue may not be something that they had even thought of on their own—and now, in the form of a question, the mediator has raised *another* issue.

The mediator could ask the question in an even more focused manner, such as "Are either of you seeking any reimbursement for separate property contributions for the down payment for the house?" The implication in the question may be that a party should ask for reimbursement or should, at the very least, use this area as a negotiating "chip." A party may also feel that he or she needs to take a position or make a commitment at this point in the mediation because the mediator has asked the question in an evaluative manner.

Depending on the tone and intonation of the question, the mediator may indeed be asking a leading question that implies that the parties should, or should not, ask for reimbursement. A mediator who is primarily interested in securing an agreement that is consistent with the divorce laws of her particular state does not hesitate to ask such a question because, to her, *not* asking the question means that a party might be making an agreement without full knowledge of all the legal ramifications. A mediator who is either uncomfortable with the evaluative approach or lacks the knowledge to raise specific legal issues would feel that the question would be inappropriate and better left to the parties' independent counsel. A facilitative mediator, aware that the question may also imply an evaluation in and of itself, may steer away from this type of question.

Asking hypothetical questions as to possible solutions and outcomes may be another strategy utilized by an evaluative mediator. She might frame a hypothetical question in a manner that implies approval or validation that the proposed outcome is reasonable and fair. The following phrasing places the mediator's validation behind the question:

> "A good idea might be to sell the house—have you considered that option?"
> "I have seen this parenting plan work before, and psychologists agree—what do you think?"
> "In my experience this possibility has a good chance of working—how do you feel about it?"

This manner of delivery can directly impact the outcome of the mediation—especially if the parties respect the mediator's position and advice. If the parties see the mediator as a person of authority who is implying, directly or indirectly, a possible preferred outcome, the parties may easily be persuaded to adopt a solution that may not be custom tailored to their own situation and therefore may not be as durable. The mediator's tone and body language can transform a seemingly hypothetical question into a leading question. Leaning forward, a nod of the head, and decisive hand gestures may add an even more evaluative tenor to the proposed outcome.

This style of questioning causes great consternation among facilitative mediators, who believe that the parties, not the mediator, should be totally responsible for the outcome. The evaluative mediator, however, sees this style of questioning as an effective method to encourage a recalcitrant or difficult party to reevaluate his or her own position through a process of guided reality testing.

In contrast to the evaluative mediator, the facilitative mediator typically would provide several different hypothetical solutions, stressing that each possibility may or may not work, and that it is important for the couple to find the outcome that is right for *them*. This mediator would not give only one option or hypothetical example because of her concern that the parties would simply choose that one suggestion. This type of mediator usually has encouraged the parties to come up with their own solutions and only raises possible outcomes if the parties appear blocked in their negotiation or need assistance in expanding the possibilities. Some facilitative mediators would not ask a hypothetical question at all, preferring that *only the parties* generate potential solutions.

Mediators often use closed-ended questions (i.e., a question that requires an answer of "yes," "no," or other extremely brief response); however, the timing of doing so is a crucial factor in the question's efficacy. Even the most facilitative mediator acknowledges that if all questions were open-ended, the mediation might never end. In my experience, parties tend to respond and gravitate to the style of question that is initially asked in the mediation sessions. Therefore, if the mediator begins with an extended open-ended question format, the parties may continue with longer, more extensive responses, even when the mediator changes to more clarifying or focused question. If the mediator wishes to shift the pattern of the responses to shorter answers, she may need to strategically ask several closed-ended questions before the rhythm of answers begins to change.

Conversely, if a mediator were to start with closed-ended questions such as, "What year did you buy your house?" "How much did you pay for it?" "What is the mortgage?" the parties are more likely to respond with short, specific answers. However, when the mediator later shifts to an open-ended question to broaden the conversation, the parties may continue to respond in a brief manner simply because of the rhythm of the previous format, in which one- or two-word answers were elicited one after the other. Therefore, the mediator may need to ask a series of open-ended questions before the party shifts from short answers to more extensive responses. The mediator could also prompt the parties to amplify their response by waiting expectantly, leaning forward with interest, not immediately asking another question, or by simply saying, "I would like to hear a bit more about that. Could you continue, please?"

The style and manner of questioning, therefore, should not only be strategic as to the substantive information that is being elicited but also strategic in where and how questions are inserted in the process.

THE ART OF LISTENING

Parties in conflict often have difficulty listening fully. During a divorce, emotions are swirling, the parties are under stress, and both are often anxious and confused. The value of good listening skills at such a time cannot be underestimated. The mediation process benefits the parties by providing a safe environment in which they can listen to one another, receive validation of their interests and feelings, and experience the building of rapport and trust with the mediator. In addition, by modeling active listening to the parties, the mediator helps them develop new communication skills that may find their way into future conversations between the parties, outside the mediation process.

Parties Listening to Each Other

Divorcing parties attempt to listen to each other through multiple filters in the form of past experiences and feelings. These filters may include family histories of divorce, guilt, shame, cultural or religious norms, and previous communication patterns with the spouse. Oftentimes, a husband or wife may hear what he or she wishes to hear or what he or she fears to hear. When parties are struggling to listen to a communication through filters that are clouded or obscured with distrust, anger, or other strong emotions, it is very difficult for them to accept intended information without suspecting some underlying subtext or hidden agenda. Sometimes listening is difficult because of the messenger and not the message. In the following dialogue, for example, Erica and Bill are discussing the proposed parenting plan for their two young children when Bill raises a question:

BILL: (*to the mediator*) What happens if one of us wants to move away with the children?

ERICA: (*heatedly*) I knew that you would try to take them away! Everyone has told me that you would do this! You are trying to use them as leverage!

BILL: (*Sits in stunned silence and finally responds*) Erica, last week you told me that *you* wanted to move back to your parents in New York. I'm scared that *you* will take the children away from *me*. I have never wanted to move away with the children!

Because of her anger toward Bill, Erica did not hear what he intended; she heard what she most feared. The mediator heard a clarifying question from Bill regarding custody rights, whereas Erica heard a threat to use her "children as bargaining tools."

As CEO of a company, Ben is dynamic, persuasive, and self-confident. He is knowledgeable in finance and has spent a great deal of time working with the parties' accountant and financial planner to fashion a settlement that he believes would be fair to both him and his soon-to-be ex-wife:

BEN: (*calmly and firmly*) Julie, I've done a lot of research on this and I've made a diagram of how we should divide the property.

JULIE: (*angry and frustrated*) Stop telling me what to do! You've done that throughout our marriage! You don't have the right to decide for me anymore!

BEN: (*to the mediator*) I would like to be able to show this to Julie, but she can't hear that this is a really good idea because I'm the one telling her about it. Could I explain what my proposal is to you in a separate session, and then you can relay it to Julie?

In caucus, Ben explained the proposal to the mediator, who then relayed it to Julie in a calm manner, without implying that Julie should or should not accept it.

JULIE: (*in caucus*) Is that what he wants to do?

MEDIATOR: Yes.

JULIE: Well, that is absolutely fair. I just couldn't hear what he was saying, because I don't want him to tell me what to do! I'll review this with my lawyer, but I think it's a really good idea.

Sometimes it is just that simple. Sometimes the problem is that the messenger epitomizes the dynamics of the now-failed marriage. The party objecting is not resisting the substance of the conversation, only the means by which the information is being presented. Therefore, changing the messenger may help to remove the nonproductive filter that has prevented the party from hearing what was actually communicated.

In other situations, it may be that the listening party has his or her own agenda regardless of who presents the information. Emily may try to mind read what Robert wants, assuming that Robert has his own hidden goals. Emily may simply be projecting what she hopes Robert wants, or, if Emily is angry with Robert, she may project that he is simply trying to deny her what *she* wants.

While parties are apparently listening to each other, they may also be planning their own response or rebuttal and therefore listening only in a peripheral way. Or they may have a prepackaged statement that they intend to make regardless of what the other person is saying.

There are several techniques to assess how the parties are listening to each other. A common strategy is to ask the listening party to summarize or paraphrase what the first party has just said. This strategy opens the door for corrective feedback; however, if not used carefully, it can feel somewhat parental and parties may feel that they are being quizzed by the mediator to see if they were really paying attention. Another technique is to ask the listening party to identify a particular portion of the speaker's message. For example:

"Chris, what was the most important part for you in what you heard Anne say?" or "Ryan, what are the areas of agreement that you heard in Sarah's summary?" or "Caitlin, what new information did you hear Robert share just now that might move us closer to agreement?" Notice that although these questions seem to address the listener's self-interest (i.e., "What was important to *you*?"), they are also a way for the mediator to assess how the listener may be hearing the messages and to let the parties know that they will be asked about what the other person has said, in a nonparental way.

Parties Listening to the Mediator

The listening filters function in all directions, including to and from the mediator for each party, not just between the husband and wife. One party may hear the mediator's words as nonjudgmental information; the other party may hear the same words and assume that the mediator has stated what the outcome should be. Factors that may impact the parties' filters as they listen to the mediator include:

- *Perception:* Do they see the mediator as a person of power or as an equal assisting them with the conflict?
- *Evaluation:* Do they see the mediator as experienced and knowledgeable, and, if so, is that affirming or threatening to them?
- *Projection:* Do they hold gender, age, racial, or cultural stereotypes and presume that the mediator's statements reflect those stereotypes?

The mediator cannot assume that what she has said is what the parties have heard. Therefore, it is important to ascertain and then acknowledge that what the parties heard is what the mediator intended for them to hear. By assisting the parties in giving feedback to the mediator, encouraging them to feel comfortable when they correct or rephrase the mediator's summaries, and closely watching the body language of the parties as they listen to her, the mediator can assess how her communication is being received.

The Mediator as Listener

Mediators also need to assess how they are listening to the parties. The benefits of active listening by the mediator cannot be underestimated; the mediator must listen beyond the parties' words to discover the unstated and to search for indications of their underlying interests, needs, and motivations.

Mediators who were previously trained as attorneys may fall into the trap of listening in an evaluative manner; for example, what are the facts, what are the inconsistencies, how can I respond to or counter that position? They are used to listening in order to *debate* rather than to *connect*. They may pass over the interest-based responses in order to catch the factual issues and information. A good trial attorney has been trained to listen to what is relevant, respond quickly, think on her feet, and offer an effective rebuttal. The attorney as mediator, therefore, may fall into the trap of planning how she is going to respond while the party is speaking. Although this manner of listening is valuable in an attorney's law practice, it is limiting to a mediator because she is listening only partly. Active listening requires a suspension of judgment and evaluation, an openness to listen to any communication without any predetermined notions. Only in this way can the mediator fully understand what the party is expressing. This ability to listen in the moment, although difficult, is extraordinarily powerful—for the parties as well as the mediator.

Mediators previously trained as therapists may be too deeply focused on mining the underlying needs. Trained to listen for unexpressed motivations or needs, with the goal of long-term behavioral change, such mediators may miss negotiation moves in their search for a comprehensive psychological understanding of the parties' personalities and conflicts. Whereas mediators previously trained as lawyers often feel more comfortable with the negotiation aspect of the mediation process, mediators trained as therapists often feel more comfortable with the communication aspect. Since negotiation and communication are interwoven throughout the mediation process, it is imperative that the mediator listen for both levels of messages.

Silence

The ability to listen also involves the ability to stay silent. Silence is not easy to manage for many negotiators. Indeed, the typical North American is used to quick responses. When a person does not respond to an offer in an expedient manner, the silence is assumed to be a tactic to make the other party uncomfortable. The "tactic" may work if the waiting party gets frustrated and begins to negotiate against him- or herself ("Well, okay, I guess that offer for the house buyout was a bit low, so how about if I add another $5,000?"), rather than wait for what they perceive is a delayed response.

However, this negative response to silence may be culturally bound. For instance, in mediation training, a member of the Lakota Sioux tribe stated that rapid responses to offers were seen as a sign of disrespect, that the listener had already made up his or her mind before the offer was presented. A truly respectful negotiation, therefore, would involve periods of silence wherein each party quietly listened and thought about the proposals on the table.

In divorce mediation, the mediator must learn that her ability to accept silence at the table is very powerful. If the mediator is uncomfortable with silence and begins to interject (e.g., "Well, Julie, how do you feel about that offer?" or "David, you seem quiet; perhaps that number was a bit high for you"), the mediator could unwittingly influence the outcome simply by inserting herself into the silence. A mediator should remember that she is not being paid for the number of words that are spoken at the mediation table—it is the art and science of *how and when words are used* that are important.

A mediator can model listening skills for the parties as well as demonstrate to them that she is actually listening to what they are saying. Verbal and nonverbal/gestural forms of affirmation can be very effective. For example, a murmur or empathetic "I see" can validate to the party that he or she is being heard. A slight tilt or nod of the head sends a similar signal. Be aware, though, that repeated nodding or rapid nodding can be construed as agreement (in Arab cultures, for example, the tilt of the head to the side means "yes") or as a prompting to move along more quickly. Leaning forward, eye contact levels appropriate to cultures, and open-hand gestures can also be effective. In addition, removing *all* distractions (e.g., cell phones, beepers, interruptions from support personnel, unless absolutely necessary) conveys that the mediator's focus is squarely on the parties.

By asking clarifying questions, providing feedback, and paraphrasing what she has heard, the mediator sends a message to the party that she is actively involved in tracking the conversation and is interested in gleaning more information. In short, the mediator is listening, with intention and focus, to what the parties are saying.

Empathy versus Sympathy

The mediator must be conscious of listening with empathy rather than listening with sympathy. *Empathy* communicates to the parties that they have come to a safe place where they will be accepted and listened to in a time of pain, frustration, and anger, and that the mediator understands their concerns. *Sympathy* may convey a sense of connectedness through the mediator's personal feelings of sadness about what she is being told. Such expressions may be easily misconstrued by a party as agreement with that party. Thus conveying sympathy can create the appearance of bias and partiality and could result in an attempt by one party to join with the mediator against the other party. This position is not healthy for the parties or the mediator. The difference between "I understand" and "I agree" is crucial. Therefore, the mediator must retain a balanced mode of response between the parties by offering empathic statements that validate each party's concerns and needs. This balance will create a feeling of acceptance and safety for both parties.

In summary, the art of listening involves the skills of knowing

- When to ask questions
- When to interrupt
- When to encourage

- When to acknowledge and validate
- When to structure or control the conversation
- When to let it flow with minimal involvement by the mediator
- When to be silent

NEGOTIATING IN THE CONTEXT OF ANGER

Parties in a divorce proceeding are frequently very angry. Anger is an extremely valuable emotion if used constructively in mediation; it can indicate (1) the depth of a party's emotions, (2) the strength of a party's convictions, or (3) even the ability or inability to effectively communicate his or her needs and wants. If the opportunity to express anger in mediation is denied or forestalled by the mediator, parties may still reach an agreement on their issues, but they may miss the chance to forge a truly integrative agreement that has more durability. Expressions of anger provide opportunities to move into relational issues that could impact the couple's agreement. Conversely, destructive or uncontrolled anger can be dangerous, disruptive, disempowering, and "freeze" all communication. The party who rages in a mediation session, using personally insulting or threatening language, creates a very different environment from a party who argues his or her needs passionately and forcefully from a place of conviction. Therefore, the mediator needs to assess the expression of anger in mediation on many levels.

The Mediator's Comfort Level with Anger

- What is my own level of comfort with the expression of anger by myself or by others?
- How do I respond when other people get angry?

If a mediator is unused to dealing with anger, she may feel personally uncomfortable when confronted with raised voices, an occasional expletive, or expressions of pent-up frustration. Mediators who are uncomfortable with anger often do not project a sense of self-assuredness when anger is openly expressed at the mediation table. They may immediately request a time-out, delay, or caucus to calm things down before continuing. If the mediator does not project a sense of calmness and control, however, the recipient of the anger may feel additional concern or fear and the angry party may assume that he or she has power or control over the process through the use of this anger. Both parties may see this lack of comfort by the mediator as a limitation; instead of competently managing it, the mediator appears to be sidestepping it in any way possible. This (mis)perception can derail an otherwise productive session. To be truly effective, divorce mediators must be comfortable with constructive expressions of anger by the parties and be able to utilize the anger to assist the party in expressing how strongly he or she feels about particular issues.

The Parties' Comfort Level with Anger

- What are the parties' levels of comfort with anger?
- Is only one party expressing anger, or is there a heated interaction?
- How does the receiving party respond?
- Is the anger constructive (i.e., does it move the parties forward in their communication) or destructive (i.e., does it create a nonproductive climate)?

It is important for mediators to have an ability to recognize and deal with the ways in which the parties respond to anger. It is helpful to observe if there are volleys of anger or if only one party is expressing it. If both parties seem to be comfortable with the angry exchange, then the mediator may decide not to intervene; however, if the anger is creating a nonproductive climate, the mediator can use a variety of techniques to change the mood and tone of the parties' exchanges.

Some parties are used to a pattern of assertive, even aggressive, communication with each other and feel stifled or frustrated if they are told they cannot interrupt each other or express their needs in strong terms. These are people who routinely engage in "ritual opposition" (Tannen, 1984). Demonstrative styles of speech may also be culturally appropriate for the couple and may include raised voices, hand gestures, exclamations, and aggressive body language.

Giorgio and Christina were a divorcing couple whose communication style was mutually loud, aggressive, interruptive, and accompanied by dramatic physical gestures. After several minutes of raised voices and forceful statements by the parties, the mediator decided to caucus to assess whether the communication style and pattern were constructive or whether either party was feeling intimidated:

MEDIATOR: Christina, how do you feel this session is progressing?

CHRISTINA: I can't believe this! He is finally listening to me! You [mediator] are a miracle worker! He is being so respectful! Thank you!

Somewhat surprised, the mediator then held a brief caucus with Giorgio.

GIORGIO: Without you in the room, she would be out of control! She is so relaxed and finally listening instead of just yelling! I think it is because we both feel so safe here.

Four sessions later, without a drop in the volume of their communication, the couple reached a mutually satisfactory agreement and were effusive in their enthusiasm about how well the process had worked for them. The parties had both expressed a comfort level with a boisterous, dynamic, in-your-face style of negotiating. Had the mediator indicated that this type of communication was inappropriate and violated some set of mediational guidelines, the parties may not have moved forward and accomplished their goals. Furthermore, the parties indicated that they had gained greater respect for each other and improved their relationship.

However, many divorcing couples do not share similar comfort levels in their tolerance for either expressing or receiving anger. This disparity can lead to a potentially difficult situation for a mediator. If a party's anger is stifled at the mediation, acting out by that party may likely occur as soon as the parties leave the session. The anger has simply continued to simmer and possibly increase. On the other hand, the receiving party should not be subjected to a mediation environment that is hostile, accusatory, scary, or unsafe.

The mediator needs to assess the comfort level of both parties. Is the body language of the receiving party indicating discomfort by inward or turned-away posture? Is his or her gaze cast downward, allowing minimal or no eye contact with the other party? Is there reticence to speak? (Some of these types of behavior may even indicate the presence of domestic violence, a topic that is beyond the scope of this chapter but is addressed in Milne, Chapter 14, this volume.) The mediator should consult with either party in caucus if she suspects any discomfort whatsoever in either party.

If one party is uncomfortable with anger, the most dramatic strategy is to separate the parties for their mediation sessions so that the anger is not expressed openly. However, although separating the parties can provide a temporary reduction in the tension level, it is also possible, as just noted, that the unaddressed anger will flare up again—often as soon as the parties leave the mediation setting. Conversely, the mediator should not be too invested in pressuring the parties to participate in joint sessions in order to express their feelings to each other, if such sessions would be too difficult for one of the parties.

Another strategy is to coach the angry party, in a caucus, on how to express his or her anger in a productive way to the other party. This can be an extremely effective technique *if* the angry party is able to absorb and process the information and exert some control over the expression of his or her anger. Possible ways of wording an intervention include the following:

"When you are angry, do you think that [name of spouse] really hears what you are saying, or do you think [he or she] is focused on the anger?"

"Your anger indicates that you feel very strongly about this issue. How could you tell [name of spouse] how important this matter is to you in a manner in which [he or she] can hear you?"

"If you are angry throughout the negotiation today, how do you think [name of spouse] will know what part of the negotiation is really important to you?"

"Do you think that [name of spouse] will think you are angry at the whole situation and that this particular issue is not more important than any other?"

"If [name of spouse] is feeling attacked, do you think [he or she] will be able to listen to you with an open mind, or will [he or she] feel defensive and self-protective in response to your anger?"

"What is your goal in expressing your anger to [name of spouse]?"

"How can you express your anger in a way that encourages [name of spouse] to hear your point of view?"

If the party is able to articulate what is causing the anger and pinpoint the important areas, he or she may then wish to practice with the mediator how to express his or her convictions strongly, yet without alienating the other party. The mediator can assist the angry party in expressing him- or herself in a way that can be received. Because the mediator is asking the angry party to do something in his or her own self-interest (i.e., create an environment in which the other party feels safe enough to listen fully to his or her needs), he or she may be more willing to make adaptations than if the mediator asked the party to "be respectful" of the other party. Sometimes divorcing parties do not want to be told that they need to be respectful or even civil, especially if they have suffered a romantic wound or betrayal of love. Changing their behavior because it is in their self-interest to do so, however, usually provides more motivation.

THE USE AND MISUSE OF REFRAMING EMOTIONAL STATEMENTS

The art of reframing communication and position is a vital component of the mediator's toolbox. The mediator may reframe a party's words in order to take personal, attacking comments and transform them into less threatening, nonlabeling language. This approach usually calms the parties and moves them from "you" statements to "I" statements that focus on the problem (rather than the people). A mediator can reframe a party's offer in neutral language so that it can be more easily heard by the spouse and, at the same time, model respect and validation to both parties.

Reframing the parties' words can be an effective tool of deescalation—or it can seem patronizing. By reducing the hostile language to more neutral or comfortable terminology, the mediator is often simultaneously reducing the intensity behind the language. An angry party may feel that the mediator is taking sides, dismissing the passion or anger behind the statement, or invalidating the seriousness of the situation. The new language may feel *neutered* rather than *neutral!* Furthermore, ineffective reframing may depersonalize the feelings so that the message is lost in the globalization of the statement. Effective reframing, in contrast, reflects the parties' needs. In the following brief exchange, the mediator's effort to reduce or smooth over the anger fails completely:

JANET: Jack, you are a lying jerk! You've cheated on me and betrayed our children! You're *no good!* I wish you were *dead!*

MEDIATOR: (*hoping to diffuse the situation, states calmly*) It appears that there is an issue of lack of trust. This is very common in divorce.

JANET: (*Displays open-mouthed astonishment, as she feels that the mediator has reduced her pain and anger to a dispassionate, global, and impersonal statement regarding issues!*)

Although the mediator obviously should not match Janet's intensity in both language and tone, the mediator's complete lack of intensity, combined with the use of impersonal language, devalue Janet's emotions and can appear patronizing and objectifying. The mediator could make a similar statement regarding trust, but lean forward and intensify her voice when doing so. Or the mediator could use slightly stronger words (e.g., "I can hear a strong sense of betrayal and anger that has been created by actions that have occurred in your marriage") but keep her tone calm. The goal of reframing is to retain the importance of the feelings behind the message while detoxifying the words, so that the receiving party can hear them in a nondefensive way.

SPEAKING TO BE UNDERSTOOD: THE CONSEQUENCES OF THERAPIST-SPEAK/LAWYER-SPEAK/MEDIATOR-SPEAK

Many divorce mediators come from the legal or mental health professions. In either case, it is all too easy to let the jargon of their former professions seep into their conversations in mediation. Mediators with legal training may use phrases such as "I would like each of you to state your position," "Each of you will have a chance to respond to the other's argument," and "Please state the facts as you believe them to be." Words such as *position, argument,* and *facts* all convey a more legalistic format for the mediation and consequently set a more adversarial tone. Mediators previously trained as therapists might say, "Please share your feelings about what Chris has said," or "I hear you saying that you have some deeper anxieties with regard to the proposed parenting plan." Words such as *share, deeper, feelings,* and *anxieties* reflect a more therapeutic approach.

Mediators may attempt to remove lawyer-speak and therapist-speak from their language by substituting other "professional" language. A young mediation intern said to a couple, "My job is to facilitate the interface between the two of you." Bewildered, the client responded, "Does that mean you'll help us talk to each other?"

The mediator's goal is to speak conversationally in a manner that is appropriate to the age, background, and culture of the parties. Certain ages and cultures may speak more formally to each other; others may be more relaxed. Mediators who see children as part of their divorce mediation practice use language with them that is obviously quite different from the words used with their parents. The mediator should be aware of the context of the communication and adapt herself accordingly.

The mediator must realize that word choice sends its own message. Using a therapeutic model with two highly competitive lawyers in a highly competitive negotiation may cause raised eyebrows and a slight smirk from at least one, if not both. Using structured, legalese language for two unrepresented parties who are suspicious of lawyers can create anxiety and a fear that they have not avoided the adversarial system after all. The mediator should meet with clients at their level, mirroring the style of speech that the clients use.

One straightforward method of matching speech patterns and creating rapport is to mirror the sensory modality that is being used by the client in his or her speech (Elgin, 1987). For example, if the client says, "It *looks* like one of those options might work," the mediator could respond, "Let's *see* what each option would look like." If the client says, "It *feels* like one of those options might work," the mediator could respond, "Let's *touch* base with each of those options." Although very subtle and probably not consciously noticed by the client, mirroring sensory modalities creates a rapport with the client (Elgin, 1987).

IT'S NOT JUST WHAT YOU SAY, IT'S HOW YOU SAY IT

Mediators should be aware that only 7% of what they communicate is transmitted through spoken words. Intonation, inflection, and stressing of words—how the voice is used—accounts for 38%, and a full 55% is nonverbally or visually communicated (Mehrabian, 1981). Clearly, it is crucial that mediators use all three dimensions effectively in order to fully communicate with the parties. The effective use includes, of course, the ability to *receive* the messages that are being sent through word, intonation, and body language.

Responding to all these levels validates the parties and assures them that the mediator is fully attending to them. Missing the cues or sending the wrong message can confuse or dismay parties who are already distraught.

The Voice

Mediators are often not aware of their own voices or speech style: the tone, speed, tension, resonance, and pitch of their voices, and their use of qualifiers, pauses, emphases, or intensity in the style of their speech. For learning purposes, mediators should tape their voices in conversation (rather than simply listening to themselves reading a speech or delivering a brief message on an answering machine). Answering the following questions can be helpful in analyzing the strengths and weaknesses of style and delivery:

- Is my voice calm? Am I breathing in a relaxed way? What is the overall speed and tone of my voice?
- Do I use direct language, or do I cushion my thoughts with the use of qualifiers such as *maybe, might, perhaps,* and *possibly?* Do I insert unnecessary and superfluous words or sounds such as *well, okay, you know, ummm, ah?*
- Do I interrupt or overlap other speakers? Can others hear emotions in my voice? Can they tell when I am smiling, insistent, assured, frustrated, or tense?

It is important to analyze if a party in conflict would feel comfortable and safe listening to the mediator's voice. The voice should convey calmness and confidence, and it should signal the mediator's thoughts through changes in volume, pacing, and pauses.

The Body

It is extremely important that the mediator present an assured, competent, and secure persona to the parties. The use of body language as a means of establishing rapport, gaining focus and attention, and providing validation is a key factor in effective communication. Body posture can convey welcome, interest, and empathy—or, in contrast, disinterest, aloofness, and distance. Even the spacing around the table in the office may convey an environment that either adds to or detracts from parties' level of comfort—for example, a close, problem-solving, more intimate approach (e.g., a small round table) or a more formal, issue-focused, structured approach (e.g., a conference table).

Hand gestures and eye contact are also essential elements of establishing rapport and providing focus. The following questions are useful for purposes of self-evaluation:

- Are my hands and arms relaxed and away from my face? Do I use my hands in conversation? For example, if I interrupt, do I use hand gestures, and if so, is it a sharp gesture with my palm outstretched, indicating *halt* (which has an aggressive feeling to it), or is the palm down and slightly bending, indicating "wait a minute, please"?
- When I am making a point, do I use props, such as holding a pencil, which can be distracting and aggressive?
- If I am establishing eye contact with one party, what am I doing to keep the other party connected to the process? Do I slightly shift my body posture toward the listening party while my eye contact stays with the speaking party? Is my eye contact culturally appropriate and affirming to both parties?
- Am I mirroring parties' body language to convey empathy and connectedness?

Communication swirls around the mediation table in the words that are used, the silences that are held, the style, tone, and intonation of the voice, and the clues sent via the physical mannerisms. The mediator should be conscious and strategic in her choice of words, delivery, and nonverbal communication. Above all, the mediator should be aware that the lack of congruence between these different dimensions can cause confusion and dismay for the listening party. For example, if the mediator states, "That is a great idea, Erica," but her arms are folded across her chest (perhaps conveying a lack of acceptance and/or a closing off) or her eyebrows are furrowed, Erica may feel even more unsure than before the meeting, from the mediator's conflicting signals. The mediator should seek congruence among all dimensions of her communication.

CONCLUSION

Effective communication is the key to unlocking the parties' interests, establishing a safe environment, modeling respectful behavior, and empowering the parties to express themselves so that they can be truly heard. Without effective communication between the parties and between the mediator and the parties, the durability of a settlement agreement (if there *is* one at all) is questionable. Perhaps more than any other area of mediation, the divorce mediator must be cognizant of the many underlying interests and concerns that can lead either to a long-term resolution or simply a legal marital settlement agreement that does not end the conflict.

Not only do the parties need to feel satisfied with the substantive outcome of their agreement, they need to feel some sense of satisfaction with the process that led to the agreement. If Mary feels that her expressions of emotion were overly restricted and not fully heard; if Paul feels that the practical and legal issues were discussed only in a global, impersonal way; or if both feel unsafe in expressing their needs, then the victory of the written divorce agreement is likely to ring hollow. In contrast, if both parties felt that they were heard and had experienced empathy from the mediator and/or the other party, then even if each did not "win" a particular issue, they both will leave the mediation process knowing that their position was respectfully discussed. In addition the dialogue felt safe and nonjudgmental, the pacing of the conversations was thoughtful and thorough, not rushed and perfunctory, and they experienced a sense of closure to their divorce process. These multilayered benefits can then lead them to move beyond the negotiation positions as they continue to heal.

REFERENCES

Elgin, S. H. (1987). *The last word on the gentle art of verbal self-defense.* New York: Prentice Hall.

Hall, E. T. (1983). *The dance of life: The other dimension of life.* New York: Doubleday.

Mehrabian, A. (1981). *Silent messages: Implicit communication of emotions and attitudes* (2nd ed.). Belmont, CA: Wadsworth.

Tannen, D. (1984). *Talking from 9 to 5: Women and men in the workplace–language, sex and power.* New York: Avon.

CHAPTER 12

Strategies for Managing Impasses

ROBERT D. BENJAMIN

Impasse analysis and management focus on exploring why the parties have reached an impasse and the techniques a mediator can use to *avoid* reaching an impasse. Robert D. Benjamin metaphorically demonstrates how managing impasse is similar to running the rapids of a river—there is no pretense that one is going to control the river (impasse), but one must instead develop a strategy to navigate the turbulence. This chapter confronts the inevitability of impasse and proposes methods a mediator can use to "read" the impasse and effectively negotiate a way through it.

The emergence of an impasse in mediation can be elusive and unexpected. It can crop up "out of nowhere" as a serious threat to settlement in a seemingly simple and uncomplicated matter. Even an expected impasse is no less disconcerting. This chapter offers a topographical "map" of the conflict terrain in which an impasse is likely to occur. This map offers both a view of the "big picture"–the theoretical frame–and a close-in practice focus. The application of the theory is essential for devising management strategies and effective techniques and skills. The map traces the systemic dimensions of the impasse experience and charts the dynamic interplay between the mediator's mindset and approach and the participants' issues, beliefs, and behaviors. Traditionally, impasse analysis and management have been limited to a focus on the parties, thereby overlooking or disregarding the mediator's contribution. This limited focus was based, in part, on an unwarranted assumption that the third-party role as a mere "objective" and "neutral" bystander is minimal.

Viewing the "big picture" is critical to avoid the pitfall of myopically limiting the view of impasse management to nothing more than the accumulation of an arsenal of "fix-it" techniques—the "here's what I always do" syndrome, ostensibly cured by the "10 tips to avoid an impasse." This kind of thinking assumes that all impasses are alike. Beyond just throwing techniques at an impasse, a theoretical frame offers a means for the reflective analysis and customized response that can address the unique aspects of a particular impasse.

Thus the chapter begins with a consideration of the potential for misdirection in how the term *impasse* is conventionally understood and applied. Greater precision in what is meant by the term in a mediation context can limit the risk of misdirection, as can ferreting out the conventional wisdom that tends to view the condition of impasse in a mostly negative light. The chapter then presents the most salient premises of field theory and systems theory and discusses their utility. Understanding the varieties of impasse also requires some examination of the underlying beliefs about the sources of conflict; the mediator's assumptions about the reasons for conflict, in general, often shape how he or she approaches and deals with a perceived impasse. Finally, the chapter provides an overview of specific techniques and skills useful in implementing an impasse management strategy and considers the nature of impasse in any dispute context, and specifically in the family and divorce context.

An impasse is a force of nature, inherently uncontrollable and unpredictable. However, the impasse condition is susceptible to some measure of effective management *if* it is "read" reasonably well and a thoughtful strategy is in place to guide the competent application of technique and skills. Indeed, managing an impasse in a negotiation can be compared to "running" the rapids of a wild river. Most people can appreciate the metaphor, whether or not they have ever gone white-water rafting. There can be no pretense of controlling the river, but I can "read" the rapids and approach the turbulence with a studied strategy and technique that lessens the risk of being dumped. Sometimes, as in conflict management, the rafter is forced to engage one obstacle—for example, a boulder in the middle of the river—to avoid a more serious risk—a sinkhole that can swallow raft and person whole. The best river runners know that a good measure of their success starts with the clear recognition that they cannot fight the river and expect to win; they can only negotiate the unique variables of the river's flow and thereby manage the energy that is all around them. Likewise, mediators need to think about their understanding of impasse to make sure they see part of the river's flow to be encountered and negotiated.

DEFINING IMPASSE: BETWEEN RESISTANCE TO NEGOTIATION AND FLAT-OUT DEADLOCK

The popular or colloquial use of the term *impasse* describes the difficult situations in a negotiation that fall somewhere between being stuck and total collapse. For some, the word carries the more final and judgmental meaning of the word *deadlock*, conveying the determination that further negotiation is futile or inappropriate (Yarn, 1999). The term *impasse* is often used loosely and imprecisely. The distinction between the level of antagonism realistically expected in most disputes and the heightened level of difficulty that characterizes an impasse can be slight. While most disputes are manageable and require little more than a touch of organization and a supportive nudge from a mediator, the risk of an impasse remains, be it striking a sensitive nerve in one or both parties or tripping over an unstated issue. Still other conflicts are more difficult and intractable from the start because the issues are more complex or carry a special gravity, the surrounding politics are especially intrusive, the timing is off, or parties are not prepared or disposed to negotiate. A persistent contributing factor to the risk of impasse is the culturally ingrained resistance to negotiation as a mode of conflict management. In Western "techno-rational" cultures in which there is a strong inclination to seek the truth and the "right" answer, negotiation and mediation are often perceived to be weak, paltry, and sometimes even immoral actions because the truth is necessarily minimized and displaced from the center of focus (Berlin, 1991; Benjamin, 1998a, 1999c).

It is important to parse out more precisely what is meant by impasse because the offhand use of the term may itself play a role in defining the situation and making it more difficult. In some instances, for example, the perceived impasse may have less to do with the participants and more to do with the mediator. His or her style may grate on, or be ill-suited to dealing with, the particular parties' personalities. Beyond personalities, the term impasse may more aptly describe the mediator's self-perception of his or her relative ability to counter the parties' resistance and move toward agreement than an intrinsic condition of the participants' dispute (J. Melamed, personal communication, 2002). In short, the mediator is stuck, or the impasse may even be mediator induced.

From whatever source—the participants or the mediator—an impasse defines the point when the negotiations have stalled and, whatever the original reasons for the conflict, there is now an added complication with the intensification of the stress and frustration level in all concerned. This much is clear: While many disputes are little more than differences of opinion or questions of interpretation over generally agreed-upon principles, an impasse describes a heightened level of difficulty; it is the point at which the collision between an irresistible force and an immovable object appears most shrill and glaring. And, while impasses occur in all dispute contexts, they are perhaps more overtly on display in family and divorce matters where, for one or more of the participants, the principle of being right is under constant attack by the pragmatic necessity for settlement. This is fertile terrain for impasses of all varieties to swell up, sometimes out of nowhere.

In addition to the perceptual distortions the term impasse can evoke, the mere idea of an impasse carries a decidedly negative tone that casts an emotional pall over the negotiation process. An impasse is either something to be avoided at all costs or to overcome as speedily as possible. The presence of an impasse, at the very least, implies the failure of the mediator to lead the parties to agreement. Just the fear of an impasse can sometimes incite its onset. Impasse, however, might be viewed more constructively, if not more positively. The occurrence of an impasse may, in fact, be useful. An impasse ought to be viewed less as an aberration and more as a normal and expected development in the progression of many disputes. An impasse is best thought of as a signal of the participants' natural resistance to change, not as an implacable obstacle, and requiring only a shift in thinking. While the mediator would still do well to strategically plan how to sidestep unnecessary conflicts and foreseeable impasses, creating strategies that can redirect the energy of impasses that will invariably arise may be more important. An analogy: A successful interior designer who regularly endures the difficulties and vagaries of clients, engineers, architects, and craftsman once offered a perspective that is apropos of a mediator in the middle of a complex matter, constantly faced with the appearance of impasses, in varying guises, that threaten agreement: "There are no mistakes, only design revisions" (R. Robertson, personal communication, 2002).

IMPASSE AS A CHAOTIC EVENT

Conflicts occur in the context of systems—families, organizations, cultures, or nations. Those systems are, by definition, nonlinear, complex, and dynamic rather than simple, predictable, mechanistic "cause-and-effect" structures. The experience of an impasse is a chaotic event, the source and appearance of which can be sudden and unexplained. As noted, the impasse can emerge at the beginning, middle, or when the end is in sight and all involved least expect to "hit a wall." While some are understandable and not unexpected, others defy explanation and cannot be traced to particular factors or to the relationships between them. The system is driven by the behavior of actors who are moved by their own incentives, goals, and calculations, with little predictability (Perrow, 1984). People who appear to be reasonable and committed to the resolution of a dispute can suddenly turn intransigent and unyielding. They just close down and draw the proverbial line in the sand—"I will go this far and no further!" Many occurrences of impasses in negotiations bear resemblance to other human as well as nonhuman, nonlinear, dynamic phenomena that are best described by chaos theory. Not unlike a traffic jam, a sudden thunderstorm, stock market fluctuation, or heart attack, they are seemingly unpredictable, random events that nonetheless have an order all their own (Gleick, 1987; Benjamin, 2000a).

Although the notion that the cause or occurrence of an impasse can be precisely predicted and controlled is naïve, there is still clear benefit to planning and preparation. As with any storm, a timely, flexible, and strategic response can make a critical difference in the long-term outcomes. An impasse unattended and unmanaged can quickly—and unnecessarily—close down the negotiation process entirely. When many unresolved impasses accumulate and calcify over time, the conflict comes to be viewed as protracted and intractable, spinning off flurries of derivative disputes. This is the "Who did what to whom?" stuff, almost impossible to unravel or move beyond, which can eclipse the primary issues and appear every bit as intense and destructive (Coleman, 2000a). Negotiating an impasse is critical because it often defines an edge, in both the participants' and the mediator's minds, on which the negotiation process either moves ahead or collapses.

THE MEDIATOR PREPARES

Impasse is the point at which mediation becomes most interesting and creative, as much or more art than science. It is also where the "mediator presence" can make an apparent difference. Managing an impasse has as much to do with how the mediator prepares intellectually, emotionally, and physically as it does with intervention skills and techniques.

A good working theory and understanding of the sources of conflict and varieties of impasse are essential but not sufficient. A mediator cannot *reason* his or her way out of an impasse. Nothing exposes the limits of a prescriptive, formulaic, by-the-book approach, or the overly orthodox adherence to a particular ideological style, faster than an impasse. An impasse is often a turning point in the conflict drama; the mediator must be ready and able to improvise, deviate from the prescribed, and often rely on sheer wit and crazy wisdom (Benjamin, 2001a, 2001b).

Left unaddressed, an impasse can quickly breed skepticism of the whole mediation process, dampen participants' belief in the potential for an agreement, and undermine their confidence in the mediator's ability. Although reaching an agreement is not the sole purpose of mediation, for many people it is a test of sorts. Especially in family conflicts, many people begin in a pessimistic state about their ability to negotiate difficulties, given their past track record. Ironically, mediation offers parties the prospect of more success in managing issues in divorce or other difficult matters than they may have had in their marriage. But for the same reasons, when an impasse does crop up, it is all the more threatening—it carries symbolic potency as a reminder of the risk of failure. To effectively manage an impasse, the mediator must demonstrate that the process offers a viable and realistic opportunity to moderate what the parties have previously considered their hopeless and futile personal discussions.

All of this—the intellectual and emotional energy to engage an impasse—requires physical stamina. Managing impasses requires the integration of intuitive, tacit knowing and gut instinct together with a studied, analytical understanding of the dynamics of conflict. The sequence of response can be organized into three levels: (1) the mediator's internal response of centering; (2) the stabilization of the mediation process; and (3) the analysis, intervention, and constructive realignment of the negotiation.

Level 1: The Mediator's Response—Centering

• *Awareness.* The mediator learns to become aware of his or her own physical sensations often associated with the stress of impasse. Before becoming mentally aware of an impasse brewing, many people notice their neck muscles tighten or a "knot in their stomach." These somatic responses are worth noting—they are the "feeling of what is" (Damasio, 1994).

• *Centering.* First, *do nothing.* The stress, frustration, and negative energy given off during an impasse can quickly envelope the mediator as well as the participants. When sensing that the parties are going around in circles or when every suggestion—theirs or the mediator's—is met with "Yes, but . . ." and an invitation for them to offer an alternative suggestion draws a blank look, the mediator can take a deep breath, relax, center him- or herself, and do nothing. The mediator particularly resists the temptation to move forward in the chair and try even harder to solve the parties' problems.

Level 2: Stabilizing the Mediation Process

• *Articulate the impasse.* Use a reflective question to probe, such as "My sense is that we continue to be tripped up by this issue of the presence of other people, with whom either of you may be involved, being around your children—is that accurate?"

• *Normalize the impasse.* Seldom is an impasse a crisis in the real sense of the term; there is no external and overwhelming threat of physical harm, like a tornado or bomb explosion. The crisis is perceptual in nature; the source of the confusion and the feeling of lack of control is internal. The mediator who takes the stance of "Every suggestion I have made over the last three sessions has been rejected—this mediation is not going to work" is likely to end up terminating many of his or her clients. In contrast, intervening with a normalizing comment to the effect that "This is not uncommon" is almost always helpful in terms of reducing the immediate tension (Benjamin, 2000d) and reminding all involved that their current experience is *normal*, not critical.

Level 3: Analysis and Intervention

• *Conduct a quick mediator self-analysis.* Running down a mental checklist can be immensely helpful for the mediator facing an impasse. Am I clearly hearing the parties concerns? Have I missed any clues about the source of resistance? How might I have contributed to this impasse? Have I missed a key step in the structure by trying to move too quickly toward solutions? Have I pushed too hard to close the deal too soon? Have I used an approach that is not compatible with the situation or the parties?

• *Map and assess the nature of the impasse.* Field theory and systems theory (both discussed below) offer a useful organizing frame within which to form and test working hypotheses about the nature of the impasse. The resistance to the negotiation process may originate in other people or circumstances, either inside or outside the immediate conflict, that need to be considered. Some sticking points may be more apparent than others. This mapping helps the mediator to anticipate potential impasses and begin, early on, to strategize about how to structure the process to avoid unnecessary difficulties.

• *Implement strategy and techniques.* At this point it is time to take action and implement the strategy and techniques deemed most likely to penetrate the impasse. With each intervention, the mediator should gauge its effectiveness in managing the impasse.

THE PRACTICAL NECESSITY OF THEORY

In the middle of an impasse, when the negotiation process appears to be near collapse, abstract, theoretical musings may seem out of place. Yet that is the time when a thoughtful organizing framework is most essential in resisting the slide into a crisis mentality. How an impasse is viewed conceptually often dictates a mediator's strategic approach. Every practitioner operates by some theory, be it de facto and unwitting or by reflective and conscious design. Unexamined working assumptions tend to allow personal beliefs and feelings about conflict, idiosyncratic anecdotal experiences, and conditioned responses from other professional training to muddle the view of the impasse. The mediator's careful reflection and conscious deliberation about his or her theory of practice is always useful, but it becomes critical when dealing with the impasse (Lang & Taylor, 2000; Schön, 1983).

Effective impasse management requires a perspective that allows the mediator to assess and develop, on the spot, a working hypothesis about the resistance encountered in order to formulate a strategic response. "The practitioner," Deutch (2000) stated, "must synthesize the knowledge from many theories and research studies; she must make a collage or mosaic of many theoretical ideas . . . rather than relying on any single one" (pp. 9–10). Pragmatism rules: "enduring truths" must necessarily yield to "useful truths" (Deutch, 2000, pp. 9–10). There is no pretense that a theory will entirely fit what is being observed, but it can offer a place to begin. Without such an overview a mediator is prone to viewing and managing an impasse in terms that merely confirm his or her personal beliefs and biases, and therefore the impasse stands a greater risk of being mismanaged. For example, not uncommonly in a divorce mediation, the man explodes in anger. The practitioner, if susceptible to conventional wisdom, might assume that behavior, intentional or not, to be an act of dominance, an assertion of power, or a play for control. Sometimes the woman feels intimidated and closes down. Depending on how it plays out, the situation could become characterized as an impasse. An overall theory allows for other plausible—and more benign (from the man's perspective)—hypotheses to be taken into account. Considering the man's hurt, fear, anger, or sense of powerlessness in the situation may give the mediator a broader view of the behavior and a broader range of motion in response.

Whereas some practitioners deny the value of any working theory and purport to be wholly eclectic, others become ideologically bound to a chosen theory. This latter group may attempt to *impose* a theoretical model on reality and employ the same technique regardless of the particular circumstances. Effective practice can be hindered by a working theory that is postulated *not* in terms of how people in conflict actually feel or behave but, rather, on how the practitioner hopes or believes the parties should feel and act (Benjamin, 1999b). In dealing with an impasse, this position can be worse than no theory at all. Sometimes an impasse may not even be connected to the identified conflict; for example, the man's explosion, described above, may be entirely unrelated to the divorce. But if the mediator believes that most conflicts are the result of peoples' inability to communicate and empathize with each other, then he or she will view any impasse in those terms, even when other factors, such as the scarcity of time or money, may be at the core of the resistance. Conversely, a seemingly straightforward and rational negotiation process that appears headed toward agreement can be quickly derailed by a party's offhand remark or a perceived "smirk" that a mediator who is focused solely on interests and needs fails to address. A functional theory, in contrast, provides a more comprehensive field of vision that encompasses both the apparent and the less obvious tensions present in most disputes and *un*tethers a practitioner from overinvestment in any particular theoretical model. Many situations veer toward impasse because the third party does not have a useful working theory or is too bound by the orthodoxy of a particular theory.

Early in their careers, many practitioners tend not to have deliberately or consciously chosen an operative theory of conflict and have instead adopted the theory to which they were first exposed or unwittingly take on an approach that is comfortable and compatible with their underlying personal, cultural, or religious values and beliefs. This is evident, for example, in the affinity displayed by many practitioners for setting rules of behavior in mediation. Some like rules and believe that technique protects and focuses disputing parties. Others shun rules and structure, concerned that those techniques are overly directive and intrusive, and stifle participants open expression, thus undermining the mediation process principle of self-determination (Benjamin, 2003).

Overactive adherence to theoretical formulations has led to clashes between mediators who view conflict from contrasting perspectives. This clash is amply illustrated in the chapters of this book and becomes more vividly apparent in the face of impasse. Ironically, in a field ostensibly dedicated to managing differences, "style wars" are common and not necessarily constructive (Coleman, 2000b, pp. 597–599; Benjamin, 2000b). Those who approach conflict as a competition for power and control are skeptical of the efficacy of those who believe communication is the root cause and therefore focus on relationships and cooperation. At the extremes, the humanists are considered to be naïve dupes and the "pure business" mediators are cast as slick, Machiavellian operators. Then there are the inveterate rationalists, who believe that conflict arises from scarce resources, and by setting aside emotion, problems can be solved by reason and logic alone. They risk being viewed as rational fools. Finally, there are those who see conflict in moral terms and consider it an opportunity to bring forward principles of social justice. These individuals can be rigid and inflexible and refuse to negotiate at all.

As a practical matter, managing an impasse does not allow much room for the luxury of attachment to a particular theory. Nowhere is an integrated, applied, and systemic theory of conflict more necessary than in the throes of an impasse. In the end, theoretical abstractions must take a backseat to the reflective consideration of the risks and advantages of a variety of strategies and techniques in managing impasses.

"MAPPING" AN IMPASSE ON THE CONFLICT TERRAIN: FIELD THEORY AND SYSTEMS THEORY

As noted, a useful practice theory offers a topographical mapping of the conflict terrain that provides a multidimensional view, including notations of elevation—those matters likely to be of higher or lower emotional intensity—which allow mediators to anticipate the potential trouble spots and where conditions are veering toward an impasse. Beyond metaphor, drawing an actual map of the conflict system is useful, if not essential, especially for complex matters such as those frequently found in the divorce and family context. Graphics, visual displays, and illustrations comprise some of the most important techniques available by which both mediator and participants can grasp the dynamics of the situation and *see* the impasse for themselves. Two theories that are especially useful for mapping the conflict terrain are field theory and systems theory. *Field theory* provides a method by which to identify forces of resistance and inducements for parties to come to agreement by allowing for change. *Systems theory* offers a view of the dynamics of any organization (business, professional, or institutional) and family groups of every description (Benjamin, 2002c).

Field Theory

Kurt Lewin's (1935) field theory has stood the test of time. For more than a half century, his concepts of tensions and force fields in social systems have continued to prove useful in understanding conflicts, in general, and the impasse, in particular. An impasse is understood as an essentially frozen state in which the forces that motivate people to change are countered or outweighed by restraining forces. In Lewin's theory, a goal gradient is used to gauge an individual's positive or negative valences for change—complete approach, complete resistance, or ambivalence. Moving beyond impasse requires an "unfreezing"—a thawing of some blockages, thereby creating openings for the parties locked in dispute to move toward something different. After the shift, there will likely be periods of "refreezing," but possibly into different kinds of behavior or actions that are more resilient and responsive to change (Lewin, 1947). The obvious inference to be drawn from field theory, directly applicable to the management of impasses, is the requirement that the mediator or facilitator devise techniques to induce or catalyze this unfreezing process.

Specific techniques, discussed more fully below, include creating a measure of confusion with regard to the parties' operative mythologies (be they conscious or unconscious) about justice, truth, rationality, and the finality of the outcome of the dispute. Resistance to negotiation must be countered if there is to be movement. Creating a measure of cognitive dissonance in the parties' thinking—unsettling them to the point that they are not so sure of what they thought they knew about the probable outcome—often depotentiates this resistance (Benjamin, 1995a). This countering technique requires a somewhat countercultural and counterintuitive approach in a techno-rational culture that tends to rely heavily on logic and rational argument. Resistance, however, can be aggravated and intensified by approaches that are too straightforward and direct. Explaining to a party why his or her long-held beliefs are inaccurate is likely to be met with rebuttal. Challenging resistance with logic or persuasion may be not only ineffectual but actually catalyze more pernicious resistance in other ways at other times (Marcus, 2000; Deutch, 1973).

In many divorce conflicts, the first impasse occurs at the very beginning in relation to the decision to mediate. For many, agreement to mediate is viewed as acceptance of the proposed divorce or separation, nor are parties typically at similar emotional "places." The person who feels left or rejected is likely to "dig in" and resist the idea of a divorce—and ergo, of using mediation for that process. The more the person motivated to move ahead (the "identified initiator") presses for change, the more the resistor is likely to balk and try to slow down or reject the mediation process. Conversely, as the resistor balks, the initiator becomes increasingly impatient and may bolt from mediation, deciding it cannot work. This dynamic is played out in couples, to varying degrees, the majority of the time.

Field theory reminds the mediator of the importance of an early assessment to determine who wants "this deal"—the divorce—and who does not. If the mediator overlooks the pressures and resistance to move ahead and simply assumes that the presence of both parties indicates a mutual desire to proceed, then an impasse might develop before the mediation process even begins. Perhaps worse, if the resistance goes unacknowledged, the person may suppress it, where it forms into a latent infection that may well surface weeks or months later in the mediation process. In a subsequent discussion of some unrelated issue, the resistant party might issue an ultimatum from seemingly "out of the blue": "If you want this divorce so bad, you'll give me . . . the house/custody/more child support!" Not uncommonly, mediators are prone to use conventional techniques, such as logic, either to convince the resistant party of the legal inevitability of divorce and the value of mediation or to encourage the initiator to reconsider the decision to divorce. Reason and logic might very well inflame the resistance and foment an impasse. Although the use of reason, logic, and persuasion is culturally embedded in our approach to conflict, doing so is the least effective means of convincing anyone of anything (Benjamin, 2000d).

Systems Theory and Effects

There is a human tendency to think about, and explain, human events and behavior in linear terms, assigning specific causes to observed effects. Borrowed from the study of interactions among organic and inorganic materials, systems theory broadened the horizon to take in many other variables beyond those immediately in view (von Bertalanffy, 1986). Viewing the phenomenon of impasses in the family conflict system requires the same broadening of perspective. Often the occurrence of an impasse is more complex than the mere idiosyncrasies and guile of the parties would suggest; it is not simply attributable to his rigidity or her anger. There are many other variables that impinge on the conflict system, some of which include other people (e.g., friends, relatives, lawyers, counselors, accountants—all with opinions and influence), timing (e.g., the duration of the dispute and status in the legal process), other systems (e.g., legal requirements), and other circumstances (e.g., the health of the parties and their immediate family members). Families are complex systems, and anything that affects one member of the family will generate a ripple effect that moves through the entire family.

Family systems theory begins with the assumption that the family is an organism in its own right, the whole of which is different from the sum of its parts—or members (Bowen, 1982). In the still all-too-common mechanistic legal view, the family is merely a biologically related group of people, each with respective rights and responsibilities that are, for the most part, interchangeable. The implication is that if the family does not work, it is due to the instability of one of the members and his or her removal will solve the problem (Benjamin, 2002c). Sometimes, though, a family composed of unstable people might function reasonably well, whereas a family of apparently stable and functioning members may make for an unstable family unit. In short, a family as a unit can have characteristics that are not easily attributable or deducible from the nature or traits of any of its component members. This unique chemistry of a family—or, for that matter, any human organization—is understood in complex systems terms as the "emergent properties" of the system. In fact, many of the characteristics of individuals are formed interactively (Jervis, 1997, pp. 15–17). Mediators should take care not to be lulled into thinking that a matter will be easy to negotiate because the participants initially appear to be reasonable and cooperative. Although each may be genuinely committed to settlement (assuming *genuineness* could be defined precisely), the negotiation may nonetheless become deadlocked. Likewise, people who might seem to be "crazy" and improbable candidates for mediation on first impression can often succeed quite well in the process.

Systems theory offers the mediator a checklist of characteristic elements common to all systems, organizations, and families. From a review of this checklist, a holistic sense of the families' dynamics, strengths, and vulnerabilities can be gleaned. Ultimately, the theory allows the mediator to clarify issues effectively; more immediately, however, it provides a means to (1) anticipate areas of potential impasses, (2) avoid the impasses, if possible, or (3) custom design a strategy to manage the situation preemptively. These characteristic elements of a system include the following:

  • *Boundaries*: who is viewed as being in or outside the boundaries of the family. The involvement of in-laws/grandparents and parents' new relationships or spouses present classic boundary issues that are threatening to family members.
  • *Transgenerational patterns*: the folklore or inherited culture of the family; "the way things have always been done around here." Departing from past traditions, which is common in divorce, is a risk factor for impasse development.
  • *Hierarchy:* who is in charge in the organization. A clear structure is required for any system to function. The family structure is one of the first casualties in a divorce, with much confusion about who is in charge. Power struggles between the parents or the outright abdication of responsibility by one or both parents is a risk factor.
  • *Interactional patterns*: how members in the family communicate with each other. Do they meet and talk with each other directly or leave written

notes for each other to read? Do they talk through other people? A ripe area for impasse is a triangulation, which occurs when a parent talks to a child about the other parent or to the other parent about a child. How do they talk? The 1979 movie *The Great Santini* (from the book by Pat Conroy, 1976) vividly illustrates a rigid interactional pattern of communication that borders on being abusive. The father (played by Robert Duvall) is a military officer who orders his family around like a military unit, formal and autocratic in the extreme.

  • *Subsystems*: within the family system are several subsystems based on gender, interest, age, and responsibility. The parents and children are each separate subsystems. These special alliances are constructive when the family is functioning well but can take on a sinister cast when the family is being restructured. The 1989 movie *The War of the Roses* provides a forceful tableau of a family divided into enemy camps, where alliances are crystallized, with mother, teenage daughter, and cat aligned against father, teenage son, and dog. In divorce, previously harmless alliances may become threatening, as members look for allies to support their positions. Such entrenchments are often the stuff of impasses, with each of the parents looking to team up with the children against the other parent.

  • *Developmental stages*: the ages of both the children and parents provide hints of possible impasse-risk areas. If the children and parents are younger, then present-day security and cash flow issues are the likely focus, whereas if they are older, then attention tends to veer toward issues around future security.

A common boundary issue that typically surfaces early in the divorce process concerns the parties' fears about other relationships and offers a good example of applied systems theory. When Frank, the husband in a divorce matter, stated that he "will not tolerate his children spending time with that man—an immoral criminal who smokes dope—in his house," the makings of a potential impasse loomed. The mediator's early awareness and articulation of the issue can make a difference. The mediator might respond: "Frank, you appear to be concerned that Susan is 'exposing' the children to outsiders, people you consider a threat to your children's welfare. This is a particularly difficult issue to address because it places each of your personal values on the line. It is hard not feeling as though you have control over the boundaries of your family. We will deal directly with this issue of how best to stabilize your family, but it will take time and won't be easy." The comment serves to take the edge off a potentially explosive issue and place it in a manageable perspective, thereby reducing the prospect of an impasse arising around it. Systems theory helps mediators to recognize, organize, and clarify impasse risk areas.

The family system is also interconnected with other systems—legal, social, health care, religious, among others—adding many more layers of complexity. The family is strongly influenced by interactions with these other systems, which have occurred at other places or times and are not usually apparent. The interconnections can be dense, indeed. The legal system offers a good example. A change in the law or the appointment of one judge instead of another to manage the matter may require, prohibit, or constrain what happens, causing ripples of consequences—some unintended—that cascade throughout the family system and all of the connected systems as well (Jervis, 1997; Elizur & Minuchin, 1952). Introducing a new element—the participation of a mediator or other third party—intended to foster agreement can paradoxically trigger an impasse. In a family in the throes of a divorce, participants' sensitivities are heightened, and even the mere idea of going to mediation may feel risky and threatening. The mediator's approach, if not carefully considered, can cause participants to be even more resistant to change—a "revenge effect"—clearly an unintended consequence. For example, a mediator who is too directive and outcome focused when one or both parties are not ready to move ahead may intensify the tension level. Conversely, a mediator who is nondirective when the participants are already confused and doubtful might inadvertently discourage them from pursuing the negotiation process (Tenner, 1996; Benjamin, 1999b).

In addition, uncontrolled legal actions, laws, regulations, court rules, and administrative policies can all trigger an impasse, as discussed in the following paragraphs:

• The intemperate or unilateral filing of formal legal actions, such as a petition, motion for discovery, or order for spousal protection, can unduly legalize a divorce action and cause an impasse. Although the intended objective might be to "turn up the heat" and push the negotiation forward, the action can have the opposite effect of increasing the level of stress and tearing down the mediation process.

• The laws, regulations, and policies—which are confusing, at best, and sometimes inconsistent and even contradictory—can immobilize the negotiation process (Elster, 1989; Howard, 1994; Benjamin, 2000c). For example, the child support laws, guidelines, and court rules in most states, though intended to clarify matters, are often so complex that they lead to more confusion. By giving the illusion of clarity—a seemingly simple mathematical calculation—these materials sometimes entrench the parties in their positions. The mediation of child support does not appear to be warranted when the "numbers speak for themselves." The benefit of uniformity, sought by child support guideline writers, can be undermined by the many permutations to the formula that are not immediately apparent. Sometimes, a state's child support legislation can be a source of more conflict in divorce, not less. Most states have laws that correlate parenting time with money—the "dollars for minutes" game—so fathers jockey for joint custody as much to pay less support as to have more time with the children. Conversely, mothers seek sole custody to justify more support money.

• Finally, stressors in and from other systems, such as schools, the workplace, or other organizations, can cause family conflict and be a source of, or intensify, an impasse. Losing a job, chronic and serious health issues, or financial difficulties can be the cause or result of a divorce and make agreement look all the more improbable.

Systems theory is necessary to design strategies that effectively manage impasse. Understanding how outside forces can grip the parties in an impasse, the mediator might paradoxically turn the situation around to use the same understanding to break the impasse. Here graphics are useful to show the parties how they are both caught and feeling controlled by outside forces, and thus must band together and forge an alliance against a mutual enemy to protect themselves and their children. Essentially, the mediator is aiding them in a conspiracy against the external system. For example, to avoid being forced to do something neither of them wants but the legal system requires, the parties will have to cooperate to beat the system (Benjamin, 1998b).

BELIEFS ABOUT CONFLICT AND VARIETIES OF IMPASSE

Because there are multiple varieties of impasses, there is no final or unifying theory that explains all, or even most, occurrences. Notwithstanding this reality, it remains common for discussions to focus on single sources, such as (1) the lack of acknowledgment and empowerment of a party, (2) insufficient clarification of issues to allow for rational decision analysis, (3) disregard of the value of forgiveness, and (4) the absence of spiritual dimension, among others. Although all of these areas are credible, none alone can explain the whole range of possible impasses, and preoccupation with one can easily blind the mediator to other and perhaps more plausible hypotheses that might better explain the resistance. Oftentimes, uninformed and unexamined beliefs about the origins of conflict color and define the individual's view of the impasse.

There are six general notions or beliefs about conflict that alone, or in combination with one other, underlie the most common varieties of impasse. Each is part of our evolutionary biology and psychology; although none is immutable, all are an ingrained part of our human nature, and not easily denied. Thus, pretending to not have a competitive streak, be it large or small, is like pretending not to have a right arm (Benjamin, 1999a, 2002a; Wright, 1994).

1. *Conflict arises out of the pursuit of power and control.* From Thucydides, the 5th century Greek historian, through Hobbes, Machiavelli, and Kissinger

in present times, many have viewed conflict as the result of the human imperative to gain power and control over others in not only their personal lives and business dealings but in politics and international relations as well. An impasse occurs when a party, group, or nation resists the ultimatums, demands, or other aggressive acts of another (Kaplan, 2002).

2. *Conflict is a reflection of evil in the world, a dislocation of the moral order.* Essentially, from a Christian theological view, conflict is thought by many to be punishment for humanity's fall from grace—our failure to maintain a moral order (Benjamin, 1998a; Pagels, 1995). This moral dimension underlies not just disputes that are overtly about values, such as interfaith disputes, but extends to many other areas as well. The moral order and sanctions for transgressions against that order are not unique to human beings (Wright, 1994). From this perspective, an impasse occurs when a party feels that any, or further, negotiation is a fundamental compromise of principle and, as such, is sinful or immoral.

3. *Conflict is the result of people's failure to communicate, empathize, or otherwise respect each other and their unwillingness to forgive and trust one another.* Just as there is an imperative to gain power and control, so too is there one to cooperate for mutual protection, gain, and the survival of the species (de Waal, 1996; Ridley, 1997). This imperative is the source of the human disposition to altruistic behavior. From this perspective, impasse occurs when there is a failure to acknowledge and validate other human beings (Bush & Folger, 1994).

4. *Conflict is the result of the allocation or misallocation of scarce resources.* This is essentially an economic view of conflict and is predicated on the belief that human beings act rationally to further their self-interests. The problem-solving approach is derived from this belief about conflict and suggests that the careful exploration of parties' interests and needs and the objective application of risk–benefit analysis can mitigate the conflict (Axelrod, 1984). In this view, an impasse occurs when there has been either an inadequate assessment or insufficient clarification of the underlying interests and needs, or a failure to separate the people from the problem, allowing emotional factors to overtake the negotiations (Fisher, Ury, & Patton, 1991).

5. *Conflict is the result of psychocultural confusion, complexity, and ambiguity.* In a fast-paced world of technology and rationality, many people feel overwhelmed, confused, and immobilized by decision making. At the same time, many traditional support systems, such as religion, cultural identity, and family networks, are also in flux (Adler, 1977; Lifton, 1993). There is for many a personal fear of taking responsibility for one's own life (Becker, 1997). Negotiation involves choices and requires taking responsibility for decisions; these elements necessarily entail taking the risk of being "played for a fool" and losing (Pagels, 1995). The perception of that risk, especially in mediation, may be far less than the actual risk, but it is still a powerful disincentive that

must be overcome. In a complex world, where professionals are often viewed as de facto gatekeepers to expertise, many people prefer to defer to them (Illich, 1976). An impasse can result when a person becomes so fragmented and insecure that he or she slips into a perceptual crisis and is unable or unwilling to make a decision (Watzlawick, 1983).

6. *Conflict is an outgrowth of unintended consequences and the operations of complex organizations and systems.* The creation of laws, rules, regulations, and policies calculated to redress a particular problem and to make societal functioning more uniform, smoother, and fairer has frequently backfired and created the opposite effect. Many laws passed to solve particular problems have not done so, but they have created other problems and led to unintended consequences (Tenner, 1996). Most states, for example, require detailed written parenting plans to be filed with the court, with the ostensible goal of clarifying arrangements and minimizing parenting disputes. Yet few parents can adhere to the written plans as a practical matter, leading to conflicts and sometimes to more litigation. In some instances, new laws are at odds with or confuse those still in effect. Mostly, however, rules and laws can undermine the exercise of individual initiative, responsibility, and discretion (Howard, 1994). If there are laws for everything, people are more hesitant to act and make their own choices—they are caught between what the law seems to require and what makes sense to them (Benjamin, 2003).

Strategically designing an approach to working with impasses necessarily requires taking into account the parties' and the mediator's beliefs about the sources of conflict. Examining the sources of the conflict can offer useful insight about how to work through the resistance. One source may predominate, but more likely there will be strains of others as well. An impasse arising from a party's personal confusion and immobilization may point to the need for a heavier dose of structure and organization. Sometimes a review of the decision analysis process is useful to assure that issues are clarified and sharply focused. Impasses over values and ideologies might require strategies that circumvent the obligation of any party to abdicate his or her beliefs.

STRATEGIC MANAGEMENT OF IMPASSES: THE PROTEAN APPROACH

Effectively managing an impasse does not allow the mediator the luxury of presuming that a particular source of conflict or theory of human nature alone will serve to explain what is going on or will provide the right strategy to overcome the resistance.

A mediator needs to draw eclectically from various theories to construct a strategy that clears a particular impasse. He or she needs to be protean; that is, the mediator needs to shift the shape of his or her approach depending on the context, situation, and parties' circumstances. In one instance, the mediator may draw from the competitive approach, acting in a calculated, possibly even confrontational, manner, and in another, draw from the humanistic approach by offering empathy and, at the proper time, analysis and objectivity. Likewise, being structured and directive are necessary and useful techniques, at times, to manage impasse, while at other times doing nothing might be most effective (Benjamin, 1995a, 1995b).

Any strategy, if it is to be useful, must allow for the greatest range of motion and flexibility. It may be that the impasse is insurmountable, the timing is simply not right, or the surrounding politics are too intrusive. However, this outcome is usually not knowable until the mediation process actually terminates. Until that time, the parties deserve every measure of diligence the mediator can muster to remove resistance and help them consider options for settling the conflict. The mediator is well served by the qualities of determination (to the point of stubbornness), physical stamina, and a disciplined *un*willingness to accept what might seem to be the obvious futility of continuing when success appears to be against the odds.

TECHNIQUES AND SKILLS FOR MANAGING IMPASSES

Specific techniques are most useful when placed in service of an overall strategy. Without such a framework, these techniques are about as helpful as knowing how to swing a bat in a football game. As well, thought should be given to the "footprint" left by a particular technique. Less intrusive tactics are generally preferred to more directive and heavy-handed ones. Presented in the order of importance and least level of intrusiveness, these techniques are as follows.

Strategic Empathy

Empathy, the ability to convey to another person the sense that he or she has been heard is reliant on effective listening—the first and most important technique. Communications and neurolinguistic theory posits that people construct their reality through their use of verbal and nonverbal language; the stories, myths, and metaphors they are prone to use; and the timber, tone, and tension of their speech pattern. A listener, by using similar metaphors, patterns, and behaviors, can synchronize or pace the rhythm and intensity of the speaker, listening not only for cognitive understanding but approximating the emotional state as well (Laborde, 1987)—in short, to figuratively enter the speaker's reality and engage or connect with him or her emotionally (Benjamin, 2000d). The listener must be able to hear the speaker's meaning, sometimes in spite of their words. The speaker may be having trouble articulating his or her thoughts and feelings clearly—which is commonly the case in conflict situations. This careful listening is especially important for two reasons, when faced with an impasse. First, a well-placed comment such as "I want to make sure I'm hearing you clearly" slows down the discussion and gives the mediator time to center him- or herself. Second, careful listening can detect the clues people almost always give, albeit in code, about the source of their fears or concerns—which is quite possibly at the root of the impasse. For example, the statement "I need to protect the children from him" may translate into "I'm afraid of being displaced and losing my kids."

Reviewing the Structure of the Mediation Process

Consider what has been done thus far and if a step has been missed or needs to be reemphasized. Often an impasse can be induced by the structure imposed by the mediator (or lack of structure). If parties are encouraged to consider options before they are ready, one or both may balk.

In an effort to problem solve efficiently—to "fix things"—there is a tendency for mediators to get ahead of themselves, In difficult cases, people cannot effectively negotiate and consider options until the following have occurred (essentially in this order): (1) They have told their stories in some fashion, and the mediator has clarified their different perceptions of the facts—how they agree or disagree; (2) *all* of the issues—the ones the parties have identified and others about which the mediator has become aware—have been clarified; (3) the options, both the obvious and crazy ones, have been identified; and (4) the risks and advantages of each option has been considered.

Altering and Shifting the Parties' Thinking Frame

This is the point where traditional approaches to impasses are most useful. Brainstorming to create options, weighing the best and worst alternatives to the negotiated agreements and sizing up the transaction costs are among the most obvious. Another is to encourage the parties to "go to the balcony" in order to gain "a distanced view of close things" (Heifetz, 1994). Asking people to switch roles, changing the environment, or any approach that encourages the parties to consider the consequences and implications of their perspective can be useful.

Using "Crazy Wisdom" to Shock or Tweak the Parties

In more difficult cases, nontraditional tactics and methods may be necessary to unsettle people who are locked into a cycle of thinking that is going nowhere fast. The mediator's unexpected expression of frustration can sometimes shake them—"I just don't think this mediation makes sense." Sometimes it is useful for the mediator to act strategically confrontational by, for example, challenging the likelihood of the differing court outcomes in which each party has expressed faith. Causing confusion by organizing papers as though to leave or wandering over to a window and gazing out in the middle of a heated discussion can be disconcerting and cause the parties to reconsider their negotiating perspectives. A well-placed piece of unexpected, even shocking, behavior can be useful. Just as Red Adair, famous for fighting runaway oil rig fires, would stuff a stick of dynamite down the well—the explosion kills the fire by depriving it of oxygen—a mediator might try to startle both parties, robbing them of the fuel for fighting, by saying gruffly, "I think you're both working with misinformation—you'd better check with your attorneys." Likewise, a paradoxical injunction can be effective: "Maybe mediation doesn't make sense for both of you—you might be better off in court." Giving people permission to do what they say they want to do—go to court—often relieves their need to actually do it (Benjamin, 1995b; Laborde, 1987; Nisker, 1990; Palazzoli, Boscolo, Cecchin, & Prata, 1978).

Caucus: Meeting Separately with Both Parties

The caucus format offers an opportunity to go into greater depth and connect with each person, examining fears and underlying concerns that might be the source of the resistance to moving forward. Caucus is especially useful when the mediator feels drawn into blaming or challenging one party more than the other, or is perceived as doing so. Entering parties' respective realities is critical to managing an impasse. Indeed, it is often the only way to gain enough momentum and trust to be able to confront and effectively plant seeds of confusion in one or both of the parties' perspectives (Benjamin, 2000d).

The Strategic Use of Time

In a culture with a strong affinity for the "fix it now," "solve the problem," "time is money" mentality, one of the most effective techniques for managing an impasse is often the least used—time. The mediator needs to set the pace and slow down the parties. The mediator can use timing to set perspective. Time can offer a salve that allows a party to move from his or her position without losing face. Neither party is willing to change his or her mind in front of the other party, nor should that be expected. In a subsequent session at another time, however, that change can occur. Haynes (1988) suggested that the mediator should never ask parties to shift their perspectives to a degree that exceeds their ability to assimilate the implied change. This understanding highlights the limitations of many court-connected or related custody mediation programs that unrealistically allot only a certain amount of time or number of sessions to the mediation of complex issues. Parenthetically, consider how using custody in the title of the program might well contribute to the parties' positioning; the term "custody" sets up a legalistic "win–lose" frame from the very start.

• *No conflict before its time.* Especially in difficult disputes, such as those involving values, a measure of aging is necessary before the dispute can be managed effectively. A proper foundation must be laid for any real discussion to occur. Those who are too rational in their approach sometimes miss the boat in these difficult cases by presuming that the problem can be solved by direct and immediate discussion.

• *Set a moderate pace.* Especially in difficult cases, do not allow the parties to do what they think they want to do—hurtle toward a solution. Although the fast solution might work, if it does not, then the mediation process will be that much harder to recover.

• *Stall parties from talking immediately about "the hardest problem."* Sometimes talking about tangentially relevant issues that surround the main issue can set the tone and lay the groundwork for the more challenging discussion to come.

• *Set time frames by which to judge progress and avoid hard and fast timetables or deadlines.* Imposing time constraints and deadlines can sometimes be useful, but it may also do more harm than good. The conventional wisdom that people will not settle unless "their feet are held to the fire" may be wrong as often as it is right. Sometimes people balk because they are being pushed too hard to settle (Moore, 1996; Benjamin, 2000d).

The Use of Experts

Depending on the nature of the impasse, suggest that the parties consult with attorneys, accountants, counselors, financial planners, or other advisors between sessions and, in some instances, consider obtaining second opinions. Calling in the experts is obviously useful when the insecurity that is blocking the negotiation concerns a lack of information. Moreover, when a party is entrenched, expert advice can be useful, paradoxically, to create more confusion. Or include experts in selected meetings, where the parties are then given an opportunity to jointly hear not only what their own advisor might be saying but the other party's as well. This gives them the opportunity and responsibility to evaluate all the advice in their dispute. The parties thereby become a de facto jury in their own situation. Hearing multiple opinions sometimes confirms for the parties that there is no single "right" answer easily available and persuades them to accept settlement with a less-than-perfect option (Benjamin, 2000d).

Considering Other Modes of Conflict Management

Arbitration or the use of a special master or fact finder to render a determination about the issue causing resistance could be useful. Whether or not the parties actually decide to use another mode is less important than the opportunity to take a break from the discussion of the issue and to scrutinize alternative modes. The mass of issues to be considered if arbitration is to be used—such as how and who to choose as an arbitrator, whether the arbitration should be binding or advisory, determining the level of formality of the arbital process (e.g., rules of evidence, presence of attorneys), and a number of other design details—might be sufficiently daunting so as to encourage their recommitment to mediation.

Using Other Modes of Conflict Management within the Mediation Context

The use of a former judge or other expert person to serve as a nonbinding arbitrator offers the parties an opportunity to observe how an outsider might view their respective positions. This aditional person can give them a sense of how their perspective might "play" in court (or another forum). The technique can be effective but requires that the mediator be clear about his or her role delineation. Some mediators have formalized this technique into a style of mediation popularly known as "med-arb": The mediator first attempts to facilitate a resolution, but at the point of impasse, becomes the arbitrator rendering a determination in the matter. Although this approach may work sometimes, there is risk. Once the mediator has become an arbitrator, he or she will be unlikely to be able to regain the mediator role—and an arbitrator, not unlike a judge, typically offends at least one party, if not both, by rendering a decision (Benjamin, 1994).

COMMON VARIETIES OF IMPASSES IN FAMILY AND DIVORCE CONFLICTS

The following impasses are especially common in family and divorce conflicts. Knowing the likelihood of encountering these "hot spots" allows the mediator the opportunity to anticipate and put in place preemptive strategies to minimize the impact of the impasse.

Personal or Relational Resistance

In mediation there are typically internal as well as external blocks to negotiation that must often be overcome. Internal resistance from within one or a number of the parties may stem from cultural, moral, or psychological antipathies to negotiation. In this culture negotiation is a sign of weakness—John Wayne would not negotiate a matter of principle (and most disputes are matters of principle). On another level, some parties believe that negotiation is tantamount to committing sinful or immoral behavior; after all, the archetype of evil in the Western world is Satan, and "his" primary *modus operandi* is to negotiate for our souls (Benjamin, 1998a). Christian theology has indeed seeped into secular cultural sensibilities and affects many people, regardless of their religious persuasion (Pagels, 1995). Finally, many people do not want to be responsible for their own lives and resist making decisions; they believe that professionals know better what is best for them than they know for themselves.

Many protest that they want to be reasonable, but the walls to negotiation start to rise with the slightest hint or suggestion of a compromise or the prospect of "giving in." The source of this impasse is usually a personal sense of confusion, lack of control, and ultimate rightness. In short, each party believes that "I am right, so I should not have to negotiate." Acting in a confrontational manner and pressing an immobilized party to consider the practical realities of the situation are seldom effective. The best techniques include stalling (e.g., giving parties time to consider their alternatives) and caucus (in which the mediator can offer strategic empathy).

At the extreme, family disputes sometimes become so protracted that they extend even beyond the lifetime of the parties and are passed on to succeeding generations for *centuries*. These types of conflict—the notorious "bad blood" disputes that escalate into geopolitical conflicts, wars, and even crusades—have a built-in impasse factor that some suggest is not susceptible to negotiation or mediation and must, albeit painfully, simply be allowed to run their course (Anderson, 1999). The Israeli–Palestinian, Serbian–Croation, Hutu–Tutsi, and Irish–English conflicts are examples. These disputes between ethnic groups can be thought of as extended family disputes in disguise. There is often a strong moral component involved, in that many of those groups identify with particular religions. Negotiations, mediations, skirmishes, violence, and impasses will cycle and recur intermittently and continually over generations, taking on strains of ideological and value conflicts as each side asserts principles of loyalty to family and faith as a pretext for continuing the conflict (Huntington, 1996). The same phrasing used to dismiss negotiation as a viable option is common to both family conflicts and this kind of geopolitical conflicts: "You cannot negotiate with someone you don't trust," or "You cannot negotiate with terrorists and madmen" (Benjamin, 2002a, 2002b; Huntington, 1996). Moreover, both family and geopolitical conflicts are further complicated by secondary acts and parties that perpetuate the wars. The memories, accurate or not, of peripheral incidents—"What your lawyer said when we met . . . your closing of the bank account . . . you failed to keep your word"—eclipse the primary dispute, which may even be forgotten. Sometimes genuine value disputes are involved; other times a communications dispute is squeezed so tightly that it *becomes* construed as a value conflict.

Many mediators, being inveterate rationalists, assiduously avoid the past, preferring instead to focus on the future. They downplay the story or the history of the conflict, fearing that focus will merely exacerbate the parties' animosities and sidetrack the mediation. Yet, while care needs to be taken not to become mired in "ancient" history, especially when negotiations are at an impasse, exploring the roots of the dispute often reveals the underlying difficulties in the conflict. John Haynes (1988), in a line that has become a favorite for many mediators, said, "I don't want to rehash the past. I want you to reshape the future." Ironically, while this statement draws applause as a logical and positivist intervention, some rehashing may be exactly what is needed.

Finally, many mediators become preoccupied with establishing trust between the parties. While trust is useful, it is not essential for effective negotiations and agreements. For many parties, their relationship has deteriorated into abject hatred on the part of one or more of those involved. And sometimes the lofty pursuit of forgiveness and apology or empowerment and recognition between the parties, although admirable, can obscure the pursuit of the more mundane but decidedly useful goal of enabling the parties to resolve their dispute, despite their continued feelings of animosity toward each other (Bush & Folger, 1994). People need not trust each other or be friendly in order to negotiate.

Ideological or Value Differences

Impasses rooted in ideological or value differences are some of the most difficult. Many mediators believe people cannot negotiate genuine value disputes at all; that belief, in itself, can foment an impasse. The "blood feuds" discussed above could just as easily qualify as this variety of impasse. The challenge is to sort out a "genuine" value dispute from one contaminated by many other concerns. There are few pure value conflicts. For example, notwithstanding the large industry that has grown up around custody mediation, and the assumption that many divorcing parents are locked into heated value conflicts, à la the movie *Kramer vs. Kramer* (1979), a good number, if not a majority of parenting value disputes, are nothing more than money disputes in disguise. The "dollars for minutes" controversy, frequently played out in divorce disputes, where he wants joint custody so that he has the children more time and is obligated to pay less, and she wants sole custody so that *she* has the children more *and* receives more money, is hard enough and can be itself the source of impasse—but it is not necessarily a value dispute.

Value disputes go to the core of each party's belief systems and are distinguishable from mere differences in style or opinion. In many ways, our techno-rational culture encourages value conflicts. Both science and religion support a quest for the truth and standing on one's principles (Berlin, 1991). For many, being right is more important than being settled. At the extreme, a true ideologue is hard to identify and cannot be easily predetermined. Some are serious when they say they are willing to die for their cause; others may be serious but will also think twice if presented with an option that appears to further their cause; still others are merely being strategic. Smith (1997) noted:

> Saint and martyr possess an inner identity that sets them off from the rest
> of mankind. . . . they are incapable of accepting compromise or accommo-
> dating to the needs of others, and more often than not their determination
> to sacrifice themselves is accompanied by an equal willingness to sacrifice
> others. (p. 15)

Ideologues may not even know, themselves, how committed they are, and
their words can be misleading. The only way for the mediator to ascertain
the level of commitment may be to play through the negotiation, watching
actions that belie words, and listening for the clues that offer options.

Strategically, dealing with the ideologue in value disputes gives rise to
the most difficult kind of impasse. Ideologues anchor themselves in the
truth and righteousness of their beliefs and often see the conflict as means
of vindication (Benjamin, 1999c). Negotiation, on the other hand, requires
the quest for the truth to be set aside long enough for the parties to focus
their attention on settlement. Good examples of classic value conflicts include disputes between parents (or other caretakers) about a child's health
care (e.g., should the child be given Ritalin for attention-deficit disorder) or
religious upbringing (e.g., "I want the children raised . . . Catholic . . . Jewish
. . . Moslem). Value disputes will continually resurface throughout the negotiation process, invading every discussion, whether child related or otherwise.

In managing potential or actual impasses, the first task is to contain the
larger issue and address the smaller issues first: For example, "We'll need to
talk about church affiliation and education, but first we need to look at the
basic living arrangement." Next, separate style issues—how each parent disciplines or manages his or her household—from genuine value disputes. Often
style issues are unwittingly or strategically presented as value disputes. The
mediator needs to ratchet down the discussion of style differences into the
less volatile domain of parents' individual choices—as opposed to being seen
as an indicator of moral fitness to parent (or not).

A tactic for managing a stubborn value dispute involves playing one
value against another. There is typically more than one value at stake. Forcing the competition of values, deciding which is primary, can sometimes
break the impasse. For example, in a dispute over children's religious affiliation, one parent's value is sharing his or her religion and tradition; the
other's value is to ensure that the children are not confused by an exposure
to different religious experiences at the same time; still another value—one
that both parents might share—is the importance of being settled. The value
of being settled can be juxtaposed to the other values.

In difficult matters, a brew combining most of the techniques suggested
above is necessary:

- Caucus to explore each parent's worst fears or strategic thinking.
- Use outside experts to offer reality checks.

- Employ timing as a strategy to allow each person a chance to reconsider his or her perspective and shift it without losing face.
- Controlled confrontation, as a last resort, may be necessary to clarify the potential consequences of the breakdown in the negotiations. A direct question can be asked: "Is this the issue you want to go down with? Is this the sword you want to fall on?"

Power and Control Impasses

Power and control impasses can be elusive. Some people operate out of the desire to control and gain the advantage over others. Behaviors expressing fear of loss and need of self-protection may resemble controlling behavior. From whichever source, the inclination to be controlling and have power does not necessarily mean there is a power imbalance, per se. Some mediators' work has a political edge to it in which there is a tendency to make judgments and identify the parties as either a victim or perpetrator based on their status (e.g., male or female, homemaker or professional), or actions (e.g., an incident of domestic violence or expression of anger) alone. In every conflict, and most apparently in family conflicts, varying leverages and entitlements are available to each party and may shift over time. The frequent reference to the "level playing field" as a requirement for mediation is dubious in theory and nonexistent in practice. Power balance is a dynamic rather than static state that shifts during the course of the negotiation process. Very seldom can a determination be made as to which party is all powerful, leaving the other powerless.

In those circumstances where there is a pressing concern about whether the parties can reach a substantially informed and consensual agreement because of a gross disparity in available resources (i.e., access to professional consultation with lawyers, counselors, financial advisors, etc.; money; or physical or mental health circumstances) the mediator may need to act to head off an impending impasse. The primary techniques include first articulating the imbalance: "Put it on the table," provide information, and use experts to bolster both parties. Both parties must feel safe. Operationally, that means every precaution should be taken to ensure neither of them feels he or she is being played for a fool by engaging in the mediation process. In the process of balancing the power, one party may need additional information, but the other party also needs protection and reassurance that the balancing is to his or her advantage as well. Using "victim/perp" labeling obviously works against this understanding of protecting both parties. Finally, a paradoxical injunction can also be useful: "If you are not feeling safe enough in mediation, perhaps we should explore your alternatives and consider terminating the process for the present time." As with the use of this intervention at any time, the mediator must have thought through the advisability of the comment thoroughly so that it sounds (and *is*) authentic (Benjamin, 2000d).

Systemic/Political Impasses

The family system is part of a web of other systems—the legal system, health care system, and educational system, to name but a few. In one sense, divorce is merely the intersection, and sometimes collision, between the family system and the legal system. To the extent that a divorce between two individuals requires the review and approval of a judge and generally must comport with law and public policy, the parties may have an impasse imposed upon them by outside forces. Options and agreements the people might want to consider may not be available. Sometimes the parties agreements can be set aside by the arbitrary and capricious whim of a judge or administrator. For example, child support guidelines, used in most states, can offer a measure of guidance, but they can also be used intrusively to effectively coerce the parties into an acceptance of an agreement that suits neither of them. Another example involves retirement assets. By federal law, retirement assets can often be constructively divided through a "qualified domestic relations order" (QDRO), but state governments can choose to opt out of such coverage—as many do—for their public workers (e.g., police, firefighters, teachers, and other civil service employees). The absence of a QDRO allows for no viable means to divide retirement assets—which, for many parties in divorce, are one of their most valuable and important resources. As a result, the parties are forced to fight each other. People, variables, and considerations outside the control of either party can create challenging impasses.

The mediator must understand the larger systemic dimensions to manage this kind of an impasse. The first step is to identify those people who could sabotage the parties' agreement and bring them into the negotiation process in some manner—if not directly and in person, then through representatives or by obtaining their commitment to the agreement terms. Second, the mediator needs to help the parties cooperate in forming a conspiracy against their common enemy—the external force or authority—be it state, judge, or both (Benjamin, 1998b).

Scarce Resources: Time, Money, and Security

The most frequent and common variety of impasse concerns money: the allocation of financial responsibilities between the parties. For the vast majority of people, the harsh reality of divorce requires a change in lifestyle, if not the standard of living, for one or both people. Simple economics dictates that two households cannot live as cheaply as one. Although many mediators continue to try and sell the idea that divorce does not have to be a "zero-sum" game, that it can be a "win/win" deal in which both parties are satisfied with the outcome, there are relatively few takers for that sales pitch. For most, divorce looks like a loss, smells like a loss, and feels like a loss. There may be some benefits to it, but these are generally apparent only in hindsight (Benjamin, 1999a).

Scratching the surface of most difficult divorces reveals money as the most contentious issue. As a generalization, the person in the wife role is worried about making ends meet, and the person in the husband role does not want to subsidize the soon-to-be ex-wife and be "on the hook" forever. Many times the parties become locked in an impasse and immobilized by fear as a result of misinformation or lack of information. Ironically, for many married couples, the first time they have ever budgeted—looked at their spendable income against their expenses—is when they are required to do so to sort out their finances in their divorce. When they are confronted with the harsh reality that their expenses significantly exceed their income, one or both is usually taken aback and overwhelmed. At that point, it is naïve to expect them to be able to approach the issues rationally. At that point, if pressed to move ahead before reality has had a chance to sink in, they may feel so frustrated that they balk and the negotiation process may well deteriorate into an impasse.

Thorough preplanning and organization are the primary preemptive techniques critical to heading off an impasse over money and resources (Benjamin, 1999d). The mediator should set incremental and realistic expectations for the process, resisting the embedded cultural tendency to "cut to the chase" and immediately attempt to answer the ultimate question "Who will pay whom how much?" too soon. Mediators contribute to the impasses of their clients by getting ahead of themselves. Structuring the process into four discrete stages is important: Make sure that both parties (1) have sufficient information, (2) substantially understand the issues and concerns, (3) have a good sense of the options available, and (4) appreciate the risks and advantages of each option. Only then are they ready to negotiate effectively. Beginning the process in the middle, without sufficient grounding, only heightens the fear and anxiety level that leads directly to an impasse. It is critical to factor in sufficient time for the parties to come to terms with the numbers. The importance of slowing down the pace cannot be overstated. Later in the process, after the parties have acquired adequate information and an understanding of the issues, the use of outside experts (e.g., accountants, financial planners, and even paraprofessionals) can be another useful technique to work through an impasse (Benjamin, 2000d).

It also bears noting that the presentation of mediation as a "win/win" proposition can be problematic in the context of the distribution of financial responsibilities and division of property. Especially around these business issues, parties often have an expectation that the outcome will be "fair" and that both will be satisfied with the result. Mediators sometimes unwittingly foster that belief. Of course, each party has his or her own preconceived notion of fairness. Fulfilling the expectation of both parties being satisfied in the division of scarce resources is not realistic. To minimize the risk of an impasse, it may be both useful and more effective as a marketing strategy to understate the goals of mediation. Instead of suggesting that everyone will be satisfied, consider presenting mediation as "good business," wherein both partners will feel safe and protected from compromising tactics and exploitation.

Mediator-Induced Impasse

The mediator can induce an impasse in at least three ways. First, a mediator who is panicked and overwhelmed by the prospect of an impasse may cause the parties to panic, pushing them closer to an impasse. Second, if the mediator lacks structure and is insufficiently organized, the parties may not gain a sense of direction or movement out of their conflict, causing them to lose hope in the process. In essence, the mediator is a leader or guide skilled in traversing the unfamiliar terrain of conflict; a leader's primary task is to provide a positive outlook—meaning the illusion of progress—so that the reality can follow. Third, if the mediator's timing and pacing are jarring or out of synch with the parties, they may balk and resist. Specifically, if the mediator moves the process along too fast or too slow, or the parties feel pressed to consider options, problem solve, and settle before they are ready, the negotiations may break down. Reviewing the mediation process structure to ensure the appropriate pacing and the strategic use of time are critical to counteract this kind of impasse.

CONCLUSION

Managing an impasse is the true test of a mediator, especially when the impasse occurs in complex disputes that evoke deeply held feelings and emotions in situations that are highly ambiguous and unstructured, such as family and divorce conflicts. Whether between families or nations, most conflicts include grievances that are compounded by newer ones that are added on over time (Ross, 1993). An impasse is the point at which the art and science of the craft of mediation intersect most vividly. Although many mediators can effectively manage disputes much of the time merely by following a basic format, moving through an impasse requires considerably more skill. In the hardest cases, neither a natural talent nor brilliant analytical acumen and skill are enough by themselves. There the mediator is obligated to perform a refined blending of both, using what might be termed "systematic intuition." This intentional oxymoron is meant to suggest the seamless integration of a disciplined, carefully designed analytical structure and strategy together with a developed sense of intuition and tacit knowing (Benjamin, 2001a).

REFERENCES

Adler, P. (1977). Beyond cultural identity: Reflections on multi-culturalism. In R. W. Brislin (Ed.), *Culture learning: Concepts, applications, and research.* Honolulu: University Press of Hawaii.

Anderson, S. (1999, December 26). The curse of blood and vengeance. *The New York Times Magazine,* p. 29.

Axelrod, R. (1984). *The evolution of cooperation.* New York: Basic Books.

Becker, E. (1997) *The denial of death.* New York: Free Press.

Benjamin, R. D. (1994, Winter). Professional and ethical issues in med-arb practice. *Mediation News,* p. 6.

Benjamin, R. D. (1995a). The constructive uses of deception. *Mediation Quarterly, 13*(1), 3–18.

Benjamin, R. D. (1995b). The mediator as trickster: The folkloric figure as professional role model. *Mediation Quarterly, 13*(3), 131–149.

Benjamin, R. D. (1998a). Negotiation and evil: The sources of religious and moral resistance to the settlement of conflict. *Mediation Quarterly, 15,* 245–266.

Benjamin, R. D. (1998b). Mediation as a subversive activity. Available: *www.Mediate.com*

Benjamin, R. D. (1999a). Guerilla mediation: The use of warfare strategies in the management of conflict. Available: *www.Mediate.com*

Benjamin, R. D. (1999b). Mediators as peacemakers: The revenge effect. *Mediation News, 18*(3), 11–12.

Benjamin, R. D. (1999c). The quest for truth and the truth of lies. *Mediation News, 18*(4), 11–12.

Benjamin, R. D. (1999d). The natural mediator. *Mediation News, 18*(1), 8–9.

Benjamin, R. D. (2000a). The physics of gridlock and the Zen of mediation. *Mediation News, 70*(1), 14–15.

Benjamin, R. D. (2000b). On being too fussy about values in mediation: Consider the hedgehog and the fox. *Mediation News, 19*(2), 9–10.

Benjamin, R. D. (2000c). Lessons from frogs. *Mediation News, 19*(3), 7–8.

Benjamin, R. D. (2000d). *Effective negotiation and mediation: Applied theory and practice handbook* (rev. ed.). Portland, OR: Mediation and Conflict Management Services.

Benjamin, R. D. (2001a, Summer). Gut instinct: A mediator prepares. *Association for Conflict Resolution,* pp. 6–7.

Benjamin, R. D. (2001b, Fall). Mediation as theatre and negotiation as performance art. *Association for Conflict Resolution,* pp. 7–8.

Benjamin, R. D. (2002a, Fall). The geopolitical factor in family mediation. *Association for Conflict Resolution,* pp. 7–9.

Benjamin, R. D. (2002b). Terry Waite: A study in authenticity. Available: *www.Mediate.com*

Benjamin, R. D. (2002c, Winter). The negotiated family. *Association for Conflict Resolution,* pp. 27–29.

Benjamin, R. D. (2003). About rules: Surveying the terrain between "don't ask/don't tell" and "zero tolerance". Available: *www.Mediate.com*

Berlin, I. (1991). *The crooked timber of history.* New York: Knopf.

Bowen, M. (1982). *Family therapy in clinical practice.* New York: Aronson.

Bush, R. A. B., & Folger, J. P. (1994). *The promise of mediation: Responding to conflict through empowerment and recognition.* San Francisco: Jossey-Bass.

Coleman, P. (2000a). Intractable conflicts. In M. Deutch & P. T. Coleman (Eds.), *The handbook of conflict resolution: Theory and practice* (pp. 428–450). San Francisco: Jossey-Bass.

Coleman, P. (2000b). Concluding overview. In M. Deutch & P. T. Coleman (Eds.), *The handbook of conflict resolution: Theory and practice* (pp. 596–599). San Francisco: Jossey-Bass.

Conroy, P. (1976). *The great Santini.* New York: Bantam Books.

Damasio, A. (1994). *Descartes' error: Emotion, reason, and the human brain.* New York: Putnam.

Deutch, M. (1973). *The resolution of conflict: Constructive and destructive processes.* New Haven, CT: Yale University Press.

Deutch, M. (2000). Introduction. In M. Deutch & P. T. Coleman (Eds.), *The handbook of conflict resolution: Theory and practice* (pp. 9–10). San Francisco: Jossey-Bass.

de Waal, F. (1996). *Good natured.* Cambridge, MA: Harvard University Press.

Elizur, J., & Minuchin, S. (1952). *Institutionalizing madness.* New York: Basic Books.

Elster, J. (1989). *Solomonic judgments: Studies in the limitations of rationality.* Cambridge, MA: Cambridge University Press.

Fisher, R., Ury, W., & Patton, B. (1991). *Getting to yes* (2nd ed.). New York: Penguin.

Gleick, J. (1987). *Chaos.* New York: Viking Press.

Haynes, J. (1988). *The case of Willie* [Videotape]. Portland, OR: Academy of Family Mediators.

Heifetz, R. A. (1994). *Leadership without easy answers.* Cambridge, MA: Harvard University Press.

Howard, P. K. (1994). *The death of common sense.* New York: Random House.

Huntington, S. J. (1996). *The clash of civilizations and the remaking of world order.* New York: Touchstone.

Illich, I. (1976). *Medical nemesis: The expropriation of health.* New York: Random House.

Jervis, R. (1997). *System effects: Complexity in political and social life.* Princeton, NJ: Princeton University Press.

Kaplan, R. D. (2002). *Warrior politics.* New York: Random House.

Laborde, G. Z. (1987). *Influencing with integrity.* Palo Alto, CA: Syntony.

Lang, M. D., & Taylor, A. (2000). *The making of a mediator.* San Francisco: Jossey-Bass.

Lewin, K. A. (1935). *A dynamic theory of personality.* New York: McGraw-Hill.

Lewin, K. A. (1947). Group decision and social change. In E. E. Macoby, T. Newcomb, & E. Hartley (Eds.), *Readings in social psychology.* Austin, TX: Holt, Rinehart & Winston.

Lifton, R. J. (1993). *The protean self.* Chicago: University of Chicago Press.

Marcus, E. C. (2000). Change processes and conflict. In M. Deutch & P. T. Coleman, (Eds.), *The handbook of conflict resolution: Theory and practice* (pp. 366–381). San Francisco: Jossey-Bass.

Moore, C. W. (1996). *The mediation process* (3rd ed.). San Francisco: Jossey-Bass.

Nisker, W. (1990). *Crazy wisdom.* Berkeley, CA: Ten Speed Press.

Pagels, E. (1995). *The origins of Satan.* New York: Random House.

Palazzoli, S. M., Boscolo, L, Cecchin, G, & Prata, G. (1978). *Paradox and counterparadox.* New York: Aronson.

Perrow, C. (1984). *Normal accidents.* New York: Basic Books.

Ridley, M. (1997). *The origins of virtue.* New York: Viking Press.

Ross, M. H. (1993). *The culture of conflict.* New Haven, CT: Yale University Press.

Schön, D. A. (1983). *The reflective practitioner: How professionals think in action.* New York: Basic Books.

Smith, L. B. (1997). *Fools, martyrs and traitors.* Evanston, IL: Northwestern University Press.

Tenner, E. (1996). *Why things bite back: Technology and the revenge of unintended consequences.* New York: Knopf.

Ury, W. (1993). *Getting past no.* New York: Bantam Books.

von Bertalanffy, L. (1986). *General systems theory: Foundations, development, applications.* New York: Braziller.

Watzlawick, P. (1983). *The situation is hopeless but not serious.* New York: Norton.

Wright, R. (1994). *The moral animal.* New York: Pantheon.

Yarn, D. (Ed.). (1999). *Dictionary of conflict resolution.* San Francisco: Jossey-Bass.

PART IV
Special Applications and Considerations

CHAPTER 13

Mediation with Never-Married Parents

JOAN K. RAISNER

The growth of never-married parents in society has led to an increasing number of these parents entering mediation to resolve disputes over custody, parental access, and decision making. Most mediators lack specific training in dealing with the unique characteristics of this population. This chapter draws on the author's extensive experience mediating with never-married parents. It examines differences between never-married and divorcing parents, events that bring never-married parents into mediation, reintroducing a parent and child, and specific strategies and interventions for mediation with parents who were never married.

The increased use of mediation by U.S. courts when parents have disputes over child custody and other parenting issues is well documented. This rapid growth is occurring in both court-connected services and the private sector. Mediation of child custody disputes was first piloted in the Los Angeles County, California, Conciliation Courts in 1973 (Thoennes, Salem, & Pearson, 1995). By the mid-1990s more than 200 court-connected programs throughout the country offered the alternative of mediation (Salem & Milne, 1995). Records from the office of the Marriage and Family Counseling Service (MFCS), the mediation service of the Cook County Circuit Court (Chicago, Illinois), indicate that the number of families referred for mediation services in that program increased nearly threefold in the last 15 years.

At the same time that the use of family mediation was spreading throughout the United States, an exponential increase in the number of out-of-wedlock births also occurred. The number of children living with a single parent *who had never married* grew from 243,000 in 1960, to 3.7 million in

1983, to 6.3 million in 1993 (Wilson, 1996), and reached 11.9 million in 1998 (Bureau of the Census, 1998). Whereas in recent years the total number of children living with single mothers has appeared to level off, the number of children living with single fathers increased by 25%, to 2.1 million, in the years between 1995 and 1998 (Bureau of the Census, 2000). The percentage of children being born to unmarried, non-Hispanic white women, especially women who have some college education, also is on the rise (Browning, Miller-McLemore, Couture, Lyon, & Franklin, 1997).

These numbers portray the rapid growth in the creation of families occurring outside of a marriage. It is not surprising, then, that an increasing number of these families are finding their way into family court systems and are being referred to court mediation services to resolve their disputes over custody, parental access, and decision making. How can family mediators be effective in serving this growing number of nontraditional families?

It is likely that most mediators received training in family mediation that was based on a tradition of mediating with divorcing families. Family mediators are likely to feel confident in assuming that some circumstances apply, in general, to many of those divorcing parents. For example, family mediators initially may assume that the divorcing parents lived together as a separate family unit; that both parents played a role in the child's life; and that the divorcing parents need help in managing the transition from their formerly intimate relationship to a new, businesslike, co-parenting arrangement that involves two homes (Ricci, 1997). And, perhaps the most significant of all, the mediator knows that these parents *fully expected to be involved with a court in order to dissolve their marriage.*

Experiences with divorcing families do not necessarily equip a family mediator to address the circumstances and the needs of the never-married parents who come to court over issues of physical custody, access, and decision making in regard to their children. What if the parents who did not marry also did not establish an ongoing relationship with each other or did not have a history of making decisions together? Perhaps someone other than either parent was involved in the routine care of the children. The family mediator may be assisting these parents to establish a businesslike parenting relationship when no personal *or* parenting relationship existed in the past (Raisner, 1997). A co-parenting arrangement may be the last thing that either parent was considering—although a family mediator should recognize that many never-married parents consider that they have, in fact, been "cooperatively parenting" in their own ways. Most important, given that the entire relationship was based on a limited or informal arrangement, did these parents have *any reasonable expectation that a court would become involved in their business?*

This chapter explores the possible characteristics and needs of these nontraditional, never-married parents and the families they create. In 2002, the MFCS department served over 2,600 families who were ordered to mediate their disputes about their children by Domestic Relations Court judges; of those families, nearly 40% were families in which the parents had never married each other. During the time that I have served as a mediator in the MFCS court mediation program, I personally have mediated more than 1,000 cases in which the parents were married to each other and at least an equal number of cases in which the parents were never married to each other.

This chapter is based on observations, experiences, and surveys of case records conducted over those years. I include some factors that appear to have an impact on parents' decisions to marry or not, because these factors also have an impact on the mediation process. I describe some of the differences that appear to exist between never-married and divorcing parents, and I suggest strategies to consider when conducting family mediation with this growing population of nontraditional families.

THE DECISION TO MARRY

A case could be made that, historically, marriage-type contracts evolved in human social groups along with the concepts of private property and primogeniture. Marital status does ensure an orderly transfer of property and social status and puts boundaries on acceptable human sexual behaviors. Each community defines who is eligible to marry and establishes appropriate rituals for that purpose.

The existence of never-married parents is not a new phenomenon. In fact, the decision of whether or not two people even *could* marry has not always been in the hands of the individuals themselves. For Catholics in 19th-century Germany, for example, the Catholic Church determined who was qualified to marry and performed all marriages. Those Catholics who lacked the necessary wealth or property to marry formed family units outside the Church and outside the formal structure in arrangements called *concubinage* (Abrams, 1993). Since individuals in these less formal unions did not meet the financial standards to marry, concubinage filled a community need, on one hand, and served to support the prevailing prejudices of that time about the perceived lack of morals and character in the poorer classes, on the other. Although not a marriage, concubinage was a recognized category and bestowed civil standing with respect to the parental rights and duties of the mothers and fathers. Marriage or concubinage legally defined the status of the children born to women and also levied a social judgment on a woman's sexuality (Abrams, 1993). Eventually, the desire to limit the drain on public funds that was necessary to support out-of-wedlock children led to a liberalization of marriage law and the end of state-sanctioned concubinage in Germany (Abrams, 1993).

Access to officially sanctioned unions has not always been available in the United States either. Due to rural and frontier conditions, in the absence of local clergy or a justice of the peace, couples could enter into a *common-law marriage* and become husband and wife simply by making a public declaration of their intentions. During the period of slavery, slave couples were forbidden to marry, so they developed their own ceremony (called *jumping the broom*), so strong was the need to be recognized as a family unit, even in the face of those inhuman conditions. Currently, our U.S. "community" is discussing whether to extend the right to marry to same-sex couples.

Other public policies can influence the decision to marry. For example, proposed legislation to replace the 1996 Welfare Reform Law—which established time limits and job training requirements for mothers who received any form of public assistance—sought, among other provisions, up to $300 million dollars for states to distribute as incentives to welfare mothers to marry. The proposed legislation generated a robust debate over whether the government should be in the business of promoting (possibly dubious) marriages, especially through what might be experienced as irresistible financial incentives to an economically disadvantaged group (Lauerman, 2002).

Obviously, marriage continues to be the golden standard, given that the full weight of legal, religious, and social norms combine to support formal marriage contracts. In light of these promarriage social pressures, what could be the even more compelling reason *not* to marry? We may more fully understand the complex dynamics of the nontraditional families established by never-married parents if we can appreciate some of the many reasons why a marriage might *not* occur.

THE DECISION NOT TO MARRY

Compared with the social stigmas of the past, U.S. society today does appear more accepting of a variety of family units. Families are families, whether they are created by same-sex parent adoptions or inseminations, or by children born through surrogate pregnancies, or by those couples who choose to remain childless, or by those couples who simply decided to live together and have children without the encumbrance of a formal marriage. A pregnancy, in and of itself, does not create the same degree of pressure on the parents to marry that it might have in years past. Single parents today appear more likely to end an unhealthy intimate relationship rather than proceed to a marriage just because they are expecting a child. In fact, parents who never married each other may have fears that now a court is going to force them into a relationship that had ended for good reasons. Like some divorcing parents, if they thought that they had "solved" their problems with the other parent by breaking off the relationship, they now will be required to address those problems—probably in a mediation session—for the sake of the child.

Many of the reasons that relationships do not proceed to marriage are personal. People often choose not to marry for the same good reasons that ultimately cause people to divorce: drug and alcohol abuse, infidelity, financial concerns, domestic violence, mental abuse, or perhaps persistent interference from other family members. Just as in divorce mediation, family mediators need to screen for the presence of this history between parents who are ordered to mediate and who did not marry each other.

A survey of 197 families of never-married parents who were served by the MFCS program over a 4-year period provides an illustration of this point. Almost 70% of those parents reported a history of some violence in their past relationship with each other (Raisner, 1997) and stated that this violent history was a factor in the decision not to marry. (However, the presence of that history did *not* appear to be a factor in their ability to reach a parenting agreement with the assistance of a mediator in a safe and fair environment. Compared to their divorcing counterparts, never-married parents even appeared to reach a settlement in mediation in somewhat greater numbers [Raisner, 1997].)

Another reason a marriage might not occur is economic. The financial ability to provide for a family is still strongly linked to eligibility for marriage, and its absence may function as a deterrent. According to one study, men who were identified as African Americans and who were employed or in the military were two times more likely to marry as similar men who were not in the work force at all. No relationship in this study, however, was found between a man's employment and his experience of fatherhood. An estimated 44% of the men in this study fathered their first child out of wedlock before their 25th birthday (Testa & Krogh, 1995). When unemployment figures for a specific group of U.S. citizens are disproportionately high, it is likely that the percentage of parents within that group who do not marry will also be disproportionately high.

Other factors contributing to the decision not to marry may be societal and/or cultural. Is the decision not to marry based on the parents' prior experiences either with divorce and/or with courts? Did specific public policies, either indirectly or directly, influence their decision of whether or not to get married? Or are they individuals who have a strong aversion to any organized or institutionalized structure? Do they experience any structure as intrusive, controlling, or limiting of their personal choices? Did these parents avoid marriage because they strongly identified with a group that has been historically marginalized or discriminated against in the United States and specifically chose not to abide by the strictures of what they feel is an unjust system?

Legal and cultural factors also can cause a breakdown in the ability of a parent—in many cases, it is the father—even to maintain a physical presence in the child's life. For example, young men in the United States of certain ethnic backgrounds will spend more time in prison than others. According to one report, nearly one in three (32%) African American men between the ages of 20 and 29 years are under some type of correctional control at any one time: awaiting trial, on probation, serving a sentence, or on parole. Many of these men also are never-married fathers. This figure compares to one in eight (12.5%) Hispanic men, and one in 25 (4%) non-Hispanic white men (Newman, 1999).

Any of these factors could have an impact on the decision of whether to marry or not to marry. However, to proceed effectively, the family mediator will find it helpful to grasp the specific reasons why any particular set of parents came to their personal decision not to marry each other. Working with parents who have made informal contracts can lead mediators toward a more creative, exciting model of family mediation.

INFORMAL CONTRACTS

What do we actually know about how unmarried couples negotiate parenthood? The following remarks are taken from an interview with Waldo Johnson, Jr., Assistant Professor in the School of Social Service Administration, University of Chicago. Professor Johnson is a principal investigator in the national longitudinal "Fragile Families and Child Well-Being Study."

> The general impression is that these fathers are not only absent, but they don't offer support . . . and don't care about their children. But a preliminary study of 20 unwed African-American mothers and 14 [unwed African-American] fathers residing in Chicago shows that the relationship is much more complex than that. The relationship can be dramatically affected by a multitude of issues, such as the father's ability to provide financial support, the relationship between the mother and father, and the relationship between the unwed parents' families. (Behan, 1998, p. 111).

A survey of the records of 267 Parentage Court families who attended mediation at MFCS during the period of 1995–1997 supports the existence and complexity of these informal commitments:

Median age of the mothers:	29 years old
Median age of the fathers:	31 years old
Median length of the relationship:	4 years
Percentage who lived together:	61%
Percentage with more than one child together:	20%

Obviously, many parents may not have married but they did form informal contracts in large numbers—including setting up separate, marital-like family units. When looking at the above list, the family mediator may notice similarities between divorcing and never-married parents—at least, that is what it may look like at first. Important clues to the underlying differences in their issues become apparent by comparing the statements of the parents themselves. Parents who are divorcing often make statements such as the following:

"I never expected that my marriage would end like this."
"What should we tell the children?"
"I want to continue to be a fully involved parent, like I was before."
"I'll agree to anything. I just want to get out!"

Although some parents who were never married to one another are in circumstances that look very similar to their divorcing counterparts, in many instances they will express their concerns in a different way. Never-married parents are more likely to make statements such as the following:

"I don't know why we are even here. We were never married."
"This is all about the money!"
"I always let him see the child, at least whenever he came around."
"Some fathers, they walk away. Not me. My child isn't going to grow up like that."
"So a court is going to tell me how to raise my child?"
"I'm just here for my rights."
"I never thought *my* child would end up in the system."

Instead of having issues about the ending of their relationship, many never-married parents are likely to have issues about finding themselves "in the system." The court is going to insist on a formal access plan and/or on collecting regular child support payments. Many nonresidential parents state that they were an active participant and/or contributor to their child's well-being in the past. Quite likely, the residential parent did make the child available on a frequent basis. Now either parent can feel indignant, resentful, or humiliated at being "hauled into court."

WHAT ISSUES BRING NEVER-MARRIED PARENTS INTO COURT?

One of the most important distinctions between divorcing and never-married parents is that never-married parents did not expect to be involved in court at all. The events that bring a set of never-married parents into court usually are not connected to the breakup of the relationship itself. What is more likely to prompt court involvement by parents who never married each other is an event that interrupted or changed their informal parenting arrangements. Court involvement may occur at the request of one parent who is responding to a sudden denial of access to the child. Anything that interrupts the informal arrangement—such as a change of employment, relocation, a change in parenting capacity, the influence of new partners—may precipitate recourse to court action. These are issues that family mediators will find familiar from their work with *postdecree* situations—issues that commonly bring divorced parents back into court long *after* the divorce.

Initially, never-married parents might direct many of their negative feelings about being in court toward the mediator—who, after all, may be an extension of the court system. Paradoxically, these same parents often react positively to the mediator as the "human face of the court system." If the never-married parents are not sophisticated users of public institutions such as the courts—and if attorneys do not represent them, as is often the case—the mediation setting can be seen as an opportunity to discuss what is going on—finally, privately. If the parents are carefully screened for safety and fairness concerns, the chance to communicate, assisted by the family mediator, can be a very welcome opportunity.

Other relatives of the never-married parent may have played a significant role in rearing the child, especially if the parent was young, still in school, etc., when the child was born (Oyserman, Radin, & Benn, 1993; Parish, Hao, & Hogan, 1991). These relatives may feel justified, whether indirectly or directly, in trying to influence the outcome of the mediation process. Does the mediator sense that someone other than the parents is trying to maintain the status quo by discouraging parental cooperation? Can the parents recognize that other persons are "present" in the mediation room? Are the parents aware that they may need to make a plan to handle that situation? Sometimes a visitation schedule is more appropriate for the grandmother than the mother, for example.

The involvement of other relatives can work in another way. For example, younger single parents often live with their family of origin for several years after becoming parents. When a single parent moves into his or her own household, it can cause new tensions, mistrust, and a sense of loss. The custodial parent who felt reassured about the level of care when sending the child to that extended family home for visits may no longer feel the child will be adequately cared for when visiting with the other parent alone in an unfamiliar space.

Many times court proceedings are initiated for financial reasons. In Illinois, for example, a woman who receives any type of public assistance for herself or her child is required to name a father. The state then proceeds with a child support collection process against that father for reimbursement of aid to the mother and child. Failure to pay eventually results in legal actions by the state against the father. Nonpayment of child support can cause a parent to be jailed for his or her debt to the state—officially called "contempt of court." Fathers and/or their relatives often believe that these legal actions originated with the mother. Conversely, the state may require a routine DNA test to verify parentage of the child, and the mother may feel that the father is trying to humiliate her or to reject the child. Until the parents sort out these issues, the entire mediation process may be stalemated.

The following are examples of some situations that brought never married-parents to court:

Father and mother, now in their early 20s, grew up and went to school together. Both live with members of their original families. Father's mother cared for the now 18-month-old child while mother worked. Father and his family paid for formula, diapers, and medicine. When mother lost her job, she applied for public aid, unaware that public aid routinely brings petitions to collect child support payments from fathers. Father and his family thought the mother brought the petition and were outraged after all they had contributed. The family cut off all informal contact with the mother and child and urged the father to file for physical custody. Family members on both sides then "talked bad" about each other in the neighborhood. Neither the mother nor the father knew what to believe.

Father is in his mid-40s, mother in her mid-20s. Father is in a 22-year marriage (with four other children); he had a relationship with the mother of this now 7-year old child during a brief separation from his wife. There was no contact between the father and child until the mother brought a recent petition for child support. Father counterfiled for weekend visitation and 10 weeks each summer with the child. The wife cannot believe this is happening,

Mother is a 26-year-old habitual drug user with no permanent residence. The child, now 6 years old, was placed with father at birth by the state and has been raised by the paternal grandmother. Mother reappeared, having completed her third rehab program. She is petitioning for overnight, weekend visitation with this child and two younger children living with other fathers. The grandmother cannot understand how a court could let this happen.

Father and mother dated briefly in their late 20s, recognized the relationship was abusive, broke up, and then moved on. Their child, now 14 years old, had very infrequent contact with father, most of which was at the home of the paternal grandparents on holidays. Mother and child had a big fight and mother took the child to father to "teach the child a lesson." Father immediately petitioned the court for custody and child support. The child cannot believe this is happening.

Mother and father, now in their mid-40s, broke off their relationship 13 years ago when their child was a toddler. Mother married and had two younger children. Father already had two older children who lived with him. This child, now 15, had never met the father but "found his name on some papers." The child decided to contact the father, initiated visitation, and eventually requested to live with him to "get to know my father while I am still a child." The mother is devastated that this is happening.

The parents, now in their mid-30s, lived together for 4 years. They recognized the relationship was not going anywhere, yet both continued to parent their two children. Now, several years later, mother is getting married and is going to have another child. Father came to court "just to get something on paper, so there are no problems in the future."

The first thing that may impress the family mediator when working with parents who did not marry each other is the complexity of the issues that lie behind the event that brought the parents to court. Although a child support petition often initiates the court process, in fact money may not be the real driving force. The underlying issues at the heart of the scenarios described above (and hundreds like them) are quite complex: a misunderstanding of the behavior of other adults; a lack of acknowledgment of the value of nonmonetary support; the sudden appearance of an absent parent; fears about parenting capacity; changes initiated by the child's age and developmental stage; or issues that may be brought up by the court process itself. Maybe it *was* just a desire to make things official.

After looking at the complex variations to be found in never-married relationships, the second thing that a family mediator might well conclude is that effective mediation will require getting specific information about the history of the never-married parents' prior relationship. Did the parents establish a home together? Did they make any decisions about child bearing and child rearing together? How has each parent participated with the upbringing of the children in the past? What is the role of a third person, such as a grandparent or a new partner? What were the parents' emotional reactions at the time their personal relationship ended? What has been the pattern of contact with the child since the breakup? How do they feel about being in court now? Are they open to updating their information? Is it even safe to exchange new information with the other parent?

FAMILY MEDIATION WITH PARENTS WHO LIVED TOGETHER

The following characteristics may be present, to some degree, in all family mediation cases, whether the parents were married or not. However, parents who lived within an informal contract may present some additional challenges.

Grief/Relief

Parents who lived together may also be feeling some of the emotional reactions that are present with divorcing parents, except that the impact and timing of these emotions is more likely to occur at the point when they have to give up the dream that they can handle everything between themselves. They previously may have felt great relief that they were "done" with each other. The mediator not only acknowledges the couple's grief and fears about the future but also facilitates a process of adjustment to the unexpected reality that they will now continue to be involved in each other's lives—because the court is insisting on it, and because their child needs them to be. The mediator can provide information on resources they can access to address the problems that undermined their relationship in the first place.

Timing

How significant is the timing of the court involvement? Like any litigants, parents who did not marry may be suspicious of each other's motives for bringing a matter to court. In addition, they may have suspicions about the timing of this parenting dispute:

"Why now?"
"Is this happening because I'm dating again?"
"Is this a power play to get back at me?"

Informal Bonds

Any formal parenting plan created by divorcing parents may reasonably discuss the possibility of continuing the child's relationships with any half-siblings, stepsiblings, or other relatives of the noncustodial parent. The child whose parents did not marry but who lived together under an informal contract may have formed other important attachments during the time that the parents were together—attachments that are not likely to be addressed by a court. Is the "brother" who lived with the child, who was the biological child from a prior relationship of one of the never-married parents, still a brother when that parent and the brother move out? Is the "grandmother" who babysat for all the children of both parents when they lived together still going to care for the nonbiological grandchild when the parents go their separate ways? The mediator needs to explore these issues with the parents; not only may their child be experiencing the same range of emotions as any child of a divorce, but their child may have many additional worries. The mediator should help the parents consider and address the question: Is the child going to avoid emotional attachments in the future?

Another possible mediation scenario: Will the parent who raised a partner's child for many years still have a presence in that nonbiological child's life after the relationship with the child's parent is over? An Illinois District Appellate Court decision in 1996 reversed the dismissal of a nonparent's claim for visitation in a case in which the man had believed he was the child's father and developed a loving relationship with the child (*Koelle v. Zwiren*, 1996). An ongoing effort to address the realities of nonbiological relationships is the proposed Uniform Parentage Act (2000), which tries to balance the claims of a biological parent with the other established relationships in a child's life. Until legislation and case law can catch up with the realities of these relationships in nontraditional families, family mediators will continue to break new ground by facilitating agreements that acknowledge these relationships.

FAMILY MEDIATION WITH PARENTS WHO NEVER LIVED TOGETHER

One of the most satisfying and challenging experiences for a mediator is to facilitate the process of putting together a realistic child-centered plan to reintroduce the child to a long-absent parent. This is especially the case when the previously absent parent is filled with a desire to make up for lost time. The dialogue may go something like this:

CUSTODIAL PARENT: Why now? You were never there for us.

ABSENT PARENT: I was young. I'm a different person now. I've got myself more together now.

CUSTODIAL PARENT: Why upset the child? I'm married now. She calls my husband "Daddy."

ABSENT PARENT: I never knew my father, and I don't want my child growing up that way.

CUSTODIAL PARENT: What if the child doesn't want to see you!

ABSENT PARENT: This is just using the child to get back at me!

A mediator will solicit proposals, of course, for structuring the permanent access plan regarding the child's time with the noncustodial parent. However, it may be necessary to start with a reintroduction process. The following steps may be helpful for a parent who had a limited prior relationship with his or her child.

If the child is an infant or toddler:

Start with brief, frequent visits in the child's home, with a trusted person present.

Build a presence in the child's life by providing photos, tapes, etc.
Take brief trips away from the child's home to familiar places.
Increase the time of visits away from the child's home, maintaining the usual routines.
Be completely flexible in response to the child's mood.
Present a pleasant, relaxed face during transfer of the child between the parents.

If the child is a preteen:

Start with brief visits to the child's home and demonstrate courtesy.
Make telephone contact at consistent and appropriate times.
Send cards, small gifts, and e-mails; attend school events.
Extend the contacts: select child-directed activities (e.g., going to movies, shopping), meet other relatives.
Set up a visit to your home. Try out occasional overnights.
Avoid being a nonstop entertainer or an instant disciplinarian.
Plan ways to communicate with the custodial parent—the child is not a messenger!
Remember, a child of this age may resent giving up status as a "junior adult."
Reassure the child that you will not take him or her away from the other parent.

Whether or not a family mediator's protocol includes any meetings with children, there are some areas a mediator may wish to explore while working on a parenting plan with never-married parents who also never established a home together:

- What was the prior contact, if any, with the nonresidential parent? What experiences did these parents have in making decisions together?
- Can the parents articulate the child's needs? How will the age of the child enter into the planning process? How will the child's preferences be incorporated into the plan?
- What support does the child need to adjust to a new person and a new family unit?
- What other kinds of help do the parents need to be successful in their efforts and in their parenting plan?

WHAT ELSE CAN A MEDIATOR DO?

The following are suggestions made by family mediation colleagues who also work with never-married families in the MFCS program. These strategies can have special effectiveness when they are adapted to the needs and concerns of families in which the parents did not marry.

Providing Education

If the parents do not have a history of working together in the past, the mediator can add a stronger informative component to his or her interactions with them in order to promote successful communication and smoother co-parenting. Employing this strategy will feel different from the mediation conducted with divorcing parents, when the mediator may have to put more effort into addressing/correcting some well-established "bad habits" that crept into their pattern of parenting together. The mediator can ask questions to assess the parents' understanding of child development and provide information and resources on how to fill any gaps. Specific steps to take include finding and sharing appropriate articles and/or sources of information on (1) single parenting, (2) the importance of grandparents, (3) activities to do with a child that do not cost much money, (4) family counseling for children of single parents, etc.

Slow the Pace

All petitioners come to court insisting on specific solutions. Most litigants are shocked by what they hear said about themselves in court. Never-married parents, in particular, may need extra time to step back from the "solutions" (e.g., supervised visitation, sole custody, parenting classes, and on and on) they brought to court and explore with the mediator what it is they really want to accomplish. They may not have a personal history with each other that will provide a moderating influence, and they often will not have attorneys to put things into perspective for them. The reasons for demanding supervised visits, for example, can be anything from poor compliance with a schedule ("He's always late"), to poor parenting skills ("He lets the child play video games all night"), to the presence of an immediate danger to the child ("She's dating a sex offender!"). The problem they are trying to solve needs to be clearly identified.

These parents may experience mediation as providing a huge safety net, a place where they can, at last, safely discuss problems, try temporary plans, review and update those plans, and even discuss their nonlegal issues. The family mediator may feel like a case manager at times, making referrals from his or her personal network of resources, coordinating the results of working with other helpers, and/or checking in to see how the introduction to a child is going. All of this takes time, and mediators need to remember to slow down the pace of mediation to reflect each family's needs.

Balancing the Power

Among the many reasons why parents may not marry, as was suggested earlier, is a desire to maintain a sense of control and prevent intrusions into their personal lives. Therefore, the extra effort taken to acknowledge and reduce parents' sense of powerlessness at being in court will smooth the process. The goal of retaining as much control as possible over the decisions made about their child will be these parents' strongest motivator to move past their suspicions and resentments of each other—because right now, the court is all in their business.

Providing Guidelines

When parents who have little or no experience with each other are asked to put together a schedule, they also may need guidelines. Although not measurable or enforceable in the same way as a schedule, guidelines can help establish the basic behaviors that form the parents' foundation for future trust and cooperation. By reaching agreement on the answers to the following types of questions, with the mediator's help, parents will be able to construct a viable parenting plan that serves themselves as well as the child:

> How will requests for changes in the schedule be handled?
> Are there any events the parents will attend together?
> How will parents communicate with the child's school? With doctors? With each other?
> What other adults will be allowed to guide and discipline the child?
> Will third parties assist the child and/or the parents?

Screening for a History of Violence

A family mediator may be the first person to ever ask about physically and emotionally abusive behavior between the parents. Abusive behavior causes physically and psychologically harmful experiences that can interfere with the victim's ability to organize his or her thoughts and speak freely. Both divorcing and never-married parents may believe that they escaped the problem with the dissolution of the relationship. However, there may be lingering effects of the past traumatic events. Being required to be back in contact with each other may trigger old memories and patterns that can interfere with the capacity to respond to mediation. Some people need the formality of the court process and the strict atmosphere of a courtroom (Grillo, 1991) in order to be protected from ongoing threats to their safety or new acts of violence.

WHAT ABOUT THE CHILDREN?

> A child-centered perspective calls for a rhetoric that
> speaks less about competing rights and more about
> adult responsibility and children's needs.
>
> WOODHOUSE, 1993, p. 17

The emotional impact on the children when their never-married parents end their personal relationship may depend on whether or not the parents ever lived together with the children. A family mediation protocol that includes talking with the children may be even more crucial with never-married parents than it is with divorcing parents to assess what the children need *now,* because now their parents are in court.

Any child of separated parents is likely to be angry at one or both parents and experience a painful conflict of loyalties. The child of never-married parents also may feel embarrassed that his or her family is different in some fundamental way from the families of other children whose parents are divorced. Perhaps the embarrassment comes in response to an awareness of social judgments about the parents' unwed status. Sometimes a child will balk at maintaining contact with a biological parent when the custodial parent marries and creates what looks to the child like a more "normal" family. The family mediator can reassure the child that every family looks different but that difference does not mean the family is not normal.

During an interview with a child, the mediator should carefully avoid questions and language that communicate any preconceived ideas about family life. Useful questions and comments elicit the child's opinions about the mediation process and any awareness of the parents' issues. For example:

> "I am a helper to your family, and you are important, so I wanted to
>   meet you."
> "Do you know why you are here today?"
> "This is not punishment—nobody's in trouble!"
> "I am not a decision maker for your parents, and you aren't either,
>   right?"
> "Do you know what 'confidential' means?"

The mediator may begin with general questions about the child's activities, friendships, school experiences, likes and dislikes. For example:

> "What grade are you in now? How is that different from last year?"
> "What is your favorite activity in school?"

"Do you have a special friend?"

"What do you like about your friends? What do you think your friends like about you?"

The mediator may begin with neutral questions about the child's daily routine and home structure. For example:

"Who gets you up in the morning?"

"How do you get to school?"

"When do you spend time with Mom? With Dad?"

"What do you like to do when you are with Mom? With Dad?"

The mediator also may inquire about the child's feelings and opinions as long as the child is assured that the child's words will be kept confidential and that he or she is not being asked to make decisions or "tattle":

"Do you have any special chores? What happens if you forget to do them sometimes? Do you know how to keep that from happening?"

"Do you have any worries? Is anything happening to you that you think is unfair? Who would you talk to if you had a big problem and needed help?"

"If you had three wishes, what would they be?"

"What would you do with that million dollars?"

The mediator shows flexibility by following the child's lead in the conversation when choosing topics, changing topics, or making comments. When the timing is right, the mediator can use humor, stories, and comparisons to relieve any misplaced guilt the child may have about being the cause of new troubles between the parents:

"Do you have a driver's license yet? No? You are not old enough yet? Well, do you think you are old enough to make grownups leave or come back? You just wish you could?"

"Lots of kids wish their parents would get back together. OK? OK."

"You can look around and decide what you want to do when you are grown up, and maybe have your own children. Oh, you are already doing that?"

WHY DO MEDIATORS LIKE TO WORK WITH NONTRADITIONAL FAMILIES?

Although most family mediation with nontraditional families continues to cluster around court programs such as MFCS, inevitably more private mediators will market their services to these clients. It makes good business sense to attract this growing population of potential clients. Some mediators really like working with these families for reasons that go well beyond building a practice. It depends on what appeals to the individual, of course; some mediators find that the dynamics of never-married parents are an unexpectedly good match with their personal style.

Many of these parents are very direct, very practical. They are unlikely to use mediation to prolong a court process, for example, just to maintain the negative intimacy with the other parent. Their ability to "cut to the chase" can be remarkable. Mediators may find that they are able to accomplish a great deal in a relatively brief time with many never-married parents. This aspect can be very satisfying.

Like any two litigants, the emotions of never-married parents may be very strong. However, they may never demonstrate a commitment to forming a co-parenting relationship, as we know it. One advantage, however, is that they may be less overwhelmed by the raw emotions that are typically present when mediating with newly divorcing parents. Since the breakup itself is not the subject of litigation, mediating with them on their issues may feel like a "cleaner process."

Many never-married parents have successfully navigated the rough waters of parting from one another, and they may have more reasonable expectations of each other. They may have developed the necessary skills to deal well with many of life's complexities. They may even be in a place where they feel emotionally generous toward the other parent. When something totally out of the blue suddenly taxes the limits of those skills and that generosity, the mediator can focus on restoring them to their previous careful balance, their former successful level of functioning—a very satisfying undertaking.

Children in these nontraditional families often feel comfortable talking to adults in a matter-of-fact way. These children may demonstrate manners and sophistication that reflect their participation in a more adult-identified world. They may express surprising insights into adult situations because their families are not typical. They may welcome a chance to talk to someone outside the family. In short, they may have a lot to say. "If you enjoyed talking to me, do you think you might like to have your own person to talk to again, like a counselor? Great!"

Whatever the outcome of their mediation—and coming to a clearer understanding of the exact issues in their dispute is considered a very successful outcome for a mediation process with any family—many never-married parents express heartfelt appreciation that they had the opportunity to meet with the mediator. Some of the parents who chose not to marry may specifically mention that they enjoyed the opportunity to discuss their situation in an environment where no one was judging them or telling them what to do. Mediation may be a unique experience for them that empowers and affirms their nontraditional parenting arrangements.

CONCLUSION

Family mediators need to appreciate the different dynamics that may exist when conducting family mediation with parents who are divorcing versus those who did not marry. The timing of their court process and the issues that bring them into court may be very different for never-married parents. It is essential to consider the impact on mediation if the parents did, or did not, establish a home together. Furthermore, a respect for, and appreciation of, the prior relationship that existed between the parents who did not marry each other, their choices, and the complex reasons for those choices are the foundation of successful mediation with this population.

Mediators must constantly examine the assumptions they have taken for granted from the model of traditional family mediation. By accumulating resources and building a network of support among other professionals who also recognize and serve these nontraditional families, mediators can increase and extend the benefits of these parents' mediation experience. Central mediation areas to address with these parents include (1) clarifying the issues that brought them to court, (2) updating their information about each other, (3) creating guidelines to build trust, and (4) refocusing the parents on their child's needs. Underlying the work of addressing these areas is respect for their former level of functioning, the role of other nonbiological relationships in their "family," and the contributions of other family members.

By fully enjoying the fresh outlooks that nontraditional families bring into the mediation environment and contributing their experiences and observations with these parents, each mediator who works with this population can add to our growing understanding of family mediation with nontraditional family units.

REFERENCES

Abrams, L. (1993). Concubinage, cohabitation and the law: Class and gender relations in nineteenth-century Germany. *Gender and History,* 5(1), 82–100.

Behan, C. (1998, March 19). Where are the fathers? *The University of Chicago Chronicle,* pp. 3, 8.

Browning, D. S., Miller-McLemore, B. J., Couture, P. D., Lyon, K. B., & Franklin, R. M. (1997). *From culture wars to common ground: Religious debate and the American family.* Louisville, KY: Westminster John Knox Press.

Bureau of the Census. (1998). Available: *www.census.gov/Press-Release/cb98-228.html*

Bureau of the Census. (2000). Available: *www.census.gov/Press-Release/www/200/cb00-175.html*

Grillo, T. (1991). The mediation alternative: Process dangers for women. *Yale Law Review, 100,* 1574–1610.

Koelle v. Zwiren, 284 Ill. App. 3d 778, 672 N.E.2d 868 (1996).

Lauerman, C. (2002, May 22). Wedding bells ring untrue. *Chicago Tribune,* Section 8, pp. 1, 8.

Newman, M. (1999, Fall). The criminal injustice system. *Chicago Media Watch Report,* pp. 1, 2, 12.

Oyserman, D., Radin, N., & Benn, R. (1993). Dynamics in three-generational families: Teens, grandparents and babies. *Developmental Psychology, 29*(3), 564–572.

Parish, W. L., Hao, L., & Hogan, D. P. (1991). Family support networks, welfare, and work among young mothers. *Journal of Marriage and the Family, 53,* 203–215.

Raisner, J. K. (1997). Family mediation and never-married parents. *Family and Conciliation Courts Review, 35,* 90–101.

Ricci, I. (1997). *Mom's house, Dad's house.* New York: Penguin.

Salem, P., & Milne, A. (1995). Making mediation work in domestic abuse. *Family Advocate, 17*(3), 34–38.

Testa, M., & Krogh, M. (1995). The effect of employment on marriage among black males in inner-city Chicago. In M. B. Tucker & C. Mitchell-Kernan (Eds.), *The decline in marriage among African Americans: Causes, consequences, and policy implications* (pp. 59–99). New York: Sage.

Thoennes, N., Salem, P., & Pearson, J. (1995). Mediation and domestic violence: Current policies and practices. *Family Conciliation Courts Review, 33*(1), 6–29.

Uniform Parentage Act. (2000). *Family Law Quarterly, 35,* 1–97. Available: *www.nccusl.org*

Wilson, W. J. (1996). *When work disappears: The world of the new urban poor.* New York: Knopf.

Woodhouse, B. B. (1993). Hatching the egg: A child-centered perspective on parents' rights. *Cardoza Law Review, 14,* 17–47.

SELECTED READINGS ON PARENTAGE

Courtesy of Mary Therese Doheny, JD, Law Offices of Wessel & Doheny, 188 West Randolph Street, Suite 1100, Chicago, IL 60601; (312) 558-3000.

Claiborne, J. (1999). From partners to parents: Toward a child-centered family law jurisprudence. *Santa Clara Law Review, 39,* 4. —This article discusses the relationship of the parents and the importance of the cooperative parental partnership in custody decisions. It is relevant because there is often a wide variance in the parental relationship, which may influence custody decisions.

Harris, L. J. (1996). Reconsidering the criteria for legal fatherhood. *Utah Law Review,* 461. —Discusses biological fatherhood in the context of custody decisions and embraces concept of "functional paternity" as a basis for establishing parental obligations and rights.

Kaplan, D. S. (2000). Why truth is not a defense in paternity action. *Texas Journal of Women and the Law, 10,* 69. —The conflict between historical presumptions about paternity and the emerging scientific (DNA) knowledge that refutes those presumptions is examined in this article. The author sees courts reacting to this conflict in three different ways. Courts have adopted different models, either highly discretionary or extreme and unforgiving, when it comes to the admittance of DNA evidence. Court responses range from always excluding DNA evidence that rebuts presumption of paternity (Pennsylvania) to always admitting evidence (Massachusetts) or excluding DNA based on best interest (New York).

Nolan, L. (1999). Children and their parents before the United States Supreme Court from Levy to Michael H.: Unlikely participants in constitutional jurisprudence. *Capital University Law Review, 28,* 1. —Reviews U.S. Supreme Court cases from 1968 to 1989 and concludes that the U.S. Supreme Court has erased most common-law disabilities for children while also recognizing a father's liberty and interest in relationship with the child.

Roberts, P. (2001). Biology and beyond: The case for passage of the New Uniform Parentage Act. *Family Law Quarterly, 35,* 41. —This article provides an overview of the history of parentage and the development of the law for parents and children. The author lists the various modern issues in parentage and discusses how the Uniform Parentage Act addresses those issues.

Williams, W. C. (1997). The paradox of paternity establishment: As rights go up, rates go down. *University of Florida Journal of Law and Public Policy, 8,* 261. —This article discusses child support and mandatory paternity establishment.

Woodhouse, B. B. (1993). Hatching the egg: A child-centered perspective on parents' rights. *Cardozo Law Review, 14,* 17–47. —This is an incredibly well written and informative article that focuses on the child's perspective and stretches the mind, particularly if the reader is an attorney who represents children. Recommended reading.

CHAPTER 14

Mediation and Domestic Abuse

ANN L. MILNE

The high incidence of domestic abuse suggests that most mediators inevitably have clients for whom domestic abuse is an issue. It is imperative that mediators understand the dynamics of domestic abuse and its potential impact on the mediation process. This chapter explores both sides of the controversy regarding whether mediation should be used in these cases and discusses the nature of domestic abuse, its impact on the mediation process, screening for abuse, mediation models, and hybrid tools and techniques.

There are nearly 6 million incidents of physical assault against women reported every year, and 76% of these are perpetrated by current or former husbands, cohabiting partners, or dates (Danis, 2003).[1] Domestic violence affects a wide range of victims regardless of socioeconomic status, ethnic heritage, race, or age (Bureau of Justice Statistics, 1995).[2] Once viewed as a private matter, domestic abuse has become front-page news:

- 37% of women who seek treatment in emergency rooms were injured by a current or former intimate partner (U.S. Department of Justice, 1997).
- More than three women are murdered by their husbands or boyfriends in the United States every day (Bureau of Justice Statistics, 2003).
- 78% of stalking victims are women (Tjaden & Thoennes, 1998).
- 80% of women who are stalked by former husbands are physically assaulted by that partner (Tjaden & Thoennes, 1998).
- 50% of men who batter their partners also abuse their children (Straus, Gelles, & Smith, 1990).

Changes in the law and the increased media attention given to domestic abuse have sensitized the public to this formerly private issue. In contrast, the use of mediation has increased significantly as a less public forum to resolve disputes between former spouses. Courts in at least 38 states have mandated that parents be referred to mediation when they are disputing custody or parental access schedules (Tondo, Coronel, & Drucker, 2001).

The use of mediation in cases involving instances or allegations of domestic abuse has been hotly debated. At some point in their career, most mediators will come face to face with these individuals and the challenges they present. The purpose of this chapter is to provide an overview of the dynamics of an abusive relationship in relation to the use of mediation in such cases involving allegations and/or instances of abuse.

UNDERSTANDING THE DYNAMICS OF DOMESTIC ABUSE

The pedagogy of domestic abuse has changed over the years from a "cycle of violence" approach—premised on a set of escalatory behaviors that result in an abusive act, followed by a "honeymoon stage" and a time of apology and contrition—to a theory of "power and control." This theory, developed by the Domestic Abuse Intervention Project in Duluth, Minnesota, considers behaviors such as verbal intimidation, threats of violence, threats to take the children, and economic control and isolation as ways of asserting control over another individual. The control is maintained by the enveloping threat and/or actuality of physical abuse (see Figure 14.1).

BATTERED WOMEN

It is a misperception that battered women are undereducated, unemployed, povery-sticken women of color with many children, living in an urban ghetto. In fact, they are professional women, factory workers, homemakers, college graduates, dropouts, wealthy, poor, African American, Caucasian, Asian, Hispanic, grandmothers and teenagers alike.

Why do these women remain in an abusive relationship? How do they make the decision to get out? Ending a relationship is very difficult for most people and even more so for a woman whose self-confidence has been diminished. Battered women report the following reasons for staying with a batterer (Stuehling & Hart, 1997; Wilson, 1997):

• *Hope for change.* An abusive partner is often remorseful, promising that it "won't happen again" or even to get counseling. A victim may be reluctant to leave when the partner is in treatment for the abuse; she wants to believe the treatment will end the abuse. Battered women are often committed

FIGURE 14.1. Power and control wheel.

to the relationship and the family and want the relationship to improve, not end.

• *Isolation.* Batterers isolate their partners in order to maintain control over them. Tactics may include censoring phone calls, cutting off transportation, and isolating them from friends and family. Often a victim feels humiliated, needs to hide the bruises from others, and lacks confidence to socialize and seek help.

• *Societal denial.* Battered women fear that no one will believe them because the batterer is often well liked. Women are reluctant to bring patterns of abuse to the attention of lawyers, let alone the judge and others who would pass judgment on them (Mahoney, 1994). They know they may not be believed. They assume that others will question why they would stay if things were that bad.

• *Impediments to leaving.* The batterer typically puts up many impediments to the possibility of the wife's leaving, such as threatening to take the children, withholding support, humiliating her in front of friends and family, and threatening to kill her and/or commit suicide.

• *Dangers in leaving.* Many battered women are convinced that a separation will not end the abuse. They fear retaliation and are not confident that separation will ensure their safety. This fear is born out by the statistics that report that separation is often the most dangerous time for a woman; the very attempt to leave incites an abusive partner (Fineman, 2002, citing Mahoney, 1994).

What factors contribute to a woman's ability/motivation to leave?

• *Economics.* The most likely predictor of whether a victim will permanently separate from a batterer is whether or not she has the economic resources to survive (Stuehling & Hart, 1997).

• *Repetitive leave taking.* Many battered women leave and return several times before they are able to separate permanently. The first time a victim leaves may be a test to see whether her husband will get some help. When he is violent again, she may leave and seek information about resources available to help her. She may return to him again and, in the interim, begin to pull together some economic, employment, or educational resources in case she must leave again. Mediators must understand that a woman's emotional and physical readiness (Stuehling & Hart, 1997; Wilson, 1997) in the leaving process may impact her ability to participate in a mediation process.

BATTERING PARTNERS

It is a misperception that batterers are thugs, knuckle-walkers, drunks, underemployed, unhappy in their jobs, poor communicators, and angry lowlifes with low self-esteem. Batterers are corporate executives, laborers, professors, police officers, high-wage earners, unemployed, college graduates, high school dropouts, Caucasian, African American, Asian, Hispanic—and your next door neighbor or best friend.

Why do these men batter women? Because they can. A batterer believes the following (Stuehling & Hart, 1997):

• He is entitled to control his partner.
• He is not a bad person even if he abuses his partner.
• He will get what he wants through the use of violence.

• He will not suffer consequences that outweigh the benefits achieved through the abuse.

There are many misconceptions about the types of men who become batterers and why they abuse their partners (Gondolf, 1988):

Myth: Batterers are men who cannot control their emotions.
Fact: Batterers choose the victim, the time, place, behavior, and severity of the abuse.
Myth: Batterers batter when they are enraged.
Fact: Many batterers acknowledge that anger is not present in all abusive incidents. A batterer's anger is aroused when their partners do not respond to the abuse or the threat of abuse.
Myth: Batterers batter because they cannot communicate effectively.
Fact: Many batterers are very good communicators, effectively using both spoken and unspoken language. Victims are acutely tuned in to the communications of their abusers.
Myth: Batterers have low self-esteem.
Fact: Research indicates that batterers do not differ from nonbatterers relative to self-esteem. However, batterers *do* have a stronger belief in their entitlement to control their partners than do nonbatterers (Gondolf, 1988).

GAY AND LESBIAN ABUSE

Gay and lesbian relationships are not immune from abuse, and a victim's sexual orientation does not preclude legal protection. Gay and lesbian partners may share children and personal property. When the relationship ends, the partners may find themselves in conflict over children, property, and finances. Until recently, courts have refused to hear these cases, claiming to have no jurisdiction over these individuals (Wisconsin Supreme Court, *In re:* Interest of Z. J. H., *Sporleder v. Hermes,* 1991). Recent decisions (Wisconsin Supreme Court, *In re:* Custody of H. S. H., *K. Holtzman v. Knott,* 1995) have changed this situation, but mediation may still be viewed as a more welcome and sensitive process, compared to the court system, by which these individuals can attempt to resolve their disputes.

Cases involving gay/lesbian partners can become more challenging when abuse is a factor in the relationship. A homophobic society, reluctance to publically disclose their sexual orientation, and a fear that their rights to protection from abuse may not be taken seriously can inhibit these victims from seeking an order of protection and can make screening for abuse difficult for a mediator.

THE LEGAL SYSTEM'S RESPONSE TO DOMESTIC ABUSE

The legal system's response to domestic abuse cases has evolved over the past two decades from a benign approach of essentially asking the parties to "cool down" by separating for the night to current responses that include mandatory arrest, civil protection and restraining orders, criminal protection orders, prosecution, shelters for battered women, and civil damage actions against the batterer. At least 20 states now direct judges to consider domestic abuse when awarding custody (Milne, Salem, & Koeffler, 1992).

The juxtaposition of strengthened court and legal interventions in domestic abuse cases with the expanded use of mediation has resulted in considerable controversy over the use of mediation in cases involving incidents and allegations of domestic abuse. Many victim advocates assert that mediation is potentially unsafe and can result in unfair agreements as the dynamics of the abusive relationship are enacted in the mediation process. Mediation proponents counter that mediation can be an empowering process and a better alternative than traditional lawyer-assisted negotiation and significantly better than litigation and adjudication. Arbitrarily prohibiting victims of domestic abuse from participating in mediation takes away choices—and taking away choices replicates the dynamics of the abusive relationship.

INTRODUCTION TO THE DEBATE

The debate has polarized the issues as well as the mediation and the domestic abuse prevention communities. A symposium convened by the Association of Family and Conciliation Courts (AFCC) in 1989 in Chicago, in an effort to surface and discuss the issues of mediation and domestic abuse, led to picketing of the hotel and angry outbursts among participants. Bread-and-butter issues, including concerns that the expansion of mediation would result in decreased funding for domestic abuse programs, have added to the conflict. Both proponents and opponents of the use of mediation in domestic abuse cases offer persuasive arguments for their positions.

In Opposition

Safety is a primary concern of those who oppose mediation in this context. Victim advocates note that the point at which partners separate is the most dangerous time for a potential or actual victim of domestic abuse (Fischer, Vidman, & Ellis, 1993). Partners who have assaulted and emotionally abused their partners during their marital relationship are most likely to assault or abuse them during and following negotiations or mediation (Ellis & Stuckless, 1996, citing Monahan, 1981; O'Leary, 1993). Mediation sessions allow the batterer to have contact with his victim and access to information that could jeopardize her safety. Furthermore, the mediation process pro-motes collaboration in an otherwise uncollaborative relationship and often results in agreements that promote continuing contact and an ongoing co-parenting relationship (Joyce, 1997). Because violent men seek new means of control when old ones fail, batterers are likely to use the legal system as a new arena of combat when they seek to keep their wives from leaving (Mahoney, 1994). Victims are likely to be fearful, compliant, and acquiescent in mediation, unable to participate effectively in the collaborative nature of the mediation process. Therefore, fairness and voluntariness—two essential components in mediation—are lacking.

The criminalization of domestic abuse was a hard-fought victory for the advocacy community. There is a concern that mediation will become a diver-sion from prosecution that will undermine the system of sanctions that many in the advocacy community believe are the only deterrents to further abuse (Fagan, 1996). The U.S. Commission on Civil Rights (1982) issued a strong statement to this effect:

> Mediation and arbitration place the parties on equal footing and ask them to negotiate an agreement for future behavior. Beyond failing to punish as-sailants for their crimes, this process implies that victims share responsibil-ity for the illegal conduct and requires them to modify their own behavior in exchange for the assailants' promises not to commit further crimes. (p. 2)

Other arguments offered in opposition to the use of mediation in cases involving domestic abuse include the dynamics of the relationship, which may preclude a victim from being able to express herself fully in the media-tion process; undetected intimidation and coercion of a victim that could re-sult in an involuntary agreement; inadequately trained mediators; the pri-vacy of the mediation process, which diminishes the public sanctions against abuse; the decriminalization of the abuse via the use of mediation as a diver-sion from prosecution; the time limitations imposed by some mediation pro-grams; the pressure on the institution to settle cases in order to justify the program's existence and, in some instances, continued funding; mediation agreements that are not commuted to a court order and are thus unenforceable; and the lack of an advocate for a victim in a mediation session.

In her seminal article "Mediation of Wife Abuse Cases: The Adverse Im-pact of Informal Dispute Resolution on Women," Lisa Lerman advocates for a "law enforcement" model that enforces formal legal action combined with punishment or rehabilitation of wife abusers. The goal is to ensure the safety of the victim and to give the abuser a clear message that society will not tol-erate his continued violence against his mate (Lerman, 1984). Advocates of the law enforcement model state that the goals of mediation—reaching an agreement, reconciling the parties, recognizing mutual responsibility for the problem, and removing abuse cases from the court system—are arguably incompatible with the law enforcement model's primary goal of stopping violence (Lerman, 1984; Sun & Woods, 1989; Charbonneau, 1992; Treuthart, 1996).

These assumptions and concerns led to positional policy recommendations, such as those that appeared in *A Mediator's Guide to Domestic Abuse*, published by the National Center on Women and Family Law: "Family law cases involving parties between whom there was or is domestic abuse should not be mediated—no matter how seemingly long ago or how seemingly slight the abuse might appear" (Sun & Woods, 1989, p. 6). These positions took on a life of their own in the ensuing debate over the use of mediation. Many mediators found themselves in positions where the mediation process, as described by some of these early opponents, was not a process with which they were familiar and would counter that opponents' assumptions about the mediation process are dramatically inaccurate.

Current arguments about the use of mediation in domestic abuse cases more accurately reflect today's view of mediation practices and do not focus so much on the mediation process itself but rather on the nature of domestic abuse and the concerns endemic to these cases. *Mediators should take these public policy concerns seriously.*

Power issues are a major concern to those who argue against the use of mediation in cases of domestic abuse. Some point to women's inherent lack of power relative to men in our society and contend that in relationships involving domestic abuse, these power differentials are even more disparate—resulting in an inequality of bargaining power in mediation that can lead to unfair agreements. Opponents believe that these power differences cannot be remedied even by a very skilled mediator (Rimelspach, 2001; Grillo, 1991; Hart, 1990).

The dynamics of a relationship in which there has been domestic abuse make mediation a troublesome venture. Such relationships are often characterized by a decided lack of honesty, trust, ability to communicate, and ability to compromise—qualities that do not make the parties good candidates for mediation. Indeed, secrecy and distortion often shroud the relationship (Gerencser, 1995). As noted in an article by Gagnon (1992): "It is difficult to imagine a batterer coming to a mutually agreeable outcome with his partner in mediation; it is equally difficult to imagine that he will comply with an agreement he believes is unfair to him" (pp. 272, 275). Victim advocates argue that women who have been in abusive relationships have been conditioned to put their spouses' needs ahead of their own needs out of necessity and are unable to break out of this habit and advocate for their own interests and that of their children in the mediation process (Hart, 1990).

Other concerns include the following:

- A mediator may not be aware of the violence and its impact on the mediation process because the parties keep it well hidden or because a victim does not identify herself as having been abused due to embarrassment or fear of public humiliation.
- A victim does not see herself as a victim and does not identify her experiences as having been abusive; some victims grew up in abusive families, and this behavior is accepted and accommodated.
- Mediation agreements may not be enforceable or may require additional steps that can be costly and time consuming in order to incorporate them into a court order.
- The mediation process lacks the power of the discovery process and cannot ensure a full disclosure of information.
- The future orientation of mediation discounts the impact of past behaviors (Rimelsbach, 2001; O'Connell Corcoran & Melamed, 1990).

Many mediators are not experts in the dynamics of domestic abuse and assume that what you see is what you get. However, a calm, composed, articulate—even charming—batterer and an agreeable victim do not equal a level playing field and a consensual relationship. As Hart (1990), a victim advocate and attorney, persuasively points out:

> The battered woman is not free to choose. She is not free to elect or reject mediation if the batterer prefers it, not free to identify and advocate for components essential for her autonomy and safety and that of her children, not free to terminate mediation when she concludes it is not working. (p. 321)

In Support

Most mediation proponents agree with the following guidelines:

- Some cases involving domestic abuse are inappropriate for mediation.
- Screening is necessary to determine which cases are appropriate.
- Mediators must be well trained in the dynamics of domestic abuse.
- Participation in the mediation process must be safe, fair, and voluntary.
- Victims of abuse should not be required to mediate.

Given these guidelines, proponents of making mediation available in cases of domestic abuse generally start with the argument of the BATMA: What is the couple's best alternative to a mediated agreement (a modification of Fisher & Ury's [1983] BATNA [best alternative to a negotiated agreement]). In short, if mediation is not used, then what? It is argued by both social science experts and legal scholars that mediation is more appropriate and effective than the adversarial process, even in cases of domestic abuse (Maccoby & Mnookin, 1992). Some have said that the adversarial process exacerbates the dynamics between partners when abuse is a factor by escalating the conflict and reinforcing the power and control differential and the win/lose aspects of the relationship (O'Connell Corcoran & Melamed, 1990).

Many feminists who take issue with the mediation process also take issue with the adversarial process and agree that women also do not fare well in the hierarchical nature of litigation (Yellott, 1990). Few judges and lawyers have expertise in the subject of domestic abuse, whereas many mediators have had training in it. Consequently, mediators are often in a better position to identify domestic abuse, help the parties determine whether mediation is an appropriate intervention, and make referrals to additional services (Rimelspach, 2001; Newmark, Harrell, & Salem, 1995).

The mediation process also provides a forum where the abuse is more likely to be disclosed by the parties. The private and confidential nature of mediation and the knowledge that the mediator is not a fact finder or judge may allow partners to discuss the concerns and look for acceptable safeguards, knowing that such disclosures will not be used against them. Furthermore, the mediation process can double as an affirmation for an abused spouse that she is no longer willing to subordinate her needs and those of the children to the batterer's. Joyce (1997) notes that "mediation empowers participants to end violence . . . by serving as a model of conflict resolution. . . . Mediation can provide a supportive, empowering environment for women who in many cases have been stripped of their identity, dignity, and self-esteem" (p. 451). In contrast, the adversarial process encourages individuals to deny or minimize past abusive behavior (Joyce, 1997; Salem & Milne, 1995; Erickson & McKnight,1990). In studies conducted in Ontario by Ellis (Ellis, 1994; Ellis & Stuckless, 1996), mediation was associated with a greater reduction in physical, verbal, and emotional abuse than lawyer-assisted settlement.

Additional support for the availability of mediation in cases of domestic abuse include the fact that time can be devoted to crafting an agreement and that short-term agreements can be put in place and reviewed periodically—weekly, if need be—whereas court procedures are often hurried and result in court orders that are difficult, time consuming, and expensive to modify. Moreover, the mediation process allows for a broader range of solutions than are typically available to a judge. Creative solutions are encouraged in mediation, and the parties can invite additional resource experts into the process, such as an advocate, counselor, or child psychologist, to help partners better understand some of the issues and explore additional alternatives.

Issues that are not necessarily "legal" ones but are important to the couple can also be discussed more readily in mediation. Working out what toys the children can take back and forth between households, the amount and timing of telephone contact between a parent and the children, and the matter of sharing clothing can often become sources of conflict that escalate into a major battle and even lead to an abusive episode if not resolved between the parties. It is unlikely that a judge will take the time to address these sources of conflict, and hiring two lawyers to negotiate over these types of matters becomes prohibitively expensive for the majority of couples.

Lastly, although most proponents of mediation do not tout mediation as therapy, the therapeutic aspect of helping people learn to be cooperative decision makers cannot be discounted. As a result of participating in a mediation process, some parents learn more collaborative and cooperative communication techniques as well as the need to focus on the future rather than the past. These skills can serve them well, help them address their concerns, and diminish conflict between them.

REFRAMING THE DEBATE

Mediation opponents and proponents would likely agree that the uneven quality of mediation provided in many communities and the number of practicing but inadequately trained mediators are obstacles to reaching consensus about the use of mediation and need to be remedied. As in any conflict, the framing of the issues is critical in order to adequately address the concerns about the use of mediation in cases involving allegations or instances of abuse. Rather than framing the question, *Should mediation be used in cases involving domestic abuse?,* a more useful framing of the issue would be: *What process can we develop that will best help individuals who have been involved in an abusive relationship address the issues between them so that they can move on with their lives without violence and without the need for ongoing court and legal interventions?* The answer to this question leads us to the matter of system design: *Can we design a dispute resolution process that addresses the concerns that have been noted by both opponents and proponents of mediation?*

UNDERLYING ASSUMPTIONS WHEN DESIGNING
A MEDIATION PROCESS FOR DOMESTIC ABUSE CASES

1. *Mediation is an option.* This statement may seem oxymoronic when used in the context of mandatory mediation. When mediation is mandated, the mandate should refer to the requirement to *offer* the service, not to accept it. Mediation should be voluntary for all participants and especially for victims and batterers. Assuming they are making an informed decision and have had an opportunity to learn what mediation is and how it works, clients should be free to refuse to participate in mediation. Furthermore, clients should be free to withdraw from a mediation process at any point in time.

Not only should mediation be voluntary for the clients at all points of the process, it should be voluntary for the mediator as well. All parties, including the mediator, should be free to withdraw or terminate the mediation process.

2. *Disallowing options is disempowering.* Restricting access to mediation through state statute or court rule because of a history of domestic abuse takes away choices—and taking away choices replicates the very same dynamics of the abusive relationship. In a pilot project to examine the use of mediation in domestic abuse cases, many victims expressed the belief that a prohibition against mediation was damaging rather than helpful. The victims believed that they should have the right to decide whether mediation is in their best interest (Thoennes, Salem, & Pearson, 1995; DiPietro, 1992).

3. *Agreements reached in mediation are voluntary.* Not only is participation in the process voluntary, but what parties leave with—the agreements—must also be voluntary. This requirement means that mediators must develop procedures to ensure that a victim is not being coerced, manipulated, or intimidated into an agreement and that mediators are not superimposing their views about outcomes on the parties.

4. *Mediation should be no less of a process than what the litigation process offers and should be better.* There is much consensus in both the legal and mental health fields, and between mediators and advocates for victims of abuse, that the adversarial process does not serve these families well. A mediation process should be designed as an improvement over what currently exists. No one wants a flawed system. Designing a system that merely substitutes one flawed system for another is not useful. This principle may require that we develop a hybrid mediation process to ensure that the interests of all parties are adequately addressed, given the special concerns presented in domestic abuse cases.

5. *A mediator is neutral, not neutered.* Power imbalances are a fact of life, but in domestic abuse cases they can be a life-threatening fact. Being neutral does not mean that the mediator is neutered. Exceptions to the confidential nature of mediation in most states require the mediator to report threatening situations to the proper authorities. So although the parties are in charge of the product, the mediator is in charge of the process. Coercive, manipulative, threatening, or other unacceptable behaviors may result in the mediator terminating the process and reporting any safety concerns.

The mediator has additional tools and techniques to facilitate informed decision making and address power imbalances. The use of a caucus, in which the mediator meets separately and privately with each participant, allows the mediator to check in with a victim of abuse to ascertain that the process is working for her and that she is not being talked in or out of anything. The mediator can serve as an agent of reality by raising questions about a tentative agreement, asking the parties to check in with their attorneys, and assigning homework (e.g., getting a second opinion about a proposed agreement, or suggesting that the parties try out the proposed agreement for a short period of time and then reevaluate the outcome). And, ultimately, the mediator can terminate the mediation process and assist the parties in securing other resources that may better address their circumstances. These referrals may include an attorney, a financial planner, an advocate for the victim, a shelter, the court system, the prosecutor's office, and the police.

6. *Not mediating entitlement to be abusive.* Mediation should not be attempted when a batterer expresses entitlement to abuse his partner. Abuse is not negotiable.

When providing mediation to batterers and victims, the following are excluded from the list of topics to be addressed:

1. *We are not mediating whether or not the abuse occurred.* Investigatory or evidentiary issues such as whether the abuse occurred, how often it occurred, and the severity of the abuse should not be mediated. Mediation is not intended to function as a determinative process, and the mediator should not be turned into a judge or jury. There are other systems designed to make determinative decisions, if needed, such as the police, the district attorney, medical personnel, and the judge.

2. *We are not mediating reconciliation.* Many women express concern that meeting with the batterer in the mediation process will make them susceptible to pleas and promises regarding a reconciliation. Batterers may attempt to use the mediation process as an opportunity to talk the victim into coming home or getting back together. Reconciliation should not be a subject of mediation. If both parties are interested in pursuing this possibility, a referral can be made to a counselor or other resource person. The mediation process is intended to focus on other issues that will not be served if they become comingled with reconciliation issues.

3. *We are not mediating fault and blame.* Mediation should not be a forum to "try the case." Storytelling, "setting the record straight," justifying behavior, defending self, minimizing, rationalizing, or blaming others should not be topics for mediation.

4. *We are not mediating punishment and consequences.* Mediation should not be used as a forum to negotiate consequences or dole out punishment for past behaviors (e.g., "He took my car keys away so he can't see the children" or "She closed our checking account so I'm not going to pay her child support"). The focus belongs on the parties' day-to-day living arrangements and in enforcing ground rules that will preclude the recurrence of past problems.

5. *We are not mediating dropping of charges, protective orders, or restraining orders.* In other words, we are not mediating "if . . . then" proposals (e.g., "If I

do this, then you will drop the abuse charges"). Prosecutorial decisions are not within the purview of the mediation process, and withdrawing protective orders or restraining orders should not be allowed to be used as leverage in the mediation process.

6. *We are not mediating contingencies or leveraging of issues.* Leveraging one behavior or concession against another is a replication of the "if . . . then" dynamic noted in point 5. Statements such as "If I can have the kids overnight for the weekend, then I'll drop the custody action" are another form of manipulating the mediation process. Once an agenda of issues is established, each issue should be mediated without linking or leveraging the outcome of one issue to another. This principle does not discount the reality that one issue may have an impact on another; who is going to stay in the house obviously will impact the parenting schedule. This contingency is best handled in mediation by agreeing to review the "big picture" at the conclusion of the process to make sure that each of the tentative agreements fits together in a manner that makes sense overall.

7. *We are not mediating court orders.* The mediation process should not be used to reopen previously adjudicated matters such as no-contact orders and custody or visitation rulings unless that is the referred issue. Attempting to insert adjudicated matters only leads to a manipulation of the mediation process. While we want the parties to remain in control of the product, we want the mediator to remain in control of the process to ensure that the process is not undermined. To repeat: Contact orders or established court determinations should not be mediated unless that is the referred issue.

8. *We are not mediating threshold issues.* Threshold issues, such as whether a parent will have access to the children, are best defined as determinative issues and left for the court to determine.

With the above procedural ground rules in place, the following areas can be effectively mediated:

1. *Terms of living apart.* Matters such as establishing a date for moving out, determining who is going to live where, division of household accessories, establishing a parenting schedule, and payment of household expenses are all day-to-day living arrangements that parties may need to address. The judge often does not have the time to take up each of these individual issues, and paying lawyers to negotiate them can be too costly for many.

2. *Parenting schedules.* Mediation allows parents to establish parental access schedules and to review them as needs may dictate. For some families it may be very helpful to mediate a schedule for the upcoming weekend and then return to mediation the following week to take stock of how the plan worked and consider any needed modifications. Living situations can be in flux, and the needs and schedules of children may also dictate the need for

short-term agreements. Returning to court to make these modifications is not always possible, given a crowded court calendar, and may also be cost prohibitive.

3. *Property division.* Mediation can be a very helpful process for dividing up personal possessions such as furnishings, household supplies, photographs, books, tools, and all the other sundry things that family members need to manage their daily lives.

4. *Financial support.* All states have child support guidelines that a judge uses when a question of child support is presented to the court. But establishing the amount of child support is only the tip of the iceberg for some parents. In addition to determining an amount, parents may also use mediation to establish what the child support will cover and reach agreements for paying for "extras" for the children (e.g., sporting equipment, school trips, lessons, camp, gifts). Mediation also allows for more creative support procedures such as establishing a central checking account from which all child-related expenses are paid. Contributions to college funds, tax deductions for dependents, and discretionary medical expenses can all be addressed in the mediation process. Financial support for an adult may also be more creatively and effectively addressed in the mediation process, where individuals can take the time to discuss their needs and look for solutions that work for everyone.

5. *Transportation of the children.* Transportation needs of the children may extend beyond pickup and drop-off times. Expanded issues may include third-party transporters, use of a car seat, insurance, public transportation, airline schedules, procedures for children who may be traveling alone, etc.

6. *Use of clothing and toys.* Power and control issues can often be played out over such things as what clothing is sent along with the children and the condition in which it arrives back home. Sending children for a weekend without adequate clothing or returning clothing torn and dirty has led to many an argument between parents. Children taking a new Christmas toy over to one parent's house and not bringing it back can lead to the same end. Although seemingly mundane and unlikely as topics for litigation, these are matters that can plague divorcing/divorced parents and can lead to serious power and control issues and ultimately abusive behaviors. Mediation often proves to be an ideal forum for resolving or preempting such disputes.

7. *Holidays and vacations.* Conflicts over holiday and vacation schedules with the children often erupt immediately before or after these occasions. Getting into court in a timely manner is not always possible, and, as a result, the conflict expands into other areas as well. Generally, parents can get an appointment with a mediator quickly and reach a resolution about the current pressing matter as well as put in place future schedules. Vacation discussions can include accompanying persons, emergency medical care, communication between the children and the other parent while away, arranging for clothing and equipment, spending money, and many other issues. Holiday

discussions can include religious activities, gifts, ground rules for extended family members, etc.

8. *Accompanying persons.* Mediation may include a discussion about the need for an accompanying person to ensure that the children are comfortable or being adequately cared for and supervised. Determining the identity of this person, his or her level of responsibility, the duration of his or her presence, and the expectations of the task can all be a subject for mediation. Other discussions about accompanying persons may focus on the presence of boyfriends/girlfriends, relatives, or friends and their behavior around the children.

9. *Activities with the children.* Mediation can be a very useful forum in which to share information about what activities the children would enjoy as well as to resolve disputes regarding activities of which a parent disapproves. Is it OK to take the children hunting? To a friend's home? To the corner tavern? Even routine activities such as meals and baths and bedtimes can become areas of conflict addressed in mediation.

10. *Phone access.* The frequency of phone contact with the children, the time of day, the duration of the conversations, and the costs of any long-distance charges may be resolved in mediation.

11. *Medical care.* Mediation can help parents make decisions about routine medical care, such as who arranges for dental and doctor checkups, as well as putting in place agreements for how to handle emergency medical care. Conflicts over paying for orthodontia or other uninsured, discretionary medical care can often be resolved in mediation. Clarifying any medications and their dosages can also be topics for mediation.

12. *School contact.* Is it OK for a parent to stop by the school to say hello to a child or to chat with the teacher? Will parents attend parent–teacher conferences together or separately? Who should the school contact regarding any behavioral or educational concerns? Will school notices and report cards be sent to both parents? Will both parents participate in children's sporting and other school events? Mediators can help parents address these issues.

13. *Child-care arrangements.* How will child-care decisions be made? How will a day-care provider be selected? Who will pay for child care? If a parent is called away from home, will the other parent be given the first opportunity to babysit? Does the other parent have a right to know who is providing substitute care for the children? Parents can more effectively discuss these issues in a mediation process.

SYSTEM DESIGN

The design and development of a mediation service should embody the principles noted above. Designing a mediation service for cases with which there are allegations or instances of domestic abuse includes (1) establishing an effective case identification or screening system, (2) refining the models of practice to address safety and decision-making concerns, (3) ensuring that participants are informed, and (4) providing specialized training for mediators.

Screening

Screening procedures should be developed that allow the parties and the mediator to determine whether mediation is the service of choice in this challenging context. Screening can be effective in excluding inappropriate cases from mediation (Chandler, 1990); it should be simple enough to utilize to ensure wide and uniform application, with precautions for each party's safety (Gerencser, 1995). The design of a screening system involves four considerations: (1) when screening is conducted, (2) who should conduct the screening, (3) screening tools and methods, and (4) ground rules for screening.

When

Screening systems need to be in place prior to the initiation of mediation as well as throughout the process. Premediation screening is used to identify the presence or history of an abusive relationship and its impact on the parties' ability to participate safely and effectively in mediation. Gerencser (1995) asserts that if premediation screening does not occur, mediation should not be required by any court (Chandler, 1990; see also Georgia Commission on Dispute Resolution, 1995).

Some couples with no history of abuse experience an abusive event during the course of the separation, while mediation is underway. In other cases, the abuse was not identified or disclosed in the prescreening process. Screening throughout mediation is used to determine (1) whether a case continues to be appropriate or should be terminated and referred to other resources, or (2) whether the mediation process needs to be modified in any way.

Who

In optimal terms, the entire service delivery system needs to participate in the screening process, including the judge, commissioner or referee, attorneys, intake officer, clerk of courts, advocates, shelter staff, and the mediator (Gerencser, 1995). Whenever abuse is identified, it should become a part of the screening process. If a judge, commissioner, or referee learns of abuse through motions presented at a preliminary hearing, this information should be noted on any referral to mediation. If lawyers are aware that there has been a history of abuse, they should disclose this information as a part of the mediation intake process and include it in the initial pleadings (Gerencser, 1995). If parties participate in some form of intake process, such as a premediation parent education program or divorce orientation program, and disclose information about abuse, the information should be included in the screening process. Filing a petition for a restraining order with the clerk of courts should result in an automatic notation that can be picked up in the screening process.

Screening Tools and Methods

Screening instruments may include a questionnaire completed by the parties prior to mediation, a follow-up phone call, a person-to-person interview or caucus, and a review of the file. (For further descriptions of screening protocols, see Ellis, 2003; Tolman, 1992; Girdner, 1990; Marthaler, 1989.) It is recommended that screening questions, whether written or verbal, begin with several general questions, proceed to inquire about specific behaviors, and conclude by asking if the interviewee has any concerns about participating in mediation (Girdner, 1990).

A written questionnaire may be sent to each of the parties and returned prior to the first mediation appointment. It is important that critical information, such as addresses and phone numbers, is not inadvertently revealed to the other party in the cover letter. The purpose of the questionnaire should be clearly stated: for example, "to assist the mediation office in determining whether mediation is an appropriate next step and whether a first appointment should be joint or separate." This is also an opportunity to provide clients with basic information about the mediation process: a description of how it typically works, the benefits of mediation, as well as reasons why mediation may *not* be appropriate. In addition to gathering basic intake information (e.g., names and ages of children, employment, legal representation), the questionnaire inquires about any indicators that could adversely impact the mediation process, including any history of abuse, drug or alcohol problems, language considerations, physical disabilities, etc. (Questions about abuse should not be limited solely to physical abuse but should investigate sexual, emotional, and other forms of abuse as well.)

The design of a written questionnaire must take into account language barriers and must address the privacy of information. Clients may be uncomfortable and reluctant to disclose sensitive information when they are not sure how the questionnaire may be used (Dutton, 1992). Correspondingly, clients may attempt to use the questionnaire as a perceived opportunity to funnel favorable information about their case or unfavorable to the other side to the mediator or to the court.

The advance questionnaire is followed by a phone call when the questionnaire raises concerns about the appropriateness or form of mediation.

The phone call can be conducted by intake or screening personnel as well as the mediator to further elicit information that might have an impact on the appropriateness of mediation as a mode of intervention. Again, as with the questionnaire, it is important that this phone call not become an opportunity for a client to funnel information favorable to his or her case or unfavorable to the other person's case in advance of the mediation session. Having someone other than the mediator make this follow-up phone call may help obviate this potential problem. It is also important to make certain that the call is made at a convenient time and place, so that the individual can talk freely without fear of being overhead (especially by the batterer).

In some programs parties fill out the questionnaire in the waiting room immediately prior to the first mediation appointment. This method must ensure that a party can complete the questionnaire in private, without the other party censoring the answers to the questions. In addition, this method may also make it more difficult to modify the format of the first session, as both parties are already present.

A review of parties' legal file, police records, and court docket may also provide information regarding abuse. The legal file may indicate the presence of a no-contact order, or abuse may be noted in the pleadings. A scan of the criminal and civil computer log of prior contacts may also note a history of abuse. This information may be readily accessed by court-connected mediation staff but may not be available to a mediator in private practice. Some court mediation programs routinely check police and court records on all referrals for mediation (Pearson, 1997).

A personal, face-to-face interview is the preferred method of screening (Tolman, 1992; Girdner, 1990; Marthaler, 1989). Girdner recommends that this screening interview be conducted by a person of the same gender. Marthaler used a male–female team, with the same gender interviewer taking the lead with the client. As noted, others recommend that the screening interview not be conducted by the mediator but rather by intake or specially trained screening personnel (Gerencser, 1995). In some programs the face-to-face screening is conducted in conjunction with attending a divorce orientation or parent education program prior to mediation (Pearson, 1997). Some programs conduct the face-to-face screening at an appointment prior to, and separate from, the first mediation appointment, whereas other programs conduct it as a part of an initial caucus with each party, immediately preceding the first mediation session (Marthaler, 1989).

The following questions are adapted from Girdner's Conflict Assessment Protocol (Girdner, 1990), which is based on dangerousness assessment research (Stuart & Campbell, 1989; Campbell, 1986; Straus, 1979):

• *General questions.* "I'd like to ask you some general questions about your relationship. How were decisions made in your marriage? What happens when the two of you fight? How does your spouse respond when angry?

How do you? How would I know if you are angry? How would I know if the other person is angry? Has anger ever risen to a level where someone is afraid?"

    • *Specific questions.* "I'd like to ask you some questions about what some people do when they are angry. Have any of these occurred in your relationship: Shouting? Name calling? Pushing? Hitting? Choking? Slapping? Biting? Have weapons ever been used, or threatened to be used, against someone in your household?"

    It should be noted that these questions address only the physical aspects of domestic abuse. Additional questions should be developed that address the other aspects of domestic abuse.[3] These might include: "Does your spouse control any of your day-to-day activities to the point that you don't feel free to come and go? Do you feel that you can disagree with your spouse without fear? Do you have access to money without having to ask permission?"

    • *Questions about participating in mediation.* "Now I'd like to ask you some questions about participating in the mediation process. Do you have any concerns about participating in mediation? Do you feel that you can freely put your concerns/issues on the table? If mediation starts going in a direction that you are not comfortable with, what would you do? Is there anything that worries you about meeting with your spouse? Do you have any suggestions about how we might best meet? Do you have any questions about the process?"

Ground Rules for Screening

    1. *Screen each party.* Screening is not intended to be done only with a victim. Both spouses should be included in the screening protocol. This inclusiveness not only embodies the balanced procedures of the mediation process but also provides the opportunity to explore potential pitfalls with each spouse.

    2. *Screen each party separately.* It is crucial that the screening and mediation processes do not revictimize the victim. A victim may not be able to disclose information or ask questions in front of the batterer for fear of further abuse or reprisal. Separate and private screening procedures must be implemented.

    3. *Define abusive behaviors.* Asking if domestic abuse has ever occurred within the relationship may not be a helpful approach. Some individuals may be embarrassed to answer such a blunt question, and others would not define what they have experienced as *abuse* (Marthaler, 1989). It is also important to investigate forms of abuse other than physical abuse. Asking about specific behaviors, as noted above, provides more useful information.

4. *Move from general to specific questions.* Moving from the general to the specific not only helps build rapport but prompts more complete disclosure of information.

5. *Confidentiality.* Both parties need to know that the screening interview is confidential, that the information will not be shared with the other party, and that any exceptions to confidentiality (i.e., instances of child abuse or danger to a party) must be reported to the proper authorities.

Triage

Screening is not an end unto itself. Its purpose is to help the screener and the participant determine, or "triage," whether (1) mediation can be conducted as usual, (2) no mediation should be provided, or (3) a hybrid model of mediation should be employed (Ver Steegh, 2003; Girdner, 1990; Straus, 1990).

- *Mediation as usual.* Traditional mediation may be considered appropriate when there is no ongoing pattern of abuse, control issues are not central to the relationship, and neither party is fearful of participating.
- *No mediation.* Mediation may be considered inappropriate, not offered, or terminated when there is (1) a pattern of ongoing and continued physical, emotional or other abuse, (2) a history of serious injury, (3) the use or threat of weapons, (4) indication that the victim puts the abuser's needs before her own, and (5) indication that the victim fears injury or abuse as the result of participating in mediation.
- *A customized model of mediation.* Mediation can be conducted using special tools or procedures when abuse has occurred, the elements of the "no mediation" condition are *not* present, and the parties voluntarily consent to mediation.

A hybrid or customized mediation process may include any of the following:

1. *Separate sessions.* Conjoint mediation sessions can be replaced by separate sessions, to which the parties come at different times or even different days. Preempting the possibility of physical and visual contact may address some of the concerns about coercion, manipulation, and safety. It may be important that the times of the separate sessions be kept confidential, so that a batterer is not able to stalk or confront a victim upon entering or exiting mediation. The mediator must structure these separate sessions to make sure that they do not turn into fact-finding quagmires, in which the mediation process becomes a test of who's telling the truth or a vehicle for either of the

parties to attempt to win over the mediator to his or her side. Carefully defining the mediator's role and the ground rules should help prevent this unwanted development.

2. *Shuttle mediation.* Shuttle mediation allows for a facilitated process without face-to-face contact. The parties are seated in separate rooms, and the mediator shuttles back and forth between them. This tactic preempts any face-to-face coercive behavior or comments, while allowing for a smoother and more efficient communication and decision-making process than may occur with the use of separate sessions.

3. *Frequent caucuses.* When a mediator chooses to meet conjointly with the parties, frequent caucuses will allow him or her to interrupt attempts to coerce or manipulate a spouse and to check in with the victim regarding her level of comfort without putting her on the spot in front of the batterer.

4. *Telephone mediation.* Mediating via conference call or sequential calls between the parties also preempts the face-to-face concerns. However, telephone mediation may inhibit the rapport building between the parties and the mediator and certainly limits the mediator's ability to observe visual cues and body language.

5. *Closed-circuit TV mediation.* Closed-circuit TV mediation is often used in remote areas or where geographical distances preclude getting together. This format of mediation allows the mediator to take in the visual cues and body language absent in telephone mediation. This adaptation may be another tool for mediating in domestic abuse cases.

6. *Including supportive third parties in mediation.* Inviting third parties, such as an advocate for each party, a counselor, or attorneys, may add a level of support when one is mediating in domestic abuse cases. In these cases, third parties should generally be limited to professionals or other neutral people; family members or new spouses or boyfriends/girlfriends are highly inadvisable.

7. *Comediation.* A male–female comediation team may also provide a measure of comfort and safety that allows mediation to move forward in domestic abuse cases.

8. *Security measures.* The physical environment and location of mediation sessions may need to be examined closely. Separate waiting rooms allow a victim to wait for her appointment without being subjected to controlling behaviors, threats, or other hostile cues that might undermine her effective participation in mediation. Scheduling the batterer to arrive first and the victim to leave the appointment first may also preempt arrival and departure confrontations. Availability of security personnel to accompany individuals to their cars, alarm systems, and metal detectors may be standard procedures and equipment available in court-connected mediation programs but may not be available in some community agencies or private practices. Alternatives include developing an alarm signaling system to alert outer-office staff

to notify the police or to activate other security measures. Providing seating arrangements that do not block exits and avoiding the use of tables that could hide kicking or tapping of a victim are other considerations.

9. *Pairing mediation with an abuser treatment program and advocacy interventions.* Some programs offer mediation in conjunction with batterer enrollment in an abuser treatment program and victim participation in a victim support and advocacy program.

10. *Completing an abuser treatment program and an advocacy program is a prior condition to participating in mediation.*

Informed Participants

An important and sometimes overlooked element of system design is making sure that the system is being used by informed participants. Many individuals are uninformed or misinformed about mediation and do not effectively make use of the process as a result. Premediation educational programs and parent education programs have been shown to be very effective methods for educating consumers about mediation and helping them decide for themselves whether the process is appropriate for them (Schepard, 2003). Printed materials, such as AFCC's brochure *Is Mediation for Us* (Milne, 2003), videos (e.g., *It's Still Your Choice,* Salem, 1990), and Internet websites (e.g., *www.mediate.com; www.acrnet.org;* and *www.wamediators.org*) can provide helpful information and educate clients about the proper use of mediation.

Mediator Training

Mediation is still largely an unregulated practice in most jurisdictions. Florida requires 4 hours of domestic violence training every 2 years to maintain a certification in mediation. Members of the Ontario Association for Family Mediation must complete 5 hours of domestic violence training as part of the basic training requirement (Landau, 1995). The Association for Conflict Resolution (ACR) requires 2 hours of training in domestic abuse within the standard training requirement to be listed as a Practitioner Family Member. The Model Standards of Practice for Family and Divorce Mediators state that "a mediator shall not undertake a mediation in which the family situation has been assessed to involve domestic abuse without appropriate and adequate training" (Standard XB; see the appendix of Schepard, Chapter 22, this volume). Mediation training should include information about the dynamics of domestic abuse, specialized mediation tools and techniques, and system design and mediation protocols (including confidentiality and the duty to warn) for domestic abuse cases.

A WORD ABOUT POWER

As a factor in all interpersonal relationships, power has been written about extensively by many others (see Lang, Chapter 10, this volume; Haynes, 1988; Mayer, 1987). However, when abuse is wielded as a source of power, the stakes are dramatically different. Court interventions, litigation, and lawyer-assisted negotiation procedures do not necessarily remedy power imbalances in domestic abuse. The mediation process can draw on risk assessment procedures and the resources offered by the community to attempt to structure a process that offers another choice.

Power is also very fluid. A batterer acquires power as a result of the abuse and the threat of abuse. A victim acquires power through legal sanctions, such as a protective order, and through disclosure of the abuse. Information or expertise can also connote power. A husband may have knowledge of the finances and, as a result, have financial power, whereas the wife may have knowledge of the children's schedules and have parental power as a result. The mediation process can track the power flow and point the parties toward win/win outcomes as opposed to win/lose.

PARENTING AGREEMENTS WHEN DOMESTIC ABUSE IS AN ISSUE

It has been suggested that customary parenting agreements may need to be modified when domestic abuse is a factor (Pearson, 1997). The potential for continued conflict and assertions of control can be minimized through the following:

• *Be specific.* Vague language such as "reasonable visitation upon reasonable notice" does not provide the specificity necessary for high-conflict couples. Detailed schedules, including days, times, transportation, presence of third parties, interim phone contacts, etc., lessen the need for communication that leads to miscommunication and eliminates the opportunity for intimidation and coercion.

• *Establish a method for dealing with schedule modifications.* Change is an inevitable—and potential—source of conflict. Identifying a method to deal with changes in schedules, rescheduling, and changed circumstances on the front end may preempt future conflicts.

• *Well-defined exceptions.* "No exceptions" to the agreements are preferable but probably unrealistic. Foreshadowing the "what ifs" (e.g., what if Grandfather is not available to pick up the children) may preempt the need for contact and possible conflict.

• *Defined methods of communication.* If verbal communication is permitted, ground rules (however unenforceable) may help establish expectations and allow a party to hang up or walk away when language becomes abusive or threatening. Alternative methods of communication, such as written notes or e-mail, should also be considered.

• *Consequences.* The consequences of not abiding by the agreement are not negotiable, nor is subsequent abuse. However, it may be useful to include the steps that will be taken should a party fail to follow the agreement or further abuse occurs.

RESEARCH FINDINGS

Quantitative longitudinal research on the impact of mediation in cases of domestic abuse is lacking. In 1993, the Association of Family and Conciliation Courts (AFCC) was funded by the State Justice Institute (SJI) to conduct a study on "Domestic Abuse and Empowerment in Custody and Visitation Cases." This study included 422 individuals from 293 families in two court settings: Minneapolis, Minnesota, and Portland, Oregon. Eighty percent of the women and 72% of the men reported that abuse had occurred in their marriage (Newmark et al., 1995).[4]

Research with human subjects requires that individuals be duly informed and given a choice to participate or not in a research experiment. Comparing outcomes in a mediation process with outcomes in a custody evaluation process required the consent of the parties before they could be randomly assigned to a mediation group or to a custody evaluation group. The AFCC/SJI research project had to be terminated prior to completion due to the failure to acquire the consent of enough individuals willing to forego the mediation process and be assigned to the custody evaluation process.

As already noted, studies by Ellis (1994; Ellis & Stuckless, 1996) found that mediation was associated with a greater reduction in physical, verbal, and emotional abuse than lawyer-assisted settlement.

Additional qualitative and quantitative research would add to the body of knowledge about the use of mediation in domestic abuse cases. It would be useful for researchers to identify the elements of a mediation process that allow a victim and a batterer to participate safely and effectively and review these outcomes over time. Furthermore, it would be useful to study the outcome for families with domestic abuse experience who did not mediate—either because the statute or court policy precluded them from doing so or mediation was not available to them—compared to families with domestic abuse experience who did mediate. For the growing unrepresented or *pro se* population of litigants, mediation may be the only consumer support available, short of litigation. Outcome studies on the impact of precluding mediation would be very illuminating.

Additional research is also needed to (1) develop effective screening tools to identify domestic abuse, (2) develop statistically significant standards to determine which cases are appropriate for referral to mediation, and (3) identify the need for specific hybrid mediation approaches. A more universally accepted screening tool would aid in the training of mediators and may assist in ensuring a standard of service throughout the field.

CONFESSIONS OF A MEDIATOR

I have been a mediator for more than 30 years and have worked in both a court-connected setting and a private practice. Over time I have come to several personal conclusions and observations about my own practices when mediating cases involving allegations or instances of domestic abuse:

1. *I am far more controlling of the process.* Whereas I normally espouse a mildly directive, facilitative style, when I am mediating in a case known to me to include allegations or instances of domestic abuse, I often find that I must be far more controlling of the process than I am in cases that do not involve such dynamics. I have learned that if the parties are to be in charge of the product, then I must be *firmly* in charge of the process. To take charge of the process may require more frequent and more assertive interventions on my part to maintain the collaborative balance that ensures that neither party is being talked in or out of something and to make sure that the mediation process is not being misused. At the same time, I need to avoid becoming enmeshed in an arm-wrestling contest with the batterer, who may attempt to take over the process.

2. *I am less concerned about maintaining rapport.* When I train mediators, I stress the importance of establishing a rapport with the clients early on as the stage is set for processing and resolving the issues. Mediation is a risk-taking process. It requires a willingness by the parties to disclose personal concerns and to put a suggestion or a proposal on the table, risking that it might be rejected. If the parties are not willing to take some risks with me, they are not likely to take risks with the other person. As simple as it sounds, liking the parties and being liked by the parties seem to be underpinnings of the rapport building that is the typical foundation of the mediation process.

However, when I am mediating in a case known to me to include domestic abuse concerns, I find that I must focus more on managing the process than being concerned about liking the parties or vice versa. Although I cannot disregard the rapport issue, when it comes to choosing who is going to control the process versus possibly stepping on a party's toes as he attempts to take over the process, I must choose to step on those toes and retain control of the process. The incentive for the batterer to accept this vesting of control with the mediator is the BATMA—the "best alternative to a mediated agreement" (Fisher & Ury, 1983) he faces if mediation does not go forward.

3. *Judgment is important.* The role of the mediator is typically described as that of a nonjudgmental neutral party. The mediator is not a judge; he or she does not judge the parties or their agreements. However, when mediating in cases of possible or known domestic abuse, I have come to believe that judgment is important. The mediator must continually reevaluate whether this case is appropriate for mediation and whether he or she has the skills needed to work effectively with this couple.

4. *Forget the balancing act.* Terms such as *maintaining balance, power balancing,* and *level playing field* are often used when describing the mediation process. However, when mediating in a case involving issues of domestic abuse, I find that I am "off-balance" much of the time because I am challenged to keep control of the process.

5. *The process is less collaborative and more of a facilitated negotiation.* To describe collaboration, Fisher and Ury (1983) use the analogy of two judges sitting on the bench together as they decide a difficult case. I often use this analogy with my clients to help them make the cognitive transition from adversarial to collaborative modes of functioning. When mediating in a case of domestic abuse, however, I find that the process becomes more of a hybrid— more one of facilitated negotiation than a collaborative one. The parties focus more on their separate interests and solutions rather than the mutual interests that I tend to focus on when abuse is not a factor.

6. *Short-term agreements.* One of the incentives to using mediation in cases involving concerns about domestic abuse is the ability to put in place agreements of a short-term nature and revisit and revise them as needs dictate. Predictability and steadfastness are not often present with these couples. Putting in place agreements or court orders that apply over the long haul is often counterproductive due to the tenuousness, volatility, and unpredictable nature of these relationships.

7. *Need for reliable resources.* The need to establish a scaffolding of support can be very important when mediating in domestic abuse cases. The support of the parties' attorneys, victim and batterer advocates, counselors, and a safety plan can all work together to facilitate the success of the mediation process.

8. *Watch your language.* Colloquialisms that I use in everyday speech can often take on unintended meanings with domestic abuse partners. Using expressions such as "Can you live with that?", "It strikes me that . . . ", or "Please cut that out" would be insensitive and inappropriate with couples who have abuse issues.

9. *Limitations on self-determination.* I often describe mediation as a process of empowering the parties and facilitating self-determination. When mediating in a case with domestic abuse concerns, however, I find that there are other persons, in addition to the principle parties, who may need to have a determinative voice. These include the parties' attorneys, advocates for the

victim and batterer, and myself as the mediator. Each of us may have a say and even a vote as to whether the mediation process goes forward.

10. *Sweat equity is a fact of life.* I usually tell my mediation students that I know something is wrong when I am working harder than the clients. I have found that, when mediating in cases where abuse concerns have been raised, my skills are challenged, there is a level of stress not found with nonabuse cases, and I work *hard* to ensure that the mediation process is serving the interests and safety of both parties.

CONCLUSIONS

The question of whether or not mediation is appropriate in cases of domestic abuse must be reframed to focus on finding an answer to the question of what kind of system we could design that would provide a safe and secure decision-making process for spouses and parents in dispute. Although a traditional mediation process may not offer the protection necessary in domestic abuse cases, dismissing mediation outright may also be a mistake. The development of hybrid mediation models that embody the self-determination principles of the mediation process while also addressing power, control, coercion, and safety issues must be the goal.

Beginning and ending mediation, and the terms of any agreement, should be a choice for the parties and the mediator. Taking away choices is disempowering. To replicate the very dynamics of an abusive relationship by taking away the opportunity to choose mediation does not serve victims well. Power is very fluid. The batterer acquires power because of his ability to control the victim. A victim acquires power as the result of the public disclosure of the abuse and the protective order and sanctions imposed on the batterer by the civil and criminal justice systems. But neither source of power resolves the ongoing day-to-day decisions that couples face in a separation and divorce. The court system's ability to decide these issues often falls short. It behooves professionals in the fields of mediation and domestic abuse to work together to design systems that support the principles of autonomy and self-determination and allow spouses to separate and divorce in a dignified and safe manner.

ACKNOWLEDGMENT

I would like to thank Kristin Koeffler, Director of the Rock County, Wisconsin, Domestic Violence Intervention Program for her review of this chapter and her helpful suggestions.

NOTES

1. The overwhelming majority of adult victims of domestic abuse are women. By a ratio of 3 to 1, wives are more likely to be killed by their husbands than vice versa (Wil-

son & Daley, 1994). Although some men are victims of abuse, this chapter refers to victims generally as women and batterers generally as men. See also Ellis and Stuckless (1996, Chap. 4) for a more thorough discussion of the asymmetry of gender in domestic abuse.

2. In this chapter *domestic abuse* is defined as a continuum of behaviors ranging from degrading remarks to cruel jokes, economic exploitation, punches and kicks, false imprisonment, sexual abuse, suffocating actions, maiming assaults, and homicide perpetrated upon a family or household member (from Stuehling & Hart, 1997).

3. Desmond Ellis, PhD (La Marsh Research Centre on Violence and Conflict Resolution, York University, North York, Ontario M3J 1P3, Canada; e-mail: *desellis@yorku.ca*) is developing a written intake assessment questionnaire (DOVE) that will measure physical and psychological forms of abuse and their impact on the mediation process.

4. In this study, abuse was defined as "intimidation" through threats, stalking, or telephone harassment; "physical abuse" such as slapping, grabbing, shoving, kicking, or punching; "severe abuse" by beating or choking; and "use of a weapon" to threaten or injure.

REFERENCES

Bureau of Justice Statistics. (1995). Violence against women: Estimates from the redesigned survey. Washington, DC: U.S. Department of Justice.

Bureau of Justice Statistics. (2003). Crime data brief: Intimate partner violence 1993–2001. Washington, DC: U.S. Department of Justice.

Campbell, J. (1986). Nursing assessment for risk of homicide with battered women. *Advances in Nursing Science, 8*(4), 36–51.

Chandler, D. (1990). Violence, fear and communication: The variable impact of domestic violence on mediation. *Mediation Quarterly, 7*(4), 344–345.

Charbonneau, P. (1992). *Mediation in cases of domestic abuse: Helpful option or unacceptable risk?* (final report of the Domestic Abuse and Mediation Project). Washington, DC: State Justice Institute.

Danis, F. (2003). The criminalization of domestic violence: What social workers need to know. *Social Work, 28*(2), 237–246.

DiPietro, S. (1992). *Alaska child visitation mediation pilot project* (report to the Alaska legislature).

Dutton, M. (1992). *Empowering and healing the battered woman: A model for assessment and intervention.* New York: Springer.

Ellis, D. (1994). *Family mediation pilot project final report.* Toronto: Ministry of the Attorney General of Ontario.

Ellis, D. (2003). *Domestic Violence Evaluation (DOVE) manual.* AFCC annual conference materials, Ottawa, Canada.

Ellis, D. & Stuckless, N. (1996). *Mediating and negotiating marital conflicts.* Thousand Oaks, CA: Sage.

Erickson, S., & McKnight, M. (1990). Mediating spousal abuse divorces. *Mediation Quarterly, 7*(4), 377–388.

Fagan, J. (1996). *The criminalization of domestic violence: Promises and limits.* Washington, DC: U.S. Department of Justice, National Institute of Justice.

Fineman, M. (2002). Domestic violence, custody, and visitation. *Family Law Quarterly, 36*(1), 211–225.

Fischer, K., Vidman, N., & Ellis, R. (1993). The culture of battering and the role of mediation in domestic violence cases. *SMU Law Review, 46,* 2117-2174.

Fisher, R., & Ury, W. (1983). *Getting to yes: Negotiating agreement without giving in.* New York: Penguin.

Gagnon, A. (1992). Ending mandatory divorce mediation for battered women. *Harvard Women's Law Journal, 15,* 272-275.

Georgia Commission on Dispute Resolution. (1995). *Mediation in cases involving domestic violence.* Atlanta: Author.

Gerencser, A. (1995). Family mediation: Screening for domestic abuse. *Florida State University Law Review, 23*(1), 43-69.

Girdner, L. (1990). Mediation triage: Screening for spouse abuse in divorce mediation. *Mediation Quarterly, 7*(4), 365-376.

Gondolf, E. W. (1988). Who are those guys?: Toward a behavioral typology of batterers. *Violence and Victims, 3,* 187-203.

Grillo, T. (1991). The mediation alternative: Process dangers for women. *Yale Law Journal, 100,* 1545-1610.

Hart, B. (1990). Gentle jeopardy: The further endangerment of battered women and children in custody mediation. *Mediation Quarterly, 7,* 317-320.

Haynes, J. (1988). Power balancing. In J. Folberg & A. Milne (Eds.), *Divorce mediation: Theory and practice* (pp. 277-296). New York: Guilford Press.

Joyce, H. (1997). Comment, mediation and domestic violence: Legislative responses. *Journal of the American Academy of Matrimonial Law, 14,* 447-453.

Landau, B. (1995). The Toronto Forum on Women Abuse: The process and the outcome. *Family and Conciliation Courts Review, 33*(1), 63-78.

Lerman, L. (1984). Mediation of wife abuse cases: The adverse impact of informal dispute resolution on women. *Harvard Women's Law Review, 7,* 57-113.

Maccoby, E., & Mnookin, R. (1992). *Dividing the child: Social and legal dilemmas of custody.* Cambridge, MA: Harvard University Press.

Mahoney, M. (1994). Victimization or oppression? Women's lives, violence, and agency. In M. Fineman & R. Mykitiuk (Eds.), *The public nature of private violence.* New York: Routledge.

Marthaler, D. (1989). Successful mediation with abusive couples. *Mediation Quarterly, 23,* 53-65.

Mayer, B. (1987). The dynamics of power in mediation and negotiation. *Mediation Quarterly, 16,* 75-86.

Milne, A. L. (2003). *Is mediation for us?* [Brochure]. (Available from AFCC, 6515 Grand Teton Plaza, Suite 210, Madison, Wisconsin 53719)

Milne, A., Salem, P., & Koeffler, K. (1992). When domestic abuse is an issue. *Family Advocate, 2,* 34-39.

Monahan, J. (1981). *The clinical prediction of violent behavior.* Washington, DC: U.S. Government Printing Office.

Newmark, L., Harrell, A., & Salem, P., (1995). Domestic violence and empowerment in custody and visitation cases: An empirical study on the impact of domestic violence. *Family and Conciliation Courts Review, 30,* 32-33.

O'Connell Corcoran K.. & Melamed, J. (1990). Coercion to empowerment: Spousal abuse and mediation. *Mediation Quarterly, 7,* 303-312.

O'Leary, K. D. (1993). Through a psychological lens: Personality traits, personality disorders and levels of violence. In R. Gelles & D. Loseke (Eds.), *Current controversies on family violence* (pp. 7-30). Newbury Park, CA: Sage.

Pearson, J. (1997). *Divorce mediation and domestic violence.* Denver, CO: Center for Policy Research.

Rimelspach, R. (2001). Mediating family disputes in a world with domestic violence: How to devise a safe and effective court-connected mediation program. *Ohio State Journal on Dispute Resolution, 17*(1), 95–112.

Salem, P. (1990). *It's still your choice* [Video]. (Available from AFCC, 6515 Grand Teton Plaza, Suite 210, Madison, Wisconsin 53719)

Salem, P., & Milne, A. (1995). Making mediation work in a domestic violence case. *Family Advocate, 4,* 34–38.

Schepard, A. (2003). *Children, courts and custody: Interdisciplinary models for divorcing families.* Cambridge, MA: Cambridge University Press.

Straus, M. (1979). Measuring intrafamily conflict and violence: The conflict tactics scales. *Journal of Marriage and the Family, 41,* 75–88.

Straus, M. (1990). The conflict tactics scales and its critics: An evaluation and new data on validity and relativity. In M. Straus & R. Gelles, *Physical violence in American families: Risk factors and adaptation to violence in 8,145 families* (pp. 49–73). New Brunswick, NJ: Transaction.

Straus, M., & Gelles, R. (1990). *Physical violence in American families: Risk factors and adaptations to violence in 8,145 families.* New Brunswick, NJ: Transaction.

Stuart, E., & Campbell, M. (1989). Assessment of patterns of dangerousness with battered women. *Issues in Mental Health Nursing, 10,* 245–260.

Stuehling, J., & Hart, B. (1997). *Domestic violence legal advocacy practice: Participant manual.* Harrisburg, PA: Pennsylvania Coalition Against Domestic Violence.

Sun, M., & Woods, L. (1989). *A mediator's guide to domestic violence.* New York: National Center on Women and Family Law.

Thoennes, N., Salem, P., & Pearson, J. (1995). Mediation and domestic violence: Current policies and practices. *Family and Conciliation Courts Review, 6,* 7.

Tjaden, P., & Thoennes, N. (1998). *Stalking in America: Findings from the National Violence Against Women Survey.* Washington, DC: U.S. Department of Justice, National Institute of Justice.

Tolman, R. (1992). *Tolman screening model* (final report of the Domestic Abuse and Mediation Project). Portland: Maine Court Mediation Service.

Tondo, C., Coronel, R., & Drucker, B. (2001). Mediation trends: Survey of the states. *Family Court Review, 39*(4), 431–453.

Treuthart, M. P. (1996). All that glitters is not gold: Mediation in domestic abuse cases. *Clearinghouse Review: Special Issues, 30,* 243–260.

U.S. Commission on Civil Rights. (1982). *Under the rule of thumb: Battered women and the administration of justice.* Washington, DC: Author.

U.S. Department of Justice. (1997). *Violence-related injuries treated in hospital emergency departments.* Washington, DC: Author.

Ver Steegh, N. (2003). Yes, no, and maybe: Informed decision making about divorce mediation in the presence of domestic violence. *William and Mary Journal of Women and the Law, 9,* 145–206.

Wilson, K. J. (1997). *When violence begins at home: A comprehensive guide to understanding and ending domestic abuse.* Alameda, CA: Hunter House.

Wilson, M., & Daley, M. (1994). Spousal homicide [special issue]. *Juristat, 14*(8).

Wisconsin Supreme Court. (1991). *In re:* Interest of Z. J. H., Sporleder v. Hermes. 1962 Wis. 2nd, 1002, 471, N.W. 2d 202.

Wisconsin Supreme Court. (1995). *In re:* Custody of H. S. H., K. Holtzman v. Knott. 193 Wis. 2nd, 649, 533 N.W. 2d 419.

Yellott, A. (1990). Mediation and domestic violence: A call for collaboration. *Mediation Quarterly, 8,* 39–50.

RESOURCES

Association for Conflict Resolution, 1015 18th Street NW, Suite 1150, Washington, DC 20036; (202) 464-9700; website: *www.acrnet.org;* e-mail: *acr@acrnet.org*

Association of Family and Conciliation Courts (AFCC), 6515 Grand Teton Plaza, Suite 210, Madison, WI 53719; (608) 664-3750; website: *www.afccnet.org;* e-mail: *afcc@afccnet.org*

Family Violence Department, National Council of Juvenile and Family Court Judges, P.O. Box 8970, Reno, NV 89507; (775) 784-6012; website: *www.ncjfcj.unr.edu*

National Coalition Against Domestic Violence, P.O. Box 18749, Denver, CO 80218; website: *www.ncadv.org.*–Provides a list of state and local organizations and other resources.

National Domestic Violence Hotline; 800-799-SAFE(7233).

CHAPTER 15

Mediating with Blended Families

LYNN CARP JACOB

The number of stepfamilies in the United States will soon outnumber all other family types. Mediators working with stepfamilies frequently face situations that are logistically and emotionally complex. This chapter examines the characteristics of blended families, common myths associated with these families, and the blended family life cycle. The impact of blended family issues on the mediation process is discussed and a model for working with blended families in mediation is presented.

Jane and Bill have been divorced for 2 years. Jane is now in a lesbian relationship. Bill has recently married a woman who has three children from her first marriage. Jane contacted a mediator. When she met alone with the mediator, she complained that since his marriage, Bill has become very rigid about issues relating to the schedule of their 8-year-old son. In the meeting with Bill and his wife, the couple explained that they wanted to have all of their children on the same schedule so that on alternate weekends they could have time as a couple with no children at home.

Ten-year-old Carrie had been talking to both of her parents for months. She has been living primarily with her mother and 15-year-old brother and wants to move in with her father, his wife, and their 1-year-old twins. The parents were unable to work this out on their own and sought the help of a mediator.

Janice called asking for a mediation session for herself and her ex-husband, Jim. Jim has remarried; Janice has not. They have two children, ages 14 and 7. The judge has ordered them to participate in mediation. There are two main problems: choosing a high school for their older child and their frequent conflict over the children's schedule.

These cases were all resolved in mediation, and all involved issues related to blended families. Little has been written about mediating with families who combine after divorce. This chapter helps mediators understand and address the unique challenges that are associated with mediating cases involving issues that arise after families combine. The first part of the chapter examines the characteristics of blended families, common myths associated with these families, and the life cycle of such families. The second part of the chapter focuses on how blended family issues impact the mediation process and provides a model and techniques for working with these families.

THE BLENDED FAMILY

What is a blended family? Definitions vary. In this chapter a blended family is defined as a committed adult couple, at least one of whom has a child from a previous marriage or relationship. The terms *blended family, stepfamily, combined family,* and *remarried family* are used interchangeably.

There is no single blended family prototype. The adults in a blended family may be married or cohabitating, opposite sex or same sex. They may include a biological or adoptive parent of a child from a previous relationship. Some blended families include households in which children are seldom present. In others children reside in the home most of the time. Sometimes the biological or adoptive parent plays an important part in a child's life; at other times, this is not the case. Blended families also vary because of their cultural backgrounds. They may include grandparents, stepchildren, step-grandparents, as well as step-aunts and step-uncles.

Using this broader definition of a blended family, the United States Census Bureau noted that over half of the entire U.S. population has been, is, or will be part of a blended family situation at some point during their lifetimes. Demographers predict that by 2010, there will be more stepfamilies in the United States than any other family type (Visher & Visher, 1998).

Even before the increase in the divorce rate in the last half century, single-parent families and stepfamilies were common, typically forming after the death of one parent. Historically, blended families have been tolerated, although regarded as atypical and somehow dysfunctional—an undesirable deviation from the nuclear, biological family ideal. According to current trends, blended families will soon become more common than biological families. With more than half of all families in blended families, the pejorative stereotype is beginning to change (McGoldrick & Carter, 1999).

CHILDREN AND STEPFAMILIES

The myth of the ideal family persists today. Children are generally surprised when they learn that their parents are divorcing. They will likely mourn the loss of the ideal intact family, even though their family may never have conformed to that ideal. They may continue to experience this loss and some of the tangible impact of the divorce, such as dealing with two homes and ongoing postdivorce conflict. It is very common for children to hold on to the fantasy that the family will reunite.

When their parents remarry, children face more changes in the form of further restructuring of their lives. Reactions to these changes, transitions, and losses vary with the personality, age, and developmental stage of the child. Children in the same family commonly have markedly different reactions to blended family formation. An oldest child can suddenly become a second child, with a possible loss of status and responsibility within the household.

Siblings also play a distinctive role in the stepfamily. Now present in the new family may be full siblings who share the same parents and half-siblings who have only one parent in common. Two children who are stepsiblings may live in the same home without any biological or legal relationship. Their parents may then decide to have their own biological child, further complicating the sibling relationships. Such a biological child tends to be helpful to the bonding process of the blended family.

Loyalty conflicts and competition exist for both adults and children in blended families. Since the parent–child relationship precedes the new spouse relationship, it is common for adults to feel caught between their children and their new partners. Their loyalties are divided between the children they brought into the marriage and the needs of the new spouse. If the remarriage is to succeed, the couple's relationship should be primary. At the same time, the emotional needs of the children require considerable attention. It is best for children when all of their parents can develop a cooperative relationship. Emily and John Visher coined the term "parenting coalition" to refer to all of the adults involved in parenting a child. They suggested that the message children need to hear is that it is acceptable to love both of their parents and to have amicable relationships with all family members (Visher & Visher, 1998).

The formation of a blended family after a death poses special challenges. When a parent dies, children may struggle with grieving the loss of the parent for a protracted period and then may come to idealize the deceased parent. The loyalty conflicts for a child accepting a stepparent into his or her life, while still honoring the memory of the deceased parent, can be profound (Ganong & Coleman, 1994).

Whether a blended family results from the death of a parent or from divorce, we know that, given their size and complexity, these families find themselves embroiled in conflict more frequently than biological families.

Changing from two minifamilies to one blended family involves a complex development of new daily as well as holiday customs and traditions. Some children decide they want a change in the amount of time they spend in their two households. Other children decide to move from the household where they had originally been spending most of their time. Working out these changes often involves conflict.

COMMON MYTHS ABOUT BLENDED FAMILIES

Numerous myths and misunderstandings abound regarding blended families. To be most helpful, it is important for mediators to understand some of the common myths.

Myth 1: Blended Families Are the Same as Biological Families

Life in blended families is quite different from nuclear families. The connectedness of the original two-parent family gradually emerges throughout the family life cycle, from courtship to marriage to parenthood. In contrast, a remarried family is formed from segments that already possess significant and distinctive links that have a previous history. In some ways this type of marriage is like the merger of two companies with different cultures and histories. Each "company" needs to adapt to the ways of the other if the two are to "work" together. Furthermore, in remarried families, in contrast to biological or adoptive families, a parent may be living elsewhere; the parent–child relationship predates the couple relationship; and the children are often members of two households.

Myth 2: Loving and Caring Develop Instantly

Loving and caring almost *never* bloom "on the spot." The process typically takes 2–5 years, and sometimes longer—or never happens. It is easier for young children (under the age of 3–5) to adapt, because they have fewer memories of the intact marriage and tend to accept the blended family as normal. Typically, the first months of blended family life are an extremely confusing time, as family members plunge into roles that normally require years to cultivate. Adults and children likely have quite different expectations. Adults often expect the new family to "make up for" everything that was missing from their first marriage. Children may feel that they have not been given a choice about the marriage and act out their angry or hurt feelings by misbehavior or disrespect toward the stepparent. It is common for the stepparent to feel hurt by the stepchild's angry and hostile behavior. During these stressful times it is especially important for the new partners to work together on their marriage so they both feel loved and cared for while they give the children time and space to adapt. Parents can certainly command respectful behavior toward stepparents, but they cannot mandate love. Even respect takes time to engender.

Myth 3: Anything Negative That Happens Is a Result of Being in a Blended Family

Although blended families are undeniably complicated units, they need not be dysfunctional. It is important to consider all areas of family life. Healthy blended families need (1) knowledge of what to expect in this type of family; (2) good couple unity; (3) space for the children to continue relationships with all of the parental figures; and (4) civil relationships between all of the parental adults. With time—and in many cases, professional help—blended families can get beyond conflict and complications to full functioning (McGoldrick & Carter, 1999).

Myth 4: All Stepmothers Are Wicked

The most difficult role noted repeatedly in the myths, fairy tales, and litera-ture of most cultures of the world is that of the stepmother. We do not yet know the precise reason for this universally pejorative view, though it is likely connected with the reality that mothers tend to be in charge of households and of "mothering"; it may also be fueled by the seemingly inherent competi-tion that exists (at least, initially) between mothers and stepmothers or by the loyalty issues of the children (Ihinger-Tallman & Pasley, 1997; Visher & Visher, 1988). In both *Cinderella* and *Hansel and Gretel* we find classic depic-tions of the wicked stepmother. The stereotype comes with being part of a blended family, and fear of being perceived this way can make new stepmoth-ers inhibited and ultimately ineffective. Stepmothers can learn to overcome these negative stereotypes, but it takes hard work, patience, and often media-tion or therapy. (See Appendix 15.1 for a sample of information provided to stepparents who are struggling with these issues in their families.)

THE BLENDED FAMILY LIFE CYCLE

The blended family is in constant flux, especially in the early stages, as family members sort through their own interests, needs, and roles. Children may feel betrayed and act out their anger or hurt feelings. Adolescents typically have a particularly difficult time because their developmental focus has shifted from one of family solidarity to separating from the family and devel-oping independent lives. As a consequence, they may have far less investment in cultivating blended family interconnectedness. It is important to note that roughly 60 percent of second marriages fail (Hetherington & Kelly, 2002). Understanding the life cycle of the stepfamily is important in putting the multiple changes attendant to stepfamily formation into perspective.

How long does it take members of blended families to bond? Throughout the literature are references to the greater ease associated with young children. Papernow (1993) proposes a continuum of cohesiveness in which it takes from 2 to 8 years for families to traverse the basic stages necessary to develop a sense of unity and loyalty. Family attachment ultimately becomes primary for all of its members, but often the process requires outside help.

Those who mediate with blended families should be familiar with these stages to help blended family members normalize their experiences and restore their often battered self-esteem. Papernow's (1993) schema for the life cycle of the remarried family consists of three main phases (see Figure 15.1). Phase One, in particular, is important for mediators to understand, as this period is most likely to lead families to mediation. In Phase One the family remains primarily divided along biological lines, functioning as two minifamilies or one minifamily and an "outsider."

Within this first phase there are three stages: (1) the fantasy period of anticipation and hope; (2) the immersion time, in which the families live together and begin to recognize their differences; and (3) the awareness stage in which conflict and dissatisfaction are likely to peak.

By the time they reach the awareness stage, family members have begun to see that changes must be made for the new family to remain viable. Awareness of problems is most likely to prompt the blended family to seek mediation or therapy. Common clash points that prompt help-seeking behavior include conflict between the biological families on child-related or financial issues, conflict between a parent or stepparent and a child, sibling conflict, and continued eruptions within the blended family.

During Phase Two of mobilization and action, the family is beginning to move toward resolution of their differences. A feeling of unity begins to develop. By Phase Three of contact and resolution, there is a bonding and a feeling of loyalty among stepfamily members. The pace through which stepfamilies move from one phase to another varies enormously.

Papernow's (1993) research suggests that healthy family development is related to the presence of support, validation, and an understanding of the intense and painful feelings involved in the early stages of blended family life.

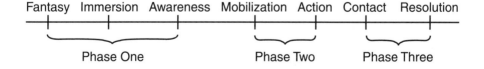

FIGURE 15.1. Stages of development in blended families.

MEDIATING WITH STEPFAMILIES

Blended families—with all their inherent conflict—have become more common in recent years. At the same time, mediation has become more widely accepted as a process for addressing family disputes. It appears that an increasing number of blended families is using mediation to resolve disputes. This is likely a natural outgrowth of the increasing popularity of mediation in combination with the pervasiveness of blended families.

Blended family disputes often involve postdecree matters related to a second marriage and children from either or both of the parents. Couples may be referred to mediation by the courts, lawyers, therapists, school counselors, or one of the parents themselves. The conflict may be presented as a concern about a child, or how family members are relating to one another, or finances.

The primary dispute, in most cases with blended families, concerns the ongoing difficulties between the former spouses, who find themselves enmeshed in conflict over various issues related to postdecree parenting. Former spouses may bring unresolved issues from previous marriages, which can impact the new blended family in a profound way. Although the parents (biological or adoptive) are typically the main players in the dispute resolution process, stepparents often play an important role in the mediation, as they voice their strong feelings about these issues.

Disputes between the biological parents regarding children may be specifically related to any of the following areas:

1. The emerging role of the stepparent
2. The amount of contact between children and the nonresidential parent
3. A child or a parent's dissatisfaction with a schedule
4. Relocation of one of the families, or a child's request to move from one household to the other
5. Financial issues

Disputes also arise when one parent is dissatisfied with the parenting style of the other. Following a remarriage, it is not uncommon for a disengaged parent to wish to reestablish contact with a child. This type of case is complicated simply because the child may not wish to have a relationship with the disengaged parent.

Within the financial arena, modification of child support is a common request. In some cases there is disagreement about funding college or selling the marital home. Couples with these disputes turn to mediation as an alternative to litigation to avoid the negative impact of the litigation process and to prevent the escalation of conflict.

Blended family issues also may trigger a need for mediation when a parent, divorcing for the second time, confronts the complications that arise because a biological child has established a meaningful relationship with the now-divorcing stepparent. In the case of a second divorce for either of the parents, it is important for the mediator to inquire about relationships with stepchildren. Unless a stepparent has adopted a stepchild, that stepparent does not have formal legal rights to the child.

When conflict over stepparent visitation is litigated, court rulings tend to favor blood ties over psychological ones. However, more judicial districts are beginning to allow stepparents visitation rights. Mediation allows couples to voluntarily establish visitation arrangements for the stepparent. These cases can be a bit more complicated from a logistical perspective.

In one such case involving a second marriage and subsequent divorce, the divorcing couple had an 8-year-old son together. The mother's 12-year-old son from her first marriage had been living with the couple, and the stepfather had a close and caring relationship with the boy—who also had a close relationship with his biological father. The stepfather expressed a strong desire to maintain a relationship with both his son, with whom he had a clear legal relationship, and his stepson, with whom he had no legal relationship. After some discussion, the divorcing parents negotiated a schedule in which both boys would be with the stepfather one overnight during the week. Both boys would then spend alternate weekends with their respective biological fathers.

Blended families pose special challenges for mediators by virtue of their complexity. Acquiring a firm grounding in existing knowledge about stepfamilies and using educative and normative interventions when needed are essential components of effective mediation in this context. Blended families place great demands on their members' problem-solving and communication skills. In addition to providing a safe setting in which to resolve disputes, mediators can discuss ways to manage the stepfamily transition process and attendant intrafamilial difficulties with stepfamily members. Mediators should also be prepared to make referrals to therapeutic and educational services when more specialized intervention is needed. The Stepfamily Association of America is an excellent resource for mediators in this regard.

STAGES OF MEDIATION: A MODEL FOR CONDUCTING MEDIATION WITH BLENDED FAMILIES

Mediation with blended families is a new and emerging field of practice, with few existing practice models targeted specifically toward this ever-growing population. With the most difficult high-conflict cases—those in which there may be physical or emotional abuse or chemical dependency (see Baris et al., 2001)—mediators may need to serve more as a child advocate or may choose to work together with therapists to help parents focus on the child's needs. This chapter does not address a process for these high-conflict families but rather focuses on the more typical blended family conflicts.

When blended families seek mediation, they often do not recognize that most of the conflict they are experiencing is related to normal life transitions, including developmental impasses in the process of blended family formation. Instead, the dispute gets transformed into a legal or quasi-legal issue. It is therefore important for the mediator to assume the roles of educator, facilitator, problem solver, and child advocate, when necessary.

The way I work with postdecree cases, in general, has changed over the years. Initially, I started by seeing the parents together and then seeing them individually or with a significant other (Jacob, 1997). Currently, I start with individual sessions with all my clients. The purpose of these meetings is to screen for abuse and intimidation, to learn from the individual ex-spouses how they see their situation and why they believe they have been unable to resolve their differences, and to determine what they believe will be the most difficult issues. I next hold a joint session and then decide, with the parents, who should be present for the negotiating session(s). The order of sessions is not rigid—if a client requests a different format, I will consider this change. I have seen couples who explain in their initial telephone call that they get along quite decently but want a neutral facilitator present to help them discuss a particular topic, such as a recent misunderstanding about their child's schedule or a concern one might have about their child's participation in a particular activity such as football. Some cases have been resolved in one or two joint sessions. In others, I have held individual sessions after the joint meeting.

Stage 1: Individual Sessions

This session serves several purposes: It is used to screen for abuse and intimidation and to determine if the parents and I feel it is appropriate to continue with mediation. I also use this time to more fully ascertain each parent's concerns and to build an alliance with each of them. The educative function of the mediator is emphasized during this session. I try to discern the parent's view of the children's relationships with the various members of the two families. I always ask myself whether these parents appear to be able to separate their needs from the needs of their children. I want to know if the parents have the emotional ability to determine how the children are functioning and what is in their children's best interest. These are subtle aspects that I determine by observing the parents and asking questions related to the children. The use of individual meetings, referred to as caucuses, will be discussed in more detail later in this chapter.

Stage 2: Initial Joint Session

The joint session is an opportunity to assess the conflict between the parents since they both have primary responsibility and decision-making power over the children. I state my role as one of facilitating their discussion and resolution of the issues, not one of making decisions for them. Rarely does the negotiation of substantive issues take place at this time. Rather, I review the mediation process, determine each parent's agenda, and obtain their agreement to mediate. I want to set a tone of balance and neutrality in which neither party feels favored. They are informed about the process together and express their intention to make use of it in a constructive way.

Stage 3: Additional Individual Sessions

Whether children are directly involved in mediation depends on their age, the nature of the conflict, and the parents' preferences. Children should be seen when the mediator believes that their input will help the family move forward toward resolution of the dispute without creating an undue burden on the children. In my experience, adolescents prefer to be seen, for they like to have a voice in issues related to them. I typically tell parents that children are welcome to give input but that parents get the final vote. I believe this frees children from what could become a loyalty conflict (Jacob, 1991). If either or both parents have a spouse or significant other, I will invite the parent to bring this person to a separate mediation session. Occasionally, when the conflict is high, I might schedule a series of alternating individual meetings. In one such situation, I negotiated a child's time in each household with one parent in my office and the other on a speaker phone.

Stage 4: Negotiations

After the individual meetings and the initial joint session, the negotiation typically begins. Several negotiating sessions may be required, and these can take place in a variety of configurations:

1. The biological parents together or in alternating individual sessions
2. The biological parents together with their respective spouses or partners
3. Alternating meetings between the biological parents and the children

If the parties all agree and seem able to negotiate flexibly and openly, both biological parents and their respective partners can be included—what has been referred to as the parenting coalition. Spouses of biological parents are often helpful in calming them and realistically appraising the situation, as well as assessing different options for resolution of the dispute. In this way, the stepparents help the mediator manage the session. Another option is to have only the biological parents present for the negotiating session. When there is major conflict or an imbalance of power, it is possible to shuttle between the biological parents, who are seated in two separate rooms, or hold alternate individual sessions. In my experience, the key to success is for the mediator to take command of the process and provide a setting that works for all of the clients.

Postdecree mediation with blended families typically requires between two and six sessions to resolve specific disputes and provide referrals to the educational and support services that are occasionally needed to help the blended family system move forward. A relatively uncomplicated blended family mediation might require initial separate meetings with the biological parents, a joint meeting, and one or more negotiation sessions. More difficult cases may require additional, or even ongoing, meetings. These are typically parents who cannot negotiate a child's schedule on their own. I have met with some parents twice a year and with others monthly. Within the bounds of a tightly structured session, these parents are able to negotiate a parenting schedule.

CORE STRATEGIES IN MEDIATION WITH BLENDED FAMILIES

Caucusing

A primary feature of postdivorce mediation with blended families is the extensive use of the caucus, a private meeting held by the mediator with an individual party or parties in dispute (Moore, 1987). The caucus may be used within a joint session or as an entire separate session. The initial meetings that I hold with each of the parents are technically caucuses. I tell the parents that I will assume that whatever is said in caucus may be shared with the other party unless they ask that specific content be kept confidential. At the end of the session, I typically ask if there is anything they would like me to keep confidential.

Caucusing can be used at different stages of the mediation process. In the early stages, I use it for screening and for engaging clients and building trust. It is also a good way for the mediator to meet with stepparents and include them in the process. In situations of conflict, in particular, the expression of strong emotions is sometimes best done within the caucus format because it allows the mediator to prevent the parties' anger and other emotions from obstructing the mediation process.

Caucusing can also be used as a break during stressful negotiations. The mediator or the parties can request such a break. When negotiations are at an impasse or strong emotions are being expressed in a way that is not helpful to the process, calling for a caucus may be highly effective in getting the parties back on track.

During a caucus, the mediator can help the parties gain insight into how the conflict is being maintained, focusing on their individual contribution to the dispute. The mediator can also educate the parties regarding blended family roles and tasks, effective problem-solving strategies, and available options for resolution.

Finally, caucusing can be used to help the parties alter their negotiating positions or to discuss an emotional issue that seems to be getting in the way of the negotiation (Moore, 1987).

Educating

Rarely are stepfamily members prepared for the multiple tasks and challenges involved in blended family formation and restructuring. Mediator monologues and brief stories are particularly useful teaching tools for conveying key pointers, such as the importance of (1) the stepparent assuming a secondary role when disciplining children, (2) allowing children to have their own space, and (3) not trying to force a relationship. The stories can also focus on the difficulties children face when they go back and forth between two homes, especially if they are caught in the middle of parental conflict. Some mediators make use of current stepfamily research and refer families to written materials. Others relate their personal or clinical experience.

It is often helpful to provide succinct educational monologues throughout the mediation process. The following are fairly typical mediation monologues that can be used at different stages of the process.

Comments to a parent and relatively new spouse:

"Your role is a particularly difficult one. Don't expect too much too soon. It may take a long time for the three [or four or five] of you to feel like a family. The best place for you to start is to try building a friendship with the child/children. It might be easier for you to try doing activities separately with each of the children."

The mediator might add later:

"In my experience there should be no contest between a parent, a stepparent, or a biological/adoptive parent. Such a competition will not be helpful. When children are born, they get one mother and one father—a stepparent will never be able to be *that* parent. The stepparent role is *different* from the parent role."

Comments about children:

"There are many stresses for children in blended families, including hearing one parent speak badly about the other, hearing their parent and stepparent fight and fearing that this marriage will break up, and adjusting to the new rules and traditions in the household."

"It is easy for stepparents to try too hard. I suggest that stepparents give their spouses their input and then let the biological parent enforce the rules. This frees the stepparent to simply develop a friendship with the children."

COMEDIATION AND CONSULTATION

Working with blended families can be challenging even for experienced family mediators. Two tools are particularly useful in combating mediator stress and burnout. Comediation allows the mediator to work in conjunction with a colleague. The two mediators can discuss each case and debrief emotions that may be stirred up by the process. Individual and group consultation provides another forum for discussing cases. Consultation also combats the isolation and frustration often experienced by stepfamily mediators, particularly those who are in private practice.

CONCLUSION

The blended family provides unique challenges for mediators. The conflict a mediator might find in a first-time divorcing couple can grow exponentially by the "second time around." The logistical issues alone can create significant conflict and challenges when multiple families are involved. In many ways, mediating with blended families is significantly different from mediating a one-family, two-parent divorce, yet there are similarities as well. Reframing issues, serving as an educator, and validating the wishes of each member of the family are a few of the interventions common to both types of family mediation.

Blended families have gradually become normative; however, they still need to *feel* normal. Mediators who have an understanding of the issues that blended families must address can be instrumental in inspiring confidence and skills that lead to attachments that help members feel related in their hearts as well as in their households.

APPENDIX 15.1. TIPS FOR STEPFAMILIES*

1. Be patient. Relationships take time to develop.
2. Accept the role of stepmother/stepfather. It is a different role from that of biological parent (more like a caring uncle or aunt), but it is very important.

3. Partners need to support one another and establish a relationship separate from the children.

4. Learn to live with the reality of ex-spouses.

5. Develop a relationship with stepchildren before attempting to discipline them. Family meetings are sometimes helpful.

6. Do not take misbehaviors personally. Every stepparent goes through a period of testing by the children.

7. It's OK to ask for courtesy and respect from your stepchildren. In return, you must be courteous to the children and treat them fairly.

8. Discuss appropriate dress, privacy, and modesty with regard to teenage children.

9. Don't expect to love your stepchildren or have the stepchildren love you instantly. Try to find special interest to share with them.

10. Don't badmouth the children's biological parent. That only hurts the children and makes them feel defensive.

11. Good communication and a sense of humor can be very helpful. Don't try too hard. Remember, you are creating a new family. It is a great deal of work but can be rewarding in the long run.

Source: Adapted from "Tips for Stepparents" handout. Airing Institute of Cincinnati, Ohio (1997).

ACKNOWLEDGMENT

This chapter is adapted from *Mediation and Conflict Resolution in Social Work and Human Services* (1st ed.) edited by E. Kruk. © 1997, with permission of Wadsworth, an imprint of the Wadsworth Group, a division of Thomson Learning; Fax 800-730-2215.

REFERENCES

Airing Institute of Cincinnati, Ohio. (1997, July 17). *Tips for stepparents.* Handout distributed at the 14th annual conference of the Academy of Family Mediators, North Falmouth, MA.

Baris, M. A., Coates, C. A., Duvall, B. B., Garrity, C. B., Johnson, E. T., & LaCrosse, E. R. (2001). *Working with high-conflict families of divorce.* Northvale, NJ: Aronson.

Ganong, L. H., & Coleman, M. (1994). *Remarried family relationships.* Thousand Oaks, CA: Sage.

Hetherington, E. M., & Kelly, J. (2002). *For better or for worse: Divorce reconsidered.* New York: Norton.

Ihinger-Tallman, M., & Pasley, K. (1997). Stepfamilies in 1984 and today: A scholarly perspective. *Marriage and Family Review, 26*(1–2), 19–40. [Copublished in I. Levin & M. H. Sussman (Eds.), *Stepfamilies: History, research and policy* (pp. 19–40). Binghamton, NY: Haworth Press.]

Jacob, L. C. (1991). Mediating postdecree disputes. *Mediation Quarterly, 8*(3), 171–183.

Jacob, L. C. (1997). Postdivorce mediation with stepfamilies: An overview of issues and process. In E. Kruk (Ed.), *Mediation and conflict resolution in social work and human services* (1st ed., pp. 81–95). Belmont, CA: Wadsworth.

McGoldrick, M., & Carter, B. (1999). Remarried families. In B. Carter & M. McGoldrick (Eds.), *The expanded family life cycle* (3rd ed., pp. 417–435). Needham Heights, MA: Allyn & Bacon.

Moore, C. W. (1987). The caucus: Private meetings that promote settlement. *Mediation Quarterly, 16,* 87–101.

Papernow, P. (1993). *Becoming a stepfamily: Patterns of development in remarried families.* San Francisco: Jossey-Bass.

Visher, E., & Visher, J. (1988). *Old loyalties, new ties: Therapeutic strategies with stepfamilies.* New York: Brunner/Mazel.

Visher, E. B., & Visher, J. S. (1998). Stepparents: The forgotten family members. *Family and Conciliation Courts Review, 36*(4), 444–451.

CHAPTER 16

Mediating Separation of Same-Sex Couples

ALLAN E. BARSKY

Institutional, social, and legal recognition of same-sex relationships include the rights and obligations that exist when partners separate. Mediators working with same-sex couples must possess a knowledge of issues and concerns that are unique to this population, while understanding that differences between same-sex and different-sex couples does not necessarily alter the basic mediation process. This chapter presents information and specific examples to demonstrate how mediators can work effectively and ethically with same-sex couples.

When family and divorce mediation first developed as a profession in the 1970s, the concept of family embraced by most mediators comprised a heterosexual man (who headed the family) and a heterosexual woman who were legally married (i.e., a different-sex couple). At the time, this conception reflected both legal definitions of marriage and psychological definitions of "normal" families. Although many jurisdictions still have laws that discriminate against same-sex couples,[1] other jurisdictions have legally recognized same-sex relationships, including the rights and obligations that accrue upon separation (Bertrand & Hornick, 1994; Diaz, 1999; Dickson, 1995). In 1973, the American Psychiatric Association removed homosexuality from the *Diagnostic and Statistical Manual of Mental Disorders* (see American Psychiatric Association, 2000, for the latest edition, DSM-IV-RT). Since that time, the American Psychological Association (1998) and the National Association of Social Workers (2000) have also declared that homosexuality is a normal expression of sexual orientation. The American Academy of Pediatrics (2002) has stated that children "born to or adopted by one member of a same-sex couple deserve the security of two legally recognized parents" (p. 339). Psychology, social work, and other mental health professions now view families headed by gay men or lesbians as valid and healthy forms of relationships (Paterson, 2001; Tye, 2003). Still, many people hold negative attitudes and beliefs about gay men and lesbians as individuals, spouses, and parents. Given mediator values related to client self-determination, mediator impartiality, and appreciation of diversity (Model Standards of Practice, 2001, Standards I, IV, and XIII; see also the appendix in Schepard, Chapter 22, this volume), mediators are professionally obliged to broaden their definition of family to embrace those headed by same-sex couples.

This chapter describes the knowledge, theories, values, awareness, and skills that mediators require in order to work effectively and ethically with same-sex couples going through separation.[2] First an overview of current legal and psychosocial perspectives on same-sex couples provides a knowledge base that mediators can draw upon when working with this population. The following section discusses ethical issues that can arise for practitioners when mediating separation of same-sex couples, as well as ways in which mediators can enhance their awareness of their own values and predilections. The next section describes specific skills and approaches to practice that mediators can incorporate into their toolkits to ensure appropriate interventions in their work with same-sex couples. The chapter concludes with suggestions for the future in terms of policy, practice, and research.

Although the focus of this discussion is on same-sex couples, the differences between same-sex couples and different-sex couples should not be exaggerated (Tye, 2003). At the same time, ignoring the differences would be an equal folly (Van Wormer, Wells, & Boes, 2000)

LEGAL KNOWLEDGE BASE

How mediators approach work with same-sex couples depends, in part, on the legal framework that governs their practice in their jurisdiction. As Mnookin and Kornhauser (1979) note, mediation clients bargain in the shadow of the law. This means that clients' choices often are affected by what a court would decide. Clients are allowed, however, to establish their own rights and obligations by contract beyond legal prescriptions, as long as they do not contravene specific legal prohibitions. Accordingly, mediators need to know the laws that govern same-sex couples, as well as how to allow their clients to mediate in relation to their underlying needs and interests rather than solely their rights (Barsky, 2000, Gordon, 2003).

Laws affecting same-sex couples differ greatly *across* countries, as well as *within* many of them. In the United States, laws vary from state to state, and even between cities within a state. Until 2003, states such as Florida had criminal laws that prohibited sodomy, child welfare laws that banned adoption by gay or lesbian parents, and case law in divorce situations where judges have used sexual orientation as a reason to deny a parent custody of a child (American Civil Liberties Union, 2002; Dickson, 1995). Although the United States Supreme Court declared laws prohibiting sodomy to be unconstitutional (*Lawrence et al. v. Texas,* 2003) and the adoption ban is currently being challenged in court, other anti-gay laws continue, and some states continue to try to delegitimate same-sex families by passing "Defense of Marriage" laws (that prohibit same-sex civil marriages) and by proposing constitutional amendments that restrict marriages to different-sex couples. In states with these types of discriminatory laws, same-sex couples might be disinclined to go to court to seek help resolving separation issues (Diaz, 1999). Although going to court and admitting a same-sex relationship no longer puts parties at peril of criminal charges for sodomy, same-sex couples understand that some judges still retain negative attitudes toward gays and lesbians. If a state has a Defense of Marriage Act, this law could also invalidate a prenuptial or marriage agreement between same-sex partners.[3]

Other jurisdictions do not necessarily have laws banning same-sex marriages but also do not offer any form of legal recognition of same-sex unions (Appleby, 2001). This means that there is no legislation governing spousal support, division of property, or other incidents of cohabitation for a same-sex couple that is separating (Human Rights Campaign, 2002). A woman who has given up her education and career to raise children, for example, would find it difficult to convince a court that she has a right to some type of support or compensation from a former female domestic partner. This situation might be particularly unfair if the employed partner were able to advance her career and financial status because the stay-at-home partner took full responsibility for child rearing. The situation is similar for unmarried different-sex partners who separate in states with no laws protecting former common-law spouses.

The problems for same-sex couples may go further should they have a dispute over custody or access to their children. Consider, for example, a gay-male couple that had a child through surrogacy, with one partner as the biological father. Upon separation, the other (nonbiological) father may have no legal standing to pursue custody or visitation of the child (Brown, 2003).[4] Although legislation in virtually all jurisdictions says that decisions on custody and visitation are to be based on the best interests of the child, some states give preference to biological parents and effectively cut off a person who has taken on parenting responsibility but has no biological connection (Human Rights Campaign, 2002; American Civil Liberties Union, 2002).[5] Another complication may arise if grandparents, out of homophobic beliefs, pursue custody of the child, so that the child is not raised in a gay, lesbian, bisexual, or transgender (GLBT[6]) home. Although all states have laws that permit grandparents or other nonparent applicants to pursue custody and access, the courts have tended to give priority to the rights of the biological parents. Still, the outcome of a case can depend upon the specific wording of legislation in the state, and whether the nonparent applicant can prove "harm" to the child if the nonparents were denied custody or visitation (Brown, 2003).

In more gay- and lesbian-friendly jurisdictions, legislation explicitly recognizes legal rights and responsibilities for same-sex couples upon separation. In Canada, for example, courts have held that laws prohibiting same-sex marriages are unconstitutional, and the federal government has drafted laws to formally recognize same-sex marriages. Unmarried same-sex partners can also be recognized as common law spouses if they are living together with the intent to cohabitate. In states and provinces that prohibit discrimination based upon sexual orientation, courts are not allowed to discriminate against lesbians or gay men during custody decisions. One might speculate that anti-gay biases affect some judge's decisions, though often such bias is difficult to prove.[7] In custody disputes between straight and gay parents, judges in some states explicitly deny custody to gay parents because they are gay (categorically excluded) or because of negative stereotypes about homosexuals (e.g., societal stigmatization, dysfunctional psychosocial development, ineffective parenting, the possibility that the child may contract AIDS, or molestation by the homosexual parent; Diaz, 1999).

The Netherlands and Denmark are other examples of jurisdictions that have more fully embraced same-sex couples as legitimate families. These countries have laws allowing same-sex couples to marry, with the same rights and obligations as different-sex couples upon divorce. Historically, U.S. courts have recognized marriages that were authorized outside the United States. Some states have passed legislation stating that they will not recognize same-sex marriages from other jurisdictions. There are currently no precedents in other states for how a court would handle a same-sex couple applying for divorce of a foreign same-sex marriage.

Cities such as Los Angeles, Ft. Lauderdale, and New York allow for registration of domestic partnerships involving same-sex couples.[8] Although the enabling laws may protect same-sex couples from some types of discrimination at the municipal level (e.g., job discrimination by the city), family law is a matter for state legislation. If the state does not recognize the relationship, then separating same-sex couples have no legal recourse for spousal support or other legal entitlements upon separation (American Civil Liberties Union, 2002).

Given the patchwork of evolving laws in different regions, mediators need to learn the laws that govern same-sex couples in their jurisdiction and to refer clients to competent lawyers for advice, as needed. For websites that provide current information about the laws affecting same-sex couples in various states, see the Resources section at the end of this chapter.

PSYCHOSOCIAL KNOWLEDGE BASE

When working with same-sex couples, mediators must ensure that the psychological and sociological theories and research that inform their practice are free from bias against lesbians and gay men (Barsky, Barsky, & Laverdiere, 2000). Although it is impossible to review all theories, some of the more common theories that inform the practice of mediation include developmental, family systems, and sociocultural variation theories (Irving & Benjamin, 1995). The following discussion deconstructs some of the concepts from the traditional versions of these theories and indicates perspectives that need to be addressed when reconstructing them to ensure that they fit the psychosocial realities of same-sex couples going through separation.

Developmental Theories

Traditional developmental theories such as Freud's Stages of Psychosexual Development or Erikson's Eight Stages of Man suggest that there is a "normal" sequence of life tasks and stages that people experience as they move from infancy through adulthood. The manner in which these tasks are experienced and resolved affects coping abilities and personalities. Traditional developmental theories suggest that normal people develop different-sex attractions and relationships, relegating homosexuality to an aberration or pathology. Since the 1970s, all major professional mental health associations have accepted homosexuality as a normal form of development and reject the notion that gays or lesbians can or should be "cured" of homosexuality (Van Wormer et al., 2000). Accordingly, traditional developmental theories must be reconstructed to incorporate the gay or lesbian reality.

An important aspect of development particular to the gay and lesbian experience is that of "coming out," which refers to an individual's process of developing an acceptance of his or her sexual and romantic attractions to others of the same sex. For individuals growing up in a family, religion, or community that is openly hostile to gays and lesbians, this process can be particularly difficult. High rates of suicide among gay teens are generally attributed to the individuals' reactions to negative family and societal attitudes and lack of perceived support (Hammelman, 1993; Tremblay & Ramsay, 1997). Mediators need to understand that coming out is a lifelong process, given that people generally assume a person is heterosexual unless the person indicates to them otherwise. Some people may be open about their sexual orientation to all people, but others choose to disclose this information only to those they believe will be accepting and supportive. Some may be open to gay acquaintances, for example, but not to close friends, colleagues at work, their religious or ethnic community, or family. Often, people find it most difficult to be open to family members, fearing rejection by those they love most (Van Wormer et al., 2000). Members of a same-sex couple may be in much different stages of coming out. In fact, differing degrees of openness is often a source of conflict leading to separation. In addition, mediated agreements may need to take into account each partner's comfort level with being out to various people involved in their lives. For example, a woman who has not told her parents about her lesbian lover may need to move in with her parents following separation, child in hand, but still not want her parents to know about her sexual orientation. The mediator's role is not to judge what is right or wrong but to validate and be supportive of the needs of all individuals. Rather than induce further guilt or stress, mediators can explore opportunities for gay or lesbian clients to continue their paths to self-acceptance, for example, by offering referrals for counseling, exploring options for coming out in a safer manner, and challenging negative stereotypes and self-images. Ultimately, each client must decide for him- or herself.

Mediation literature recognizes that the impact of divorce depends on the family unit's stage within the family life cycle: for example, a short-term marriage with no children, a long-term marriage with adolescent children, or an empty-nest couple (Irving & Benjamin, 1995; Ahrons & Rodgers, 1987). This research must be viewed with caution, however, when inferring implications for work with same-sex couples. The meaning of being childless, for example, may have different implications for a different-sex couple than for a same-sex couple. Families and society, in general, tend to have strong expectations for married couples to have children, whereas families and society are less likely to expect same-sex couples to have children (indeed, they may oppose the possibility). Family mediators must strive to understand each family in light of its unique wishes and experiences, which may or may not include expectations to have children. For same-sex couples that have had children through adoption, surrogacy, or donor insemination, their decision to have children was very deliberate and often required the parents to overcome incredible logistic, legal, and financial hurdles to be able to have children in these ways (Tye, 2003). Though all parents experience emotional stress over their parenting roles during separation, same-sex parents of children through adoption, surrogacy, or donor insemination may have particular emotional issues to work through when facing the prospect of separation and how to reinvent themselves as co-parents.

The still-prevailing notion of marriage "until death do us part" means that divorcing couples may experience social stigma and strong feelings of guilt. The stereotype that intimate gay relationships are unstable and short lived might mean that gay individuals experience less stigmatization when they terminate their relationship. On the other hand, many same-sex couples feel the obligation of looking "normal" or "healthy" to the non-GLBT world and feel a particularly strong sense of failure when their relationships break down. Mediators can help parties process these feelings of failure and offer the prospect of redeveloping a healthy family configuration through a constructive mediation agreement. Children and teenagers raised by same-sex couples may also experience separation differently from children raised by different-sex couples (Diaz, 1999; McIntyre, 1994). Some studies, for instance, have found that children of lesbian couples are more accepting of their mother's new partners than children of different-sex couples. On the other hand, children of same-sex couples who are separating may face additional stress because of peers who tease or stigmatize them about being from a gay family (Diaz, 1999). Mediators who are sensitive to these issues can help parents explore whether these issues affect their particular family and, if necessary, how best to deal with them.

Reliable social science research on the life cycle of families headed by same-sex couples has been limited. Researchers and funding bodies essentially ignored this area until the 1980s, and it is still difficult to obtain a representative sample—given prevailing societal discrimination and the ensuing reluctance of many same-sex couples to identify themselves publicly. A national survey of 560 gay male and 706 lesbian couples (Bryant & Demian, 1994) sheds some light on the nature of same-sex couples. For example, the average length of current relationships was 6 years, even though the average age of research participants was only 35 years. About 65% of couples jointly owned or rented their residence. Some participants, though considering themselves a couple, had never cohabited together on a full-time basis. Whereas newspapers and media often refer to members of same-sex couples as "long-time companions," most participants preferred the terms "lovers" or "life partners."[9] About 91% of lesbians and 63% of gay men reported that they were in an exclusive sexual relationship. Same-sex couples were most likely to report that they got support for their relationships from gay and lesbian friends and gay-positive[10] organizations. They were most likely to report low levels of support and high levels of hostility from relatives and religious institutions (primarily churches). Although laws in many states provide little or no protection for same-sex spouses, only 43% of same-sex couples had any legal documents protecting their spousal interests, such as a will, a power of attorney, or a living-together (partnership) agreement. Approximately 21% of lesbians and 9% of gay men reported being a caregiver for their children. Although mediators must be careful not to generalize from these types of statistics, the following suggestions seem warranted:

- Mediators should not make assumptions or sweeping generalizations about same-sex couples, including whether they have children, whether they have exclusive sexual relationships, or whether they have lived together. Diversity among same-sex couples is as broad as diversity among different-sex couples (Greene, 1997; O'Neill, 1999).
- Mediators should broaden the concept of family to one that embraces people who live together or provide care and support, rather than simply those who are related by blood or by marriage.

- Mediators should be sensitive to sources of conflict that are external to the couple relationship (e.g., anti-gay attitudes and beliefs from extended family and religious communities).
- Mediators should explore the unique life courses of same-sex couples, including their life expectations, life experiences, and challenges with separation, given their current life stage and social context.

Family Systems Theories

Various mediation models[11] have been based on family systems theories, including Structured Family Therapy, Strategic Family Therapy, Milan Family Systems Model, and Bowenian Family Therapy (Diaz, 1999; Gold, 1997; Irving & Benjamin, 2002). Essentially, family systems theories suggest that each member of a family has an impact on other members of that family and that a practitioner needs to intervene with the family as a whole as opposed to each individual separately. Although these concepts apply equally to same-sex couples and to different-sex ones, the notions of roles, expectations, and boundaries within family systems can be quite different. Traditional family systems theories, for example, suggest that, in order to be functional, a family should have clear delineation of roles; for example, a mother as the emotional care provider and manager of the household, a father as the financial provider and disciplinarian, and children as the recipients of support who tend to model themselves after, and align with, the parent of the same sex. While these traditional sex-typed roles have been challenged for different-sex couples, mediators need to appreciate the even greater differences for same-sex couples. When a family is headed by two women, for example, the role traditionally assumed by a father may be shared by both parents or may be assumed primarily by one parent. Furthermore, some roles may be held by a male from outside the household (e.g., the biological father, an uncle, a grandparent, or a close family friend). For mediators who are helping parents to focus on the best interests of a child, it is crucial to explore caretaking roles with an open frame of reference, rather than stereotyping who can perform what types of caretaking roles for children.

In traditional family systems theories, functional families are defined as having clearly defined, flexible boundaries. Boundaries that are too rigid, disengaged, permeable, or enmeshed are viewed as problematic (Zastrow, 1999). Some families headed by same-sex couples might be considered to have overly rigid boundaries because they are secretive about the fact that they *are* a same-sex couple; that is, there is an informal but powerful policy of "Don't ask, don't tell" within the extended family and community. A mediator or other practitioner must be careful about encouraging the family to open up its boundaries, given the stages of coming out for family members. A family's fears about negative responses from people outside the immediate family system may be realistic, and family members may not currently possess coping skills for dealing with homophobic neighbors, employers, schools, etc. Rather than judging what a same-sex couple "should do," mediators need to help such clients explore stresses, risks, and options by beginning with a validation of the clients' subjective perspectives.

Some family systems issues for same-sex couples are related to gender rather than sexuality. Given that women are socialized to be nurturing and other-focused, professionals who are trained primarily to work with different-sex couples might view some lesbian couples as too enmeshed, psychologically fused, overly restricted in their individuality, or having such a large investment in the relationship that breakup is particularly difficult (Van Wormer et al., 2000). Rather than pathologize this type of relationship, mediators can help these lesbian clients separate emotionally by validating their history of caring and mutual investment, thus giving them permission to move on. Mediators should recognize that many lesbians desire to maintain a close relationship with their former partners, given the social networks and intimacy they shared during their cohabitation as domestic partners (Felicio & Sutherland, 2001). In contrast, given that men are socialized to be independent, mediators may find that some gay-male clients desire a complete termination of their relationship with a former partner. Mediators must avoid simply applying heterosexual norms or expectations about the types of relationships that same-sex couples "should" have following separation. Clients must determine their own preferred postseparation relationship.

Another example of potential gender-based differences relates to the tendency for men in U.S. culture to be socialized as competitive and authoritarian. Gay men, for example, tend to be stricter than lesbians in their parenting roles (Tye, 2003). In relationships, men learn how to be in control, territorial, or expressive of anger, and to initiate sex. They may not learn to be nurturing, empathic, expressive of tender emotions, or proficient at household duties such as cooking, cleaning the house, and doing laundry (Brown, 2003). If both men in a couple reflect this type of socialization, it may lead to breakdown in the relationship and affect how well the men can work toward an amicable dissolution. Although the "queen" and "fairy" stereotypes of gay men suggest that they possess feminine qualities, in reality gay men can reflect masculine *or* feminine qualities, and likely a combination of both. Similarly, whereas the "dyke" stereotype of lesbians suggests that they possess masculine qualities, lesbians (like all people) reflect varying combinations of feminine and masculine qualities. Rather than relying on gender or sexual orientation-based stereotypes, it is wiser for mediators to assess each client system—gay or straight—on an individual basis, including preferred roles, communication styles, expectations, and desired boundaries.

Sociocultural Variation

When the first family mediation textbooks and journal articles appeared in the 1970s, the primary models were billed as "one size fits all." In other words, proponents of mediation implied that their models applied equally to all people. Since the 1980s, there has been growing awareness of the importance of factoring cultural and ethnic diversity into the way that mediation services are conceptualized and delivered (Lederach, 1995; LeBaron, 1997). Since the 1990s, scholarly publications have also addressed issues related specifically to mediation with gay and lesbian clients (Campbell, 1996; Felicio & Sutherland, 2001; Freshman, 1997; Gunning, 1995; McIntyre, 1994; Townley, 1992; Walsh, Jacob, & Simons, 1995). Unfortunately, there is still very little mediation literature on the impact of diversity within same-sex couples. Just as there are great cultural, social, religious, and other differences between different-sex couples, there are also great variations between same-sex couples. Even the notion of sexuality varies between cultures.

Among many traditional Native American cultures, for instance, sexual identity is not limited to being gay or straight. Although in some literature the Native construct of "Two-Spirited" is associated with being gay, the concept more accurately refers to a person who possesses both male and female spirits, incorporating aspects of social identity from both genders in a fluid manner. Within this culture, a variety of expressions of sexuality is considered normal. In contrast, within some traditional Asian cultures, the concept of sexual expression of any type is such an intensely private matter that any discussion of sexuality is treated as taboo (Greene, 1997). When working with same-sex clients from different cultures, a mediator must be cautious of misinterpreting culturally based information. For instance, when a Hispanic man who has sex with other men refuses to describe himself as gay, this refusal may not be an indication of denial but rather a lack of identification with the mainstream American concept of what it means to be gay.

In order to take sociocultural variations among same-sex couples into account, mediators should consider the following steps:

- Educate themselves[12] not only about same-sex couples but also about issues related to the specific religious, cultural, ethnic, gender, and socioeconomic characteristics of the clients with whom they will be mediating.
- Help clients explore both cultural sources of conflict and strengths within their cultures to support their processes of separation and parenting.
- Become aware of their own cultural biases and perspectives, to reduce the chances of making false assumptions about clients from different cultures.

ETHICS, VALUES, AND SELF-AWARENESS

Mediator codes of ethics state that mediators should be impartial, neutral, and respect clients' rights to self-determination (e.g., Model Standards of Practice, 2001, sections IV and XIII; see the appendix in Schepard, Chapter 22, this volume). It is easy for mediators to *say* they support these pronouncements, but in the context of work with same-sex clients and putting these principles *into practice,* the following issues may pose ethical dilemmas for mediators: mediators who have negative attitudes or beliefs toward lesbians or gays; a client's involvement in unsafe sexual practices; intimate partner abuse; and closeted clients who fear being "outed."

Negative Attitudes and Beliefs

It is unlikely that a same-sex couple would seek the services of a mediator who outwardly expresses homophobic attitudes toward gay men or lesbians.[13] Ethical dilemmas are more likely to arise when negative attitudes are less overt. Anti-gay biases and attitudes (e.g., use of heterosexist language that excludes or demeans gay and lesbian clients) can affect a mediator's interventions, even if the mediator sees him- or herself as impartial or gay-positive. Homophobia is so entrenched in U.S. culture that even mediators who are gay or lesbian themselves may have remnants of internalized homophobia.

For mediators and other professionals, the key to dealing with internalized homophobia is to become aware of its possible sources (Bryant, 1992; Van Wormer et al., 2000). For some, negative attitudes toward gay and lesbian individuals stem from what they have learned from their religions. Rabbi Harold Kushner notes that some people quote the Bible as saying that homosexuality is an abomination; he suggests that the Bible was written originally in Hebrew, and people would need to read the *original quotations* in their *original context* to understand them accurately. He further suggests that people are entitled to have religious beliefs that view homosexuality as immoral, but he adds, "Don't make other people miserable because of your religious beliefs" (Kushner, 2001). Mediators are obviously entitled to their own views of homosexuality, but in a professional role, they are ethically obliged to serve clients without judgment or prejudice and without imposing values or beliefs.

If a mediator is unable to deal with same-sex couples in a nonjudgmental, competent manner, then it is incumbent on that mediator not only to terminate the mediation but to refer the clients to a mediator who can provide nonjudgmental and competent services for them (Hartman & Laird, 1998). Gay and lesbian community centers, local "Pink Pages" directories, and websites often provide lists of gay-positive professionals, including mediators. Although some writers suggest that GLBT mediators are generally best equipped to serve GLBT clients (Walter, 2003), the sexual orientation and gender expression of the mediator may or may not be the most important factors to GLBT clients who are selecting mediators. GLBT clients should be encouraged to select mediators based upon their knowledge, values, and skills, some of which may be particular to the GLBT community.

Unsafe Sexual Practices

Although the rates of HIV infection and AIDS are disproportionately high among gay men in the United States, mediators must not treat AIDS as if it were a "gay disease" or stereotype gay and lesbian individuals as promiscuous. The issues of AIDS and unsafe sex apply to both same-sex and different-sex couples; however, because of the numbers of gay-male couples affected by AIDS (Brown, 2003), it is important to acknowledge the issue in this chapter. Still, mediators must not assume that a client is at high risk of AIDS or other sexually transmitted diseases just because he is gay. Many same-sex couples are monogamous and sexually safe. Even if clients have had an open relationship with multiple sexual partners, the mediator must be careful not to judge or impose values.

Consider a situation where one client (Clive) divulges that he is HIV-positive or has been engaging in unsafe sexual practices. What are the mediator's ethical obligations to the former partner (Paul) if he has not been informed? The mediator's duties depend on the nature of the HIV transmission risks (if any), how the mediator explained confidentiality (including its limitations), and the types of legal reporting requirements for professionals with clients who might be putting others at risk of HIV transmission. If contraction of HIV has occurred after the relationship terminated and the clients are not having sexual relations, then Paul has no right to know this information. However, the mediator could be caught in an ethical dilemma if it is possible that Clive put Paul at risk. Does the obligation to keep information confidential supercede Paul's right to know if he has been put at risk of HIV? Although the mediator's code of ethics may not address this specific situation, the mediator can preempt this type of dilemma by explaining limitations on confidentiality at the beginning of mediation and by including his or her ethical obligation to act on information indicating the possibility of serious risk of harm to another. When Clive privately discloses being HIV positive and asks the mediator not to tell Paul, the mediator should first explore Paul's reasoning. Perhaps Clive is concerned about Paul's reaction or whether this development will affect their decision on where their child should live. By working through these issues, the mediator might be able to help Clive disclose the information in a constructive manner. If Clive still refuses to disclose the information to Paul directly, the mediator could contact the Department of Health to determine whether there is a reporting requirement in this particular situation. In some states, the Department of Health (or similar agency) takes responsibility for advising people who may have been put at risk of HIV.[14]

Intimate Partner Abuse

Another issue that is not specific to same-sex couples is that of intimate partner abuse (Lundy & Leventhal, 1999). Although mediators need to screen for abuse and take appropriate safeguards for all clients who may be at risk (Landau, Wolfson, Landau, Bartoletti, & Mesbur, 2000), certain concerns relating to same-sex couples may be different. First, mediators should not assume that intimate partner abuse does not occur within same-sex couples or that it is any less severe among same-sex couples just because the partners are physically similar. Intimate partner abuse can include physical, emotional, verbal, or economic mistreatment. Among same-sex couples, one source of emotional abuse may be threats to "out" the other partner to family, friends, or employers. A closeted partner may be particularly vulnerable to extortion by an angry former partner who threatens disclosure unless the closeted partner agrees to certain demands, such as custody of a child. During screening for abuse, mediators should consider levels of outness of both clients and the possibility of coercion by the client who is more out.

Fear of Outing

Fear of outing comes in many forms and from several levels (e.g., family, work, neighbors, society at large). Mediators must pay attention to options considered in mediation that might put one partner, both partners, or the child at risk of hate crimes or other types of discrimination. Consider, for instance, a lesbian couple that has a child in day care. While cohabiting, the biological mother takes the child to and from day care. During mediation, the parties consider a plan in which the nonbiological parent would pick up the child from day care. In order for the day care to release the child to the nonbiological parent, the day-care staff will need some type of documentation authorizing this person to pick up the child. A mediator might view this transaction as a simple matter of the biological mother writing a letter stating that both parents share custody or parenting responsibilities. For a family that is not "out" to the day-care staff, this letter may have the effect of outing them. The clients need to come up with their own solution, taking into account their perceptions of risks. For example, a client who has been a victim of gay bashing usually finds it very difficult to trust others and take further risks of disclosure.

Although issues such as homophobia, abuse, and HIV are salient realities within the gay and lesbian communities, mediators also need to focus on the strengths within these communities (Van Wormer et al., 2000). For example, these communities have developed very strong support systems for people with AIDS and advocacy for women's concerns, such as funding for research on breast cancer. As minority groups that have suffered from oppression for a long time, many gay men and lesbians have learned to respond with humor, resiliency, self-confidence, strong relational competencies, ingenuity, and other positive forms of coping (Felicio & Sutherland, 2001). Mediators can help their clients build on these strengths as same-sex couples face the challenges of separation.

SKILLS AND APPROACHES TO PRACTICE

Given the diversity among same-sex couples and the lack of empirical research to demonstrate which model of mediation works best with which types of family dynamics, we cannot say that a particular model of mediation is most appropriate for mediation with same-sex couples. In one of the few published studies on the use of particular models of mediation with same-sex couples, Diaz (1999) found that Therapeutic Family Mediation was effective with high-conflict lesbian couples in terms of reducing conflict between them and improving their children's behavior. Although this study used pre- and postmediation tests, there were no control groups, making it impossible to compare the effectiveness of different models.

For couples that simply want to resolve financial or property issues and go their separate ways, a task-oriented approach might be preferred. For couples that plan to have an ongoing relationship as co-parents or friends, a process-oriented approach (such as transformative or therapeutic mediation) might be preferred. These considerations are similar for different-sex couples. (One difference, however, may arise from the likelihood of contact: Clients active within the gay or lesbian community are more likely to have contact with each other on an ongoing basis, since the gay/lesbian community is smaller than the general community.) Rather than trying to evaluate which model of mediation is more appropriate for same-sex couples, this section examines particular skills and approaches to practice that should be considered at each stage of a mediation process in order to ensure that it is appropriate for the particular needs of same-sex couples who are separating. The seven phases of mediation discussed here include preparation, orientation to mediation, issue definition, exploring interests and needs, negotiation and problem solving, finalizing an agreement, and follow-up (Barsky, 2000).

Preparation

The mediation process starts prior to referral. Before even coming close to working with a same-sex couple, mediators need to ensure that their brochures, promotional material, policies, procedures, intake forms, and standard contracts use language that is inclusive of same-sex couples. Using terms such as *marriage, divorce, husband,* and *wife* implies that the mediator works only with different-sex, married couples. Using terms such as *cohabitation, separation, spouses,* and *life partners* (in addition to, or instead of, the prior terms) encompasses same-sex and different-sex couples, regardless of marital status. Although this linguistic point may seem trite, consider how you would feel if you were lesbian and the only space on an intake form for your name, given that your partner is the biological mother of your child, was under the title of "husband/father." Different language may be preferred in different locations. For example, in cities that allow for registration of "domestic partnerships," the preferred term may be *domestic partners.* If you are not familiar with preferred terminology in your area, check with local family counselors or social service agencies that work with same-sex couples.

If you want to reach out specifically to same-sex couples, prepare a separate set of promotional material. In this material, you could note specific issues that are relevant to same-sex couples. Noting your familiarity with laws affecting same-sex couples, for example, suggests that you are informed and that you have gay-positive attitudes. If you are lesbian or gay, you may want to indicate this in your materials. Although mediators need to be impartial, some potential clients feel more comfortable with a mediator who is lesbian or gay. However, whereas some mediators favor self-disclosure about their sexual orientation, others decide that such disclosure violates the notion of a mediator as a neutral third party. To promote your services in GLBT communities, you can advertise in their web-based and paper directories, newspapers, radio programs, and other media. To make more direct contact, offer free informational sessions on legal or psychosocial issues for GLBT clients going through separation.

When a client or lawyer calls requesting mediation services, you will not know initially how open the clients are concerning their sexual orientation. Using inclusive language and a matter-of-fact tone of voice may increase their comfort and trust levels. Rather than assuming that a potential client is married or has children, ask open-ended questions such as "Who was living in the family home prior to separation?" If you do not feel comfortable mediating with a same-sex couple, ensure that you have a list of appropriate mediators or other resources that you can use for referrals.

Orientation to Mediation

Many same-sex couples have had negative experiences with law, lawyers, or the justice system generally (e.g., lack of protection from discrimination or gay bashing, lack of legal recognition of their relationships, lack of access to court to pursue their rights). Although mediation offers such clients an opportunity to work out their own solutions in a confidential setting, mediators must be careful not to feed into a total disregard for the legal system. In some cases, same-sex couples are able to work through separation issues without the aid of lawyers. In cases involving significant legal issues, however, it is incumbent upon the mediator to stress the importance of obtaining independent legal advice. In order to ensure access to legal advice, locate the gay-positive lawyers in your community.[15] You can provide a list of such lawyers to your clients so that they have some measure of assurance that the lawyers they contact will be amenable to serving them respectfully and competently.

Confidentiality issues may be of particular importance to some same-sex clients (Walter, 2003). Ask clients if they have any concerns related to privacy. Let them know how you intend to deal with these issues. Describe the different possibilities for formalizing an agreement, once it has been reached. For example, asking for a court order on consent would make the agreement a public document, whereas a lawyer-drafted agreement signed by the clients is a private document. The parties may need to discuss these issues with lawyers to learn about pertinent legal issues and consequences. Lawyers might advise, for example, that the child support agreement be incorporated into a court order so that the clients can use a support enforcement agency to receive and disburse child support payments.

When deciding who may need to be included in mediation, remember to allow the clients to define their family. Ask, for instance, "Who are the people involved in your son's day-to-day care?" or "Who has been involved in the major decisions about your child's medical care?" The important decision makers and caretakers in their families may not be limited to people related by blood or marriage (e.g., a good friend who plays a grandmotherly role given that the client's biological family has cut all ties).

Issue Definition

In the issue definition stage, clients relate their stories or concerns and the mediator helps them identify issues. Regardless of whether the clients come from a same-sex or different-sex couple, the clients are responsible for determining the issues that they want to resolve. During this stage, clients may use legal terminology that may not fit from a strict legal perspective. For example, they may identify "spousal support" in a jurisdiction that does not recognize spousal support obligations between same-sex couples. If possible, try to use plain language that can be understood by all. If clients are comfortable using the term "spousal support" during mediation discussions, you might inform them that it is not technically spousal support and when they come down to writing an agreement, the terminology may need to be altered (e.g., "Cayla will provide Joan with $200 per month for 12 months to help Joan pay for her job-training course").

Exploring Interests and Needs

During this stage, the mediator helps the parties define their needs and interests, including their mutual interests. For same-sex couples, an interest-based approach to mediation is preferable to a rights-based approach, particularly in jurisdictions that do not provide adequate rights of protection for them. By focusing on their needs, interests, and relational issues, clients can address matters of concern to them in a way that works for them—as opposed to merely accepting the current law's definition of their rights. Although joint problem solving based on the parties' mutual interests can be beneficial, facilitating this approach can be particularly challenging for a mediator when one party seems to have all the rights on his or her side.

Consider, for instance, a case where Donna asks Blythe to move in with her. Blythe agrees, selling her condo, and getting rid of all the furniture and possessions that will not fit into Donna's house. Blythe uses the proceeds of the sale of her condo to help Donna pay the mortgage on Donna's house. Four years later, they split up. In mediation, Blythe asks Donna for some type of compensation to help her set up a new home. Legally, Blythe may have no right to compensation because she sold her home voluntarily, there is no concept of division of marital property for same-sex couples, and there was no agreement between them about what would happen if they separated. A court would probably consider Blythe's contributions to Donna's mortgage payments to be a gift. If Donna takes a rights-based approach, she will argue that she does not owe Blythe anything. If the mediator can focus the parties on interests (e.g., an "amicable solution") or needs (e.g., Blyth's need for financial support to establish her separate home), then they may be able to arrive at a solution based on fairness and consensus rather than one based on legal rights.

In another example of how a rights-based approach might work against fairness and the joint interests of the parties, laws regarding custody and visitation often favor a biological parent over a nonbiological parent. Here, the shadow of the law creates a power imbalance between the parties. The mediator may need to use empowering or other methods of addressing power imbalances to ensure that the parties perceive the mediation process as fair.[16] The dilemma for the mediator is that the biological parent may view the mediator as biased if the mediator tries to rebalance the distribution of power, but the nonbiological parent may view the process as unfair if the mediation focuses solely on legal rights. Ideally, the mediator can help the parents focus on the best interests of the child. From a psychosocial perspective, a child's attachment to, and connection with, a parent is based on who takes care of the child (Irving & Benjamin, 2002; Rosen & Burke, 1999), rather than who has the biological connection. In a family headed by a same-sex couple, the child may have strong attachments to one or both parents, depending primarily on the quality and duration of caregiving by each parent (Riggs, 2003).

Negotiation and Problem Solving

During this phase of mediation, one of the key techniques for the mediator is to encourage creativity. To facilitate brainstorming, a mediator might provide suggestions based on experiences with other clients in similar situations. Solutions that have worked for different-sex couples may or may not work for same-sex couples. Consider the issue of child care in a situation where both parents work full-time. With a different-sex couple, the mediator might assume that there is a positive relationship with the grandparents and that they can offer child-care help. Although this may be a false assumption even for an different-sex couple, mediators need to demonstrate a heightened sensitivity to this issue when working with same-sex couples that may have been shunned by their relatives. Rather than ask if grandparents could help out, the mediator could ask about people in their lives who are a source of support, or about people in their lives whom they consider to be family.

To help parents identify creative solutions or objective criteria for deciding between options, the mediator could refer the clients to resources for lesbian and gay individuals (e.g., bookstores with gay and lesbian literature sections, websites with dependable information for gay or lesbian parents, and self-help groups for gays or lesbians who are going through separation). If a lesbian mother asks, "Does a boy need a father figure?" the mediator might not know the answer. The mediator would be better advised to refer the parents to literature on this subject rather than feign an answer. Even if the mediator thinks he or she knows the answer, the mediator must be careful not to impose personal beliefs on the clients. Ideally, the mediator has experience working with same-sex couples and can draw from both practical and book knowledge on the issues that face separating same-sex couples and their children. If a mediator offers information or options for a solution, the mediator must ensure that the parties feel free to accept or reject that information or options he or she provides, given their unique situation and beliefs.

If the clients seem to be reaching an impasse, the mediator can help them explore what might happen if they have to go to court, including the potential benefits and risks for themselves, the child, and the GLBT community. The risks include the obvious emotional and financial costs of litigation, as well as potential for increasing animosity and conflict. What may be less obvious, initially, are the consequences to the GLBT community of having one member of a same-sex couple go to court to deny that the other person was a "real partner" or a "real parent" to the child. Although the person denying these relationships might "win" the court case, this type of litigation could feed into legal and social stereotypes that diminish the perceived integrity of relationships of families headed by same-sex couples (Walter, 2003). Certainly, the mediator should not impose beliefs about the dangers of this type of litigation to the GLBT community, but it may be appropriate to encourage the parents to explore the consequences of this type of litigation from community as well as individual and family perspectives.

Finalizing an Agreement

Once the parties reach an understanding about how to deal with the issues that brought them into mediation, they need to decide whether the understanding needs to be formalized into a legally enforceable agreement or court order. There may be a number of reasons why separating same-sex couples do not want to go to court. They may be in the closet and do not want to air their issues in a public court; the laws in their jurisdiction may discriminate against gay men and lesbians; or they may have had negative prior experiences with the legal system. A separation agreement affords them privacy, but only to a point. If one person alleges the other has breached the contract, then that person may need to go to court to enforce the contract. If the first person does not want to go public, then, from a practical perspective, he or she cannot enforce the agreement.

Legal advice for same-sex couples may be particularly important in jurisdictions with anti-gay laws. In a jurisdiction that prohibits same-sex marriages, for instance, the courts might refuse to enforce a separation agreement that refers to dissolution of a marriage between two men or two women. Some lawyers suggest that separation agreements between same-sex couples in such jurisdictions be drafted as general agreements rather than agreements under family law. A division of property agreement, for instance, could look like a commercial agreement to buy, sell, or divide property interests, without mention of the prior marriage. If the couple has children, the parenting agreements could be written on a separate contract, without mention of the marriage, division of property, possession of the home, spousal support, etc. To protect a nonbiological parent's relationship with the child,[17] the parties might agree to a second-parent adoption.[18] The situation can become more complicated if a same-sex couple legally marries in Canada but lives in the United States and then tries to obtain a divorce. A U.S. court might refuse to accept the divorce case if the state does not recognize the marriage. A Canadian court might also refuse to hear the case because the parties are not residing in Canada. Given the uncertainties in the law and differences among jurisdictions, mediators should refer clients for legal advice on these issues.

Some same-sex couples might ask a mediator to facilitate a "legal separation." The mediator should ask what the couple means by this—there may be no such official possibility as a "legal separation." The parties might be thinking that they need something akin to a divorce decree or a court order stating that they are separated—which is not legally possible. The mediator might be able to help the parties and their lawyers devise a separation agreement, which gives the parties a document that says that they have "terminated their relationship" or that they "acknowledge their separation."

For clients who cannot or do not want to go to court to enforce agreements,[19] the mediator can stress the advantages of a self-enforcing agreement; that is, an agreement that includes terms that encourage compliance and discourage breaches of the agreement. If one parent has agreed to make child-support payments, for instance, the parties can reduce the risks of late payments by having the payer's employer deposit part of the paycheck directly into the payee's bank account. The mediator can also instill commitment to the agreement by helping the parties understand the costs to all parties, particularly the child, of noncompliance. One of the most serious problems for children of separated parents is the level of conflict between the parents following separation (Wallerstein, 1991). If mediators can help parents understand the impact of their conflicts on the children, they may be more motivated to make the mediated agreement work to avoid causing further harm to their children.

Follow-Up

During follow-up, which can occur through telephone contact or a face-to-face meeting, the mediator checks with the clients to see how well the mediated agreement is working. For same-sex couples that do not want to go back to court, mediation is also the first alternative to consider should future issues arise. Follow-up not only shows the clients that the mediator cares about their postmediation progress but also provides the mediator with an opportunity to learn from the feedback: which of the mediator's interventions contributed in a positive way; what could the mediator have done differently? Since research on mediation with same-sex couples is sparse, mediators should also consider participating in research in order to improve the state of the knowledge in this area.

Another aspect of follow-up may include referring clients to community resources for assistance with ongoing psychosocial issues that cannot be handled in mediation. The mediator should be aware of gay-positive therapists and support groups for issues such as coming out, people with HIV or AIDS, and gay or lesbian parents. Mediators could also have gay-positive literature available in their waiting rooms or offices (e.g., a directory of services for the GLBT community, a GLBT newspaper or magazine,[20] children's books with GLBT-positive messages,[21] and flyers for specific support groups).[22]

CONCLUSIONS

Although this chapter focuses specifically on same-sex couples, mediators must remember that generalizations are just that. Each client brings unique features and dynamics to mediation, regardless of the client's sexual orientation or definition of family. Knowledge and skills to work with diverse clients can be learned, provided that mediators bring values such as acceptance, openness, and respect to their work. All of us have preconceptions and biases about the nature of family, what is "good" for separating couples and their children, and what types of parenting rights and responsibilities society "should" promote. As family mediators working with same-sex couples, it is imperative to be aware of our preconceptions and biases, ensuring that these do not inhibit our ability to practice in an impartial, respectful, and client-centered manner.

As part of the family law system, family mediators also have a moral obligation to ensure that family laws are inclusive and fair. In jurisdictions where family laws discriminate against same-sex couples, family mediators should encourage their agencies and organizations to promote law reform. Laws that deprive same-sex couples of rights affect mediation in a negative manner, even if mediators are able to focus the parties on interests rather than rights. In order to support law reform, mediators could work together with some of the existing organizations that advocate for rights of GLBTs.[23]

Mediators also need to work with researchers to improve the state of knowledge about separation and mediation with same-sex couples. What is the nature of power dynamics between same-sex couples in mediation? How prevalent is violence between same-sex couples upon separation? How does the presence of AIDS within the family affect the mediation process?[24] Mediators also need to learn how to track their own cases in a strategic manner in order to learn from their own best (and less than best) practices. We must also develop mediation training materials (Barsky, 2000) and offer training programs that are inclusive of same-sex families. Conference organizers and regulatory bodies also need to be more inclusive.[25]

Mediation issues regarding gay, lesbian, bisexual, and transgender individuals go far beyond the issues for same-sex couples described in this chapter. What are the implications for mediation when a couple has a child who is GLBT? How does a mediator deal with issues that arise when a different-sex couple separates upon one partner's finding out the other is GLBT? How can mediation assist the processes of adoption or surrogacy by a same-sex couple? How might mediation assist with the estate planning issues for same-sex couples? What forms of mediation might be appropriate for handling hate crimes against GLBTs? What models of parent–youth mediation would be appropriate when a GLBT child runs away or is forced to leave the family?

Certainly, we have far more issues than answers. The good news for mediators is that the profession of mediation has a history of innovation, openness, and respect. We learn from our clients, and they have much to teach us.

APPENDIX 16.1. CHECKLIST OF LEGAL QUESTIONS
REGARDING SEPARATION OF SAME-SEX COUPLES

Because family law varies from state to state and because many laws are changing, it is impossible to summarize the current laws for all 50 states. When researching local laws or consulting with a lawyer, consider the following questions:

1. Do the laws of my jurisdiction recognize same-sex relationships? If they do, then what rights and obligations, if any, do these laws create regarding:
   a. Division of family property or other assets upon separation?
   b. Financial support of a former same-sex spouse?
   c. Possession of the family home?
2. Do local laws allow a same-sex partner who is not a biological parent to apply for:
   a. Visitation?
   b. Custody (including primary residence and parenting responsibility)?
   Do theses laws give preferential treatment to the biological parent?
3. What are the financial obligations, if any, of a same-sex spouse who assumed financial and emotional parent responsibilities for a child during cohabitation but is not the child's biological parent?
4. Do local laws prohibit same-sex marriages or domestic partnerships?
5. Do local adoption laws allow for:
   a. Second-parent adoptions (i.e., the spouse of a biological parent can adopt a child without the other spouse losing his or her parenting rights)?
   b. Adoption by a gay or lesbian parent?

Depending on the particular situation, it may also be important to understand tax and estate planning issues for same-sex couples, pension and survivor benefits, grandparent rights, and whether local laws protect GLBT individuals from discrimination in housing and in the workplace.

NOTES

1. The term "same-sex couple" is used rather than "homosexual couple" to connote a couple that has either two women or two men, regardless of their sexual orientations (e.g., a different-sex married couple could involve a closeted lesbian and a straight man, or a same-sex couple could be composed of two bisexual men).

2. Although this chapter focuses on same-sex couples composed of two gay men or two lesbians, mediators also need to be aware of other family compositions where sexuality and gender considerations need to be taken into account; for example, separation between a man and woman when one partner is gay, lesbian, bisexual, or questioning (Campbell, 1996); separation when one person is transgender; and separation when one child of the relationship is gay, lesbian, bisexual, transgender, or questioning (Hammelman, 1993).

3. Even in states that have Defense of Marriage laws, same-sex couples can still have a marriage performed by a minister, rabbi, or other clergy person from a religious denomination that accepts same-sex marriages. Defense of Marriage laws say that even if the state does not recognize these marriages, it does not criminalize them. If a mediator is helping a couple develop a prenuptial or marriage agreement in a jurisdiction with Defense of Marriage laws, the mediator might use terms such as partnership agreement, cohabitation

agreement, or living together arrangement (Walter, 2003), so that the agreement does not talk about marriage, and courts might be more likely to enforce the agreement should the need arise. On November 18, 2003, the Supreme Judicial Court in Massachusetts held that laws prohibiting state recognition of same-sex marriage are discriminatory and unconstitutional (*Goodridge vs. Department of Health*, 2003). The court ordered the state legislature to amend its laws to allow same-sex civil marriages, though the state is also considering a constitutional amendment to permit exclusion of same-sex couples from the right to civil marriage.

4. Some states, including New York, California, and Vermont, permit second-parent adoptions for same-sex couples. If a male partner of the biological father adopts the child under a second-parent adoption, then the adoptive father and biological father have equal standing under the law in regard to custody and visitation.

5. For a discussion of both sides of this issue from a legal perspective, see the majority and dissent judgments of the Supreme Court of New York Appellate Division in *Alison D. v. Virginia M.* (1990).

6. GLBT is used here to include people who are also questioning their sexuality or gender identity; some use the term GLBTQ to include those who are questioning.

7. In some cases, the anti-gay bias of a particular judge is readily apparent. A judgment of the Supreme Court of Alabama, for example, recently held: "Homosexual conduct is and has been, considered abhorrent, immoral, detestable, a crime against nature and a violation of the laws of nature and of nature's God upon which this Nation and our laws are predicated . . . the courts of this State have consistently held that exposing a child to such behavior has a destructive and seriously detrimental effect on the children. It is an inherent evil against which children must be protected" (Ex parte H.H., 2002).

8. See *http://www.aclu.org/issues/gay/dpstate.html* for a list of states and cities that register domestic partnerships, including same-sex partnerships.

9. To promote equal recognition with different-sex marriage, some gay-rights advocates suggest using the conventional labels of *husbands, wives,* or *spouses* for members of a same-sex couple.

10. *Gay-positive* refers to individuals, groups, or organizations that are open, respectful, and supportive to people who are gay, lesbian, bisexual, or transgender.

11. Particularly therapeutic and process-oriented family mediation models; task-oriented mediation models, including evaluative mediation or conciliation, are less likely to employ family systems theories.

12. For example, through readings, consultation with cultural interpreters (professionals from the same background as the client), or ongoing contact and involvement with the culture.

13. During a session on mediation with gays and lesbians at an Academy of Family Mediators conference, the session leaders assembled an e-mail listserve for people interested in further information on these issues. Because of a typographical error, a mediator who had not signed up for this list began to receive e-mails from this group. He e-mailed not only the group, telling them how immoral it was for them to condone homosexuality, but he also contacted the conference session's employer to complain. The virulent homophobia expressed in his e-mails punctuated the need for stronger policies and education concerning mediation with gay men and lesbians. Conference sessions on gays and lesbians tend to attract people who are already somewhat knowledgeable or gay-positive in their attitudes. Among more than 20 national and international mediation conferences attended by this writer, none has had a conference-wide session or keynote address highlighting gay and lesbian issues. They tend to be relegated to side or special interest issues.

14. For a more comprehensive discussion of issues related to HIV, reporting, and confidentiality, consult an ethics text from social work, psychology, or another discipline

where these issues have been analyzed more thoroughly (e.g., Corey, Corey, & Callahan, 1998; Loewenberg, Dolgoff, & Harrington, 2000).

15. Initially, it is easy to obtain names from a GLBT directory or a GLBT community center. In either case, be sure to talk directly to the lawyers you intend to put on your list so that you are confident that these people will work with GLBT clients appropriately and competently.

16. For further information on addressing power imbalances, see Lang (Chapter 10, this volume).

17. Other possible documents to support a nonbiological parent's rights and obligations include a "Guardianship Agreement" that would apply if the biological parent dies and "Consent to Medical Care" that informs health care providers that the nonbiological parent has the biological parent's consent to authorize health care for the specified child.

18. For a list of states that allow and disallow second-parent adoptions by same-sex partners, see Human Rights Campaign (2002). If the client's state does not permit second-parent adoptions for lesbian or gay individuals, it might be possible for them to apply for an adoption in another state that does allow it. Although their home state may not allow them to adopt, their state should recognize an adoption from the other state.

19. As noted earlier in this chapter, gay and lesbian clients may not have access to courts for either legal or emotional reasons. Legally, for example, some states do not allow nonbiological parents to contest custody against biological parents, effectively prohibiting the same-sex partner of a child's biological parent from going to court to enforce a custody agreement (Human Rights Campaign, 2002; Hunter, Michaelson, & Stoddard, 1992). From an emotional perspective, a gay or lesbian client may fear homophobic responses from a judge or from the community if he or she participates in a public court hearing to enforce an agreement.

20. For example, the *Advocate* (*http://www.advocate.com*) or *Gay Parent* (*http://www.gayparentmag.com*).

21. For example, *Asha's Mums* (Elwin & Paulse, 1990) by Women's Press in Toronto, or *Heather Has Two Mommies* (Newman, 1999) by Alyson Wonderland in Los Angeles.

22. For example, Parents and Friends of Lesbians and Gays (*http://www.pflag.org*).

23. For example, the Human Rights Campaign (*http://www.hrc.org*), Lambda Legal Defense and Education Fund (*http://www.lambdalegal.org*), National Center for Lesbian Rights (*http://www.nclrights.org*), or Gay and Lesbian Advocates and Defenders (*http://www.glad.org*).

24. Some issues to consider include dealing with grief and loss; child-care provisions for when one or both parents become too ill to continue particular parenting responsibilities; provisions for end-of-life decision making, wills, and estate planning; mental competence of a person with AIDS-related dementia and the possible need for substitute decision makers in mediation; and employment capacity and power imbalances related to the relative health of the clients.

25. I have attended a number of mediation trainings where the role-play exercises dealing with same-sex couples were filled with stereotypes and the trainers themselves laughed at these stereotypes. *Training the trainers* is another priority.

REFERENCES

Ahrons, C. R., & Rodgers, R. H. (1987). *Divorced families: A multidisciplinary developmental view*. New York: Norton.

Alison D. v. Virginia M., 155 A.D.2d 11, 552 N.Y.S.2d 321 (1990).

American Academy of Pediatrics. (2002). Coparent or second-parent adoption by same-sex parents. *Pediatrics, 109,* 330–340.

American Civil Liberties Union. (2002). Facts and quotes: Rights denied to gay Americans. Available: *www.aclu.org*

American Psychiatric Association. (2000). *Diagnostic and statistical manual of mental disorders* (4th ed., text rev.). Washington, DC: Author.

American Psychological Association. (1998). Answers to your questions about sexual orientation and homosexuality. Available: *www.apa.org/pubinfo/answers.html*

Appleby, G. A. (2001). Lesbian, gay, bisexual, and transgender people confront heterocentrism, heterosexism, and homophobia. In G. A. Appleby, E. Colon, & J. Hamilton (Eds.), *Diversity, oppression, and social functioning: Person-in-environment assessment and intervention* (pp. 145–178). Boston: Allyn & Bacon.

Barsky, A. E. (2000). *Conflict resolution for the helping professions.* Belmont, CA: Brooks/ Cole.

Barsky, A. E., Barsky, S. A., & Laverdiere, A. (2000). Crisis intervention with a gay Irish-American man: Social work and interprofessional responses. In E. Geva, A. E. Barsky, & F. Westernoff (Eds.), *Interprofessional practice with diverse populations: Cases in point.* Greenwich, CT: Greenwood.

Bertrand, L. D., & Hornick, J. (1994). *Changing definitions of the family: A social science perspective.* Invited paper presented at the annual meeting of the Canadian Bar Association, Toronto.

Brown, L. S. (2003). Relationships more enduring: Implications of the *Troxel* decision for lesbian and gay families. *Family Court Review, 41*(1), 60–66.

Bryant, A. S., & Demian. (1994). Relationship characteristics of American gay and lesbian couples: Findings of a national survey. *Journal of Gay and Lesbian Social Services, 1*(2), 101–117.

Bryant, S. (1992). Mediation for lesbian and gay families. *Mediation Quarterly, 9*(4), 391–395.

Campbell, A. (1996). Mediation of children issues when one parent is gay. *Mediation Quarterly, 14*(1), 79–88.

Corey, G., Corey, M. S., & Callahan, P. (1998). *Issues and ethics in the helping professions* (5th ed.). Belmont, CA: Brooks/Cole–Wadsworth.

Diaz, T. (1999). Therapeutic mediation in lesbian headed families. *Dissertation Abstracts International* (UMI Order No. 9945950; available: *www.umi.com/hp/Products/Dissertations.html*)

Dickson, D. T. (1995). *Law in the health and human services.* New York: Free Press.

Elwin, R., & Paulse, M. (1990). *Asha's mums.* Toronto: Women's Press.

Ex parte H. H. (In re: D.H. v. H.H.) (2002). Ala. LEXIS 44 (1002045) (Supreme Court of Alabama).

Felicio, D. M., & Sutherland, M. (2001). Beyond the dominant narrative: Intimacy and conflict. *Mediation Quarterly, 18*(4), 363–376.

Freshman, C. (1997). Privatizing same-sex "marriage" through alternative dispute resolution: Community-enhancing versus community-enabling mediation. *University of California Los Angeles Law Review, 44,* 1687–1771.

Gold, L. (1997). Marriage and family: Mediation of couple and family disputes. In E. Kruk (Ed.), *Mediation and conflict resolution in social work and the human services* (pp. 19–35). Belmont, CA: Brooks/Cole.

Gordon, R. (2003). *Mediation of gay/lesbian marriages not found in court.* Available: *http:// www.mediate.com/articles/gordon.cfm*

Goodridge vs. Department of Health. (2003, November 18). 9927103 10-176-03 (MA Supreme Judicial Court). Available: *http://www.lawyersweeklyusa.com/archives/ma/opin/ sup/1017603.htm*

Greene, B. (Ed.). (1997). *Ethnic and cultural diversity among lesbians and gay men*. Newbury Park, CA: Sage.

Gunning, I. R. (1995). Mediation as an alternative to court for lesbian and gay families: Some thoughts on Douglas McIntyre's article. *Mediation Quarterly, 13*(1), 47–52.

Hammelman, T. L. (1993). Gay and lesbian youth: Contributing factors to serious attempts or considerations of suicide. *Journal of Gay and Lesbian Psychotherapy, 2*(1), 77–89.

Hartman, A., & Laird, J. (1998). Moral and ethical issues in working with lesbians and gay men. *Families in Society: The Journal of Contemporary Human Services, 79*, 263–276.

Human Rights Campaign. (2002). *State of the family: Laws and legislation affecting gay, lesbian, bisexual and transgender families*. Available: *www.hrc.org/familynet/documents/SoTF.pdf*

Hunter, N. D., Michaelson, S. E., & Stoddard, T. B. (1992). *The rights of lesbians and gay men*. Carbondale, IL: Southern Illinois Press.

Irving, H. H., & Benjamin, M. (1995). *Family mediation: Contemporary issues*. Thousand Oaks, CA: Sage.

Irving, H. H., & Benjamin, M. (2002). *Therapeutic family mediation*. Thousand Oaks, CA: Sage.

Kushner, H. (2001, December 24). *Diane Rehm Show*, National Public Radio.

Landau, B., Wolfson, L., Landau, N., Bartoletti, M., & Mesbur, R. (2000). *Family mediation handbook* (3rd ed.). Toronto: Butterworths.

Lawrence et al. v. Texas (2003). United States Supreme Court, No. 02-102, decided June 26, 2003. Available: *http://caselaw.lp.findlaw.com/scripts/getcase.pl?court=US&vol=000&invol=02-102*

LeBaron, M. (1997). Intercultural perspectives: Mediation, conflict resolution, and multicultural reality: Culturally competent practice. In E. Kruk (Ed.), *Mediation and conflict resolution in social work and the human services* (pp. 315–335). Belmont, CA: Brooks/Cole.

Lederach, J. P. (1995). *Preparing for peace: Conflict transformation across cultures*. Syracuse, NY: Syracuse University Press.

Loewenberg, F., Dolgoff, R., & Harrington, D. (2000). *Ethical decisions for social work practice* (6th ed.). Itasca, IL: Peacock.

Lundy, S. E., & Leventhal, B. (1999). *Same sex domestic violence: Strategies for change*. Thousand Oaks, CA: Sage.

McIntyre, D. H. (1994). Gay parents and child custody: A struggle under the legal system. *Mediation Quarterly, 12*(2), 135–149.

Mnookin, R., & Kornhauser, L. (1979). Bargaining in the shadow of the law: The case of divorce. *Yale Law Journal, 88*, 960–997.

Model Standards of Practice for Family and Divorce Mediation. (2001). Symposium on standards of practice. *Family Court Review, 39*(1), 121–134.

National Association of Social Workers. (2000). Position statement: "Reparative" and "conversion" therapies for lesbians and gay men. Available: *www.socialworkers.org/diversity/lgb/reparative.asp*

Newman, L. (1999). *Heather has two mommies* (10th ed.). Los Angeles: Alyson Bookstore.

O'Neill, B. (1999). Social work with gay, lesbian, and bisexual members of racial and ethnic minority groups. In G. Y. Lie & D. Este (Eds.), *Professional social service delivery in a multicultural world*. Toronto: Canadian Scholars.

Paterson, C. J. (2001). *Lesbian and gay parenting*. American Psychological Association Online: *www.apa.org/pi/parent.html*

Riggs, S. (2003). Response to *Troxel v. Granville*: Implications of attachment theory for judicial decisions regarding custody and third party visitation. *Family Court Review, 41*(1), 39–53.

Rosen, K. S., & Burke, P. B. (1999). Multiple attachment relationships within families with mothers and fathers with two young children. *Developmental Psychology, 35*(2), 436–444.

Townley, A. (1992). The invisible –ism: Heterosexism and the implications for mediation. *Mediation Quarterly, 9*(4), 397–400.

Tremblay, P. J., & Ramsay, R. (1997). *Gay and bisexual male youth: Overrepresented in suicide problems and associate risk factors.* Paper presented at the Third Bi-Regional Adolescent Suicide Prevention Conference, Breckenridge, CO. Available: *www.virtualcity.com/youthsuicide/colorado.htm*

Tye, M. C. (2003). Lesbian, gay, bisexual, and transgender parents: Special considerations for the custody and adoption evaluator. *Family Court Review, 41*(1), 92–103.

Van Wormer, K., Wells, J., & Boes, M. (2000). *Social work with lesbians, gays and bisexuals.* Boston: Allyn & Bacon.

Wallerstein, J. (1991). The long-term effects of divorce on children: A review. *Journal of the American Academy of Child and Adolescent Psychiatry, 30,* 349–360.

Walsh, F., Jacob, L., & Simons, V. (1995). Facilitating healthy divorce processes: Therapy and mediation approaches. In N. S. Jacobson & A. S. Gurman (Eds.), *Clinical handbook of couple therapy* (pp. 340–365). New York: Guilford Press.

Walter, B. J. (2003). Lesbian mediation: Resolving custody and visitation disputes when couples end their relationships. *Family Court Review, 41*(1), 104–121.

Zastrow, C. H. (1999). *The practice of social work.* Belmont, CA: Brooks/Cole.

RESOURCES FOR MEDIATORS WORKING WITH SAME-SEX COUPLES

Education and Support Groups

Gay, Lesbian and Straight Education Network (including books and videos for parents and children that can be purchased online): *http://www.glsen.org*

Family Pride Coalition: *http://www.familypride.org*

Lambda GLBT Community Services (including domestic violence information and suicide hotlines): *http://www.lambda.org*

National Association of Lesbian, Gay, Bisexual and Transgender Community Centers: *http://www.lgbtcenters.org/home.htm*

Parents, Family and Friends of Lesbians and Gays: *http://www.pflag.org*

Legal Information and Advocacy Organizations

American Civil Liberties Union (including current family law issues for GLBTs): *http://www.aclu.org/issues/gay/hmgl.html*

Equality for Gays and Lesbians Everywhere (Canada): *http://www.egale.ca*

Human Rights Campaign (including state-by-state laws and public policy initiatives): *http://www.hrc.org*

Lambda Legal Defense (including issues for GLBTs and people with AIDS): *http://www.lambdalegal.org*

National Center for Lesbian Rights: *http://www.nclrights.org*

CHAPTER 17

Mediating in the Shadow of an Affair[1]

EMILY M. BROWN

Affairs may be either the result of a dissolving relationship or the cause. Either way, after disclosure of an affair, emotions are heightened and the relationship becomes more complex. Mediating in the shadow of an affair, although challenging, can be of particular help in moving a divorcing couple past rage, blame, and guilt, in order to make necessary decisions about the divorce. In this chapter, Emily M. Brown provides a systemic approach to understanding the "exit affair" and offers mediative strategies to defuse the obsession it creates. She also provides an example of how to reframe the issues and emphasizes the mediation of parenting arrangements when an affair is part of the picture.

Traditionally the legal system has viewed an affair as a cause of divorce: the betraying partner deserved to be punished, and adultery was used as the basis for making decisions about parenting and financial matters. The adoption of no-fault divorce in California in 1969 marked a change in the legacy of adultery. Currently 12 states still allow a spouse to sue for a divorce on the basis of adultery (Butler, 2000). In states that have only no-fault statutes for divorce, the legacy of adultery lives on in the punitive aspects of some attorney-negotiated agreements and in some judicial decisions[2] about parenting and financial arrangements. Public opinion also supports this view. Thinking of affairs in terms of the innocent victim and the heartless betrayer helps distance the pain and anger that occur and is seen as settling the score.

An affair adds a difficult dimension to the process of working out decisions about parenting arrangements, finances, and property. An affair that occurs as the marriage is already coming apart creates such emotional chaos that other issues tend to get lost in the turmoil.

Most mediators are aware that the blame and punishment endemic in the adversarial process of divorce hinders the ability of divorcing families to plan effectively for their future. Mediation of divorce issues replaces blame and punishment with a problem-solving approach. Mediation reframes *right and wrong* to *options and choices.* The very premises of mediation imply that there is no right way "to be a family" and focus on the normality of differences among family members. When an affair is part of the picture, mediation is the ideal process because it helps the parties move beyond rage, blame, and emotional impasse rather than use the affair to punish, moralize, or exercise personal bias.

Mediating in the shadow of an affair, however, is especially difficult. The emotions are heightened and volatile. The betrayed spouse is usually in the obsessive phase of dealing with the affair. The recent dishonesties have greatly impaired the trust between the spouses. Parents are likely to have already pressured their children to take sides. Family and friends are present as a shadow chorus, providing the betrayed spouse with all sorts of advice, most of it bad. Even when the affair is over, the third party is another shadow presence. Key issues to be addressed in mediation in these cases include (1) the betrayed spouse's obsession with the affair, (2) the couple's avoidance of the issues of ending, and (3) future contact between the children and the third party.

The affair and what it represents emotionally are superimposed on the normal separation process, which is difficult enough without the presence of an affair. Communication between divorcing spouses tends to be angry or defensive, and more often than not, garbled. With an affair, the betrayed spouse's obsession and the betraying partner's rejecting stance ensure fireworks that further impede the communication process and can undermine the separation.

A SYSTEMS APPROACH TO AFFAIRS

For mediation to be successful, it is essential that the mediator understand the characteristics and dynamics of the exit affair. This understanding provides the context for considering mediator strategies and interventions. This approach is based on systems theory: actions taken by one part of a system are influenced by and stimulate responses in other parts of the system (Karpel & Strauss, 1983; Papp, 1977; Kerr & Bowen, 1988). For example, a man who works long hours attending to his career may not pay much attention to his wife's loneliness and her requests for time because he believes that his financial support of the family is more important. His wife deals with her loneliness by going shopping. The husband's comment is an absentminded "That's nice" when she shows him the dress she bought. The wife encounters an old male friend. They do a lot of talking, and he listens to her. Before long she is having an affair with him. While she is the one who chose to have an affair, both spouses cooperated to make enough room in their marriage for an affair to occur by avoiding their deeper problems. And so it is with all types of affairs. Both spouses collude to set the stage for an affair by not addressing the issues at hand. This systemic concept is central to considering what strategies to use in mediation.

THE EXIT AFFAIR

The exit affair is the most common kind of affair encountered in mediation.[3] Contrary to popular belief, the exit affair is not the reason the marriage is ending. One spouse has already decided to end the marriage but cannot decide how to do it or is afraid to tell the other spouse of that decision. Instead, an affair is the vehicle used to slide out of the marriage. When the affair is disclosed, a common statement made by the betraying partner is "I love you, but I'm not *in* love with you." Being in love with someone described as "my friend" who "understands" is used as justification for ending the marriage. At some level the betraying partner hopes the affair will provoke the betrayed spouse to do the hard work of ending the marriage. Usually, however, the betrayed spouse does not cooperate and instead rages and obsesses about the affair.

Understanding and knowing how to work with the dynamics of the exit affair are essential to the success of the mediation process. Characteristics of the exit affair include the following:

- Both spouses duck difficult issues, avoid talking about the deterioration of the marriage, and avoid conflict in general.
- Both spouses have unfinished business from childhood about loss and endings.
- The affair is used to justify leaving the marriage because the betraying partner does not want to take responsibility for ending the marriage.
- Both spouses are invested in making the third party the bad guy (e.g., "It's only because of [Jane/John] that our marriage is ending. It's nothing *I* did."
- The affair is of recent origin—6 months or so.
- The betraying partner wants to end the marriage and is acting accordingly. (This is not the type of affair in which the betraying partner is attached to both the spouse and the third party and cannot decide between the two.)
- Trust issues often get played out in destructive, defensive maneuvers, such as hiring a private investigator, emptying bank accounts, or retaining a piranha-like attorney.

• The gender of the betraying partner does not make much difference in the mediation process, unless the betrayed spouse is male and comes from a culture that advocates punishment of women who have affairs, such as some Arabic, Asian, or Hispanic cultures (e.g., "honor killings" of women who are judged to have shamed the family still occur frequently in Pakistan [Beattie, 1999]; Jordan [Mann, 2000]; Bangladesh [Constable, 2000]; and Argentina).

The characteristics and dynamics of the exit affair are exacerbated when the spouses have unresolved childhood wounds, are experiencing other current losses, or utilize extremely dysfunctional coping styles.

THE OBSESSIVE PHASE

The betrayed spouse, on learning of the partner's affair, usually goes through a brief period of numbness or shock, followed by an obsessive phase that consists of raging, crying, blaming, attacking, and asking thousands of questions about the details of the affair. Attempts are made to "make things go back the way they were." Often the betrayed spouse rages at the third party as well and sometimes informs the third party's spouse of the affair. The betrayed spouse may tell everyone—parents, children, friends, and neighbors—what the betraying partner has done. Some betrayed spouses become violent.

Alternatively, the betrayed spouse may hibernate and tell no one, becoming more depressed by the moment. Nothing the betraying partner says or does helps in either situation, because the betrayed spouse can no longer trust the betraying partner.

The function of obsession is to hold the pain, fear, and helplessness at bay. Despite the decibel level and tone of voice, obsessive behavior is generated by a ruminating thought process and is not an expression of genuine emotion. As long as the betrayed spouse is obsessing, he or she can avoid feeling the pain of betrayal and delay facing the difficult issues of ending the marriage.

Although the obsessive spouse may appear to be expressing emotions, much of what transpires is an attack on, or an inquisition of, the betraying partner. If the betrayed spouse does express emotion, it is usually anger, but the spouse is not in touch with the deeper emotions about what is happening. It is important to remember that anger is a secondary emotion that offers a defense in the face of danger. (Primary emotions in this situation tend to be pain, fear, or helplessness, or a combination of these). The sound and fury of anger camouflage the pain. However, the obsession about the affair inhibits the grieving process that must occur to heal from a spouse's affair or the end of the marriage.

To get beyond the obsession, the betrayed spouse needs to be in touch with emotional reality. Pain, fear, and helplessness are at the core of this emotional reality. These are the feelings the mediator will need to access if mediation is to be successful.

MOTIVATIONS FOR MEDIATION

What would lead a separating couple who have experienced an affair to mediation? Both spouses may be motivated by the desire for privacy. The betrayed spouse often feels a sense of shame and engages in self-blame about what he or she did or did not do that could have led to the affair. This focus on self-blaming is commonly part of the obsession. The betraying partner may also experience shame at having chosen this route out of the marriage. Mediation offers greater privacy than negotiation between attorneys and much less exposure than litigation.

These couples may choose mediation for all the reasons other couples do: to maintain control of the decision-making process, reduce the conflict and acrimony, and limit the costs of splitting up. They may see mediation as the best way to help their children through the separation and divorce, particularly if parenting has been one of their strong points.

OBSTACLES TO MEDIATION

The biggest obstacle to choosing mediation is the betrayed spouse's desire to publicly avenge the wrong by hiring a piranha-like lawyer to punish the betraying partner. Other obstacles to mediation are the betrayed spouse's distrust of the betraying partner and his or her sense of powerlessness. When obsession is constant, the betraying partner may also feel powerless.

Trust and betrayal issues surface in statements such as "This marriage has never been any good" or "Jane has always put her needs first—she's *never* listened to what I want." Such verbalizations are attempts to simplify the situation by denouncing the spouse or the marriage as totally bad. If the situation is totally bad, then nothing can be done and the painful process of letting go of the good parts of the relationship can be bypassed—or so the couple hopes. In other words, each spouse is afraid to be emotionally vulnerable with the other. Both fear that listening to the other spouse will leave them feeling far too vulnerable, overwhelmed, and in too much pain.

ISSUES FOR THE MEDIATOR

Mediating in the shadow of an affair can be difficult for the mediator as well as for the couple. Dealing with the betrayed spouse's obsession takes tremendous concentration and energy. The emotions are intense, especially those of the betrayed spouse. The betrayed spouse's emotions may be heightened if the betraying partner's affect is one of cool distance, void of emotion. The betrayed spouse is often looking for some sign of caring and gets angrier and more frantic when none is shown. If any caring is shown, it is dismissed as not enough or not genuine.

The mediator must observe and listen to both spouses, assessing the emotional content to determine what is fear driven, what is pain driven, and what is reality. Fighting and blaming are usually driven by denied feelings of pain, fear, or powerlessness. People who end their marriage with an affair are usually trying to avoid the normal pain and loss that is part of ending a marriage. They want to hang onto their dreams and make them come true. The betrayed spouse hangs onto the belief that this marriage can be saved if only the partner would change. The betraying partner also hangs onto the old dreams but believes switching partners will now make the dreams a reality. The more one spouse attempts to make the dreams come true, the more the other spouse counters those efforts. Feelings of powerlessness increase and are defended against with commensurate anger. This dynamic creates the very contention and powerlessness that the couple hoped to avoid.

The mediator, too, may hold beliefs and emotions that interfere with the mediation process. Some mediators are judgmental about spouses who have an affair. Others find it too easy to fall into the traps of feeling sorry for the betrayed spouse or judging the betraying partner's behavior and letting those perceptions distort the mediation process. Distortions may show up in the form of subtly or openly taking sides, assuming that the "innocent victim" should be compensated, believing that it is harmful for the children to spend time with the parent having the affair, and making negative remarks to colleagues about one or both spouses.

It is helpful for the mediator to recognize that affairs do not happen in marriages that are working well. They occur when both spouses have set the stage for an affair by not attending to the marital issues. Exit affairs indicate that the marriage has eroded significantly and both spouses are avoiding addressing the erosion and the diminishing viability of the marriage.

Mediators who are judgmental about those involved in an affair or overly sympathetic to the betrayed spouse need to evaluate their ability to mediate effectively or whether they should refrain from taking these cases. Mediators who have personally experienced being part of an affair triangle, currently or in the recent past, should abstain from mediating these cases until their own situation is thoroughly resolved.

ADDRESSING EMOTIONS IN MEDIATION

Dealing with emotions in mediation can be challenging. Common mediator wisdom has held that highly volatile cases cannot be mediated. Yet the primary reasons for reaching an impasse in mediation are the emotional issues that underlie the conflict. The ending of a marriage is an emotional process. Fights about property, money, and parenting are, at their core, emotional issues. The emotional core needs to be addressed in order to achieve a long-lasting resolution of the practical issues. (However, in cases of serious mental illness or substance abuse, addressing emotions is best left for the therapist; presumably these cases are screened out of mediation.)

The goal of mediation when the marriage is ending with an affair is to help the couple talk about and resolve the issues that will enable them to establish a workable structure for the future. Hiding behind the affair impedes the partners' ability to settle the practical and parenting issues and move through the grief process.

Effective tools are necessary to resolve disputes about parenting, finances, and property. The classic mediation techniques, such as reframing or focusing on the children's needs, are often ineffective in dealing with the intense emotions generated by an affair. Other tools that address the emotions are needed. The mental health professions have developed some very useful methods that mediators can adopt and use—without learning to do therapy. Using a technique in mediation that is drawn from the therapy arena requires that the mediator learn how to identify and address the underlying emotional issues that are interfering with resolution of the practical issues. Achieving this goal may require listening to fears expressed by a spouse or gaining an understanding of family dynamics.

Bush and Folger (1994) talk about "bringing out the intrinsic goodness that lies within the parties as human beings" in their model of transformative mediation (p. 82). In mediation, accessing the pain, fear, and powerlessness underlying the betrayed spouse's obsessive anger helps humanize the situation. The obsession may have so obscured the real emotions that the betraying partner may be hearing the betrayed spouse's pain for the first time. Hearing and connecting with the real pain opens a pathway between the spouses that helps them talk about where they are and what they need to do.

When mediation is progressing well, it is not necessary to inquire about emotions. When the obsession surfaces or an impasse develops, it is time to address the underlying emotional problem. This focus is usually necessary when the mediator is dealing with the betrayed spouse's obsession, discussing issues pertaining to loss and the ending of the marriage, or talking about the children's future contact with the third party.

MANAGING THE OBSESSION

Simply put, the mediator must get the obsession under control in order to make space to mediate. In an effort to be compassionate, it can be tempting

to listen to the story of the affair and the accompanying obsessive rumina-
tions and to sympathize with the betrayed spouse. However, this approach
can "kill" the mediation. The betrayed spouse is saying, in effect, "I have no
responsibility for what has happened; it is all my partner's fault." This is the
statement of a person who is *feeling* powerless. It does not necessarily mean
the person *is* powerless.

Part of our work as mediators is to help the spouses access their own
power. Listening to the obsession has the opposite effect: It encourages the
betrayed spouse to define him- or herself as a victim, and it fuels more obsession. The chaos that results can defeat the mediation (and the mediator). If
the mediator allows the obsession to dominate the sessions, the betraying
partner will not be willing to continue mediation.

Instead, the mediator must teach the spouses to slow down, feel their
powerlessness (or other emotion), and only after the emotion ebbs away, go
back to the task at hand. Experiencing the pain, fear, and powerlessness is
grounding for the betrayed spouse and frees that spouse to work on the tasks
of mediation. Hearing the real emotions that have been generated by the affair is sobering for the betraying partner as well.

Addressing the emotions in mediation is done differently than in therapy. In mediation, emotions are addressed directly only when they present a
problem. Stay with the practical task when that is working. When emotions
are getting in the way, it is necessary to address them. To do so, the mediator
needs to be emotionally present and to connect with each spouse during the
mediation process. This connection can be conveyed via a tone of voice, a
look, or other gesture that demonstrates a personal and empathic response.
Connecting requires listening (but not to the obsessing), acknowledging, and
questioning.

For example, when a spouse is starting to obsess, the mediator might
say, "I can see that you're really hurting, but right now we need to talk about
how the children will be cared for after school." Such an acknowledgment of
the person's emotional state helps build rapport. If this kind of comment
does not stop the obsession, immediately try another variation of that statement. If *that* does not work, it is time to ask, "What are you feeling right
now?" A typical response is, "Angry!" Then ask, "Under the anger, what are
you feeling?" You might hear, "I feel that she's a bitch!" Respond with,
"That's not a feeling . . . what are you feeling?" Follow through with this until
the person is able to tune into what he or she is feeling. This approach works
only if the mediator is truly concerned and open to hearing about the person's pain, fear, or helplessness without trying to fix it.

The mediator's overall strategy is one of shifting the focus from the affair to the fact that the marriage is ending and there are issues to be resolved.
To shift the focus, start by acknowledging the emotion that is being displayed, as in the following conversation:

ANNE [betrayed spouse]: I just don't see how he could have done it—how *could* he just go and have an affair with some bimbo from work? Don't you think what he did is wrong? (*angry, accusing tone*)

JENNIFER [mediator]: Anne, I can hear that you're really upset. And I can understand your being upset. But the affair happened, and none of us can change that, and right now we need to talk about how the two of you are going to move ahead from this point. Right now we're focusing on the home that the two of you have lived in and what the possibilities are for keeping it.

ANNE: But don't you think what he did is wrong?

JENNIFER: It doesn't matter what I think. Right now we need to get on with our task for today so that you can begin to get an idea of what your options are for your house.

ANNE: I just can't think about the house when I'm so upset! Rob, why don't you just admit you screwed up big time and just let me have the house (*angry voice*).

ROB: Anne, I've told you I'm sorry (*little emotion other than impatience*). Let's just get this process over with.

JENNIFER: Anne, I know you're upset. I want to know what you're feeling right now, under the anger.

ANNE: I'm angry, that's what I'm feeling!

JENNIFER: I know you're angry, but you've got some deeper feelings under the anger.

ANNE: Feelings about. . . ?

JENNIFER: Not *about* anything. Just what are you feeling at this moment in time, under the anger?

ANNE: What do you mean, "under the anger"? I'm angry!

JENNIFER: See what your body is telling you about what you feel. What are you feeling in your stomach, or maybe in your chest, or your neck and shoulders?

ANNE: (*long pause*) Hurt, just so much hurt. I'm hurt that he . . .

JENNIFER: Stay with your hurt. Just feel it for a minute. You don't have to say or do anything while you feel it. (*silence of a minute or 2 until Anne's body language indicates she's shifted gears*) Noticing your hurt is important. Even though it hurts, it's grounding. (*pause*) Let's get back now to thinking about the house.

At this point Anne is better able to participate in the mediation process. She will obsess again, maybe in the next few minutes, but gradually, as the mediator continues using this process to help Anne get to the emotions underneath her anger, the obsession will decrease in frequency, duration, and intensity. That diminishment gives the mediator time to work with both of them on the tasks they have brought to the table. When Anne gets into her obsessive mode again, the mediator will quickly ask her what she is feeling "right now," and as before, once Anne identifies her feeling, the mediator will ask her to stay with it for a minute or so. When Anne shifts gears, the mediator can get back to the task at hand. The mediator can expect to move back and forth repeatedly between emotions and mediation tasks during the session.

The mediator needs to be aware that moral judgments, statements about the motivation of another, verbal attacks, and comments that begin with "I feel that you . . ." are not statements about what one is feeling. Comments such as "I feel betrayed" need to be taken to a deeper level. *Betrayed* relates to an action *someone else* has taken; the mediator redirects the focus by asking, "How do you feel when you've been betrayed?" With an affair, the emotions expressed are typically some variant of pain, fear, or powerlessness, as noted. The advantages of using this technique to shift away from obsessive rumination include the following:

- The betrayed partner's emotions may be painful, but they are also grounding and thus calming.
- Experiencing emotions rather than the chaos of obsession helps the betrayed spouse focus on the work of mediation.
- If the betraying partner can hear the betrayed spouse's real pain, it helps him experience her as another human being, not just someone who rages and attacks. This may boost his willingness to discuss and negotiate issues with her.
- It helps the mediator stay sane and in control of the session.

FACILITATING A POSITIVE EMOTIONAL EXCHANGE

Issues that may appear easy to the mediator but are difficult for the couple usually have an emotional base. The mediator may see practical opportunities for tradeoffs, but underneath the stated practical issue lies an unresolved emotional problem.

One of my early and memorable cases presented such an issue. The couple had been referred to mediation by their attorneys, two of the most expensive attorneys in town. The spouses were arguing over $3,000 worth of household property. The nature of the issue did not match the intensity of their conflict, nor did it make sense that each had paid their attorney as much as the property was worth. Thus the issue had to be an emotional one. I stated, "I know you want something from each other, but I don't think it's the property. I think it's something emotional." At first it was as if I were speaking Greek.

As I persisted with this approach, I suggested that not only was it something emotional but something very important. The woman was the first to pick up on what I was saying. I worked with her, in the presence of her husband, to formulate what she wanted from him. She wanted to know if he felt she had been a good wife to him during the early part of their marriage, before she had had the affair. I asked her to hold her question while I worked with him about what he wanted from her. He, too, wanted validation for his role as husband in the early part of their marriage. She then asked him her question, and he was very generous in his answer. He followed by asking her his question, and she was just as generous. In the next 10 minutes they decided what to do with their property, and the mediation was completed. What they really needed from the mediation was validation from each other. The elements that make this strategy work include the following:

- Shifting from the practical issue to the emotional issue
- Persisting with the idea that the issue is an emotional one
- Working with each partner until the identified desire becomes a real possibility
- Establishing mutual vulnerability
- Framing the issue in a positive way (i.e., in terms of what each wants)
- Facilitating a positive exchange

Some spouses feel too vulnerable to work on identifying what they want emotionally in the presence of the other spouse. In that case, the mediator may choose to caucus with each spouse to uncover the unresolved emotional issues and options that would lead to resolution. The mediator should make sure that what they identify is a realistic possibility. Neither money nor punishment resolves emotional issues. Resolution requires an emotional acknowledgment or affirmation of the underlying emotional issues. It is highly unlikely that resumption of the marriage is a viable possibility. The mediator needs to prepare each spouse to discuss the emotional issue and its resolution in the next session.

When the spouses cannot take in what the other is saying, the mediator needs to listen to, validate, and acknowledge what is being said. The mediator may also need to translate information and emotional content—as if the spouses were speaking different languages.

TRUST ISSUES

Often the earlier dishonesty about the affair has seriously impaired trust. Can or should the mediator help the betrayed spouse believe anything the betraying partner says? The mediator needs to toss this issue back to the couple. Help them identify areas where trust still exists, based on their experience with each other. Ask questions such as "In what areas has your spouse always been dependable?" or "What do you and your spouse agree are the important elements of parenting?" "What would ensure that you will follow through with what you have decided?" When trust is weak, the mediator can help the couple develop backup plans that protect against further betrayal regarding finances, parenting, or other matters. For example, spousal support might be paid by an automatic bank transfer from the payor's bank account to that of the payee. Or conflict in front of the children can be lessened when one parent takes the children to school and the other parent picks up the children after school on transfer days.

MEDIATING PARENTING ARRANGEMENTS

When an affair is part of the picture, parenting issues are often the most difficult to mediate. For example, a betrayed spouse may pursue sole custody to prevent feeling lonely. The meta-message is "He has a girl friend, so I need the children so I'm not all alone." Some betrayed spouses want to prevent any contact between the third party and the children by severely limiting the children's contact with the betraying partner. A desire to punish the betraying partner may be played out regarding parenting or financial support issues. Many betrayed spouses invite the mediator to take sides and join in punishing the betraying partner. Traps for the mediator are presented at every turn. The mediator needs to focus on the children's needs and disallow efforts to link parenting arrangements and custody to the affair.

If it is not already too late, the mediator should ask the parents not to say anything to their children about the impending separation or the affair until an agreement has been reached in mediation about how best to talk about the situation. The mediator can educate parents about children's emotional needs by assigning reading such as *Mom's House, Dad's House* (Ricci, 1997) and *Affairs* (Brown, 1999), and referring them to well-conceived and well-presented courses on parenting after separation and divorce.

Much of the conflict about parenting arrangements is related to fear. Often it is fear of losing the love and affection of the children to the other parent or the third party. The mediator should ask each spouse to identify his or her fears. Spouses may discover they have the same fears or be intrigued by the differences in their fears. The mediator can acknowledge their fears and then ask each what they do now that contributes to their child's love for them. What could they do that would make their children *not* love them? What kind of legacy do they want to give their children? If they continue to be unable to reach agreement on key parenting issues, the mediator should ask questions that tap into the underlying emotional issues. These issues may have more to do with experiences in the family of origin than with the spouse, or the spouse's behavior may echo experiences in the family of origin. The mediator can ask the spouses what kind of relationship they had as a child with each of their parents. What worked well in that family? If the spouses could change one thing about their relationship with each parent, what would it be? Did he or she feel secure as a child? If not, why not? Does each spouse want to do better by the children? What would each like to be different for the children? If possible, the mediator should do this work while both parents are present. If either spouse feels too vulnerable to discuss this in the presence of the other parent, the mediator can caucus with each and then bring them back together to discuss what kind of assurances they need from the other in order to proceed with mediation.

The "hot potato" in discussing parenting arrangements is usually the children's contact with the third party. The mediator can suggest to parents that children need time to grieve for their family as they have known it before having to deal with the third party. The issue is not that the third party is a secret but that the children need "protected time" to recover from their parents' separation before having to deal with parents' new relationships. Most parents who agree to establish "protected time" set a period of 6 months, during which the child will have no contact with the third party or with any other new romantic partner. At the end of that period, the parents discuss and decide whether the children are ready for contact with the third party or any other person with whom a parent may become involved. By the end of this 6-month period, many exit affairs are over, their purpose having been served. If the affair is continuing, parents are generally better able to work out a plan for gradual contact between the children and the third party than they were earlier. The amount of time the children need to grieve for the family they have known corresponds roughly to the time it takes most spouses to move beyond the worst of the obsession. The parents may want to include in their agreement restrictions on children spending the night when a third party is present.

OTHER MEDIATION MODELS

Irving and Benjamin (1989) make extensive use of techniques drawn from the mental health field to address emotional issues. Their therapeutic family mediation process expands the mediation model still further. An assessment process is used to differentiate between those couples who are ready for mediation, those who should not use mediation, and those who, with help, may be able to mediate successfully. The latter group is offered premediation services to produce a change in patterns of marital interaction. Premediation is brief, usually one to four sessions, with the specific goal of moving the spouses to a point of readiness for mediation. Irving and Benjamin (1989) assert:

There is no inconsistency about using therapeutic methods in dispute resolution since failure in mediation can often be traced to relational dysfunction. . . . Only the resolution of underlying emotional issues will ensure an
agreement that is likely to remain intact and functioning despite the many
predictable vicissitudes of client postdivorce adjustment. (pp. 122, 128)

A similar approach is used by Pruett and Johnston in mediating with
high-conflict families (see Chapter 5, this volume; see also Johnston & Campbell, 1988). Prenegotiation counseling is offered to the spouses individually
before moving into the negotiation phase of mediation. Johnston also advocates the use of an extensive assessment of high-conflict divorcing parents,
which is designed to pinpoint the specific issues in dispute and their history,
assess the parenting ability and the parent–child relationship, and clarify the
current situation, including family strengths and resources.

Johnston holds strategy conferences with the other professionals involved with the family, such as teachers, guidance counselors, and therapists.
She sometimes involves other professionals who are working with the family
in the mediation sessions themselves so they can offer support to each of the
spouses. Johnston clearly states that this model of mediation is therapeutic,
blurring the boundary between mediation and therapy, and that the mediator is not neutral but is an advocate for the child (Johnston & Campbell,
1988).

EMOTIONS AND THE MEDIATOR'S JUDGMENT

It is the mediator's judgment call regarding how far to go in addressing the
emotions in mediation. Most mediators are too cautious. Being overly cautious may be due to a lack of training or to training that focuses on the rational and practical issues and excludes interventions that address emotions.
Other mediators are not comfortable addressing emotions.

When addressing emotional issues in the shadow of an affair, the mediator must be clear about what is emotion, what is a thought or a belief, and
what is obsessive rumination. There is no room in mediation for emotional
attacks that come veiled as an expression of emotions. Should a mediator address emotions in mediation? This depends on the following factors:

- The mediator's comfort level with anger, tears, and other strong emotional displays
- The mediator's understanding of the differences between thoughts,
  expressions of emotion, and obsessive rumination
- The mediator's personal reactions to affairs, which could unduly influence the mediation process
- The mediator's training

SUMMARY

- Focus on the task at hand; when that is not working, address the betrayed spouse's emotions.
- Acknowledge feelings, not obsessive rumination.
- Keep in mind that pain, fear, and powerless feelings are grounding. Obsessive anger is chaotic. Maintaining a victim stance means staying stuck.
- Cut off obsessive ruminating immediately, using interventions that help the betrayed spouse get to the emotions underlying the obsession.
- Always maintain tight control of the session; emotional attacks must be stopped—they are *not* an expression of the underlying emotions.
- Allow no moralizing about the affair; concerns about morality cannot be mediated, and affairs do not happen unless *both* spouses make room for them.
- Never take a position when asked whether you believe affairs are wrong.
- Emotional vulnerability needs to be mutual for both spouses, although not necessarily equal.
- Get underneath the betrayed spouse's obsession by focusing on the emotions underneath the anger and the obsessive questioning.
- Ask the betraying partner to listen to the betrayed spouse when he or she is expressing real emotion.
- Do not focus more attention on the betrayer than on the betrayed (although the reverse is workable).
- Consider whether delaying sessions might give the betrayed spouse time to move beyond the obsessive preoccupation with the affair, especially if that spouse has just begun therapy.
- Help the couple talk about ending their marriage.
- Use reframing and a reality perspective to help the betrayed spouse shift from blame to facing the end of the marriage.
- Be conscious of your own feelings while mediating. Can you use your own responses productively in the mediation without getting caught up in the talk or the emotions of the affair? If this is a problem, discuss the situation with a consultant who is knowledgeable about addressing emotions in mediation.

Mediation and mediators can help reframe the way people think about divorce and the way they go about divorcing, particularly those couples who divorce in the shadow of an affair. Rather than proving who is right and who is wrong, divorce could become a process of acknowledging that "Yes, right now we are very hurt and angry, and we need distance from each other, but we don't have to be obsessed with hate and blame, or with proving the other is wrong in order to end our marriage. We can feel our pain and our sadness, and even be angry, *and* we can build upon our strengths."

NOTES

1. The title of Mnookin and Kornhauser's (1979) article, "Bargaining in the Shadow of the Law: The Case of Divorce," has stayed with me over the years, and my chapter title is a play on theirs.

2. As examples, see Dockins v. Dockins, 475 So. 2d 571 (Ala. Civ. App. 1985): mother denied custody—entertained lover in home when children were present; Adam v. Adam, 436 N.W. 2d 266 (S.D. 1989): mother's extramarital affair deemed harmful to 5-year-old child.

3. For a description of other types of affairs, see Brown (1999), written for the general public, or Brown (2001), written for mental health professionals.

REFERENCES

Beattie, M. (1999, June 3). Honour killings continue to punish Pakistani women. *Globe and Mail*, p. A13.

Brown, E. M. (1999). *Affairs: A guide to working through the repercussions of infidelity*. San Francisco: Jossey-Bass.

Brown, E. M. (2001). *Patterns of infidelity and their treatment* (2nd ed.). Philadelphia: Brunner-Routledge.

Bush, R. A. B., & Folger, J. P. (1994). *The promise of mediation: Responding to conflict through empowerment and recognition*. San Francisco: Jossey-Bass.

Butler, M. (2000). Grounds for divorce: A survey. *Journal of Contemporary Legal Issues, 11*, 166–173.

Constable, P. (2000, May 8). In Pakistan, women pay the price of honor. *The Washington Post*, pp. A1, A16.

Irving, H., & Benjamin, M. (1989). Therapeutic family mediation: Fitting the service to the interactional diversity of client couples. *Mediation Quarterly, 7*(2), 115.

Johnston, J. & Campbell, L. (1988). *Impasses of divorce: The dynamics and resolution of family conflict*. New York: Free Press.

Karpel, M. A., & Strauss, E. S. (1983). *Family evaluation*. New York: Gardner Press.

Kerr, M. E., & Bowen, M. (1988). *Family evaluation: An approach based on Bowen theory*. New York: Norton.

Mann, J. (2000, February 2). A desperate woman is denied asylum. *The Washington Post*, p. C15.

Mnookin, R. H., & Kornhauser, L. (1979). Bargaining in the shadow of the law: The case of divorce. *Yale Law Journal, 88*, 950–997.

Papp, P. (1977). The family that had all the answers. In P. Papp, *Family therapy: Full length case studies* (pp. 143–165). New York: Gardner Press.

Ricci, I. (1997). *Mom's house, Dad's house* (2nd ed.). New York: Simon & Schuster.

PART V
Mediation in the Court Context

CHAPTER 18

Court-Based Mandatory Mediation

Special Considerations

ISOLINA RICCI

Mandated mediation of child-related issues in court-based programs presents challenges beyond those encountered in private sector mediation. This chapter describes the philosophical and practical questions inherent in a statewide mandate and explores the history, clientele, statutory framework, purpose, and economics of court-connected family mediation. Isolina Ricci, a leader in the development of court-based mediation in California, describes and discusses both the confidential and recommending models of mediation and offers examples of mediation including those with issues of violence. Dr. Ricci urges greater attention to the needs of diverse client populations, to the roles of management and the judiciary, and further refinement and implementation of standards of practice.

When family mediation becomes mandatory, mediation is transformed from a privately ordered dispute resolution process to one that must now be accessible to all, visibly accountable, and, arguably, more structured. This broader vision includes mediation with non-English-speaking litigants, those living in indigent conditions, and those with complex family structures. Since court-based mandatory mediation nearly always includes disputes over children, mediation participants and mediators usually are expected to do more than address the dispute. They also may take a close look at what constitutes the best interests and needs of the children, how conflict between parents affects children, and the desirability of maintaining an ongoing relationship for child rearing. To address the major dimensions of court-based mandatory mediation, this chapter offers several perspectives:

- The influence of the historical context on the practice of court-based mediation.
- The challenges inherent in working with mediation clients from a broad range of backgrounds.
- The key roles of statutes, rules of court, and standards of practice in defining and structuring the mediation process.
- The purpose of mediation and the mediator's role.
- The "confidential" and "recommending" models of mediation.
- The economics of mediation and access to different mediation models.

This chapter also addresses the need for client orientation and education, the use of mediation when issues of domestic violence are present, and the court's expanding responsibilities for program operations. Examples of two major models of court-based mediation are provided and issues raised by current practices are explored. This chapter does *not* discuss various views of neutrality, problem solving, or philosophies of mediation, as these are covered elsewhere in this volume. Instead the practical matters of providing accountable and competent mandatory child custody mediation in the context of a contemporary family court system are the focus. The following discussion is primarily based on research and the experience with California's[1] 58 different family-court mandatory mediation models. Many of the issues and circumstances central to court-based family mediation, however, are not limited to one state or region but often apply to other jurisdictions.

HISTORICAL CONTEXT FOR COURT-CONNECTED MANDATORY FAMILY MEDIATION

Each region or state often has a historical context that has influenced or shaped its practice of court-connected mediation. This historical context is an important force that can determine the scope of mediation and its status within the family court system. The use of court-based family mediation began in the early 1970s, when several courts in California, Minnesota, and Wisconsin began referring certain contested family cases to their conciliation courts for custody counseling as an alternative to the adversary system (Elkin, 1977). Similar efforts to humanize the divorce process and reduce parental acrimony were also being developed in the private sector. The concept of a neutral third party who would facilitate a "parenting agreement" and a "business-like working relationship" between parents was developed (Ricci, 1975, 1980). Across the country, the concept of "self-determination" gained prominence (Milne, 1978), as did "structured mediation" (Coogler, 1978). The early mediation programs in California courts in the 1970s were characterized by two distinct practices and philosophies, popularly called the "confidential" model and the "recommending" models (Duryee, 1989; McIsaac,

1981). To this day, these two approaches continue to develop in parallel, albeit with controversy, reflecting the influence of the local court's history and its legal culture.

In 1980, California became the first state to mandate all parents in the state with custody or visitation disputes to participate in family mediation either prior to, or concurrent with, the court hearing.[2] All Superior Courts were directed to provide these mediation services.[3] Disputants could choose to use either court-based or private mediators. With some caveats, the research shows that California's mandatory court-based mediation program has been a success (Center for Families, 2000a). Most states today have developed statutes and court policies governing family mediation. An estimated 12 states currently mandate family mediation when there are disputes over custody or visitation, as do a number of local jurisdictions. Nearly all courts have discretion to order mediation in selected cases (Tondo, Coronel, & Drucker, 2001).

THE WIDE RANGE OF COURT MEDIATION CLIENTS

A court-based family mediator in a mandatory program has the opportunity to work with a broad client base representing a wide range of issues and circumstances. Court mediation clients can include parents who were never married to one another, stepparents, grandparents, guardians, as well as currently married and formerly married parents.[4] In California, a state where no ethic group is in the majority, court mediation clients come from many different ethnic, cultural, economic, and educational backgrounds. Nearly 38% of parents has a high school education or less, and 26% has an income of less than $800 per month. An estimated 20% of parents is unemployed, and in 64% of families one or both are not represented by attorneys. About one-half (52%) of the children involved in custody and visitation disputes are between the ages of 5 and 12, and 32% are 4 years of age and younger (Center for Families, 2000a). The majority of mediation clients identify themselves as belonging to a wide range of ethnic groups. Non-Hispanic white clients are in the minority, and a significant number of clients do not speak English. The court mediation staff, however, is predominately non-Hispanic white and speaks only English. Unfortunately, certified interpreters for family court are often in short supply (Center for Families, 2001c). These circumstances are discussed later in this chapter.

Custody and visitation disputes are often embedded in families' difficulties with their environment and with personal and interpersonal functioning. These nonlegal issues often need to be addressed in mediation in parallel with the legal issues, in order to aid the family in developing a better environment for child rearing. Research on families using court-based mediation in California identifies the many challenges faced by these parents and their children.

- In 44% of the families, there was either a current or a previous domestic violence restraining order.
- In 41% of the families, children have witnessed violence in their homes.
- In 67% of the families, parents expressed serious concerns about their children's well-being, especially their emotional adjustment.
- In 39% of the families, parents raised concerns over their children's safety.
- In 25% of all cases, families had been investigated by Child Protective Services at one time.
- In 59% of the mediation sessions, one or more serious issues were raised, including domestic violence, substance and alcohol abuse, maligning the other parent, harassing the other parent, and stalking (Center for Families, 1996, 2001a).

A court mediator, therefore, must be skilled in assessing the family's circumstances as well as addressing allegations and counterallegations by mediation clients about illegal or dangerous behavior.

The prevailing sentiment in the field is that it is not enough to provide mediation or adjudication without considering the influence of the family context on the desired outcome. If a client is burdened with difficult environmental or personal circumstances, the client may not be able to participate fully in mediation or fully implement a mediated agreement. Although it is not the purpose of the court to seek and identify nonlegal problems, it must nonetheless attempt to deal with them when they are brought before it, especially when these problems raise questions about a child or victim's health and safety or the best interest of the child. Court hearings are not designed for the dynamic development of parenting plans or client self-determination, and most California courts do not have the resources to provide full child custody evaluations for complex cases at low or no cost.

When families require specialized interventions, the family and the court look to the community and social service agencies for assistance. If these services do not exist, are uncoordinated, or the family does not qualify for a service, children and family are left without options. In the words of one mediation services director, "For many clients, the court and the mediation service is their last resort for help with their problems. They have no place else to go."[5]

Many courts have attempted to marshal both community and internal resources for families by developing additional court services or procedures and actively promoting collaborations with community organizations and government agencies. These clusters and networks of courts and community agencies working together in a spirit of collaboration have been labeled "therapeutic court services." They mirror the procedures and services that characterize "therapeutic courts" and are marked by flexibility and ongoing involvement of the court and case monitoring (Ricci & Depner, 2000). As a natural outgrowth of this case coordination, a court-connected mediation service may also be the first to identify and coordinate files in a family law case where at least one of the family members has a case in another department. For example, in a divorce case where there are three children, a father may have a history of driving while intoxicated, a teenage son may have a pending case in juvenile court, and a grandparent may have quietly filed for guardianship of the youngest child. When mediation is mandated prior to the court hearing, this information may be identified by the case management system and collected for the mediator's review prior to the mediation session. Once the mediation is complete, the bundled files with the mediation report are given to the judge.

STATUTES, CODES OF ETHICS, AND RULES OF COURT

When mediation is court based or court connected, the standards of practice for mediation extend beyond mediators and mediation participants to include the court itself. Courts, rather than their mediators, are now ultimately responsible for the quality and scope of their mediation programs and the competency of their mediators. A mandate that requires mediation carries with it an obligation for accessibility and consistency of service across jurisdictions. The history and customs of a jurisdiction or an individual court, while important, should not override the intentions of statewide statutes or standards. Furthermore, since mediation as a discipline differs from that of court management as well as that of the bench, there are often competing principles at work. Mediation requires adequate preparation and time for deliberations and negotiations. The principles of court management, in contrast, may emphasize efficiency and a speedy case resolution. Standards of practice are therefore necessary to clearly articulate principles and boundaries for mediation that will cut across the different disciplines by setting requirements for the court as well as for the mediators. Hence, statutes, rules of court, and codes of ethics for the conduct of mandatory programs and for the certification of mediators may become quite detailed.

Statutes, Rules of Court, and other standards of practice are dynamic. Often, they are shaped and modified by prevailing political climates, special interest groups, and the shifting needs of the families entering the family courts. For example, the first standards of practice in California were "highly advisory" and supplemented the mediation laws.[6] The current mediation uniform standards of practice are now a mandatory Rule of Court.[7] These new standards address the pressing challenges of providing high-quality me-

diation services in the face of rising caseloads, steep increases in clients without attorneys, significant numbers of clients with serious problems, and the
rise in numbers of non-English-speaking clients.

THE PURPOSE OF MEDIATION AND THE MEDIATOR'S ROLE

When mediation is mandatory and court based, its purpose may be defined
in a court rule as well as in statute. In California, the purpose of mediation is
more than the facilitation of a self-determined agreement on child custody
or visitation. It is marked by a focus on the child's "best interests," a term
that is defined by law.[8] The California standards of practice, which extrapo-
late on the law, provide an extensive list of expectations for the active involvement of the mediator. For example, although mediators are expected to assist the parties in developing a written parenting plan without injecting any
undue influence or personal bias in the discourse, the mediator's role (as defined below) may become directive, even in a "confidential" model. The California court-based mediator is expected to facilitate the development of a
parenting plan that "protects the health, safety, welfare and best interest of
the child and that optimizes the child's relationship with each party." The
mediator is charged with aiding the parties to create an agreement that addresses each child's current and future developmental needs. This agreement should ensure the child's frequent and continuing contact with both
parents, as long as this arrangement is in the best interests of the child.[9]

The Rule of Court expects the mediator to include, as appropriate, provisions for supervised visitation in high-risk cases and designations for
parenting time and decision making. The mediator is to include "a description of each party's authority to make decisions that affect the child; language that minimizes jargon; a detailed schedule of the time a child is to
spend with each party, including vacations, holidays, and special occasions
and times when the child's contact with a party may be interrupted."[10] In addition to issues of custody and access, the mediator's role is to facilitate the
family's transition and to reduce acrimony that may exist between the parties
by helping them improve their communication skills. The mediator is directed to focus on the child's needs and areas of stability, to aid the family to
identify its strengths, and to refer, when needed, to local counseling or other
services.

The mediator is expected to control for potential power imbalances between the parties during mediation and to terminate mediation if this balance cannot be achieved. Furthermore, the mediator is required to suspend
or terminate mediation if a client makes allegations of child abuse or neglect
or the circumstances could heighten threats or risks of violence. In cases
with a history of domestic violence, a statute provides for separate sessions at
separate times (discussed in greater detail later in this chapter). The Califor-

nia statute permits the mediator, when necessary and appropriate, to interview the child, and to exclude counsel and domestic violence support persons. The mediator may also recommend to the court that an investigation be conducted or that other services be offered to assist the parties, and that restraining orders be issued "pending determination of the controversy" in order to protect the child.[11] Mediation concludes with a written Parenting Plan that encompasses the parents' agreement and a written or oral description of any subsequent case management or court procedures proposed for resolving outstanding custody or visitation issues. These instructions could include information on obtaining temporary orders and returning to court to resolve future custody or visitation disputes. Given these directives, it is not surprising that the practice of court mediation in California has evolved as a specialty distinct from private family mediation (Ricci, 1992, 1998).

DIFFERENCES BETWEEN PRIVATE AND COURT-CONNECTED MEDIATION

Most mandatory statewide programs provide court-based mediators or have panels or lists of court-approved private mediators that meet the state's formal qualifications and certification requirements. Litigants in some states are required to pay either for court-connected or private mediation services, unless payment would pose a hardship. California law, on the other hand, requires the courts to provide mediators free of charge.

State law may limit the scope of court-based mediation to issues of custody, visitation, and other issues that pertain solely to children and parenting. Private mediators, in contrast, may have the flexibility and freedom to mediate all issues, unless the court has referred a case to them for a specific reason. Court-connected mediators or other certified private mediators must usually meet pertinent statutory requirements and standards of practice, including those for eligibility, education, experience, supervision, ongoing training, and continuing education in specified areas.

Many states do not have formal criteria for private-sector mediators, even those who receive referrals from the court. In these states, a private mediator may choose to meet all of the same requirements as a court mediator but is not bound to do so. If unschooled in what to expect in mediation, a potential client may not be aware of what constitutes a competent mediator, whether or not certification or qualifications are required, or what they have a right to expect from the mediation process. Clients, then, must rely on the training and experience of the private-sector mediator they select and on the accuracy of the orientation, education, or information they are given regarding mediation.

Unlike court-based mediators, private mediators are not usually supervised. They rarely are subject to formal performance reviews or disciplinary action but may sometimes have actions taken against them by clients who attempt to sue or file complaints with their licensing boards. It is important to note that for a private practitioner there is no built-in economic incentive to provide efficient services, especially when a couple has generous financial resources. Couples unaware of the terms of the state or local mandate may not question attending regular mediation sessions for 6 or 8 months, assuming that long-term negotiations are expected by the state mandate. Although national professional organizations and mediators upholding their national standards have made impressive strides in addressing issues such as these, most of the attention has been centered not on the private practitioner but on the court mediator. Although court-based mediation is less flexible and more abbreviated than private mediation, it currently may be more accountable to the public than is private mediation.

Court-based mediators are required to understand and uphold the foundations of law, ethics, and principles that are set forth in statutes, Rules of Court, and the Court's Code of Ethics. They must be especially conversant with legal practices and the local legal conventions, because they are representatives of the legal system. In California, court mediators must have, at a minimum, a master's degree in a behavioral science, 2 years of prior mediation experience, knowledge of the court system, family law procedures, community resources, as well other areas beyond the practice of mediation.[12] Most court mediators are licensed mental health professionals with over 5 years of court experience, and 44% have more than 10 years experience. Most of these child-custody mediators also have other duties, primarily guardianship mediation, partial and full custody evaluations, and special procedural responsibilities in cases involving domestic violence (Center for Families, 2000b). A court-based mediator in a mandatory mediation program, therefore, usually has expertise far beyond the scope of the traditional clinical training provided for private mediation (Ricci & Radloff, 1995).

CLIENT ORIENTATION AND EDUCATION CLASSES

Clients entering the legal system and the mediation process need to know what to expect and how to prepare for negotiations. Courts may not rely solely on their mediators to educate the clients in session; some make available, or mandate, brief orientation and parent education programs prior to mediation so that clients are informed about the process. When clients enter the legal system without legal counsel, orientation and education classes are the prime means of providing them with information that otherwise may not be readily available to them.[13]

Clients should receive the necessary information well before the mediation session so that they can prepare for negotiations and fully participate in mediation. Written materials mailed to clients prior to the class and additional materials distributed in class can be quite useful for the client. Not only can clients gain knowledge from the materials they receive in advance, but they can also prepare questions for the class presenters. In addition, clients can benefit by sharing and discussing the information with their advisors and family members prior to the mediation session.

Court-sponsored orientation classes typically meet once (sometimes twice) and can include presentations by mediators, videotapes, illustrations, questions and answers, written materials, and group exercises. Parent education classes are more focused on children's needs and the parenting relationship and may involve two to six meetings (Ricci, 1998). Although evaluation research on the long-term effectiveness of parent education programs is in its early stages, methodologically there is reliable evidence that orientation and parent education programs are well received by attendees (Haertel, 2000).

Curriculum content for these parent programs may or may not be predefined. In California certain basic education goals and content are set forth in the mandatory standards of practice. These programs are designed to aid parents in (1) understanding their children's current and future developmental needs; (2) evaluating the pertinence of research and professional opinions for their own circumstances; and (3) addressing their communication problems and their co-parenting relationship. Some courts also refer families to groups designed specifically for children, for parenting, or for families with high levels of conflict.

The goals for orientation and education include providing information "that facilitates the parties' informed and self-determined decision making about the types of disputed issues generally discussed in mediation and the range of possible outcomes from the mediation process."[14] Along with explaining the mediation process and the mediator's role, education must include the "circumstances that may lead the mediator to make a particular recommendation to the court, limitations on the confidentiality of the process; and access to information communicated by the parties or included in the mediation file."[15] In short, the standards of practice expect that court-based orientation and education be of the highest quality.

DOMESTIC VIOLENCE

Unlike most states, which exempt cases from mediation when there are issues of family violence, California's statutes allow mediation to occur, with provisions for separate sessions at separate times,[16] and allow the presence of a support person in mediation.[17] Separate sessions are offered when a restraining order is in effect or when the client expresses concern for his or her safety. In addition, California has enacted a statutory presumption against awarding either sole or joint legal or physical custody to a perpetrator of domestic violence.[18] Mediators are required to receive advanced training each year on issues of domestic violence,[19] and cases with issues of violence are to be handled in accordance with a separate written protocol, required by the Judicial Council of California, the policy-making body for the judicial branch.[20] This separate protocol supplements other mandates. If there is a restraining order in place, the issues that can be mediated are circumscribed by the terms of the restraining order and the safety of the victim and the child. The issue of domestic violence can never be mediated.

THE COURT'S RESPONSIBILITIES FOR PROGRAM OPERATIONS

The court has the ultimate responsibility for ensuring the quality of its mandatory mediation program. Courts can help assure a quality mediation program by staffing their program with mediators who are impartial, ethical, competent, and conversant with the law, the purposes of mediation, and the Rules of Court. Promoting mediator competency and accountability involves more than proper training and mentoring. Also needed are continuing education, peer consultation, knowledgeable supervision, and regular performance oversight. There should be a sufficient number of mediators to meet the demand for mandatory services. When the number of mediations increases without a commensurate increase in staff, waiting lists for mediation may result and certain aspects of mediation may be hurried in order to meet the court hearing date.

In addition to ensuring the services of an adequate number of capable mediators, other elements necessary for an accountable mandatory program include (1) a setting for mediation and orientation that is safe and conducive to negotiations; (2) formal and accessible grievance procedures; (3) trained personnel to conduct intake procedures that screen for restraining orders and other safety-related issues; and (4) methods for accurate and efficient collection of statistics, including information on client issues and client satisfaction with the mediator and the service. When court resources are not readily available to meet all of these needs, the mediator, the court, the mediation program, and the client may be at a disadvantage. A court should design its case management and case-processing procedures so that there is sufficient time for parties to receive orientation and prepare their cases. The process leading up to mediation and the time allotted for the mediation session should promote a sense of fairness and the opportunity for clients to participate fully.

There is some evidence to suggest that mediation prior to the first hearing reduces subsequent court hearings (Fairbanks & Street, 2001). When there is a generous time interval between the first mediation session and the court hearing, the parties have a greater opportunity to measure and deliberate their issues and to be better informed when they enter mediation.

THE "CONFIDENTIAL" AND "RECOMMENDING" MODELS OF MEDIATION

Few subjects in mediation have sustained the intense polemic as has the debate about whether or not mediators should make recommendations to the court. The controversy, not unique to family mediation, usually centers on the varied philosophies of mediation, the degrees of self-determination, mediator neutrality, the degree to which the circle of confidentiality is extended (Duryee, 1989), child and victim safety issues, the balance of power between parties, and the participants' needs for and trust in the process itself (McIsaac, 2001). The recommending mediation model is not limited to California; variations are found in other court settings and may be referred to as "open" (Duryee, 1989) or "evaluative" mediation (Shienvold, Chapter 6, this volume). (Some of the concerns expressed in this debate are similar to the issues raised in Part II, "Models of Practice," of this volume.)

Both the recommending and confidential models of mediation are utilized in California courts. The majority of mediation programs provide recommending mediation, but nearly half of the mediations conducted in the state are in courts that use confidential models of mediation. Two important distinctions should be made about these models. First, *recommending* and *confidential* are umbrella terms for a number of individualized programs that process cases somewhat differently (Center for Families, 2000b). Second, a court can change from a recommending to a confidential mediation model at will. The bench and court administration may decide to shift models to accommodate changes in court philosophy or to respond to what it believes are the changed needs of the litigants. Third, some courts use both models. Of interest is the reaction of mediation clients to each model. With some exceptions, clients give both models high marks, with most clients stating that they would recommend the process to their friends (Center for Families, 2000a).[21]

Both approaches to mediation must follow the principles set forth in the Rule of Court and statutes. For example, if there are five issues to be addressed in mediation and four of them are settled by agreement, mediators in both models are required to write out the agreement on the four issues either as a Parenting Plan that is attached to the court order or written as a stipulation on a court-order form. Mediators in both models may recommend further action to the court, as described in the statutes and the Rule of Court. For example, the mediator might recommend that the court appoint an attorney for the child or that a child custody evaluation be conducted. In both models, the attorneys are intended to have sufficient time to review the outcome of mediation and to confer with their clients prior to a settlement conference or a court hearing. However, mediators approach the resolution of the unresolved issue differently.

In a confidential model, the mediator makes no recommendation as to the preferred outcome of any unresolved issues, either verbally or in writing. Instead, the mediator notes the remaining issues to be addressed and for-

wards it to the court for further assignment, or the case may proceed to a settlement conference. The attorneys receive a copy of both the agreement and
the document that states which issues remain in dispute. The mediator does
not suggest solutions or resolutions to the outstanding issues but may recommend a brief assessment, an investigation, an evaluation, or the appointment
of an attorney for the child if the circumstances warrant.[22] The matter may
also be returned to the court in order to schedule a contested hearing.

In contrast, under the recommending model, mediators may be asked
to make a recommendation regarding the unresolved issues in a written report to the court for the judge's perusal. Courts that use the recommending
approach are required to advise their clients prior to the beginning of mediation that if and when their negotiations reach an impasse, the mediator may
carry out a dual role of mediator and evaluator. Mediation participants are
to be told about this dual role in written materials, again in the orientation
sessions, and again by the mediator at the beginning of the session. If the negotiations reach an impasse, the mediator informs the parties of his or her
shift in role. If issues still remain after further discussion, the mediator may
elect to terminate the mediation and begin the recommendation process or
refer the case back to the court for further deliberations or evaluation.

The recommending phase of mediation is not uniformly defined across
courts or jurisdictions. Different courts follow somewhat different procedures. Nonetheless, if the mediator must make a recommendation on the
resolution of the outstanding issue, he or she is expected to collect information on the case, beyond the content of the mediation session itself, by examining court records and the party declarations. Typically this type of review
occurs when there are no major conflicts about parental behavior and both
parties appear to be competent parents.

If the case warrants further investigation due to allegations of substance
abuse, child abuse, psychological problems, or neglect of the child's educational needs, the mediator may also obtain signed releases from the parents
to collect information from other sources such as day-care providers, teachers, doctors, therapists, agencies such as Child Protective Services, or services connected to social welfare or mental health. In jurisdictions where the
court either encourages or requires mediators to collaborate on case outcomes with Social Services, the law regulates any information received by the
mediator. Since the recommending process is not detailed in the California
Rule of Court for mediation, some courts structure their recommendation
process by following the laws regulating child custody investigations and
evaluations and the Rule of Court for "partial" child custody evaluations.[23]
The child custody evaluation Rule of Court applies to all practitioners, both
in the public and private sector, who conduct any child custody evaluation. A
partial evaluation is defined as an "examination of the health, safety, welfare,
and best interest of the child that is limited by court order in either time or
scope." This rule requires that a recommendation include "data collection

and analysis that allow the evaluator to observe and consider each party in comparable ways and to substantiate interpretations and conclusions regarding each child's developmental needs, the quality of attachment to each parent and that parent's social environment; and the child's reactions to the separation, divorce or parental conflict."[24] This rule also states that any recommendations made to the court must be made only for parties who have been interviewed and evaluated.

Clients receive their recommendation from the mediator in a variety of ways. Some courts make the recommendations available a number of days before court. Other courts provide the parties with the mediator's recommendations only a day or two before the hearing; some courts, on the day of the hearing. The mediator may meet with the parties after the information gathering has been completed but before a recommendation is made. The mediator calls this meeting so that the parents can be informed of the reports the mediator has collected from different contacts. Sometimes the new information clarifies matters for the parents, and they negotiate and reach agreement on most or all of the issues prior to their court hearing. In other courts, the mediator may have no further contact with the family. At the hearing, the mediator's recommendation, along with other evidence, is considered by the judge. In some instances, the judge may consider the recommendation to fashion a final order, but in many other cases, the recommendation is considered for a temporary order pending further deliberation or until the next mediation appointment. Although the judge may or may not use the mediator's recommendation in rendering a judgment, the common belief is that a judicial officer always reviews the mediator's recommendations. When a mediator makes a recommendation, the mediator may be called to testify before the court.

AN EXAMPLE OF MEDIATION WITH LOW RISK TO THE CHILD

Stanley and Sara are divorced parents disputing a schedule change and have come to the court for mediation. Stanley wants 3 more hours of time with his sons, ages 6 and 7, twice a month. Sara thinks that this additional time would disrupt the boys' school night schedule and is standing firm on her position. Prior to the mediation session, the parents will receive detailed information on mediation and other related topics and will be expected to attend an orientation class and probably a parent education class (Ricci, 1998). Stanley and Sara will be expected to complete an intake form that elicits a social history and attempts to screen for serious problems, including family violence. Their case appears to be a straightforward dispute that presents no undue risk to the child or to a possible victim.

The mediation session with Stanley and Sara lasts 2 hours, during which they reach an agreement. Typically, sessions last 1½–3 hours, and couples attend just one session. (However, some couples may attend up to six sessions, but rarely more.) When the mediation results in an agreement, the agreement is put in writing and submitted for review by the parties and their attorneys. For example, in one large court that uses a confidential model of mediation, the agreement is written up on a court-order form and the parties are given 20 days to reconsider.[25] If they do not submit any objections in writing during that time frame, the court order goes forward. If objections are raised, the parties are expected to return for further mediation, or the judge may hear the case. In some other courts, the parties pick up their agreement after their mediation, sometimes on the same day. In other courts, the agreement is sent by mail.

At the end of the mediation or several weeks later, clients may be asked to fill out a client form registering their level of satisfaction with the mediation and the mediator. In some courts, the parties may agree to return to mediation after several months to discuss how the plan is serving the children or to aid the parents with its implementation.

AN EXAMPLE OF A MEDIATION WHEN A QUESTION OF RISK EXISTS

Because California mediation programs do include cases with issues or incidences of domestic violence, the following example is included to illustrate how such a mediation process can be used to aid the family and protect the alleged victim and children. Linda has filed for divorce and full custody of their two children, ages 9 and 11, stating that Mike, the children's father, is abusing alcohol and has slapped her on several occasions over the past 3 months. Mike contends that Linda abuses painkillers and is a poor parent. Linda has a temporary restraining order in effect, issued by the family court, which includes a "stay away" order from the family home. Mike asserts that he will dispute the temporary restraining order and contests Linda's request for full custody.

The presence and terms of a temporary restraining order severely restrict what can be negotiated in mediation. For example, although custody is an issue with Linda and Mike, it cannot be negotiated in mediation because of the restraining order and the allegations of violence. A restraining order is issued by the court on behalf of the person who is asserting the allegations (i.e., the protected party). The order restrains certain actions by the alleged batterer. The mediation process cannot be used to dismiss any restraining order or to negotiate the issue of violence. In this case, mediation may be useful in other ways. For example, the mediator can assist with immediate needs, such as safety planning and possibly a temporary supervised visitation arrangement, and can determine whether he or she will want to interview the children. Mediation can also help by providing referrals to community resources that specialize in serving families with issues of domestic violence.

When Linda fills out the mediation service intake form, she notes the incidents of violence and the restraining order and alleges Mike's alcohol abuse. She also states that she is in poor health and jobless. When violence is an issue, the victim or threatened party can request separate mediation sessions at separate times. When there is a temporary restraining order that includes a "stay away" order, separate sessions may be required. Like Stanley and Sara, Linda and Mike will be expected to attend a parent education or orientation program prior to mediation. However, because of the temporary restraining order, Linda will attend a separate session at a different time from Mike's session. Linda could also request the presence of a support person in the mediation session.[26]

Linda and Mike meet with the mediator separately on different days to reduce the possibility of stalking. Information regarding the day and times of their appointments is kept confidential. The mediator isolates the issues in individual sessions with each of them and aids them in exploring their options. Over the course of the mediation process, the parents do agree to supervised visitation so that the children can see their father during the course of the restraining order. The mediator meets with the children. She observes that they appear anxious and want to talk about the slapping incidents, their father's absence, and their mother's illness.

In a confidential model, the mediator usually writes up the issues on which the parties agree, then itemizes the remaining issues in dispute without making any recommendation as to their resolution. In this case, the mediator could recommend referrals to community services or interventions to address the violence, the children's needs, and the mother's ill health. These recommendations could even include recommending an attorney for the children or a full custody evaluation. This memo is sent to the parents and their attorneys (if they have counsel). The memo is the basis for their further deliberations and possibly a settlement conference. However, since there are issues of risk, Mike and Linda will probably be referred first for a family assessment process with a different mental health professional.

In some family courts that use recommending models, the mediator is the court's primary resource for neutral information regarding risk factors and children's needs. For example, in one court, the mediator would prepare a confidential report to the judge that listed first the parents' mutual agreements, followed by a narrative about the unresolved issues. Finally, the report would list any recommendations reached by the mediator after his or her discussions with collateral contacts—including, when necessary, a recommendation for a psychological evaluation, specialized information from a doctor or therapist, or a restraining order. The mediator may be more likely to conduct an assessment or brief investigation under the label of a *recommendation* when the court does not have separate child custody assessment or evaluation resources and when parents do not have legal representation or the resources for private evaluation services.[27] For cases with these complex circumstances, the mediator should be cross-trained to carry out both assessment and mediation functions.

If Linda and Mike's agreement for supervised visitation becomes a court order, the mediation program should aid them in enrolling for this service. The court may also provide Linda and Mike with follow-up sessions or case management services with the mediator or a court counselor.

WORKING WITH CLIENTS FROM DIVERSE BACKGROUNDS

Mandatory mediation, by its very nature, includes all disputants regardless of cultural or ethnic background. As a result, court-based mediators work with clients who represent a broad range of cultures, languages, customs, levels of acculturation, education, and status. The customs and beliefs of the client may depart significantly from those of the mainstream culture, including those that define the role and place of women, children, the use of physical force, respect or resistance to authority, and knowledge of and respect for American laws and the legal system. For many, the law and the legal system are at best confusing, more often anxiety provoking and mysterious. This mix of uncertainty and threat is especially onerous when the law and the representatives of the law speak a different language and operate within a traditional Caucasian perspective (Sanchez & Taylor, 1991). Language and terminology provide the context for understanding expectations and experiences, just as learning styles and ways of interacting are expressions of a culture. In a state such as California, where no one race or culture is in the majority (Center for Families, 2001c) and 224 languages are spoken, significant numbers of non-English-speaking clients must participate in the mandated mediation program (Center for Families, 2001b).

For mediators to be "culturally competent," especially with non-English-speaking clients, they must be aware of, and have an appreciation for, each client's personal experience as well as his or her ethnic heritage. Each client will have a unique worldview shaped by his or her level of acculturation, traditions, and values that will influence the negotiations and the client's ability to adequately express and promote his or her views. Moreover, mediators should be able to facilitate referrals for family members to outside services (Waldman, 1999) and help clients understand how state policies can be viewed as compatible with their traditional beliefs (e.g., laws that protect parental rights or the safety of children).

Ideally, mediators should either speak the language or have enough understanding of the language to follow an interpreter's translation. However, because of insufficient resources, courts and mediators must often rely on a mutually acceptable member of the cultural community to translate the issues and negotiations. These ad hoc interpreters may pose a risk to the governing principle of neutrality, because they may not be monitored or screened for bias. As an alternative, courts could also contract with mediators and agencies already established in ethnic or culturally defined communities, so that the mediation could take place in the community rather than in the court setting.

Client education programs for those litigants inexperienced with the court system must take special care to describe the steps in mediation, the responsibilities of the parties in the negotiations, options following unsuccessful negotiations on all issues, the court hearing, and the implementation of the mediated agreement. The forms, codes, rules, legal terms, procedures, and educational materials should also be made available in the languages most common in the jurisdiction.

THE ECONOMICS OF MANDATORY MEDIATION

When decision makers are charged with constructing a funding base for mandatory mediation, a key question to explore is whether it is ethical or appropriate to charge citizens for a mandated service. Many courts have answered "Yes," whereas others, such as those in California, have answered "No."[28] Depending on the state and jurisdiction, mediation may be free; may be fee based, computed on a sliding scale in relation to the client's ability to pay; or it may be based on the full fee customarily charged by private mediators. Adequate financial support for a court-based mediation program is essential but not always forthcoming. Furthermore, the source of financing can shape a mediation program model and determine who can use the service.

If permitted, courts can obtain some or most of the needed funding by charging fees for the services they provided. Courts can also expect litigants to find their own private mediators and negotiate their own fees. When court-based mediation is free to the client, however, the court takes on the full responsibility of funding the program. The court can provide this free service at the court, using court staff trained as mediators, or it can contract with outside providers. Compensation for outside court-connected providers also varies. Some courts offer their contractors a flat fee for each mediation they conduct, whereas others offer a set hourly rate. Contracting for services can release the court from overhead costs of providing an in-house service, because mediators on contract usually conduct the sessions in their own private offices. Although the use of contract mediators is common, the trend in California has moved toward more in-court staff. This shift may be due to the higher level of risk inherent in conducting mediations without access to secure offices and security personnel, the desire to have expert staff in residence, as well as the court's desire to provide greater oversight and accountability.

Unless client fees cover all program costs, court-based mediation programs must compete with other worthwhile programs for local and state resources. Mandatory mediation programs are not automatically exempt from this competition because of their mandate, unless they have a protected and adequate funding stream. All court-based services experience both the constraints and benefits of being part of a court, including the court's level of success in procuring adequate funding for its operations.

ACCESS TO DIFFERENT MEDIATION MODELS

Different funding and fee models can heavily influence variations in mediation services. In many jurisdictions, there are differences in the duration of mediation, the issues that can be mediated, the availability of appointments, and the level of compliance by the mediators and the programs to existing rules or standards of practice. A court-based mediation may be completed in one or two sessions for several reasons: (1) mediation may be limited to custody and visitation disputes, (2) parents may wish to negotiate only one or two issues rather than a full parenting plan, or (3) the court does not have the resources to provide more than one or two sessions. Private mediation, on the other hand, (1) addresses a wide range of issues, (2) often attracts clients who seek to develop a full parenting plan, and (3) offers the potential for ongoing mediation sessions. Courts, unlike private practitioners, typically do not have the freedom to offer evening or weekend appointments, and their mediators must follow state standards. Private mediators may offer a wide variety of appointment options, may not be required to follow standards of practice, and are usually sole proprietors or in practice with one or two partners.

Both systems of providing mediation, although different, can be both useful and helpful. However, the different models are not equally accessible to all citizens. The private mediation model is out of the reach of less financially endowed clients, whereas the court-based model is open to all. In short, a litigant's access to different mediation models is usually determined by the ability of the litigant to pay for the service.

Mandatory mediation should be characterized by consistency and fairness of service delivery to citizens of all incomes. As a rule of thumb, if the population using court-based mediation reflects the economic composition of the community, then an egalitarian mediation system has probably been achieved. However, if a court-based mediation program serves a disproportionate number of citizens who are near or below the poverty line, as is the case in so many California courts, then a dual system may exist. When evaluating mandatory mediation, important questions to include are "Do clients have choices between systems of mediation?" and

"Are the indigent limited to the court model while the affluent have a choice of models?"

CONCLUSION

Despite the many challenges they face in delivering a competent service, court-based mandatory mediation programs have established themselves as a unique branch of family mediation. They offer an important and valued service to families from all backgrounds. Litigated custody cases have been reduced, and, at least in California, most court-based litigants are satisfied with the service. Without the mandate to mediate, people in the heat of conflict would not voluntarily take the time to engage in a new process that expected them to communicate respectfully and find compromises. Mandatory mediation has helped countless families settle their differences, focus on their children's needs, and reduce the need for court-based actions. It has greatly increased the public's awareness of alternatives to adjudication and may be the underlying reason for the overall growth and acceptance of family mediation, in general. A number of states has taken the bold step of mandating mediation. It is open to debate whether this step reflects primarily a utilitarian need for less costly and swifter resolution of family conflict or a belief that mediation has better short- and long-term outcomes for the family than does the traditional court process.

As mandatory mediation becomes more widespread, it is important to vigorously pursue in greater depth those philosophical and practical issues inherent in its practice and in the management needed to deliver that service. This includes those courts that are moving toward the coordination or unification of complex family law cases with crossover matters in domestic violence, juvenile dependency, illegal substance abuse, and probate guardianship.

First, mediators, judges, managers, and supervisors of mediation programs should explore avenues for the continuing review and modifications of the standards of practice as the clients' needs change, new laws are enacted, and case coordination between court departments becomes more common. While the current standards provide a necessary and purposeful structure, the mediation process and the case preparation for mediation nonetheless remains dynamic.

Second, courts should redouble their efforts for ensuring that their mediation service is accessible and useful to people from all backgrounds and economic means. This may require a court to provide specialized orientation procedures and educational programs as well as multilingual mediators and materials translated in several languages. Third, courts should further explore and refine hybrid models for complex and high-risk cases: for example, models that use mediation approaches in phases of child custody evaluations; models for conducting emergency assessments or triage; or models that combine the process of mediation, assessment, and case coordination, as illustrated in Shienvold, Chapter 6, this volume.

Fourth, more attention needs to be paid to the role of the judiciary and court management in the effective delivery of a mandated service. While a dedicated and well-trained mediation staff is the core of a quality mandatory mediation program, an effective program requires both adequate funding as well as decision makers who understand that mediation can, in many cases, offer the potential for better family outcomes than adjudication does. The court must provide trained managers and supervisors attuned to this unique service,[29] the concepts of court–community partnerships for service referrals, and the coordination of complex cases within its court-connected services. Lastly, the prevailing political climate plays a significant role in determining a successful mandatory program. To procure the opportunity to continue to serve the general public, managers of court-based mediation programs need a place at their court's decision-making table, and policy makers who support a mediation approach to resolving conflict must maintain a persuasive presence in the overall political arena.

ACKNOWLEDGMENT

This work was supported in part by the Rockefeller Foundation, Bellagio Scholar-in-Residence program.

NOTES

1. The California mandatory mediation program serves an estimated 91,500 cases a year, involving more than 140,000 children. The program is documented in a set of large-scale longitudinal and representative studies that make up the database of the Statewide Uniform Statistical Reporting System (SUSRS). This database contains information on more than 18,000 mediation participants garnered from nine studies. Statewide studies must meet two fundamental criteria: (1) All eligible parties across the state have an equal opportunity to be included in the research, thereby ensuring representation of the full range of cases across the state; and (2) the research includes enough cases to permit reliable inferences from the data. Research reports are available online at *www.courtinfo.ca.gov/programs/cfcc/resources/publications/articles.htm*.

2. Senate Bill 961 mandated child custody mediation and was carried by Senator Alan Sieroty. This bill was chaptered in 1980 and became effective January 1, 1981.

3. All references to the California mediation statutes can be found in the California Family Code, Chapter 11, "Mediation of Custody and Visitation Issues," §§3160–3186.

4. California Family Code, §3178(b).

5. Despite chronic lack of revenues, many courts seek to generate a creative and effective response for families in need. A few examples include the Unified Family Court of Yolo; the "HOPE" Court; Butte Superior Court; the "Comprehensive Services Program of Interventions for the Diverse Needs of Families in the Family Court System"; Santa Clara

Superior Court; and specialized programs for high-conflict families pioneered in Los Angeles and Alameda Superior Courts.

6. California Standards of Judicial Administration, adopted 1992, §26. Also see Norton, Weiss, Ricci, and Fielding (1992).

7. California Rule of Court, rule 5.210, "Court-Connected Child Custody Mediation," has been in effect since July 1, 2001.

8. California Family Code, §§3011, 3020, 3161.

9. "Best interest of the child" in California is defined in California Family Code §§3011 and 3020.

10. California Rule of Court, rule 5.210.

11. California Family Code, §§3181, 3182, 3183.

12. Court-based mediators in California are expected to have knowledge of adult psychopathology and psychology of families, child development, child abuse, clinical issues, effects of divorce, effects on children, domestic violence, and child custody research sufficient to enable assessment of children's mental health needs. (California Family Code §§1815, 3164[b]).

13. Eighty-seven percent of California mediation programs reported that parent education programs are provided to mediation clients either through the court or an outside agency contracted by the court. Source: "Administrative Court Services Available to Families," (November 2000), Center for Families, Children and the Courts, Judicial Council of California.

14. California Rule of Court, rule 5.210.

15. California Rule of Court, rule 5.210.

16. California Family Code, §3181.

17. California Family Code, §6303.

18. California Family Code, §3044.

19. California Family Code, §1816.

20. California Family Code, §3170(b), and Rule of Court, rule 5.215(j).

21. Seventy-seven percent of clients in California's recommending mediation models and 79% of clients in confidential mediation models said that mediation was a good way to resolve their issues. Although this is a strong approval rating, the fact remains that 23% and 21% of clients were critical of the process. Seventy-three percent of clients in recommending mediation models and 79% in confidential models said that the other parent did not have an unfair advantage in the session; 84% of clients in recommending mediation models and 90% of clients in confidential models said that they would recommend this process to their friends if they had a custody or visitation dispute. It is important to note that clients rated the two models slightly differently (from 2 to 6%) and that there is a significant number of clients who are not satisfied with court-based mandatory mediation. Source: Personal communication to the author from Don Will at the Center for Families, Children and the Courts. Also see Center for Families, Children and the Courts (2001a).

22. California Family Code, §§3180, 3183(b).

23. See, for example, the San Diego Superior Court Mediation Program.

24. California Rule of Court, rule 5.225, "Court-Ordered Child Custody Evaluations."

25. Santa Clara Superior Court's mediation program policy.

26. California Family Code, §6303.

27. A child custody evaluation, if performed by the court, costs litigants $150–$600, depending on its scope. If a private evaluator performs the evaluation, the cost (in California) can be extensive and charges of $3,000 or more are common. The court may be reluctant to order such studies if it has few or no court-based evaluators.

28. In California, the appellate court rendered a decision prohibiting courts from charging the public for mandatory mediation services (*Hogoboom v. Superior Court* [1996]).

29. Over the past 11 years, the National Association of Court Management (NACM) has developed curriculum guidelines to define core competencies for presiding and supervising judges, court managers, and court administrative staff in ten areas of management. NACM's "Ten Core Competencies" include a competency in "Essential Elements," a category that includes the management of mediation and other court services. The NACM core competencies can be viewed on the association's website, *www.nacmnet.org.*

REFERENCES

California Rules of Court. (2001). *Court connected child custody mediation (rule 5.210).* San Francisco: Judicial Council of California.

California Rules of Court. (2002). *Domestic violence protocol for family court services (rule 5.215).* San Francisco: Judicial Council of California.

Center for Families, Children and the Courts. (1996). *Statewide and local statistical profiles: Child custody mediation cases.* San Francisco: Administrative Office of the Courts, Judicial Council of California.

Center for Families, Children and the Courts. (2000a). *Client ratings of mediation services by recommending and non-recommending courts in California.* San Francisco: Administrative Office of the Courts, Judicial Council of California.

Center for Families, Children and the Courts. (2000b, November). *Providers of family court services: The 1999 service providers survey.* Paper presented at the Statewide Conference for Directors and Administrators of Court Services, San Francisco.

Center for Families, Children and the Courts. (2001a). *1999 Client baseline study.* San Francisco: Administrative Office of the Courts, Judicial Council of California.

Center for Families, Children and the Courts. (2001b). *Family law interpreter pilot program: Report to the legislature.* San Francisco: Administrative Office of the Courts, Judicial Council of California.

Center for Families, Children and the Courts. (2001c). *Research update: Custody mediation and ethnic diversity in California.* San Francisco: Administrative Office of the Courts, Judicial Council of California.

Coogler, O. J. (1978). *Structured mediation in divorce settlement: A handbook for marital mediators.* Lexington, MA: Lexington Books.

Duryee, A. M. (1989). *Open family mediation in the court: A systemic view.* Oakland, CA: Alameda County Superior Court.

Elkin, M. (1977). Post-divorce counseling in a conciliation court. *Journal of Divorce, 1,* 55–65.

Fairbanks, G. C., & Street, I. C. (2001). *Timing is everything: The appropriate timing of case referrals to mediation–a comparative study of two courts.* James City, Ninth Judicial District, VA (State Justice Institute, grant SJI-99-N-224).

Haertel, D. G. (2000). *A review of parent education program evaluations.* San Francisco: Administrative Office of the Courts, Judicial Council of California.

Hogoboom v. Superior Court, 51 Cal. App. 4th 653.59 Cal. Rptr. 2d 254 (1996).

McIsaac, H. (1981). Mandatory conciliation custody/visitation matters: California's bold stroke. *Conciliation Courts Review, 19*(2), 73–77.

McIsaac, H. (2001). Confidentiality revisited, California style. *Family Court Review, 39*(4), 405–414.

Milne, L. A. (1978). Custody of children in a divorce process: A family self-determination model. *Conciliation Courts Review, 16,* 2–12.

Norton, E., Weiss, W., Ricci, I., & Fielding, R. (1992). Development of uniform standards of practice for court-connected child custody mediation in California. *Family and Conciliation Courts Review, 30*(2), 217–228.

Ricci, I. (1975). *The single-parent experience*, UCLA Extension, graduate level. University of California, Los Angeles.

Ricci, I. (1980). *Mom's house, Dad's house: How parents make two homes for their children after divorce.* New York: Macmillan.

Ricci, I. (1992). Implementing a legislative mandate for services and coordination to California's court-connected family mediation and conciliation courts. *Association of Family and Conciliation Courts Review, 30*(2), 169–184.

Ricci, I. (1998). Parent education in California family courts. *Family Futures, 2*(3), 21–27.

Ricci, I., & Depner, E. C. (2000, March). *New frontiers in family courts: Court-community alliances and therapeutic conflict resolution models.* Paper presented at the Conflict and Cooperation in Families Conference, Bethesda, MD.

Ricci, I., & Radloff, S. (1995). MFTs and family law. *Family Therapy News, 26*(1), 13.

Sanchez, E., & Taylor, A. (1991). Out of the white box: Adapting mediation to the needs of Hispanic and other minorities within American society. *Family and Conciliation Courts Review, 29*(2), 114–128.

Tondo, C. A., Coronel, R., & Drucker, B. (2001). Mediation trends: A survey of the states. *Family Court Review, 39*(4), 431–453.

Waldman, F. (1999). Violence or discipline? Working with multicultural court-ordered clients. *Journal of Marital And Family Therapy, 25*(4), 503–515.

CHAPTER 19

Reconciling Self-Determination, Coercion, and Settlement in Court-Connected Mediation

NANCY A. WELSH

Self-determination is considered a central characteristic of the mediation process. However, the definition of self-determination may vary significantly, resulting in very different mediation processes. This chapter examines definitions of self-determination, how it evolved in court-connected mediation, and threats to self-determination in this context. Professor Nancy A. Welsh then explores how the state of Florida addressed the question of self-determination in its ethical guidelines and presents alternative mechanisms for protecting party self-determination.

Ethical codes for mediators consistently describe party self-determination as the "fundamental" principle underlying mediation (Joint Committee of Delegates, 1994, Standard 1; American Bar Association, 2001, Standard 1). One commentator has said that self-determination is "the heart and soul of mediation as a dispute resolution procedure" (Watson, 1998, p. 14). Arriving at a precise definition of self-determination and an effective means to protect it, however, have proven problematic, particularly as mediation has become an integral part of court operations.

This chapter begins by discussing the vision of self-determination that dominated the original mediation movement and inspired its broadly facilitative approach, then considers the vision revealed in the evolution of court-connected family mediation. Next, the chapter briefly describes one influential state's approach to safeguarding self-determination in court-connected mediation and assesses the likely effectiveness of this approach. Finally, the chapter discusses and evaluates various other means of protecting self-determination and preventing coercion in mediation, with particular focus on a proposal for a nonwaivable cooling-off period.

A VISION OF SELF-DETERMINATION ANCHORED IN PARTY EMPOWERMENT

Much of the support for the "contemporary mediation movement" (Bush & Folger, 1994, p. 1) and the vision of self-determination that accompanied it arose out of dissatisfaction with the legal system's perceived mistreatment of disputants (Folberg, 1983; Kovach & Love, 1998). Commentators of the time argued that the legal system mistreated litigants by depriving them of control over the resolution of their disputes. This criticism was particularly potent when it was directed at the courts' traditional handling of the very personal and highly traumatic issues of child custody and visitation (Milne, 1978). Obviously, disputants' loss of control occurred when their cases went to trial. However, mediation proponents pointed out that, even before trial, the litigation process took "much of the decision making . . . out of the hands of the clients, as the attorneys engage[d] in battle within the legal system" (Haynes, 1981, p. 3). Because the civil litigation system forced disputants to delegate their disputes "to lawyers for expression and [to] judges for decision" (Rogers & McEwen, 1994, §5.2, n. 10), some commentators argued that disputants inevitably felt excluded from the resolution of their disputes in the courts, regardless of whether that resolution occurred at trial or through settlement (Folberg & Taylor, 1984).

Commentators thus "urged that dispute resolution should more fully involve the participants in disputes" (Folberg & Taylor, 1984, p. 6). In sharp contrast to the traditional litigation process, then, mediation was conceived as a disputant-centered, disputant-dominated process (Folberg, 1983; Milne, 1978). It relied on the disputants' active and direct participation in the mediation process and in decision making (Folberg & Taylor, 1984; Milne, 1978). Mediation offered all disputants a means to wrest control over both the dispute resolution *process* and the dispute resolution *outcome* from legal and counseling professionals (Rifkin & Sawyer, 1982). In the family context, the process permitted divorcing parents to reclaim responsibility for "planning for the future of [their] family in its newly organized state" (Milne, 1978, p. 1). Ultimately, advocates argued that mediation offered the potential to nurture "self-determination" (Folberg & Taylor, 1984, pp. 34–35; Milne, 1978, p. 1).

Mediation advocates also rejected the notion that the law should serve as the exclusive determinant of the substantive norms used to control discussion and decision making in the dispute resolution process (Felstiner, Abel, & Sarat, 1980–1981; Folberg, 1983; McThenia & Shaffer, 1985). Instead, these advocates argued that the disputants could and should define fairness for themselves (Folberg & Taylor, 1984; Kovach & Love, 1998). Control of the substantive norms to be applied to the discussion and decision-making process was integral to the originally dominant vision of self-determination. Thus, many mediation advocates envisioned party self-determination as involving much more than just the disputants' passive ability to respond to the particular settlement proposal put before them. Rather, self-determination in mediation "restor[ed] to individuals . . . a sense of their own value and strength and own capacity to handle life's problems" (Bush & Folger, 1994, p. 2). It placed the disputants themselves at the center of the mediation process in nearly every way. They were the principal actors and creators within the process.

Self-determination promised disputants the opportunity to (1) participate actively and directly in the process of resolving their dispute, (2) control the substantive norms guiding their discussion and decision making, (3) create the options for settlement, and (4) control the final outcome of the dispute resolution process. This vision of party self-determination assumed that at the conclusion of a mediation, the parties would and should feel that the agreement they reached was theirs, warts and all. This vision did not anticipate that parties would (or should) feel forced to agree to accept or offer a settlement that reflected someone else's—namely, a third party's—norms, experience, or will. Ultimately, then, the principle of self-determination in mediation was intended to foster party empowerment (Buss, 1999; Folberg & Taylor, 1984; Grillo, 1991; Merry, 1994; Riskin, 1996).

THE MEDIATION MODEL AS A MANIFESTATION OF SELF-DETERMINATION

Not surprisingly, the mediation model that arose at this time manifested an empowerment-oriented vision of self-determination. Mediation was voluntary. Mediation advocates argued that people should participate in mediation only if they chose to do so (Beer, 1982; Grillo, 1991; Katz, 1993; Shonholtz, 1984). Mediation required that each party become "an active part of the communication" (Folberg & Taylor, 1984, p. 41). The disputants were supposed to do the talking in mediation. The mediator's job was to make sure that each had a chance to speak, that no one dominated the session, and that disputants listened to each other's perceptions and focused on underlying needs (Community Dispute Resolution Center, 1989; Neighborhood Justice Centers of Atlanta, 1987). The mediator's role was to "validate and encourage parties throughout the process" (Community Dispute Resolution Center, p. 4) and to use both the mediation structure and a variety of techniques to enable the parties' individual and joint will to emerge, thus permitting them to exercise their self-determination (Beer, 1982; Community Dispute Resolution Center, 1989; Milne, 1978).

Mediation's form fit its function rather elegantly, and it appeared that this form was quite effective in enabling disputants to reach resolution and in generating high participant satisfaction (Tyler, 1989). Unfortunately, however, few disputants elected to use this new process (Rogers & McEwen, 1994). Most disputants continued to turn to the courts for resolution of their disputes. Somewhat ironically then, despite mediation's genesis out of dissatisfaction with the judicial process, mediation proponents began advocating for the institutionalization of mediation—particularly mediation of small claims and custody disputes—*within* the courts because that was where disputants and their disputes could be found.

THE VISION OF SELF-DETERMINATION REVEALED IN THE EVOLUTION OF COURT-CONNECTED FAMILY MEDIATION

In order to understand the evolution and eventual narrowing of the vision of self-determination in the court-connected context, it is useful to recall why the courts chose to embrace a process that arose out of frustration with litigation. Accurately or not, judges—including the Chief Justice of the U.S. Supreme Court—and attorneys perceived that the courts were facing increased dockets and reduced resources, while litigants were enduring longer waiting periods for trial (Burger, 1977). Some of the claimed by-products of mediation—the ability to save time and money—responded directly to these concerns. Mediation advocates, meanwhile, highlighted the high levels of party satisfaction achieved through the use of mediation (Keilitz, Daley, & Hanson, 1992; McEwen & Maiman, 1981; Pearson & Thoennes, 1989).

In the divorce and child custody area, mediation held additional attractions. As laws and attitudes regarding divorce changed, the courts were confronted with an increasing number of custody contests. Many judges and attorneys were uncomfortable dealing with divorcing spouses' strong emotions (Kisthardt, 1997), and family court counseling staff expressed frustration with "having to agonize over other people's life decisions" (Milne, 1978, p. 1). The courts were searching for a means of aiding parents in developing new relationships to serve the best interests of their children (Kisthardt, 1997; Milne, 1978). To some, mediation may have appeared as a timely and very attractive antidote to the perceived ills of the judicial system. It was a process that could *simultaneously* increase efficiency, better serve children, *and* improve litigants' satisfaction with their treatment in court. Understood in this way, it seems almost natural that courts embraced divorce and child custody mediation and made it an integral part of the litigation process.

Importantly, early court-connected family mediation programs focused very consciously on fostering "family self-determination" (Milne, 1978, p. 1). As was true for the community mediation programs described earlier, disputants' participation was voluntary. Mediation sessions were structured to enhance parents' communication, the respectful discussion of their feelings, and joint work toward meeting the children's needs (Milne, 1978). These programs were designed to permit and even encourage divorcing spouses to take their rightful role as the parents who would and could determine what was best for their children, rather than relinquishing that responsibility to "a judge who may never lay eyes on the children and doesn't have to live with the decision on a day in and day out basis" (Milne, 1978, p. 2).

Evidence confirms that court-connected family mediation, as practiced today, remains faithful in many key respects to the vision of self-determination that inspired the contemporary mediation movement. Empirical data clearly show that the disputants themselves attend these mediation sessions (Wissler, 1999). They are directly involved in the discussion of the disputed issues. They express their feelings, hear the mediator acknowledging what they said, and are involved in developing their own settlement agreements (Keilitz et al., 1992; McEwen, Rogers, & Maiman, 1995; Wissler, 1999). Indeed, comparisons between traditional court litigation and mediation have revealed that disputants who participate in family mediation generally perceive the process as fairer than the court experience, more protective of the disputants' rights than court, and exerting less pressure to reach agreement quickly or to agree to unwanted terms (Keilitz et al., 1992). Lawyers, who attend many more family mediation sessions now than they did in the 1970s—and in some states, such as Maine, accompany their clients "almost always" (Kisthardt, 1997; McEwen et al., 1995; Wissler, 1999)—also seem to appreciate the opportunity presented by mediation for clients' self-determination. Research indicates that attorneys value their clients' participation in the process and view themselves as playing supporting roles (McEwen et al., 1995).

Other evidence, however, signals that there is some narrowing of the vision of the self-determination principle that underlies court-connected family mediation. First, because few parties chose to enter into family mediation when participation was voluntary (Shaw, Singer, & Povich, 1992; Pearson & Thoennes, 1989; Society of Professionals in Dispute Resolution, 1991), mediation in many courts is now mandatory. At least 33 states now mandate family mediation in contested custody or visitation disputes, and court-connected family mediation is used in a total of 38 states as well as the District of Columbia (Ricci, Chapter 18, this volume; Salem & Milne, 1995). Thus, many disputants *must* enter mediation, even when they might otherwise choose not to do so. Obviously, such a mandate is not consistent with a vision of self-determination that is grounded fully in the goal of party empowerment.

Second, the pressure upon court-connected mediation programs to reduce court caseloads has resulted in certain process adaptations that trigger concerns regarding the protection of disputants' self-determination. For example, whereas early models of court-connected family mediation involved 6–8 weeks of mutual education and decision making (Milne, 1978), more recent research indicates that most court-connected cases are mediated in 3 hours or less (Pearson & Thoennes, 1989). Some court-connected models of mediation provide for even less time. The standard mediation in San Diego Superior Court, for example, has been reported as lasting only 1½ hours (Cohen, 1991). Disputants' self-determination is likely to suffer if they are given inadequate time to discuss and thoughtfully consider how to resolve difficult personal issues.

Third, the mediators in court-connected family mediation have never been wholly disinterested third parties, and they become directly involved in shaping mediated outcomes. From the inception of court-connected custody mediation programs, many courts made their mediators directly responsible for the quality of the agreements, particularly those terms relevant to the protection of children's best interests (Ricci, Chapter 18, this volume; Waldman, 1997). Even those family mediators committed to ensuring self-determination were, and are, equally committed to being "direct and forthright in defining the children's emotional and physical needs" (Milne, 1978, p. 5) and guiding the parents' decision making. Indeed, there is substantial evidence that both early and current family mediators could be characterized as "active and directive" (Pearson & Thoennes, 1989, p. 16) in structuring the process, evaluating the merits of the disputants' cases, advocating on behalf of the children, and suggesting and even recommending agreement terms (Pearson & Thoennes; Wissler, 1999). Analysis of family mediation sessions has revealed that mediators are "responsible for making most of the proposed solutions" (Pearson & Thoennes, p. 17). The most dramatic evidence that family mediators are directly involved in the creation of outcomes is the fact that many courts permit, or even *require,* the mediators to provide the court with recommended resolutions if the disputants are unable to reach agreements on all of the issues in mediation (Cohen, 1991; Dennis, 1994; Ricci, Chapter 18, this volume). Although these actions by mediators produce settlements, they are not wholly consistent with a vision of self-determination that emphasizes the *disputants'* communication, negotiation, selection of norms, and creation of options.

Finally, evidence suggests that the growing presence of attorneys at family mediation sessions impedes the operative vision of self-determination. For example, even though attorneys value family mediation for the opportunity it provides to their clients to participate in discussion and decision making, mediators indicate that the disputants' participation is less active when their attorneys are present (Wissler, 1999). Attorneys may affect mediators' behavior as well. Attorneys rely on the mediators to help their clients become more realistic, and they expect mediators to provide "second opinions" regarding likely outcomes (McEwen et al., 1995). Thus, the presence of attorneys may heighten the frequency, intensity, and significance of mediators' evaluative interventions.

This brief summary of the current practice of court-connected family mediation reveals a vision of self-determination that continues to value disputants' participation and empowerment, but the practice of family mediation also demonstrates a reduction or constriction of that vision. Perhaps due to the need to conserve judicial resources or the courts' obligation to protect the welfare of children or the involvement of professionals in most court-connected mediation sessions, the current model of family mediation clearly does not place all of its trust in the *disputants'* self-understanding and judgment, or *their* control over the norms used to guide decision making, or *their* active and direct participation in the communication needed to achieve shared understanding and negotiation, or, ultimately, *their* control over the final decision. Instead, as evidenced by the extent of mediators' direct involvement in the creation, evaluation, and selection of solutions, the vision of self-determination that is operative in court-connected family mediation assumes that the disputants need access to the *mediator's* knowledge, experience, and judgment. The mediator joins the disputants on center stage to ensure that they have the information they need to make a final decision that is informed and "rational" (Moberly, 1997). The disputants' control at the moment of decision making thus becomes the focus of this narrowed vision of their self-determination.

Is there anything wrong with such a focus and the desire to inform the disputants' decision making? Importantly, disputants themselves express more favorable assessments of the mediation process when mediators suggest possible settlement options, evaluate the merits of the case, and advocate on behalf of the children (Wissler, 1999). These research results appear to contradict those who have argued that " 'evaluative' mediation is an oxymoron" (Kovach & Love, 1996, p. 31). Rather, disputants' reactions seem to support those commentators who have emphasized the courts' obligation to facilitate fair and just results (Stempel, 1997), disputants' right to explore the application of legal norms to their cases (Stark, 1996), and the need for disputants to understand the consequences of their best alternative to a negotiated agreement (or BATNA; Stempel; Mnookin & Kornhauser, 1979). Implemented as respectful elective education, evaluative interventions by mediators need not impair even the more expansive vision of disputants' self-determination. Instead, at their best, such interventions can enhance disputants' discussion, deliberation, and creativity—and thus their self-determination (Moberly, 1997).

Unfortunately, though, the constriction of an empowerment-based vision of disputants' self-determination also has the potential to invite trouble, especially when combined with time reductions in the length of the mediation sessions and the courts' need to reduce their dockets. Furthermore, not all mediators' evaluations are designed to enhance disputants' discussion, deliberation, and creative problem solving. Sometimes evaluative interventions are meant to do no more than produce a decision—and, in particular, a decision to settle. And, sometimes, mediators simply go too far.

TAKING THE NARROWED VISION TOO FAR: THREATENING SELF-DETERMINATION IN COURT-CONNECTED FAMILY MEDIATION

Even the scholars and practitioners who support mediator evaluation admit that "in some instances, 'evaluative' mediators undoubtedly need to be reined in to prevent mediation from being converted to arbitration and to prevent the evaluative mediator who jumps to conclusions from bullying one or both parties into an unsatisfactory resolution of a controversy" (Stempel, 1997, p. 969). Mediators who rely *predominantly* on an evaluative approach (Kovach & Love, 1998) or those who use the *most aggressive* of the possible evaluative strategies (i.e., "predicting outcomes of court or other processes" and "urging or pushing the parties to settle or to accept a particular settlement proposal or range"; Riskin, 1994, p. 111) threaten even the limited vision of disputants' self-determination. Nonsettling disputants in family cases, for example, have questioned the fairness of the mediation process when mediators go beyond suggesting options to recommending particular settlements (Wissler, 1999). And, increasingly, disputants are claiming that mediators' aggressive evaluation had the effect of coercing them into agreements.

A recent case in Florida offers one vivid example of possible "muscle mediation" in a court-ordered family mediation. The *Vitakis-Valchine v. Valchine* (2001) case involved the disposition of frozen embryos as well as the distribution of a couple's assets. The couple reached an agreement in a court-ordered mediation session. Subsequently, however, the wife filed a motion to set aside the settlement agreement, alleging, among other claims, that the mediator had been coercive. Describing the wife's allegations, the court wrote:

> With respect to the frozen embryos, which were in the custody of the Fertility Institute of Boca Raton, the wife explained that there were lengthy discussions concerning what was to become of them. The wife was concerned about destroying the embryos and wanted to retain them herself. The wife testified that the mediator told her that the embryos were not "lives in being" and that the court would not require the husband to pay child support if she were impregnated with the embryos after the divorce. According to the wife, the mediator told her that the judge would *never* give her custody of the embryos, but would order them destroyed. The wife said that at one point during the discussion of the frozen embryo issue, the mediator came in, threw the papers on the table, and declared "that's it, I give up." Then, according to the wife, the mediator told her that if no agreement was

reached, he (the mediator) would report to the trial judge that the
settlement failed because of her. . . .

With respect to the distribution of assets, the wife alleges that the mediator told her that she was not entitled to any of the husband's federal
pensions. She further testified that the mediator told her that the husband's pensions were only worth about $200 per month and that she would
spend at least $70,000 in court litigating entitlement to this relatively mod-
est sum. The wife states that the mediation was conducted with neither her
nor the mediator knowing the present value of the husband's pensions or
the marital estate itself. The wife testified that she and her new attorney
had since constructed a list of assets and liabilities, and that she was
shortchanged by approximately $34,000—not including the husband's pen-
sions. When asked what she would have done if [the mediator] had told her
that the attorney's fees could have amounted to as little as $15,000, the wife
stated, "I would have took [sic] it to trial."

Finally, the wife testified that she signed the agreement in part due to
"time pressure" being placed on her by the mediator. She testified that
while the final draft was being typed up, the mediator got a call and she
heard him say "have a bottle of wine and a glass of drink, and a strong
drink ready for me [sic]." The wife explained that the mediator had repeatedly stated that his daughter was leaving for law school, and finally said
that "you guys have five minutes to hurry up and get out of here because
that family is more important to me." The wife testified that she ultimately
signed the agreement because "[I] felt pressured. I felt that I had no other
alternative but to accept the Agreement from the things that I was told by
[the mediator]. I believed everything that he said." (*Vitakis-Valchine v.
Valchine,* 2001, at 1097)

This disputant's complaint is not an isolated example. Other discon-
tented disputants involved in divorce and child custody mediation sessions
have brought grievances alleging that the mediator:

- "assumed the role as a judge meeting privately with the attorneys,"
  "repeatedly spoke in a threatening and manipulative manner," "never
  . . . allowed [the disputant] to discuss the division of assets directly
  with [her] husband" and "made the decisions and divisions of assets
  without [the disputant's] input or financial considerations" (letter to
  Office of the Executive Secretary of the Supreme Court of Virginia,
  personal communication, November 3, 1996).
- was "abusive ('yelled, pointed his finger in [the complainant's] face
  and threw papers during the session') . . . inappropriately prolonged
  the session . . . 'dictated the solution he envisioned' . . . and attempted
  to intimidate the complainant" (Florida Mediator Qualifications
  Board Case No. 98-009, 1998).
- "during caucus . . . used coercion and threats to garner the agreement
  and told the complainants to be more cooperative since 'they would

not be pleased with [the judge in the case]'s decision' " (Florida Mediator Qualifications Board Case No. 11, 1994).

- "threatened [the disputant] with contempt of court, coerced her into staying past the time when she could bargain effectively, . . . would not allow her to obtain food when she requested, and used verbal assaults to obtain agreement" (Florida Mediator Qualifications Board Case No. 97-003, 1997).

There is no evidence that family mediators regularly engage in the deplorable tactics described in these excerpts. Nonetheless, if the allegations of these mediation participants are taken as true—and, admittedly, this is a major assumption—the conduct challenges the complacent assumption that the principle of party self-determination guides every mediator's choices and actions.

FLORIDA'S APPROACH TO PROTECTING SELF-DETERMINATION

Florida, a leader in the institutionalization of court-connected mediation, is one state that has grappled with questions raised by mediator evaluation and, particularly, the need to protect party self-determination from overaggressive mediator evaluation. Florida courts have had the authority to refer all, or any part, of a filed civil action to mediation since January 1, 1988. Florida's first set of ethical guidelines for its court-connected mediators, the Florida Rules for Certified and Court Appointed Mediators, became effective in May 1992. In part, due to the emergence of allegations regarding mediator coercion, as described above, the Florida Supreme Court Committee on Arbitration and Mediation embarked on a year-long study in 1997 "to determine if Florida's ethical rules for mediators would benefit from review and revision" (Florida Proposed Rule, 1998, R. 10.031).

The Committee developed and distributed a proposal to explicitly permit mediators to provide "professional advice or information"—but only to the extent that it did "not violate . . . self-determination of the parties" (Florida Proposed Rule, 1998, R. 10.037(a) option two). Other proposed revisions explicitly defined self-determination as "decision-making" (Florida Proposed Rule, 1998, R. 10.031) or making "a free and informed choice to agree or not to agree" (Florida Proposed Rule, 1998, R. 10.031, committee note).

The committee also proposed to protect self-determination by specifying what mediators could *not* do. These proposed provisions prohibited mediator coercion or improper influence (Florida Proposed Rule, 1998, R. 10.031), as well as mediators' "attempt[s] to interfere with a party's self-determination by offering professional or personal opinions regarding the outcome of the case" (Florida Proposed Rule, 1998, R. 10.031). Proposed Rule 10.030, meanwhile, summed up the "mediator's responsibility to the parties" as including "honoring their right of self-determination; acting with impartiality; and avoiding coercion, improper influence, or conflicts of interest" (Florida Proposed Rule, 1998, R. 10.030).

In response to the committee's request for comments regarding these proposals, some respondents clearly expressed fears that important elements of self-determination would be lost if mediators were given explicit permission to provide professional advice and opinions. For example, one opponent predicted:

> The proposed rule revision will indirectly serve to unnecessarily reduce the active participation of the parties in mediation. . . . The potential for a negative evaluation by the mediator would likely lead parties to be encouraged to take a less active role in mediation and let their attorneys, if present, to take the lead. . . . Empowerment involves both active involvement in the 1) process of mediation (negotiation) and 2) outcome of mediation (acceptance or rejection of a final agreement). The proposed rules, while generally preserving self-determination, seem likely to have a chilling effect [on] . . . the parties' participation in mediation. . . . The mediator will have more freedom to deviate from the existing rules while the parties will feel less freedom to freely, actively, and openly exercise their right to freely participate in mediation. We will have empowered the mediator to stray from mediating, while disempowering the parties. (Letter from Gregory Firestone to Sharon Press, September 29, 1998)

Other opponents feared that if mediators were permitted to evaluate cases, "a party would become reliant on information provided by an 'expert' mediator and acquiesce to a settlement based upon what a mediator states" (memo from Deborah Deratany to Sharon Press, February 18, 1998). These commentators wanted to be sure that "responsibility [was kept] squarely upon the parties to be the evaluators of the fair, proper or likely court outcome" (letter from Lela Love to Lawrence Watson, February 24, 1998). The vision of self-determination revealed by these comments is reminiscent of the vision that inspired the contemporary mediation movement: Both focus on the disputants' self-understanding, their control over the norms to guide decision making, the need for their active and direct participation in the communication to achieve shared understanding and negotiation, and, ultimately, their control over the final decision.

Those who took the opposite position and supported permitting mediators to provide professional advice and opinions were just as deeply committed to self-determination. But rather than viewing the parties as the primary participants in the process and the creators of their own substantive norms and settlement options, these commentators emphasized the disputants' control over the final outcome of the mediation session and their need to "thoroughly understand their options" (memo from John Lande to Sharon Press, February 12, 1998), as well as their need for "qualified, legal opinion and understanding" and "objective criteria" to allow them "to make their decisions and compromises" (letter from Michael Mattson to Florida Dispute Resolution Center Rules Committee, March 16, 1998). Indeed, some of these commentators argued that if mediators were not permitted to evaluate, they would become mere dreaded " 'message carriers' who simply repeat what they have been told and offer no new input to the process" (letter from Tom Arnold to Elizabeth Plapinger, January 27, 1998), and the mediation process would be "sterilize[d] . . . into impotence" (Watson, 1998, p. 15). This second vision of self-determination tended to place the parties in the role of consumers who require externally generated information to inform their "rational" decision making, as they choose among several prepackaged settlement options (memo from Reverend Dr. David P. Juwal to Sharon Press, February 14, 1998).

The latter vision—in which disputants' self-determination largely begins and ends with their control over the decision "to agree or not to agree" (Florida Proposed Rules, 1998, R. 10.031) to the mediators' proposals—is consistent with the traditional operation of the courts and lawyers. Indeed, as attorneys negotiate on their clients' behalf, they are ethically bound to communicate settlement offers to their clients (American Bar Association, 2002, R. 1.4, C.1) and to abide by their clients' decisions to accept or reject such offers (American Bar Association, 2002, R. 1.2[a]). No agreement can be reached without the clients' consent. But it is usually the attorneys, not their clients, who are the active participants in the process of negotiation and in the shaping of an agreement.

The Supreme Court Committee on Arbitration and Mediation ultimately embraced the vision of self-determination that focused on the disputants' control over the decision "to agree or not to agree" (Florida Proposed Rule, 1998, R. 10.031) to enter into a particular settlement. Although the committee's final recommendations clearly acknowledged the importance of self-determination, the participatory vision of this concept disappeared. The Florida Supreme Court promulgated revisions are based on the Committee's recommendation that permit mediators to offer their personal or professional "opinions" and to engage in evaluation, ranging from the provision of "information" to pointing out possible outcomes of the case and discussing the merits of a claim or defense (Florida Rules for Certified and Court-Appointed Mediators, 2000, R. 10.370). The final rules require the mediator's evaluation to be "consistent with the standards of impartiality and preserving party self-determination" (Florida Rules for Certified and Court-Appointed Mediators, 2000, R. 10.370). The rules also identify two specific situations in which offering a personal or professional opinion would violate self-determination, per se. The mediator is prohibited from offering a "personal or professional opinion as to how the court in which the case has been filed will resolve the dispute" (Florida Rules for Certified and Court-Appointed Mediators, 2000, R.

10.370) and from offering a "personal or professional opinion intended to coerce the parties, decide the dispute, or direct a resolution of the issue" (Florida Rules for Certified and Court-Appointed Mediators, 2000, R. 10.370).

Although the committee cautioned that "special care should be taken to preserve the parties' right to self-determination if the mediator provides input to the mediation process" (Florida Rules for Certified and Court-Appointed Mediators, 2000, R. 10.310), the revised rules evidence the committee's (and, ultimately, Florida's) adoption of the narrower vision of self-determination and a faith that self-determination can be protected by asserting its importance *and* specifically banning mediator coercion. Unfortunately, such faith may be misplaced. Indeed, it is instructive to review courts' handling of coercion claims by other neutral third parties—specifically, judges and magistrates. Such a review suggests that within the courts the value of settlement can trump the value of self-determination.

THE COURTS' PROTECTION OF SETTLEMENTS

Courts have declared that settlements represent the "best justice" (*Cottman Transmission Sys., Inc. v. Metro Distrib. Inc.,* 1993) and that judicial deference to litigants' agreements is appropriate because "the parties to the dispute are in the best position to determine how to resolve a contested matter in a way which is least disadvantageous to everyone" (*United States v. City of Miami,* 1980, at 1322). This language suggests that the courts, like the governing bodies that regulate mediator ethics, are concerned about party self-determination—the parties' direct involvement in, and control over, assessing their interests and options and ultimately shaping a settlement agreement that meets those interests or, at the very least, is "least disadvantageous to everyone."

It seems reasonable that if the courts defer to settlements *because* they express the parties' self-determination, then the courts must be sure that the settlements *actually express* such self-determination. Courts, however, hold a nearly unshakable presumption that settlements—nearly all settlements—have been "freely entered into" (*Casto v. Casto,* 1987, at 334) and that parties' "manifestation of assent" (Restatement (Second) of Contracts, 1981, §164, 175) to a settlement agreement results from the exercise of their "free will." Indeed, it is the party who claims that he or she was deprived of the exercise of his or her free will in entering into a settlement agreement who bears the burden of proof (*Petracca v. Petracca,* 1998). The power to exercise free will is accompanied by responsibility for the consequences—for good or for ill. The courts do not permit parties to rescind agreements simply because they are suffering "buyer's (or seller's) remorse" (*Rosevear v. Rosevear,* 1998), had a "change of heart" (*Ovidiah v.*

N.Y. Ass'n for New Americans, 1997), or have become "unhappy" (*Stoelting v. Stoelting,* 1987) with the poor bargain that they struck (*Petracca v. Petracca,* 1998, at 910; *Casto v. Casto,* 1987, at 334).

Of course, disgruntled parties may claim they were coerced into an agreement, and the law recognizes this argument as a valid defense (Restatement, §175; *Machinery Hauling, Inc. v. Steel of W. Va.,* 1989). Nonetheless, it remains very difficult for parties to overcome the presumption that they exercised free will. It becomes even more difficult when a party claims that his or her agreement was coerced—or his or her free will was overcome—by the language or behavior of a court official, such as a judge or a magistrate in a settlement conference.

The courts often explain their hesitation to permit rescission of a settlement agreement by finding that the complaining party's allegation of coercion, duress, or pressure "falls well short of demonstrating by clear and convincing evidence that [the complaining party] was 'deprived of the exercise of . . . free will' " (*Porter v. Chicago Bd. of Educ.,* 1997, at 1129). In other words, the courts are unlikely to brand anything as coercion unless they can "see" it in the record. Courts *have* been able to "see" such coercion when judges have sanctioned parties for their failure to accept the settlement the judge had suggested (*National Ass'n of Gov't Employees, Inc. v. National Fed'n. of Fed. Employees,* 1988) or to settle by the judge's deadline (*Newton v. Keene Corp.,* 1990), or when judges have accelerated the date of trial because a party refused to settle (*Wolff v. Laverne Inc.,* 1962; *Innis v. Innis,* 1993; *Chomski v. Alston Cab Co.,* 1969; *Mitchell v. Iowa Cab Co.,* 1968). Importantly, when parties have alleged, and been able to show, that judges engaged in these and other explicitly coercive behaviors for the purpose of coercing settlement or punishing a failure to settle, appellate courts have been willing to vacate the sanctions—and, occasionally, to vacate settlement agreements.

However, appellate courts have been much less willing to recognize and provide relief when parties have claimed more subtle, implicit coercion by a judge. For example, courts have not found it coercive when judicial officers have predicted to unrepresented parties that they will lose their lawsuits and their businesses will be closed (*Cottman Transmission Sys., Inc. v. Metro Distrib., Inc.,* 1993); when parties have alleged that the judicial officer presiding over a settlement conference made them feel that they must make an immediate decision regarding settlement (*Porter v. Chicago Bd. of Educ.,* 1997); when a trial judge excluded parties' attorneys from his settlement discussions with the parties (*Dutton v. Dutton,* 1998, at 14); or when unsophisticated parties, who were excluded from the judicial settlement conference, were forced to testify regarding their understanding of, and assent to, settlement just minutes after their attorney informed them of the settlement and before they had had any opportunity to confer with the attorney (*Associates Financial Services Company of Hawaii, Inc. v. Mijo,* 1998).

If a trial judge's evaluation of, and advocacy for, a particular settlement are not viewed as coercive, it is hard to comprehend how even the evaluative interventions used by the family mediator in the Florida case of *Vitakis-Valchine v. Valchine* (2001) could be deemed coercive. Under these circumstances, Florida's (and other states') choice to protect self-determination by repeatedly asserting the importance of this principle and banning coercion appear well meaning but seriously flawed.

ALTERNATIVE MECHANISMS FOR PROTECTING PARTY SELF-DETERMINATION

Finding an effective means of protecting self-determination and preventing coercion requires acknowledgment that high-pressure tactics—or muscle mediation—is not effective in a vacuum. Rather, these tactics *derive* their effectiveness from the framework within which they operate. They are effective because (1) self-determination is now understood quite narrowly as a party's power to choose to agree, or not to agree, to a settlement; (2) this narrowed vision is consistent with courts' and attorneys' understanding of parties' free will; (3) courts are eager to enforce settlements and hold a strong presumption that a settlement reflects the exercise of parties' free will (or self-determination); and (4) courts require a strong showing to overcome this presumption and generally perceive coercion only in its most blatant forms. These current realities suggest that in order to protect parties' self-determination in mediation—even the narrower vision—modifications must be made within this framework. What follows are several options that have been proposed or attempted.

Option 1: Clarifying the Definition of Self-Determination in Mediation

As described earlier, mediation proponents have varying understandings of the core principle of self-determination. This variation is, in part, the result of unclear wording in statutes, rules, and ethical guidelines. In some statutes, mediation is defined as facilitation of "settlement," whereas others describe it as facilitation of "communication between the parties" in order to discuss settlement. Different definitions can lead to different perceptions regarding the appropriate goal and role of mediators. Similarly, ethical guidelines seem to define "self-determination" solely as the ability of a party to decide to agree or not to agree—making this concept synonymous with free will—whereas many mediation proponents view self-determination as something more.

If there are concerns that the original rich vision of self-determination is being lost, there may be a need to rewrite statutes, rules, and ethical guidelines to revise the definition of self-determination and clearly differentiate it from "free will": Self-determination in the mediation context requires more protection than traditional negotiation and judicially hosted settlement conferences have accorded to parties' free will. Specifically, statutes, rules, and ethical guidelines regarding the governing principle of self-determination could be rewritten to include the following provisions:

- Active and direct party participation
- Communication and negotiation by the disputing parties
- Parties' identification and selection of the interests and substantive norms that should guide the creation of settlement options
- Parties' creation of potential settlement options
- Parties' control over the final outcome

In other words, the definitions should reference the indicia of party empowerment.

There is reason to suspect, however, that these semantic changes are unlikely to have much effect in the end—and will lead to new questions of interpretation. For example, questions will arise as to how much direct participation by parties will be considered sufficient, how the system will judge whether a mediator adequately solicited parties' interests and norms, or what will constitute adequate consideration of parties' interests and norms in the creation of a settlement. Ultimately, it is unclear how this redefinition of self-determination would be enforced. These are significant concerns and lead to the conclusion that focusing on changing the language in statutes, rules, and ethical guidelines is unlikely to succeed in safeguarding self-determination.

Option 2: Clarifying the Definition of Mediation and Self-Determination by Educating the Public

Frequently, mediators speak of the need for more extensive and effective public education as a means to ensure that disputants understand the mediation process. Obviously, such public education would incorporate a vision of self-determination. The concept of increased public education has tremendous appeal, particularly for mediators who are concerned about, and wish to serve, the public good. However, proponents of this strategy ignore the difficulty of reaching a mass audience and delivering a rather subtle message. To date, mediation has been institutionalized most effectively by reaching and responding to the needs of society's professional gatekeepers—lawyers, judges, counselors, therapists, ministers, managers—who then educate their clients, congregants, or employees. These gatekeepers bring their own professional biases, which tend to influence the message. It is unlikely that attempts to provide public education regarding the meaning of self-determination would ever reach a mass audience effectively. Therefore, this option also appears unlikely to safeguard self-determination.

Option 3: Clarifying the Relationship between Self-Determination and Mediator Evaluation by Educating Mediators

Some mediators believe that the key to safeguarding self-determination lies in teaching their own professional members techniques designed to protect and nurture self-determination. Indeed, the number of articles published and sessions held that teach effective evaluation by mediators (Aaron, 1996) testify to this burgeoning focus. The authors of these articles and the leaders of the workshops are quick to stress the importance of party self-determination in mediation. As a result, they advocate evaluation designed to "educate" the parties, not to coerce them into an agreement.

Unquestionably, mediators have much to learn from these articles and workshops, from research exploring the effect of particular evaluative tools (Wissler, 1999), and from research and articles examining lawyers' and parties' decision making (Birke & Fox, 1999). By themselves, however, these workshops, articles, and research projects can do no more than establish an informed, aspirational standard for mediator conduct. They cannot regulate mediator conduct or be used directly to protect party self-determination. Indeed, the mediators most likely to violate self-determination are least likely to read such articles or attend such workshops. Thus, this third option, by itself, cannot effectively safeguard self-determination.

Option 4: Modifying the Presumption against Coercion

Currently, as we have seen, the courts prefer settlement and presume that a settlement agreement represents the expression of free will. The party alleging coercion bears the burden of producing enough evidence to persuade the court that the coercion occurred. A party's subjective feeling that he or she did something he or she did not really want to do is not enough.

A fourth option for protecting a richer version of party self-determination is to modify the burden of proof that is borne by the party alleging coercion. First, the burden might be changed to require only that the party alleging coercion make a showing that satisfies a probable cause standard. A party's subjective feeling that he or she was coerced, coupled with evidence of a mediator's negative evaluation or strong support for a particular settlement proposal, might be able to meet this standard. If the court found probable cause, the court could require the mediator to prove either that he or she did not engage in coercive behavior or that the party's agreement was free and voluntary (*Casto v. Casto*, 1987).

Obviously, this modification would reduce the burden currently borne by parties alleging coercion and acknowledge that mediators can engage in effective and coercive manipulation without making outright threats or imposing sanctions. However, this provision could have several very unfortunate consequences. Fewer people might be willing to serve as mediators if they might be forced to prove that they did not coerce parties into settlement. Mediation itself could become the source of much litigation. Finally, it is difficult to imagine how confidentiality could be protected under these circumstances (*Olam v. Congress Mortgage Co.*, 1999). For all of these reasons, this option would probably not be most effective in safeguarding self-determination.

Option 5: Changing the Focus from Coercion to Undue Influence

Another, related contract defense that parties may use to void a contract, known as the defense of "undue influence," may apply quite well to mediation, particularly if mediators are considered to have a fiduciary relationship with the parties (Nolan-Haley, 1999). Undue influence is "unfair persuasion of a party who is under the domination of the person exercising the persuasion or who by virtue of the relation between them is justified in assuming that person will not act in a manner inconsistent with his welfare" (Restatement, 1981, §177). Mediators are supposed to honor, protect, and nurture parties' self-determination. Mediation—and the mediator presiding over this process—is supposed to "empower" the parties, "enable" them to be "ultimate decisionmakers" and "satisfy" them (Rosenberg, 1991, p. 467). Under these circumstances, it would not be unreasonable for parties in a mediation to assume that their mediator has a type of fiduciary relationship with them. The existence of this relationship could help to explain how "the free play of a man's will [might be] overborne" (*Odorizzi v. Bloomfield School District*, 1966, at 539) by a mediator's repeated and insistent evaluation, even though the mediator made no threats and imposed no sanctions. All of this suggests that mediator codes of ethics might be revised to prohibit undue influence by the mediator and to make it clear that such undue influence would constitute a violation of party self-determination.

Despite the apparent suitability of the defense of undue influence and the difference between the evidence required to substantiate coercion versus undue influence, recent cases (*Olam v. Congress Mortgage Co.*, 1999) suggest that, in practice, courts and ethical boards do not distinguish between these defenses as they work to preserve settlement agreements, particularly if they find that the settlement agreements are not unreasonable. In addition, the option of using an undue influence standard raises the likelihood of the same unfortunate consequences that plague the proposal to modify the burden of proof borne by parties alleging coercion. Mediation itself—and particularly the mediator's actions or statements allegedly designed to persuade a party to change his or her position—would become the cause of litigation. Courts have already demonstrated the difficulty of protecting the confidentiality of communications and conduct occurring during a mediation session when they must determine whether a mediator (or other parties to a mediation) engaged in undue influence (*Olam v. Congress Mortgage Co.,* 1999). Although this option—prohibiting undue influence by the mediator—has some appeal, its effectiveness is also questionable.

Option 6: Modifying the Presumption That a Mediated Settlement Agreement Is Immediately Binding

Many mediation advocates have urged courts to treat settlement agreements arising out of mediation processes in precisely the same way that they treat settlement agreements arising out of unassisted negotiation between litigants and/or their attorneys. Many mediators have bristled at additional requirements that legislators and courts have imposed on mediated settlement agreements before they are considered enforceable, such as (1) requiring that mediated settlement agreements be in writing (*Ryan v. Garcia,* 1994; *Murphy v. Padilla,* 1996), (2) requiring stipulations regarding the binding nature of the agreement (Cal. Bus. & Prof. Code, 1980, §467.4; Fla. Stat. Ann., 1988/2000, §723.038(2)), or (3) requiring the agreements to be signed by all parties *and* their attorneys (*Gordon v. Royal Caribbean Cruises, Ltd.,* 1994). Perhaps many mediators have reacted negatively to these requirements because they have perceived them as implying a skepticism—even outright distrust—by legislators, lawyers, and judges.

In their eagerness to attain legitimacy, however, many mediators have assumed too quickly that the enforcement of mediated agreements must be made in the image of negotiated agreements. "Self-determination" is *not* part of the lexicon regarding the enforcement of negotiated settlement agreements, and the standards currently used to determine whether parties exercised their free will in reaching a negotiated agreement are likely to fall short in protecting the fundamental principle of self-determination. Therefore, it may be necessary to *embrace and advocate for* a protection that holds court-connected mediation to a higher standard than traditional negotiation. The protection that may be most effective is the imposition of a 3-day nonwaivable cooling-off period before mediated settlement agreements, whether oral or written, become binding.

Cooling-off periods are not new. They are used in contexts in which it has become clear that high-pressure sales tactics are being used to persuade unwilling parties to "manifest" their "assent" to contracts. For example, in the home solicitation context, legislators and regulators concluded that "in a significant proportion" of these sales, "consumers had been induced to sign a sales contract by high pressure techniques" (U.C.C.C., §2.501, 1968, comment 1) and therefore provided consumers with a 3-day cooling-off period, during which they have the unilateral right to rescind their purchase agreements without penalty (C.F.R. §429.1, 429.2; U.C.C.C. §2.502(1); U.C.C.C. §3.502(1); Mo. Ann. Stat. §407.710; Neb. Rev. Stat. §69-1604; N.Y. Pers. Prop. Law §425; N.C. Gen. Stat. §25A-39). Cooling-off periods have also been applied to particular types of mediation. In Florida, for example, court rules provide for a 10-day cooling-off period for agreements reached in family mediation, if attorneys do not accompany the disputants (Fla. Family L. R. P. 12.740(f)(1), 1996). Many other states also impose a sort of cooling-off period on divorce and child custody agreements reached in mediation by providing that an agreement does not become binding until the disputants' attorneys have an opportunity to review it.

It is fairly easy to anticipate the objections to wider use of cooling-off periods for mediated agreements. Some will argue that a mediator—even a mediator using muscle mediation tactics—cannot be compared to a "pitchman" in a home solicitation sale. Nevertheless, we must remember that some mediators do indeed describe their task as "selling" a settlement proposal. The distinction between such a mediator and a pitchman may be difficult to draw. Furthermore, we must remember that mediation has often been described to litigants as a process that will "promote mutual respect" while also "empowering" them (Florida Rules for Certified and Court-Appointed Mediators, 1992, R. 10.060) and allowing them "to reach agreements that take into account important facts that are often ignored in judicial decision making" (Rosenberg, 1991, p. 467). These descriptions are unlikely to prepare disputants for the tactics of the muscle mediator.

By far, however, the most significant objection to the imposition of a cooling-off period is that it would permit disputants to back out of agreements much more easily, possibly based only on buyer's or seller's remorse. Such ease of rescission could reduce mediation settlement rates, which may, in turn, lead to reduced use of mediation. This concern squarely raises the challenge of "walking the talk" of self-determination.

If self-determination, not settlement, is the fundamental principle underlying mediation, then the benefits provided by this cooling-off proposal would clearly outweigh the possible risks. Unlike many of the other options discussed earlier, a cooling-off period is relatively straightforward, easily administrable, and unlikely to invite litigation and/or intrusions on the confidentiality of mediation. Much more important, however, this option would reward mediators who view their role as primarily facilitative and penalize mediators who use techniques designed to force an agreement. Mediators who use facilitative techniques are more likely to build disputants' investment in, and likely compliance with, a settlement that they view as *theirs*—truly an expression of *their* self-determination. The disputants would be less likely to rescind their agreements during the cooling-off period, even if they could do so without penalty. Evaluation would be one of the tools in these mediators' toolboxes, but they would have an incentive—keeping their settlements—to use this tool so that it supports (rather than threatens) party self-determination. The cooling-off period would discourage mediators' coercive use of evaluation, or muscle mediation, because these behaviors would be more likely to result in parties' repudiation of their agreements. Ultimately,

this option has the potential to be quite effective in reducing coercive mediation and, as importantly, in protecting *both* the currently narrowed
understanding of self-determination and the broader understanding that
first inspired many to join the contemporary mediation movement.

CONCLUSION

Self-determination has been identified as the fundamental, core characteristic of the mediation process. Nonetheless, the existence and meaning of self-
determination cannot be taken for granted. Indeed, current trends in the
institutionalization of court-connected mediation are challenging courts and
mediation advocates to clarify the meaning of *self-determination* and to develop effective mechanisms to protect it. If mediation advocates and courts
fail to develop these mechanisms, the heady principle of self-determination
will become a largely irrelevant relic from the early days of the contemporary
mediation movement. On the other hand, if courts and mediation advocates
act now to define and protect the enactment of self-determination as central
to mediation, then mediation may yet become a process that is qualitatively
different from, and better than, the traditional dispute resolution processes
found within the courts. The days of romance for mediation advocates and
the courts are not over (Menkel-Meadow, 1997), but, as with most
relationships, we must be willing to make the choices and undertake the
work required to keep the flame alive.

ACKNOWLEDGMENT

This chapter is based, in large part, on Welsh (2001). Copyright 2001 by the Program on
Negotiation and by The President and Fellows of Harvard College. I wish to extend my
heartfelt thanks to Geoffrey Sawyer for his research assistance.

REFERENCES

Aaron, M. (1996). ADR toolbox: The highwire art of evaluation. *Alternatives to the High Cost
of Litigation, 14*, 62–64.
American Bar Association. (2001). Model standards of practice for family and divorce mediation. *Family Law Quarterly, 25*, 27.
American Bar Association. (2002). *Model rules of professional responsibility: Rules 1.2(a), 1.4–
comment 1.* Chicago: Author.
Associates Financial Services Company of Hawaii, Inc. v. Mijo, 950 P.2d 1219 (Haw. 1998).
Beer, J., with Stief, E. (1982). *Peacemaking in your neighborhood: Mediator's handbook* Philadelphia: New Society.
Birke, R., & Fox, C. (1999). Psychological principles in negotiating civil settlements. *Harvard Negotiation Law Review, 4*, 1–57.

Burger, W. (1977. Fall). Our vicious legal spiral. *Judge's Journal*, 22–24, 48–49.

Bush, R. B., & Folger, J. (1994). *Promise of mediation.* San Francisco: Jossey-Bass.

Buss, E. (1999). Confronting developmental barriers to the empowerment of child clients. *Cornell Law Review, 84*, 895–966.

Cal. Bus. & Prof. Code §467.4 (1980).

Casto v. Casto, 508 So.2d 330, at 333, 334 (Fla. 1987).

C.F.R. §429.1, 429.2 (1999).

Chomski v. Alston Cab Co., 299 N.Y.S.2d 896 (N.Y. App. Div. 1969).

Cohen, L. (1991). Mandatory mediation: A rose by any other name. *Mediation Quarterly, 9,* 33–46.

Community Dispute Resolution Center. (1989). *Mediation training manual: Six stages of mediation.* Author.

Cottman Transmission Sys., Inc. v. Metro Distrib., Inc., No. Civ. A. 92-2131, 1993 WL 481555 (E.D. Pa. Nov. 19, 1993).

Dennis, D. (1994, Spring). The advantages of having mediators conduct custody evaluations. *Association of Family and Conciliation Courts Newsletter, 13*(2), 6.

Dutton v. Dutton, 713 N.E. 2d 14, at 14 (Ohio App. Dist. Ct. 1998).

Felstiner, W., Abel, R., & Sarat, A. (1980–1981). The emergence and transformation of disputes: Naming, blaming, claiming . . . . *Law and Society Review, 15,* 631–654.

Fla. Family L. R. P. 12.740(f)(1) (1996).

Fla. Stat. Ann. §723.038(2) (1988 & Supp. 2000).

Florida Mediator Qualifications Board Case No. 11, 1994.

Florida Mediator Qualifications Board Case No. 97-003, 1997.

Florida Mediator Qualifications Board Case No. 98-009, 1998.

Florida Proposed Rule Changes for Certified and Court-Appointed Mediators. (1998, January), *Resolution report,* 13, 18, R. 10.030.

Florida Proposed Rule Changes for Certified and Court-Appointed Mediators. (1998, January), *Resolution report,* 13, 18, R. 10.031, committee note.

Florida Proposed Rule Changes for Certified and Court-Appointed Mediators. (1998, January), *Professional advice and opinions,* R. 10.370, committee note.

Florida Proposed Rule Changes for Certified and Court-Appointed Mediators. (1998, January), *Resolution report,* 13, 18, R. 10.037(a) option two.

Florida Rules for Certified and Court-Appointed Mediators. (1992). R. 10.060.

Florida Rules for Certified and Court-Appointed Mediators. (2000). *Self-determination.* Florida Statutes Annotated Mediator Rule, R. 10.310, committee note.

Florida Rules for Certified and Court-Appointed Mediators. (2000). *Professional advice or opinions.* Florida Statutes Annotated Mediator Rule, R. 10.370.

Folberg, J. (1983). A mediation overview: History and dimensions of practice. *Mediation Quarterly, 1,* 3.

Folberg, J., & Taylor, A. (1984). *Mediation: A comprehensive guide to resolving disputes without litigation.* San Francisco: Jossey-Bass.

Gordon v. Royal Caribbean Cruises Ltd., 641 So. 2d 515 (Fla. Dist. Ct. App. 1994).

Grillo, T. (1991). The mediation alternative: Process dangers for women. *Yale Law Journal, 100,* 1547–1610.

Haynes, J. (1981). *Divorce mediation* (Vol. 3). New York: Springer.

Innis v. Innis, 616 N.E.2d 837 (Mass. App. Ct. 1993).

Joint Committee of Delegates from American Arbitration Association, American Bar Association, and Society of Professionals in Dispute Resolution. (1994). *Model standards of conduct for mediators.* Washington, DC: American Arbitration Association.

Katz, L. (1993). Compulsory alternative dispute resolution and voluntarism: Two-headed monster or two sides of the coin? *Journal of Dispute Resolution, 1993*(1), 1–55.

Keilitz, S., Daley H. W. K., & Hanson, R. (1992). *Multi-state assessment of divorce mediation and traditional court processing.* Williamsburg, VA: National Center for State Courts.

Kisthardt, M. K. (1997). The use of mediation and arbitration for resolving family conflicts: What lawyers think about them. *Journal of the American Academy of Matrimonial Lawyers, 14,* 353–392.

Kovach, K., & Love, L. (1996). Evaluative mediation is an oxymoron. *Alternatives to the High Cost of Litigation, 14,* 31–32.

Kovach, K., & Love, L. (1998). Mapping mediation: The risks of Riskin's grid. *Harvard Negotiation Law Review, 3,* 71–110.

Machinery Hauling, Inc. v. Steel of W. Va., 384 S.E.2d 139 (1989).

McEwen, C. A., & Maiman, R. J. (1981). Small claims mediation in Maine: An empirical assessment. *Maine Law Review, 33,* 237–268.

McEwen, C. A., Rogers, N. H., & Maiman, R. J. (1995). Bring in the lawyers: Challenging the dominant approaches to ensuring fairness in divorce mediation. *Minnesota Law Review, 79,* 1317–1411.

McThenia, A., & Shaffer, T. (1985). For reconciliation. *Yale Law Journal, 94,* 1660–1668.

Menkel-Meadow, C. (1997). Ethics in alternative dispute resolution: New issues, no answers from the adversary conception of lawyers' responsibilities. *South Texas Law Review, 38,* 407–454.

Merry, S. (1994). Albie M. Davis: Community mediation as community organizing. In Deborah Kolb & Associates (Eds.), *When talk works: Profiles of mediators* (pp. 245–277). San Francisco: Jossey-Bass.

Milne, A. (1978). Custody of children in a divorce process: A family self-determination model. *Conciliation Courts Review, 16,* 1–10.

Mitchell v. Iowa Cab Co., 294 N.Y.S.2d 749 (N.Y. App. Div. 1968).

Mnookin, R., & Kornhauser, L. (1979). Bargaining in the shadow of the law: The case of divorce. *Yale Law Journal, 88,* 968–970.

Mo. Ann. Stat. §407.710 (West 1990).

Moberly, R. (1997). Mediator gag rules: Is it ethical for mediators to evaluate or advise? *South Texas Law Review, 38,* 669–678.

Murphy v. Padilla, 49 Cal.Rptr.2d 722 (Cal. Ct. App. 1996).

National Ass'n of Gov't Employees, Inc. v. National Fed'n. of Fed. Employees, 844 F.2d 216 (5th Cir. 1988).

N.C. Gen. Stat. §25A-39 (1999).

Neb. Rev. Stat. §69-1604 (1996).

Neighborhood Justice Centers of Atlanta. (1987). *Training manual for mediators.* Atlanta, GA: Author.

Newton v. Keene Corp., 918 F.2d 1121 (3rd Cir. 1990).

Nolan-Haley, J. (1999). Informed consent in mediation: A guiding principle for truly educated decision making. *Notre Dame Law Review, 74,* 775–840.

N.Y. Pers. Prop. Law §425 (1992).

Odorizzi v. Bloomfield School District, 54 Cal.Rptr. 533, at 539, 540, 542 (Cal. Ct. App. 1966).

Olam v. Congress Mortgage Co., 68 F. Supp.2d 1110, at 1110, 1149 (N.D. Cal. 1999).

Ovidiah v. N.Y. Ass'n for New Americans, Nos. 95 Civ. 10523(SS), 96 Civ. 330(SS), 1997 WL 342411 (S.D.N.Y. June 23, 1997).

Pearson, J., & Thoennes, N. (1989). Divorce mediation: Reflections on a decade of research. In K. Kresselin & D. Pruitt (Eds.), *Mediation research: The process and effectiveness of third-party intervention* (pp. 16–19). San Francisco: Jossey-Bass.

Petracca v. Petracca, 706 So.2d 904, at 910, 912 (Fla. Dist. Ct. App. 1998).

Porter v. Chicago Bd. of Educ., 981 F.Supp. 1129, at 1129 (N.D. Ill. 1997).

Restatement (Second) of Contracts §164, 175, 177 (1981).

Rifkin, J., & Sawyer, J. (1982). Alternative dispute resolution: From a legal services perspective. *NLADA Briefcase, 39,* 20–26.

Riskin, L. (1994). Mediator orientations, strategies and techniques. *Alternatives to High Cost Litigation, 12,* 111–114.

Riskin, L. (1996). Understanding mediators' orientations, strategies, and techniques: A grid for the perplexed., *Harvard Negotiation Law Review, 1,* 7–51.

Rogers, N., & McEwen, C. (1994). *Mediation: Law, policy and practice* (2nd ed.). New York: Clark, Bordman, Callaghan.

Rosenberg, J. (1991). In defense of mediation. *Arizona Law Review, 33,* 467–507.

Rosevear v. Rosevear, 76 Cal.Rptr.2d 691, at 691 (Cal. Ct. App. 1998).

Ryan v. Garcia, 33 Cal.Rptr.2d 158 (Cal. Ct. App. 1994).

Salem, P., & Milne, A. (1995). Making mediation work in a domestic violence case. *Family Advocate, 17,* 34–38.

Shaw, M., Singer, L. R., & Povich, E. A. (1992). *National standards for court-connected mediation programs.* Washington, DC: Center for Dispute Settlement and The Institute of Judicial Administration.

Shonholtz, R. (1984). Neighborhood justice systems: Work, structure, and guiding principles. *Mediation Quarterly, 5,* 22–23.

Society of Professionals in Dispute Resolution. (1991). *Mandated participation and settlement coercion: Dispute resolution as it relates to the courts* (Report No. 1). Washington, DC: Law and Public Policy Committee.

Stark, J. (1996). Preliminary reflections on the establishment of a mediation clinic. *Clinical Law Review, 2,* 457–521.

Stempel, J. (1997). Beyond formalism and false dichotomies: The need for institutionalizing a flexible concept of the mediator's role. *Florida State University Law Review, 24,* 949–984.

Stoelting v. Stoelting, 412 N.W.2d 861, 864 (N.D. 1987).

Tyler, T. (1989). The quality of dispute resolution processes and outcome: Measurement problems and possibilities. *University of Denver Law Review, 66,* 436.

U.C.C.C. §2.501, comment 1 (1968).

U.C.C.C. §2.502(1) (1968).

U.C.C.C. §3.502(1) (1974).

United States v. City of Miami, 614 F.2d 1322, at 1322 (5th Cir. 1980).

Vitakis-Valchine v. Valchine, 793 So.2d 1094, at 1097, 1099 (Fla. Dist. Ct. App. August 22, 2001).

Waldman, E. (1997). Identifying the role of social norms in mediation: A multiple model approach. *Hastings Law Journal, 48,* 730–769.

Watson, L., Jr. (1998, January). Advice and opinions from mediators: A rational analysis. *Florida Dispute Resolution Center: Resolution Report, 13,* 13–15.

Welsh, N. A. (2001). The thinning vision of self-determination in court-connected mediation: The inevitable price of institutionalization? *Harvard Negotiation Law Review, 6,* 1–96.

Wissler, R. L. (1999). *Trapping the data: An assessment of domestic relations mediation in Maine and Ohio courts.* Supreme Court of Ohio, SJI grant No. 95-03C-A-152.

Wolff v. Laverne Inc., 233 N.Y.S.2d 555 (N.Y. App. Div. 1962).

PART VI
Developing the Profession

CHAPTER 20

Research on the Impact
of Family Mediation

CONNIE J. A. BECK
BRUCE D. SALES
ROBERT E. EMERY

This chapter takes the proclaimed benefits of mediation and subjects them to the eyes of the researcher to reveal some of the flaws and shortcomings of the findings. This pragmatic review of the research will help a mediator more fully understand the substantiated benefits of mediation, the impact they can have on the development of the field, and their implications for social policy and practices.

In less than two decades, divorce mediation has grown from a novel idea to a widely implemented alternative for settling divorce and child custody disputes (Elrod & Spector, 1996; Emery, 1994; Hendricks, 1993–1994). The rapid development of mediation has been spurred by broad concerns that the adversarial settlement of divorce disputes, whether through attorney negotiations or litigation, creates problems both for the administration of justice and for the well-being of divorced families, especially children. Adversarial procedures in divorce cases repeatedly have been criticized as expensive, time consuming, and divisive. Divorce mediation has been promoted as a way of increasing efficiency in the dispute resolution process, improving party satisfaction, and raising compliance with divorce agreements (Emery & Wyer, 1987a; Irving & Benjamin, 1995; Kelly, 1996). Divorce mediation also has been described as a way of helping families to negotiate agreements and renegotiate relationships in a more adaptive manner than adversarial procedures (Emery, 1994). In comparison to adversarial settlement,

mediation has been hypothesized to promote individual well-being and preserve family relationships that continue despite the end of the marriage (Emery, 1994). When viewed through the lens of scientific objectivity as opposed
to advocacy based on belief and opinion, this is a long and lofty list of claims.

This chapter views these claims as hypotheses about the benefits of mediation relative to adversarial settlement and objectively evaluates the existing research evidence that supports, or fails to support, the benefits put
forth by mediation advocates. Carefully conducted empirical research is essential to assess the strength of the support for these and other strongly held
convictions about divorce mediation. Indeed, the importance of the relationship between research and practice applies in every field. The challenge of
understanding this relationship in divorce mediation, however, is significant
because it is a relatively new field, with mediation research conducted by
scholars from many different disciplines (e.g., lawyers, psychologists, social
workers, sociologists). In addition, mediation practice is conducted by mediators from many different disciplines (e.g., psychology, social work, counseling, law, and nonprofessional volunteers), in different settings (e.g., private
offices and courts), and under different conditions (e.g., all issues considered, limited issues addressed).

To evaluate the current state of knowledge about family mediation, we
first review the state statutes and local court rules concerning mediation,
looking for basic premises and assumptions underlying these laws and rules.
We then identify and review research that applies to these premises and assumptions, placing ourselves in the position of a "devil's advocate" by seriously questioning the underlying assumptions (Sales, 1983). We identify
many benefits associated with family mediation, not the least of which is that
mediation researchers can be credited with undertaking some of the first rigorous empirical assessments of the *adversarial* settlement of family disputes
as well as of the mediation alternative. Nevertheless, empirical support for
the mediation alternative falls well short of the long list of hypothesized benefits and, as we point out, most research to date is flawed or incomplete in
many respects. In pointing to the limits and weaknesses of the research base,
we hope that our review will stimulate both researchers and practitioners to
continue refining their methods of practice and research designs, and to collaborate in the effort of improving mediation practices and social policies in
the future. Without this collaboration, both research and practice suffer
(Honeyman, McAdoo, & Welsh, 2001a, 2001b).

This chapter is organized around four topics: efficiency of the legal process, client satisfaction with mediation, effects on mental health and family
relationships, and mediation process characteristics. *Efficiency of the legal process* affects both clients and the legal system, because it directly speaks to the
costs incurred by the clients and the state. *Client satisfaction with mediation* is
important because of its presumed effect on compliance with agreements
and the perceived legitimacy of mediation and the legal process. Given the
short- and long-term anger and frustration that can occur for parents and

children of divorce, mediation's effects on *client mental health and subsequent family relationships* are essential to consider. Lastly, *mediation process characteristics* (i.e., clients discussing their concerns fully, having a neutral third person mediate these discussions, and having this discussion occur in a less adversarial forum) are important because they define how mediation should operate and why mediation should facilitate a positive divorce solution without litigation.

EFFICIENCY OF THE LEGAL PROCESS

The efficiency of the legal process is a major concern for the judicial system as well as for the all taxpayers who support the operation of this system. One of the goals of mediation has been to decrease costs for both litigants and the system. These costs include real dollars spent by the legal system and the litigants, time spent by litigants, and emotional costs incurred by litigants. We reserve discussion of the third type of costs to the section on client mental health and subsequent family relationships, because it is a qualitatively different type of cost than dollars and time spent.

Financial Costs

Costs for Litigants

Legal fees for divorces can be very high, particularly for couples with modest incomes (Sales, Beck, & Haan, 1993a, 1993b; Schlissel, 1992); thus, some proponents of mediation have argued for its value by maintaining that mediation reduces the financial burden on litigants. There is research to support this position. Kelly (1990a, 1990b) found that couples mediating their dispute incurred only 50% of the costs of litigating couples. Pearson (1994) also found a substantial financial benefit for mediating couples when the mediation was successful in reaching a settlement. Part of the financial benefit appears to relate to the decreased use of attorneys and consequent savings of attorneys fees (Kelly, 1990b; Pearson & Thoennes, 1982, 1988a). When mediation is unsuccessful in reaching a settlement, these benefits were found to disappear (Pearson, 1994).

Despite the logic of these findings, research also has found no or minimal cost savings for mediating couples (Bahr, 1981; Ellis, 1990; Keilitz, Daley, & Hanson, 1992). What may be occurring in some cases is that couples continue to rely on legal advice during the mediation process, which results in ongoing attorneys fees. In addition, in those jurisdictions where there are no court-sponsored programs, it is possible that clients pay both mediator and attorney fees. Another possible factor compounding the complexity of calculating costs for mediation is that attorneys often use a flat-fee billing procedure for divorce cases. The fact that some clients mediate a portion of their divorce (e.g., custody and visitation) does not greatly reduce the flat fee to be charged by their attorney (Keilitz et al., 1992).

It appears that if there are any cost savings for litigants, they are likely to flow to clients from higher socioeconomic levels who opt for voluntary, fee-for-service, comprehensive mediation to resolve all of their disputed issues (Kelly, 1990b). Complex cases involving substantial disputed property and custodial interests can involve substantial attorney fees, if litigated. In addition, local court rules and state statutes may limit the types of contested issues that can be resolved through the court-sponsored mediation program (e.g., custody/visitation vs. all issues). The result is that clients must use both mediation and litigation to resolve all issues (e.g., financial matters), which increases the cost of fully resolving the dispute.

Costs for the Court System

One assumed benefit of devoting resources to mediation programs is that these programs will save money for the court system in processing divorce cases. Although some researchers have made optimistic projections concerning cost savings to the courts (Bahr, 1981; Doyle & Caron, 1979; McIsaac, 1981; Milne, 1978; Pearson, 1981; Pearson & Thoennes, 1982; Weiss & Collada, 1977), other researchers have not been as optimistic in their projections (Cohen, 1982, cited in Pearson & Thoennes, 1988a; Fix & Harter, 1992; MacCoun, Lind, Hensler, Bryant & Ebener, 1988; Pearson, 1994). The discrepancies in these findings relate to the costs included when calculating the cost projections (Beck & Sales, 2001). By including all costs associated with maintaining a dual system for processing divorces (i.e., court-sponsored mediation and litigation programs), the court expenditures for processing cases on a per case basis is actually likely to increase (Fix & Harter, 1992). This increase in overall court expenditures has also been found for other types of alternative dispute resolution programs (MacCoun et al., 1988; Hensler, Lipson, & Rolph, 1981). In an evaluation of the New Jersey Automobile Arbitration Program, for example, it was found that increases in the use of an arbitration program offset the gains from less use of litigation. The program also did not reduce the length of time to case resolution or produce savings in legal fees (Tyler, 1997). In another evaluation of a court-annexed arbitration program, results indicated that two tradeoffs in costs occurred: (1) the costs were reduced for the clients but increased for the state, and (2) costs were reduced for the counties but increased for the state (Esser, 1989; Hensler et al., 1981). An important question then becomes: Are reduced costs for one player appropriate and/or acceptable "benefits" if these costs then are passed on to another?

Many variables affect costs associated with maintaining mediation programs. For example, *when* the cases are diverted to mediation (e.g., immediately upon receipt of filings, referred at a judge's discretion, or undertaken voluntarily by the parties) has enormous consequences in terms of costs. In addition, jurisdictions differ in whether multiple court hearings prior or subsequent to mediation are required or merely allowed. Obviously, the number of hearings involved can increase the costs to the system (Fix & Harter, 1992). Finally, there appears to be a tradeoff between costs borne by the litigants and those borne by the state in processing divorce cases. For example, clients working with attorneys bear a higher cost burden but may reduce the overall cost for the courts by having fewer pretrial hearings (Beck & Sales, 2001; Esser, 1989).

Costs for High-Conflict Families

One conclusion that is uncontroversial is that the most time-consuming and costly cases for both the litigants and the court system are those divorce cases that include a high degree of conflict (Fix & Harter, 1992; Johnston & Campbell, 1988; Johnston, Campbell, & Tall, 1985; Wingspread Conference Report, 2001). These are cases in which the parents do not trust each other, hold a high degree of anger toward each other, and have mental health and/or substance abuse problems. Often these individuals are willing to continue fighting each other and engage in repetitive litigation. Costs for the court system associated with these cases include increased judicial and court time. Developing methods for handling these cases has always been challenging. Recently, specialized programs that provide immediate assistance to these families have been created in a number of states (Brandt, 2000; Elrod, 2001; Johnston & Roseby, 1997; Johnston, 2000; Kenney & Vigil, 1996; Schepard, 2000). These programs include appointment of a "family court advisor," "special master," or "co-parenting arbitrator" who is available to the family to resolve minor conflicts that arise. These advisors are either mental health professionals or lawyers who have varying degrees of legal and binding decision-making authority. Initial evaluation reports concerning these services are generally encouraging (Mitchell, 1998); however, no studies have empirically evaluated these programs for cost effectiveness, decreases in disputes, benefits to children, increased skills in co-parenting, and quality of parent–child relationships (Johnston, 2000). Whatever the costs might be, the costs associated with providing these additional services must also be considered in the total system expenditures.

Time Costs

The time it takes to resolve divorce disputes through litigation can be significant. Thus, one compelling reason for advocating mediation over litigation is the belief that cases will move faster. And, in fact, several researchers have found this to be true (Emery & Wyer, 1987a; Trost, Braver, & Schoeneman, 1988). The time savings result from (1) the presence of both parties in the same room working toward a solution, (2) both generally inclined toward reaching an agreement, as well as (3) the readier access to mediation appointments versus court dates, which often must be set many months in advance. Mediation is not necessarily faster for all cases, however. Mediation has been shown to be faster only when it successfully produced an agreement (Pearson, 1994). Cases moved the slowest when the parties were unsuccessful in reaching agreement in mediation and then had to resort to litigation to resolve the remaining disputed issues.

This conclusion is probably only partially correct. In a multijurisdictional study (Keilitz et al., 1992), only three of the four sites studied indicated that mediation proceeded faster than litigation. Further analysis was then done by examining solely the mediation category and dividing it into the various types of outcomes (i.e., settled prior to mediating, discontinued mediation before beginning it, reached agreement or partial agreement, or did not reach agreement). This analysis found that for two jurisdictions, cases that reached agreement had faster case-processing times than cases in which no agreement was reached. But in two other jurisdictions, cases that reached agreement had longer case-processing times than cases that did not reach agreement. The researchers concluded that the method of dispute resolution (i.e., mediation vs. litigation) has much less effect on case-processing times than do other confounding social, legal, and economic factors. For example, local court procedural rules determining the point at which cases are referred to mediation have a significant impact on how long a case takes to work its way through the legal process (e.g., whether hearings must be held in court prior to cases being referred to mediation or whether they are referred immediately).

Reducing Initial Court Hearings and Relitigation

Reducing the number of initial hearings and relitigation in divorce cases was a major goal of early mediation programs (Keilitz et al., 1992), and the majority of the research efforts to date have been spent assessing these two issues. Reductions in initial hearings are often measured in terms of settlement rates, and relitigation is often measured in terms of postdivorce returns to court. Some research on these issues is very encouraging (Clement & Schwebel, 1993; Depner, Cannata, & Simon, 1992; Emery, Laumann-Billings, Waldron, Sbarra, & Dillon, 2001; Emery, 1994; Emery, Shaw, & Jackson, 1987; Irving & Benjamin, 1995; Kelly, 1990a, 1990b, 1996; Kelly & Duryee, 1992; Margolin, 1973; Pearson & Thoennes, 1989; Smoron, 1998). The rate of cases settling in mediation ranges from 50 to 85% for both court-sponsored and volunteer programs (Depner et al., 1992; Emery, 1994; Irving & Benjamin, 1995; Kelly & Duryee, 1992; Kelly, 1996; Pearson, 1994). Furthermore, those couples who use mediation to resolve their divorce return to court less often than litigating couples, at least when measured up to 2 years postdivorce (Clement & Schwebel, 1993; Pearson & Thoennes, 1982). Unfortunately, the differences in relitigation rates between mediating and litigating clients disappear after 2 years postdivorce (Kelly, 1990b; Pearson & Thoennes, 1989). In a 9-year follow-up study, for example, Dillon and Emery (1996) found that there were no short- or long-term differences on the number of changes attempted or made on custody, visitation, and support arrangements, or on the forum used to make those changes. Interestingly, in looking at the same cases 12 years postdivorce, Emery and his colleagues found that mediation families made more changes in primary residence over the 12 years, but these were typically made informally and did not utilize court services (Emery et al., 2001). These researchers concluded that this finding indicates either a sign of continued cooperation and flexibility between the parents or instability for the child(ren). Future research will clarify the appropriate conclusion to be drawn from this finding. Although mediation may not be effective in reducing relitigation, research also shows it does not increase it (Pearson, 1994).

Compliance with Court Orders

Mediation involves a cooperative process. It is hoped that giving parents responsibility in making decisions will also lead to increased compliance with the resulting agreements. From the perspective of the client as well as the court system, compliance with court orders is essential (Beck & Sales, 2001).

Clients' compliance with child support agreements is particularly important in that it reduces the economic distress experienced by custodial parents after divorce (Dillon & Emery, 1996). Compliance is also a benefit for the court system because it reduces the costs associated with additional court hearings or other state involvement in these cases (e.g., child support enforcement proceedings associated with Aid for Dependent Children funds, now called Temporary Aid for Needy Families, and "special master" programs for high-conflict cases). Some research modestly supports the notion that mediation enhances compliance with agreements (Bautz & Hill, 1989; Emery, Matthews, & Wyer, 1991; Kelly, 1990b; Pearson & Thoennes, 1985b, 1986), but, unfortunately, these increased rates do not extend over time (Pearson & Thoennes, 1988c). In a study of matched pairs of custodial/noncustodial parents, only 47–66% of noncustodial parents paid all that they owed in child support, and 4–13% paid nothing (Braver, Fitzpatrick, & Bay, 1991). Any short-term benefits of mediation may not extend to long-term compliance, which appears to be controlled by variables outside the methods used to resolve the custody issues (e.g., mediation vs. litigation; Braver et al., 1991; Pearson & Thoennes,1985a). For example, two studies found that compliance with child support orders had less to do with the dispute resolution method than with several other variables: the degree of conflict in the marriage, level of anger with the ex-spouse 2 years postdivorce, the ex-spouses' income prior to the divorce, and the payer's current employment (Kelly, 1990a, 1990b; Braver et al., 1991).

CLIENT SATISFACTION WITH MEDIATION

The research concerning client satisfaction in mediation is voluminous and important to understand in order to evaluate the presumed benefit of mediation in supposedly increasing the satisfaction of divorcing couples with the legal process. Increased satisfaction, in turn, is presumed to increase respect for the legal process, the legal actors, and the outcome of the legal proceeding (e.g., the agreement produced from mediation) and increase the likelihood of compliance with the results.

The reported rates of client satisfaction with mediation vary broadly: 33–90%, when all mediation clients are surveyed (Pearson & Thoennes, 1982; Irving & Benjamin, 1992; Kelly & Gigy, 1989; Kelly, 1989); 60–80%, when only clients who reach agreement are considered; and 30–61% for clients who do not reach agreement (Pearson & Thoennes, 1986; Kressel, Frontera, Florenza, Butler, & Fish, 1994). With one exception (Emery, discussed below), these data are either not compared to litigation control groups or are compared to a single combined litigation control group. Results from these comparison studies show that 30–50% of litigation clients report satisfaction with their experiences (Pearson & Thoennes, 1982, 1989; Kelly, 1989). Because these ranges are so broad, it is important to assess possible reasons for the discrepant findings. A set of research design issues provides a likely explanation.

Comparison Goups

For comparison groups to be meaningful as research design components, it is important to compare like groups. For example, if we compared a combined mediation group with a combined litigation group, the results would differ dramatically from a comparison using a mediation group composed of only those clients who reached an agreement. This point is particularly important when evaluating how clients respond to mediation, because clients who reach agreement are fundamentally different from those who do not. For example, many of the positive claims associated with mediation (e.g., compliance rates are higher, satisfaction rates are higher) only apply to those who reach agreement (Pearson & Thoennes, 1984a, 1984b).

A similar compelling logic argues for dividing the litigation group (Beck & Sales, 2001; Kressel, 1985; Levy, 1984). For example, researchers have noted that a combined litigation group includes a diverse collection of cases, ranging from those cases where an agreement was reached in negotiations between lawyers prior to any hearings to those that needed custody evaluations and full hearings with complete judicial determinations (Kressel, 1985; Levy, 1984; Pearson & Thoennes, 1984a, 1984b). Given this variation, a fairer comparison would be, for example, to compare mediator-negotiated agreements to lawyer-negotiated agreements, wherein no hearings or custody evaluations were needed, or, as Emery and Wyer (1987a) have done, to *not* divide up either group. In these comparisons, clients randomly assigned to mediation have, on average, reported greater satisfaction than those who proceeded with adversarial settlement in areas reflecting the process and outcome of dispute settlement and the effects on self, children, and relationship with the former spouse. Two qualifications on these findings are noteworthy: (1) Satisfaction with both mediation and adversarial settlement declined over time (but differences between the groups were still found 12 years after dispute settlement), and (2), as discussed shortly, men reaped more of the benefit in added satisfaction in comparison to women (Emery, 1994, Emery et al., 2001).

Finally, it is critical to identify all of the dimensions along which mediation and litigation cases might vary so that comparison groups are appropriate. Stated another way, it is important to compare groups possessing similar characteristics (Beck & Sales, 2001; Kressel, 1985; Levy, 1984). For example, cases likely vary along an "adversarialness" continuum (Pearson & Thoennes, 1984a, 1984b). If this mediation continuum could be operationalized and measured in mediation and litigation, it would then allow for mediation and litigation groups to be compared using like cases along the continuum.

Meaning of Satisfaction and Dissatisfaction

Once the need for appropriate comparison groups is addressed, it is important to unpack the term *satisfaction/dissatisfaction* as it is used in the mediation literature. Client satisfaction/dissatisfaction in mediation research has addressed numerous specific targets (e.g., clients' satisfaction or dissatisfaction with the mediator, the process, the outcome, their experience generally), not all of which directly measure all meanings of satisfaction or dissatisfaction. Unfortunately, mediation researchers have combined this plethora of targets under the general heading of *satisfaction* when analyzing the data (Pearson & Thoennes, 1984b, 1986; Keilitz et al., 1992). Recommendations to others to use mediation, for example, may indicate less about satisfaction or dissatisfaction with the process than the perceived ability to get more of what is wanted in this process. Furthermore, measures of satisfaction or dissatisfaction do not tell us if the remaining respondents were satisfied/dissatisfied or neutral about their experience, and with what aspect of that experience in particular. For example, those who litigate their divorces are not necessarily dissatisfied with the entire court process (Dingwall & Eekelaar, 1988; Pearson & Thoennes, 1988a, 1989), but they are very dissatisfied with court hearings, in particular, and for several reasons: The hearings expose private issues in a public forum, "criminal" overtones permeate the context, the court hearings are totally impersonal in nature, and the legal actors in the system hold too much control (Pearson & Thoennes, 1988a, 1989).

Assessments of satisfaction/dissatisfaction must also control for/account for other variables. Since mediation clients engaged in disputes over issues other than custody and visitation also need to use the litigation system (Kelly, 1991; Kressel; 1985; Pearson & Thoennes, 1985b), a reasonable question is whether clients are able to separate their experiences to a point that the experience in one system does not cloud the experience in the other. This issue has not been explored empirically (Kelly, 1991). In addition, the type of mediation program (court annexed or private fee-for-service), client characteristics (e.g., demographics, anger between clients), and the issues being addressed (e.g., custody/visitation vs. all issues) also warrant consideration, if the data are to be meaningfully interpreted.

Gender Differences

Gender differences in satisfaction have been noted in several studies. For example, one research group found that fathers were much more satisfied with mediation than with litigation whereas mothers were equally satisfied with both (Emery et al., 2001). In another study, the relative importance of the process (litigation or mediation) versus outcome (terms of settlement reached) for determining satisfaction also differed depending on the disputant's gender (Kitzmann & Emery, 1993). For fathers, the fairness of the procedure was more important to overall satisfaction, whereas for mothers, obtaining the desired outcome was more important. Consistent with the analogous literature on procedural justice (Lind & Tyler, 1988), Kitzmann and Emery argued that the importance of participating in a fair process was very important to the fathers in their study given that the outcome generally favored the mothers. That is, if you win, it does not matter how you win. However, if you lose, it is important to your satisfaction that you see the dispute resolution process as being fair.

Women and men who mediated and litigated were also asked if they "won what they wanted." For women and men who mediated, the responses were similar (Emery, 1994). For women and men who litigated, however, the responses were quite different. Women reported that they won "quite a bit" versus men who reported they won "a little" (Emery, 1994). When women who mediated were compared to women who litigated their dispute, women who litigated reported winning "quite a bit" whereas women who mediated reported winning only "somewhat." This difference is understandable in that mediation focuses on "win/win" solutions that demand compromise (Emery, 1994; Kitzmann & Emery, 1993). These researchers also pointed out that the biggest differences in satisfaction rates were not between men and women but between mens' rating of mediation versus mens' ratings of litigation (Emery & Wyer, 1987b; Pearson, 1994). Men in this study were extremely dissatisfied with litigation as a method of dispute resolution, most likely because mothers typically won physical custody of their children.

A second research group found similar satisfaction rates for men and women concerning the division of property, child support, and willingness to recommend mediation (Pearson & Thoennes, 1988a, 1989). These researchers also assessed variables concerning the experience of mediation. Women reported both more positive and negative responses to mediation than did men. For example, women reported that mediation helped them better understand their spouse's point of view, focused attention on the children, kept discussions on track, identified problems, and helped them better understand their own feelings. Women also reported feeling pressured into an agreement by the ex-spouse, never feeling comfortable expressing their feelings, being tense and angry during the sessions, and feeling that the mediator directed the terms of the agreement (Pearson & Thoennes, 1988a, 1989; but see Kelly & Duryee, 1992).

A third research group found that there were gender differences in satisfaction rates concerning the outcome of mediation similar to that found in the Emery study noted above (Kelly & Duryee, 1992). Whereas 43% of the men reportedly were dissatisfied with the outcome, only 17% of the women reported being dissatisfied (Kelly & Duryee, 1992). Both research groups (Emery's and Kelly's) have speculated about the reasons regarding the gender differences in satisfaction with outcome of custody disputes. Although Emery's research was conducted in Virginia, where there is a cultural and judicial preference for mother custodians, and Kelly's research was conducted against a backdrop of "gender neutrality" in California, the reality is that in both studies, results indicated a clear preference for mother custody, regardless of cultural backdrops and legal custody standards.

Passage of Time

Immediately after divorce and during the first year postdivorce, rates of satisfaction with mediation are high (70–90% for those who reached agreement, and 50–82% for those who did not reach agreement but were glad they tried the process) (Cauble, Thoennes, Pearson, & Appleford, 1985; Lyon, Thoennes, Pearson, & Appleford, 1985; Little, Thoennes, Pearson, & Appleford, 1985; Pearson & Thoennes, 1986). In terms of dissatisfaction, Little et al. (1985) reported that only 20% of the clients not reaching agreement reported that they regretted trying mediation. Satisfaction rates dropped dramatically during the ensuing years. Five years postdivorce, approximately 65% of those clients who reached agreement in mediation remained satisfied, whereas only 40% of those who did not reach agreement were still satisfied. The complex nature of postdivorce parenting and relationships may cloud the initial good feelings parents had concerning the dispute resolution method they chose to resolve their divorce (Pearson & Thoennes, 1986).

In a 12-year follow-up study, satisfaction rates reported by both men and women declined over time but did so for both mediation and litigation groups (Emery et al., 2001). Men who mediated remained more satisfied than men who litigated 12 years earlier. Women remained significantly more satisfied with the outcome of dispute resolution and its impact on the co-parental relationship and the children.

Number of Sessions

An important finding is that programs that severely limit the number of sessions (i.e., one or two) do not produce satisfied customers who fully understand the issues involved (Pearson, 1993, 1994). For example, research conducted in Delaware found that when mediation was limited to one 45-minute session, structured to calculate child support payments based on legal guidelines, the clients were not particularly satisfied. Over half of the clients (56%) stated that mediation was not better than a hearing with a judge (Pearson, 1994). Trying to save time or money with mediation may come at a high cost to client satisfaction.

Compliance and the Validity of Self-Reports

As noted earlier, understanding the causes of compliance is a complex undertaking that includes variables beyond litigant satisfaction with the process and outcome (e.g., degree of conflict in the marriage, level of anger 2 years postdivorce, ex-spouse income before divorce, and payor's current employment status). Thus, not surprisingly, satisfaction, although important, has not been found necessarily to correlate with positive outcomes concerning compliance with court orders. This result has been reported in a number of studies wherein social science researchers asked parents about satisfaction levels with a program provided and then also evaluated more objective measures (Kidder, Judd, & Smith, 1986; Gutek, 1978). These researchers concluded that although research subjects do report high satisfaction ratings on programs, what they are basically telling researchers is that they appreciate the researchers' good intentions, the special attention, and the investment of resources. Gutek (1978) concluded that both subjective and objective ratings of satisfaction are important but must be considered separately. In addition, overall satisfaction should not be confused with an objective evaluation of the quality of services provided (Kressel, Pruitt, & Associates, 1989).

EFFECTS ON MENTAL HEALTH AND FAMILY RELATIONSHIPS

Divorce is an emotionally difficult process that affects both parents and children. A presumed benefit of mediation, compared to litigation, is that it leads to reduced adversarialness and parental conflict. Not surprisingly, many clients would prefer mediation if they could be promised these results.

One major contributor to adversarialness is argued to be the presentation of competing positions by lawyers as they attempt to resolve family disputes (Coogler, 1978; Ellis, 1990; Emery et al., 1987; Gerber, 1990; Marlow & Sauber, 1990; Mnookin, 1975; Rich, 1980; Schlissel, 1992), which is then said to create lasting psychological distress (Bloom, Asher & White, 1978). It seems reasonable that a mediation process, focused on cooperation as opposed to competition, would lessen these negative effects (Coogler, 1978; Ellis, 1990; Emery et al., 1987; Gerber, 1990; Kelly, 1991, 1996; Marlow & Sauber, 1990; Mnookin, 1975; Pearson & Thoennes, 1985b, 1989; Rich, 1980; Schlissel, 1992).

Sources of Adversarialness

Adversarialness or acrimony is discussed in the mediation literature in relation to three litigation processes: (1) parents negotiating through intermediaries; (2) the presentation of competing positions through which "justice" is supposed to emerge; and (3) solutions defined by lawyers based on individual "rights."

Parents in litigation are required to negotiate through their lawyers, which reduces direct communication between the parents. The result can be increased distrust of the other spouse and an inability to work through that distrust. There is some research that addresses this point. A long tradition in social psychological research indicates that a message passed through several sources has a tendency to be altered (Allport & Postman, 1975). Interestingly, in the mediation literature, there is little research that addresses whether and how this process occurs in litigation, and if it does, what are the indicators that it has a negative impact on parents and/or their children. One logical source to investigate would be the attorneys' choice of negotiation strategies (Mnookin, 1993). There is some support for the notion that argumentative and hostile negotiation strategies might lead to increased acrimony between the clients. However, divorce lawyers reported that obnoxious and argumentative strategies are easier to use in telephone conversations with opposing counsel or in documents than when they are in face-to-face meetings with the clients present (McEwen, Rogers, & Maiman, 1995). In addition, there is no empirical support for the notion that most or all divorce lawyers conduct business in this way and are thus responsible for the trademark acrimony between divorcing parents. Indeed, the few qualitative studies available of lawyer conduct indicate the opposite. Obnoxious, argumentative strategies are used only in the minority of cases (Felstiner & Sarat, 1992; Griffiths, 1986; McEwen et al., 1995; Sarat & Felstiner, 1986, 1989, 1995). The professional norm is that of a "reasonable lawyer" who seeks to reach a divorce settlement by avoiding inflation of client demands, informing clients of the risks and likely outcomes of unrealistic demands, limiting expectations, overcoming resistence of angry clients, while asserting clients' interests and responding to new information (Levy, 1984; McEwen et al., 1995; Sarat & Felstiner, 1986). Thus, the notion that negotiating through intermediaries causes increased acrimony, although intuitively appealing, is not well supported by empirical findings.

Litigation is premised on the adversarial approach to dispute resolution, which includes the presentation of competing facts and arguments. This method of dispute resolution is assumed to increase the distance between the spouses and the acrimony between them. Again, there is little empirical or qualitative research to support this notion. For example, there is little research outlining specifically (1) how this process occurs in litigation, (2) how many families are affected by this problem, (3) what specific variables indicate its causal and negative impact on parents and/or their children, and (4) the number and/or percent of lawyers that focuses on presenting competing positions and refuses to settle amicably for what is fair (Beck & Sales, 2001). Again, the qualitative research that exists has actually shown the opposite. Both nationally (Bryan, 1994; Felstiner & Sarat, 1992; Mather, McEwen, & Maiman, 2001; McEwen et al., 1995; Sarat & Felstiner, 1986, 1989, 1995) and internationally (Griffiths, 1986), the objective of most divorce lawyers is a "reasonable divorce." This information is critical in assessing the viability of the commonly held notion that the presentation of competing positions necessarily and causally increases acrimony in a divorcing couple's relationship.

Finally, lawyers as representatives of each parent are typically seen as ending up defining the goals for the divorce or redefining the initial position of each spouse. Once again, the argument is that the spouses move further apart psychologically and come to believe that the other spouse is becoming more adversarial, uncaring, hostile, and selfish—which, in turn, creates more adversarial behavior. The research that addresses this point indicates that the negotiations between clients and lawyers are complex and control over decision making is not always easy to predict at any given time (Felstiner & Sarat, 1992; Levy, 1984). These researchers argue that the client and attorney must work together to negotiate a settlement. While attorneys have expertise in defining legal entitlements, clients have expertise in determining the ex-spouse's reactions to the various proposals that are available (Felstiner & Sarat, 1992). In addition, lawyers with clients of similar social status are less able to control the negotiations and are more likely to take orders from the clients than are lawyers with clients from a lower social status who are also emotionally distraught and unable to make considered decisions about their future (Felstiner & Sarat, 1992). Yet, even in the latter situation, lawyers must act as counselors, helping their clients to "cool off" emotionally so that they are less angry at their spouse and thus present less polarized positions (McEwen et al., 1995; Mather et al., 2001). Lawyers use a variety of strategies (e.g., "yes . . . but"; procrastination) to slow the process until angry clients can reach more "reasoned" decisions regarding demands.

Lawyers also typically look to the clients' goals for defining the shape and structure of their legal representation (McEwen et al., 1995; Mather et al., 2001). In comparing this research to that of mediators, even when mediation is provided by mental health professionals, it can be perceived as tension filled and adversarial (Pearson & Thoennes, 1985a, 1986, 1988b, 1989). Mediators in both mandatory and voluntary programs are encouraged to, and do, develop active, directive strategies to control both the process of mediation as well as many of the terms reached in these agreements (Cobb, 1993, 1994; Cobb & Rifkin, 1991a, 1991b; Dingwall & Greatbatch, 1991; Greatbatch & Dingwall, 1989; Kressel et al., 1994; Rifkin, Millen, & Cobb, 1991; Pearson & Thoennes, 1988b, 1989; Silbey, 1993). The result is that it is unclear in which process, litigation or mediation, clients are actually given more responsibility in making decisions.

Effect of Adversarialness on Disputants

Competition regarding who can best meet the needs of the children and the need to establish how big of a share of the marital assets each deserves are believed to foster negative emotions such as anger, depression, frustration, and worry. Thus, the emotional reactions of parents may be determined by individual psychological functioning (e.g., anger, depression, frustration, worry), couple interactions (e.g., the initial level of conflict between divorcing parents), and the legal processes used in obtaining the divorce.

Individual Psychological Functioning

Resolution of emotional problems associated with divorce is a long process that extends well beyond the legal resolution of divorce-related issues (Emery, 1994). Pearson and Thoennes (1985b) found that even among couples who reached an agreement in mediation, one-third of the parents still maintained that they had made little or no progress in their divorce. Dillon and Emery (1996) also found that 9 years postdivorce, parents reported continued problems associated with parenting and emotional issues. Whether a couple uses mediation or litigation to resolve a divorce dispute, divorce continues to have an impact on parents and children for many years (Dillon & Emery, 1996; Laumann-Billings & Emery, 2000).

The emotions associated with the divorce process include anger, depression, frustration, worry, and continued attachment to the former spouse. Anger is a well-documented variable in the research literature. Kelly and her colleagues (Kelly, Gigy, & Hausman, 1988) found that a majority (nearly 60%) of the clients in their study reported moderate to extreme anger at their spouse. Breaking down the category, 28% reported high/extreme anger, 30% reported moderate levels of anger, and 40% reported mild to no anger. Those clients reporting high levels of anger also reported that they perceived their spouse as also very angry. Not surprisingly, anger was highly correlated with other negative outcomes (e.g., stress, uncooperativeness, conflict, tension). However, anger may be both a liability and an asset for divorcing couples. Emery (1990, 1994) theorized that anger assists people in creating emotional distance and decreasing the chance of depression caused by the breakup of a relationship and the dreams associated with it. Emery (1990) suggested that the key may be to feel anger but behave cooperatively. Unfortunately, there is little research support for the notion that mediation has any ability to alter the anger couples direct at one another (Dillon & Emery, 1996). There is also little research support that mediation directly and positively changes any of the other individual-level variables noted above (depression, frustration, worry, and continued attachment to the former spouse) (Emery et al., 2001; Emery, 1994; Emery & Wyer, 1987a; Kelly, 1990b; Kelly et al., 1988; Kitzmann & Emery, 1994).

Why is it, then, that mediators recognize intense and difficult emotions in the couples they are seeing whereas mediation researchers find little evidence of these in their studies? One possibility is that the measures used to detect these various emotions are traditional measures of psychopathology, designed for psychiatric populations, not for relatively normal individuals experiencing a particularly difficult period. It may be that although mediation does not significantly impact full-blown clinical disorders, it can positively impact strong emotions that are painful and uncomfortable. In a recent study designed to measure painful memories concerning parents' divorce, Laumann-Billings and Emery (2000) found that although the young adults of divorced parents did not significantly differ from those of married parents on clinical measures of depression and anxiety, there were significant differences between the groups on measures of painful memories associated with their childhoods (e.g., childhoods were harder, wanted more time with their father, wondered if their father loved them). It may well be that similar instruments could be constructed to measure the strong emotions of divorcing parents and their children, as distinct from mental disorders, so that the effect of mediation on emotions and mental health could be fully studied.

Couple Interactions

Clearly, divorcing couples come to the divorce process with individual emotional problems. Research also suggests that they arrive with a well-entrenched pattern of relating, including established strategies for resolving (or not resolving) conflict. These patterns of relating have been identified and documented (Akister, 1993; Fitzpatrick, 1988; Fisher, 1995; Fowers, 1996; Gottman, 1993; Lavee, 1993). Researchers have also identified parenting relationship patterns that exist after divorce (Ahrons, 1995; Ahrons & Rodgers, 1987; Maccoby, Buchanan, Mnookin, & Dornbush, 1993). Each type of couple identified in these various typologies is defined by the manner in which emotion is expressed, the levels of conflict existing in the relationships, and the strategies used by the couple to resolve (or not resolve) conflict. The typologies of couple relationship patterns in marriage, not surprisingly, are very similar to the parenting typologies found postdivorce.

In better understanding the range of possible couple relationship patterns of the clients entering mediation, Gottman's (1993) findings regarding marital couple types are informative. Gottman asked subjects to come to his laboratory and discuss an ongoing problem area in their relationship for 15 minutes. He then tape-recorded the conversation, coded the recorded interactions between the couple, and analyzed the data. From these data he arrived at five couple types. "Validating" couples express emotion easily and calmly. There is a sense that they are working together, even though each is contentious in supporting his or her position on the issue under discussion. "Volatile" couples express a high level of both positive and negative emotion. Each person attempts to persuade without really listening to the other, and a premium is placed on arguing. "Avoider" couples express little emotion, either positive or negative. They emphasize common ground as opposed to differences and do not use specific strategies to resolve conflict. Instead, these couples rely on the passage of time to resolve issues. "Hostile" couples frequently express negative emotion and engage in a good deal of direct conflict. Blaming, defensiveness, verbal contempt, and disgust are common strategies used to resolve conflict. "Hostile/detached" couples do not express either positive or negative emotions and are not involved listeners. They experience periods of attack and defensiveness but, in general, are not involved with each other. In addition, Gottman (1993) found that three of the relationship types tended to be relatively stable over time, and the couples tended to stay married (i.e., "validating," "volatile," and "avoider") whereas the remaining two couple types tended to be relatively unstable and divorce often (i.e., "hostile" and "hostile/detached"). Thus, mediators are likely to face a range of interaction patterns, and the last two types are likely to be most represented in the divorcing population.

Ahrons and Rodgers (1987; Ahrons, 1995) identified five divorced-couple interaction patterns. It is interesting to note that the divorced couple patterns correspond well to Gottman's marital couple interaction patterns. For example, Ahrons and Rodgers also identified five typologies. "Perfect pals" continue to be friends, discuss personal as well as parenting issues, spend holidays together with friends and family, and share decision making and parenting. "Cooperative colleagues" are much like "perfect pals" but do not remain close personal friends or continue to see their in-laws. These two types of couples correspond to Gottman's "validating" couple type. "Angry associates" remain angry and bitter and continue to wage long legal battles over financial matters, custody, and visitation. Anger remains a strong motivator for remaining connected. They are able to parent, but the children often get caught in the parent's relationship struggles. "Fiery foes" are much like "angry associates" but are unable to respect each other as parents and undermine each other's parenting efforts. Visitation with the nonresidential parents generally declines, and divorces are marked by continuing litigation. Gottman's "volitle" or "hostile" couple types correspond well to Ahrons and Rodger's "angry associates" and "fiery foes," in that the couples are driven by anger to a large extent. "Dissolved duos" sever contact, and one parent generally leaves the geographical area. Although the parent who leaves may reappear, usually they do not do so for several years. This couple type is much like Gottman's "hostile/detatched" typology. It is hypothesized that most couples likely continue the same or a similar pattern of interaction developed during the marriage during their divorce (Beck & Sales, 2001) and thereafter.

It may be that the couple relationship and parenting patterns interact with the legal procedure used to divorce (Beck & Sales, 2001). There is research support for the notion that the more cooperative couples (e.g., Gottman's "validating" or Ahrons's "perfect pals" or "cooperative colleagues") are able to benefit from a private, informal, cooperative process (Kressel, Jaffee, Tuchman, Watson, & Deutsch, 1980). The more conflict-ridden couples with enmeshed relationships (e.g., Gottman's "volitile," "hostile," or "hostile/detached" and Ahrons's "angry associates" or "fiery foes") do not do as well in traditional mediation (Kressel et al., 1980). These parties remain bitter, dissatisfied with the settlement, and the conflict tends to continue postdivorce with postmediation lawsuits (Kressel et al., 1980; see also Bickerdike, 1998). Additionally, the majority of research evaluating court-sponsored mediation programs indicates that traditional mediation has an extremely limited ability to alter basic relationship patterns existing in couples (Emery & Wyer, 1987b; Johnston et al., 1985; Irving & Benjamin, 1995; Keilitz et al., 1992; Pearson & Thoennes, 1985a).

There are, however, several studies that reported findings concerning improvement in ex-spousal relationships (Irving & Benjamin, 1995; Kelly, 1990b, 1991; Pearson, 1994). An important distinction of these studies is that they evaluated private, voluntary, fee-for-service programs that address all issues, offer many sessions, and when needed to accomplish a settlement, provide referrals to psychotherapy. The clientele and the services in these private programs are very different from court-sponsored programs. First, the clients who attend these programs tend to be better educated and of higher socioeconomic status than the vast majority of clients who are referred to court-sponsored programs in states where they are mandated to attend (Emery & Wyer, 1987a; Irving & Benjamin, 1995; Kelly, 1990b). The clients of the private services also tend to be more cooperative generally (Emery & Jackson, 1989; Irving & Benjamin, 1995). And at least one set of researchers, who reported positive effects of mediation on couple interaction, used a therapeutic mode of mediation that includes a long period of as-

sessment, referral of clients who do not appear "ready" to proceed in mediation to therapy sessions to resolve emotional issues, and specifically
addresses conflict between the couple (Irving & Benjamin, 1995). These
findings are therefore difficult to generalize to a larger population of court-
referred clients. Additionally, positive changes found immediately
postmediation do not remain over time. Both Pearson (1994) and Kelly
(1990b, 1991, 1996) reported that in follow-up assessments 2 to 5 years
postmediation, there were no differences between the mediation and litigation groups on positive changes in the clients' relationships reportedly due to
participating in mediation. Emery and his colleagues found similar results in
a 12-year follow-up study (Emery et al., 2001). At 12 years postdivorce, these
researchers found that there were no significant differences between parent-
reported problems associated with co-parenting between those who litigated
versus mediated their divorces. The encouraging news from this study is that
those nonresidential parents who mediated their divorces remained more
involved with their children without increased levels of conflict (Emery et al.,
2001).

Legal Process Used to Divorce

The inherent competitiveness of litigation is believed to increase conflict
between divorcing parents (Johnston & Campbeli, 1988; Saposnek, 1983),
and this conflict is reported likely to continue after the divorce (Emery,
Matthews, & Kitzmann, 1991), because litigation is argued to promote hostile negotiations concerning the major issues to be resolved (e.g., custody,
visitation, property, and division of assets; Maccoby et al., 1993; Somary &
Emery, 1991). Alternatively, mediation is seen as a consensus-building process that thus has a less detrimental impact on parents' psychological well-
being by encouraging cooperation in meeting the needs of the family
jointly (Dillon & Emery, 1996; Emery & Wyer, 1987b; Kitzmann & Emery,
1994).

Why is it, then, that studies rarely find positive changes in basic couple
communication patterns and psychological functioning in mediation cases?
The answer might lie in the fact that mediation is a time-limited, goal-oriented
intervention for developing custody and visitation agreements (Pearson &
Thoennes, 1988b). It was not designed to assess and provide family-therapy-
oriented interventions for the underlying psychological problems of families
(Pearson & Thoennes, 1985b, 1988a, 1989). Even when such interventions are
assessed, the changes that might be seen to accrue from such assessment are
few and far between: Research has shown that changing basic underlying couple interaction patterns is very difficult to do (Jacobson & Addis, 1993; Johnson & Lebow, 2000). Even under very good conditions (e.g., willing participants for as many sessions as required), the family therapy models tested leave
many couples unimproved or still distressed (e.g., 60–65% of couples some-

what distressed or unchanged by treatment; Jacobson & Addis, 1993; Johnson & Lebow, 2000). Follow-up studies report a troublesome trend that treatment gains are not maintained over time (Gottman, 1994; Johnson & Lebow, 2000). Without continued effort to maintain change in a relationship, couples are easily drawn back into familiar and negative interaction patterns. In the case of divorcing couples, there is less motivation to work together on maintaining change (Beck & Sales, 2001). Thus, those mediation programs that are likely to create changes in couple relationship patterns are those that (1) use a therapeutic model of mediation that focuses on conflict between the spouses, (2) allow as many sessions as needed to accomplish the desired changes, and (3) require follow-up telephone calls to clients by the mediator and/or follow-up "booster" sessions with the mediator to resolve any problems that arise in the first several months after divorce (Beck & Sales, 2001; Felstiner & Williams, 1980; Kitzmann & Emery, 1994). Ongoing support for families postmediation is also a critical component to continued amicable negotiations of contentious issues that arise in the normal course of life (e.g., child support, visitation, education, religion, role of new partners, developmental issues; Felstiner & Williams, 1980; Pearson & Thoennes, 1989).

Next, we turn our attention to the effects of the dispute resolution process on the amount of time nonresidential parents willingly spend with their children. Because many courts are very reluctant to force unmotivated parents to visit their children or unwilling children to visit their parents, we see visitation as more related to family relationships than to compliance with formal court orders. A potential benefit of mediation would be a reduction in the number of emotional barriers experienced by nonresidential parents, so that they would be more willing to visit their children. In one study, Kelly (1990b) found a significant difference in the rates of compliance with visitation at the initial point of divorce, with the adversarial group complying 70% of the time, whereas the mediating group complied 88% of the time. Unfortunately, Kelly did not provide figures for compliance with visitation agreements when she again collected data from these subjects 2 years postdivorce. Emery and his colleagues corrected for this problem. In a follow-up study of their mediating and litigating clients 12 years postdivorce, they found that nonresidential parents who used mediation saw their children significantly more often and had more frequent telephone contact than did the nonresidential parents in the litigation group (Emery et al., 2001).

MEDIATION PROCESS CHARACTERISTICS

To conclude our review of the empirical research comparing mediation and litigation, we now turn to assessing some of the core assumptions underlying mediation. In this section we carefully examine the characteristics that have been proposed as unique to mediation and assess whether these characteristics operate in practice as they are assumed or intended. In other words, we compare general mediation practice to the proposed ideal mediation practice. Rather than comparing mediation directly to litigation via the findings of empirical studies, as we did in the previous sections, in this final section we compare mediation practice to the ideal mediation practice and assess the relevant literature that bears on the questions posed.

Mediation process characteristics in the ideal mediation practice include (1) full discussion of issues by both parties, (2) the presence of a neutral mediator, and (3) the experience of reduced adversarialness in the dispute resolution process. These components have been assumed to be important sources of the success of mediation programs. This section discusses the first two process characteristics. We do not reconsider the assumed characteristic of reduced adversarialness for mediation, because we considered this topic in our prior discussion of the effects on mental health and family relationships and sources of adversarialness. As that section concluded, although rhetoric asserting a prevailing adversarialness in litigation is persuasive, research findings do not present a clear picture of which process, litigation or mediation, is more adversarial or the specific variables and processes that cause the adversarialness.

Airing Concerns

Being able to thoroughly discuss issues ideally should increase both disputants' perceptions that their story is being fully heard, which, in turn, should increase the chances for a successful long-term outcome. Pearson and Thoennes (1985b, 1986), for example, reported that for 70–80% of those studied, airing concerns was a high priority for them. Nevertheless, there are reasons to question whether these goals are being achieved for all couples in mediation. For example, some parents report feeling rushed during mediation, both because of the unique characteristics of the mediation program and because of the limited number of sessions allowed during their mediation (Pearson, 1993).

Less obvious factors also militate against the possibility of disputants in mediation airing their concerns fully. For example, couple-level and individual-level variables have been shown to negatively affect the airing of concerns in mediation, with airing concerns reported as contraindicated for families with certain dynamics. The clearest of these are those cases described as "Culture of Battering" relationships (Fischer, Vidmar, & Ellis, 1993), in which one partner is physically abusing the other and where the pattern of abuse (e.g., emotional and physical) is such that the abusing partner dominates and controls the other when present, leaving the abused spouse feeling socially isolated, depressed, and incapable of standing up for self-interests. In addition, these relationships are characterized by the party's denial that abuse has been occurring, or a minimization of it when it is recognized. In such situations, bringing the spouses into forced contact opens the opportunity for the abusing spouse to reinitiate the pattern of emotional control, which negates the possibility of a genuine airing of concerns and provides another opportunity for continued control or emotional violence (Alaska Judicial Council, 1992; Fischer et al., 1993; Newmark, Harrell, & Salem, 1995; Pearson, 1991, 1993).

In recent years, the pressing issues domestic violence presents have been taken seriously by mediators, who have produced a proliferation of information in response. Despite the conflicting or apparently counterproductive attributes of mediation as a container for domestic violence issues, a significant number of such cases ends up in mediation. A survey of 200 mediation programs nationwide was conducted by Thoennes, Salem, and Pearson (1995). Estimates of the percentage of cases in mediation that contains some level of domestic violence ranged from 50–80% (Pearson, 1997). No programs surveyed estimated the incidence at less than 50%. An earlier study found that 68% of the couples that requested mediation were experiencing, or had experienced, domestic violence and were then, by statute, excluded from mediating their disputes (Alaska Judicial Council, 1992). We also know that approximately 80% of mediation programs report screening for domestic violence, but unfortunately only about 50% use separate, private interviews, the preferred method for obtaining accurate information (Pearson, 1997). The research also indicates that 20% of the programs surveyed do not use any screening measures to detect domestic violence behaviors, 30% state that the mediation staff receive no training in assessment of domestic violence, and 30% report they do not use special mediation techniques (e.g., shuttle mediation and comediation) to ensure the safety and fairness of the process (Thoennes et al., 1995; Pearson, 1997).

Fortunately, large court-annexed mediation programs (where the vast majority of mandatory mediation occurs) have the highest percentages of mediators receiving specialized training in assessing domestic violence, and nearly all use special techniques to promote safety and fairness in the negotiation process (Thoennes et al., 1995). These techniques include the use of separate waiting rooms; separate mediation rooms, with mediators shuttling between rooms; security guards; escort services to parking structures; in-person, private screening and male–female comediation teams; victim advocates allowed in sessions; termination by the mediator if sessions lead to unsafe agreements; and referrals to shelters and counseling programs (Thoennes et al., 1995; Pearson, 1997). Innovative programs that address couples who have violent components in their relationships are also being developed. Many of these programs address important safety issues immediately and directly, and develop agreements and/or temporary court orders specifying measures that will be taken, if needed, to protect the safety of women and their children while the divorce is pending (Pearson, 1997). These measures are encouraging, and evaluating their effectiveness is critical (Thoennes et al., 1995).

Much of the vociferous debate concerning whether women are better or worse off by virtue of mediating issues continues without the benefit of any hard data. For example, there is little empirical research exploring and documenting the specific behaviors that occur in relationships referred/mandated to mediation. In addition, no research has documented the frequency of violent behaviors over the course of the relationships referred to mediation, these couples' interaction patterns, or the mediation outcomes that relate to different behavior patterns in these cases. Until these variables are understood and the additional safety measures noted above are evaluated, it is difficult to state with assurance that women and children are more protected in mediation than in litigation. However, given the high rates of self-representation occurring in these cases and the serious lack of state-sponsored legal representation for these women and children, the same criticisms are true concerning litigation (Pearson, 1997; Sales et al., 1993a). Financially strapped victims of domestic violence have few options that ensure their protection when they decide to divorce their abusers.

The problems domestic violence presents to professionals are not unique to mediators. The underreporting of domestic violence in couple therapy is noted as a major finding in the psychotherapy research literature that has emerged in the last decade (Johnson & Lebow, 2000). Many psychotherapists also have substantial problems identifying the presence of abuse even after detailed pretreatment assessments (Aldarondo & Straus, 1994; O'Leary, Vivian, & Malone, 1991). Solving the problem for mediators is not simple because there are no clinical criteria available to determine what level of violence precludes the usefulness of mediation with these couples. Couple therapy researchers also assert that designing well-defined assessment procedures and specific treatment strategies for the levels of violence found in these relationships are major challenges of the new century (Bograd & Mederos, 1999; Johnson & Lebow, 2000). One line of research that might be very helpful in developing these criteria is the research that identifies patterns of violent behavior and distinguishes between those patterns that are more amenable to psychotherapy treatment and those patterns that are particularly lethal to the victims (Aldarondo & Straus, 1994; Berns, Jacobson, & Gottman, 1999; Holtzworth-Munroe, Beatty, & Anglin, 1995; Jacobson & Gottman, 1998).

Fully airing concerns is also problematic for couples exhibiting particular patterns of enmeshed interactions (Mathis & Yingling, 1990). For example, some of these couples can become stuck in endless disputing simply for the sake of arguing with each other without any real intent of reaching a mediated settlement (Ricci, 1980; Jones, 1994). Emery argues that these couples remain intimately involved through their acrimony and are not yet willing to break this bond, even though they are involved in the divorce process (Emery, 1994). Thus, airing concerns allows these couples to replay their pathological pattern of interaction rather than negotiate the creation of a lasting settlement. Other examples of enmeshed interactions that are contraindicative of mediation are presented by couples who have extreme ambivalence about the divorce decision (Kressel et al., 1980), couples who cannot communicate or discuss their conflict because of their underlying anger and hurt feelings (Kressel et al., 1980), and couples where one partner demands behavioral changes from the other partner, only to have the other defend his or her behavior or withdraw completely from the discussion (demand–withdraw interactions; Berns et al., 1999; Shoham, Rohrbaugh, Stickle, & Jacob, 1998; Christensen, 1987, 1988).

Beck and Sales (2001) have argued that these types of enmeshed interactions could interact negatively with the type of mediation intervention offered. For example, those mediators who use a form of mediation that is high on structure and directiveness (e.g., structured mediation) may well find that airing concerns is unlikely to occur with couples entrenched in demand–withdraw interaction patterns. Once the mediator attempts directive intervention strategies, it may be interpreted as a demand that stimulates one of the spouses to withdraw—and a full airing of concerns is no longer likely.

Moreover, predicting the success of mediation for particular couples requires a sensitivity to mediation intervention variables (e.g., directiveness of mediator style), couple interaction variables (e.g., communication styles), and individual variables (e.g., level of depression, anger, and withdrawal) that interact to determine when, and under what conditions, mediation is likely to promote the goal of both individuals completely airing their concerns. For example, Bickerdike (1998) tested Emery's (1994) theory of grief in divorce, which predicted that one partner's response to divorce is inextricably woven with the other's response. Bickerdike reported that the dynamic of one party pushing for the divorce and the other pushing against it can negatively affect constructive problem solving and the possibility of reaching a settlement.

In addition, understanding the potential individual-level variables, such as anger, is critical to developing mediation approaches that can effectively help couples with, for example, one angry partner, achieve a successful outcome (Bickerdike, 1998). In some cases, one of the partners negotiates in "bad faith." Psychological dysfunction or unresolved marital attachment seems to be associated with the fact that the goal of these negotiators is not to achieve a successful resolution but instead to continue the conflict (Kressel et al., 1989). These individual-level characteristics do not necessarily mean that the mediation is likely to fail, but they do lead to complexities in the mediation process and require the mediator to respond differently than he or she would to couples who wish to see the marriage successfully terminated. For example, individuals who have unresolved attachment to the partner may fail to keep appointments, come in late for sessions, revise positions that were held in previous meetings, and introduce new concerns just when the mediator might have anticipated that a resolution was in sight.

Mediator Neutrality

One of the goals of mediation is to return control of the settlement process to the parties. In order to accomplish this goal, mediation statutes may define the role of the mediator as someone who is neutral in regard to the parties' interests and whose purpose is to facilitate the attainment of parties' goals, whatever they may be. Neutrality therefore becomes a critical assumption of the mediation process that research and scholarship have addressed.

Neutrality as Impartiality

Neutrality can be seen as *impartiality* on the part of the mediator toward both parties. Under this definition, there should be an absence of mediator bias, such that his or her attitudes and values do not impinge on the mediation process or settlement agreement. The question becomes: Are mediators likely to achieve this goal? Social psychological research has a shown that impartiality is most likely to be achieved during interpersonal communication when an individual's cognition (thoughts), affect (feelings), and behavior are neutral. Specifically, the mediator should hold no prior attitudes toward the couple or issues in the divorce, have no preexisting negative or positive feelings concerning the mediation process with the couple or the specifics of the proposed divorce, and no prior experiences relevant to the mediation.

None of these three contingencies is likely to occur in mediation. Mediators *do* have prior experiences, thoughts, and feelings that all have been shown to influence their mediation responsibilities (Dingwall & Greatbatch, 1991; Folger & Bernard, 1985). Mediators work with divorcing couples every day, expressing attitudes and building cognitions—which make these two individual-level variables most likely to predict mediator behavior (see Taylor, Peplau, & Sears, 1997). With repetition, these attitudes and cognitions become easily accessible to the mediator and are likely reflected in his or her work. This is a problematic dynamic; as Downing, Judd, and Brauer (1992) pointed out, attitudes often become more extreme when they are expressed frequently.

Mediator values and attitudes undermine impartiality for another reason. Attitudes and values indeed change a person's perception of the available information; this perceptional change, in turn, affects the mediator's interactions with the couples. The mediator may feel pulled by these attitudes and values to behave directively and therapeutically in his or her interactions with the couple—which is actually the opposite of neutral behavior (Taylor, 1997). Some mediators have been hesitant to acknowledge what is occurring and label their nonneutral interventions with euphemisms such as "expanded" neutrality (Taylor, 1997). At this point, the label of neutrality becomes functionally meaningless. Several mediation researchers have abandoned the notion of impartiality and advocate for the expanded mediator role. Indeed, this role is more consistent with what we know from social psychology about the nature of interpersonal communication.

One subgroup of mediators assumes the role of impartial focus on achieving a settlement agreement but leaves underlying causes for conflict unaddressed. Despite the fact that these types of mediators place great weight on impartiality, their focus on achieving a settlement may inadvertently lead them to push couples toward a particular result. Not surprisingly, the settlements coming out of this type of mediation are less durable and result in more postmediation litigation (Kressel et al., 1994).

An alternative mediator style has been characterized as problem-solving mediation. In this approach, the mediator is active, investigates the causes of problems, and directs the parties toward particular discussions that can lead to solutions. Once again, the mediator may perceive him- or herself as acting with neutrality, but clearly such behavior is *not* impartial. These mediators actively seek to solve the underlying problems so that a result can be achieved. Despite the loss of impartiality, problem-solving mediation produces sessions that result in more durable settlements and more favorable attitudes on the part of the parties toward the mediation experience (Kressel et al., 1994).

Ultimately, practice style may best serve clients when it is simply responsive to their needs. For example, Pruitt (1995) suggests that when couples have a positive or neutral relationship, it is easy for the mediator to be neutral because the couple is capable of handling that neutrality and motivated to reach a fair solution. When the relationship is filled with conflict, neutrality in mediation is unlikely to be helpful. What these couples might need is an active, direct mediator style that can contain the conflict and adequately investigate proposed solutions.

Neutrality as Equidistance

Neutrality in mediation also may be viewed as the responsibility of the mediators to hold themselves equidistant from each of the parties. Thus, neutrality as equidistance is a relational process between the parties and the mediators and may result, at any given moment, in the mediator favoring one side or the other in order to achieve a balanced outcome (Cobb & Rifkin, 1991b). The dilemma with this approach is that there is no guidance in the mediation literature that clearly identifies when a power difference is occurring or when to shift mediator favor to one side or the other.

There has been some scholarly discussion of this issue. For example, Mnookin (1984) identified five elements that define power in a relationship: (1) the legal rules governing the distribution of the marital property, the provision of alimony, and the decision about child support; (2) the parties' evaluation of alternative outcomes; (3) the level of risk that each person is willing to assume; (4) the parties' abilities to pay lawyers or other professionals to aid them in the dispute process; and (5) the parties' support for their position and their willingness to manipulate each other to gain advantage. Although these factors can produce different "weightings" for each of the parties, resulting in different power balances, how the mediator ascertains the presence of these factors, their extent, and their result are not discussed in the literature. Another mediation scholar (Haynes, 1981, 1988) presented another list of factors to consider, but the same problem exists in determining when these problems are occurring. Although some scholars note that mediators have the capability to redress imbalances (e.g., by providing information, assisting in organizing the weaker party's material to present a more effective case, limiting discussion of certain issues, ending the sessions, or advising a party to seek expert assistance; Emery, 1994; Grillo, 1991; Kelly, 1995), none of their suggested factors or interventions has been tested empirically or cross-validated to ensure effectiveness. As Brodsky (1990) noted, the result is that mediators rely on their own intuitive sense—which translates as relying on their biases or values.

Client Perceptions of Nonneutrality

Although litigants have expectations about what mediation will be like, and one of those expectations is that the mediator will assume a neutral stance, this expectation is probably fueled, in large part, by the orientation the mediator provides for the clients. If, for whatever reason, litigants presume mediator neutrality but then perceive mediator bias at one or many points throughout the process, their level of frustration and dissatisfaction with the process is likely to increase substantially.

The expectation of mediator neutrality is likely enhanced once mediation begins, if mediators present themselves in an informal, intimate, and supportive way to litigants (Kelly, 1993). Typically, mediators sit close to parties and engage in conversations about the most intimate details of litigants' lives. But behaviors in private meetings with one of the clients, although enhancing that client's need for privacy and personal support, can lead the other client to feel that the mediator has violated the promise of neutrality. Ironically, both litigants may end up equally distrusting of and frustrated by the mediator, if he or she engages in these apparently highly supportive private conversations with one or both of the parties. Perceived violations, therefore, of promised mediator neutrality can indeed strike parties very hard.

Unfortunately, there is little research that directly assesses client perceptions of mediator neutrality. However, the problem has been recognized in
policy discussions about mediation. Several commentators have argued that
mediators should develop and provide to litigants an accurate statement of
their goals, values, and methods, so that clients do not develop inappropriate
expectations or feel misled during the mediation process (Dingwall &
Greatbatch, 1991; Maxwell, 1992; Menkel-Meadow, 1993).

CONCLUSION

Our review of the extant research suggests that often the idealistic assumptions of mediation proponents are not often supported scientifically. Despite
this lack of empirical substantiation, however, we know from reported experiences that mediation has helped many families through exceedingly difficult periods in their lives. We applaud the efforts of mediators, court administrators, judges, and the staff of domestic relations courts, whose efforts
have made such a significant difference to these families. Many mediation
clients have described their experiences in mediation as positive and the
information and skills obtained as long lasting.

Nevertheless, we should never be content simply to believe that our well-
intended interventions are maximally effective and create the least possible
negative sequellae. We enthusiastically agree with Honeyman, McAdoo, and
Welch (2001a, 2001b), who contend that, to truly inform social policy, mediators, the courts, and mediation researchers need to work closely together, in
a careful and systematic manner, to assess the variables that affect the mediation process and outcome. Only through methodologically sound empirical
research will we learn what specific behaviors and processes facilitate appropriate mediation outcomes and what factors inhibit mediation practitioners
from achieving their goals.

REFERENCES

Ahrons, C. R. (1995). *The good divorce.* New York: HarperCollins.
Ahrons, C. R., & Rodgers, R. H. (1987). *Divorced families: A multidisciplinary developmental view.* New York: Norton.
Akister, J. (1993). The spouse subsystem in the family context: Couple interaction categories. *Journal of Family Therapy, 15*(1), 1–21.
Alaska Judicial Council. (1992, February). *Alaska Child Visitation Mediation Pilot Project: Report to the legislature.* Anchorage, AK: Author.
Aldarondo, E., & Straus, M. A. (1994). Screening for physical violence in couple therapy: Methodological, practical, and ethical considerations. *Family Process, 33,* 425–439.
Allport, G., & Postman, L. (1975). *The psychology of rumor.* New York: Holt.
Bahr, S. (1981). An evaluation of court mediation: A comparison in divorce cases with children. *Journal of Family Issues, 2,* 39–60.

Bautz, B. J., & Hill, R. M. (1989). Divorce mediation in New Hampshire: A voluntary concept. *Mediation Quarterly, 7,* 33–40.

Beck, C. J. A., & Sales, B. D. (2001). *Family mediation: Facts, myths and future prospects.* Washington, DC: American Psychological Association.

Berns, S., Jacobson, N., & Gottman, J. (1999). Demand/withdraw interaction patterns between different types of batterers and their spouses. *Journal of Marital and Family Therapy, 25*(3), 337–347.

Bickerdike, A. J. (1998). *Conflict resolution in divorce mediation: The impact of the divorce adjustment process and negotiation behaviour on mediation outcome.* Unpublished doctoral dissertation, La Trobe University, Bundoora, Victoria, Australia.

Bloom, B. L., Asher, S. J., & White, S. W. (1978). Marital disruption as a stressor: A review and analysis. *Psychological Bulletin, 85,* 867–894.

Bograd, M., & Mederos, F. (1999). Battering and couples therapy: Universal screening and selection of treatment modality. *Journal of Marital and Family Therapy, 25,* 291–312.

Brandt, E. B. (2000). Essay: The challenge to rural states of procedural reform in high conflict custody cases. *University of Arkansas at Little Rock Law Review, 22,* 357–368.

Braver, S. L., Fitzpatrick, P. J., & Bay, R. C. (1991). Noncustodial parent's report of child support payments. *Family Relations, 40*(2), 180–185.

Brodsky, S. L. (1990). Professional ethics and professional morality and the assessment of competence for execution: A response to Bonnie. *Law and Human Behavior, 14*(1), 91–97.

Bryan, P. E. (1994). Reclaiming professionalism: The lawyer's role in divorce mediation. *Family Law Quarterly, 28,* 177–222.

Cauble, A. E., Thoennes, N., Pearson, J., & Appleford, R. (1985). A case study: Custody resolution counseling in Hennepin County, Minnesota. *Conciliation Courts Review, 23*(2), 27–35.

Christensen, A. (1987). Detection of conflict patterns in couples. In K. Hahlweg & M. J. Goldstein (Eds.), *Understanding major mental disorders: The contribution of family interaction research* (pp. 250–265). New York: Family Process Press.

Christensen, A. (1988). Dysfunctional interaction patterns in couples. In P. Noller & M. A. Fitzpatrick (Eds.), *Perspectives on marital interaction* (pp. 31–52). Clevedon, UK: Multilingual Matters.

Clement, J. A., & Schwebel, A. I. (1993). A research agenda for divorce mediation: The creation of second order knowledge to inform legal policy. *Ohio State Journal on Dispute Resolution, 9*(1), 95–113.

Cobb, S. (1993). Empowerment and mediation: A narrative perspective. *Negotiation Journal, 9,* 245–259.

Cobb, S. (1994). A narrative perspective on mediation: Toward the materialization of the "storytelling" metaphor. In J. P. Folger & T. S. Jones (Eds.), *New directions in mediation: Communication research and perspectives* (pp. 48–63). Thousand Oaks, CA: Sage.

Cobb, S. (1997). The domestication of violence in mediation. *Law and Society Review, 31*(3), 397–440.

Cobb, S., & Rifkin, J. (1991a). Neutrality as a discursive practice: The construction and transformation of narratives in community mediation. *Studies in Law, Politics and Society, 11,* 69–91.

Cobb, S., & Rifkin, J. (1991b). Practice and paradox: Deconstructing neutrality in mediation. *Law and Social Inquiry, 16*(1), 35–62.

Cohen, S. (1982). *The diversion study: A preliminary report.* Unpublished report of the Clackamas Circuit Court, Oregon City, OR.

Coogler, O. J. (1978). *Structured mediation in divorce settlement: A handbook for marital mediators.* Lexington, MA: Heath.

Depner, C., Cannata, K. B., & Simon, M. B. (1992). Building a uniform statistical reporting system: A snapshot of California Family Court Services. *Family and Conciliation Courts Review, 30*(2), 185–206.

Dillon, P. A., & Emery, R. E. (1996). Divorce mediation and resolution of child custody disputes: Long-term effects. *American Journal of Orthopsychiatry, 66*(1), 131–140.

Dingwall, R. (1988). Empowerment or enforcement? Some questions about power and control in divorce mediation. In R. Dingwall & J. M. Eekelaar (Eds.), *Divorce, mediation and the legal process* (pp. 150–167). Oxford, UK: Clarendon.

Dingwall, R., & Eekelaar, J. (1988). A wider vision. In R. Dingwall & J. Eekelaar (Eds.), *Divorce mediation and the legal process* (pp. 168–182). Oxford, UK: Clarendon.

Dingwall, R., & Greatbatch, D. (1991). Behind closed doors: A preliminary report on mediator/client interaction in England. *Family and Conciliation Courts Review, 29*(3), 291–303.

Downing, J. W., Judd, C. W., & Brauer, M. (1992). Effects of repeated expressions on attitude extremity. *Journal of Personality and Social Psychology, 63,* 17–29.

Doyle, P. M., & Caron, W. A. (1979). Contested custody intervention: An empirical assessment. In D. H. Olson, M. Cleveland, P. Doyle, M. F. Rockcastle, B. Robinson, R. Reimer, J. Minton, W. Caron, & S. Cohen (Eds.), *Child custody: Literature review and alternative approaches* (pp. 137–190). Monograph for the McKnight Foundation, Hennepin County Domestic Relations Division, St. Paul, MN.

Ellis, D. (1990). Marital conflict mediation and post-separation wife abuse. *Law and Inequality Journal, 8,* 317–339.

Elrod, L. D. (2001). A Minnesota comparative family law symposium: Reforming the system to protect children in high conflict custody cases. *William Mitchell Law Review, 28,* 495–570.

Elrod, L. D., & Spector, R. G. (1996). A review of the year in family law: Children's issues take the spotlight. *Family Law Quarterly, 29,* 741–774.

Emery, R. E. (1990). Divorce mediation: A practice in search of a theory [Review of *Divorce mediation: Theory and practice*]. *Contemporary Psychology, 35*(4), 373–374.

Emery, R. E. (1994). *Renegotiating family relationships: Divorce, child custody, and mediation.* New York: Guilford Press.

Emery, R. E., & Jackson, J. A. (1989). The Charlottesville Mediation Project: Mediated and litigated child custody disputes. *Mediation Quarterly, 24,* 3–18.

Emery, R. E., Laumann-Billings, L., Waldron, M. C., Sbarra, D. A., & Dillon, P. (2001). Child custody mediation and litigation: Custody, contact and coparenting 12 years after initial dispute resolution. *Journal of Consulting and Clinical Psychology, 69*(2), 323–332.

Emery, R. E., Matthews, S. G., & Kitzmann, K. M. (1991). Child custody mediation and litigation: Parents' satisfaction one year after settlement. *Journal of Consulting and Clinical Psychology, 62*(1), 124–129.

Emery, R. E., Matthews, S. G., & Wyer, M. M. (1991). Child custody mediation and litigation: Further evidence on the differing views of mothers and fathers. *Journal of Consulting and Clinical Psychology, 59*(3), 410–418.

Emery, R. E., Shaw, D. S., & Jackson, J. A. (1987). A clinical description of a model of child custody mediation. In J. P. Vincent (Vol. Ed.), *Advances in family intervention, assessment, and theory* (Vol. 4, pp. 309–333). Greenwich, CT: JAI Press.

Emery, R. E., & Wyer, M. M. (1987a). Child custody mediation and litigation: An experimental evaluation of the experience of parents. *Journal of Consulting and Clinical Psychology, 55,* 179–186.

Emery, R. E., & Wyer, M. M. (1987b). Divorce mediation. *American Psychologist, 42*(2), 472–480.

Esser, J. (1989). Evaluations of dispute processing: We do not know what we think and we do not think what we know. *Denver University Law Review, 66*(3), 499–562.

Felstiner, W. L. F., & Sarat, A. (1992). Symposium: Enactments of power—negotiating reality and responsibility in lawyer–client interactions. *Cornell Law Review, 77,* 1447–1498.

Felstiner, W. L. F., & Williams, L. A. (1980). *Community mediation in Dorcester, Massachusetts.* Washington, DC: U.S. Department of Justice, National Institute of Justice.

Fischer, K., Vidmar, N., & Ellis, R. (1993). The culture of battering and the role of mediation in domestic violence cases. *Southern Methodist University Law Review, 46,* 2117–2174.

Fisher, L. (1995). An empirically derived typology of families: I. Relationships and adult health. *Family Process, 34*(2), 161–182.

Fitzpatrick, M. A. (1988). *Between husbands and wives: Communication in marriage.* Newbury Park, CA: Sage.

Fix, M., & Harter, P. (1992). *Hard cases, vulnerable people: An analysis of mediation programs at the multi-door courthouse of the Superior Court of the District of Columbia.* Washington, DC: State Justice Institute, Urban Institute.

Folger, J. P., & Bernard, S. E. (1985). Divorce mediation: When mediators challenge divorcing parties. *Mediation Quarterly, 10,* 5–23.

Fowers, B. J. (1996). Predicting marital success for premarital couple types based on PRE-PARE. *Journal of Marital and Family Therapy, 22*(1), 103–119.

Gerber, R. J. (1990). Recommendation on domestic relations reform. *Arizona Law Review, 32,* 9–19.

Gottman, J. M. (1993). The roles of conflict engagement, escalation, and avoidance in marital interaction: A longitudinal view of five types of couples. *Journal of Consulting and Clinical Psychology, 61*(1), 6–15.

Gottman, J. M. (1994). *What predicts divorce?: The relationship between marital process and marital outcomes.* Hillsdale, NJ: Erlbaum.

Greatbatch, D., & Dingwall, R. (1989). Selective facilitation: Some preliminary observations on a strategy used by divorce mediators. *Law and Society Review, 23*(4), 613–641.

Griffiths, J. (1986). What do Dutch lawyers actually do in divorce cases? *Law and Society Review, 10,* 135–175.

Grillo, T. (1991). The mediation alternative: Process dangers for women. *Yale Law Journal, 100,* 1545–1610.

Gutek, B. A. (1978). Strategies for studying client satisfaction. *Journal of Social Issues, 34*(4), 44–56.

Haynes, J. M. (1981). *Divorce mediation: A practical guide for therapists and counselors.* New York: Springer.

Haynes, J. (1988). Power balancing. In J. Folberg & A. Milne (Eds.), *Divorce mediation: Theory and practice* (pp. 277–296). New York: Guilford Press.

Hendricks, C. L. (1993–1994). The trend toward mandatory mediation in custody and visitation disputes of minor children: An overview. *Journal of Family Law, 32,* 491–510.

Hensler, D., Lipson, A., & Rolph, E. (1981). *Judicial arbitration in California: The first year.* Santa Monica, CA: RAND Institute for Civil Justice.

Holtzworth-Munroe, A., Beatty, S. B., & Anglin, K. (1995). The assessment and treatment of marital violence: An introduction for the marital therapist. In N. S. Jacobson & A. S. Gurman (Eds.), *Clinical handbook of couple therapy* (2nd ed., pp. 317–339). New York: Guilford Press.

Honeyman, C., McAdoo, B., & Welsh, N. (2001a). Not quite protocols: Toward collaborative research in dispute resolution. *Conflict Resolution Quarterly, 19*(1), 75–88.

Honeyman, C., McAdoo, B., & Welsh, N. (2001b). Here there be monsters: At the edge of the map of conflict resolution. In S. Morokuma (Ed.), *The conflict resolution practitioner: Bridging theory and practice.* Atlanta, GA: Office of Dispute Resolution.

Irving, H. H., & Benjamin, M. (1992). An evaluation of process and outcome in a private family mediation service. *Mediation Quarterly, 10*(1), 35–55.

Irving, H. H., & Benjamin, M. (1995). *Family mediation: Contemporary issues.* Thousand Oaks, CA: Sage.

Jacobson, N. S., & Addis, M. E. (1993). Research on couples and couple therapy: What do we know? Where are we going? *Journal of Consulting and Clinical Psychology, 61*(1), 85–93.

Jacobson, N. S., & Gottman, J. (1998). *When men batter women.* New York: Simon & Schuster.

Johnson, S., & Lebow, J. (2000). The "coming of age" of couple therapy: A decade review. *Journal of Marital and Family Therapy, 26*(1), 23–38.

Johnston, J. R. (2000). Essay: Building multidisciplinary professional partnerships with the court on behalf of high-conflict divorcing families and their children: Who needs what kind of help? *University of Arkansas at Little Rock Law Review, 22,* 453–490.

Johnston, J. R., & Campbell, L. E. G. (1988). *Impasses of divorce: The dynamics and resolution of family conflict.* New York: Free Press.

Johnston, J. R., Campbell, L. E. G., & Tall, M. C. (1985). Impasses to the resolution of custody and visitation disputes. *Journal of Orthopsychiatry, 55,* 112–129.

Johnston, J. R., & Roseby, V. (1997). *In the name of the child: A developmental approach to understanding and helping children of high conflict and violent divorce.* New York: Free Press.

Jones, T. S. (1994). A dialectical reframing of the mediation process. In J. P. Folger & T. S. Jones (Eds.), *New directions in mediation: Communication research and perspectives* (pp. 26–47). Thousand Oaks, CA: Sage.

Keilitz, S. L., Daley, H. W. K., & Hanson, R. A. (1992). *Multi-state assessment of divorce mediation and traditional court processing.* Paper prepared for the National Center for State Courts, Alexandria, VA.

Kelly, J. B. (1983). Mediation and psychotherapy: Distinguishing the differences. *Mediation Quarterly, 1,* 33–44.

Kelly, J. B. (1989). Mediated and adversarial divorce: Respondents' perceptions of their processes and outcomes. *Mediation Quarterly, 24,* 71–88.

Kelly, J. B. (1990a). Is mediation less expensive?: Comparison of mediated and adversarial divorce costs. *Mediation Quarterly, 8,* 15–25.

Kelly, J. B. (1990b, December). *Mediated and adversarial divorce resolution processes: An analysis of post-divorce outcomes–final report.* Prepared for the Fund for Research in Dispute Resolution, Washington, DC.

Kelly, J. B. (1991). Parent interaction after divorce: Comparison of mediated and adversarial divorce processes. *Behavioral Sciences and the Law, 9,* 387–398.

Kelly, J. B. (1993). Current research on children's postdivorce adjustment: No simple answers. *Family and Conciliation Courts Review, 31*(1), 29–49.

Kelly, J. B. (1995). Power imbalance in divorce and interpersonal mediation: Assessment and intervention. *Mediation Quarterly, 13*(2), 83–98.

Kelly, J. B. (1996). A decade of divorce mediation research: Some answers and questions. *Family and Conciliation Courts Review, 34*(3), 373–385.

Kelly, J. B., & Duryee, M. A. (1992). Women's and men's views of mediation in voluntary and mandatory mediation settings. *Family and Conciliation Courts Review, 30*(1), 34–49.

Kelly, J. B., & Gigy, L. L. (1989). Divorce mediation: Characteristics of clients and outcomes. In K. Kressel, D. G. Pruitt, & Associates (Eds.), *Mediation research* (pp. 263–283). San Francisco: Jossey-Bass.

Kelly, J. B., Gigy, L., & Hausman, S. (1988). Mediated and adversarial divorce: Initial findings from a longitudinal study. In J. Folberg & A. Milne (Eds.), *Divorce mediation: Theory and practice* (pp. 453–474). New York: Guilford Press.

Kelly, J. B., Zlatchin, C., & Shawn, J. (1985). Divorce mediation: Process, prospects, and professional issues. In C. P. Ewing (Ed.), *Psychology, psychiatry, and the law: A clinical and forensic handbook* (pp. 243–279). Sarasota, FL: Professional Resource Exchange.

Kenney, L. M., & Vigil, D. (1996). A lawyer's guide to therapeutic interventions in domestic relations court. *Arizona State Law Journal, 28,* 629–672.

Kidder, L. H., Judd, C. M., & Smith, E. R. (1986). *Research methods in social relations* (5th ed.). New York: Holt, Rinehart & Winston.

Kitzmann, K. M., & Emery, R. E. (1993). Procedural justice and parents' satisfaction in a field study of child custody dispute resolution. *Law and Human Behavior, 17*(5), 553–567.

Kitzmann, K. M., & Emery, R. E. (1994). Child and family coping one year after mediated and litigated child custody disputes. *Journal of Family Psychology, 8,* 150–159.

Kramer, K. M., Arbuthnot, J., Gordon, D. A., Rousis, N. J., & Hoza, J. (1998). Effects of skill-based versus information-based education programs on domestic violence and parental communication. *Family and Conciliation Courts Review, 36*(1), 9–31.

Kressel, K. (1985). *The process of divorce: How professionals and couples negotiate settlements.* New York: Basic Books.

Kressel, K., Frontera, E. A., Florenza, S., Butler, F., & Fish L. (1994). The settlement-orientation vs. the problem-solving style in custody mediation. *Journal of Social Issues, 50*(1), 67–84.

Kressel, K., & Hochberg, A. M. (1987). Divorce attorneys: Assessment of a typology and attitudes towards legal reform. *Journal of Divorce, 10*(3/4), 1–14.

Kressel, K., Jaffee, N., Tuchman, B., Watson, C., & Deutsch, M. (1980). A typology of divorcing couples: Implications for mediation and the divorce process. *Family Process, 19,* 101–116.

Kressel, K., Pruitt, D. G., & Associates. (Eds.). (1989). *Mediation research: The process and effectiveness of third-party intervention.* San Francisco: Jossey-Bass.

Laumann-Billings, L., & Emery, R. E. (2000). Distress among young adults from divorced families. *Journal of Family Psychology, 14*(4), 671–687.

Lavee, Y. (1993). Seven types of marriage: Empirical typology based on ENRICH. *Journal of Marital and Family Therapy, 19*(4), 325–340.

Lawyers see rise in anger of parties in domestic disputes. (1996, May 8). *Los Angeles Daily Journal,* p. 1.

Levy, R. J. (1984). Comment on the Pearson–Thoennes study and on mediation. *Family Law Quarterly, 17*(4), 525–533.

Lind, E. A., & Tyler, T. (1988). *The social psychology of procedural justice.* New York: Plenum Press.

Little, M., Thoennes, N., Pearson, J., & Appleford, R. (1985). A case study: The custody mediation services of the Los Angeles Conciliation Court. *Conciliation Courts Review, 23*(2), 1–13.

Lyon, M., Thoennes, N., Pearson, J., & Appleford, R. (1985). A case study: The custody mediation services of the Family Division, Connecticut Superior Court. *Conciliation Courts Review, 23*(2), 15–26.

Maccoby, E. E., Buchanan, C. M., Mnookin, R. H., & Dornbusch, S. M. (1993). Postdivorce roles of mothers and fathers in the lives of their children. *Journal of Family Psychology, 7*(1), 24–38.

MacCoun, R. J., Lind, E. A., Hensler, D. R., Bryant, D. L., & Ebener, P. A. (1988). *Alternative adjudication: An evaluation of the New Jersey Automobile Arbitration Program.* Santa Monica, CA: RAND.

Margolin, F. M. (1973). An approach to resolution of visitation disputes post-divorce: Short-term counseling. *Dissertation Abstracts International, 34*(4-B), 1754.

Marlow, L., & Sauber, S. (1990). *The handbook of divorce mediation.* New York: Plenum Press.

Mather, L., McEwen, C. A., & Maiman, R. J. (2001). *Divorce lawyers at work: Varieties of professionalism in practice.* New York: Oxford University Press.

Mathis, R. D., & Yingling, L. C. (1990). Recommendations for divorce mediation with chaotically adaptable family systems. *Mediation Quarterly, 8*(2), 125–136.

Maxwell, N. G. (1992). The feminist dilemma in mediation. *International Review of Comparative Public Policy, 4,* 67–84.

McEwen, C. A., Rogers, N. H., & Maiman, R. J. (1995). Bring in the lawyers: Challenging the dominant approaches to ensuring fairness in divorce mediation. *Minnesota Law Review, 79,* 1317–1411.

McIsaac, H. (1981). Mandatory conciliation custody/visitation matters: California's bold stroke. *Conciliation Courts Review, 19*(2), 73–81.

Menkel-Meadow, C. (1993). Commentary: Professional responsibility for third-party neutrals. *Alternatives, 11*(9), 129–131.

Milne, A. (1978). Custody of children in a divorce process: A family self-determination model. *Conciliation Courts Review, 16*(2), 1–10.

Mitchell, F. (1998). The dispute resolution continuum: A diversity of new ideas. *Diversity Update, 4*(3), 2–3.

Mnookin, R. H. (1975). Child-custody adjudication: Judicial functions in the fact of indeterminacy. *Law and Contemporary Problems, 39,* 226–292.

Mnookin, R. H. (1984). Divorce bargaining: The limits on private ordering. In J. M. Eekelaar & S. N. Katz (Eds.), *The resolution of family conflict: Comparative legal perspectives* (pp. 364–383). Toronto: Butterworths.

Mnookin, R. H. (1993). Why negotiations fail: An exploration of barriers to the resolution of conflict. *Ohio State Journal on Dispute Resolution, 8,* 235–241.

Newmark, L., Harrell, A., & Salem, P. (1995). Domestic violence and empowerment in custody and visitation cases. *Family and Conciliation Courts Review, 33*(1), 30–62.

O'Leary, K. D., Vivian, D., & Malone, J. (1991, October). *Assessment of physical aggression in marriage.* Paper presented at the annual meeting of the Association for the Advancement of Behavior Therapy, San Francisco, CA.

Pearson J. (1981). Child custody: Why not let the parents decide? *Judges Journal, 20*(1), 4–10, 12.

Pearson, J. (1991). The equity of mediated divorce agreements. *Mediation Quarterly, 9*(2), 179–197.

Pearson, J. (1993). Ten myths about family law. *Family Law Quarterly, 27*(2), 279–299.

Pearson, J. (1994). Family mediation. In S. Keilitz (Ed.), *A report on current research findings–implications for courts and future research needs* (pp. 53–75). Washington, DC: State Justice Institute.

Pearson, J. (1997). Mediating when domestic violence is a factor: Policies and practices in court-based divorce mediation programs. *Mediation Quarterly, 14*(4), 321–335.

Pearson, J., & Thoennes, N. (1982). The mediation and adjudication of divorce disputes: The benefits outweigh the costs. *The Family Advocate, 4,* 26–32.

Pearson, J., & Thoennes, N. (1984a). Dialogue: A rely to Professor Levy's comment. *Family Law Quarterly, 17*(4), 535–538.

Pearson, J., & Thoennes, N. (1984b). Mediating and litigating custody disputes: A longitudinal evaluation. *Family Law Quarterly, 17*(4), 497–524.

Pearson J., & Thoennes, N. (1985a). Mediation versus the courts in child custody cases. *Negotiation Journal, 1,* 235–244.

Pearson, J., & Thoennes, N. (1985b). A preliminary portrait of client reactions to three court mediation programs. *Conciliation Courts Review, 23*(1), 1–14.

Pearson, J., & Thoennes, N. (1986). Mediation in custody disputes. *Behavioral Sciences and the Law, 4*(2), 203–216.

Pearson, J., & Thoennes, N. (1988a). Divorce mediation: An American picture. In R. Dingwall & J. Eekelaar (Eds.), *Divorce mediation and the legal process* (pp. 71–91). Oxford, UK: Clarendon.

Pearson, J., & Thoennes, N. (1988b). Divorce mediation research results. In J. Folberg & A. Milne (Eds.), *Divorce mediation: Theory and practice* (pp. 429–452). New York: Guilford Press.

Pearson, J., & Thoennes, N. (1988c). Supporting children after divorce: The influence of custody on support levels and payments. *Family Law Quarterly, 22*(3), 319–339.

Pearson, J., & Thoennes, N. (1989). Divorce mediation: Reflections on a decade of research. In K. Kressel, D. G. Pruitt, & Associates (Eds.), *Mediation research: The process and effectiveness of third-party intervention* (pp. 9–30). San Francisco: Jossey-Bass.

Pruitt, D. G. (1995). Process and outcome in community mediation. *Negotiation Journal, 11,* 365–377.

Ricci, I. (1980). *Mom's house, Dad's house.* New York: Macmillan.

Rich, W. (1980). The role of lawyers: Beyond advocacy. *Brigham Young University Law Review, 1980,* 767–784.

Rifkin, J., Millen J., & Cobb, S. (1991). Toward a new discourse for mediation: A critique of neutrality. *Mediation Quarterly, 9*(2), 151–164.

Sales, B. D. (1983). The legal regulation of psychology: Professional and scientific interactions. In C. J. Scheirer & B. L. Hammonds (Eds.), *The master lecture series. Vol. 2: Psychology and the law* (pp. 5–36). Washington, DC: American Psychological Association.

Sales, B. D., Beck, C. J., & Haan, R. K. (1993a). Is self-representation a reasonable alternative to attorney representation in divorce cases? *Saint Louis University Law Journal, 37*(3), 553–605.

Sales, B., Beck, C. J., & Haan, R. E. (1993b). *Self-representation in divorce cases.* Chicago: American Bar Association.

Saposnek, D. T. (1983). *Mediating child custody disputes: A systematic guide for family therapists, court counselors, attorneys, and judges.* San Francisco: Jossey-Bass.

Sarat, A., & Felstiner, W. L. F. (1986). Law and strategy in the divorce lawyer's office. *Law and Society Review, 20*(1), 93–134.

Sarat, A., & Felstiner, W. L. F. (1989). Lawyers and legal consciousness: Law talk in the divorce lawyer's office. *Yale Law Journal, 98,* 1663–1688.

Sarat, A., & Felstiner, W. L. F. (1995). *Divorce lawyers and their clients.* New York: Oxford University Press.

Schepard, A. (2000). Essay: The evolving judicial role in child custody disputes: From fault finder to conflict manager to differential case management. *University of Arkansas at Little Rock Law Review, 22,* 395–428.

Schlissel, S. W. (1992). A proposal for final and binding arbitration of initial custody determinations. *Family Law Quarterly, 26*(1), 71–84.

Shoham, V., Rohrbaugh, M., Stickle, T., & Jacob, T. (1998). Demand–withdraw couple interaction moderate retention in cognitive-behavioral vs. family-systems treatments for alcoholism. *Journal of Family Psychology, 12*(4), 1–21.

Silbey, S. S. (1993, October). Mediation mythology. *Negotiation Journal,* 349–353.

Smoron, K. A. (1998). Conflicting roles in child custody mediation: Impartiality/neutrality and the best interests of the child [Co-winning essay: 1997 Law School Essay Contest]. *Family and Conciliation Courts Review, 36*(2), 258–280.

Somary, K., & Emery, R. E. (1991). Emotional anger and grief in divorce mediation. *Mediation Quarterly, 8*(3), 185–197.

Taylor, A. (1997). Concepts of neutrality in family mediation: Contexts, ethics, influence, and transformative process. *Mediation Quarterly, 14*(3), 215–236.

Taylor, S. E., Peplau, L. A., & Sears, D. O. (1997). *Social psychology.* Upper Saddle River, NJ: Prentice Hall.

Thoennes, N., Salem, P., & Pearson, J. (1995). Mediation and domestic violence: Current policies and practices. *Family and Conciliation Courts Review, 33*(1), 6–29.

Trost, M. R., Braver, S. L., & Schoeneman, R. (1988). Mandatory mediation: Encouraging results for the court system. *Family and Conciliation Courts Review, 26*(2), 59–65.

Tyler, T. R. (1990). *Why people obey the law.* New Haven, CT: Yale University Press.

Tyler, T. R. (1997). Citizen discontent with legal procedures: A social science perspective on civil procedure reform. *American Journal of Comparative Law, 45,* 871–904.

Weiss, W. W., & Collada, H. B. (1977, October). Conciliation counseling: The court's effective mechanism for resolving visitation and custody disputes. *Family Coordinator,* pp. 444–446.

Wingspread Conference Report. (2001). High-conflict custody cases: Reforming the system for children. *Family Court Review, 39*(2), 146–157.

CHAPTER 21

Certifying Mediators

PEGGY ENGLISH
LINDA C. NEILSON

Peggy English and Linda C. Neilson were integral to the design and implementation of Family Mediation Canada's (FMC) certification program for family mediators. Their wealth of experience is presented in this chapter, where they discuss the how-tos of assessing a mediator's knowledge base and ability to implement skills, as well as provide a learning tool for those who participate in the certification process.

"I found the certification to be the most rigorous and rewarding achievement of my career as a family mediator. The beauty of it is that is not only confirms you as a competent mediator, but it also 'grows' you!"[1]

"The certification process itself was a tremendous learning experience for me."[2]

"The approach should be aspirational, not prescriptive; it should encourage learning, creativity, and professional development, not the attainment of a particular set of standards. A process that supports inventiveness, continued learning, and movement toward artistry will serve the field well."[3]

In "The Role of Interest-Based Facilitation in Designing Accreditation Standards: The Canadian Experience" (Neilson & English, 2001), we discussed methodological and theoretical issues associated with the design and implementation of Family Mediation Canada's[4] (FMC) national certification process for mediators. In this chapter, we build upon those discussions. More particularly, the chapter demonstrates how the core mediation values, principles, and methodologies that guided the creation and implementation of the certification process are woven throughout that process. Thus the chapter begins with a brief discussion of the development of the certification process and describes how interactive assessment tools and certification processes designed for FMC actually work. Central to the process is the engagement of assessors with mediators in an assessment process that incorporates interactive learning, self-reflective growth, and professional development. Finally, we present an analysis of the current certification process and discuss some of the never-ending issues and challenges that, when addressed, allow such processes to mirror the evolution of knowledge within the mediation community and society as a whole.

It is important to note, before we begin, that attempting to describe, in a linear medium, the interactive assessment process used by FMC to evaluate mediators is rather like trying to describe the complex relationships of matter in particle physics. Particles are interconnected and interrelated; they cannot be measured or understood in a straight line, independently of each other. So too do the particles (i.e., skills, knowledge, techniques, abilities, personal qualities) mediators bring to the mediation table operate in a reciprocal fashion. None can be understood, assessed, or measured independently of each other, of the process, or of the interactive, interpersonal, cultural, and even social context in which mediation takes place. Thus an effective evaluation of a mediator's performance must take place as part of an interactive interplay between assessor and candidate. That interplay must incorporate and balance objective observation with dialogue and the exchange of understandings and perspectives on what occurred during the mediation process. Consequently, FMC's certification process is nonlinear and is qualitative as well as quantitative.

During FMC's certification process, assessors work with applicants to unravel, identify, understand, and assess applicant skills and abilities. Assessors elicit from applicants their understandings and explanations of how they link mediation theory to practice—or, in lay terms, why they work with clients in mediation the way they do. Effective mediators draw from a variety of theories and associated skills and techniques; there is no single model of mediation that has been established as the correct way to do mediation (Moore, 1996; Lang & Taylor, 2000; MacFarlane, 1999, Chap. 3; Morris & Pirie, 1994; Menkel-Meadow, 1995). Skills and techniques that suit one mediation session do not necessarily suit other clients, with different needs, in another mediation session. FMC's certification process has been designed to respect and honor diversity in mediation practice, while enacting the fundamental values and principles of the discipline.

All models of mediation include disputants and a third party or parties who help disputants understand, negotiate, manage, and resolve conflict. Mediators do not, generally, have or impose decision-making power.[5] Moreover, we and FMC endorse Morris's (1997) assertion that "the most important point for discussion . . . in mediation is the fact of human interdependence" and three universal principles: respect, caring, and procedural fairness.

Over the course of 10 years, we have facilitated the design and implementation of FMC's practice standards and certification process. We believe that assessment processes for mediators ought to adhere to the fundamental values of mediation identified previously. As is the case in a mediation process, assessors have an obligation to gain candidate trust and to establish a mutual commitment to the certification assessment process. The result is that FMC's assessment process provides more than a pass/fail exercise. Candidates are offered an opportunity to participate in collaborative, personalized self-reflection as part of the process and are given written feedback and suggestions for their professional growth.

HISTORY

From its beginnings in 1984, FMC has been committed to developing standards of practice that promote high-quality specialized family mediation services for the public. Throughout the 1980s and 1990s, we engaged in research and extensive participatory, action-oriented consultation processes with mediation practitioners and trainers—at first individually (English, 1993, 1994a; Neilson, 1992)[6] and then together on behalf of FMC—in order to explore practice, education, training, and assessment issues. From 1993 to 1996, we[7] engaged in face-to-face interviews, e-mail and telephone consultations, written correspondence, and "town hall meetings" with mediators and mediation trainers at numerous mediation conferences in every province and territory in Canada (and in many states in the United States) in order to facilitate the development of standards of practice[8] and, later, a certification process for mediators. From the beginning, the goal was to facilitate the development and design of practice standards and accreditation processes from the "ground up," inductively[9]—from practice to theory[10]—by working with mediation practitioners in the design of the certification process. Subsequently, the process was pilot tested, evaluated, and verified by an independent researcher (Neilson & English, 2001, note 4).

During the early 1990s in Canada, as the public, courts, and government agencies began to endorse and promote family mediation, practitioners became increasingly concerned about professional accountability issues, given the proliferation of programs and practitioners in the field. More particularly, practitioners became convinced that,[11] if the field of mediation were to remain a respected and viable alternative to litigation and courts, the mediation community would have to develop a mechanism to promote highly competent specialized family mediation practitioners. Practitioners considered it important that the mediation community set its own standards and assessment processes rather than have them imposed by judicial, administrative, or governmental bodies that possessed little specialized knowledge of the field.

As a result, in 1996, FMC's general membership directed FMC to explore and develop accreditation options for mediation practitioners.

DEVELOPMENT

In 1987, the Society for Professionals in Dispute Resolution (SPIDR) in the United States established a qualifications committee to (1) determine what constitutes a "neutral" role in a conflict resolution process; (2) identify core competencies; (3) develop principles, processes, and policies to be used to establish, assess, and monitor those competencies; and (4) educate the mediation community and consumers about those competencies (Society of Professionals in Dispute Resolution, 1989). In 1995 I (English) represented Family Mediation Canada as an "observer" at the SPIDR Commission II (Society of Professionals in Dispute Resolution, 1995) and was invited to take the SPIDR recommendations back to FMC and use the principles identified in the development of an evaluation or certification process for family mediators. The principles generated by SPIDR became operational guidelines for the FMC certification project (English, 1997):

1. Root the certification process in the values and culture of family mediation in Canada.
2. Maintain the self-determination of practitioners and keep the process voluntary.
3. Respect that the development of the certification process was as important as the finished product.
4. Recognize that the certification process must reflect the changes in the practice and knowledge of mediation as the field develops and grows.
5. Define a process that supports and encourages the practitioners to improve their skills.
6. Involve a wide group of practitioners to reflect the diversity of gender, style, geography, age, culture, language, discipline, and experience.
7. Develop standards that are attainable and reflect a minimum level of preparation.
8. Define ways to promote and continue the growth of the practitioner following his or her certification.

Thus the seeds of the FMC National Certification Pilot Project, 1997–1999, were sown. FMC received financial assistance from the Federal Department of Justice, and the Law Foundation of the Northwest Territories and formed a partnership with the Family Justice Division of the Ministry of Attorney General of British Columbia[12] to develop national certification standards for family mediators. An implementation team chaired by one of us (Neilson) worked with the other project manager (English), throughout the certification development and implementation process.

Town Hall conference sessions, telephone, e-mail, and written consultations with practitioners continued throughout the 1990s. In the beginning, members of the mediation community were somewhat apprehensive about the establishment of certification assessment processes for family mediators. Some of the concerns we encountered in Canada in the early 1990s are still heard today:

1. Certification and accreditation processes contradict basic mediation philosophies, such as the principle of inclusion and respect for diversity of perspective and practice.
2. Premature establishment of standards and methods to measure performance would limit the innovative, creative nature of the process.
3. Certification requirements would create barriers to entry into the field.
4. Certification would encourage a monopoly on practice—an exclusive grouping and a bureaucratic structure—that would be similar to and would reproduce public complaints about the cumbersome adversarial/judicial system.
5. Setting standards without research identifying the best model of practice could limit excellence in the expanding field.
6. Increasing educational and practice requirements would limit diversity among practitioners.
7. Not enough is known about mediation in relation to minority groups, power imbalances, and issues of diversity to allow the establishment of inclusive standards that are culturally and gender sensitive.
8. It is not possible to measure or assess mediator performance because we do not know yet how to measure mediation success (is success satisfied clients, durability of agreement, rate of settlement, changed society?).[13]
9. Different models of mediation require different evaluation tools.
10. It is not possible to design an interactive assessment process that could produce consistent, measurable results.
11. Mediation practitioners come from many fields, and certification processes must respect and recognize these diverse origins.

These concerns and the interests they represent are valuable; they should not, in our view, be dismissed. Instead, in true mediation fashion, we have attempted to embrace them and incorporate them into FMC's certification process. Thus, in recognition that mediation is an art and an interpersonal process grounded more in "the innate personal quality to manage effectively complex human interactions" (Neilson & English, 1996, section 4.6) than in professional orientation, professional status was not made a prerequisite for practice or certification. In recognition of the notion that national practice and certification standards ought to be inclusive and that certification should enhance, not inhibit, entry into the discipline or the development of mediation services, FMC's certification process was made inclusive and voluntary. FMC members are not obligated to engage in the certification process as a condition of membership or practice—although all FMC members are obligated to adhere to FMC Standards of Practice and its Code of Professional Conduct.

In connection with diversity of practice and perspective, the certification process was designed to respect different theoretical and methodological approaches. The research to date suggests that it has been successful in this regard. (We return to this issue later.) Furthermore, FMC's certification process assesses mediator responses to power imbalance, as well as sensitivities to, and understandings of, issues associated with gender and culture.[14] The assessment process assigns extra weight to these issues.[15] Still, work on these high-priority issues is continuing[16] and much remains to be done. We simply disagree, however, with the notion that standards of professional practice and certification assessment processes must await expert–researcher determination of the best model of practice for a number of reasons: (1) searching for a single best, "one-size-fits-all" model of mediation practice is misguided; (2) inhibiting disciplinary development and evolution is wrong; (3) responding to different clients with different conflicts in different contexts in different ways ought to be encouraged; and (4) adjudicating or evaluating debated claims is contrary to the fundamental principles of mediation.[17] In our view, it is better to concentrate on areas of agreement within the discipline than on the areas of debate; it is also better to work with practitioners as facilitators—to identify the state of the discipline today and the personal qualities, knowledge, and skills necessary to perform it—than to engage in judgment. Thus FMC's *Practice, Certification and Training Standards* became the product *of* practitioners *for* practitioners.

DEVELOPMENT OF THE MEDIATOR SKILLS ASSESSMENT TOOL

Practitioners agree that family mediation is not only a skill but an interactive art and that substantive knowledge serves no useful purpose unless it can be used effectively in a facilitative, interactive context of conflict resolution. Thus central to FMC certification are completion of a practicum (as part of the learning process) and an interactive, skills-based evaluation (as part of the assessment process).

It is important to note that the FMC's (and the Ministry of Attorney General of British Columbia)[18] interactive, skills-based assessment process was designed primarily by practitioners. A team of highly experienced mediation practitioners, employed by the Ministry of Attorney General of British Columbia, worked closely with English (an experienced practitioner representing FMC), a human resource person, and a union representative also from the Ministry of Attorney General of British Columbia, in consultation with an academic/researcher/lawyer (Neilson, representing FMC) to develop the interactive skills assessment tool. The team studied, and was influenced by, assessment models developed in Canada, the United States, and England but opted to develop a new assessment tool. Because the goal was to design a tool that could respond effectively and fairly to a variety of models of mediation, the committee opted to define the work of a mediator in terms of the primary and secondary tasks performed by all mediators. The thesis was that embedded in each of these mediation tasks are the values and skills necessary to work effectively with clients. Yet it would be inaccurate to give the impression that skills could be isolated, observed, and measured independently of each other. Instead, experienced mediation practitioners contend that "fundamental to an understanding of mediation is the importance of appreciating the reciprocal relationships among knowledge, skills, process and context" and that, in interactive settings, each identifiable skill and method alters the nature and meaning of the other and thus can only be understood and assessed in connection with each other and in context (Neilson, 1992, note 9; Neilson & English, 2001, note 4; English et al., 1999). Indeed, as they conducted the assessments, the assessors found that skills do not and cannot stand alone. In fact, the "particles" of mediation overlap the process categories and change in relevance depending on when and how they are used in the context of the mediation.

In the beginning, the primary and secondary mediator tasks were defined as follows:

1. Managing the relationships during the mediation:
   a. Establishing and maintaining a respectful, trusting relationship with the participants (answering the question "Does the mediator form an effective relationship with the participants?").
   b. Facilitating a collaborative relationship between the participants (answering the question "Does the mediator promote the clients' cooperative efforts and mutual understanding?").
   c. Managing the power imbalances (answering the question "Does the mediator facilitate opportunities for full participation?").
2. Managing the process of the mediation:
   a. Attending to and exploring the participants' interests (answering the question "Does the mediator help the participants identify underlying interests?").
   b. Managing conflict appropriately (answering the question "Does the mediator help the participants engage productively?").

   c. Evaluating ongoing process (answering the question "Does the mediator monitor and work with the participants to continually adapt the process?").
   d. Conducting the mediation ethically (answering the question "Does the mediator work with the participants in a professional manner?").
3. Managing the content or information in the mediation:
   a. Helping the participants identify and manage information (answering the question "Does the mediator provide a framework to gather and track information?").
   b. Helping the participants apply interest-based solutions (answering the question "Does the mediator help the participants generate options and apply interest-based solutions?").

The decision to incorporate certain secondary tasks into the primary tasks of managing relationships and process was hotly debated. Because the skills and knowledge associated with the tasks (e.g., power balancing, respect for client self-determination, and transitional skills) span all task categories, it was an arbitrary committee decision to include power balancing in the "relationship management" category and conflict management skills, such as elicitation of interests, and monitoring and adapting skills in the "process management" category.

The union representative of the skills assessment design team was helpful in keeping the committee focused on the necessity of identifying and including concrete, observable communication behaviors that could be verified and justified, using objective criteria. Thus the committee first identified observable mediation behaviors that could be associated with each of the defined tasks. It then became apparent to the committee that the behaviors identified represented different *levels* of skills. Then began the task of categorizing skills into levels of mediator ability, from poor to outstanding. It is at this point—identification of level of skill—that the professional expertise of the FMC assessor comes into play, because how each behavior is rated depends on the context in which the behavior is demonstrated. It has become increasingly clear to the assessors that observed behaviors can only be assessed in the context of each other and of the mediation process as a whole, because it is the interactive nature of the mediation that gives each skill and observed behavior relevance and significance. Indeed, the assessors found that attempting to isolate and quantify skills out of the context of other skills or the mediation process as a whole produced inappropriate evaluations. For instance, the same power-balancing method—say, encouraging one party to speak and asking the other party to paraphrase what was heard—may produce an alignment with one party in one context, be culturally inappropriate in another context, and be an effective method to balance differing levels of power in yet another context. Assessors using FMC's skills-based assessment tool, therefore, assess mediator knowledge and skills in the context of each other and in the context of the process as a whole.

The question of "weighting"—giving more value to certain tasks and their supporting skills—was discussed at length. At first the committee was resistant to this notion, given the interdependence of mediation skills and knowledge and thus the inability to consider any in isolation from the other. It was only after completing the pilot project and using the interactive skills assessment tool to evaluate over 150 candidates (166 applied; 136 were successful) that it was recognized, as recommended by Desmond Ellis (1999, note 17), who was hired to serve as an external evaluator of the certification process, that "performing ethically" and "managing power imbalance" ought to be assessed independently as well as in the context of the mediation demonstration as a whole. Thus, in recognition of the fundamental importance of mediators *not* causing interpersonal or social harm, FMC changed the certification process to require all mediators to pass the power imbalance[19] and ethics portions of the assessment process in order to attain certification. It was interesting to note that, although the assessment tools did not, as they were originally designed, weight power imbalance skills and ethical conduct more heavily than other aspects of the assessment process, research data from the independent evaluation (Ellis, 1999, note 26) demonstrated that such assessments were strong predictors of overall success or failure. In other words, all those who failed the skills assessment also failed "balancing power" and "performing ethically." Failure in these categories seemed to predict or indicate limited mediation ability. Consequently, although mediator responses to power imbalance and ethical conduct issues are still assessed in context (of other skills and the process as a whole), rather than independently, acceptable performance in these two categories is now a condition of certification.

Figure 21.1 illustrates the skills-based procedural assessment checklist used by FMC assessors[20] in the FMC certification program today.

DEVELOPMENT OF THE SUBSTANTIVE KNOWLEDGE WRITTEN EXAMINATION

Preparation, design, pilot testing, and revisions (revisions continue today) of examinations that could test for substantive knowledge drawn from the disciplines of law, social work, psychology, and conflict resolution, while still respecting the culture and vocabulary of the variety of disciplines from which mediators come, proved a Herculean task (Neilson & English, 2001, note 4, p. 228). The FMC examination team included a social worker/lawyer working with a lawyer/academic, a provincial court judge, an academic/lawyer/ sociologist and the project manager, occasionally operating in the role of mediator. Each examination was pilot tested on two mediators, one with a legal and another with a mental health background, in each of the 10 prov-

I. MANAGING THE RELATIONSHIPS IN MEDIATION	EXAMPLES OF OBSERVABLE BEHAVIORS	LEVEL
A. Establishes and maintains a respectful, trusting relationship with the participants. Does the mediator form an effective relationship with the participants? *OBSERVED BEHAVIORS*	**1. NO SKILLS DEMONSTRATED** • Treats participants in a disrespectful manner. • Makes no attempt to develop trust or rapport. **2. INADEQUATE SKILLS DEMONSTRATED** • Demonstrates uncertainty, lack of confidence in the mediation process. • Establishes minimal relationship with participants. • Expresses own views, imposes own decisions, and disregards those made by participants. • Forces participants to disclose feelings which expose and make them feel more vulnerable. **3. SATISFACTORY SKILLS DEMONSTRATED** • Is "present" and attentive. • Builds rapport and confidence in mediation process and self. • Demonstrates ability to be nonjudgmental and to keep an open mind. • Encourages open expression of views. Uses language both can understand. • Acknowledges what participants express as important to them. • Uses humor appropriately. **4. STRONG SKILLS DEMONSTRATED** • Protects and affirms participants' right to self-determination. • Maintains and supports participants' integrity. **5. OUTSTANDING SKILLS DEMONSTRATED** • Continually demonstrates predictability and accountability in all aspects of the working relationship. • Participants able to work with risks and creativity because of quality of trust in the mediator and the mediation process.	

(continued)

FIGURE 21.1 *(continued)*

| B. Facilitates a collaborative relationship between the participants

Does the mediator promote clients cooperative efforts and mutual understanding?

OBSERVED BEHAVIORS | 1. NO SKILLS DEMONSTRATED
• Actively discourages dialogue and distrust between participants.
• Participants have a worse relationship at end of session than at the beginning.

2. INADEQUATE SKILLS DEMONSTRATED
• Fails to establish effective guidelines for communication.
• Continually cuts off participants when they are engaged in productive discussion.
• Insists on controlling all dialogue through mediator, thus promoting dependency on mediator.
• Does not mutualize.

3. SATISFACTORY SKILLS DEMONSTRATED
• Engages both participants in the discussions.
• Encourages the participants' cooperation and partnership in the process.
• Promotes each participant's understanding of the other's point of view of the conflict.
4. STRONG SKILLS DEMONSTRATED
• Works with participants to promote mutual understanding, insight into and empathy for the other.
• Helps participants find a mutual definition of the problem.
5. OUTSTANDING SKILLS DEMONSTRATED
• Enhances participants' commitment to their new collaborative working relationship. | |
| C. Manages power imbalances

Does the mediator facilitate opportunities for full participation?

OBSERVED BEHAVIORS | 1. NO SKILLS DEMONSTRATED
• Ignores one party completely or diminishes the importance of what he or she says.
• Does not recognize unequal power balance.
2. INADEQUATE SKILLS DEMONSTRATED
• Uses the participants' positional, emotionally laden, inflammatory language.
• Allows one participant to dominate the session.
• Aligns with one of the participants.

3. SATISFACTORY SKILLS DEMONSTRATED
• Ensures equal communication opportunities which both understand.
• Uses appropriate body language and eye contact.
• Ongoing screening for safety.
• Ensures both agree with process decisions.

4. STRONG SKILLS DEMONSTRATED
• Works with participants to develop a process that creates and ensures equal opportunities for involvement. | *NOTE: A failure in this category (less than 3) means a failure overall.* |

(continued)

FIGURE 21.1 *(continued)*

5. OUTSTANDING SKILLS DEMONSTRATED
• Establishes and maintains a working environment based on equality with all participants able to give and receive appropriate, constructive comments/feedback.

II. MANAGING THE PROCESS OF THE MEDIATION	EXAMPLES OF OBSERVABLE BEHAVIORS* *You are not expected to demonstrate every one of these behaviors.	LEVEL
A. Attends to and explores participants' interests Does the mediator assist participants to identify underlying interests? *OBSERVED BEHAVIORS*	1. NO SKILLS DEMONSTRATED • Entrenches participants in their positions. • Accepts statements at face value; no questions or probes. • Imposes mediator's interests. 2. INADEQUATE SKILLS DEMONSTRATED • Minimal exploration of positions and without exploring interests before moving to solutions. • Ignores/mishandles statements of feelings. • Allows assumptions and misunderstandings. 3. SATISFACTORY SKILLS DEMONSTRATED • Allows sufficient time for each participant to express his or her positions and explore his or her interests. • Reframes positions and probes for underlying interests. • Acknowledges the p+articipants' feelings. • Clarifies misunderstandings and assumptions. • Ensures children's interests are addressed. 4. STRONG SKILLS DEMONSTRATED • Identifies mutual and individual interests. • Is able to differentiate and connect interests of the participants. 5. OUTSTANDING SKILLS DEMONSTRATED • Works with the participants to identify principles based on their underlying interests.	
B. Manages conflict appropriately Does the mediator assist the participants to engage productively? *OBSERVED BEHAVIORS*	1. NO SKILLS DEMONSTRATED • Oblivious to or extreme unease with conflict. • Neither participant feels emotionally or physically safe in the mediation. • No screening for safety. • Terminates unsafely. 2. INADEQUATE SKILLS DEMONSTRATED • Ignores or mismanages emotionally damaging statements. • Negatively reframes statements which serve to escalate, maintain, or entrench the participants' positions.	

(continued)

494

FIGURE 21.1 *(continued)*

3. SATISFACTORY SKILLS DEMONSTRATED
- Provides ongoing screening for safety.
- Works with the parties to develop their communication guidelines.
- Establishes and maintains (redirects, refocuses) constructive negotiations.
- Establishes an emotionally and physically safe atmosphere.
- Ensures focus is on the problem not the people.
- Acknowledges and normalizes the participants' conflict.

4. STRONG SKILLS DEMONSTRATED
- Uses interventions to seek clarification.
- Confronts discrepancies.
- Uses immediacy to attend to nonverbal cues.
- Reframes statements to defuse and gain consensus.

5. OUTSTANDING SKILLS DEMONSTRATED
- Appears comfortable with conflict and to assist the participants to deal with their conflict in a healthy, healing manner.
- Facilitates the participants' ongoing positive communication patterns.

C. Evaluates ongoing process Does the mediator monitor and work with participants to continually adapt the process? *OBSERVED BEHAVIORS*	1. NO SKILLS DEMONSTRATED • Overwhelmed and confused by the process and takes no action. • No control over process with no established and respected guidelines. 2. INADEQUATE SKILLS DEMONSTRATED • Unaware of participants' resistance to process. • Does not solicit or respect the participants' input into the process. • Lacks awareness of the contentiousness of the issues. • Allows participants to focus on past behaviors which are unrelated to the issue at hand. 3. SATISFACTORY SKILLS DEMONSTRATED • Respects each participant's different needs for time to process decisions. • Maintains optimism and forward movement. • Monitors participant's readiness to move productively through the process. • Demonstrates adequate understanding of issues. • Comfortable with silence. • Participants feel safe and understand what is happening.

(continued)

FIGURE 21.1 *(continued)*

- Helps generate an agenda and prioritizes it.
- Works with the participants to develop a process that respects their culture and their uniqueness.

4. STRONG SKILLS DEMONSTRATED
- Helps participants focus on issues to be addressed based on individual and mutual interests.
- Seeks clarification and direction from the participants in the process design, adapts agenda, and makes procedural changes as necessary.
- Tracks body language as well as verbal cues and attends to nonverbal cues.
- Encourages them in their capacity to work through the issues.

5. OUTSTANDING SKILLS DEMONSTRATED
- Consistently works with the participants to ensure that they are engaged in a mediation process that meets their particular needs with predictable transitions and structure and a pace they are both comfortable with.

D. Conducts the mediation ethically

Does the mediator work with the participants in a professional manner?

OBSERVED BEHAVIORS

1. NO SKILLS DEMONSTRATED
- Sets up or continues with an unsafe meeting endangering one or more of the participants.
- Violates code of ethics/professional standards of practice.

2. INADEQUATE SKILLS DEMONSTRATED
- Fails to discuss confidentiality.
- Gives wrong information or gives legal advice.
- Imposes solutions.

3. SATISFACTORY SKILLS DEMONSTRATED
- Explains confidentiality and deals with any immediate concerns around it.
- Monitors participants' readiness and safety before mediation and as an ongoing process.
- Evaluates need to include others or refer out.
- Acts within own area of ability and mandate.
- Discloses mediator biases/conflicts of interest.
- Maintains the children's best interests.
- Ensures full disclosure of information.

4. STRONG SKILLS DEMONSTRATED
- Ensures decision-making power remains with participants.
- Encourages feedback from participants on mediator impartiality.
- Preserves self-determination even when impasse is reached.

NOTE: A failure in this category (less than 3) means a failure overall.

(continued)

496

FIGURE 21.1 *(continued)*

5. OUTSTANDING SKILLS DEMONSTRATED
  • Continually engages participants in a process with integrity and respect, guarding their rights and maintaining their self-determination.

III. MANAGING THE CONTENT OF MEDIATION	EXAMPLES OF OBSERVABLE BEHAVIORS* *You are not expected to demonstrate every one of these behaviors.	LEVEL

A. Assists participants to identify and manage information

Does the mediator provide a framework to gather and track information?

OBSERVED BEHAVIORS

1. NO SKILLS DEMONSTRATED
  • Lacks interest and skill in soliciting information.
  • Deliberately misuses and mismanages information.

2. INADEQUATE SKILLS DEMONSTRATED
  • Does not provide appropriate information (role and process of mediation, pertinent issues).
  • Poor listening skills and does not capture the essence of what is being communicated.
  • Lacks knowledge of stages of children's growth and development, grieving cycle, community resources, etc.

3. SATISFACTORY SKILLS DEMONSTRATED
  • Defines the mediation process and the roles of the mediator and the participants.
  • Uses a variety of questions to generate information.
  • Tracks, uses, and summarizes information accurately.
  • Provides appropriate and correct information and/or refers to helpful resources.
  • Encourages full disclosure of information needed to make decisions.
  • Appears to understand case facts.

4. STRONG SKILLS DEMONSTRATED
  • Assists participants to organize information.
  • Works with participants to aid their ability to see new information and information links.
  • Helps the participants develop a framework to gather and track their needed information.

5. OUTSTANDING SKILLS DEMONSTRATED
  • Assists the participants to apply interest-based criteria in judging usefulness or relevance of the information.
  • Works with the participants to ensure the information is integrated throughout the process.

(continued)

FIGURE 21.1 *(continued)*

B. Assists participants to apply interest-based solutions

Does the mediator assist the participants to generate options and apply interest-based solutions?

OBSERVED BEHAVIORS

1. NO SKILLS DEMONSTRATED
   • Forces parties to a decision not of their making.
   • Frames issues as positional and the negotiations become positional bargaining.

2. INADEQUATE SKILLS DEMONSTRATED
   • Parties appear ready and express need to proceed with options, but mediator postpones despite time to do so.
   • Allows premature decisions based on insufficient information.
   • Does not summarize where they leave off.
   • Limits creation of options.
   • Allows unrealistic and unworkable decisions.

3. SATISFACTORY SKILLS DEMONSTRATED
   • Assists participants to explore and evaluate options.
   • Accurately summarizes progress.
   • Breaks solutions down into manageable portions.
   • Works with participants to build interim measures to assist until next session.
   • Promotes participants' ability to define their own outcomes or solutions.
   • Encourages and commends the participants' efforts.

4. STRONG SKILLS DEMONSTRATED
   • Helps the participants identify principles and criteria that will guide their decision making.
   • Assists participants to select a wide variety of creative options which best address their mutual as well as individual interests.
   • Provides an opportunity for participants to test the reality of their decisions.
   • Provides for options if agreement is not reached or breaks down.

5. OUTSTANDING SKILLS DEMONSTRATED
   • Works with the participants to develop their own principles to evaluate their solutions.
   • Encourages the participants' belief in their ability to use their own criteria to develop interest-based solutions for the present mediation and for their future negotiations.

inces and one of the territories of Canada. Results, comments, and suggestions from all geographical areas of Canada were collected, examinations were rewritten, and tested again by members of the committee. FMC now processes a test bank of substantive knowledge exams, albeit in a constant state of revision.

These examinations proved to be a source of great anxiety to certification candidates. Yet, although they are comprehensive and lengthy (they take 3–4 hours to write), the pass rate was high (Ellis, 1999, note 26),[21] probably, in part, because most of the mediators who applied for certification during the pilot implementation project were highly skilled; many, 12.5%, were mediation trainers and/or administrators of mediation programs. FMC is monitoring the situation to determine whether or not the pass rate for the examinations, currently set at 60%, should be reassessed.

OVERVIEW OF FMC'S CERTIFICATION PROCESS

The FMC family mediator certification assessment process begins with a five-page application and letters of reference, including a personal profile assessment, a practicum supervisor's report, and verification of specified hours of training (180 hours for family relations or financial mediators; 230 hours for comprehensive mediators, plus completion of a supervised practicum or peer review and continuing education).[22] The certification process is voluntary; it is designed to assess mediators who have already received training and accumulated experience. Certification assessments operate independently of training in order to offer an objective professional evaluation. The application is reviewed and assessed by the administrator of the certification program. Once the application is accepted and the candidate has paid the cost of the assessment, he or she is sent a *Certification Candidate's Manual,* designed to familiarize the candidates with all the steps and expectations of the assessment process. The manual includes detailed instructions and copies of the assessment tools, such as the skills assessment checklist discussed earlier.

Precertification workshops were designed for FMC. These 2-day workshops provide an opportunity for candidates to discuss the assessment process, work with the skills assessment checklist, and use video equipment to make videotapes of mediators demonstrating mediation skills. During the pilot evaluation of FMC's certification process, precertification workshops (to be discussed shortly) were offered by FMC certification assessors. Participants reported that their fellow classmates in the workshops provided support and valuable feedback on their mediation skills. In order to preserve the independent, arms-length integrity of the certification process, these 2-day workshops are now offered by independent mediation trainers licensed by FMC. These workshops, though recommended by FMC, are not a requirement for certification. During the pilot evaluation of the certification process, five candidates who had not attended the workshops applied for certification; using only the *Candidate's Manual* for guidance, four completed the process successfully.

Role-playing mediation scenarios that are adaptations of actual mediation cases are included in the *Candidate's Manual.* The scenarios were chosen for their realism and complexity to give mediation candidates an opportunity to demonstrate a variety of skills in handling multiproblem, highly emotional, family law conflicts. Candidates are asked to videotape a 1-hour demonstration[23] of their mediation abilities, as identified in the skills assessment checklist, using the role-play scenarios provided. That said, candidates have the option of submitting live mediation sessions with clients for assessment, provided that they have a signed release from their clients allowing them to do so. Our experience, however, is that this is not the best option. During the pilot project, only one candidate chose to submit a live mediation for assessment. The assessors found that using a live mediation was less than fully satisfactory, as the clients obviously had their own needs in the mediation: Mediators are required ethically to respond to clients' needs, and these needs do not always coincide with the mediator's need to demonstrate a variety of skills in a 1-hour framework. Presumably, using live mediation sessions might work if each assessor could review tapes of a whole mediation process (or 3–12 hours of tape) for each candidate.[24] Asking candidates to edit hours of mediation tape to produce a single-hour demonstration is also unlikely to work, given the importance of assessing skills in context. The experience has led FMC to discourage the presentation of live mediations for assessment.

FMC chose to promote the use videotaped simulated mediations rather than live demonstrations so that candidates would have more control over the assessment process. This method allows candidates to make as many tapes as they like until they create one they think is a good example of their work. It also allows candidates from remote regions of Canada to participate in certification, since they do not have to finance the cost of travel to a central "testing" center. Furthermore, the use of videotapes enables assessors to replay portions of the tape in order to review parts of the mediation process, so they can reassess prior assumptions and skill evaluations in the context of the mediation session as a whole. This procedure provides more reflective and comprehensive assessment than would be possible in a live assessment.

As part of the skills demonstration tape, candidates are asked to include feedback from the role-playing mediation clients about their understandings and perspectives on what occurred during the simulated session. This feedback is to occur immediately following the conclusion of the session. The role players are instructed to discuss the parts of the mediation done well and any parts that appeared to challenge the certification candidate.

The next step is a reflective, self-evaluative assessment. Before candidates submit the video for assessment, they are asked to review their own tape and to complete a self-assessment and reflective analysis of their own work. In particular, they are asked to answer questions about style or model of practice and to identify their own strengths as a mediator displayed in the demonstration tape, as well as shortcomings with better practice alternatives. Candidates are also asked to provide examples from the demonstration tape of techniques used to: (1) maintain a positive relationship with participants, (2) maintain a collaborative atmosphere between or among participants, (3) encourage participants to abandon positions in favor of interests, (4) promote participant transition (i.e. expanded understanding of the other participant, the problem, or the solutions), and (5) assist the participants in managing the content of the session. After completing this task, candidates are asked to review and rate their own demonstration tape using the FMC's skills assessment checklist in Figure 21.1. These documents are then sent to the assessors with the demonstration tape for evaluation.

The self-evaluation component of the certification assessment process serves educational as well as assessment functions. It encourages mediators to (1) reflect on their own theories, methodologies, and styles of practice and (2) think about how they connect theory to practice. This component also allows the assessors to consider the theoretical and thus methodological orientations of candidates when assessing skills demonstrations.

ASSESSMENTS USING THE SKILLS ASSESSMENT TOOL

Each assessment tape is viewed independently by two assessors. The first step is watching the entire skills-based assessment tape and writing down the mediation dialogue. (After 100 assessments, assessors learn to write quickly in shorthand!) Next the assessor reviews the dialogue to identify observed communication behaviors associated with each required skill and task; these are highlighted on the dialogue sheet and then transferred, as illustrations, onto the skills assessment checklist, thereby illustrating the reasons for the assessor ratings in each category. The communication behaviors are then assigned a numerical value (embedded in the assessment checklist in Figure 21.1). Candidates must achieve a score of 60% overall and a score of 60% in categories C ("manages power imbalances") and D ("conducts the mediation effectively") in order to pass the skills portion of the certification assessment process. Prior to finalizing the scores, assessors review candidates' self-reflective assessments in order to ensure that they have taken into account candidates' theoretical and methodological orientations. The assessors then consult each other and compare assessments.

FMC assessors have found that candidates readily understand FMC's skills checklist and that use of the tool helps to focus subsequent discussions with candidates in the next stage of the process and allows assessors to give concrete examples of behaviors assessed. These discussions serve two functions: They help the assessors (1) better understand candidates' theoretical and methodological underpinnings, and (2) coach candidates through their critical learning process, should improvement be necessary.

Candidates are provided with a written assessment identifying levels of accomplishment and matters that require attention. Figure 21.2 presents a composite of written feedback sent to a number of candidates who required more work in order the achieve certification.[25] The assessors have found that it is vitally important to provide information about strengths as well as limitations in order to encourage continuing learning and reapplication.

It is important to note that the assessors identify the location of the behaviors they cite in the evaluation from the demonstration tape. This specificity allows the candidate to review a copy of the videotape while reviewing the written assessment in order to enhance learning.

FIGURE 21.2. Family Mediator Skills Assessment. Examples of assessment feedback for candidates who were rated as "more work needed."

	Demonstrates required skills/ more work needed
I. MANAGING THE RELATIONSHIPS IN MEDIATION	
A. Establishes and maintains a respectful, trusting relationship between participants and the mediator. *Does the mediator form an effective relationship?* CANDIDATE A: Friendly, confident manner. Uses encouraging language. Needs to listen closer to the participants' priorities and respect their agenda (e.g., both parties wanted to talk about parenting and the mediator pushed them to talk about the house until they assertively said no). Needs to emphasize the process is theirs and respect their self-determination. Watch putting your hand over your mouth; this makes it hard for the clients to hear and physically limits your connection with them. Works hard to build empathy by acknowledging Harry's pain (e.g., "It is very difficult for you to accept what has happened") but at times the mediator's comments come across harshly and seem to limit the development of the mediator client relationship (e.g., "You have to get a grip on yourself").	Needs to maintain and support participants' integrity.
B. Facilitates a collaborative relationship between the participants. *Does the mediator promote client's self-determination and mutual understanding?* CANDIDATE B: Controls all of the dialogue through the mediator. Cuts off communication between the parties and limits their interaction. Need to be aware of leading, misstating, or misrepresenting (e.g., Mediator: "The best plan is an after-school regime with daddy rather than the facility care plan"; here "best" is the mediator's word . . . Sarah rejects this idea and attacks the mediator's neutrality).	Needs to minimize interruptions by the mediator and monitor use of divisive language.

(continued)

FIGURE 21.2 *(continued)*

C. Manages power imbalances. *Does the mediator facilitate opportunities for full participation?* *CANDIDATE A:* Works hard to try to give equal communication opportunities to both parties. Harry dominates the beginning of the session and spending time acknowledging and exploring his concerns could be helpful here. Be careful with agreeing with statements made by the parties because of perceived alignment (e.g., with Jeanie with her idea of talking to her father [@ 18 minutes] without checking with Harry). The idea may be fine, but saying "That is an excellent suggestion" may be viewed by the participants as siding with one over the other. When the mediator ends up in a discussion about Jeanie's psychological state, demonstrates very good recovery skills (e.g., @ 28 minutes, acknowledging and asking Jeanie "How can we get back on track?").	Needs to be more careful in agreeing with a party and accepting statements at face value with no questions or probes.
II. MANAGING THE PROCESS OF MEDIATION	
A. Works with the participants to develop and work through the mediation. *Does the mediator assist participants to identify underlying interests?* *CANDIDATE B:* Demonstrates strong skills in using hunches regarding the participants' positions (e.g., @ 8 minutes, "Sounds like you are feeling disadvantaged?"). Uses some good open questions (e.g., @ 25 minutes, "Tell me what is it like to be a mom or dad"). Needs to be careful that the questions are not positional questions (e.g., @ 59 minutes, Sarah says "You can't undermine my relationship with the girls," and the mediator replies, "How do you respond to that, George"—this just keeps George in his position). Use of reframing would assist them to move more quickly to interests (e.g., George could respond to Sarah's interests rather than her position, such as "So for you, Sarah, the plans that you and George will make need to include ways to ensure and maintain solid parenting relationships with the girls. How do you respond to that, George?"). Demonstrates good skills in acknowledging feelings. Needs to go one step further with that and explore the "why" (e.g., "George, this is scary for you," but also they both need to know why—what are his interests such as concerns, fears for future—so more probing and clarifying would help move George and the mediation along).	Use more reframing to neutralize the parties' statements and move the parties off their positions.
B. Manages conflict appropriately. *Does the mediator assist the participants to engage productively?* *CANDIDATE A:* Use of more immediacy and talking about the "old" way versus the "new" way to communicate may have prevented so many interruptions. Also helpful to give some information on different stages in the grief cycle of separation. By spending time in the beginning to establish "their" guidelines for the sessions and gaining permission for the mediator to intervene, would enable the mediator to be more effective in dealing with the conflict. Needs to develop more intervention techniques to manage conflict (e.g., reframing, refocus on children, immediacy, and confronting). At times appears to be oblivious to the unease and frustration level of the clients; needs to observe and acknowledge some of their nonverbal behaviors.	Needs to develop a repertoire of skills to manage conflict.

(continued)

FIGURE 21.2 *(continued)*

C. Evaluates ongoing process. *Does the mediator monitor and work with participants to continually adapt the process?* *CANDIDATE C:* Tries to track the negative communication patterns and respectfully asks permission to be able to direct the discussion. Nice work in demonstrating ability to stop the parties from looking for immediate solutions before they explore all possibilities. Participants express frustration at not getting on with the issues. Seems to lack structure in the process; needs to summarize more frequently and help them clarify what they have agreed to and what is next on the agenda.	Needs to be more assertive and clearly establish an agenda and work with them to prioritize their issues.
D. Conducts the mediation ethically. *Does the mediator work with the participants in a professional manner?* *CANDIDATE A:* Supports the participants' decision to work in mediation and keep this out of court. Encourages consultation with lawyers—this is especially important in dealing with financial issues. Mediator should not be in the decision-making role (e.g., @ 63 minutes, "I remind you that the three of us will make the decisions") and (@ 40 minutes, mediator suggests they sell their house) and then build the process on the mediator's suggestion (e.g., @ 44 minutes, "You decided to sell your house so now where are you going to live?"). It is important to help the participants to remember the needs of the children.	The mediator does not make decisions for the clients.

III. MANAGING THE CONTENT OF MEDIATION

A. Assists participants to identify and manage information. *Does the mediator provide a framework to gather and track information?* *CANDIDATE C:* Appears confused by the facts of the case and the volume of information. Sometimes uses closed questions in an interrogative manner; a more curious tone would draw out the parties more effectively.	Needs to develop a repertoire of questions to gather information and a system of organizing data.
B. Assists participants to apply interest-based solution. *Does the mediator assist the participants to generate options and apply interest-based solutions?* *CANDIDATE B:* Assists them to understand from the outset that they have many choices (e.g., @ 9 minutes, "You have two different options and two choices and in between are more scenarios"). Manages to get an interim agreement. Needs to assign homework (e.g., "Write down how you would see the involvement of both sets of grandparents in a way that would be good for the children and acceptable to the other parent") instead of the mediator taking on the assignment of writing down the grandparent involvement.	Needs to keep the work in the hands of the participants.

Figure 21.3 presents an actual report to an outstanding candidate for certification. It is important to note here the interdependence of the mediator's skills and process evaluated during the assessment process.

After the written assessment has been sent to the candidates, assessors contact by telephone candidates who submitted poor or inadequate demonstrations in order to help them gain an understanding of their styles of practice, goals, and objectives as mediators and to coach them in the pursuit of their critical learning needs. The goal of the process is to encourage continuing professional growth and development and eventual certification. Candidates who fail the skills-based demonstration may repeat this step after *thoroughly* discussing their first demonstration with an assessor and clearly understanding the requirements needed to upgrade the skills demonstration. Assessors may require candidates to engage in more practice experience or in more training in specified fields before submitting another demonstration.

Candidates who fail a second demonstration are required to successfully complete a supervised practicum and to submit a report from their practicum supervisor before they submit a third skills demonstration. Since the goal is to encourage professional growth and development of mediators, rather than to limit entry into the field, FMC certifying assessors are committed to helping candidates find the best course of study and practice to suit their candidate's individual needs.

Candidates who pass the skills-based assessment must also take a 3–4 hour invigilated substantive knowledge examination discussed earlier that includes questions drawn from law, mental health, and conflict resolution fields and questions that assess for issues associated with mediator sensitivities to vulnerabilities produced by gender, culture, sexual orientation, and abuse.

Candidates must pass each stage of the assessment process (the skills-based checklist and the substantive knowledge exam) and the power imbalance and ethical conduct assessments in order to become certified.

INDEPENDENT RESEARCH EVALUATION OF FMC CERTIFICATION PROCESS

Prior to its implementation, the certification assessment process was pilot tested and evaluated in four Canadian jurisdictions—New Brunswick, Ontario, Manitoba, and British Columbia (with spaces reserved for applicants from other jurisdictions)—by an independent, external researcher: Dr. Desmond Ellis of York University. After collecting data from each site and from 120 of the total 136 candidates for certification, Ellis reported his conclusion that FMC's certification process is reliable and recommended national implementation. A few of the findings from the pilot study are discussed here. First, Ellis analyzed the skills-based assessment scores of the two FMC assessors on a per-candidate basis. He found that the assessment scores

FIGURE 21.3. Family Mediator Skills Assessment. Example of feedback for "outstanding skills demonstrated."

I. MANAGING THE RELATIONSHIPS IN MEDIATION

A. Establishes and maintains a respectful, trusting relationship between participants and the mediator.

Does the mediator form an effective relationship?

Warm, engaging, open manner. Very attentive to the parties—listens carefully and watches intently—100% present with her clients. Acknowledges that what they say is important. Nonjudgmental and empathetic. Establishes and maintains a trusting relationship throughout the mediation by being accountable and predictable in the process. High energy. Uses down-to-earth language. Phrases such as "sounds like" could be used less.

B. Facilitates a collaborative relationship between the participants.

Does the mediator promote client's self-determination and mutual understanding?

Engages both the parties early in the session by using their common interest of their daughters, "Tell me about the girls." Uses every opportunity to mutualize their concerns (e.g., "Both your families have supported you with money and help with the children," "Both of you are going back to your roots," and "You both come with different views about what is the best outcome"). Continually establishes a mutual definition of their problems (e.g., "Your two key areas are a parenting plan for your children and what to do about your house," and "The girls will have a home with both of you, and so you have to find living arrangements that work for your girls"). Respects and acknowledges their uniqueness (e.g., "You see it as wrong from your perspective and Jeanie sees it as right from her perspective").

C. Manages power imbalances.

Does the mediator facilitate opportunities for full participation?

Recognizes and attempts to correct the power imbalance between Harry and Jeanie. Demonstrates a wide variety of skills for managing power imbalances (e.g., supporting Jeanie's ability to speak, affirming her right to self-determination, and acknowledging her struggles as "equal to" Harry's). Does not align with Harry when he tries to co-opt the mediator around the issues of financing of the house. Affirms both parties' ideas in a nonjudgmental and normalizing way (e.g., "Both of you are going back to your roots. It seems most natural").

II. MANAGING THE PROCESS OF MEDIATION

A. Works with the participants to develop and work through the mediation.

Does the mediator assist participants to identify underlying interests?

Strong demonstration of working with the participants to identify, understand and use their underlying interests to generate some resolutions based on their mutually validated interests (e.g., helps them move from "I want the girls and money" to "we need to discuss a parenting plan based on stability and continuity for the girls and make some decisions about how we both can have homes that meet high standards for the girls"). Continually ensures that the girls' interests are addressed. Acknowledges and normalizes their feelings (e.g., "You all pulled together."). Helps the parties differentiate (e.g., Harry values Calgary and his history and Jeanie needs to go back to Kelowna) and connect their interests (e.g., both need to return to their roots and support from their parents).

B. Manages conflict appropriately.

Does the mediator assist the participants to engage productively?

Engages the parties in an atmosphere of respectful cooperation, so they did not demonstrate much conflict. Uses positive reinforcement for their patience and for the

506

way they are communicating (e.g., "Thanks for waiting. You clearly have lots to talk about" and "I commend you for trying to make it work; your girls are lucky to have you as parents"). Reframes statements to defuse and gain consensus (e.g., regarding parenting arrangements, "You both have come with different views of an outcome. It is normal to have lots of work to do" and regarding the financial decisions about housing, "Looking at options to financing for fairness").

C. Evaluates ongoing process.

Does the mediator monitor and work with participants to continually adapt the process?

The session moves along by the optimism and enthusiasm of the mediator. Needs to monitor the pacing and allow for occasional pauses so that the participants can process the information and dynamics of the session. Continually checks with both parties in developing a process that works for both of them (e.g., "How will that work for you?" and "What do you want to talk about first?"). Encouraging (e.g., Jeanie expresses her doubts about succeeding in the mediation, and mediator replies, "There are a number of approaches you can try out"). Always reframes statements to gain consensus (e.g., "You understand it as OK as long as it is temporary," and "This is your chance to negotiate something for you and your children").

D. Conducts the mediation ethically.

Does the mediator work with the participants in a professional manner?

Gives legal information about Harry's misunderstanding and is very clear about her mandate (e.g., "It is not my role to give you tips"). Encourages independent legal advice. Consistently ensures that the decision-making power remains with the participants. Gives excellent explanation of confidentiality issues. Discusses need for "other support people," and acknowledges Jeanie's work done in counseling.

III. MANAGING THE CONTENT OF MEDIATION

A. Assists participants to identify and manage information.

Does the mediator provide a framework to gather and track information?

Clearly comfortable with managing the facts of the case (e.g., tracks and accurately summarizes their issues). Strong skills in using a variety of questions to generate information (e.g., "How can you get what you want and give the girls a family and continuity?", "What do they need for their well-being?" and "How can it work for your whole constellations?"). Helps them identify new information (e.g., why they need an appraisal) and the mediator then sits back and lets them work it out. Assists them in defining interest-based criteria to judge their resolutions (e.g., "stability and continuity" in their parenting plans for the girls).

B. Assists participants to apply interest-based solution.

Does the mediator assist the participants to generate options and apply interest-based solutions?

Strong demonstration of summarizing their progress. Provides opportunities for the parties to test the reality of their decisions (e.g., asks consequential questions regarding the best interests of the children, "Sounds like you need some exploration, but how does that play out for the girls?"). Works to build interim measures (e.g., to appraisal of house, holiday to Kelowna) that bridge until the next session. Breaks down solutions into manageable portions and reassures (e.g., "You don't have to settle everything right now"). Could have suggested an interim agreement to be drawn up. Very empowering and encouraging in her belief that they have the ability to work out their own solutions in the mediation and in the future.

were highly consistent and concluded that the assessment tool was reliable (Ellis, 1999, note 26; Neilson & English, 2001, note 4, p. 232).

Another interesting finding was that candidates for certification who rated their own performance more highly than the assessors tended to have lower assessment scores than those who were more self-evaluative and critical (Ellis, as quoted by Neilson & English, 2001, note 4, p. 236). In "The Role of Interest-Based Facilitation in Designing Accreditation Standards: The Canadian Experience," we speculated that this finding may be a function of the important influence of mediator personality on mediation performance as well as the importance of critical self-evaluation in professional development (Neilson & English, 2001, note 4, pp. 236–245). FMC assessors have found the FMC assessment process—particularly the inclusion of specific examples of communication behaviors—invaluable when dealing with overconfident candidates who lack critical self-evaluation skills.

Finally, in connection with diversity in professional and theoretical orientation, the evidence so far, as reported in Neilson and English (2001) and in English et al. (1999, Appendix 14)[26] is that the certification process is able to respond effectively to applicants who come to the certification process from different professional backgrounds and from different theoretical perspectives, using different methodologies.[27] During the pilot study 136 mediators successfully completed the certification process. Comparison of the skills assessment scores for lawyer (22) and social worker (33) applicants[28] revealed that they had similar assessment scores[29] (average scores from assessor's A and B). Social workers scored an average of 32.94, lawyers, an average of 34.74 (English et al., 1999, Appendix 14, note 4).[30] The finding is consistent with mediation research that indicates profession of origin is not a reliable predictor of mediation skill (Elwork & Smucker, 1988; Kochan & Jick, 1978; Pearson, Thoennes, & Vanderkoi, 1982; Society of Professionals in Dispute Resolution, 1988).

CONTINUING CHALLENGES

Although FMC's certification process appears to have addressed a number of challenges and concerns confronting the discipline, its "job" is far from done. Indeed, professional standards and certification processes for mediators must stay vibrant and alive. They can only do so if their overseers remain receptive to the changing needs and interests of the discipline. Some of the major challenges that lie ahead include keeping professional and certification standards current and responsive to theoretical and methodological developments in the field. This is no easy task for an organization, such as FMC, which must rely on donations of professional expertise. Current challenges include ensuring that mediation assessment processes assess mediator responses to vulnerabilities produced by abuse, disability, and culture, as knowledge in these fields continues to evolve. In October, 2003, Family Mediation Canada revised its *Standards of Practice and Certification*[31] to restrict the use of face-to-face mediation in partner abuse cases and to address a number of practice issues associated with mediation and culture. No doubt, additional changes will be needed in the future. Responding to culture, in particular, will be a continuing challenge.

We know that culture affects perceptions of conflict and thus the appropriateness of conflict methodologies. On the one hand is the importance of respecting and honoring the development and use of nonmediation alternatives more appropriate than mediation in certain cultural contexts; on the other is the importance of mediators responding to cultural needs and interests in an appropriate manner. Although it is questionable that we could or should attempt to create a generic conflict resolution process applicable to all cultures, since such an approach fails to honor self-determinism and cultural integrity, much work has been done in this area and far more remains to be done. Unanswered but highly salient questions include the following:

- How do we ensure that mediators understand and are able to circumvent the "cultural blind spots" of mediation, such as the field's emphasis on:
  - Individual interests and needs
  - Face-to-face negotiations
  - Cultural assumptions about gender, children, and the nature of family
  - Communication skills that promote forthright discussion, summarizing, and questioning to elicit feelings
- How do we ensure that cultural knowledge enhances mediator sensitivity to the nature, meaning, and implications of culture as experienced and understood by participants so that it does not result in overgeneralization and/or imposition of the mediator's understandings of culture?
- How do we ensure that assessment processes fairly and accurately assess mediators who work in different cultures?
- How do we ensure that certification processes are accessible to mediators who work in a variety of cultures that use a variety of languages and techniques?

Other challenges on the immediate horizon include: (1) resisting demands to simplify the field, (2) resisting requests for texts candidates can memorize in order to pass the substantive knowledge examination (the danger is that candidates will study to pass the test rather than seek more complete knowledge of the field), (3) resisting pressure to create single-model assessments of mediation practice, (4) resisting claims of disciplinary ownership of the field, and (5) resisting problems associated with computer-assisted conflict resolution.

In closing, although we like to think that FMC's *Standards of Practice and Certification* and its certification process are a good beginning, we recognize they are merely that: a beginning. Our hope is that the approaches we have taken and the product produced will prove useful to the mediation community, in Canada and the United States, as the discipline continues to evolve and develop.

NOTES

1. M. Guravich, Certified Family Relations Mediator (FMC), Operational Consultant, Program Support, Court Services Division, Department of Justice, Province of New Brunswick, comment on Family Mediation Canada certification process, 1999.

2. J. Maresca, family lawyer and Certified Comprehensive Family Mediator (FMC) comment on Family Mediation Canada certification process, 1999.

3. Lang and Taylor (2000, p. 239).

4. Family Mediation Canada (FMC) was created in 1984. Its objects are: (1) to provide a Canadian forum for the exchange of ideas, experiences, research, and opportunities relating to all aspects of family mediation through newsletters, conferences, and seminars; (2) to develop and encourage a code of ethics and standards of practice; (3) to develop and encourage training and a continuing education program; (4) to encourage and conduct research into all areas of family dispute resolution; (5) to provide consultation to provincial mediation associations and other interested agencies, groups, and individuals; and (6) to inform the Canadian public about the advantages of mediation. From its inception, FMC was committed to advancing family mediation by developing standards of practice to ensure quality mediation services for the public.

5. Although evaluation and arbitration processes are commonly annexed to mediation processes, once a third party offers pure evaluation or arbitration, he or she is offering expert evaluation or arbitration, not mediation. See, for example, Boskey's comments in Love and Boskey (1997).

6. Neilson's dissertation was the product, in part, of in-depth interviews with 102 practicing mediators, 17 administrators, and 17 registrars and observation of 61 mediation sessions in the Greater London region of England.

7. In 1993 Peggy English literally drove across Canada, from Vancouver in British Columbia to the Atlantic Provinces, in order to consult mediators, mediation trainers, lawyers, and judges on a personal basis about education, training, practice, and certification issues.

8. Suggestions and comments of practitioners and trainers were incorporated into FMC documents. The result was numerous revisions and drafts of Practice and Training Standards, a product that continues to undergo development. (English, 1993, 1994b; English & Neilson, 1995; Neilson & English, 1996).

9. Basically, when using an inductive approach one gathers information or data about what is in order to generate theory. Subsequently, the validity of the theory or hypothesis is tested, assessed, and then, if necessary, revised. Researchers and academics

adopting deductive approaches start with a theory or hypothesis about what is (or what should be) and then set out to prove or disprove it. Both approaches have their place: inductive methodologies generate new theories and knowledge; deductive approaches test their validity.

10. Thus, English, a well-known and respected mediation practitioner with extensive experience, joined forces with Neilson, a legal academic. We believe that the involvement of the mediation community in developing practice and accreditation standards, not as subjects but as co-architects, and the use of interest-based facilitative, rather than expert-evaluative, methodology has been central to FMC's success. Inclusive, participatory approaches take longer than evaluative approaches—in our case, 10 years—yet we believe the approach is essential if practice standards and accreditation processes are genuinely to reflect the principles and values of the mediation discipline.

11. Obviously, we encountered numerous differences of opinion as we worked with practitioners to develop standards of practice and, later, an accreditation process. From 1993 to 1996 we listened carefully to such differences and concerns and repeatedly incorporated practitioner and trainer suggestions into the practice and accreditation documents. Numerous revisions were necessary to accommodate cultural and regional, urban, and rural concerns. In many respects, the 1996 document was different from the 1993 and 1994 versions. After years of consultations, the membership of FMC finally was ready to endorse the 1996 standards and directed FMC to explore accreditation options.

12. The actual costs of FMC's certification project have been valued at well over $1.5 million, as follows: a $150,000 grant from the Department of Justice, Canada; $350,314 in kind support from the Ministry of Attorney General of British Columbia; a $3,000 grant from the Law Foundation of the Northwest Territories; and $1,072,064 financial costs and professional time contributed by (donated to) Family Mediation Canada. In addition, the Province of New Brunswick, Department of Justice, assumed costs associated with the certification of court social workers in that area, law firms donated the use of meeting rooms, and the law firm of Fraser Milner donated legal assistance throughout the project and assumed some of the costs of the project. See English and Neilson with Hacking (1999).

13. FMC's certification process does not use any of these measurements because they are assessments of result, not necessarily of mediator skill or performance. FMC's certification process has been designed to ensure that assessment of skills operates independently of client response.

14. *Culture* includes religion, national and cultural affiliation and identity, sexual orientation, socioeconomic status, and region (urban and rural).

15. Mediators who do not pass the power imbalance and ethics portions of the certification assessment process are not certified, even if their other assessment scores are within an acceptable range.

16. For example, Neilson (2001) raises serious concerns about mediator and lawyer responses to women and children in partner abuse cases. Consequently, FMC's certification committee, chaired by Carole McKnight, has passed amendments that limit the use of face-to-face facilitated mediation in partner abuse cases.

17. For further discussion of last point, see Neilson and English (2001, note 4).

18. The Ministry of Attorney General of British Columbia partnered with FMC in design of the Certification Process.

19. Power imbalances commonly reflect vulnerabilities and/or special social challenges produced by factors such as abuse, culture, sexual orientation, socioeconomic status, or mental and physical disability.

20. FMC assessors are experienced mediators who have been certified by FMC and who have completed a mentored assessment training process.

21. The majority of candidates received marks of 90% or more.

22. For example, the minimum training set out for an Applicant Seeking Certification as a Comprehensive Family Mediator is as follows:

(1) AT LEAST 80 hours of basic conflict resolution and mediation theory education and skills training, including cultural training; and

(2) AT LEAST 150 hours of further related education and training including:

(a) AT LEAST 35 hours of training on the family dynamics of separation and divorce including:

(i) the psychological effects of family breakdown on family members;

(ii) stages of the separation and divorce process;

(iii) appropriate custody, access and visitation arrangements by age and maturity of the child;

(iv) child development issues as those relate to the specifics of family reorganization and parenting plans;

(b) AT LEAST 21 hours on child law—custody, access, guardianship, support, child protection and abduction law;

(c) AT LEAST 21 hours of training on abuse and control issues including instruction on power imbalances, the dynamics and effects of abuse on family members, indicators of danger in abuse cases, child protection matters associated with family abuse and violence, safety issues in mediation, the use of tools and techniques to detect and assess family abuse before and during mediation, the use and application of assessment tools to screen inappropriate family abuse cases from mediation, referral techniques, and information about sources of help for abused family members in communities;

(d) AT LEAST 42 hours training on legal and financial issues relating to separation, divorce and family reorganization, including: the law with respect to the division and allocation of the family's income and property on separation and divorce; income tax law with respect to transfers of money and property between family and former family members; a basic understanding of joint and separate liability for family debts; a basic understanding of company and partnership law; of appraisal and valuation methods; of insurance, trust and inheritance law and finally, enough evidentiary and property law to enable mediators to cope with disclosure problems;

(e) AT LEAST 7 hours of training on ethical issues relating to the mediation process;

(f) AT LEAST 3 hours on drafting memoranda of understanding; and

(3) Completion of an approved mediation practicum in accordance with FMC standards as set out in section 5.7 below, or, if the applicant has been a practicing family mediator for at least two years, in lieu of completion of a practicum, the applicant may submit two positive peer evaluations from referees competent to assess mediation and conflict resolution work who can attest to the applicant's mediation skills, knowledge and experience; and 20 hours of continuing family mediation education each year; with at least 14 hours of conflict resolution or mediation skills training in the last three

years. Other continuing family mediation education and training may include teaching and coaching, writing, reading, taking relevant courses, doing relevant volunteer work and attending relevant conferences (Neilson & English, 1996; Family Mediation Canada, 2003).

23. Review and assessment of each hour of a demonstration tape takes 2–4 hours— and more, when the skills demonstrated are borderline or poor. Consequently, allowing tapes of more than 1 hour is cost prohibitive.

24. Originally, we contemplated assessing live mediation demonstrations, but it quickly became apparent that, given Canada's geography, doing so would be cost prohibitive. Today we realize that live assessments would have been a mistake. The role plays in the live mediation were carefully developed to provide complexity and challenges required to elicit from mediators the knowledge, skills, and techniques being assessed. However, since, as noted, during live mediation, mediators must ethically respond to participant needs and interests, such needs and interests will not usually require a full range of knowledge and skill from a mediator in a single mediation session. Consequently, mediators found it difficult to demonstrate a broad range of skills in a live mediation session. Most chose the role-play option.

25. Candidates are given detailed written feedback but not the assessment scores. The skill level scores are generated merely for assessment and comparison purposes.

26. See also Neilson and English (1996, Section 4.6).

27. We are often asked if FMC's process can accommodate the assessment of mediators from different theoretical perspectives who use a variety of models, such as evaluative and transformative mediation. Although a complete answer warrants a more detailed discussion, our initial answer is "yes," provided that such processes respect the fundamental values and principles of mediation. Methods that are purely evaluative, that fail to offer respect to clients or a level of autonomy appropriate to client needs in the context of the conflict, that are not caring, that do not offer procedural fairness, or that do not promote conflict resolution would not pass the FMC assessment process.

28. Included in the social work category are applicants who list themselves as social workers and those who list professional training as a social work degree. The lawyer category includes applicants who list LLB training and those who list "lawyer" as professional of origin. One applicant, who was both a lawyer and social worker, was counted twice. Other applicants for certification included family justice counselors without social work degrees, psychologists, family and marriage counselors, criminologists, academics, a psychiatrist, an accountant, and a minister.

29. Some candidates were assessed twice. In these cases averages were taken from the second set of assessment scores, since these were the final scores for purposes of certification.

30. Candidates who did not complete the assessment process were excluded from the analysis.

31. The Standards document was also renamed; the earlier title was *Practice, Certification and Training Standards*.

REFERENCES

Ellis, D. (1999). Family Mediation Canada Certification Implementation Project Evaluation Report. In P. English & L. Neilson with W. Hacking (Eds.), *Family Mediation Canada National Certification Implementation Pilot Project Report 1997–1999*. Kitchener, Ontario, Canada: Family Mediation Canada.

Elwork, A. & Smucker, M. (1988). Developing training and practice standards for custody mediators. *Conciliation Courts Review, 26*(2), 21–31.

English, P. (1993). *The Standards and Certification Project.* Kitchener, Ontario, Canada: Family Mediation Canada.

English, P. (1994a). *Qualifications and evaluation process for the position of Family Justice Mediator in Community Family Justice Centres in the Pilot Project for Family Justice Reform in British Columbia.* Report to Wendy Hacking, Director of the Family Justice Reform Project, Ministry of Attorney General, Province of British Columbia.

English, P. (1994b). *A model standard of practice, certification of competency and training.* Kitchener, Ontario, Canada: Family Mediation Canada.

English, P. (1997). *Report to the Certification Implementation Committee.* Kitchener, Ontario, Canada: Family Mediation Canada.

English, P., & Neilson, L. (1995). *Standards and Certification Report.* Kitchener, Ontario, Canada: Family Mediation Canada.

English, P., & Neilson, L., with Hacking, W. (Eds.). (1999). *Family Mediation Canada National Certification Implementation Pilot Project Report 1997–1999.* Kitchener, Ontario, Canada: Family Mediation Canada.

Family Mediation Canada. (2003). *Standards of practice and certification.* Kitchener, Ontario, Canada: Author.

Kochan, T., & Jick, T. (1978). The public sector mediation process. *Journal of Conflict Resolution, 22*(2), 209.

Lang, M., & Taylor, A. (2000). *The making of a mediator: Developing artistry in practice.* San Francisco: Jossey-Bass.

Love, L., & Boskey, J. (1997). Should mediators evaluate?: A debate between Lela P. Love and James B. Boskey. *Cardozo Journal of Conflict Resolution, 1*(1). Available: *http://www.cardozo.yu.edu*

MacFarlane, J. (1999). *Dispute resolution readings and case studies.* Toronto: Edmond Montgomery.

Menkel-Meadow, C. (1995). The many ways of mediation. *Negotiation Journal, 11,* 217–230.

Moore, C. (1996). *The mediation process.* San Francisco: Jossey-Bass.

Morris, C. (1997). The trusted mediator: Ethics and interaction in mediation. In J. MacFarlane (Ed.), *Rethinking disputes: The mediation alternative* (pp. 301–347). Toronto: Edmond Montgomery.

Morris, C., & Pirie, A. (Eds.). (1994). *Qualifications for dispute resolution: Perspectives on the debate.* Victoria, British Columbia, Canada: University of Victoria, Institute for Dispute Resolution.

Neilson, L. (1992). *Development of family mediation: Practitioner perspectives on education.* PhD dissertation, University of London.

Neilson, L. (2001). *Spousal abuse, children and the legal system: Final report for Canadian Bar Association Law for the Futures Fund.* Fredericton, New Brunswick: Muriel McQueen Fergusson Centre for Family Violence Research. Available: *http://www.unb.ca/arts/CFVR/spousal_abuse.pdf*

Neilson, L., & English, P. (1996) *Family Mediation Canada Practice, Certification and Training Standards.* Guelph, Ontario: Family Mediation Canada.

Neilson, L., & English, P. (2001). The role of interest-based facilitation in designing accreditation standards: The Canadian experience. *Mediation Quarterly, 18*(3), 221–248.

Pearson, J., Thoennes, N., & Vanderkoi, L. (1982). Mediation of child custody disputes. *Colorado Lawyer, 2*(2), 335.

Society of Professionals in Dispute Resolution. (1988). *Issue paper on qualifications.* Washington, DC: National Institute for Dispute Resolution.

Society of Professionals in Dispute Resolution. (1989). *Qualifying neutrals: The basic principles: Report of the SPIDR Commission on Qualifications.* Washington, DC: National Institute for Dispute Resolution.

Society of Professionals in Dispute Resolution. (1995). *Ensuring competence and quality in dispute resolution practice: Report No. 2 of the SPIDR Commission on Qualifications.* Washington, DC: Author.

CHAPTER 22

The Model Standards of Practice for Family and Divorce Mediation

ANDREW SCHEPARD

Andrew Schepard served as Reporter for the development of the Model Standards of Practice for Family and Divorce Mediation. This chapter recounts the historical development of the Standards and discusses how they address professional and ethical issues germane to good practice.

The rapid growth of private and public family and divorce mediation services has created a need for quality control to protect consumers as well as to protect the credibility of an evolving profession. Unprofessional mediation practice can cause serious damage to participants and the profession. A demand for quality control, in turn, means that interested stakeholders and the public recognize that mediation is a valuable partner with courts and lawyers in the process of resolving family disputes (Schepard, 2000).

Creating quality control means that someone has to define what constitutes good mediation practice. The profession itself recognized the importance of undertaking that task, in consultation with other interested mediation stakeholders, such as the bar and family violence groups, by creating a process for dialogue that ultimately led to the *Model Standards of Practice for Divorce and Family Mediation (Model Standards)*. (See Appendix 22.1 at the end of this chapter for the full text of the *Model Standards*.)

Development of the *Model Standards* helps the mediation profession because the document provides guidance as to what constitutes high-quality practice that meets the special needs of participants and children involved in family and divorce disputes. Mediators working with this population face numerous special challenges. Children exposed to continuing parental conflict are predictable casualties of family disputes; in no other area is the welfare of so many morally innocent and socially important nonparticipants so regularly at stake. Important legal rights such as custody, child support, and property distribution are affected by agreements reached in mediation. Family disputes often produce especially intense emotional stress, which can cloud participants' judgment. The context of a family dispute can include domestic violence, child abuse, participant incapacity due to mental illness or substance abuse, and cultural differences between family members and between participants and the mediator. For the first time in the history of the mediation field in the United States, the mediation practitioners, whatever their profession of origin, can seek guidance on the generally agreed-upon and recommended approaches to performing their role in these especially intense circumstances.

This chapter has a modest aim: to introduce the *Model Standards* to those not familiar with them. It provides an overview of the standards, the process of developing the documents, and their most important themes. Family and divorce mediation is a complex and evolving field; this comparatively brief article thus cannot touch on all of the issues and problems addressed by the *Model Standards*. Many of the other chapters in this volume elaborate on the subjects mentioned here in more detail and nuance.

WHAT ARE THE *MODEL STANDARDS*?

The *Model Standards* contain consensus standards for good family and divorce mediation practice and thus provides a concrete and concise definition of the mediator's role. The document consists of 13 general principles followed by specific, detailed practice considerations regarding the implementation of each principle. The *Model Standards* are designed to provide guidance to family and divorce mediators on problems that are encountered in day-to-day practice, as well as to serve as a primer for training current and future mediators. Furthermore, the document is intended to help the public and allied professionals in the courts, law offices, therapy centers, and community groups clarify what they and their clients can expect from a family and divorce mediator.

The *Model Standards* apply to mediators working in both private practice and court-based mediation programs. (The document includes a special appendix of provisions that is particularly applicable to court-based programs.) The standards also apply to all mediators—lawyers and therapists alike—regardless of their profession of origin. A comprehensive definition of "family disputes" to which the standards are applicable is not attempted. Most mediation in court-based programs occurs in response to disputes between parents arising out of separation and divorce. Private mediation practitioners often mediate divorce- and separation-related financial issues in their practices. The *Model Standards* can also be applied to mediation in grandparent visitation disputes, child protection mediation, and any other family dispute.

A standard was included in the *Model Standards* only if symposium participants (described in the next section) reached a consensus that it encapsulated desirable practice norms. As a result, the *Model Standards* do not address some controversial questions, such as the appropriate balance between "facilitative," "evaluative," and "transformative" approaches to mediation—a subject of much discussion in the mediation community and addressed elsewhere in this volume. The *Model Standards* leave this, and similar practice issues on which the mediation community has reached no consensus, to the judgment of the mediator and the marketplace in which consumers choose mediators; these consumers will, we hope, choose wisely and with ample information about their chosen mediator's approach to mediation. When a consensus develops on this topic, old standards can be modified and new ones created.

The *Model Standards* are an aspirational resource document for organizations and individuals that wish to adopt them voluntarily. The profession itself has established a recommended code of ethics. Sanctions for violations are provinces of the organizations that adopt the *Model Standards*. This document is *not* a restatement of the law of family mediation for purposes of determining malpractice liability in civil or regulatory proceedings. Nor is it designed to be applied by administrative agencies that regulate mediators or the various professions from which mediators originate. Legislatures, courts, and voluntary professional organizations that do regulate mediation practice may, of course, find the *Model Standards* a useful starting point for creating their own standards. The guidelines have not, however, been created for that purpose.

HOW WERE THE *MODEL STANDARDS* CREATED?

The *Model Standards* were developed through a process begun by the Family Law Section of the American Bar Association and facilitated by the Association of Family and Conciliation Courts (AFCC). The process of drafting and redrafting the standards was collaborative and infused with substantial expertise, including consultation with as many interested constituencies as was feasible. The process encouraged communication and bridged differences between the family mediation community, the bar, and domestic violence advocates.

Creation of the *Model Standards* is the latest milestone in a nearly 20-year-old effort by the family mediation community to develop and refine standards of practice. Between 1982 and 1984 AFCC convened three national symposia on divorce mediation standards. The result of the efforts was the 1984 *Model Standards of Practice for Family and Divorce Mediation* (Symposium on Standards of Practice, 1984; hereafter referred to as "1984 *Model Standards*"), which also served as a resource document for state and national mediation organizations whose members included many nonlawyer family mediators and those in court-based programs.

In tandem with the process convened by AFCC, the Family Law Section of the American Bar Association created their own document, *Standards of Practice for Lawyer Mediators in Family Law Disputes* (American Bar Association, 1984; hereafter referred to as "1984 ABA Standards"). The 1984 *ABA Standards* were developed for lawyers who wished to be mediators—at that time, a role some thought inconsistent with governing standards of professional responsibility for lawyers (Silberman, 1982). The 1984 *ABA Standards* helped define how lawyers could serve as family mediators and still stay within the ethical guidelines of their profession.

Following promulgation of the 1984 *Model Standards* and 1984 *ABA Standards,* interest in mediation in all fields—and family mediation, in particular—burgeoned. Interested organizations created their own standards of practice for mediation generally.

In 1996, the Family Law Section concluded that a fresh look at the 1984 *ABA Standards* was in order. It created the Task Force on Standards of Practice for Divorce Mediation (later renamed the Committee on Mediation; hereafter referred to as "ABA Committee") to review the 1984 *ABA Standards* and make recommendations for changes and amendments. From the outset, the project was conceived as a collaborative effort with other interested groups; membership on the ABA Committee included nonlawyer mediators and liaisons from AFCC, the Academy of Family Mediators, and the Society for Professionals in Dispute Resolution.

After intensive review and study, the ABA Committee concluded that although the 1984 *ABA Standards* constituted a major step forward in the development of divorce and family mediation practices, they needed to be replaced by a new set of standards for several reasons. First, the 1984 *ABA Standards* did not address many critical issues in mediation practice that had arisen since 1984. The document applied only to mediators whose profession of origin was law, but many nonlawyers also practiced mediation. The standards did not distinguish between mediators in private practice and those in court-connected programs, nor did they deal with domestic violence, child abuse, and the mediator's role in helping parents define the best interests of their children in their postdivorce parenting arrangements. Furthermore, the document contained no mention of the need for special expertise and training in mediation, or about family violence and the need for sensitivity to cultural diversity.

Second, the 1984 *ABA Standards* used different language in some areas than guidelines for the conduct of mediation subsequently promulgated. The ABA Committee believed that uniformity of mediation standards among interested groups was needed to provide clear guidance for family mediators as well as the public. Uniformity and clarity could not, however, be provided within the framework of the 1984 *ABA Standards*.

The ABA Committee then examined all available standards of practice, conducted research, and consulted with a number of experts on family and divorce mediation. Committee members focused on the heretofore over-looked issues of domestic violence and child abuse, consulting with experts about the appropriate role of mediation when family situations involved violence or the allegations of these conditions.

The council of the ABA's Family Law Section reviewed the ABA Committee's first draft of new standards of practice in November 1997. It reaffirmed the conclusion that the 1984 *ABA Standards* should be replaced and invited other interested mediation organizations to participate in the process of drafting new standards. It specifically requested that the ABA Commission on Domestic Violence be included in the consultation process.

AFCC then offered to reconvene the Model Standards Symposium, which had last met in 1984, using the draft Standards of Practice created by the ABA Committee as the beginning point of the discussion. The aim of reconvening the Model Standards Symposium was to develop a single set of revised standards of practice applicable to *all* family mediators, regardless of profession of origin. The Family Law Section and the National Council of Dispute Resolution Organizations[1] joined AFCC in convening the Model Standards Symposium.

In October 1998 the Model Standards Symposium met in Orlando, Florida, to review the draft standards created by the ABA Committee. Representatives of more than 20 family mediation and legal organizations reviewed the ABA Committee draft, line by line, during an all-day session. A draft of revised *Model Standards* resulted, which was published in the *Family and Conciliation Courts Review* (since renamed *Family Court Review*; Symposium on Standards of Practice, 2000). The draft *Model Standards* were also posted on the websites of AFCC, the Family Law Section, and the ABA Section on Dispute Resolution. Presentations discussing the draft *Model Standards* were made at numerous national conferences. In addition, the draft *Model Standards* were mailed to more than 90 local and national mediation groups for comment.

In response, the symposium received comments and more than 80 proposals for changes in the draft *Model Standards*. The symposium met again in February 2000 in New Orleans and August 2000 in Chicago to consider these comments and proposals. Attendees at these meetings again included family mediators, family lawyers, and judges in family court from across the nation with years of experience in the field. Many of the participants are leaders in national or local family bar, mediation, and dispute resolution organizations. In addition, the American Bar Association's Commission on Domestic Violence again participated in the symposium as an expert consultant (Schepard, 2001).

The *Model Standards* were revised yet again and approved by the members of the symposium. Their final product was then submitted to the various organizations interested in adopting the *Model Standards*. The governing Councils of the Family Law Section and the Section on Dispute Resolution of the American Bar Association unanimously approved the *Model Standards* and submitted them to the American Bar Association's House of Delegates (its overall governing body), which adopted them in February 2001. AFCC and other family mediation organizations also have adopted the *Model Standards*. Thus, as of this writing, the *Model Standards* have been adopted by a number of groups, including the American Bar Association, AFCC, Connecticut Council for Divorce Mediation, Family and Divorce Mediation Council of Greater New York, Mediation Association of Northwest Ohio, Michigan Council for Family and Divorce Mediation, and the Wisconsin Association of Mediators.

THE IMPORTANCE OF FAMILY AND DIVORCE MEDIATION

The *Model Standards* (reproduced at end of chapter, Appendix 22.1) begin with a definition of mediation, including a statement of what it is and what it is not:

> Family and divorce mediation ("family mediation" or "mediation") is a process in which a mediator, an impartial third party, facilitates the resolution of family disputes by promoting the participants' voluntary agreement. The family mediator assists communication, encourages understanding, and focuses the participants on their individual and common interests. The family mediator works with the participants to explore options, make decisions and reach their own agreements.
>
> Family mediation is not a substitute for the need for family members to obtain independent legal advice or counseling or therapy. (p. 533, this volume)

The *Model Standards'* basic assumption is that mediation is a dispute resolution process and should be distinguished from, and not confused with, mental health therapy, counseling, or legal representation. Under the *Model Family Mediation Standards*, mediators have a special responsibility to make participants aware of the distinction between the mediator's craft and that of other professionals who might be involved in the family dispute resolution process (Standard IIIA[2 and 4], p. 535, this volume). Even if a mediator is a therapist and uses some techniques in mediation that can be found in therapy textbooks, the service offered—mediation—is different from therapy. The mediator aims to facilitate negotiation between participants to resolve a dispute rather than to effect long-term behavioral change. Similarly, if a mediator is also a lawyer, as a mediator he or she does not represent or provide legal advice to clients. He or she is a neutral facilitator of negotiations without the professional allegiance to a single client required in the lawyer–client relationship. A participant who wants individual therapy or independent legal advice must retain a separate professional to do so.

The *Model Standards* continue with an affirmation of the useful role mediation can play in the resolution of family disputes:

> Nor is it appropriate for all families. However, experience has established that family mediation is a valuable option for many families because it can:
>
> - increase the self-determination of participants and their ability to communicate;
> - promote the best interests of children; and
> - reduce the economic and emotional costs associated with the resolution of family disputes. (p. 533, this volume)

The *Model Standards* then recognize that "[s]elf-determination is the fundamental principle of family mediation. The mediation process relies upon the ability of participants to make their own voluntary and informed decisions" (Standard IA, p. 534, this volume).

Mediators who adhere to the practices in the *Model Standards* thus serve vitally important social goals by promoting participant self-determination and voluntary settlement of family disputes. Voluntary settlements through mediation reduce the emotional and economic transaction costs of resolving family disputes. Reducing those costs, in turn, increases the capacity of mediation participants to function as parents, employees, and citizens. Voluntary settlements through mediation (1) limit the intrusion into family autonomy that results from judicial decrees and allow participants to shape their agreements to reflect their own cultural values; (2) reduce prolonged parental conflict, which causes great damage to children; and (3) give participants "voice" in the process, which makes them more likely to adhere to agreements reached and feel more respect for the process and the society that authorized mediation to occur.

The *Model Standards'* premise is that most participants in most family disputes benefit from mediation, as does the overloaded court system. That judgment, however, is not a blanket condemnation of litigation, but a call for a diversified dispute resolution system that carefully directs participants to a family dispute process that best serves their needs. Litigation serves vital social purposes. As is discussed shortly, the *Model Standards* recognize that mediation is not appropriate for all family disputes, particularly those involving domestic abuse. Courts articulate and apply principals of law and resolve factual conflicts. They provide a measure of predictability in outcome by application of precedent and procedures rooted in due process. They can require discovery of information that one side wants to keep from the other. They protect the vulnerable and weak against the manipulative and powerful by orders that can be enforced with sanctions. Participants and children in some family disputes need these benefits, despite the heavy emotional and financial costs that litigation imposes. Recognizing that some disputes should be litigated, however, does not mean *all* of them should be. The overall social policy question is how to balance mediation and litigation, not how to eliminate one or the other.

ENTRY INTO MEDIATION

The choice to participate in mediation belongs to the participants. To make that choice intelligently, participants must be aware that mediation is an alternative to litigation and that it has particular benefits and costs. The mediator's authority to perform his or her craft comes from the consent of the participants to enter into mediation, even in court-based programs where participants are compelled to attend a mediation session. The participants may be compelled to attend, but they are not compelled to speak or agree to anything.

The *Model Standards* thus create requirements of "informed consent" for a participant's entry into mediation. The mediator must ensure that participants are fully informed about the nature of the process and consent to participate. Standard III requires the mediator to "facilitate the participants' understanding of what mediation is and assess their capacity to mediate before the participants reach an agreement to mediate" (p. 535, this volume). The mediator is required to provide an overview session with the participants before they begin mediation. The *Model Standards* list what the orientation session must include: a detailed description of what mediation is; how it differs from other dispute resolution processes; that it is voluntary and confidential; exceptions to confidentiality; when and how separate sessions with the participants can be conducted; that court approval may be required for their agreements; that participants are entitled to seek independent advice from lawyers, other professionals of their choice during the mediation process, as well as religious figures and elders, etc. (Standard IIIA[1–9], pp. 535–536, this volume). The *Model Standards* also encourage the participants to sign a written agreement to submit their dispute to mediation within a reasonable time after first consulting the family mediator (Standard IIIB, p. 536, this volume). The written agreement should contain terms that describe the mediation process in a way similar to the overview session.

WHO SHOULD MEDIATE?

The *Model Standards* define the qualifications for family mediators in functional terms, not by professional education or background. The qualifications recognize that family disputes have legal, mental health, dispute resolution, and cultural dimensions and that a mediator must be familiar with all of them. The *Model Standards* identify four basic qualities a mediator should possess: (1) knowledge of family law; (2) knowledge of, and training in, the impact of family conflict on parents, children, and others, including knowledge of child development, domestic abuse, child abuse, and neglect; (3) education and training specific to the process of mediation; and (4) the ability to recognize the impact of culture and diversity (Standard IIA[1–4], p. 535, this volume).

Family and divorce mediators thus need education, training, and experience beyond that provided by law, mental health, or general mediation training to meet the criteria established by the *Model Standards*. A therapist who takes a general mediation training program is not qualified to conduct family and divorce mediation because of his or her lack of familiarity with family law. A lawyer is not qualified to mediate family and divorce disputes without a mediation training program that includes ample information about family dynamics and the impact of culture and diversity on family disputes (Weller, Martin, & Lederach, 2001).

The *Model Standards'* stringent requirements should alleviate any remaining fear among lawyers, courts, and the public that mediators are not qualified to help resolve family disputes. In an Appendix of Special Policy Considerations, the *Model Standards* go even further to urge states and local courts to set standards and qualifications for family mediators, including procedures for evaluations and handling grievances against mediators, in consultation with appropriate professional groups, including professional associations of family mediators (pp. 541–542, this volume).

The *Model Standards* do not directly address the question of whether a nonlawyer mediator is practicing law or a lawyer mediator is practicing therapy, leaving that subject to regulatory bodies and future task forces (Schwartz, 1999; Beyer, 1998). They do, however, prohibit a mediator from providing therapy or legal advice (Standard VIA, p. 537, this volume). The *Model Standards* rely on the distinction between a mediator's provision of individually applicable advice (whether legal or therapeutic) versus general information, in stating: "Consistent with standards of impartiality and preserving participant self-determination, a mediator may provide the participants with information that the mediator is qualified by training or experience to provide" (Standard VIB, p. 537, this volume). Thus, a lawyer mediator would be able to provide the participants with general legal information, and a mediator whose profession of origin is in mental health would be able to provide participants with information he or she is qualified to provide, if otherwise appropriate.

The *Model Standards* also permit the mediator to "document the participants' resolution of their dispute" with the agreement of the participants. Thus, the participants can agree that a mediator will prepare a first draft of a written settlement resulting from their deliberations. The *Model Standards* go on, however, to remind the mediator to "inform the participants that any agreement should be reviewed by an independent attorney before it is signed" (Standard VIE, p. 537, this volume).

CONFIDENTIALITY

Communications between mediation participants and the mediator must be confidential for the same reason that communications between a patient and a doctor or an attorney and a client are confidential—to promote candor and frank discussion. Family and divorce disputes often involve intense emotions; otherwise sensible parents say things about themselves, each other, and their children in mediation that could come back to haunt them, if disclosed. Parents (and their lawyers) mediating a custody dispute must have confidence that their frustrations, hopes, and dreams will not be revealed to a court or the media.

Confidentiality also helps ensure that mediation serves its purpose of promoting participant self-determination. A mediator who knows that he or she may be subpoenaed to testify about what a parent says or to make a recommendation to the court for a custody arrangement is likely to gather information to support a position rather than facilitate discussion of shared interests. Participants who know that a mediator might testify or make a recommendation to a court are likely to try to seduce the mediator to join their side. Confidentiality thus helps ensure that mediation does not degenerate into adversarial warfare under another name.

Standard VII of the *Model Standards* recognizes the importance of confidentiality in mediation by directing the family mediator to "maintain the confidentiality of all information acquired in the mediation process, unless the mediator is permitted or required to reveal the information by law or agreement of the participants" (p. 538, this volume). This basic statement of principle, however, also recognizes that mediation confidentiality is subject to exceptions required by other compelling social policies. A distinguished group from two organizations, the National Commission on Uniform State Laws and the American Bar Association, is currently collaborating on a *Uniform Mediation Act.*[2] Unlike the *Model Standards,* which are practice guidelines directed to family and divorce mediators, the *Uniform Mediation Act* covers mediation in all subject matter areas, not just family and divorce disputes, and is designed to be enacted by state legislatures. Both the *Model Standards* and the *Uniform Mediation Act,* however, aim to guarantee confidentiality in mediation. Both also recognize exceptions to confidentiality for other pressing social values. The Reporter's Notes to the current draft of the *Uniform Mediation Act* state:

> As with other privileges, the mediation privilege must have limits, and nearly all existing state mediation statutes provide them. Definitions and

exceptions primarily are necessary to give appropriate weight to other valid justice system values. . . . They often apply to situations that arise only rarely, but might produce grave injustice in that unusual case if not excepted from the privilege.[3]

The most important social policy weighing against confidentiality in family and divorce mediation is the need to protect victims of domestic violence and detect child abuse and neglect. There is a strong social consensus that protection of children justifies mandatory child abuse reporting statutes, which radically transform traditionally confidential relationships such as that between doctor and patient. Similar policy considerations justify an exception to the confidentiality privilege for mediation. Furthermore, a mediation participant threatened by violence cannot be said to be engaged in a process of self-determination because of the coercion the threat creates.

The *Model Standards* make an exception to the basic principles of mediator confidentiality to protect the safety of participants and children. The mediator is required to report "a participant's threat of suicide or violence against any person to the threatened person and the appropriate authorities if the mediator believes such threat is likely to be acted upon" (Standard VIIC, p. 538, this volume). A mediator is thus required to report any credible threat made by a batterer against a victim of domestic violence. The *Model Standards* also require mediators to inform participants of any ethically or legally mandated reporting requirements, such as the obligation to report child abuse and neglect, before mediation begins (Standard VIIB, p. 538, this volume).

The Uniform Mediation Act contains a similar exception to confidentiality for threats of violence. Its Reporter's Notes set forth the reasoning behind the exception:

> The policy rationales supporting the privilege do not support mediation communications that threaten bodily injury. To the contrary, in these cases disclosure would serve the public interest in safety and the protection of others. Because such statements are sometimes made in anger with no intention to commit the act, the exception is a narrow one that applies only to the threatening statements; the remainder of the mediation communication remains protected against disclosure. . . .
>
> State mediation confidentiality statutes frequently recognize a similar exception. An exception for child abuse and neglect is common in domestic mediation confidentiality statutes, and the Act reaffirms these important policy choices states have made to protect their citizens.[4]

IMPARTIALITY

The *Model Standards* establish an expectation that the mediator functions with impartiality in two respects: toward the parties and toward the outcome in mediation (Standard IV, pp. 536–537, this volume). *Impartiality toward the parties* means that the mediator does not have any real or potential conflict of interest (Standard IVB, p. 536, this volume). A mediator should not mediate a dispute involving a business partner or family member for fear of being perceived as favoring one party over the other. The impartiality principle also means that a mediator should not provide mediation services to clients for whom he or she has provided other professional services in the past, such as marriage or individual counseling or legal services. While an experienced mediator may be able to separate prior professional services rendered from those now offered in mediation, the possibility of parties' misperception is just as important as the reality of the mediator's ability to function effectively, despite serving in a previous role. A mediator's prior relationship with a participant may haunt the mediation process, if another participant perceives that the mediator is not acting in an impartial fashion due to information gleaned from the prior relationship. For example, a lawyer who has drafted a will for one or both of the participants may have had access to financial information that one participant believes may prejudice the mediator's views about property division resulting from divorce. Likewise, a mediator who provided marriage counseling may be perceived by a participant as having information about the personality and behaviors of an individual that may color the mediator's views about his or her participation in mediation.

Impartiality toward the outcome means that a mediator does not have any preconceived views about a particular settlement. A mediator should not lead the parties toward a particular outcome, such as selling the house or joint custody. The participants are responsible for the outcome, not the mediator.

ENSURING MINIMUM FAIRNESS IN FACILITATED NEGOTIATIONS

Impartiality, however, does not imply that the mediator is some kind of blank slate. A mediator has a special responsibility to ensure that the mediation process is fundamentally fair and that options are carefully evaluated and considered. For example, a mediator should not sit idly by while one party attempts to intimidate the other party into a settlement by threats of violence, nor should a mediator passively facilitate an agreement that violates fundamental legal or moral norms.

The *Model Standards* articulate standards of practice to ensure the use of fundamentally fair bargaining procedures between the participants. The mediator, for example, "should be alert to the capacity and willingness of the participants to mediate before proceeding with the mediation and throughout the process" (Standard IIIC, p. 536, this volume). This provision is designed to ensure that the mediator assesses participants' willingness and ability to mediate before the process begins and throughout its progression. A

DEVELOPING THE PROFESSION

mediator who believes, for example, that a participant is suffering from a mental illness or is under the influence of drugs or alcohol should not go forward with the mediation session, until the incapacity is recognized and addressed.

The *Model Standards* also require the mediator to "facilitate full and accurate disclosure and the acquisition and development of information during mediation so that the participants can make informed decisions. This may be accomplished by encouraging participants to consult appropriate experts" (Standard VIA, p. 537, this volume). The purpose of this provision is to ensure that the participants have roughly equal access to information (such as information about income and assets and medical information about children) essential to fair negotiations and decision making. A mediator must thus be aware of the applicable financial disclosure requirements for divorce disputes and ensure that the participants are also aware of them. Failure to ensure minimum disclosure of necessary information puts potential agreements at greater risk of later challenge and invalidation in court.

The *Model Standards* do not require, however, that participants must receive exactly the same information during mediation that they do through the discovery process of depositions and document disclosure in litigation. They require only that the mediator ensure minimum disclosure for fairness; participants are entitled to decide, using the advice of outside counsel, if they wish, that the costs of additional disclosure are too great to warrant it. Similar judgments are made in lawyers' offices every day.

The *Model Standards* also require the mediator to consider suspending or terminating the mediation process if "the participants are about to enter into an agreement that the mediator reasonably believes to be unconscionable" (Standard XIA[4], p. 540, this volume). *Unconscionability* is a familiar standard in both contract and family law and has a procedural and substantive aspect. This provision imposes a requirement on the mediator to ensure that an agreement is not so unfair that it "shocks the conscience" in the manner in which it was entered (e.g., through threats of physical violence or economic coercion or a complete unwillingness to disclose vital financial information) or because the substantive terms are so wildly unfair that no reasonable person would enter into them (e.g., a complete waiver of child support by a parent who has two children to support and no other source of income). The mediator should apply the unconscionability standard with great restraint, however, in recognition of the importance of self-determination by the parties and maintaining stability in settlement agreements. This standard is designed to ensure that the mediator recognizes that a settlement agreement must satisfy minimum standards of fairness; it does not require that the terms of a mediated agreement be identical to those that would be achieved in a court order after years of discovery and litigation.

The *Model Standards* are particularly concerned with assuring that the mediator informs participants of their right to consult independent counsel and to have counsel participate in mediation, if they so desire. The *Model Standards* build on the research-based insight that the more that lawyers participate in the mediation process, the more that they support it by developing more settlement-oriented attitudes and filing fewer motions (Mcewen, Rodgers, & Maiman, 1995). The *Model Standards* document should expunge any lingering belief in the family law bar that mediators are anti-lawyer. They provide, for example, that "[b]efore family mediation begins, a mediator should . . . [inform] the participants that they may obtain independent advice from attorneys . . . during the mediation process" (Standard IIIA[4], p. 535, this volume). The mediator "should recommend that the participants obtain independent legal representation before concluding an agreement" (Standard VIC, p. 537, this volume) and "[i]f the participants so desire, the mediator should allow attorneys, counsel or advocates for the participants to be present at the mediation sessions" (Standard VID, p. 537, this volume).

Although mediators have some responsibility under the *Model Standards* to help ensure minimum fairness in both the process of bargaining and the substantive outcomes, mediators are not seen as ensurers that agreements resulting from mediation satisfy the preferences of any participant or that the agreement, as a whole, parallels what a court would award. The tradeoffs between issues and preferences in settlement of a family dispute are too complex, and most substantive family law standards too discretionary, to allow for such routine second guessing of mediated settlements.

What *Model Standards* can do, however, is provide assurances to the public and the legal community that the family mediation profession is willing to assume responsibility for ensuring fundamental fairness in facilitated negotiations. While preserving the mediator's role as an impartial one, the *Model Standards* codify good practices in mediation that make it less likely (though, of course, not impossible) for unscrupulous participants to take advantage of the mediation process.

MEDIATION AND THE BEST INTERESTS OF CHILDREN

There is no longer much debate that prolonged parental conflict arising from divorce or separation can seriously damage children emotionally, educationally, and economically (Schepard, 1998; Stern et al., 2000). A major innovation of the *Model Standards* is that they impose an obligation on the mediator to "assist participants in determining how to promote the best interests of children" caught in the middle of such family conflict (Standard VIII, p. 538, this volume).

The mediation process generally provides the best interests of children because it emphasizes self-determination and voluntary agreements and helps parents manage their conflicts responsibly (Schepard, 1985). Most children benefit from having a continuing relationship with both parents after divorce or separation if it is safe for them to do so; mediation is perhaps the best dispute resolution process available to help parents achieve that goal through self-determined agreements.

The *Model Standards* provide concrete suggestions for how mediators can help parents best utilize mediation to promote the best interests of children. However, they do not endorse any particular kind of postdivorce or separation parenting plans (e.g., joint custody, sole custody, or some variation). That decision is for the parents to make with the help of the mediator and their advisors.

Thus, the *Model Standards* suggest that the mediator encourage parents to obtain information about child development and any pertinent community resources to help their children through the difficulties of family reorganization. The *Model Standards* also suggest that parenting plans resulting from mediation contain appropriate levels of detail in provisions regarding children's residence and decision-making responsibilities rather than leave parents guessing about matters likely to result in later conflict. It is suggested that the participants address the need to revise a parenting plan over time, as their children's developmental needs change, and to create a process now to resolve future disputes (Standard VIIIA[1–5], pp. 538–539, this volume).

Other provisions of the *Model Standards* address questions of whether and how the children should participate in the mediation process. The *Model Standards* do not definitively answer these sensitive questions, instead leaving them for determination by parents in consultation with the mediator. They reinforce parental authority by stating that, except in extraordinary circumstances, children should not participate in the mediation unless both parents and the court-appointed representative of the child(ren) consent (Standard VIIID, p. 539, this volume). The *Model Standards* also indicate that the mediator should inform the parents about the full range of options available for how children might participate (e.g., direct participation in a mediation, an interview with a mental health professional or the mediator, a videotaped statement) and the costs and benefits of each (Standard VIIIE, p. 539, this volume).

One of the most difficult questions in drafting the *Model Standards* was to define the relationship between the mediation process and the representative of the children. Many states do not require representatives to be appointed for children in all disputes. In some states, nonlawyers can serve as children's representatives, and their obligations of confidentiality to the child are somewhat undefined. In many states, furthermore, lawyers for children in child custody disputes have ambiguous roles. They may represent a child's best interests (and thus have no obligations of confidentiality to the child) or may serve as a traditional advocate for the preferences of the child (with confidentiality obligations to the child).

In light of this complexity and confusion about the role of a child's representative, the *Model Standards* do not take a position on whether the representative must be included in the mediation process. The document simply imposes an obligation on the mediator to inform a child's representative of the mediation. If the representative of the child chooses to participate in the mediation, the *Model Standards* also impose an obligation on the mediator to discuss the effect of the representative's participation on the confidentiality of the process with the participants. If agreements result, the mediator should provide the child's representative with them, insofar as they relate to the child (Standard VIIIC, p. 539, this volume).

DOMESTIC ABUSE, CHILD ABUSE AND NEGLECT, AND FAMILY MEDIATION

Another major innovation of the *Model Standards* is the concrete guidance provided for family mediators who confront domestic abuse and child abuse and neglect in their practices. Abuse of a participant and danger to children significantly challenge the mediator to shape the process in a way that promotes safety (Hart, 1990; Treuthardt, 1996).

The *Model Standards* do not require any victim of violence or abuse to enter into mediation. Indeed, they define "domestic abuse" more broadly than physical violence—the typical legal definition of domestic violence—to include "issues of control and intimidation" (Standard XA, p. 540, this volume) and explicitly acknowledge that "[s]ome cases are not suitable for mediation because of safety, control, or intimidation issues" (Standard XC, p. 540, this volume). The *Model Standards* do require the mediator to adapt a four-part approach to the problem of family violence: training, screening, assuring safety, and reporting.

First, the *Model Standards* require mediators to have special training in recognizing and addressing domestic violence and child abuse and neglect before undertaking any mediation in which those elements may be present (Standards IIA[2], IXB, and XA, pp. 535, 539, and 540, respectively, this volume). The family mediation community has thus imposed upon itself a higher obligation to understand and cope with family violence than the organized bar or the family court judiciary. Although both have recognized that training in family mediation is desirable, neither has imposed a specific obligation on its membership to receive training in that area.

Second, the *Model Standards* require mediators to make reasonable efforts to screen for domestic abuse. There are recognized symptoms that characterize victims of domestic abuse. This form of abuse is defined as "a pattern of assaultive and coercive behaviors, including physical, sexual, and psychological attacks, as well as economic coercion that adults . . . use against their intimate partners" (Fantuzzo & Mohr, 1999, pp. 21–22). A family and divorce mediator should be trained to recognize those symptoms and respond with appropriate safety measures. A mediator is not required, however to follow any particular method of screening, because the drafters of the *Model Standards* were not aware of any method that has attained universal validity and could be accomplished with reasonable effort by the mediator. Nor do the *Model Standards* impose an obligation on the mediator to screen a family for child abuse and neglect—a task that requires a professional with special expertise and which results from an in-depth evaluation of the family, particularly for sexual abuse. Children rarely participate personally in mediation sessions (per Standard VIIID, p. 539, this volume). The drafters felt it was unreasonable to impose a screening obligation for child abuse and neglect on mediators when they do not usually have the opportunity to personally observe the physical and emotional conditions of participants' children. The *Model Standards* do require, however, that if the mediator reasonably believes that child abuse and neglect exist, he or she must comply with applicable child protection reporting laws (per Standard IXC, p. 539, this volume).

Third, the *Model Standards* require mediators to take steps to shape the mediation process to assure the physical safety of mediation participants. If domestic abuse exists, the *Standards* give the mediator a list of possible ways to assure victim safety during the mediation process including:

1. establishing appropriate security arrangements;
2. holding separate sessions with the participants even without the agreement of all participants;
3. allowing a friend, representative, advocate, counsel or attorney to attend the mediation sessions;
4. encouraging the participants to be represented by an attorney, counsel or an advocate throughout the mediation process;
5. referring the participants to appropriate community resources;
6. suspending or terminating the mediation sessions, with appropriate steps to protect the safety of the participants. (Standard XD[1–6], p. 540, this volume)

The *Model Standards* do not require the mediator to take any of these alternative courses of action. Rather, the mediator is required to consider these alternatives, and any other that might be appropriate, to respond to domestic abuse in a manner that ensures safety. The mediator is also required to facilitate the development of parenting plans that "protect the physical safety and psychological well-being of [participants] and their children" (Standard XE, p. 540, this volume).

The *Model Standards* provide fewer options for a mediator to respond to a situation where the mediator reasonably believes child abuse or neglect exists. The mediator, as mentioned above, is obligated to comply with applicable child protection laws. The mediator is also asked to encourage the participants to explore appropriate services and to consider suspending or terminating the mediation process in light of the allegations of child abuse and neglect (per Standard IXC[1–2], p. 539, this volume).

Finally, as previously discussed, the *Model Standards* modify the requirement of confidentiality in the mediation process in light of the vital public policy to protect against family violence. They require mediators to inform participants of any ethically or legally mandated reporting requirements, such as the obligation to report child abuse and neglect, before mediation begins (per Standard VIIB, p. 538, this volume). The *Model Standards* also require mediators to report "a participant's threat of suicide or violence against any person to the threatened person and the appropriate authorities if the mediator believes such threat is likely to be acted upon" and the disclosure is otherwise permitted by law (per Standard VIIC, p. 538, this volume). Finally, mediators should consider suspending or terminating the mediation process if "the safety of a participant or the well-being of a child is threatened" by its continuation (Standard XIA[1], p. 540, this volume).

CONCLUSION

The *Model Standards* are a commitment by the mediation profession to excellence in professional practice to benefit families and children. The court system, the bar, and the public increasingly recognize that participants in family disputes benefit from participation in these standards. The mediation profession's voluntary adherence to the *Model Standards* that it developed itself will accelerate and strengthen that trend.

APPENDIX 22.1. MODEL STANDARDS OF PRACTICE FOR FAMILY AND DIVORCE MEDIATION

Overview and Definitions

Family and divorce mediation ("family mediation" or "mediation") is a process in which a mediator, an impartial third party, facilitates the resolution of family disputes by promoting the participants' voluntary agreement. The family mediator assists communication, encourages understanding and focuses the participants on their individual and common interests. The family mediator works with the participants to explore options, make decisions and reach their own agreements.

Family mediation is not a substitute for the need for family members to obtain independent legal advice or counseling or therapy. Nor is it appropriate for all families. However, experience has established that family mediation is a valuable option for many families because it can:

- increase the self-determination of participants and their ability to communicate;
- promote the best interests of children; and
- reduce the economic and emotional costs associated with the resolution of family disputes.

Effective mediation requires that the family mediator be qualified by training, experience and temperament; that the mediator be impartial; that the participants reach their decisions voluntarily; that their decisions be based on sufficient factual data; that the mediator be aware of the impact of culture and diversity; and that the best interests of children be taken into account. Further, the mediator should also be prepared to identify families whose history includes domestic abuse or child abuse.

These *Model Standards of Practice for Family and Divorce Mediation* ("*Model Standards*") aim to perform three major functions:

- to serve as a guide for the conduct of family mediators;
- to inform the mediating participants of what they can expect; and
- to promote public confidence in mediation as a process for resolving family disputes.

The *Model Standards* are aspirational in character. They describe good practices for family mediators. They are not intended to create legal rules or standards of liability.

The *Model Standards* include different levels of guidance:

- Use of the term "may" in a *Standard* is the lowest strength of guidance and indicates a practice that the family mediator should consider adopting but which can be deviated from in the exercise of good professional judgment.
- Most of the *Standards* employ the term "should" which indicates that the practice described in the *Standard* is highly desirable and should be departed from only with very strong reason.
- The rarer use of the term "shall" in a *Standard* is a higher level of guidance to the family mediator, indicating that the mediator should not have discretion to depart from the practice described.

Standard I

A family mediator shall recognize that mediation is based on the principle of self-determination by the participants.

A. Self-determination is the fundamental principle of family mediation. The mediation process relies upon the ability of participants to make their own voluntary and informed decisions.
B. The primary role of a family mediator is to assist the participants to gain a better understanding of their own needs and interests and the needs and interests of others and to facilitate agreement among the participants.
C. A family mediator should inform the participants that they may seek information and advice from a variety of sources during the mediation process.
D. A family mediator shall inform the participants that they may withdraw from family mediation at any time and are not required to reach an agreement in mediation.

E. The family mediator's commitment shall be to the participants and the process. Pressure from outside of the mediation process shall never influence the mediator to coerce participants to settle.

Standard II

A family mediator shall be qualified by education and training to undertake the mediation.

A. To perform the family mediator's role, a mediator should:
   1. have knowledge of family law;
   2. have knowledge of and training in the impact of family conflict on parents, children and other participants, including knowledge of child development, domestic abuse and child abuse and neglect;
   3. have education and training specific to the process of mediation;
   4. be able to recognize the impact of culture and diversity.

B. Family mediators should provide information to the participants about the mediator's relevant training, education and expertise.

Standard III

A family mediator shall facilitate the participants' understanding of what mediation is and assess their capacity to mediate before the participants reach an agreement to mediate.

A. Before family mediation begins a mediator should provide the participants with an overview of the process and its purposes, including:
   1. informing the participants that reaching an agreement in family mediation is consensual in nature, that a mediator is an impartial facilitator, and that a mediator may not impose or force any settlement on the parties;
   2. distinguishing family mediation from other processes designed to address family issues and disputes;
   3. informing the participants that any agreements reached will be reviewed by the court when court approval is required;
   4. informing the participants that they may obtain independent advice from attorneys, counsel, advocates, accountants, therapists or other professionals during the mediation process;
   5. advising the participants, in appropriate cases, that they can seek the advice of religious figures, elders or other significant persons in their community whose opinions they value;
   6. discussing, if applicable, the issue of separate sessions with the participants, a description of the circumstances in which the mediator may meet alone with any of the participants, or with any third party and the conditions of confidentiality concerning these separate sessions;
   7. informing the participants that the presence or absence of other persons at a mediation, including attorneys, counselors or advocates, depends on the agreement of the participants and the mediator, unless a statute or regulation

    otherwise requires or the mediator believes that the presence of another person is required or may be beneficial because of a history or threat of violence or other serious coercive activity by a participant.

    8. describing the obligations of the mediator to maintain the confidentiality of the mediation process and its results as well as any exceptions to confidentiality;

    9. advising the participants of the circumstances under which the mediator may suspend or terminate the mediation process and that a participant has a right to suspend or terminate mediation at any time.

B. The participants should sign a written agreement to mediate their dispute and the terms and conditions thereof within a reasonable time after first consulting the family mediator.

C. The family mediator should be alert to the capacity and willingness of the participants to mediate before proceeding with the mediation and throughout the process. A mediator should not agree to conduct the mediation if the mediator reasonably believes one or more of the participants is unable or unwilling to participate.

D. Family mediators should not accept a dispute for mediation if they cannot satisfy the expectations of the participants concerning the timing of the process.

Standard IV

A family mediator shall conduct the mediation process in an impartial manner. A family mediator shall disclose all actual and potential grounds of bias and conflicts of interest reasonably known to the mediator. The participants shall be free to retain the mediator by an informed, written waiver of the conflict of interest. However, if a bias or conflict of interest clearly impairs a mediator's impartiality, the mediator shall withdraw regardless of the express agreement of the participants.

A. Impartiality means freedom from favoritism or bias in word, action or appearance, and includes a commitment to assist all participants as opposed to any one individual.

B. Conflict of interest means any relationship between the mediator, any participant or the subject matter of the dispute, that compromises or appears to compromise the mediator's impartiality.

C. A family mediator should not accept a dispute for mediation if the family mediator cannot be impartial.

D. A family mediator should identify and disclose potential grounds of bias or conflict of interest upon which a mediator's impartiality might reasonably be questioned. Such disclosure should be made prior to the start of a mediation and in time to allow the participants to select an alternate mediator.

E. A family mediator should resolve all doubts in favor of disclosure. All disclosures should be made as soon as practical after the mediator becomes aware of the bias or potential conflict of interest. The duty to disclose is a continuing duty.

F. A family mediator should guard against bias or partiality based on the participants' personal characteristics, background or performance at the mediation.

G. A family mediator should avoid conflicts of interest in recommending the services of other professionals.

H. A family mediator shall not use information about participants obtained in a mediation for personal gain or advantage

I. A family mediator should withdraw pursuant to Standard IX if the mediator believes the mediator's impartiality has been compromised or a conflict of interest has been identified and has not been waived by the participants.

Standard V

A family mediator shall fully disclose and explain the basis of any compensation, fees and charges to the participants.

A. The participants should be provided with sufficient information about fees at the outset of mediation to determine if they wish to retain the services of the mediator.

B. The participants' written agreement to mediate their dispute should include a description of their fee arrangement with the mediator.

C. A mediator should not enter into a fee agreement which is contingent upon the results of the mediation or the amount of the settlement.

D. A mediator should not accept a fee for referral of a matter to another mediator or to any other person.

E. Upon termination of mediation a mediator should return any unearned fee to the participants.

Standard VI

A family mediator shall structure the mediation process so that the participants make decisions based on sufficient information and knowledge.

A. The mediator should facilitate full and accurate disclosure and the acquisition and development of information during mediation so that the participants can make informed decisions. This may be accomplished by encouraging participants to consult appropriate experts.

B. Consistent with standards of impartiality and preserving participant self-determination, a mediator may provide the participants with information that the mediator is qualified by training or experience to provide. The mediator shall not provide therapy or legal advice.

C. The mediator should recommend that the participants obtain independent legal representation before concluding an agreement.

D. If the participants so desire, the mediator should allow attorneys, counsel or advocates for the participants to be present at the mediation sessions.

E. With the agreement of the participants, the mediator may document the participants' resolution of their dispute. The mediator should inform the participants that any agreement should be reviewed by an independent attorney before it is signed.

Standard VII

*A family mediator shall maintain the confidentiality of all information acquired in the media-
tion process, unless the mediator is permitted or required to reveal the information by law or
agreement of the participants.*

A. The mediator should discuss the participants' expectations of confidentiality
with them prior to undertaking the mediation. The written agreement to mediate should include provisions concerning confidentiality.

B. Prior to undertaking the mediation the mediator should inform the participants
of the limitations of confidentiality such as statutory, judicially or ethically
mandated reporting.

C. The mediator shall disclose a participant's threat of suicide or violence against
any person to the threatened person and the appropriate authorities if the mediator believes such threat is likely to be acted upon as permitted by law.

D. If the mediator holds private sessions with a participant, the obligations of confidentiality concerning those sessions should be discussed and agreed upon prior
to the sessions.

E. If subpoenaed or otherwise noticed to testify or to produce documents the mediator should inform the participants immediately. The mediator should not testify
or provide documents in response to a subpoena without an order of the court if
the mediator reasonably believes doing so would violate an obligation of
confidentiality to the participants.

Standard VIII

*A family mediator shall assist participants in determining how to promote the best interests of
children.*

A. The mediator should encourage the participants to explore the range of options
available for separation or post divorce parenting arrangements and their respective costs and benefits. Referral to a specialist in child development may be appropriate for these purposes. The topics for discussion may include, among
others:

1. information about community resources and programs that can help the participants and their children cope with the consequences of family reorganization and family violence;

2. problems that continuing conflict creates for children's development and what
steps might be taken to ameliorate the effects of conflict on the children;

3. development of a parenting plan that covers the children's physical residence
and decision-making responsibilities for the children, with appropriate levels
of detail as agreed to by the participants;

4. the possible need to revise parenting plans as the developmental needs of the
children evolve over time; and

5. encouragement to the participants to develop appropriate dispute resolution mechanisms to facilitate future revisions of the parenting plan.

B. The mediator should be sensitive to the impact of culture and religion on parenting philosophy and other decisions.

C. The mediator shall inform any court-appointed representative for the children of the mediation. If a representative for the children participates, the mediator should, at the outset, discuss the effect of that participation on the mediation process and the confidentiality of the mediation with the participants. Whether the representative of the children participates or not, the mediator shall provide the representative with the resulting agreements insofar as they relate to the children.

D. Except in extraordinary circumstances, the children should not participate in the mediation process without the consent of both parents and the children's court-appointed representative.

E. Prior to including the children in the mediation process, the mediator should consult with the parents and the children's court-appointed representative about whether the children should participate in the mediation process and the form of that participation.

F. The mediator should inform all concerned about the available options for the children's participation (which may include personal participation, an interview with a mental health professional, or the mediator reporting to the parents, or a videotape statement) and discuss the costs and benefits of each with the participants.

Standard IX

A family mediator shall recognize a family situation involving child abuse or neglect and take appropriate steps to shape the mediation process accordingly.

A. As used in these Standards, child abuse or neglect is defined by applicable state law.

B. A mediator shall not undertake a mediation in which the family situation has been assessed to involve child abuse or neglect without appropriate and adequate training.

C. If the mediator has reasonable grounds to believe that a child of the participants is abused or neglected within the meaning of the jurisdiction's child abuse and neglect laws, the mediator shall comply with applicable child protection laws.

1. The mediator should encourage the participants to explore appropriate services for the family.
2. The mediator should consider the appropriateness of suspending or terminating the mediation process in light of the allegations.

Standard X

A family mediator shall recognize a family situation involving domestic abuse and take appropriate steps to shape the mediation process accordingly.

A. As used in these Standards, domestic abuse includes domestic violence as defined by applicable state law and issues of control and intimidation.

B. A mediator shall not undertake a mediation in which the family situation has been assessed to involve domestic abuse without appropriate and adequate training.

C. Some cases are not suitable for mediation because of safety, control or intimidation issues. A mediator should make a reasonable effort to screen for the existence of domestic abuse prior to entering into an agreement to mediate. The mediator should continue to assess for domestic abuse throughout the mediation process.

D. If domestic abuse appears to be present the mediator shall consider taking measures to insure the safety of participants and the mediator including, among others:
   1. establishing appropriate security arrangements;
   2. holding separate sessions with the participants even without the agreement of all participants;
   3. allowing a friend, representative, advocate, counsel or attorney to attend the mediation sessions;
   4. encouraging the participants to be represented by an attorney, counsel or an advocate throughout the mediation process;
   5. referring the participants to appropriate community resources;
   6. suspending or terminating the mediation sessions, with appropriate steps to protect the safety of the participants.

E. The mediator should facilitate the participants' formulation of parenting plans that protect the physical safety and psychological well-being of themselves and their children.

Standard XI

A family mediator shall suspend or terminate the mediation process when the mediator reasonably believes that a participant is unable to effectively participate or for other compelling reasons.

A. Circumstances under which a mediator should consider suspending or terminating the mediation, may include, among others:
   1. the safety of a participant or well-being of a child is threatened;
   2. a participant has or is threatening to abduct a child;
   3. a participant is unable to participate due to the influence of drugs, alcohol, or physical or mental condition;
   4. the participants are about to enter into an agreement that the mediator reasonably believes to be unconscionable;
   5. a participant is using the mediation to further illegal conduct;
   6. a participant is using the mediation process to gain an unfair advantage;
   7. if the mediator believes the mediator's impartiality has been compromised in accordance with Standard IV.

B. If the mediator does suspend or terminate the mediation, the mediator should take all reasonable steps to minimize prejudice or inconvenience to the participants which may result.

Standard XII

A family mediator shall be truthful in the advertisement and solicitation for mediation.

A. Mediators should refrain from promises and guarantees of results. A mediator should not advertise statistical settlement data or settlement rates.
B. Mediators should accurately represent their qualifications. In an advertisement or other communication, a mediator may make reference to meeting state, national, or private organizational qualifications only if the entity referred to has a procedure for qualifying mediators and the mediator has been duly granted the requisite status.

Standard XIII

A family mediator shall acquire and maintain professional competence in mediation.

A. Mediators should continuously improve their professional skills and abilities by, among other activities, participating in relevant continuing education programs and should regularly engage in self-assessment.
B. Mediators should participate in programs of peer consultation and should help train and mentor the work of less experienced mediators.
C. Mediators should continuously strive to understand the impact of culture and diversity on the mediator's practice.

Appendix: Special Policy Considerations for State Regulation of Family Mediators and Court Affiliated Programs

The *Model Standards* recognize the *National Standards for Court Connected Dispute Resolution Programs* (1992). There are also state and local regulations governing such programs and family mediators. The following principles of organization and practice, however, are especially important for regulation of mediators and court-connected family mediation programs. They are worthy of separate mention.

A. Individual states or local courts should set standards and qualifications for family mediators including procedures for evaluations and handling grievances against mediators. In developing these standards and qualifications, regulators should consult with appropriate professional groups, including professional associations of family mediators.
B. When family mediators are appointed by a court or other institution, the appointing agency should make reasonable efforts to insure that each mediator is qualified for the appointment. If a list of family mediators qualified for court appointment exists, the requirements for being included on the list should be made public and available to all interested persons.

C. Confidentiality should not be construed to limit or prohibit the effective monitoring, research, evaluation or monitoring of mediation programs by responsible
individuals or academic institutions provided that no identifying information
about any person involved in the mediation is disclosed without their prior written consent. Under appropriate circumstances, researchers may be permitted to
obtain access to statistical data and, with the permission of the participants, to individual case files, observations of live mediations, and interviews with
participants.

ACKNOWLEDGMENTS

The views expressed in this chapter are my own; they have not been approved by the
American Bar Association, AFCC, or any of the other groups or individuals who participated in the symposium or any group that has adopted the *Model Standards*. This chapter is
adapted from Schepard (2001). Adapted by permission of the American Bar Association
Section of Family Law.

NOTES

1. The National Council of Dispute Resolution Organization is an umbrella organization that includes the Academy of Family Mediators, the American Bar Association Section of Dispute Resolution, AFCC, Conflict Resolution Education Network, the National
Association for Community Mediation, the National Conference on Peacemaking and
Conflict Resolution, and the Society of Professionals in Dispute Resolution.

2. *Uniform Mediation Act* (May 4, 2001 Draft). More information about the *Uniform
Mediation Act* can be obtained at *www.pon.harvard.edu/guests/uma.*

3. *Uniform Mediation Act*, section 2(1), working note on importance of candor (May 4,
2001 draft).

4. *Uniform Mediation Act*, working note on subsections 7(a)(3) and 7(a)(5) (May 4,
2001 draft).

REFERENCES

American Bar Association. (1984). Standards of Practice for Lawyer Mediators in Family
    Disputes. In *Dispute resolution: Negotiation, mediation, and other processes* (pp. 469–474).
    Boston, MA: Little, Brown.
Beyer, J. (1998). Practicing law at the margins: Surveying ethics rules for legal assistants
    and lawyers who mediate. *Georgia Journal of Legal Ethics, 11,* 411–420.
Fantuzzo, J. W., & Mohr, W. K. (1999). Prevalence and effects of child exposure to domes-
    tic violence. *The Future of Children: Domestic Violence and Children, 9,* 21–32.
Hart, B. (1990). Gentle jeopardy: The further endangerment of battered women in custody
    mediation. *Mediation Quarterly, 7,* 317–330.
Mcewen, C. A., Rogers, N. H., & Maiman, R. J. (1995). Bring in the lawyers: Challenging
    the dominant approaches to insuring fairness in divorce mediation. *Minnesota Law
    Review, 79,* 1317–1411.

Schepard, A. (1985). Taking children seriously: Promoting cooperative custody after divorce. *Texas Law Review, 64,* 687–788.

Schepard, A. (1998). Parental conflict prevention programs and the unified family court: A public health perspective. *Family Law Quarterly, 32*(95), 103–105.

Schepard, A. (2000). The evolving judicial role in child custody disputes: From fault finder to conflict manager to differential case management. *University of Arkansas at Little Rock Law Review, 22,* 395–428.

Schepard, A. (2001). Model standards of practice for family and divorce mediation: The symposium on standards of practice. *Family Court Review, 39,* 121–134.

Schwartz, J. (1999). Laymen cannot lawyer, but is mediation the practice of law? *Cardozo Law Review, 20,* 1715–1745.

Silberman, L. (1982). Professional responsibility problems of divorce mediation. *Family Law Quarterly, 16,* 107–145.

Stern, H., P., Mellon, M. W., Butler, B. O., Stroh, S. E., Long, N., & Jones, J. G. (2000). Battered child syndrome: Is it a paradigm for a child of embattled divorce? *University of Arkansas at Little Rock Law Review, 22,* 335–355.

Symposium on Standards of Practice for Family and Divorce Mediation convened by the Association of Family and Conciliation Courts. (1984). *Model standards of practice for family and divorce mediation.*

Symposium on Standards of Practice for Family and Divorce Mediation convened by the Association of Family and Conciliation Courts. (2000). Model standards of practice for divorce and family mediators. *Family and Conciliation Courts Review, 38,* 106–122.

Treuthart, M. (1996). All that glitters is not gold: Mediation in domestic abuse cases. *Clearinghouse Review, 30,* 243–260.

Weller, S., Martin, J. A., & Lederach, J. P. (2001). Fostering culturally responsive courts: The case of family dispute resolution for Latinos. *Family Court Review, 39,* 185–202.

CHAPTER 23

Establishing a Mediation Practice

FORREST S. MOSTEN

The demand for mediation has not always kept up with the supply of new mediators, and few mediators have been able to make a living exclusively from the practice of mediation. Today an increasing number are able to work as mediators full-time. Forrest S. Mosten, the guru of mediation practice, shares practical and proven advice on how to set up a practice and make a living as a family mediator. This chapter helps mediators avoid reinventing the private practice wheel and assists them in framing and answering the essential questions necessary for financial success as a mediator.

If you want to make mediation your day job, you need both competent skills at the table and a flow of clients. Regardless of your marketing acumen, the key to any thriving practice is the continuing good will that results in referrals that can only come from satisfied clients and colleagues who respect your work. This chapter is intended to give you a jump-start to building your own practice in an increasingly mediation-receptive environment.

USE YOUR KNOWLEDGE OF MEDIATION AS A FOUNDATION
TO PRACTICE BUILDING

If you fit the profile Laurence Boulle (1996) offers in his *Mediation: Principles, Procedures and Practice,* you may have some or all of the following personal attributes:

Listen well   Empathic
Effective communicator   Persistent

Patient	Trustworthy
Tolerant	Flexible/creative
Able to handle conflict	Positive/optimistic

Note that strategic business planning, marketing, or management skills are not on this list. Mediation practice is a small business that requires the skills and knowledge base that are taught in business schools—not mediation training classes. Yet, you know (or should know) your product well: the product of working peacefully and collaboratively with families in conflict or with those attempting to avoid conflict.

Go with your strength. Use your expertise in family conflict resolution to define your practice development. The first place to start is to pull out your basic mediation training course manual and attempt to translate the key lessons of skill building into *practice building*.

The late Dr. John Haynes said, "The mediator's silent prayer is: What can I do differently?" (Haynes, 1997). Haynes was addressing strategy formation at the table when parties seem to be stuck. This maxim works equally well in practice development. If the phone isn't ringing, ask yourself, "What can I do differently?" If you seem to be having trouble converting initial consultations into paying cases, you might ask yourself, "What can I do differently?" If you find that you are working 12-hour days at the table but do not have enough money left to pay your mortgage, ask yourself, "What can I do differently?" The mediator's prayer works in practice building, too.

Another strategy is to adapt mediation theory to practice building theory. One of our greatest mediation thinkers, Christopher Moore, of CDR Associates in Boulder, Colorado, unveiled his now famous "pizza pie" teaching aid in a chapter he wrote for Folberg and Milne's *Divorce Mediation: Theory and Practice* (Moore, 1988). Moore's pie illustrates the five sources of conflict: values, structure, relationships, interests, and data. In my training classes, I challenge students to use Moore's five sources of conflict to develop working hypotheses and strategic interventions to resolve disputes. Using the mediator's skill of looking beyond a current perspective, we can adapt Moore's five sources of conflict to five areas of practice building:

1. *Values.* Attempt to clearly articulate your own personal values and how they are present in the way you arrange to have your phone answered, your office decorated, your fees structured, and your work with referral sources.
2. *Data.* Track your time spent and the source of telephone calls, and budget and analyze your financial trends.
3. *Interests.* How are your clients' and your own underlying interests met by your refund policy?

4. *Structure.* Assess whether your office hours, its location, and its legal structure (corporate, partnership, etc.) are contributing to your bottom line.
5. *Relationships.* Monitor how your relationships with staff and referral sources impact your practice.

DON'T REINVENT THE WHEEL

Obviously, you are not the first family mediator to establish a practice—learn from the efforts of others in the field. As a group, mediators are quite generous and collaborative in sharing their experience and in offering help. Identify a role model in your community and interview him or her. Just as you learned from your mediation trainer's demonstration of how to conduct a successful caucus or make an effective opening statement, articulate for yourself what your role model does well and try to replicate it. Perhaps you will have the fortune (as I have) of encountering a role model who is willing to mentor you. Mentors are invaluable—and the benefits go both ways. Some benefits of mentors include: serving as a model for values, work ethics, and skills, as well as a source of practical advice and emotional support.

Another avenue to pursue for accumulated wisdom is that of venturing outside our young profession to learn from the work in other professions—particularly, from law practice management and small business literature. The American Bar Association's Law Practice Management Section (*www.aba.lpm.org*) is a treasure trove of books, tapes, and practice-building materials, which often adapt well to mediation practice. The ABA's number-one bestseller, *How to Start and Build a Law Practice* (Foonberg, 1999) can be applied to your mediation work. Go to your local bookstore and head for the business section. You will be amazed how much has already been published on the strategic planning, marketing, and cost-effective management of small businesses.

IS PRIVATE PRACTICE RIGHT FOR YOU?

Before leaving your day job and investing the significant money and time necessary to succeed in private practice, stop a moment and consider (just like you ask mediation parties to do): "If I get what I think I want, will I want it?" Do you really want to leave a job that provides a steady paycheck and a community of colleagues? Are you ready and able to wait months or years to replace your existing income and savings (if you ever do)? Are you willing to perform the selling and bookkeeping tasks that do not seem to escape any small business owner?

The best decision you might make is to keep family mediation as your weekend/evening avocation and retain the illusion (rather than the harsh reality) of operating your own practice. The current conflict resolution system in the United States and many other countries depends on the millions of hours of volunteer time from mediators who earn their paycheck in different day jobs.

If you are still convinced that a family mediation practice is for you, let's look at some basic practice preparation strategies.

DEFINE YOUR MEDIATION SIGNATURE

What is your mediation signature?

If you have trouble answering this question, imagine the difficulty that potential clients and referral sources might have in determining that you are the right mediator for their job. Your mediation signature allows clients and referral sources to differentiate you from all those others in the marketplace. What services you offer, what market you service, and the special qualities about you and your practice that both stand on their own and compare favorably with other "competitors" in the marketplace—all these are conveyed by your mediation signature. Specific aspects of your mediation signature can include:

• *Your style at the mediation table.* Do you adhere to one model of mediation (e.g., facilitative, transformative, evaluative), or do you have a full toolbox of techniques borrowed from several approaches?

• *Your target market.* Do you mediate for anyone who walks in the door, or do you service a primary demographic market such as the elderly, the Hispanic population, gay or lesbian individuals, the working poor, the rich, the middle class? Do you limit your practice to a single geographical locale, or are you willing to take your practice on the road?

• *Your field of expertise.* Do your specialize only in family mediation, or will you handle any type of dispute? If you specialize in family mediation, do you subspecialize in child custody, or even sub-subspecialize in geographical relocations, parenting plans for young children, or other delimited areas?

• *The types of services that you offer.* Do you limit your mediation practice to the common service of resolving current disputes, or do you also offer other services for which you are trained? Some of these other services might include preventive mediation (premarital agreements, estate planning, surrogate adoptions), mediated case management, dispute resolution systems design, unbundled coaching and/or representation of one side for parties in mediation, teaching, group facilitation, convening, or other services that contribute to your signature.

• *Your personal attributes and experience.* Do you have a unique background in business or taxes, working with children, or vocational placement that sets you apart from others in your community? Do you have particular personal qualities, such as patience, creativity, or perseverance, that would attract clients and referral sources? Do you have life experiences that help identify you with a client group with similar experiences (e.g., surviving a life-threatening illness, raising a disabled child, or being a victim of child abuse)?

You must be able to articulate your own mediation signature before you can expect clients and referral sources to know it and use it. The mediation self-survey in Appendix 23.1 will help you think through the variables that constitute your signature. Once you are clear on what your signature is, you can then create brochures that convey it, and you can communicate it in your one-to-one interactions with potential referral sources and clients.

WHERE WILL YOUR PRACTICE BE LOCATED?

Will you have a commercial office or will you practice out of your home? Will you locate your office in a professional building, or will you open a storefront? Will you practice in your neighborhood or in the city center?

Your choice of where you practice may be born of necessity—but it also can be strategically planned. If you practice out of your home, you can be like Jamie Johnson Palmer of Batavia, Illinois, who invites divorcing couples to walk through her lush garden, sit for a moment in her gazebo, and then proceed through the private entrance of her office and be treated to hot cappuccino and fresh homemade muffins.

Some mediators choose to do their marketing and office work out of their homes but see clients at lawyers' offices or rent a conference room when needed. Another approach is to locate your office strategically in an office building housing potential referral sources such as lawyers and therapists. Although a long lease offers you the security of being able to establish a geographical identity, it also brings higher financial risk if your financial projections don't work out. Negotiate for an escape clause that will permit you to cancel the lease with an agreed-upon notice and penalty (e.g., 3 months' rent in advance) that would meet both your needs and that of the property manager.

Choosing a particular geographical location in your community can also involve strategic factors. While few of us opt for a long daily commute, establishing your practice across town, in an area that is underserved in conflict resolution, might be worth it to you—or you could consider relocating your home.

CHOOSING OFFICE COLLEAGUES

Many mediators find that sharing space or even establishing a partnership or group helps to launch their practices. If you opt to share space, consider if you need your own office, or could you alternate days or days/evenings with an office mate to lower your rent? Do you want to sublease from other mediators or from professionals in a different background? In forming a group or partnership, will you team up with peers or with a mentor?

Deciding whether to join a mediation provider organization (MPO) or a private/court panel also calls for strategic thinking. Some MPOs demand exclusivity and take higher percentages of fees for their marketing and administrative support—yet, at the same time, they might provide you with the promotion and caseload you need to energize your peacemaking career. Panels are often cheaper to join and rarely require exclusivity, but they may not provide you with much business. Regardless of your choice, plan on staying with a chosen path for a significant period of time—you do not want to get a reputation for hopping around.

PRACTICE NAME

Most mediators practice under their own name because they want any current reputation or marketing efforts to translate into calls to them rather to an organization. If your name is difficult to spell or to remember, however, you may want to consider a different strategy.

If you practice in one area of a city or state, geographical names might work: for example, Northwest Peoria Mediation Center or Twin Cities Mediation. You might also consider a generic name, such as Family Mediation Services Group, or a descriptive name, such as Transformative Mediation, Peacetalk Mediation, or another name that reflects your style or values. If you choose a name other than your own, make sure that your referral sources also know your name—just in case you decide to discard the name or leave the organization. Check to be sure that a generic or descriptive name does not violate the ethical code of your profession of origin and register it as an assumed business name.

SET UP A MEDIATION-FRIENDLY OFFICE

My mentor Professor Louis M. Brown often said that "client waiting time can be client learning time." Since mediation clienthood is not a genetic condition, most mediation parties need to learn about their new role. Your office design can contribute to this goal.

Give your office the client impact test. Pretend you are a participant in mediation. Is the waiting room comfortable? Does it offer educational materials? Is your mediation room equipped with a round table, flip chart, food/ water, and the forms that you will need (so that you do not have to pop out of the session)? Do you have adequate breakout rooms for caucuses or party meetings with lawyers?

Most importantly, if facilitating your clients' informed decision making is your goal, perhaps you could provide information that is accessible and convenient. A client learning center/library, where mediation parties can observe videotapes, read lay-friendly books, and prepare documents, offers both client education and empowerment.

Your client-friendly atmosphere need not be expensive. If you do not have an extra room for a client library, simply buy an inexpensive VCR and one or two videotapes (*Mediation: It's Up to You* [Association for Conflict Resolution, 1991] and *Children: The Experts of Divorce* [Hickey, 1994] are my favorites). Place the VCR and some tapes into your existing client waiting room, accompanied by a set of earphones to reduce noise pollution. Buy a few key books or transfer them from your private library—then add additional offerings slowly. If you do not have room for a round table, consider buying a desk with a rounded side as a mediation table. In setting up your office, there is no one recipe—only your clients' needs and your own sensibilities.

DEVELOP A MARKETING STRATEGY

Walk into almost any bookstore, and you will find dozens of books on how to market a small business. You can discover tips galore: Market every day; keep track of your marketing time; always send a thank-you note—and more. Some of these tips make sense—but they are not enough. I have found that if you develop an overall marketing strategy that works for you—and stick with it over time—your practice will benefit.

One irrefutable strategy is to build from the client base that you already have and do everything in your power to increase client satisfaction. In his classic, *Thriving on Chaos*, marketing guru Tom Peters (1987) claims that it costs five times as much to acquire a new client as it does to keep the clients you have. Peters offers many insights: Here are just two: (1) Be obsessive about the quality of your work, and (2) use client complaints to strengthen the relationship with both clients and referral sources by handling the problem well. Let's explore these two nuggets a bit more deeply.

1. *Be obsessive about quality* Your work at the table in resolving disputes and the paperwork that follows should demonstrate this obsessive attention to detail. See yourself as a lifelong learner who is constantly seeking to im-

prove your craft. This mind-set is called *kaisen* by the Japanese. You can use *kaisen* in your marketing as well. If you have printed brochures that have a typo or other error, find a way to fix it (e.g., use Wite-Out or a label) or discard the brochures. If you are sending out a client information packet, make sure that the photocopies are first generation and visually appealing. You are the quality monitor of your practice. This is one area where you might give in to your obsession—without ever becoming abusive to staff!

2. *Use client problems as an opportunity to strengthen the relationship.* As a peacemaker, you can "walk the walk" by handling trouble early, directly, clearly, and finally. If you overbilled, don't just reverse the questioned charges, add some billing credit as well. If you show up late for an appointment, consider giving an equal amount of tardy time without charge—or even donate the entire session as reparation for your late show. Clients rarely demand mistake-free service—and they greatly appreciate a mediator who will own up to a mistake and rectify it beyond their expectation.

Another form of marketing strategy is to correlate the cost of your marketing efforts with the possible rewards. A low-risk approach is to market mediation services (e.g., resolution of current disputes) to your existing client base. Another slightly riskier (yet still very safe) initiative is to offer new services (e.g., preventive mediation of relationship formation, such as premarital or adoptive ones) to your current clients. You already have a reputation of competence and integrity with your current clients; adding mediation services will probably be welcomed, and the marketing cost is minimal. You can even enclose a brochure or letter about your mediation work in a current bill or regular client newsletter. This approach will cost you little and help you slowly build your mediation practice.

A riskier strategy still is offering your current services to potential new clients. It is always more expensive to market to people whom you do not know. It is even costlier to market cutting-edge services to potential clients who do not already know and respect you. Although this riskier strategy will cost more on the front end, if pursued over time, you will greatly accelerate your goal of working as a full-time peacemaker (see Karlson, 1996). Figure 23.1 provides a graphic summary of these four strategies.

USE CLIENT INTAKE AS YOUR PRIMARY MARKETING STRATEGY

Ten marketing experts may have 11 opinions as to the best marketing and advertising options. Lawyers have found the Yellow Pages to be a cost-effective way of targeting people who have a current need (American Bar Association Commission on Advertising, 1992). A website might not bring in much new business, but it can significantly affirm your credentials and bolster a potential client's inclination to hire you. Dignified print ads in professional jour-

Low Risk	Moderate Risk
Mainstream Mediation Services to Current Clients: Status Quo and Low Cost	Mainstream Mediation Services to Potential Clients: Moderate Cost and Growth
Low Risk	High Risk
New Mediation Services to Current Clients: Significant Growth and Moderate Cost	New Cutting-Edge Mediation Services to Potential Clients: Slow Growth and High Cost

FIGURE 23.1. Marketing strategies. From Mosten (2001). Copyright 2001 by Jossey-Bass. Reprinted by permission of Jossey-Bass, Inc., a subsidiary of John Wiley & Sons, Inc.

nals over a sustained time period may bring long-term referral flow from fellow professionals who can provide multiple clients. Postcards and other direct mail can target your efforts on an economic basis. One-on-one meetings or business meals help forge relationships that can build your practice one case at a time. The marketing and advertising options you can employ to open up client flow are only limited by your own creativity and budget.

Ultimately, your best strategy is to provide quality service that produces high satisfaction for your existing clients. Ranked a close second is the ability to convert telephone calls of inquiry from potential clients into paying cases. Whatever your favorite marketing strategy, your ultimate goal is the ringing of your phone. In marketing parlance, the caller is your "highest targeted prospect." Whether it is your past quality service to others, brilliant advertising, or a crisis, telephone callers are aware that they have a current demand for your services and have made a tentative decision to select you as the service brand of choice (at least, for the duration of the phone call!).

Compare this "hot" caller to the hundreds or thousands of potential clients you are paying to reach in a newspaper print ad. After you pay for ad space and production costs, most of the potential clients do not read your ad. Even if they do read it, they probably do not have an immediate need for conflict resolution. And even if they have a need, most will not act on your ad or might choose another service (lawyers, therapist, document preparer) or another mediator. If direct mail response to a targeted audience can be expected to bring a 1–3% response rate, a print ad will bring even lower response—and radio or TV, still lower (Crandall, 1997).

Concentrate on the people who do actually pick up the telephone (or e-mail) to contact you. These "hot" leads are your best opportunity to build a practice—the rest is up to you.

Even when the telephone rings frequently, mediators building their practices convert only one of 10 calls to a paying case. Why? For every 10 calls, at least four or five are from people who have a current need but do not want mediation even after you spend money or time to educate them. They really want a lawyer or other professional—or only want to talk to someone to complain about their problem.

This leaves five to six potential clients. Remember, unlike a potential law client or dental patient, the caller cannot make a unilateral decision to hire your services—it takes two (or more) to agree to mediate and then to agree on the selection of mediator. Many of your callers want mediation, but the other parties know nothing about this call. Even if the other side is well acquainted with mediation, he or she still may not want to mediate. Therefore, your ability to effectively convene a high percentage of these five or six callers for mediation may make the difference between staying in mediation practice and working at another day job. To be more concrete, if one of 10 callers turns into a paying case, you are probably on track. If two of 10 result in an opened file, your call-to-case ratio improves to five calls per case—and your income doubles!

ESTABLISH AN INTAKE MODEL

Review your intake procedures: What model do you use for case intake? Who handles the initial telephone calls or web inquiry? What steps do you and your staff take following that inquiry? What is the conversion rate of inquiries to opened case files in your office? What are the sources of those inquiries? How are referral sources recognized? Can you articulate your intake model? Four general mediation intake models are described below. Review them to identify either the workable model that you now have in place or to find a better method.

Short Intake: Mediator Talks Directly with Potential Client

Short means 1–10 minutes, maximum. The purpose of the call is to provide personal answers to the caller's basic questions, with the goal of following up by sending a mediation marketing packet or referring the caller to your website. Your challenge is to stay focused on the process of mediation rather than delve into the facts or personal concerns of the caller (this takes practice). In this call, you provide information about yourself, the types of mediation you offer, your fees, and your availability.

You want to stay brief for two reasons. First, your follow-up marketing packet and/or website will answer most questions. Second, you are "off-clock" and want to keep your time investment to a minimum. Most mediators who utilize this model also offer a free office consultation for 30–45 minutes. The free consultation then leads to private individual sessions or joint sessions "on the clock."

By the end of this short intake, presumably the caller will have confidence in your tone and information and provide contact information for sending the marketing packet. Be careful to send a packet to the other party only if you are sure that the other party is expecting it. You also might ask if the parties are represented by attorneys and if they want the lawyers to receive their own marketing packets. Remember, your credibility and neutrality as a mediator are conveyed (or not) by the way you handle these delicate issues from the first point of contact—the phone call.

In this model, you might not have any contact with the noncalling party until the first mediation or orientation session. It's often a good idea for you to call the noncalling party before this session to become acquainted with the other side of the story. In this way, both parties are assured of your neutrality going into the first mediation session.

Short Intake: Mediation Assistant Talks Directly with Potential Client

Everything about this model is the same as the short intake that you handle yourself except that another staff member takes the call. You should instruct your assistant to alert you if the caller insists on speaking with you. (Most callers are willing to speak with an assistant, if that is the procedure the mediator has established, in the same way that we accept the nurse who takes our blood pressure or temperature at a doctor's office.) You need to have an established office policy about whether you will speak to an insistent caller or have your assistant explain that, in order to preserve your neutrality, you do not talk to either party until both parties come to your office for the free orientation session. Both of these policies are used throughout the field. See Figure 23.2.

Long Intake: Mediator Talks Directly with Potential Client

Using this model, you would speak separately with each party for 15 minutes to an hour, without charge, followed by a working session with both parties "on the clock." See Figure 23.3. Most mediators who utilize this model do not necessarily send marketing materials after the telephone calls, due to the time spent on intake—but this is changing as more mediators are developing marketing materials to supplement their direct contact with potential clients.

Unlike the short-intake model in which the caller(s) do not reveal facts, relationship dynamics, or other concerns, such revelations are precisely the purpose of the long-intake model. This approach gives you the opportunity to showcase your craft as well as to bond with each party on the telephone. By taking a factual history and learning more about the conflict, you can also prepare for the joint working session and give parties information and guidance.

The major downside to this model is that after spending 1–2 hours on the telephone, the parties may never schedule an appointment. In addition,

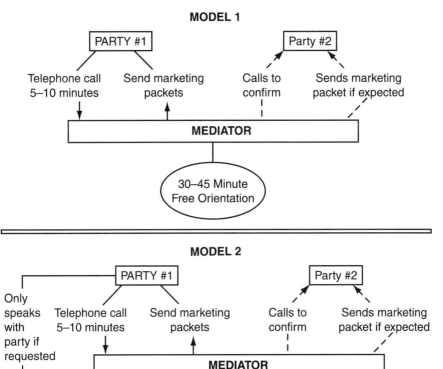

FIGURE 23.2. Mediation intake—short. From Mosten (2001). Copyright 2001 by Jossey-Bass. Reprinted by permission of Jossey-Bass, Inc., a subsidiary of John Wiley & Sons, Inc.

you may be concerned about perceptions regarding your neutrality (or lack thereof), since you will not have met or necessarily spoken with both parties prior to conducting these long intake sessions.

Long Intake: Conducted by Mediator Assistant or Case Manager

This model works best when the dispute resolution assistant or case manager is highly experienced in intake and convening procedures. See Figure 23.3.

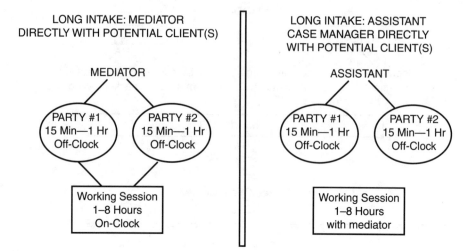

FIGURE 23.3. Mediation intake—long. From Mosten (2001). Copyright 2001 by Jossey-Bass. Reprinted by permission of Jossey-Bass, Inc., a subsidiary of John Wiley & Sons, Inc.

The telephone calls must be followed by a detailed memorandum from the intake professional so that the mediator can be fully briefed before the working session. Obviously the bonding and personal relationship between you and the parties are sacrificed in this model, and you must decide if that loss is outweighed by your timesaving methods.

Intake with Counsel

Whether long or short or handled by you or your assistant, designing intake when lawyers are involved requires special preparation. See Figure 23.4. Since lawyers are becoming more sophisticated consumers, they often do not require an extensive orientation about the process of mediation, in general. Rather, you need to educate them about particular aspects of your process, which may include:

- Use of private sessions and or conference calls prior to the date of mediation.
- Use of premediation briefs, what the briefs should include, and whether the briefs are confidential with the mediator or shared with the other parties and counsel.
- Hours of the session and how meals and snacks will be handled.
- How offers will be presented: by you or by the lawyers themselves.
- Presession sharing of boilerplate release language.

You may need to be particularly adaptable when deciding your method of intake with counsel. Some lawyers are accustomed to dealing with dispute resolution assistants or case managers working with both private mediators and mediation provider organizations, such as the Judicial Arbitration and Mediation Service (JAMS), American Arbitration Association, or National Mediation Centers. Other lawyers are concerned about the delicacy of their case and insist on speaking directly with you, either together or individually.

OFFER BOTH SINGLE-SESSION AND SEQUENTIAL-SESSION FORMATS

Traditionally, most civil mediations are set up so that the parties expect to meet and work out a settlement in a single session. Sometimes these sessions

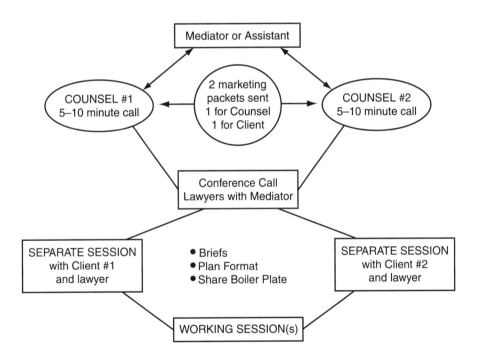

FIGURE 23.4. Intake with counsel. From Mosten (2001). Copyright 2001 by Jossey-Bass. Reprinted by permission of Jossey-Bass, Inc., a subsidiary of John Wiley & Sons, Inc.

last days and nights—exhaustion often contributes to settlement as much as your skill.

A second model, favored in family mediation, is to hold a series of shorter sessions (2–4 hours each) that are set by agreement of the parties. These sessions are often followed by a mediator's summary letter that serves as minutes of the session and outlines agreements made and issues still open for resolution. The parties continue to meet until an agreement is reached or the mediation is terminated by one or both of the parties.

In planning your sessions, you can offer either model or a hybrid. In the hybrid model, parties usually start with sequential sessions until an agreement is reached or impasse develops. The parties can then try a marathon single session to try to bring closure to the dispute. See Figure 23.5.

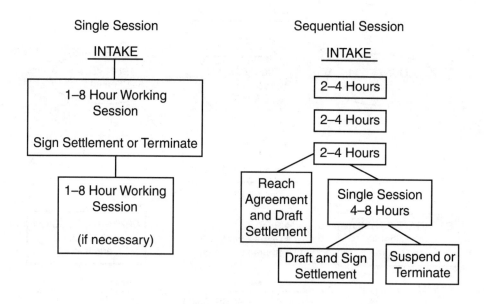

FIGURE 23.5. Mediation formats. From Mosten (2001). Copyright 2001 by Jossey-Bass. Reprinted by permission of Jossey-Bass, Inc., a subsidiary of John Wiley & Sons, Inc.

CUSTOMIZE YOUR WRITTEN MEDIATION CONTRACT

Most mediation professional standards highly recommend use of a written mediation contract, signed by parties prior to a mediation. This written agreement provides informed consent for consumers as to the mediation process services offered and fees charged. The contract also covers rules for confidentiality and inadmissibility of communications and documents prepared for the mediation in future court proceedings. You may want to have a standard agreement, but make it clear in your intake that the parties may modify it if they wish.

Your agreement may call for a 7-day, or longer, notification of cancellation, and the parties may want to be able to cancel within 24 hours. Such requested modifications force you to recognize that you may have conflicting needs with one or more of the parties. It's a tough balance. Like working out fee and payment arrangements, you must protect your own interests while remaining neutral and client centered in your approach. My mentor Louis M. Brown, the father of preventive law, always said that a client should talk with a second lawyer before making a fee arrangement with the first lawyer! It is not so different when potential clients who need to trust you are negotiating with you at the same time. You must do your best to acknowledge your own needs and still remain neutral and client centered in your focus.

CLEARLY STATE YOUR FEES

Since saving money is a prime motivation for many consumers to try mediation, you have a professional duty to be crystal clear about how much you charge and what services you offer. Agreement on fees should be part of the written agreement to mediate.

Hourly Fees

Charging by the hour is still the prevalent method, since we can never predict how long a matter will take. Furthermore, mediators may provide services between sessions, such as writing session summary letters, arranging for neutral experts, or handling emergency telephone calls; charging by the hour accommodates billing for these services.

Daily or Session Rates

You may decide to charge a flat daily rate or set rate for a multihour session. Many mediators add out-of-session charges to these flat fees; others set a flat rate and do not charge for out-of-session time. You also must set a policy for what you will do if the parties settle before the end of the arranged time. In the same way, if the session goes overtime, do you have a flat fee or do you charge by the hour, and if so, at what rate?

Flat Fees

You may wish to offer a flat rate to mediate an entire matter—no matter how many or few hours it takes. This method is certain and clear—but it sets up a conflict of interest between you and your clients. You have an economic motivation to rush a settlement to maximize your hourly return, and the parties do not have a dollars/hour motivation to accelerate their settlement. One way to reduce this problem is to arrange for a flat fee that incorporates a reduced hourly fee for a set time period and then charge hourly thereafter. For example, if your customary hourly rate is $150, you might offer a flat rate of $1,000 for the first 10 hours of mediation and $150 per hour thereafter.

PROVIDE EASY PAYMENT OPTIONS

Think through how consumers can pay for your services. Your hourly or daily rate might be competitive, but if you do not demonstrate flexibility in your methods of payment, you might find that potential clients will go elsewhere.

Payment by the Session

One way to maintain a competitive advantage in the marketplace is to unbundle payment for your mediation services. Instead of requiring parties to pay the whole bill at the end or to pay a retainer up front, they can pay as they go. This arrangement generally means that you get paid every time they meet with you—which eliminates billing altogether.

If you don't charge for time you spend on the case outside of sessions, calculating your bill will be a snap. You either bill for the flat session amount or tote up the number of hours that you are with the parties. If you do charge for out-of-session work, add up the time between sessions and have an invoice ready at the beginning of the next session. Although many mediators collect fees at the end of a session (partly because it may be unclear how long a session will last), I prefer to collect at the beginning of the session to alleviate last-minute hassles if (when!) parties bring up issues in the last 5 minutes or there is a stormy ending to the session. You don't want to be in the position of chasing parties into the parking lot in order to get a check. In addition, set clear boundaries that provide simple structure, and think about setting an ending time for the sessions, even if you have time open afterward. This measure also allows you to collect a calculated fee at the beginning of a session.

Retainers

The retainer method of payment entered mediation practice through the many mediators who come from law practice backgrounds, where payment of an up-front retainer is common. A retainer is a deposit paid at the outset of the services to ensure payment for part or all of the expected services. There is no recipe for setting the right amount. If you set it too high, you could scare away potential clients. If you set it too low, your time billed could vastly exceed the amount deposited, clients will owe you money, and you may have a risk of collection. If you have to err, nevertheless, err on the low side. Research has shown that mediation participants experience high levels of satisfaction—and satisfied customers usually pay their bills (Beck & Sales, 2002).

One way to keep your retainer low and still ensure full payment is to use what is called a "replenishable retainer." Unlike a traditional retainer, in which the fees you accrue are deducted from the retainer until the retainer is exhausted and the clients owe you money, with a replenishable retainer the deposit remains in full until the end of your services. Clients pay you regularly for the services that you render, and those payments are not deducted from the retainer. Rather, the payments replenish the original amount of the retainer. The retainer deposited is applied to the amount of the final bill. If there is still money owing after the retainer is applied, the parties receive a final billing for the additional fees. If there is a credit balance (more funds in the retainer account than in the bill for services charged), the client is sent a refund check.

Credit Card Payments

A consumer-friendly way to help parties finance mediation services is to offer them the option of paying by credit card. In fact, instead of having to ask for any retainer or payment at the end of a session or billing cycle, you can ask parties to authorize charging services as they are incurred, with the right to question any charge after receiving a bill itemizing your services. Clients like this option because they can receive services without paying a deposit up front and can pay off the mediation charges as another credit card obligation.

OFFER SEVERAL METHODS TO ALLOCATE YOUR FEES

It is part of mediation lore that the parties must equally split the fee in order for the mediation to proceed with no apparent grounds for mediation bias. Equal payment does often encourage a level playing field and equal commitment to the process. However, there are many alternatives to equal payment, and it is to your benefit to adapt to other arrangements.

Particularly in divorce mediations, the parties may share the mediator's fee unequally due to differences in ability to pay. You should always assure the parties that your neutrality will not be affected by who writes your check. More importantly, by modifying the equal payment rule, you will be making mediation services affordable and accessible while building your practice at the same time.

CONCLUSION

The purpose of this chapter is to provide an overview of the essential business components of establishing a mediation practice. After defining your mediation signature, setting up a mediation-friendly office, and developing an effective intake system and fee structure, you are now ready for the exciting challenge of funding your strategic plan, marketing to obtain clients, and constantly improving your services to maximize competence and client satisfaction. Do you recall how excited you were initially to discover the magic of mediation and how stimulating it was to help resolve conflict? Successful practice building is more than making money: It can be personally fulfilling to build your own business. Furthermore, making mediation your day job ensures that you can be available as a peacemaker to help resolve conflict for society's underserved—which can make a difference today and beyond.

APPENDIX 23.1. MEDIATOR SELF-SURVEY

I. Current Marketing Practices

1. What services do I offer as a private mediator?
2. What is the target market for my services?
3. How do I communicate the availability and nature of my services to my target market?
4. How do my services provide improvement or diversity from other mediators in the same market?
5. What is my involvement with organized professional associations in my trained profession?
6. What is my ongoing involvement with other mediators? How is such involvement "cost effective"?
7. To which professional journal subscriptions and software do I subscribe?
8. What is my involvement with statewide and national mediator organizations?
   a. How is this involvement cost effective?
9. What is the extent of my volunteer work for the community?
10. How do I help other mediators/professionals develop their professional craft or practices?

II. Financial Investment and Performance of the Practice

11. What out-of-pocket capital have I invested to develop my mediation business?
12. How much is budgeted for the next 12 months in direct capital outlay?
13. How much professional time have I invested to develop my mediation business?
14. What is the value of that time in foregone income?
15. What is my budget for professional time in the next 12 months?
16. What is the rate of economic return on my capital and professional time investment?

III. Fee Charging and Collection Practices

17. What is my record for being paid fairly, adequately, and on time for my mediation services?
18. How do I collect my unpaid fees?
19. What is the rate and timing of collection?
20. What are my practices in respect to my willingness to arbitrate or litigate to collect fees?
    a. What are my criteria for arbitrating or litigating fee collection?
    b. If I do not arbitrate or litigate, what corrective steps am I making to reduce unpaid fees?
    c. What are my criteria for writing off a fee?
21. What is contained in my written mission statement about my mediation practice?
22. What is contained in my written business plan to financially develop my mediation practice?

IV. Management of Practice

23. Do I want to have a mediator partner? (Or steady co-mediator?) If so, why? If not, why not?
24. What is my contribution to the growth of mediation through training?
25. What is my contribution to the growth of mediation through articles?
26. What is my contribution to the growth of mediation through development of materials?
27. How do I work with the following experts:
    a. Forensic accountants:
    b. Actuaries:
    c. Real estate appraisers:
    d. Business appraisers:
    e. "Industry" specialists:
    f. Child development experts:
    g. Children, extended family members:
28. How does my mediation contract inform and educate clients as to:
    a. My services?
    b. Rules of my practice?
    c. Financial requirements?

29. How does my contract protect me:
    a. Financially?
    b. From malpractice claims?
30. What do I or my staff do to educate (potential) clients about mediation?
31. What procedures have I developed in the office for:
    a. Mailing:
    b. Display:
    c. Showing videos:
    d. Helping clients prepare and succeed at mediation?
32. What is my policy in helping spouses locate consulting counsel?
33. Will I mediate by conference call? If so, what is my procedure?
34. How do I communicate outside of session with:
    a. Parties?
    b. Counsel?
    c. Experts?
35. What role do I play in:
    a. Mediation session summary letters?
    b. Drafting agreements?
    c. Interim court orders?
    d. Filing legal documents?
36. Do I permit counsel to attend sessions?
37. What role will counsel play?
38. How are their procedures set up?
39. Once the presenting problem is resolved, what preventive planning do I conduct for the spouses?
40. What follow-up do I perform in monitoring compliance with mediated agreements?
41. What type of tickle system have I set up to keep mediators on track and to follow up on future developments?
42. How do I stay in touch with mediation clients?
43. What procedures do I have for initiating wellness (annual) mediation checkups?
44. How do I engage in preventive mediation?

V. Training

45. What are my goals for training?
46. What skills do I focus on in training?
    a. What role will I play in training?
    b. What role will the supervisor play in training?
47. What areas of economic practice development do I wish to focus on in training?
48. What training format do I believe will most help me?
49. What obstacles do I believe will hinder my training?
    a. What will I do to overcome these obstacles?
    b. What do I want the supervisor to do in helping me overcome obstacles?

50. What issues or techniques do I wish to focus on in my training?
51. What type of supervisory style do I believe would be most effective in my training?
52. What type of supervision format do I believe would be most effective in my training?

ACKNOWLEDGMENT

This chapter includes excerpts adapted and reprinted from Mosten (2001). Copyright 2001 by Jossey-Bass. Reprinted by permission of Jossey-Bass, Inc., a subsidiary of John Wiley & Sons, Inc.

REFERENCES

American Bar Association Commission on Advertising. (1992). *Yellow pages advertising: An analysis of effective elements.* Chicago: Author.

Association for Conflict Resolution. (1991). *Mediation: It's up to you* [Videotape]. Washington, DC: Author.

Beck, C. J. A., & Sales, B. D. (2001). *Family mediation: Facts, myths, and future prospects.* Washington, DC: American Psychological Association.

Boulle, L. (1996). *Mediation: Principles, process, and practice.* London: Butterworths.

Crandall, R. (1997). *10 Secrets of market success.* Corte Madera, CA: Select Press.

Foonberg, J. (1999). *How to start and build a law practice* (4th ed.). Chicago: American Bar Association.

Haynes, J. (1997, July). *Family mediation beyond divorce.* Academy of Family Mediators Conference, Cape Cod, MA.

Hickey, E. (1994). *Children: The experts of divorce* [Videotape]. Hyattsville, MD: Children's Rights Council.

Karlson, D. L. (1996). *Marketing your counseling or professional services.* Menlo Park, CA: Crisp Learning.

Moore, C. W. (1988). Techniques to break impasse. In J. Folberg & A. Milne (Eds.), *Divorce mediation: Theory and practice* (pp. 251–276). New York: Guilford Press.

Mosten, F. S. (2001). *Mediation career guide.* San Francisco: Jossey-Bass.

Peters, T. (1987). *Thriving on chaos: Handbook for a management revolution.* New York: HarperCollins.

CHAPTER 24

Divorce Mediation and the Internet

JAMES C. MELAMED

The Internet has changed the way we communicate, and it is also changing the way we mediate. In this chapter, James C. Melamed, the founder of *Mediate.com,* explains the "why" and "how" of using the Internet to enhance mediation. Beyond facilitating communication when divorcing parties cannot mediate face-to-face, the Internet offers unique qualities, including asynchrony, easy access to an expanded knowledge/database, and increased capacity for each party to effectively participate. Facilitating use of the Internet for enhanced communication is a way for mediators to offer a value-added service and to distinguish themselves in this digital age.

The Internet is changing the way divorce mediation is practiced and experienced, as it becomes an ever more integral part of effective and affordable divorce mediation services and programs. The following uses of the Internet are common and increasing:

- Participants seek mediators through Internet search.
- Mediators and programs describe their services through professional websites.
- Participants and their attorneys exchange information about possible mediators by exchanging links to mediator websites.
- Mediators distribute information to clients by e-mailed attachments and links to Web pages.
- Mediators and participants correspond, separately or jointly, by e-mail.
- Mediators use e-mail mailboxes as a filing system.

- Mediators receive faxes as attachments to e-mail.
- Draft agreements may use "track changes" features to show changes.
- Mediators utilize Web resources to obtain information and educate participants.
- Participants and mediators obtain statutory, regulatory, child support, and other information online.
- Participants and mediators perform child support calculations online.
- Mediators engage in professional education online.
- Mediators and participants utilize secure discussion environments.
- Participants may utilize online resources to help them implement their agreement.

Adapting Internet technologies to mediation is not accidental. Increased use is based upon the effectiveness, convenience, and affordability of various Internet strategies. In addition to enhanced communication capacities, the Internet offers mediators and participants a vast knowledge base as well as extensive discussion communities. For many, the Internet is a comfortable, if not preferred and empowering, means of research and communication. It is also relatively free of safety concerns—perhaps because it is impossible to receive a bloody nose over the Internet, and certainly because Internet communications are memorialized, which creates a measure of accountability.

BEYOND FACE-TO-FACE DIALOGUE

Does all this mean that the Internet soon will replace face-to-face divorce mediation? The end of face-to-face divorce mediation does not loom, at least, not in the short term. Current utilization of the Internet in the divorce arena is evolving more as an augmentation than replacement of face-to-face discussions. We can, however, envision a day when the context and medium for mediation discussions may, in fact, become primarily electronic, with face-to-face meetings being the augmentation, perhaps even the exception.

Although this course of events may sound somewhat futuristic, it is already happening in Singapore, for example, where the country is fully connected by broadband and there are substantial traffic and congestion obstacles to offering mediation services downtown. Use of the Internet will continue to grow, based on such factors as ease, economy, and capacity. All said, the communication, capacity-building and participatory qualities of the Internet are wonderful extensions of the face-to-face mediation process. Few wise mediators would resist additional process options, and in the Internet we have a number of newly available approaches that can meaningfully enhance the practice and experience of divorce mediation.

Example: It is now common for mediators to direct clients to the mediator's website, to send information as an e-mail attachment, or to send information by fax, rather than using "snail mail." In fact, failing to deliver information expeditiously to potential clients may jeopardize the mediator's job chances. In addition to its immediacy, the Internet offers the additional cost bonus of requiring a small flat fee (usually about $20/month for the carrier or $40/month for DSL) regardless of the volume of information delivered over it. Client expectations are rapidly shifting toward the availability of complete information, and the enterprising mediator and program are responding with swift Internet speed. A user-friendly website and effective Internet use are emerging as standard components of effective divorce mediation practice.

Legitimate questions can and should be raised about Internet security, confidentiality, and the "digital divide" (those with lower incomes having less access to the Internet). In examining these issues fairly, we also need to examine the security, confidentiality, and distribution of non-Internet communications and services. The digital divide is, in fact, less of an issue every day, as computers are rapidly becoming as ubiquitous as phones (not to mention the Internet access provided by many libraries and schools, at no cost). Indeed, we may well find the Internet to be an effective means of delivering mediation services to places and people that have heretofore been unserved. Although mediation on the Internet may be imperfect, it may be no more imperfect than other processes—and surely better than no mediation at all.

Utilized well, the Internet offers a vital bridge between the mediator and participants. Internet use especially makes sense when there is difficulty in scheduling meetings due to work shifts, geography, animosity, fear, or other obstacles. In these situations, the Internet may be the only effective and affordable means of delivering services. Use of the Internet in divorce mediation should be viewed as a set of opportunities that are available to mediators and participants for enhancing and, in some cases, replacing face-to-face mediation discussions.

THE JOY OF ASYNCHRONOUS COMMUNICATION

Perhaps the most notable quality of most Internet communications is the common "asynchronous" nature of the communication. This means that most e-mail and Web-based communications are not a live "real-time" experience; rather, the message is crafted and only sent when the sender is ready to do so. Thoughtful, crafted messages and responses are gems to the mediator and the mediation process. The impulsive responses that often take place in real-time face-to-face mediation discussions fly, unedited, from the sender's mouth to the recipient's ears, whereas asynchronous Internet communication fosters composition, rewrites—and deletes!

Experienced mediators are well aware of the benefits of asynchrony. Indeed, these benefits are one reason that many mediators "caucus" (meet separately) with participants. Here mediators want to slow down the process and assist participants in crafting more effective proposals. Surely, the Internet works capably as an extension of the individual party caucus format and is remarkably convenient and affordable. Internet communications take little time to read—and clients do not hear a ticking of the billing meter. When the Internet is utilized for caucus, the noncaucusing participant does not need to sit in the waiting room or library, growing resentful or anxious at being ignored.

Although there is much to recommend about the Internet, its limitations and risks must also be recognized and addressed. For example, without a real-time Internet hookup (chat, audio, or video), the mediator is not able to "interrupt" a participant's (possibly foolish or incendiary) presentation; the participant may go off on long tangents that are not particularly helpful or perhaps are even destructive. There are also meaningful issues of security and confidentiality, discussed below. Some users also contend that text-based Internet communication is not good for effectively developing rapport. This may change as the Internet becomes more "real" with audio and video communications as part of the expansion of broadband connectivity.

THE DEVELOPMENT OF RAPPORT

Without rapport, the mediator has nothing. Experienced mediators know the critical importance of developing rapport with participants early in the process. One challenge to using the Internet for divorce mediation is the difficulty of achieving this much-needed rapport. At least at present, face-to-face meetings take place in a richer sensory environment. The rapport-building capacity of the face-to-face environment, and also of a phone conference call, is important for the online mediator to note. It may be worthwhile for a group that intends to work online to hold one or more face-to-face meetings to clarify process, develop rapport, consolidate progress, and agree on the means of continuing an effective dialogue while online. Mediators who want to do as much as possible online should consider using an initial face-to-face meeting or phone conference call to add "feeling" to online discussions and then whenever deemed helpful as the online mediation progresses.

When thinking about the Internet, it is important to avoid thinking in "either/or" terms. We can build rapport in person, by phone, and on the Internet. There is no reason to limit our modalities of communication. If we are wise, we will be responsive to the participants' desired ways of communicating. We are likely to work with an increasing number of participants who choose to use the Internet in the mediation process.

All mediators benefit from a quality website and responsive and capable e-mail and Web-related practices. Assuming that the Internet is within participants' comfort zones, the mediator's capable Internet performance enhances participants' respect and admiration for the mediator and is likely to improve their experience of the mediation process.

Assuming the benefits of face-to-face meeting, particularly for joint discussions, it is also worth noting that the face-to-face benefit likely lessens over time. Once rapport is in place, there are few issues that cannot be discussed and agreed upon over the Internet. When it comes to decision making, the unrushed Internet environment may, in fact, be preferable to the pressure of the face-to-face environment.

DISTANCE AND POSTDECREE MODIFICATION

This use of the Internet is particularly compelling when participants live at a distance. The relative cost savings of Internet communications becomes greater as the distance between participants increases. The Internet is especially capable of dealing with postdecree adjustments regarding parenting and support agreements. The Internet may be a safer and less pressurized environment in which to consider possible changes than a single "crisis" mediation meeting. Thus, the Internet may be especially worth considering for postdecree modifications. With familiarity presumably in place and the divorce somewhat in the past, more participants are using the Internet to consider modifications to their arrangements, especially when parents live at a distance. The reality is that many divorced parents are already using e-mail as the primary means of communicating about their ongoing parenting relationship. Extending this venue to host mediation discussions is an increasingly natural step to take. We will find more and more modification discussions taking place online, especially if getting together is in any way difficult or costly.

USING THE INTERNET BETWEEN FACE-TO-FACE MEETINGS

Internet communications can be the glue and grease that keep a dialogue effectively moving forward between face-to-face meetings. Channels of communication can be opened with each individual participant (an extension of the caucus) and with the parties jointly (an extension of joint discussions). The Internet is also particularly good for assigning and completing individual or joint homework. Homework assignments can support incremental progress toward agreement.

Some might say that the Internet is the mediator's new best friend. The Internet allows the mediator to send correspondence to participants in a flash, attach resource documents or a draft agreement, and direct participants to check out valuable resources on the Web by providing Web links. Wow!

It is also common in divorce mediation, once an e-mail channel has been created and rapport is in place, for either the mediator or a participant to engage in an e-mail "stream of consciousness" series of communications.

Participants tend to share their thinking "out loud" and "run it by" the mediator in terms of reasonableness, benefits, and costs. The mediator and participant can engage in an ongoing dialogue about perceptions, interests, options, means of improving the presentation, and the like. The mediator is similar to a pen pal assisting participants with their thoughts and moving them forward. It is noteworthy that many participant communications are generated during the late evening, after the children have been put to bed and participants are alone with their thoughts at the end of a long day. Not only do these Internet communications assist participants to move forward in their thinking, however incrementally, they are also convenient, efficient, and affordable.

EMPOWERMENT OF PARTICIPANTS

The Web is a seemingly unlimited resource for empowering mediation participants. Needless to say, mediators want participants initially to review the professional information posted on their website. Mediators can also use the Web as a means of assisting clients to locate information about mediation, conflict resolution, and divorce issues. (See the resources appendix at the end of this chapter.)

If nothing else, the Internet offers participants sources of information that can empower and assist them to normalize their experience. Participants quickly learn that they are not the first ones to undergo the seeming tortures of the divorce process and that there are lots of resources available on divorce issues. Participants may benefit from online divorce discussion groups and from divorce adjustment and parenting information and classes that can be located locally or offered online. The Internet is also a wonderful opportunity for participants (and the mediator) to research issues and cultivate the capacity to consider options—attributes certain to benefit decision making.

THE CREATION OF INTERNET CAPACITY FOR EACH PARTICIPANT

In pre-Internet days, a sign that a divorce was moving forward was the establishment of separate bank accounts. Today, it is the establishment of separate e-mail accounts. Whereas a single e-mail account and computer may work well enough when a couple is married, at the point of separation the time for a shared Internet resources has come to an end. Hence, it is common for a divorce mediator to ensure that participants who want to utilize the Internet each have separate and private Internet capacity.

This discussion is itself intriguing. It is common that one spouse has taken the Internet lead in the marriage. This spouse, usually out of a spirit of kindness and generosity, may offer to "set up" the other spouse with an e-mail address and/or separate computer. While in many situations this approach seems to make good sense (because of one spouse's knowledge, cost, convenience, and perhaps an overall atmosphere of trust), it is also important for both participants and the mediator to recognize the possibility that this disparity could result in compromising the less savvy participant's electronic security. Obviously, we do not want to become paranoid or induce paranoia in participants; still, it is not unreasonable for a mediator to suggest that it may be best for each participant to have truly independent Internet capacity. This establishment of independent Internet capacity and proficiency can be, especially for the less Internet-savvy spouse, a meaningful and valuable accomplishment not only for mediation discussions but for exploration and development of his or her postdivorce life.

CONFIDENTIALITY AND SECURITY

It is important to distinguish between issues of confidentiality and security that relate to mediation and those that pertain to the Internet. Maintaining confidentiality in mediation requires protecting mediation communications in all forms from being offered as evidence in any court or other due process hearing. From a confidentiality perspective, online communications are an extension of face-to-face communications (as are phone, fax, and hard-copy communications), and, therefore, traditional rules would seem to apply. Mediators first need to understand these statutory and regulatory provisions for mediation confidentiality in their state and then to consider augmenting these understandings to encompass their intended use of the Internet.

For example, participants may want to use Internet communications exclusively as part of their mediation and to not copy any of those communications to anyone other than the other participant and the mediator. Mediators are advised to think about how they intend to utilize the Internet and to specifically address the confidentiality and security of these communications in their Agreement to Mediate contract. Once communications are digitalized, there is also the question of how long these records will be maintained by participants, the mediator, a mediation program, and an Internet service provider. Although it may not be possible to anticipate all issues that may arise, participants and the mediator would be wise to ask themselves whether they want to form any written agreements about the limited distribution or limited perpetuation of online mediation communications and records.

It is also important to consider issues of security (as opposed to confidentiality). *Security* refers to the issue of the degree to which mediation communications are protected from being seen by, or shared with, unintended third parties. An example of a security system is a website that requires assignment of a user identification number and password; only those individuals who are authorized by the parties can access the discussion and resources. This user I.D./password system is the most common type of

Internet security. Note that issues such as how to assign a user I.D. number and password and how the mediator, the parties, and attorneys store this information must also be addressed. Participants must consider if it would be helpful to set up a system in which passwords could be changed, and if so, by whom. There is also the legitimate question of just how interested the rest of the world is in a particular divorce mediation online discussion. We should note that communication by other means, including hard copy, fax, phone, and voice mail, is far from fully secure. Any imperfections in Internet security should be evaluated not against a standard of perfection but in comparison to the other communication modalities that are available, each with its own imperfections.

So, what *is* the mediator to do about security? First, it is suggested that this issue should be directly addressed in the first mediation session and in educational and contractual materials given to the participants. A provision such as the following might be inserted into the Agreement to Mediate contract:

> The mediator and participants agree that e-mail and other Internet means of communication may be utilized for ongoing mediation communications without limitation and as part of the confidential mediation discussions. This usage includes attachments, links, faxes, any and all file types, and all means of Internet and other electronic communication. Participants will not forward or otherwise further distribute any Internet or other electronic communication to anyone who is not directly participating in the mediation. These online communications are as confidential as permitted under the law. If desired, participants understand that they may request that a more secure user identification and password system be utilized for their mediation Internet communications.

E-MAIL COMMUNICATION BETWEEN PARENTS AND CHILDREN

As more and more parents use e-mail at work and for their family communications, it is not surprising that e-mail communication is used increasingly by parents communicating with one another following their divorce, especially regarding parenting and support arrangements. Parents may also utilize e-mail, the Web, instant messaging, and chat options for communicating with children when they are at the other parent's home. These modern-day realities are best brought directly into the mediation discussions. The parties are advised to explicitly discuss any and all protocols for their Internet communication as well as their abilities and limitations on communicating with children when at the other parent's home. The communication capacity of the Internet is useful for divorcing parents and their children, and the capable mediator can assist participants to identify—as well as circumscribe—these opportunities.

There are a number of issues to consider when parents send Internet communications to their children at the other parent's home, most notably issues regarding whose computer is being used and who has access to the information. Children may have their own computer, be given a "section" of a parent's computer, or perhaps be given a laptop that they can take with them to each parent's home. Although technically it is not difficult to create a separate identity and security for a child on a parent's computer, a determined parent (as the computer's administrator) can almost always figure out ways to access information if he or she wishes to do so. This is perhaps as much an issue between each parent and their children as between the parents, but it is worth noting and discussing so as to clarify everyone's expectations.

Parents who are often online may also choose to link up with the other parent or with their children through "instant messaging," such as that offered by Yahoo, MSN, ICQ, or AOL. Instant messaging allows the sender to "interrupt" the recipient (usually with a flashing icon and/or beep) to say that a message is waiting. These "intercom" technologies, which also include real-time "chat," are bringing families closer to one another, divorced or not. These systems now include real-time audio and Web cam capacities. The divorce mediator can build upon these resources to assist families to communicate—plus, some of them are really "cool"!

CHILD SUPPORT INFORMATION AND CALCULATION

The Internet can be a very effective tool in the area of child support. Child support negotiations are dominated by the reality of child support guidelines. Federal law requires each state to provide guidelines for the calculation of child support to create predictability and consistency in the application of child support. The calculated guideline for child support is the "presumed" amount of child support—which can, if desired, be rebutted and modified for a variety of reasons that are established by state law.

Most jurisdictions provide child support information on the Internet, and some do a very good job of it. They know that parents with clear information and the ready ability to calculate are more likely to agree. A number of states now provide child support calculators online, and some websites provide a number of state calculators. Mediators need to be sure that they and participants are operating with the most recent state guidelines available. It is best to start out searching for formal state resources.

The divorce mediator can also develop form e-mail letters (often called "forms" or "stationery") that include valuable child support and other resource links. Clients will appreciate having this valuable information made available to them.

Similarly, by using a search engine such as Google, mediators and participants can find valuable information on parenting, financial management, property and debt division, tax laws relating to divorce, etc. The amount of information that is available on the Web for education, empowerment, normalization, calculation, consideration, comparison, etc., is truly amazing. Participants understandably look to their divorce mediator to provide guidance to resources during what is often a disorienting and crazy time. Divorce mediators are wise to do a bit of research on parenting, support, property, tax, and other resources in their state or province and to make these resources readily available to participants. This is an opportunity to be viewed as knowledgeable and as a source of valuable assistance.

DISTRIBUTION OF PROGRESS SUMMARIES, HOMEWORK, AND DRAFT AGREEMENTS

Compared to "snail mail," it is cheaper and faster to communicate by e-mail and attachment. This method of delivery also allows participants more involvement in the drafting process. This involvement promotes a sense of ownership, and participants are more likely to embrace the completed agreement when they and their lawyer can electronically exchange drafts for review and input.

A written summary of progress made during each session accomplishes three tasks. It (1) identifies interests, options, and points of apparent and possible agreement; (2) offers a list of "homework" (things to think about and do in preparation for a next meeting); and (3) suggests agenda items for the next meeting. If we were to compare participants' response to receiving this information a few days after the mediation session (if sent by snail mail) to their response when receiving the same information digitally an hour or two after the session, we would likely see evidence in favor of the swifter and more empowering Internet distribution. Using e-mail and attachments as a basic method of communication saves time, money, and the environment. Most important, it impresses participants and assists them to move forward capably, expeditiously, and economically.

THE MOVING-ON PROCESS

The Internet offers divorcing spouses opportunities for healthy independence, communication, and personal development. Mediators are wise to recognize the many opportunities for participants and their children to communicate on the Internet following divorce. When it comes to implementing parenting arrangements, more and more parents are saying "thank heaven for the Internet." To the extent that the Internet benefits parental communications, the beneficiaries surely also include the children. The Internet takes the pressure off parenting transitions and inconvenient and difficult phone calls, offers parents the opportunity to slow down and to be at their thoughtful best, and better allows parents to "be there," even when they cannot fully be there.

CONCLUSION

Participants, mediators, and mediation programs are already engaging in mediation communications over the Internet. The reasons are obvious: effectiveness, speed, convenience, affordability, and capacity, to name but a few. In addition to acting as an extension of face-to-face joint and caucus discussions, the Internet offers unique qualities such as asynchrony, a vast knowledge base, and party ability to participate in drafting agreements. Just as mediators have aptly integrated the phone, fax, and word processor into practice, they are now integrating the Internet. Use of the Internet is especially compelling when participants are comfortable with, and desirous of, digitally communicating and when participants are at a distance or getting together is otherwise difficult. Even if it is easy to get together, utilizing the Internet as an augmentation of face-to-face discussion makes sense if only for reasons of speed, ease, and economy. Effective integration of the Internet is a means for divorce mediators to distinguish themselves in the marketplace and to offer additional valuable service to participants.

APPENDIX 24.1. RESOURCES

Leading online mediation sites include:

- *www.mediate.com*
- *www.afccnet.org*
- *www.crinfo.org*
- *www.acrnet.org*
- *www.odr.info*

Leading divorce information sites include:

- *www.divorceinfo.com*
- *www.divorcesource.com*
- *www.divorceonline.com*
- *www.divorcenet.com*
- *www.divorcelawinfo.com*
- *www.divorcing.com*
- *www.thedivorcesite.com*
- *www.divorcehelp.com*
- *www.divorcehq.com*
- *www.ourfamilywizard.com*

Index

"f" following a page number indicates a figure; "n" following a page number indicates a note.